# Qualitative Research
# in Education and Social Sciences

# QUALITATIVE RESEARCH

## in Education and Social Sciences

### Second Edition

**DANICA G. HAYS & ANNELIESE A. SINGH**

cognella®

SAN DIEGO

Bassim Hamadeh, CEO and Publisher
Amy Smith, Senior Project Editor
Jeanine Rees, Production Editor
Emely Villavicencio, Senior Graphic Designer
Kylie Bartolome, Licensing Associate
Stephanie Adams, Senior Marketing Program Manager
Natalie Piccotti, Director of Marketing
Kassie Graves, Senior Vice President, Editorial
Jamie Giganti, Director of Academic Publishing

3970 Sorrento Valley Blvd., Ste. 500, San Diego, CA 92121

For Grace Caroline and Charlotte Harper, who shaped my heart and fill it abundantly every day.

And for the one who is forever in my soul—this is for you.

DGH

For Lauren Lukkarila—light of my life, holder of my heart, reminder of all things courage and integrity. I love you forever and ever ... and beyond.

For my mom—who taught me that rules can be transformed and that we should all live like we are in heaven on earth. I love you!

AAS

# Brief Contents

# Detailed Contents

# Preface

Welcome to *Qualitative Research in Education and Social Sciences*!
This text is about planning, conducting, and reporting qualitative research to inform our professions, communities, and scholarship as a whole. At its core, however, it is about cultivating relationships with others and ourselves as we navigate complex questions that impact us professionally and personally. Relationships are central to how we interact as professionals in education, clinical, and other social science settings with those with whom we work. Because qualitative research involves building relationships, qualitative inquiry provides immense potential for positive growth and liberation for the people we work with along the way—and also for ourselves. This potential can feel overwhelming for researchers who are new to qualitative research. However, we encourage you to remember that qualitative research is less overwhelming and more of an adventure when you build the relationship with your topic one step at a time. And this text is here to serve as a step-by-step guide to support you.

Research *is* practice; that is, it is important to conduct research that benefits clients and/or students across disciplines. This work can relate to training practitioners, developing or improving interventions, and building theory and giving voice to underresearched populations, to name just a few examples. We still attend to the importance of application and context when reporting or presenting findings in the research we have published since our graduate training, which involves a broad range of research traditions and topics.

It has been about a decade since we published the first edition of this text. Within the past decade, there have been several advances in qualitative research, which we will share in this edition. Thus, some of our early perspectives toward qualitative research have also changed. This second edition of the text reflects a more multidimensional perspective of the role of the qualitative researcher, a restructured presentation of qualitative research paradigms and traditions, and a continuing eye toward empowerment and advocacy within the research conducted with participants and communities. Throughout the last decade, we have also conducted qualitative research with diverse populations and topics, using innovative and diverse data collection methods and tools that have informed several chapters in the revised text. Other new components of this edition are as follows:

- Greater attention to Indigenous and participatory approaches in qualitative research
- Expanded discussion of ethical considerations from feminist and Indigenous research
- Discussion of ethical issues related to online research
- Greater attention to sampling, sample size, and saturation
- Inclusion of fieldwork considerations for online research
- Expanded discussion of trustworthiness strategies
- Additional data collection methods and strategies related to interviewing, online media, and other data sources

- New information on funding qualitative research
- A new chapter on the role of qualitative research in community and legislative action
- Inclusion of more perspectives from practitioners and educators and their qualitative research activities
- Updated citations

We invite you to become immersed in this text and explore the noteworthy ideas of traditional scholars, radical thinkers from a variety of education and social sciences backgrounds, and our beloved colleagues and students. A focus on shared power, collaboration, and personal and political activism is infused in our research approach and recommended often throughout the text.

This text is written at a level most suitable for graduate-level students, practitioners, and educators in a variety of social science and education disciplines. For graduate students, this book is structured to include proposal development exercises, in-class and field activities, journal exercises, and other tools that build upon one another to complete a quality proposal or report. We include a glossary of key terms and an appendix of sample qualitative proposals for your reference as you embark on (probably) unfamiliar research territory. For practitioners and educators, this text also offers several case examples, perspectives, and activities aimed toward enhancing one's research agenda. For all, the overarching goal is development as a culturally relevant scientist-practitioner conducting qualitative inquiry.

While we believe that qualitative inquiry is by no means a linear process, an aim of this text is to present material that builds upon one another, beginning with foundational material as you consider what your initial research design and process will look like. Then we move into discussions of things you might actually do in qualitative inquiry, the hands-on work with data. As you will hopefully find in this text, we intentionally focus on the foundations of research first and the performance of research second. We wanted to create a text that addresses issues, reflections, and actions throughout the research process; however, this text is by no means a comprehensive model for qualitative inquiry. To this end, we refer you to various readings to supplement your understanding of each chapter. We have attempted to simplify complex constructs and present them in an organized way, and we hope that you will find this helpful.

We use diverse examples of works, as we believe that the research process, shared perspectives, and lessons learned from any one discipline may be readily applied to your project. Part of our choice in including several disciplines—rather than just our own home disciplines—is to highlight the notion that researchers from various backgrounds can learn from one another when addressing a research problem.

We assume that the reader has some basic background knowledge in quantitative research and the scientific method. While we mention quantitative research throughout the text, our intention is not to fully describe the characteristics of this approach.

Now, we will provide an overview of how the text is organized.

# Part I: Foundations of Qualitative Inquiry

The first part of the text offers some of the foundations of qualitative research: key characteristics and uses of qualitative research, research paradigms and traditions, and research ethics. This part introduces the use of clusters for research design considerations (Part II) as well as data collection, management, analysis, and reporting (Parts III and IV).

Chapter 1, "The Qualitative Researcher's Role," outlines four foundational components of the qualitative researcher's role: equity and advocacy, participant voice, researcher reflexivity, and researcher subjectivity. We then introduce the researcher-practitioner-advocate model and discuss how the model can be integrated into various researcher activities. These activities include evaluating clinical and educational practices, building a research agenda, seeking external funding, and developing and managing a research team.

Chapter 2, "Characteristics of Qualitative Research," describes the features and history of qualitative research. We articulate five philosophies of science that inform several qualitative research paradigms to begin building a research orientation: ontology, epistemology, axiology, rhetoric, and methodology. These paradigms include positivism, post-positivism, constructivism, critical research paradigms, and Indigenous research paradigms. General contributions of qualitative research are also presented.

Chapter 3, "Ethics and Qualitative Research," introduces the reader to Western, feminist, and Indigenous influences on research ethics. We then outline some of the major ethical concepts that influence the entire qualitative research process. In addition to metaethical principles that frame ethical decision-making, the concepts of informed consent, confidentiality, multiple relationships, and competence are presented. Finally, additional considerations regarding various design components are outlined.

Chapter 4, "Qualitative Research Traditions," outlines research traditions that help to further shape qualitative design decisions. We present 12 qualitative research traditions across five clusters: case study, grounded theory, phenomenology, heuristic inquiry, consensual qualitative research, life history, narratology, ethnography, ethnomethodology, autoethnography, participatory action research, and community-based participatory research.

# Part II: Qualitative Research Design

With a sense of the value of conducting qualitative inquiry and a primer on research paradigms and traditions, Part II moves forward with some behind-the-scenes aspects of qualitative inquiry. These activities include selecting a topic, entering the field, and establishing trustworthiness. They are considered "behind the scenes" for two reasons:

- They are heavily considered and strategized upon before any data collection occurs.
- They are at the forefront of the researcher's mind throughout data collection and analysis.

To help you understand them more clearly, Part II treats each of these components as separate goals in qualitative inquiry and are therefore discussed in separate chapters. However, these goals and aspects occur interdependently in actual practice. Qualitative researchers are constantly reflecting on the relationship among the three components described in this part, asking themselves:

- How is my research topic affected by the literature as well as the research questions I am using as a lens through which to study that topic?
- How does my topic yield various sampling and fieldwork decisions?
- What role do I and others play in the study as well as topic selection and sampling methods?
- What strategies can I use now as well as plan for maintaining a rigorous research design with valid findings?

Based on the complexity of these ongoing reflections, one can see that qualitative inquiry is an active decision-making process that begins even before the first data collection.

Chapter 5, "Selecting a Topic," addresses using literature and other sources of information to arrive at a general research topic and more specific research questions. In this chapter, we explore four facets of topic selection: research goals, conceptual framework, purpose statement, and research questions. In addition, considerations for selecting a mixed methods approach are offered.

Chapter 6, "Entering the Field," describes the actions involved in launching the study within a physical and/or visual site. In this chapter, we discuss sampling and purposive sampling methods, sample size considerations, as well as steps for selecting, entering, and exiting a site. The role of gatekeepers, stakeholders, and key informants is also discussed.

Chapter 7, "Maximizing Trustworthiness," presents a general discussion of what constitutes qualitative research. We present four positions for establishing rigor and outline several criteria and strategies of trustworthiness.

## Part III: Data Collection and Analysis

The first two parts of the text serve as a backdrop for what we actively do as a qualitative researcher: collecting and analyzing data derived from a sound research design. Although data collection and analysis are presented as separate topics, we emphasize that they should occur simultaneously. Furthermore, neither can occur without proper data management along the way.

Chapter 8, "Observations and Interviewing," presents a description of observations and individual, dyadic, and focus group interviews. Fieldwork activities, observation and interview protocols, the observation continuum, and strategies for engaging successfully in these data collection methods are outlined. Recording, managing, and transcribing interview data are also discussed.

Chapter 9, "Online Media and Other Data Sources," reviews the use of various online media, including social media, blogs and vlogs, and audiovisual media. Other data sources, such as journals and dairies, personal and public documents, genealogy, and archival data, are also presented.

Chapter 10, "Basics of Qualitative Data Management and Analysis," outlines some typical steps of qualitative data analysis, several coding considerations, and qualitative data management strategies. Special attention is given to a key data management strategy used in data collection and analysis: the case display. Qualitative data software is also discussed.

Chapter 11, "Qualitative Data Analysis by Research Tradition," reviews the differences and similarities of data analysis among the research traditions. Five categories of analytic approaches are highlighted: case study, experience and theory formulation, the meaning of symbol and text, cultural expressions of process and experience, and research as a change agent.

## Part IV: The Qualitative Research Proposal and Report

The last part of the text represents the culmination of the work of qualitative researchers: using the qualitative proposal and report as a tool for communicating societal needs as well as advances in local and academic knowledge from clinical and educational disciplines. Building upon the foundations of qualitative research, elements of the qualitative research design, and data collection and analysis, this part provides strategies for communicating the value of the work qualitative researchers do to advance scholarship and community-embedded work.

Chapter 12, "Writing, Presenting, and Funding Qualitative Research," articulates the distinctions of qualitative research writing, with particular attention to writing and presentational components. In addition, the role of grant funding and strategies for effective grant proposals are provided.

Chapter 13, "Qualitative Research and Community and Legislative Action," covers strategies and steps that qualitative researchers can take to engage in community and legislative action. In this chapter, the link between social, legislative, and professional advocacy is demonstrated.

Now, let's begin the adventure of qualitative research. We hope you have a sense of the organization of the text, beginning with foundational elements of qualitative research, traveling through components of qualitative research design and data collection and analysis, and continuing on to data reporting and further advocacy work. We are encouraged that your journey into qualitative research will allow for deeper relationships with your research interests, research participants and communities, research teams and peers, and, most important, yourself. Enjoy the ride!

# Acknowledgments

We thank Kassie Graves at Cognella Academic Publishing for believing in this book, trusting us, and providing us space to shape it. What a wonderful experience and privilege it has been writing this book with you by our side! We are grateful as well to Amy Davis.

We thank our colleagues and students, who inspire us, share their ways of knowing to inform and at times dismantle our own, and remind us of the value of qualitative research in our practice, pedagogy, and scholarship.

Finally, the way we approach qualitative research is largely in response to those marginalized in our communities and the ones we have lost too soon. We are accountable to you in our work and hold your place in this world sacred.

# PART I

# Foundations of Qualitative Inquiry

## CHAPTER 1

# The Qualitative Researcher's Role

---

## CHAPTER PREVIEW

Welcome to the journey of becoming a qualitative researcher! In this chapter, we start to dive into the role you have as a qualitative researcher: connecting your research to practice and advocacy, building a research agenda, seeking external funding to support your work, and developing and managing research teams. We are deeply honored to go on this journey with you step by step as you become a qualitative researcher.

You, as a qualitative researcher, are an integral part of research design decisions as an instrument of the research process itself. As such, we begin this text by describing how you can influence the qualitative research process and outcome. In this chapter, we discuss several aspects to consider as you engage in the role of a qualitative researcher. With a foundational understanding of the qualitative researcher's role, we then discuss using a researcher-practitioner-advocate (RPA) model to frame qualitative research, including its use in building a research agenda, seeking external funding, and developing and managing a research team.

## The Qualitative Researcher's Role

There are four primary components related to your role as a qualitative researcher. These include a commitment to equity and advocacy, the inclusion of participant voice in the research process and report, and attention to researcher reflexivity as well as researcher subjectivity (see Figure 1.1). At the end of this section, review students' perspectives on their role as a qualitative researcher (see Perspectives 1.1).

### Equity and Advocacy

Qualitative research is unique and powerful. We can quickly transform settings in which we work and live in terms of our research activities, and we can be transformed by these settings. Therefore, attention to principles of equity and advocacy are very important.

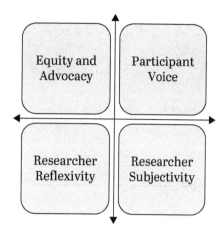

**FIGURE 1.1** The Qualitative Researcher's Role

The World Health Organization (WHO, n.d.) defines **equity** as "the absence of avoidable or remediable differences among groups of people, whether those groups are defined socially, economically, demographically or geographically" (para. 1). Within professional and personal settings, we see inequities existing due to racism, sexism, heterosexism, classism, ableism, xenophobia, linguistic discrimination, and other systems of oppression.

Equity is different from equality. Whereas equality refers to giving all groups the same resources, equity refers to the reality that oppressive systems drive differential access to important resources in society, such as health care and education. Therefore, engaging in equity means we are also engaging in the advocacy necessary to address the gaps in access to important institutional resources. As a qualitative researcher, you have the opportunity to engage in equity and advocacy at every step in your research—from beginning, to middle, and end. For instance, you can ask yourself:

- How does my research topic relate to equity? Who will be included in my sample?
- Who may have difficulty participating in my study and/or may not have been included because of a marginalized identity (e.g., Black, Indigenous, and People of Color [BIPOC], lesbian, gay, bisexual, transgender, and queer individuals [LGBTQ+], those who identify as living with a disability, etc.)?
- What am I learning about myself in terms of my experiences of privilege and oppression as I engage in research?
- How can I connect my research findings to advocacy strategies?
- How can I collaborate with community partners to address issues of equity and advocacy throughout the research process?

We will return to these issues of equity and advocacy throughout this book. There is potential for transformation of ourselves as researchers along with how the phenomena studied are conceptualized. Educators and social scientists interact daily with students, clients, peers, colleagues, and administrators and encounter phenomena that need to be understood in context to guide their work and influence policy. Our professional disciplines thus parallel the purposes of qualitative research quite well: Qualitative inquiry involves remaining flexible to the environment, attending to cultural and equity considerations, understanding another's perspective, building trust and rapport, and relying on techniques that elicit participant meanings and understandings.

------------------------------------------------------------------

## PERSPECTIVES 1.1. RESEARCHER ROLE: STUDENT PERSPECTIVES

Two doctoral students share their thoughts about the importance of thinking intentionally about the role of the qualitative researcher:

> I never realized how important my role as a researcher was until *after* my study was complete. I investigated how students of color from impoverished backgrounds in urban settings were being "lost" in the educational system around late-middle school. I started keeping a reflexive journal because my professor had recommended it. I was hesitant at first, because I had never journaled before and really didn't like the thought of writing long journal entries. Then, I realized I didn't have to write full sentences in the journal. I just wrote words, phrases, and brief thoughts. It wasn't as difficult as I thought it would be, and it worked for me to have paper journal since I was in the schools so much. Unfortunately, I didn't consider the journal as data as much as I thought of it as my own comfort zone as a researcher. I could write anything I wanted in there! After I completed my research, I went back and looked at the journal, and there were several key themes that I could have explored further if I had my research team code my journal. My advice is to keep a reflexive journal and analyze it along the way in your study!
>
> *—educational policy student*

> There are so many things to consider about your role as a researcher in qualitative studies. I studied the experiences of microaggressions by lesbian, gay, and bisexual people. I am straight, so I thought long and hard about why the research was important to me and the reactions people might have to me along the way. I was glad to have a research team of both straight and lesbian women. We were able to check in with one another whenever we had questions, felt lost, or just overwhelmed. It was important for me as a straight person to consistently check in with myself about how I was learning and growing as a person doing this study. I didn't feel like I had anti-gay biases when I started the study, but my research team was able to help me see things that I just couldn't see without them—from LGBT slang to LGBT experiences I just never had been exposed to before as a straight person. I was really motivated to give participants a "voice" after spending so much time with them. I discussed this desire with my team, and they pointed out that I was seeing the participants as more vulnerable and helpless than for who they were. Then, I started peer debriefing after my interviews, and realized my enthusiasm to give them voice made me ask more questions in interviews and not listen as much. I don't know what I would have done without my research team.
>
> *—counseling psychology student*

## Participant Voice

Qualitative researchers approach research with an intention to become immersed and rid themselves of an expert status. They are accepting of and empathic toward individuals, groups, and communities within that context. They listen to accounts of a phenomenon, engaging actively and integrating new perspectives into their own ways of understanding the participants, context, or phenomenon—or all three. Miles et al. (2020) referred to this as *local groundedness*: studying phenomena in context rather than at a distance. Direct, sustained experience with participants in context becomes a critical source of knowledge. The guiding purposes of qualitative research in generating knowledge, then, are description, attention to process, and collaboration within a social structure and with its people.

Hence, a major component of the qualitative researcher's role is to seek to understand the "voice" of the participants in qualitative research. When considering participant voice, you should address issues of accuracy, completeness, and emotional content. In terms of *accuracy*, you will make decisions about the transcription of the actual words of participants. For instance, if there is a section of a transcript that is difficult to understand, it might be important to revisit the participant and ask about this section of the transcript. This is a form of member checking that we will discuss further in Chapter 7. In terms of *completeness*, you must decide how "complete" the voice of your participants is. The issues involved in this determination range from the comfort level of participants in sharing about their experiences to whether enough time is provided to capture participants' sharing on the research phenomenon. Regarding *emotional content*, there are numerous participant experiences of a phenomenon where the emotions expressed are an important aspect of the voice of participants. Because emotional content may be conveyed without words, capturing this content may include observing the emotions, asking specifically about the emotions, and ensuring this content is included in data analysis.

Faithfully representing participant voice will become an important endeavor for you as you engage in qualitative research. You may feel pressure to "get it right" in terms of your interpretation of what your participants share with you. Mazzei and Jackson (2009) edited a book on voice in qualitative research, compiling various views on this topic in the field. Indeed, it is no simple feat to manage the task of representing participant voice.

Beginning in the mid-1980s, the challenges and seeming impossibility of representing participant voice accurately was the dialogue leading to the "crisis of representation" historical period in qualitative research (see Chapter 2). As this dialogue continued, qualitative researchers began to take such approaches as including participants' words from transcribed interviews, even documenting paralinguistic cues (e.g., pauses, silences, starts) as integral elements to an audience understanding participant voice. Documenting in this manner became a focus of ethnomethodology techniques, and the goal was to understand the meanings revealed by language structures. For instance, Garfinkel (1967), who largely influenced the field of ethnomethodology, studied the social and medical transition of a trans woman and the multiple processes in which she engaged to be able to "pass" as a woman in society. The language she used, the pauses in her transcripts, and the inclusions and omissions of words were all identified by Garfinkel to make meaning of her experience. Another example is Freebody's (2001) study of the practical reading practices used in homes and schools through examining reading session transcripts, where the communication patterns and learning process of students with both teachers and parents were the study's focus. Other researchers have responded to the crisis of representation by "recogniz[ing] the dangerous assumptions in trying to represent a single truth (seemingly articulated by a single voice) and have therefore pluralized voice, intending [to] highlight the polyvocal and multiple nature of voice within contexts that are themselves messy and constrained" (Mazzei & Jackson, 2009, p. 1).

Mazzei and Jackson (2009) acknowledge these responses to the crisis of representation. However, the authors also suggest these responses do not address the core problem with seeking to represent participant voice. They seek to interrupt this notion that voice is "there to search for, retrieve, and liberate" (Mazzei & Jackson, 2009, p. 2). Importantly, they assert that even if the raw data of a transcription are provided to an audience, it does not acknowledge the influence of the researcher on that particular piece of participant text or "voice." The authors cite Lather's (2007) encouragement that qualitative researchers do not seek out a simplistic path to the issue of voice but rather seek to "trouble" traditional notions of voice in qualitative inquiry that claim to represent a single and/or accurate voice of participants.

So, how will you address the complex issue of voice in your study? Mazzei (2009) guides the researcher to interact with participant texts in multiple ways, immersing with the text to "relisten" to its voice to identify new ways of understanding. Mazzei (2009) shares a transcript of an interview with a teacher in her study, with probes (included in boldface) that she might have used to understand elements of the participant's voice that were not as evident:

> Anne: I never really saw myself as prejudiced, but then I never really had to deal with any "other people." **[Other people? Who do you mean by other people?]** So I was raised this way and now I've come to a *very, very,* very liberal, *very* open-minded understanding as far as my friends. **[When you say liberal, you mean ...?]** I'm also a single mother, as far as people who I go out on dates with, political views, everything and it's very, *very* conflicting with my parents. **[How is that conflict lived out in your relationship with them?]** (pp. 55–56)

Mazzei's transcript provides a good example of the opportunities to embrace the challenges voice brings to a study in qualitative research. Had she asked the questions in bold brackets as probes, the less evident voice of the teacher would have emerged. We hope this example encourages you to reflect on what your role as a researcher is in portraying the voice of the participants in your study.

In addition to attending to participant voice during qualitative research, presenting that voice in the qualitative report is another consideration. Once you have obtained authentic participant data, you can decide the degree to which verbatim data are presented. For example, some researchers may present participant voice by providing individual narratives for participants. Other researchers may provide several direct participant quotes to more thoroughly describe a theme or code. However, other researchers may limit or avoid use of participant quotes or attention to individual participants yet still provide voice to a phenomenon. Your decision for how to present participant voice may be based on your research tradition, restrictions on page limitations by journal editors, complexity of research topic, and sample size, to name a few considerations.

## Researcher Reflexivity

There are multiple opportunities to deeply self-reflect on who we are and are becoming as qualitative researchers. We enter settings with a set of assumptions about a phenomenon, for instance, and our interactions with others in our research activities continuously require us to consider a new set of assumptions and understandings. **Researcher reflexivity** is defined as the active self-reflection of an investigator on the research process. Because the thoughts and feelings of the researcher, including one's reactions to and interpretations of the data, are part of the research process, reflexivity of the researcher becomes a lens into the research process itself. Therefore, it is not surprising that researcher reflexivity becomes one of the benchmarks for how trustworthy a qualitative research design is for its audience (see Chapter 7). Researcher reflexivity is one of the most challenging concepts to understand and put into action while conducting qualitative inquiry. Therefore, we will discuss the foundations of reflexivity and provide examples as well. Then we ask you to complete Activity 1.1 to identify evidence of researcher reflexivity in a qualitative article in your discipline.

One can turn to the mental health fields for some hints as to how a researcher can more fully grasp the foundations underlying reflexivity. In particular, Carl Rogers, a well-known psychotherapist, inspired the humanistic movement in counseling and psychology with his book *On Becoming a Person* (1961). In this book, Rogers made the case for a new paradigm of psychotherapy and counseling that moved away from one previously focused on behavior change. In this model, the counselor strove to meet three core conditions in their counseling work: authenticity, unconditional positive regard, and empathy. So, you may ask, what does a humanist have to do with qualitative research? Rogers's core conditions provide a guideline—or a "gut check"—for your own use of reflexivity in your research.

Rogers (1961) defined *authenticity* as the congruence between the inner and outer world. As a qualitative researcher, authenticity becomes a mirror through which to interpret data. For instance, if you are conducting a qualitative inquiry of teachers and their thoughts on the educational policy implications of the Every Student Succeeds Act of 2015, it is very likely

**ACTIVITY 1.1.** IDENTIFYING AND UNDERSTANDING RESEARCHER REFLEXIVITY

Select a qualitative journal article and identify the reflexivity of the author(s). Consider the following questions in your review:

1. Is researcher reflexivity explicitly or implicitly shared?
2. How could the researcher(s) be more forthcoming about their reflexivity?
3. Are the author(s) outsider or insider researcher(s)?
4. If you were writing this article, how would you approach researcher reflexivity? In other words, how would you convey your reflexivity to your audience in a similar article?

that you may have strong thoughts and opinions about the act—or at the very least be aware of the debate within education on the benefits and challenges of this legislation. In terms of authenticity, reflexivity would mean identifying your authentic thoughts and feelings about the legislation prior to engaging in the research process.

Rogers (1961) described *unconditional positive regard* as creating a space of acceptance of a client's true thoughts and feelings, without judgment. In terms of reflexivity, unconditional positive regard can assist qualitative researchers in delving deeply into their expectations and convictions about their research topic that may be controversial or previously not acknowledged. An example would be a researcher examining perpetrators of intimate partner violence who in the middle of their study discovers they are developing strong thoughts and feelings of doubt about the rehabilitation of perpetrators. Unconditional positive regard would allow this researcher to welcome these reactions during the research process in addition to being accountable for how this shapes their interpretation of the data.

Finally, Rogers (1961) described *empathy* as the counselor's ability to accurately identify the thoughts and feelings of the client. For the reflexive researcher, empathy generates more meaningful and in-depth reflexivity. Let's say a qualitative researcher is studying teacher-parent interactions in a rural elementary school setting. They begin coding the first interview transcription they conducted with a teacher-parent pair, and they notice they asked leading prompts that were not on the interview protocol. Generating empathy for themselves will provide the road they need to examine the "why" and "how" in regard to leaving the interview protocol. This researcher can use these reflections to anticipate the urge to use leading prompts in their next interviews, as opposed to discovering this impact on the research process later. Although it is certainly true that qualitative research is not counseling, you can use Rogers's core conditions to assist you in becoming a better, more reflexive researcher. See Table 1.1 for an expanded list of questions to guide you in advance of your study, during your study, and after the completion of your study.

**TABLE 1.1**  Using Rogers's Core Conditions in Researcher Reflexivity

| Core condition | Reflexive questions |
| --- | --- |
| Authenticity | What are my thoughts about my research topic? |
|  | How do I feel about my research topic in terms of quality and degree of feeling (positive, negative, neutral)? |
|  | What do I expect to find in the data from my participants? |
|  | How will these expectations shape how I interpret the data? |
| Unconditional positive regard | Are there reactions I have about my topic area and/or what I am discovering about my participants that are surprising me? |
|  | What judgments do I have about my participants and/or topic area? |
| Empathy | Are there reactions I am having to my study that I am not identifying or not wanting to accept or acknowledge? |
|  | How am I "seeing" the data in my study in ways that are either aligned or not aligned with what participants actually said in their own words? |

Because the concept of reflexivity is complex, Hellawell (2006) wrote about a heuristic device he uses with graduate students beginning qualitative studies to assist them in thinking about their role as a reflexive researcher. When mentoring students in qualitative designs, Hellawell first describes the notions of "insider" and "outsider" research to stimulate students to consider what position they may have. He cites Merton's (1972) definition of **insider research**: research where the investigator is not necessarily part of an organization and/or the phenomenon of inquiry but rather has knowledge of the organization and/or phenomenon prior to the study's commencement. He then describes **outsider research** as studies where the investigator has no prior intimate experience with the participants or topic area of interest. Hellawell (2006) then asks the following five heuristic questions of students regarding their qualitative studies:

1. How many of you consider you're doing insider research?
2. How many of you think you're doing outsider research?
3. How many think you're doing both?
4. How many think you're doing neither insider nor outsider research?
5. How many of you simply don't know where your research fits into this debate? (p. 488)

Interestingly, Hellawell (2006) notes that students often respond that they fit into the second option listed above: They identify as outsider researchers. He then provides an example of graduate students in education who believe they are outsider researchers because they are examining school settings of which they are not a part. He challenges these students to consider whether they are truly outside of those educational organizations by asking the following question: "Would you not be much more of an outsider were you to be researching into the perceptions of, for example, workers on a car assembly track in the motor manufacturing industry?" (Hellawell, 2006, p. 489). Locating your position as a researcher as an insider or outsider is an important task to develop skills as a reflexive investigator.

While Hellawell (2006) encourages students to identify their location as a qualitative researcher, Fawcett and Hearn (2004) insist that investigators must think of the concepts of "insider" and "outsider" not merely in terms of organizations and phenomena but also in terms of the researcher's social locations (e.g., gender, race/ethnicity, disability, etc.). The authors ask, "Can men research women, white people, people of color, or visa versa?" (Fawcett & Hearn, 2004, p. 201). These questions demand a discussion of the "otherness" of participants and the role of the researcher in relation to participants and identify four types of **otherness** that interact with one another: epistemological otherness, societal otherness, practical otherness, and local otherness. *Epistemological otherness* and *practical otherness* refer to the distance between the researcher and the participant within the research context, whereas *societal otherness* and *local otherness* refer to the social context that privileges or diminishes people—researchers and participants alike—in terms of social power. Fawcett and Hearn suggest that otherness does not eradicate understanding or potentiality of examining a phenomenon in a faithful manner. Rather, they argue that "it is how the research project is conducted, how the participants are involved, how attention is paid to ethical issues, and the extent of critical reflexivity, that have to be regarded as key factors ... [and] need to be subject to ongoing critical appraisal at each stage of the research" (Fawcett & Hearn, 2004, p. 216). They provide the following suggestions for addressing issues of otherness in qualitative research:

- consideration of historical and sociopolitical context
- researcher self-reflexivity
- awareness of social locations of researcher, participants, and phenomenon of inquiry
- attention to how knowledge is socially constructed
- alignment with empirical inquiry while refraining from asserting or speculating about participants or the phenomenon of inquiry (Fawcett & Hearn, 2004, p. 418)

## Researcher Subjectivity

While reflexivity in qualitative designs assists the qualitative researcher in self-reflection on the research process, the concept of subjectivity is just as important. **Subjectivity** is defined as the internal understandings of the qualitative researcher of the phenomenon they are studying (Schneider, 1999). Subjectivity, like reflexivity, is an important concept that distinguishes qualitative research from quantitative research. While quantitative studies discuss issues of validity and controlling variables, qualitative researchers discuss researcher subjectivity as a factor to either minimize or embrace. Qualitative researchers seeking to minimize subjectivity in their studies tend to advocate, for example, that data from participants be analyzed only based on the transcribed text from their interviews or other data sources. More recent trends in qualitative research have criticized this approach (Denzin & Lincoln, 2011), asserting that attempting to minimize subjectivity aligns qualitative approaches too closely with quantitative paradigms of "objective" science. Instead, they advocate for researchers to view their subjectivity as an indication of being closer to their study. Subjectivity then becomes a way to understand the phenomenon more intimately, and one can embrace this connection rather than keeping one's distance from the topic.

Peshkin (1988) used the phrase **virtuous subjectivity** to convey the idea that researcher subjectivity should be embraced. He discussed the importance of both individual and multiple subjectivities involved in qualitative research. Peshkin discloses his own subjectivity as well. Peshkin, a self-identified Jewish man with a liberal political perspective, conducted research on a high school community founded in fundamentalist Christian values. Acknowledging his subjectivity, Peshkin struggled with the tension between his values and the values espoused by his subject matter. He ultimately reasoned he was able to write a more nuanced account of his subject matter because he experienced this tension and struggle, acknowledged its impact on the research, and sought to share with his audience how his subjectivity influenced his interpretation of his topic. Yet Peshkin also acknowledged that a researcher with different values—say a fundamentalist Christian—would have produced a very different data set and interpretation of the same topic area. He believes this perspective would be just as valid as his own study's findings. It becomes clear to see, then, that a researcher's subjectivity paves the road for a study's outcome. This is even more reason to see subjectivity in qualitative inquiry as virtuous, not something to be overamplified or even overindulged, but rather as a critical role of the researcher that becomes the framework for a study's process.

Discussion surrounding the role of subjectivity in the research process intensified within the qualitative research field in the mid-1980s during the crisis of representation historical period (see Chapter 2). Particularly, the field began to explore the opportunities, limits, and challenges that exist when researchers seek to understand the lived experiences of participants. Because of the subjective nature of truth, how could researchers ever accurately portray the lives of their participants? In terms of accuracy, was this even a realistic goal for qualitative inquiry? If the accurate portrayal of participants was not a realistic goal, then what was the goal of qualitative designs? These questions undergirded the crisis of representation, demanding that researchers acknowledge their inability to ever truly document the participants' lived experiences of a phenomenon. In doing so, the complexity of qualitative research was deepened, and the discussion of this crisis continues to this day.

Being aware of the crisis of representation provides the opportunity for the student researcher to learn the inseparability of researcher and participant. Remembering this inseparability, researchers can search for ways to more faithfully represent their participants as experts in the phenomenon of inquiry. Morrow (2005) explained that taking the stand of naïve inquirer is "particularly important when the interviewer is an 'insider' with respect to the culture being investigated or when she or he is very familiar with the phenomenon of inquiry" (p. 254). Another strategy she identified as being important is to conduct participant checks, where the researcher shares their interpretations and findings with participants to gauge how aligned they are with the participants' lived experiences. The strategies of being a naïve inquirer and proactively engaging in participant checks both build the trustworthiness of a qualitative study (termed "validity and reliability" in quantitative research). Table 1.2 provides strategies for addressing researcher subjectivity. In Chapter 7, we expand discussion of these strategies when we discuss approaches to maximizing trustworthiness. For now, it is important that you understand that the need to establish trustworthiness emerges from the role concepts such as reflexivity and subjectivity play in qualitative research and the tension surrounding these concepts.

## Top 10 Strategies for Facilitating the Qualitative Researcher's Role

In this first section of this introductory chapter, we have outlined four components of the qualitative researcher's role. As we conclude this section, we present common pitfalls related to the qualitative researcher's role (see Wild Card 1.1) along with an opportunity to consider how your role as a qualitative researcher may include a study you are considering conducting (see Proposal Development Activity 1.1). First, we provide a top 10 list of tips

**TABLE 1.2**   Strategies to Address Researcher Subjectivity in Qualitative Research

- Take up issues of equity and advocacy at the start of your research subjectivity reflections to ensure you are "facing complex social problems fearlessly" (Staller, 2019, p. 194).
- Reflect on your culture and ask, "What values and beliefs do I bring from my cultural background that will shape how I engage in my study?"
- Approach your study by leading with your curiosity rather than with your "expertise" as a researcher. This entails asking questions, questioning your assumptions about your study, and even developing rival hypotheses that might counteract your previous analyses.
- Use participant checks throughout your study to determine the alignment of your interpretation of the meaning of the data with your participants' lived experiences of the phenomenon of inquiry.
- Have experts in the field of your phenomenon of inquiry review your findings and provide feedback on how your findings relate to findings of other similar studies.
- Build a research team to conduct data analysis and come to consensus on their interpretation of the findings.
- Triangulate data collection techniques and other research processes to build trustworthiness.
- Use a discussant or peer debriefer during the data collection and analysis process. You may consider adding a peer who has does not have an investment in the process or outcome of the study.
- Actively counteract groupthink and acknowledge research team member "roles" in the study. With any group, there is bound to be some version of groupthink that emerges. Stay on top of this by having healthy dialogues and debates, endeavoring to have divergent views of the data explored and analyzed. Also, are all the voices of your research team contributing to the analysis, or are some heard or valued more than others? Seek to value every team member's contribution in a consistent manner.
- "Wave the red flag," or note any time you and/or your coresearchers—and even your participants—use words such as "never" or "always" and questioning these instances. In addition, explore the instance where the word "sometimes" is used, as it is typically a rich information source of participants' experiences.
- Consider checking in with your participants during the data collection and analysis in order to ensure research interpretations are consistent with participants' interpretations and understandings of their own data.

Sources: Bhattacharya (2017), Corbin and Strauss (2015), Drapeau (2002), Lincoln and Guba (1995), Morrow (2005), and Staller (2018)

for addressing your role as a qualitative researcher, including examples to illustrate the strategies (Ahern, 1999):

1.  Identify some of the personal and professional issues that you might take for granted in undertaking this research (e.g., gaining access, cultural variables, power): For instance, if you have never worked with children before and your study involves middle school students, you will need to take some time to reflect on how your lack of experience will affect your interactions. You may also have differences with your participants in terms of race/ethnicity, gender, educational attainment, sexual orientation, socioeconomic

**WILD CARD 1.1.** PITFALLS TO AVOID IN YOUR QUALITATIVE RESEARCHER ROLE

There are multiple important considerations regarding your researcher role in qualitative studies! Review the following list to ensure you are paying close attention to how your role can influence your study:

- Understand, reflect, and be able to articulate how you will build reflexivity into your study.
- Do not assume a reflexive journal will provide adequate attention to reflexivity in your study. Incorporate peer debriefing pairs and/or groups throughout your study.
- Address subjectivity in your research. From the researcher-as-instrument perspective, how are you influencing the research process?
- Consider how your position as a researcher falls along the insider–outsider continuum. Do not assume you are an outsider researcher just because you are not involved in a certain organization or topic of inquiry.
- Make sure to address contextual factors and social locations of privilege and oppression as you seek to understand the relationships between yourself and your participants.
- Do not assume you as the researcher are "giving voice" to participants. Understand the problematic notions of this assumption and seek to interrupt any tendency you or your research team members have to view participants in this light.
- Plan ahead to use peer debriefing in your study and be open to the opportunities that arise along the research process to further incorporate peer debriefing sessions in your study.
- Do not use peer debriefing without documenting how the sessions influenced the process of your research.
- If it is feasible for you to build a research team and you select to work with a research team, do not take the task of building a research team lightly. Put considerable thought into your working style in groups, the role of team members, and the length and frequency of your team meetings. If you are conducting qualitative research without a team, have a strong rationale as to how and why this is important, in addition to addressing your researcher reflexivity and subjectivity.

status, disability status, and so on. These differences influence who we are personally and professionally. Note how it will influence your interaction with your study.

2. Clarify your personal value systems and acknowledge areas in which you know you are subjective: One might argue that values and subjectivity are involved in everything we do as researchers—from the data we collect to how we approach analysis and write up our studies. Related to our discussion in Number 1 above, how do these variables influence the lens you use to view your study?

**PROPOSAL DEVELOPMENT ACTIVITY 1.1.** YOUR ROLE AS A QUALITATIVE RESEARCHER

Write 1–2 paragraphs discussing your role as a researcher in your study. Answer the following questions in your discussion:

1. To what extent do you see your role as a researcher attending to equity and advocacy? What would that look like?
2. What are your thoughts, feelings, and expectations about your topic? To what extent do you think these will change throughout the research process? How?
3. What are your perspectives on reflexivity, subjectivity, and voice in your topic area?
4. What have been the perspectives of previous researchers on your topic in terms of reflexivity, subjectivity, and voice?
5. To what degree will your presence, interests, and motivations for conducting a study in your area of interest play out in your role as a researcher?

3. Describe possible areas of possible role conflict: There may be times your role as a researcher intersects with your study. In one qualitative study I (Anneliese) conducted on LGBTQ+ bullying, one of the students selected for the study by the school counselor was the child of a close neighbor. You may have conflicts that are more serious than this example. Regardless, you should be aware of these and describe them to others.

4. Identify gatekeepers' interests and consider the extent to which they are disposed to be favorable toward the project: An example of this might be a case study of a rural mental health center where they may have limited resources and/or high investment in being understood and/or portrayed in a certain light. This can influence your study's findings.

5. Recognize thoughts and feelings that could obscure your ability to listen and really hear what participants are sharing: It is more than likely that you will be moved by what participants share with you during your research. You should not feign objectivity or neutrality but you should also not give over to letting your study be driven only by your emotions.

6. Is anything new or surprising in your data collection and analysis? Research can and should be about discovery! What are the aspects of your study that are unexpected, that you did not account for, and possibly that you cannot describe? These aspects will ultimately enrich your study.

7. When blocks occur in the research process, reframe them: How could your methods change and be viewed as an opportunity? Obstacles can and will arise during research. Make sure your decisions about how to address them are guided by the spirit of your research tradition. If you are unable to conduct a focus group due to difficulty recruiting participants, how might your research tradition in tandem with your research question guide you to find another source of data collection? So much of getting unstuck involves getting grounded in your overall conceptualization of your study topic, including

previous literature related to your topic, theory, and research tradition (see Chapter 5). You might examine secondary data collection methods that we discuss in Chapter 9.

8. Even when you have completed your analysis, reflect on how to write up your account: You have spent time and energy in the data collection and analysis process. Use the same care and attention in representing this research process in your final description of the study's participants.

9. Consider whether the supporting evidence in the literature is really supporting your analysis or is just expressing the same cultural background as yourself: This really translates into challenging yourself along the road of your research study. Revisit the literature in your discipline often. Ask yourself if you are resonating with or not connecting with various aspects of this literature and consider how this may affect your study.

10. Counteract analytic neutrality: Asking the question of how you as a researcher may be either masking or avoiding addressing an aspect of your data collection and analysis is the process of counteracting analytic neutrality. Overall, good reflexivity assumes there will be masked aspects of your study of which you are not aware. Your job as a researcher then becomes to develop a plan to actively address these areas. For instance, in a qualitative study of how families interact with school personnel in after-school programs, you could plan to actively generate questions as a researcher about how you are defining what a "family" is throughout the research process.

## Researcher-Practitioner-Advocate Model

Often when we engage in qualitative research, we face challenges of what might seem like the competing roles of researcher, practitioner, and advocate. We call this the **researcher-practitioner-advocate (RPA) model**. The advocate role in this model is a more newly articulated one. However, scholars such as Fryer who titled her 2004 article "Researcher-Practitioner: An Unholy Marriage?" have explored the advantages and challenges of the interplay between research and practice. It is indeed true that as individuals, we may feel more aligned, competent, comfortable, and prepared to take on one of these two roles over the other. At the same time, however, how can one truly "backseat" one role over the other when in both counseling and educational settings we have training in both roles? In addition, because of the pervasive and persistent educational and clinical inequities that exist in society, we must also address the interplay of research, practice, and advocate identities. Therefore, although you may be naturally drawn to one of the three roles more than the others, we encourage you to engage in all three roles as you conduct qualitative research.

Finding a balance among the three roles of researcher, practitioner, and advocate is important. Elliott (2003) explored the space between researcher and practitioner and found ways to strike this balance. She discussed drawing from her wisdom gained as a practitioner and the authority she gained as a new academic to find this balance. Elliott resolved to not "remove" herself within her researcher role, seeking to understand the emotions of her participants while also using her wisdom as a practitioner to build trusting, ethical relationships with them. She also described the value of being present with both herself and her participants as a helpful tool with which to maintain that balance between the voice of the practitioner who is immersed in their settings and the voice of the researcher whose role may include a variety of aims (to understand, interrogate, challenge, support, etc.). You can note that one cannot realistically build ethical relationships with participants as a researcher and practitioner if there is little attention to the advocacy voice needed to contextualize and understand the experiences of participants.

There are ethical issues with respect to managing this balance among the three roles (discussed further in Chapter 3). From a nursing perspective, Arber (2006) discussed how she leveraged her role as a practitioner to help illuminate for the participants and the audience of her study that she had a familiarity with the context of medical care in which her participants (nurses and patients) were situated. On the one hand, her credibility as a researcher was enhanced because of her practitioner background. At the same time, a significant ethical challenge was maintaining boundaries in terms of where the role of researcher and practitioner began and ended. In both counseling and educational settings, we are working with people. We hold some knowledge about what may or may not be helpful in terms of their needs, in addition to standards and competencies in the field. Much of our own qualitative research has been with girls, women, BIPOC, and LGBTQ+ survivors of trauma. As we seek to further understand the experiences of participants, we are naturally also tapping into both our innate and acquired skills as practitioners that could (and do) pull us out of that researcher role; however, we were also collaborating with community members to ensure we are using our findings to advocate for changes in educational and clinical inequities for these groups. Our advocate role has also been present in ensuring we are addressing how systems of oppression have impacted the foci of our studies.

Adherence to the RPA model as a qualitative researcher is integral to fostering professional identity and ethical integrity. We use the American Educational Research Association's (AERA, 2011) ethical principles as an example to illustrate the alignment of the RPA model with ethical practice:

- *professional competence:* We operate within our professional competence as qualitative researchers, knowing our limitations and always operating for the benefit of our clients, students, and research participants. We continuously ask ourselves, "How am I centering the margins?" (hooks, 2003) in participant criteria and sampling and considering how advocacy can be linked to our ultimate findings as we engage in research and keep in mind our clinical and professional bounds.
- *integrity:* We live our value of integrity throughout all of our research activities, increasing the trust our clients, students, and research participants have in us, and avoid any activity that might jeopardize our clients, students, and research participants. We understand that the SPA model is not words listed on a page but rather roles we bring to life throughout every stage of our research activities.
- *professional, scientific, and scholarly responsibility:* We strive to meet the highest standards we can in qualitative inquiry as an additional way to increase trust with our clients, students, and research participants, and we are continuously responsible for our behavior

and avoid unethical conduct with our clients, students, and research participants. Along the way, we are prepared and ready to address any advocacy needs our participants may have (e.g., referral to needed resources).

- *respect for people's rights, dignity, and diversity:* We understand our clients, students, and research participants bring a wide range of multiple identities and experiences of interlocking advantages and disadvantages. So we avoid bias and discrimination in our research activities while also respecting the rights of our clients, students, and research participants to make decisions about their participation while we treat them with the utmost respect, dignity, and value. We know that when participants interact with us, we represent a collection of advantages and disadvantages based on our privilege and oppression experiences. We seek to share power and build authentic interactions with participants.
- *social responsibility:* We strive as qualitative researchers to enact social responsibility by sharing the data we gathered with our clients, students, and research participants to public and other settings where this information can be used to improve science, practice, advocacy, and the intermingling of each of these.

In the next few sections, we show how the RPA model can be applied to evaluating professional practices, building a research agenda, and developing and managing a research team.

## Evaluating Professional Practices

**Evaluation** is a term that refers to many activities. We often want to learn what the lived experience is of a clinical intervention, educational strategy, or social practice, so we may evaluate a program in various settings to understand a phenomenon. For instance, as we engage in antiracism work in our fields, we can use focus groups to explore the experiences of systemic racism for BIPOC and also conduct focus groups with White antiracist leaders to learn what the common strategies are for interrupting systemic racism in a particular practice setting. Evaluation is also a specific action embedded in all qualitative research. As qualitative researchers, we are continuously evaluating—or analyzing—data from our participants (e.g., interviews) and data from ourselves (e.g., reflexive journal). Throughout these evaluative activities, we are connected with our practitioner identities in order to contextualize the research in which we are engaged. As advocates, we notice the times in evaluation where we must pause and address an issue of inequity for a participant (e.g., a participant does not have money for transportation to participate in a study) and/or advocacy on a larger issue of inequity that arises during the study (e.g., we notice that there is not a gender-neutral bathroom in the setting where our clinical or educational research occurs that makes it less equitable for trans and nonbinary participants, so we bring this to the attention of relevant leaders who can make changes). These continuous evaluative processes in qualitative research are intricately linked to the power of research to not only learn about specific phenomena in practice settings but also leverage these understandings to enact rapid and powerful change in our activities—especially when linked to a clear research agenda, which we talk about more in the next section.

# Building a Research Agenda

Right from the start, we want to trouble the idea of who can and cannot build a research agenda. Sure, there are some important realities to acknowledge. We might think of research agendas as the domain of educators and scholars. We understand why this happens. Practitioners may not have enough time, energy, and support necessary to take their important research to the publication stage. However, some of the most transformational research conducted is led by practitioners, and when we do not get to see this research in published form we are losing out on important knowledge that has the potential to significantly impact our everyday practice settings. We see this as a social justice issue in our settings. So, whether you are a clinician or educator, we want to invite you to consider that building a research agenda is intricately linked to practice (Moore-Lobban et al., 2021). As a reminder, our role as an advocate is continuous throughout our research activities, so we ask ourselves consistently, "How is our research agenda linked to advocacy on relevant societal inequities?"

The generation of research is both an inductive and deductive process. Inductively, one may gather and explore data and generate a theory based on these data. Deductively, one may begin with an established theory and then seek to understand data through this lens. Qualitative research is primarily an inductive process. Building a research agenda, however, can be a deductive or inductive process (or both). Regardless, we encourage you to consider the larger context within which your qualitative study is conducted. Qualitative work, at its heart, is quite an intimate act. Participants share the salience of their lived experiences with us as researchers. Therefore, we believe it is important to generate knowledge (i.e., publish!) in order to honor the time and energy of participants as well as to be in line with the ethics standards of research within education and counseling settings.

A good place to begin in building a research agenda is to think about why you have engaged in the research process in the first place. What phenomenon are you seeking to understand? How possible is it to study this phenomenon? What relevance does this phenomenon hold for you personally? What has the literature in your field established (or not established) about this phenomenon? Your research agenda can be more of a deductive one or an inductive one—or have both approaches to generating knowledge. For example, you may be beginning with a theory of resilience and seeking to apply that theory to students or clients (deductive). Or you may begin to collect some data with these same students or clients and from this data generate hypotheses and theories (inductive). Your research agenda can also seek to be a combination of inductive and deductive processes.

Regardless, a large component of establishing a research agenda is thinking ahead of where you are now as a researcher. For instance, where do you see your research going in 1 year, 5 years, or more? And we are not just saying this for those who want to be faculty or work in another research institution. Keeping the values of the researcher-practitioner in mind, for those of you who are interested in careers in practice, it is also important to think ahead in terms of how you will build a research agenda that informs your practice. Within both research and practice settings, a research agenda should not be rigid. Rather, your research agenda should make room for "surprise" turns in focus. If you stringently stay on one path of a research agenda, then your practice and your research becomes in danger of becoming stale. A strong research agenda allows for and welcomes creativity and new lines of inquiry. This creativity should not translate into a scattered focus, however. A simple test for whether you have a solid focus in your research agenda is whether you can describe your research agenda in a short "elevator speech." In this elevator speech, how do you articulate important issues of equity and advocacy?

Once you start down the road of research, stop along the way to reflect on your research agenda. What has gone well in your research agenda? What might have gone better, or what might you want to shift? Who are the people who have most influenced your research agenda? Are there researchers in the field you would like to talk with in order to clarify a component of your research agenda or even with whom you might collaborate? What are the best next steps, considering what your findings have been so far? Taking time to consider the answers to these questions ultimately will help you strengthen your research agenda and become a more effective researcher-practitioner. In Perspectives 1.2, we discuss how we have established a research agenda, developed a publication record, and reflected on the next steps of our research process.

## PERSPECTIVES 1.2. BUILDING A RESEARCH AGENDA: AUTHORS' PERSPECTIVES

It's funny looking back at my earlier qualitative work now. I was so excited about qualitative inquiry and its potential for social change that I did not really stop to think about establishing a research agenda. I had been a community organizer for so long, and the practitioner role in my approach to investigating phenomena was more salient than the researcher role. I also was thinking I would be a practitioner and had no idea I would eventually work as a faculty member. As a student, I found myself getting more and more involved in qualitative research due to my interest in historically marginalized groups. I also had training as a traumatologist. I knew from the moment I engaged with participants that I would commit to publish the findings they share with me because I felt an ethical responsibility to do so. I also had some clear advocacy goals developed in collaboration with the communities I partnered with in various studies (e.g., moving from a deficit model of service provision with trans and nonbinary communities to a strength-based and liberatory model of mental health services with trans and nonbinary people). Once I understood the ins and outs of publishing, things like cover letters, revisions of manuscript, and understanding how to find a good outlet for my work became like second nature to me. Reflecting on my research agenda, it is interesting how there is a strong theme throughout all of my work. The "elevator speech" about my research agenda goes something like this: I investigate the resilience and coping of historically marginalized communities, with a specific interest in BIPOC and LGBTQ+ communities. I didn't much plan for this line of inquiry, although looking back I wish I had thought more about the specific steps of building a research agenda. There are certainly areas of inquiry I might have pursued further or avoided altogether.

—A. A. S.

I second Anneliese's reflection that a research agenda was developed over time; through a process of doing research it became clearer. As a graduate student my interest in social justice issues in counselor preparation was most salient. Specifically, I conducted studies on how trainees and new professionals thought about their cultural privilege and oppression. Back then, it didn't feel like "enough" to just ask about their conceptualization of social justice issues. However, I couldn't figure out how to make the research I was doing feel more comprehensive. Then, my clinical experience in a psychiatric hospital and addictions agency really tuned me into assessing and labeling clients with mental and substance abuse disorders, and how much the assessment and diagnosis process influenced client treatment and outcome. In my clinical work and training I was also exposed to traumatology and its prevention and treatment, and I developed an interest in domestic violence. Over the years with each new clinical, academic, and/or research experience I reflected on my evolving research agenda that included these three interest areas: privilege and oppression, assessment and diagnosis, and domestic violence. Over time, my research agenda both expanded and integrated these areas and became more directly applicable to the clients and students with which I work. In addition, I have used my scholarship to advocate for domestic violence survivors as well as those at risk for dating violence on college campuses. While it is still evolving, I see the work I do having some direct impact, confirming for me even more the value of qualitative research.

—D. G. H.

## Seeking External Funding

If it feels a little overwhelming to begin thinking about building a research agenda and qualitative inquiry as a core research competency—especially when you may just be beginning your journey as a researcher-practitioner-advocate—get ready to think about money! Money is an important consideration in qualitative research. Of course, we are talking about external funding for your qualitative research projects. We have found that early investigators spend most of their time learning how to engage in research design and related data collection and analysis activities, but that funding is an afterthought.

We understand why external funding is something we do not commonly bring front and center early in our research design. Those of us who undertake qualitative research often fund this research out of our own pockets and do not account for the time it takes to engage in qualitative research for our participants and ourselves. Some of the neglect we have in addressing issues of funding in our research comes right back to the relationship we may already have with money in our personal lives. Take a moment to think about these quick questions:

- What is your relationship with money?
- Is this relationship positive, negative, or somewhere in between (neutral)?
- Who or what in your life influenced this relationship with money?
- How do each of your answers to the above relate to issues of equity and advocacy?

We have a feeling you are having some "aha" moments after answering these questions. We also have a feeling that unless you were raised in a family and community where you did not have to worry about financial resources, that you may have a complicated relationship with money. We encourage you to continue digging into this relationship. Your mentors and your discipline likely have many sources of external funding. However, we have found as mentors that our mentees are more likely to submit applications for these pots of money when they have self-efficacy (i.e., "I can do this!") and not only know that they are worthy of applying but also know the "hows" of applying. We will talk more about external funding in Chapter 12.

## Developing and Managing a Research Team

Your decision of whether or not to use a research team is less a function of your researcher role than of the focus, goals, and needs of your research. However, we wanted to discuss the use of research teams in this chapter, exploring the researcher's role, because we see the decision you will make regarding the use of research teams as being closely related to your role as a researcher. For instance, if you decide that your qualitative study of how long-term couples manage conflict in their relationships requires multiple members of a research team in order to make the data collection feasible over a short period of time, the needs of your research should drive you to build a research team. Once you make that decision to have a research team, then there are additional decisions you make in your role as a researcher, such as whether the research team solely collects data or meets regularly throughout the research process. With the RPA model, you also may have some important considerations about how practice and advocacy will (and should) influence the selection of research team members. Activity 1.2 provides an opportunity for reflection as you build a research team.

**ACTIVITY 1.2.** BUILDING YOUR RESEARCH TEAM

Identify peers and/or colleagues who will be involved in your study and discuss the following with them:

1. What do you and your research team members see as their potential role and influence in the study?
2. To what degree do you and your research team members see themselves being involved in data collection and analysis?
3. How will you and your research team members address the four components of the qualitative researcher's role (i.e., equity and advocacy, participant voice, researcher reflexivity, researcher subjectivity)?
4. How often and for how long will your research team meet?

It can also seem like a luxury to think about building a research team for your qualitative study. However, you may also decide that, based on the focus, goals, and needs for your study, it will be beneficial to take the time, energy, and resources needed to build a research team. We want to note that a research team is not a prerequisite to strengthening the trustworthiness of your study; however, when it makes sense for your study and you decide to use a research team, it has the potential to become an additional method of trustworthiness for your study (as we will discuss further in Chapter 7). For instance, a research team may be necessary to manage the amount of data generated by a qualitative study. Research teams are also a good strategy to address issues such as researcher reflexivity and subjectivity during your study. Using research teams—also referred to as "triangulation of investigators" (also discussed in Chapter 7)—is thus an important component of establishing rigor in qualitative research.

There also may be instances where you would like to use a research team but are unable to build one or accomplish each of the steps in organizing a research team (see below). In these situations, you can adapt your approach to data collection and analysis accordingly. One example of such a situation is a study I (Anneliese) worked on where a colleague had expedited IRB approval and the opportunity to collect data about the sexual orientation identity development of trans men at a U.S. conference. My colleague collected the data in a 1-day period by individually interviewing nine participants. However, he solicited the help of another colleague and myself (who had expertise in trans research and qualitative designs) to analyze the data as peer debriefers. In another situation, you might not have the luxury of having another set of eyes on your data collection and analysis so you are unable to build a research team. However, there might be a way to involve others to help you with specific aspects of the project. Often, we find students are willing to support one another in swapping data analysis duties with one another's projects.

Remember that using a research team should be a decision based on the study's context and purpose, and your decision in this regard does not determine whether or not your research is "good." For some areas of inquiry, there simple may not be the need for a research team. An example would be if you were conducting an autoethnography of your own experiences as a person going through a divorce. For other researchers who are working outside of academic settings or in academic/community collaborations, there may be decisions made about the people involved in the research that most closely match the study's goal. An example might be a grant-funded study of Native American families and their children's experiences in middle school. If the requirements of the grant or the access to participants would be best facilitated by the primary researcher who also shares the same tribal heritage as the participants, then a research team may not be needed for this study. Perspectives 1.3 provides one testimony regarding the decision to use a research team.

## Research Team Steps

Developing and managing a research team to maximize its success involves several interdependent steps (see Figure 1.2). Although we present these steps linearly, you may have to cycle through previous steps as issues arise in the research process.

## PERSPECTIVES 1.3. HIV/AIDS RESEARCH AND WORKING ON A RESEARCH TEAM

A lot of times when I am doing formative research—conducting focus groups and key informant interviews and doing literature reviews—for my studies in HIV/AIDS, I definitely want to work with a research team. We have about five of us that work together, and we are a mix of qualitative and quantitative researchers. I think one of our strengths is that we come from a variety of backgrounds when researching HIV/AIDS. We have folks with backgrounds in social work, public health, and even business! Some of us have worked in the HIV/AIDS community, and others really have never been out of academia and worked "on the ground." The variety of these perspectives on the research team is invaluable. There are so many contextual factors influencing risky behaviors that lead to HIV/AIDS infections, and it is important to not treat individuals like they. We have quantitative researchers who look at the numbers and run mathematical models we need to look at behaviors that can be measured, and then our qualitative designs allow us to examine the contextual factors that you could never measure. We need that mixed method approach in our line of inquiry. The most important part of working on a research team is taking your own agenda and ego out of it: It's not about you. Your expertise is valuable. But realizing that you are just one person on the team is important too—that helps create the space for as many quality perspectives and direction for the research. A challenge in working on research teams is to really keep your goal in mind, or those different perspectives can have you heading off in a scatter-brained way—or worse head in the direction of only one person's perspectives on the team. One more thing: Be open. Be open to learning new things. That's the best part of being on a research team.

—*Mac McKleroy*

We believe a good first step to building your research team is to self-reflect on group dynamics (i.e., how groups function as a unit). These dynamics should also include special attention to equity and advocacy. Each of your team members will certainly bring different cultures to a research team (Bhatttacharya, 2017), but you each will also bring different identities and

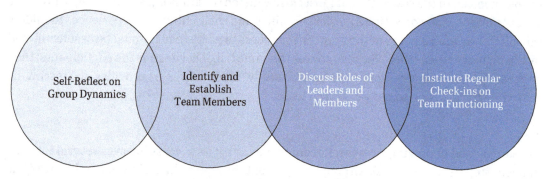

**FIGURE 1.2** Developing and Managing Your Research Team

experiences related to privilege and oppression that are important to explore to ensure you are building an equitable team that can function with equity and advocacy at its core. It can be important to reflect on how you have functioned in groups in the past since a research team is a group of people with different personalities and perspectives. For example, if you have had negative experiences in group projects, what have been the typical issues? Have you typically been a leader or a follower when you have worked in groups? Does the idea of participating in a group project (e.g., in a class) excite you because of the multiple perspectives and shared workload, or does the prospect bring up concerns about who will get "stuck" doing most of the work? Have you had predominately negative experiences in groups, or have your group experiences been mostly positive? Your answers to these questions can provide key insights as to what you may want to do in the process of building your research team. We provide these questions not to prescribe what your answers should be but rather to support you in developing your awareness of how you work in groups and to help anticipate what it will be like to work within a group for a potentially significant period. Additionally, theories of group dynamics remind us there are discrete and predictable stages of how a working group functions together (Gladding, 2020). So your self-reflection on group dynamics should also include how you see your research team forming, working, and ending the study.

A second step in building your research team is a concrete one: Identify and establish team members for your study. There are several strategies you can consider in this step. Ideally, your research team members will be interested in your study, understand the important link to equity and advocacy of your study, able to meet in person during the research process, and able to participate in the study through its completion. However, you may only be able to realistically identify research team members who fit a few of these important categories. When identifying potential team members, as a student, think about who is in your cohort and/or research network who would be a good fit for your study. In these situations, there may be a way you can collaborate. For example, a fellow student in your cohort may be on your research team, and you can offer to be a team member on their study in exchange. Another strategy could be talking with your research mentor or advisor: Would your mentor be willing to be a team member? Also, are there people who share interest in your study area who would make sense to invite into your study? These people may or may not be located in the same city as you. If the person is not in your same city, how will you manage the distance factor in the research process? Finally, you will want to think about how many team members you would like to have. While there is not a set or ideal number of people on a qualitative research team, it is important to consider how many people would make sense, considering the scope and needs of your topic of inquiry. In our experience, research teams average between two and five people in order to conduct the necessary steps of a study.

Once you have identified and established your research team, a third step is to discuss the roles of leaders and members within a study. We cannot overestimate the importance of having discussions about the roles of you as the leader and the members of your research team. Typically, when group experiences go badly, there has been role confusion (e.g., leader not identified), a lack of attention to structure that groups need to function well, and/or inattention to the strengths and challenges each person brings to a group project. Therefore, having an initial meeting with the research team members where you clarify each team member's role will be important. Below are some questions to consider as you discuss roles in your research team:

- What is the role of the leader in your team?
- What are the various roles members will play on the team?
- How often and over what length of time will the group meet? What are the different cultural orientations to time, and how can your meetings be culturally responsive for each of the team members?
- How will you address issues of equity and advocacy as you build your research team and conduct future meetings and research activities together?
- What are the anticipated challenges the group members and leader may face? How does the team want to anticipate and address these challenges?

Again, we provide these questions as a general guide to what you may want to explore. You may decide to use all these questions, only some, or generate your own. The idea is not to develop an authoritarian structure of how your research team will function but instead to provide opportunities for your research team members to build a strong foundation upon which to support and challenge one another during the research process. This is a crucial point related to equity and advocacy: When we do not move through these steps with intention, we often still operate with unnamed approaches to teamwork that are grounded in systems of dominance (e.g., White supremacy, cisgender supremacy, heterosexual supremacy, male supremacy).

After you have discussed the roles of the leader and members, a fourth step in building your research team is to institute regular check-ins with the team. How will you know if your research team is functioning well? How will you alter the functioning of the research team should unavoidable challenges arise? How often will you assess the functioning of the team? Will it be at each research team, monthly, or on another schedule?

## Inclusion of Participants on Your Research Team

An important decision that you will make within the RPA model is if, how, and when you will include participants as collaborators. For instance, participatory action research (PAR) approaches typically actively include participants from the beginning of generating a research question to the development of findings and advocacy strategies after the research has concluded (Benjamin-Thomas et al., 2018). We will cover PAR more thoroughly in Chapter 6. However, researchers can also include a participatory component to their research in other ways:

- meeting with participants to collaboratively determine a research question that would benefit communities
- developing a community advisory board of participants who receive stipends to provide feedback on research activities
- working with participants individually or in focus groups to review their initial transcripts and/or data analysis and findings
- identifying implications for research, practice, and advocacy related to the research topic in collaboration with participants

Indigenous research methods (Chilisa, 2020) can help refine these participator components through also encouraging researchers to:

- Select theoretical frameworks that encourage collaboration with participants (e.g., critical theories, postcolonial Indigenous feminist theory, Borderland-Mestizaje feminism, African and Black feminism healing methodologies, etc.).
- Consider the role of transformation in participatory approaches (e.g., what will really change as a result of collaboration with participants?).
- Create a community action plan that clearly states in accessible ways how, when, and why participants will be included in the overall research project and identifies the people who are responsible for ensuring these activities happen, how necessary resources are obtained for the research project, and that a clear evaluative framework is established.

## CHAPTER SUMMARY

This chapter has addressed four components of the qualitative researcher role. First, we discussed the importance of integrating the values of equity and advocacy in research. This involves intentional attention to issues of power within the research process as well as society in general. Furthermore, it requires us to consider how the research we conduct is inclusive and seeks to serve as a tool for advocacy to enact change. Second, we explored the problematic issue of voice in qualitative inquiry, encouraging you to seek to interrupt notions that your role as a researcher allows you to portray a singular truth of participant voice. Third, researcher reflexivity was reviewed, including its influence on the research process and using reflexive journals to document your study's reflexivity. The final component we discussed related to embracing the role researcher subjectivity plays in a qualitative study and how to seek to understand one's position along the insider–outsider continuum and its impact on your study.

These four components of a qualitative researcher's role are embedded within the RPA model. We then introduced this model and highlighted how it links to evaluating practice, building a research agenda, seeking external funding, and developing and managing a research team.

## Review Questions

1. How do the four components of the qualitative researcher role inform each other?
2. How do the four components of the qualitative researcher role relate to being a researcher-practitioner-advocate?
3. Why is building a research agenda an important component of engaging qualitative research? What are some considerations for doing so?
4. What are important funding considerations for qualitative researchers?
5. What are key considerations when using a research team for your study?

## Recommended Readings

Bhattacharya, K. (2017). *Fundamentals of qualitative research: A practical guide.* Taylor & Francis.

Jackson, A. Y., & Mazzei, L. A. (2009). *Voice in qualitative inquiry: Challenging conventional, interpretative, and critical conceptions in qualitative research.* Routledge.

Peshkin, A. (1988). Virtuous subjectivity: In the participant observer's I's. In D. Berg & K. Smith (Eds.), *The self in social inquiry: Researching methods* (pp. 267–281). Sage.

## CHAPTER 2

# Characteristics of Qualitative Research

## CHAPTER PREVIEW

In this chapter, we introduce the characteristics of qualitative research. Then we discuss the history of qualitative research and the subsequent development of various research paradigms as well as the ways in which qualitative researchers can conceptualize science from that history. We conclude the chapter with a brief discussion of qualitative research's contributions to scientific inquiry today.

## Characteristics of Qualitative Research

Chapter 1 of this text provided an important foundation for qualitative researchers to consider concepts such as equity and advocacy, participant voice, and researcher reflexivity and subjectivity. Thus, how we conceptualize, conduct, and report qualitative research is largely a function of the intersection of societal and researcher worldviews: "Qualitative research is much more than methods, procedures, and techniques. It is in fact an entire worldview" (Brinkmann et al., 2014, p. 20). In this section, we identify key characteristics of qualitative research:

- inductive and abductive analysis
- naturalistic setting
- person in context
- the humanness of research
- purposive sampling
- thick description
- interactive, flexible research design

After reviewing these characteristics, refer to Case Example 2.1 to see how they were infused in a study exploring academic leadership development.

Hays et al. (2021) conducted a grounded theory study with 20 counselor educators to identify a theoretical model of academic leadership engagement. The following central research question was addressed: What factors influence whether counselor educators engage in and sustain academic leadership positions? Here are examples of how qualitative research characteristics are present in the study:

- *inductive and abductive analysis:* The research team over 22 months triangulated data across participants, interviews, and analysts. Through independent analysis as well as analysis by consensus across 14 research team meetings, they identified preliminary codes and themes, then identified more complex themes to develop a high-level description of the core category (i.e., academic leadership). Researcher reflexivity and taking time away from the study allowed further refinement of the theory until the research team reached saturation and developed the final theoretical model.

- *naturalistic setting:* They developed interview questions that would solicit detailed information about the participants' academic settings and how those settings influenced their entering and remaining in leadership positions. They also collected demographic information to provide a description of those settings and participants' academic leadership experiences.

- *person in context:* The research team developed interview questions to query about participants' sequenced actions in terms of academic leadership and how those actions informed their meanings. In addition, the research team made efforts to strengthen the researcher–participant relationship, which allowed for more credible interviews.

- *the humanness of research:* The research team attended carefully to grounded theory principles and procedures when designing, implementing, and reporting data. They identified their assumptions and positionality as research team members and engaged in ongoing reflexivity. Further, they were intentional about the inclusion of multiple and diverse voices when selecting participants and sharing representative quotes to illustrate the theoretical model.

- *purposive sampling:* Using criterion, snowball, and theoretical sampling methods, they identified a sample that met the following selection criteria: doctoral-level counselor educator employed full time in a university setting and with current or previous service as a program coordinator, as a department chair, or in another academic leadership position (e.g., associate dean, dean).

- *thick description:* They provided details about several study components so that readers of the report could determine the extent to which findings might transfer to their personal and/or professional experiences. These components included participant characteristics and recruitment procedures; interview content and duration; research team composition, study assumptions, and leadership experiences; descriptions of themes with representative participant quotes and frequency counts; data analysis steps; and strategies used to establish study rigor.

- *interactive, flexible research design:* At the outset of the study, the research team identified the study goals and conducted a literature review to understand previous scholarship related to counseling leadership and academic leadership. Furthermore, the research question anchored their study as they collected and analyzed data concurrently. Several strategies for study rigor were also employed throughout the research process and reporting: member checking, triangulation, reflexivity, thick description, persistent observation, prolonged engagement, and use of an audit trail.

Source: Hays, D. G., Crockett, S., & Michel, R. (2021). A grounded theory of counselor educators' academic leadership development. *Counselor Education & Supervision, 60*(1), 51–72. https://doi.org/10.1002/ceas.12196

## Inductive and Abductive Analysis

Because qualitative research is exploratory in nature, oftentimes researchers use inductive analysis, or a "bottom-up" approach. **Inductive analysis** refers to the notion that data drive theory or a deeper understanding of an issue or phenomenon. The research process involves collecting data to refine research questions and build theory. As the research study progresses, patterns and themes are identified and a phenomenon is understood more fully. The research process, however, is not entirely inductive. Patton (2014) noted qualitative research is inductive and recursive, involving both discovery and verification and moving back and forth between the research process and reflection on the process and findings. Furthermore, given their existing beliefs and worldviews, qualitative researchers cannot start off a study with a blank slate of no previous knowledge or worldview.

An example might help illustrate inductive analysis. Suppose a community agency administrator notes several substance abuse counselors have left the agency within a year and decides they want to investigate what factors promote retention of substance abuse counselors. Since there is minimal literature on the topic and qualitative inquiry is warranted, the administrator collects pilot data, makes adjustments in their design, and generates an initial list of factors. With more data collection and analysis, a theory of what factors promote retention is identified. Additional adjustments are made in the research process to verify that the theory holds for future data. Specifically, the administrator queries for instances when identified factors may not yield counselor retention. Through attempting to disconfirm the identified factors, the theory is strengthened.

Qualitative research is also characterized by abductive analysis, an integral part of inductive analysis. **Abductive analysis** refers to researchers' immersion in and deliberate moving away from inductive and emerging deductive analysis to be open to new insights. It can support qualitative researchers to deeply engage in the data and avoid quick interpretation and theory development. Rinehart (2020) identified three facilitative conditions for qualitative researchers to engage in abductive analysis: (a) taking time away from the research to intentionally get "off-task" (e.g., engaging in a wellness activity); (b) allowing themselves to take note of informal prompts from their personal and professional experiences; and (c) using backward mapping to track an idea in hindsight. The sequencing of these conditions allows qualitative researchers, once they have familiarized themselves with their research activities, to intentionally take pauses to deliberate and reflect upon their data, consider outside material (e.g., their existing beliefs, views of the world, previous theory and knowledge) to inform their findings, arrive at revised understandings, and then reconstruct findings for reporting. That is, temporary detachment from the work allows time and space for hunches, intuition, and/or new external experiences to lead researchers to rethink and reorganize the narrative they report.

As qualitative researchers arrive at new insights about their research, Rinehart (2020) suggests reflecting on these questions:

- Does this idea fit the evidence?
- Does this idea make sense of the evidence?
- Given what I know of other possible explanations including those in theory and literature: How strong is my argument for this interpretation? (Try it out on friends, colleagues, and then at a conference.)
- How does this idea/way of conceptualizing what is happening "help" the participant community?
- Could this contribute something to the research community and others who might care about this situation? (p. 309)

Perspectives 2.1 illustrates how Rinehart engaged in abductive analysis for a study with principals.

-----------------------------------------------------------------------

## PERSPECTIVES 2.1. HOW LONG WALKS AND A SWIM RESHAPED A PRINCIPAL STUDY

In a 2013 dissertation study, Rinehart (as cited in Rinehart, 2020) conducted three individual interviews, each with six principals, recording and transcribing the interviews and keeping researcher journals and field memos throughout the study.

### Condition 1: Taking Time
As he arrived inductively at findings, he intentionally took time to return to the data sources over several weeks, reading them several times and developing additional notes about the story he identified from the data. This process involved familiarizing and defamiliarizing himself with the data. He took long walks and read passages aloud, considering how his assumptions and position as an educator influenced the way he viewed participants and interpreted the interview transcripts. He also considered how jargon tied to the education discipline might have left particular interview questions unasked and/or unanswered. From these walks, he reported becoming more confident about what was important from the evidence as well as what may be additional limitations of the study.

### Condition 2: Attending to Informal Prompts
Rinehart (2020) conceptualized this condition, encouraging a step out and over the artificial boundary between research tasks and his "other" life activities. An example

prompt he shared came from his reading of a John Steinbeck novel, *Travels with Charlie*. Steinbeck asks, "What are Americans like?" Rinehart adapted this question to "What are principals like?" and considered individual and collective characteristics of principals and began to reshape his data interpretation around this central purpose. Specifically, through a series of prompts generated from ideas from the novel, Rinehart presented the principals' comments on their self-assessment directly in the report.

During a later swim, Rinehart (2020) noted that he reflected on the notion that how individuals think about their jobs can have more impact on their understanding of their work than what they actually "do," that the proportion of time spent on different responsibilities was not an indication of the respective value the principal participants placed on those activities.

### Condition 3: Backward Mapping

From these reflections during a swim, Rinehart (2020) reexamined participants' transcripts and his memos to identify more clearly how they prioritized different aspects of their work. Specifically, the swim reportedly assisted him to realize that focusing on school principal activities or how they are appraised may not indicate what they actually value in their work. Thus, he went back to the evidence to look for participants' comments on what took up principals' time and what they reported was important or valuable. He noted that administrative requirements were rated low as a priority and making a difference for children was the participants' sense of purpose. He also discovered how much time participants spent maintaining a safe and positive learning environment and sustaining good relations with the school's community. Insights from abductive analysis led him to reshape his final argument around principals' identities and values.

## Naturalistic and Experimental Settings

Qualitative researchers investigate phenomena primarily in social settings, where participants—sometimes referred to as *informants* or *coresearchers*—interact with their environments to derive personal meaning. Qualitative research in a **naturalistic setting** is important, as researchers are interested in the role of context. The naturalistic setting affords practitioners and researchers with opportunities to examine how individuals interact with their environment through symbols, social roles, social and power structures, and so forth. It is also true that not all qualitative research is conducted in a naturalistic setting. Qualitative approaches may also be integrated into experimental research designs—namely in some forms of mixed method designs (Creswell & Plano Clark, 2017). An **experimental setting** that integrates qualitative research, for instance, might be a classic experimental-control quantitative research design where an experimental group receives some type of treatment and a control group does not in order to measure the effect of that treatment.

Qualitative researchers immerse themselves in the culture being studied, and time is invested in participants and the community. Data collection tends to occur in places where they spend their time normally: a classroom, neighborhood, counseling office, university, hospital, and so on. Hence, qualitative researchers are often able to sustain contact with participants and their communities before, during, and after a study period. Qualitative research as a naturalistic inquiry means, then, that practitioners and educators study the real world as it unfolds for participants in their everyday environments. Naturalistic inquiry involves having a discovery-oriented approach and being open to ongoing change as it happens within a setting. Terms used to describe this work include *fieldwork, prolonged engagement, qualitative interviewing,* and *participant observation.* These terms are discussed in more detail in Chapter 8.

## The Importance of Context

Take a moment to think about your experiences in graduate school. Perhaps think even more specifically to sitting in a qualitative research course and spending week after week learning about the topic. If you are currently enrolled in such a course, you probably expect that your experience in that course will be affected by many things, including time and location of the course, course setting, course content, course activities, and interactions among peers as well as with the instructor, to name a few. If we were investigating your experiences in a graduate level qualitative research course, we could make the assumption that your experience is affected by the environment, that to understand your perspective we should also understand what the course and perhaps the graduate program is like.

Thus, the **importance of context** as a characteristic of qualitative research refers to how participants create and give meaning to social experience. Phenomena are created and maintained by those in an environment, and social settings are self-organized in a manner that activities are structured for themselves. "By observing the sequential actions ... the investigator is able to witness how they understand each other's prior actions and what they do with that understanding in their subsequent actions" (Patton, 1991, p. 393). To this end, individuals in context interact with one another and patterns emerge that illustrate phenomena.

The importance of context also includes the research context itself: That is, our ability to collect and interpret data fully relies on the researcher–participant relationship and situational constraints and opportunities of the design. Practitioners and educators are sensitive to the natural and research environment when collecting and analyzing data as well when determining the degree to which findings are transferable (Patton, 2014). Participants and researchers cannot be understood in isolation from the research relationship and design. It is also essential to recognize that participants may not only be comprised of individuals but also may be conceptualized as groups, families, partnerships, and communities. Understanding a phenomenon fully may entail that the qualitative researcher thinks broadly about who the participants are within a certain context.

A key assumption of the importance of context characteristic is that participants are best understood holistically versus as a sum of their parts. While in qualitative research you often "lose control" of variables by not isolating them or manipulating conditions, adding contextual data provides a more comprehensive picture to address a research problem. Some answers in clinical and education settings cannot be directly observed and measured, and these unquantifiable data are only accessed by exploring participants' perspectives through interacting with them or examining traces (e.g., letter, photographs, etc.) in their environments. Just as when you read an article in a local newspaper, or hear a client's story, or evaluate a student's behavior in a classroom, you understand that the "truth" of that perspective or action is bound by the time and context in which it was observed as well as how others may perceive it. Taking things out of context only leads to limited and often inaccurate interpretations. The wide variety of ways in which researchers can explore phenomena allows better understanding of how participants make meaning of themselves, their environment, and some social phenomena.

## The Humanness of Research

The fact that we as researchers are human, that we allow our subjectivity to be integrated with our skill set in qualitative inquiry, is both a great strength and a challenge. We refer to this characteristic as the **humanness of research,** or *Verstehen*. It relates to researcher competence and researchers' impact on the design and participants—essentially, the nature of being studied and studying humans (Patton, 2014).

A researcher has direct contact with people and settings and is therefore an instrument of the study. Patton (2014) noted that the credibility of qualitative methods is highly linked to the researchers' competence for conducting a rigorous study. Qualitative researchers are an important part of the design itself and thus are to have a wide range of interpersonal, organizational, and technical skills. Some of the key skills qualitative researchers are to possess include the following (Morrow, 2007; Patton, 2014):

- attending to a rigorous research design, including a focus on research paradigms and traditions throughout the study
- using a multitude of strategies, techniques, and approaches in a creative and innovate manner to explore a phenomenon
- displaying understanding and care and being nonjudgmental to participants and their experiences
- reflecting on the research process and being mindful of voice and representation
- valuing a research relationship that promotes egalitarianism, cultural sensitivity, collaboration, and respect
- understanding that knowledge presented to researchers in the research process is ultimately represented by us and that self-reflection is necessary to recognize the benefits and challenges of subjectivity

## Purposive Sampling

Since participants are experts for a phenomenon and thus are partners in qualitative research, educators, practitioners, and social scientists seek information-rich cases that will best address a research question. The intention in **purposive sampling**, then, is to select participants for the amount of detail they can provide about a phenomenon, not simply selecting participants to meet a certain sample size.

Sample size in purposive sampling is relative to the research goals and tradition; thus, it is very difficult to establish the "right" number of participants. Typically, you need more participants if you are interested in theory development and/or heterogeneity in perspectives. Purposive sampling is discussed in more depth in Chapter 6.

## Thick Description

**Thick description** refers to providing detail about the research process, context, and participants. Qualitative researchers aim for insight and deeper understanding to illustrate a phenomenon intensely and the transferability of knowledge to other settings (i.e., depth versus breadth). The end goal of thick description is to provide enough detail that the reader can have enough information to generalize findings to a narrowed context or replicate the study in another setting. The truth is that qualitative research can be so descriptive and systematic that collection methods and findings may be easily replicated and generalized to a specific setting.

Qualitative research is named for its reference to "quality," or the detailed accounts and description of data. Qualitative researchers are interested in the who, what, when, where, why, and how of a phenomenon. Thus, the detailed report typically involves words and pictures more so than numbers. The report typically describes and tells a story, often including participant quotes. Depending on the paradigm employed, thick description can also include identifying participants, initiatives, and communities. Thick description is discussed in Chapter 7.

## An Interactive, Flexible Research Design

Designing qualitative research is not a linear, sequential process. Patton (2014) described this process as being open to discovering new paths. Maxwell (2013) also argued it should be reflexive and that different components of the design are reactive to the ongoing research process. A design should interact with the environment, with them mutually influencing each other. Maxwell developed an interactive model to qualitative research design that we believe best captures the evolving nature of qualitative inquiry. There are five major, interrelated components (see Figure 2.1):

- *goals:* the intention and focus of the research study and how the expected outcomes might affect various stakeholders. Three goals for the researcher are identified and are discussed in more detail in Chapter 5: personal, practical, and scholarly goals. Additionally, participant concerns and funder goals influence research design goals.
- *conceptual framework:* a network of significant constructs from guiding theories from personal and professional experience as well as previous literature. Essentially, the conceptual framework constitutes an evolving literature review and theoretical model of personal and professional assumptions that collectively build a study rationale. Personal experience, existing theory and prior research, exploratory and pilot research/ preliminary conclusions, and thought experiments are primary contextual factors that influence (and are influenced by) the conceptual framework and are further discussed in Chapter 5.
- *research questions:* Referred to as the "hub" of the interactive model, research questions are the "What do you want to know?" component of qualitative research design. They

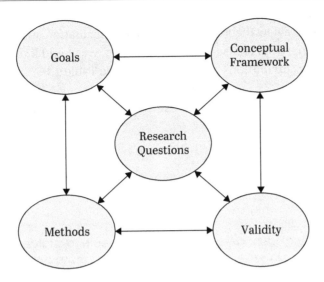

**FIGURE 2.1** The Interactive Model of
Qualitative Research Design

are influenced by the other four components and related contextual factors. Research questions are discussed primarily in Chapter 5.

- *methods:* actions taken in the design. Methods involve four components: the research–participant relationship (see Chapters 1 and 5); site and participant selection (sampling; see Chapter 6); data collection methods (see Chapters 8 and 9); and data analysis (see Chapters 10 and 11).
- *validity:* the limitations or "how you might be wrong" aspects of research design. Commonly referred to as "trustworthiness," validity impacts primarily data collection, management, and analysis. Validity is discussed further in Chapter 7. (Maxwell, 2013)

We will address each of these components as well as the contextual factors associated with the model in more detail throughout this text. Finally, Maxwell (2013) noted that ethics is a component of the model that is infused in all other components. Ethics in qualitative research design is discussed further in Chapter 3.

One way qualitative research is increasing recognition in traditionally quantitative designs is by contributing to mixed methods studies. Creswell and Creswell (2017) highlight four mixed methods strategies:

- Qualitative and quantitative data is continuously collected and integrated.
- There is continuous qualitative data collection, with intermittent "waves" of quantitative data collection.
- Qualitative data is collected first to explore, followed by quantitative data, then qualitative data again to deepen and verify findings.
- Quantitative data is collected first, then qualitative data, and then quantitative data.

We encourage you to review their text for additional information on these strategies. While the mixed methods approach is discussed in Chapter 5, we would like to highlight some of qualitative research's contributions to this approach (see Table 2.1).

**TABLE 2.1**  Contributions of Qualitative Research in Mixed Methods Studies

- Planning of research for quantitative data collection, data analysis, and data reporting and communication of results
- Giving voice to underrepresented or underresearched individuals
- Providing context for a sample
- Taking account how people feel about and construct their experiences
- Developing observation protocols that may be used for more quantifiable observations
- Using qualitative findings to develop surveys to distribute to a larger sample
- Providing information in experimental designs as a first phase of research, a component of a trial, or to help explain the findings (e.g., "piloting" the trial, understanding the clinical trial postintervention, etc.)
- Formulating interventions
- Contributing to community engagement and social change
- Determining what scale points mean (i.e., judgments about categories)
- Exploring surprising findings or unexpected results
- Stimulating theory development for various phenomena to be tested later or refined using quantitative methods
- Explaining quantitative findings
- Helping to explain mechanisms behind relationships
- Exploring constructs or variables that are unknown
- Exploring or confirming research areas

Sources: Creswell and Creswell (2017), Ercikan and Roth (2006), Mertens (2017), and Morrow (2007)

# A History of Qualitative Research

Key historical moments or phases of qualitative research exist within social, economic, historical, and cultural contexts and must be understood in relation to these. Thus, definitions and characteristics of qualitative research vary depending on the historical moment. It is important to think of these moments not as a linear progression of history but as lessons that researchers come back to as we move toward the future. That is, we revisit and celebrate the contributions of these moments.

There are different histories of qualitative research based on discipline, with greater attention historically in fields such as anthropology and communications and less so in health sciences, social sciences, and education. It is also important to underscore that our understanding of the history of qualitative research is limited and flawed, defined by those whose voice and representation of the method have been privileged (e.g., men of European American descent). Thus, contributions from women and those with other minoritized statuses are largely absent in this reporting, and our representation of history here is a truncated version.

Although the term "qualitative research" was rarely used until the 1970s, scientific inquiry has referenced the term "qualitative" when describing data as early as the 17th century. For example, philosophers such as John Locke, René Descartes, and David Hume categorized qualities of things as primary (i.e., objective and independent of observation) and secondary (i.e., subjective and dependent of interpretation). Interestingly, the term "qualitative" was used in the natural sciences (e.g., chemistry, physiology) since 1900, yet discussions about qualitative methodology were limited until the mid-20th century to topics such as interviewing and fieldwork (Brinkmann et al., 2014).

The history of qualitative research has been chronicled in different ways. For example, Brinkmann et al. (2014) highlighted contributions to qualitative research as a method through three philosophical foundations: (a) the German tradition of *Verstehen* and the development of hermeneutics; (b) the phenomenological tradition; and (c) North American traditions such as pragmatism and the Chicago School, symbolic interactionism, and ethnomethodology. Another example is Denzin and Lincoln (2011), who conceptualize the history of qualitative research in eight historical moments based on previous works (Lincoln & Guba, 1995; Vidich & Lyman, 2001). You will note that they label the first few moments of qualitative research as "ethnography" since this was the primary tradition used. In this section, we attempt to weave together these approaches (see Table 2.2). To these sources we add Indigenous contributions

**TABLE 2.2** Key Historical Moments in Qualitative Research

|  | Timeframe[a] | Key events | Contributions |
|---|---|---|---|
| **Early ethnography** | 15th to 17th centuries | Detached and objective study of diversity in "uncivilized" societies using a Eurocentric view of diversity; development of theories of human diversity | Beginnings of fieldwork |
| **Colonial ethnography** | 17th to 19th centuries | Two camps of ethnographers, with a focus either on colonization or liberation; introduction of constructivism and hermeneutics | Some attention within one camp to local context in studying groups |
| **Hermeneutics** | Early 19th to mid-20th century | Interpretation of sacred texts; interpretation of human experience by participant, researcher, and reader | Greater attention on human need to understand and interpret individual and collective experience; attention to reflexivity |
| **Traditional period** | Early 1900s to mid-1940s | Classic ethnography shifting to modern ethnography; focus on decolonization abroad and colonization and conversion within the United States; expansion of hermeneutics and introduction of critical theory paradigms and phenomenology | Greater emphasis on conducting fieldwork, taking field notes, and writing theory |

*(continued)*

**TABLE 2.2**   Key Historical Moments in Qualitative Research   (*Continued*)

| | Timeframe [a] | Key events | Contributions |
|---|---|---|---|
| **Phenomenology** | Early 20th to early 21st century | Development of three strands of studying direct lived experience: descriptive, hermeneutic, and idiographic | Attention to bracketing and individual experience |
| **Pragmatism and the Chicago School** | 1910s to 1960s | Study of human desire to understand daily problems and develop solutions | Increased attention to everyday slices of life within urban sociology |
| **Modernist** | 1940s to 1970s | Emergence of grounded theory, semiotics, ethnomethodology, and feminism; increased value on rigor (i.e., golden age of qualitative analysis). | Introduction of additional qualitative methods and strategies, including symbolic interactionism |
| **Blurred genres** | 1970 to 1986 | Blurring of humanities with other disciplines; introduction of narratology and case study traditions | Attention to interpretivism and the qualitative report; emergence of qualitative research in education and social sciences |
| **Crisis of representation** | Mid-1980s | Increased attention to feminism, constructivism, and critical theory paradigms; view of writing and fieldwork as integrated | Development of evaluation standards; increased view of phenomena as dynamic social systems influenced by cultural and political factors; discussion of researcher positionality (e.g., researcher bias) |
| **Triple crisis** | Mid-1980s to mid-1990s | Questions over the best way to represent, evaluate, and report findings | Attention to the power of disseminating findings and representation |
| **Postexperimental inquiry and beyond** | Mid-1990s to present | Sophistication of methods and focus on alternative and non-Western approaches to qualitative research design | Introduction of novel forms of data reporting |
| **Indigenous contributions** | Early 2000s to present | Greater attention to colonizing aspects of Western research on Indigenous populations; consideration of Indigenous and postcolonial paradigms | Focus on the 4 Rs of research |

Note. [a]= Timeframe per phase is approximated, and there is some overlap of phases.

as a final historical contribution. Due to space limitations, we direct you to texts in the Recommended Readings section at the end of this chapter for additional information on the history of qualitative research. After reading this section, complete Reflexive Activity 2.1 to consider how your selected topic could have been approached within each historical moment.

**REFLEXIVE ACTIVITY 2.1.** QUALITATIVE RESEARCH ACROSS HISTORICAL MOMENTS

Identify a topic of interest. Consider how the topic would have been approached from each of the historical moments in this section.

- What are some strengths of each historical moment for studying your research topic?
- What are some challenges of each historical moment for studying your research topic?
- To what extent does each historical moment sequentially inform how you approach your research topic?

## Early Ethnography

The **early ethnography period** (15th–17th centuries) is a historical moment that involved a comparison of diversity throughout the globe against an established theory of human diversity, beginning as early as the time of Columbus and colonialism efforts (Denzin & Lincoln, 2011). Vidich and Lyman (2001) defined *ethnography* as a description of individuals and their social contexts, and in this moment, descriptions were made of how non-Western societies diverged from the "civilized" European nations. Thus, the first ethnographic methods were reported in texts that reflected Western interests in understanding others and their communities. This interest was motivated by a need to classify human diversity across the world. During this period inquiry was conceptualized as atheoretical, primarily concerned with description of non-Western countries by Western (European) countries. Terms such as "savage" and "primitive" were used to describe individuals from non-Western societies.

## Colonial Ethnography

The **colonial ethnography period** (17th–19th centuries) reflects a time of complexity in qualitative research, with one camp of researchers with an interest in studying and colonizing the "primitives" and another camp with an interest in liberating colonized peoples. Thus, ethnographies from this period tell readers much about the values and perspectives of those studied as well as the Western researcher (Vidich & Lyman, 2001). During the first part of this period, explorers, guided by what was later described as positivism and postpositivism paradigms, searched for scientific "truth" through observation and comparison. These researchers asserted that knowledge was acquired through direct experience and observation of facts.

Uncovering truth was influenced by an agenda of colonization of non-Western peoples and often interpreting data through a Christian lens.

During the latter part of this period, there was a division of camps that led to value conflicts and moral dilemmas among ethnographers. Those in the second camp of liberation began to attend to the importance of the local context of those studied in understanding findings, not the context and standards of Western societies. Researchers were beginning to consider the idea of multiple truths and the notion that context influenced individuals' reality. The work *Critique of Pure Reason* by Immanuel Kant (1787) laid the foundation for constructivism and thus influenced the division among ethnographers during this period (Vidich & Lyman, 2001). Constructivism, a paradigm that served as an important groundwork for a majority of qualitative research to come later, is described in Chapter 4.

While there is some division among researchers in notions of what constitutes truth and from whose perspective and standard this should be determined, most of the ethnographers in this period continued to see the mission of their research as efforts to judge the outsider or "other" against some European standard. We continue to see this in the traditional period as qualitative research spreads throughout the world as well as extends to the United States.

## Hermeneutics

In the early 19th century, Friedrich Schleiermacher developed **hermeneutics** as a methodology of interpreting "sacred" texts, such as religious documents, mythology, history, art, and political artifacts. Although the philosophy and approach originated from scriptural interpretations, philosophers such as Wilhelm Dilthey extended it in the late 19th century to the interpretation of individual and collective human experience, and Martin Heidegger and Hans-George Gadamer described it in the early and mid-20th century, respectively, as an interpretation of interpretations, highlighting the innate human drive to understand and interpret.

The concept of reflexivity, introduced in Chapter 1, is prominent in more recent hermeneutic philosophy. That is, several layers of interpretation are inevitable as we make observations of written text, narratives, and/or human experiences in general. These layers are as follows:

- Research participants function with often passive self-interpretations of their actions and experiences.
- Researchers then interpret these interpretations and apply to a current context, concept, or theory.
- Finally, readers of the qualitative report reflects upon researchers' interpretations within the context that the findings were identified in as well as the current context of which readers live.

Thus, there is a mutuality of interpretation, and qualitative researchers engage in reflexive thinking about their observations, as knowledge is dependent on background, contextual, and largely cultural factors. Therefore, interpretation is a constantly evolving and fluid process.

In practice, aligning with a hermeneutic stance means that qualitative researchers navigate and identify these layers of interpretation and reflect both the cultural context they are in at the time of observation and reporting as well as the cultural context in which data (e.g., texts, interviews) were created. They move back and forth between parts of and the whole text or narrative for understanding while extending the meaning of the data to apply to phenomena in counseling and education. One historical figure in counseling and psychology who has served as the subject of this approach is Sigmund Freud. Bonomi (2005) reviewed a text that comments on one of Freud's essays related to self-analysis. Bonomi examined how Freud's original essay sparked commentaries among a new wave of psychoanalysts in the 1960s. The cultural and historical contexts of when both the original essay and text were written are discussed. Also, Bonomi emphasized that Freud's essay and resulting commentary heavily influenced the psychoanalytic community.

## The Traditional Period

The **traditional period** extends from the early 1900s to the mid-1940s (Lincoln & Guba, 1995; Denzin & Lincoln, 2011). We consider it one of the most foundational periods of qualitative research, as it sees the greatest amount of growth in ideas and traditions across a variety of disciplines. Classic ethnography is prevalent at the beginning of this period, slowly shifting to what is known as modern ethnography. A major contribution of this period included a greater emphasis on conducting fieldwork, taking field notes, and writing theory. Classic ethnography continued the "objective" reports from what has often been termed the "lone ethnographer," the expert fieldworker returning home with stories of the other (Lincoln & Guba, 1995).

In England an anthropological school of qualitative research known as the **British School** emerged in the 1920s and 1930s. The British School is credited with the fieldwork method, and Bronislaw Malinowski, the first major fieldworker, spoke of the importance of looking at culture from the native's point of view through sustained contact. Malinowski spent two years in the Trobriand Islands, and this research yielded the work *Argonauts of the Western Pacific: An Account of Native Enterprise and Adventure in the Archipelagoes of Melanesian New Guinea* (1922/2002). The British School scholars conceptualized ethnography as being in the presence of the people one is studying, not just their texts or artifacts. They asserted it was important to evaluate based on behavior versus just verbal statements; have prolonged, active engagement; and consider behaviors in a larger social context. The British School also conducted works within England, examining conflict, urbanization, and imperialism (MacDonald, 2001).

Vidich and Lyman (2001) noted during this period a focus on the American Indian and the idea of "saving the Indian" by converting them to Christianity and thus colonization, as well as decolonization movements in Africa and Asia. Therefore, during the early part of this period, there is an increased value on decolonization efforts abroad and thus a focus more on local context in research and more attention to colonization efforts in the United States. Worldwide, the term "primitive" was slowly replaced by "underdeveloped" and access to tribal societies became more and more difficult.

Within this period, qualitative research emphasized participant observation and fieldwork as an important way to gain information about people within their communities. Margaret Mead wrote of applied educational phenomena in other parts of the world compared to those in the United States (e.g., *Coming of Age in Samoa* [1928], *Growing Up in New Guinea* [1930], *Continuities in Cultural Evolution* [1964]). And George Herbert Mead discussed in his *Mind,*

*Self, and Society* (1934) how the social nature of self, thought, and community was a product of human meaning and interaction.

This period marks the emergence of critical theory paradigms from the Institute of Social Research in Frankfurt with theorists Max Horkheimer, Theodor Adorno, and Herbert Marcuse and a growing assumption that researcher's values are important to the task, purpose, and methods of research. Increased attention to qualitative methods in the form of detailed observations, use of diaries, and case study interviews become prevalent in psychology in Europe, with scholars such as Jean Piaget, Freud, Karen Horney, Abraham Maslow, and Carl Rogers.

## Phenomenology

**Phenomenology** as a philosophical contribution examines the role of human experience as an object of study. A *phenomenon* refers to a first-person experience, process, or relationship by which qualitative researchers try to capture to identify meanings and interactions with others within the environment. Strands of phenomenology have been introduced from the early 20th Century until the early 21st century and include descriptive phenomenology, hermeneutic phenomenology, and idiography (later referred to as interpretive phenomenological analysis [IPA]). Thus, we see hermeneutics extending into phenomenology to inform one of these strands. In Chapter 4, we discuss phenomenology in more detail as a research tradition and highlight in Chapter 11 how methodological advances of philosophers from these strands influenced qualitative data analysis.

The descriptive phenomenology strand has been defined primarily by Edmund Husserl, Amadeo Giorgi, Clark Moustakas, Paul Colaizzi, and Adrian Van Kaam. *Descriptive phenomenology* prioritizes description of the human experience as it is presented, without researcher interpretation. The assumption is that a generalized description is possible (i.e., essence) and that qualitative researchers can suspend or bracket their knowledge. Husserl is credited as the founder of phenomenology and articulated that psychological processes of the human experience (e.g., perception, awareness, consciousness), resulting from them interacting on an environment, can be described to identify the *life-world*, or a structural whole that is both socially shared and individually experienced (Welton, 1999). The life-world assumes that the object of study existed prior to interpretation of the experience with that object. For example, Brinkmann et al. (2014) use the metaphor of maps and territory to differentiate between object (i.e., life-world) and interpretation: Territory (object) is always in existence, and science gives us maps (interpretations) of the territory, which can be adapted over time.

The second strand of phenomenology, hermeneutic phenomenology, has been influenced by Heidegger, Jean-Paul Sartre, Maurice Merleau-Ponty, Hans-Georg Gadamer, Paul Ricouer, and Max Van Manen. With the historical influences of hermeneutics, Heidegger emphasized that scientific inquiry should search for meaning of human experience beyond the essence conceptualized by Husserl. He noted human experience as "being-in-the-world," which means that humans cannot extract themselves from the environment in which they are embedded. Humans can only be understood as a function of environments that influence them; thus, they do not simply act upon their environments. This strand also emphasizes the interaction of the research-participant life-worlds as well as the role of researcher interpretation and the related difficulty of bracketing, or suspension of researcher knowledge. Thus, *hermeneutic phenomenology* is defined as the description of a phenomenon or construct whereby the description is influenced by the contexts of the research and participant, as well as the research-participant social interaction.

The third phenomenological strand, idiography, is a more recent addition from scholars such as Jonathan Smith, Michael Larkin, and Paul Flowers. *Idiography* focuses on the specifics of human experience, delving deeply into analysis of that particular experience: It highlights intensive and detailed analysis of the accounts produced by a comparatively small number of participants (Larkin & Thompson, 2012). With this strand, qualitative researchers have an active role, engaging with each participant's reflections, and anchor findings firmly in direct quotes, applying specific participant accounts to larger theory.

## Pragmatism and the Chicago School

**Pragmatism**, a North American contribution of the 1910s–1960s that eventually spread to influence Western European philosophy, refers to the focus on outcomes of human behavior, based on the assumption that humans, as they engage in reflective interactions with others, have a natural desire to seek meaning and develop solutions to everyday problems they experience (Brinkmann et al., 2014). The end product of pragmatism is to develop scientific knowledge that can be applied to daily life situations. Some of the proponents of pragmatism include Charles Sanders Peirce, William James, John Dewey, and G. Mead.

Pragmatism heavily influenced a movement within sociology in the United States to examine "slices of life" in the Chicago area, known as the **Chicago School**. Through the use of participant observation, scholars studied social life directly, with some examining city life to determine and promote social reform. The first generation of Chicago School scholars included Robert Park, Ernest Burgess, Florian Znaniecki, William I. Thomas, and Jane Addams. Some salient Chicago School concepts are local studies of the natural areas or urban structures of the city; natural history of collective behavior; and radical, social change as natural patterns. The American city, then, became an ideal outlet for examining social behavior through fieldwork in specific locations. Fieldworkers explored aspects of ordinary life for various urban cultural groups who were typically marginalized by society. Social interaction was the source of various realities for urban subgroups, and lived experiences were best understood from their perspectives. With the Chicago School, ethnography was becoming more localized.

Park and Burgess had a major influence on several core ethnographies and often wrote introductions to the studies. Some of the core ethnographies of the Chicago School included:

- The study of the Polish peasants and successors to America: *The Polish Peasant in Europe and America, 1918–1920* by Thomas and Znaniecki (1927)
- Clifford Shaw's focus on juvenile delinquency: *The Jack Roller* by Shaw (1930), *The Natural History of a Delinquent Career* by Shaw and Moore (1931), and *Brothers in Crime* by Shaw (1938)
- Frances Donovan's study of women and the changing division of labor: *The Woman Who Waits* (1920) and *The Saleslady* (1929)

- Race relations and the melting pot idea: *The City* by *Park* et al. (1925), *Negro Politicians: The Rise of Negro Politics in Chicago* by Gosnell (1935), *The Etiquette of Race Relations in the South* by Park and Doyle (1937), *Race and Culture* by Park (1950), and *Society* by Park (1955).
- Medical education: *Boys in White* by Becker et al. (1961)
- General neighborhood and community studies: *Street Corner Society* by Foote Whyte (1943), *Middletown* by Lynd and Lynd (1929), and *Middletown in Transition: A Study in Cultural Conflicts* by Lynd and Lynd (1937).

## The Modernist Phase

The **modernist phase** (1940s–1970s) primarily involved the emergence of several new approaches as well as the increased attention to rigor and quality and was referred to as the "golden age of qualitative analysis" by Lincoln and Guba (1995). That is, the increasing attention to U.S. society as culturally diverse called for a need to adapt and develop qualitative methods and procedures for more complex questions. Students of the first generation of the Chicago School (e.g., Charles H. Cooley, Everett C. Hughes, Howard S. Becker, Herbert Blumer, Norman K. Denzin) began to develop the concept of symbolic interactionism in the 1940s.

**Symbolic interactionism**, a term coined by Blumer (1969), involved three central tenets:

- Humans act toward things on the basis of meanings they perceive that things have for them.
- The meaning of such things is derived from social interactions they have.
- These meanings are handled in and modified in an interpretative process.

Symbolic interactionists believe that only through social experience can individuals become self-identified. Thus, individuals interpret their experiences and identities based on social interactions. They actively interact with their environments, making sense of and responding to symbols, including things like language, signs, and cultural artifacts (Brinkmann et al., 2014).

Symbolic interactionism has its roots in social psychology and is greatly influenced by the pragmatism of G. Mead, who believed that the self was defined primarily through social and behavioral methods with a need for external examination and validation. Thus, Mead (Mead & Schubert, 1934) viewed individuals as comprised of a unique self that considers social interactions in defining the self. Through the consideration of social context, a shared meaning among individuals arises. This shared meaning leads to social organization and an understanding of various social rules and symbols. Thus, personal and shared meanings are created within and derived from social interactions. This meaning becomes individuals' reality of phenomena and creates a cycle where they act upon things based on their meanings of them, which are based on earlier interactions.

Language is a particularly important symbol for this approach because how individuals label things or processes greatly influences the way they interact and interpret them. "We can never get beyond our language ... all the questions we ask and words we use to articulate our understandings are embedded in culture" (McLeod, 2011, p. 56). As an illustration, consider the language clinicians and educators have used to describe significantly lower intelligence over the past century. Language describing these individuals has evolved from earlier terms such as "moron" and "imbecile," to "mental retardation," to an evolving term, "intellectual disability." With changes in language, changes in meaning and general attitudes toward these individuals have occurred for more sensitive assessment and educational practices.

Vidich and Lyman (2001) divided this phase into two periods: (a) ethnography of the "civic other," or community studies/ethnography of the early American immigrants (early 20th century–1960s) and (b) studies of ethnicity and assimilation (1950s–1980s). For the former period, they noted that, similar to the American Indian ethnographies, researchers sought during this phase to assimilate African, Asian, and European immigrants into Christianity. In fact, there was a surge of survey methods by churches to understand immigration trends as immigration increased. For the latter phase, scholars begin to challenge Park's melting pot idea (Vidich & Lynam, 2001).

From the tenets of symbolic interactionism came a need to study the overlooked rituals and norms of human interaction, an approach known as "ethnomethodology." Harold Garfinkel (1967) in his *Studies of Ethnomethodology* sought to examine routine actions and document what individuals do when they encounter each other. At times, this meant implementing breaching experiments to provoke social disorder to be able to understand social order. According to Garfinkel (1967), disrupting norms "should tell us something about how the structures of everyday activities are ordinarily and routinely produced and maintained" (p. 38). Conversation analysis, initially studied by Harvey Sacks and Emanuel Schegloff, was developed as a strand of ethnomethodology to study more explicitly verbal and nonverbal communication within human exchanges. Ethnomethodology, considered one of the qualitative research traditions, is discussed in further detail in Chapter 4.

## Blurred Genres

The **blurred genres period** occurred from 1970–1986 (Denzin & Lincoln, 2011). The golden age of researchers as cultural romantics was over, and greater attention was given to the act of writing itself. That is, reports were no longer being viewed as a report free from the researcher's values; instead, reports were now considered interpretations of interpretations. Clifford Geertz, in *The Interpretation of Cultures* (1973) and *Local Knowledge* (1983), two works that seem to sandwich this historical moment, best articulates this when he argues for more interpretive approaches to qualitative research that include thick descriptions of events and rituals to maximize the representation of participants' stories.

Genres such as social sciences and humanities were being blurred, giving rise to new scholars and approaches from education and social sciences disciplines. Contemporary scholars such as Harry Wolcott, Egan Guba, Robert Stake, and Yvonna Lincoln emerge in education. Research sprouts in education and social sciences disciplines, including social work, psychology, and counseling. Before this period the term "qualitative research" was virtually nonexistent in education and social sciences (Brinkmann et al., 2014; Rennie et al., 2000). With this blurring of disciplines, we see the tradition of narratology develop, shaped by Foucalt's work on narratives as a result of cultural and political practice. Furthermore, case study research in clinical and educational settings started to become more formalized. Narratology and case study as qualitative research traditions are discussed further in Chapter 4.

## Crisis of Representation

In the mid-1980s qualitative research enters the historical period termed the **crisis of representation**. In this period there is a rise in feminism, constructivism, and critical theory paradigms. The crisis comes as a result of an increased realization that qualitative researchers may not be representing themselves and their participants in an accurate way. They realize they are not experts, and there is an erosion of the notions of objectivism, structured social life, and ethnographies as museum pieces (Denzin & Lincoln, 2011). "No longer would ethnography have to serve the interests of a theory of progress that pointed toward the breakup of every ethnos" (Vidich & Lyman, 2001, p. 87).

During this historical moment, researchers began to examine more closely the role of gender, class, and race in their own lives as well as the lives of participants. They questioned their writings and saw that fieldwork and report writing are blurred activities influencing one another and are thus difficult to separate. During this phase, researchers were exposed to new evaluation standards of credibility, dependability, transferability, and confirmability (see Lincoln & Guba, 1995). Trustworthiness criteria and strategies are discussed further in Chapter 7.

## A Triple Crisis

A **triple crisis** (mid-1980s to mid-1990s) as a historical moment refers to the postmodern period of ethnography and other forms of qualitative research, a time of struggling with how to best represent the other (Denzin & Lincoln, 2011). Representations of phenomena in the forms of grand narratives about social structures were replaced by context-specific cases. The three crises that made up this moment are the following:

- There is the realization that lived experience cannot be directly represented, because it is re-created as it is written (i.e., *representational crisis*).
- The legitimacy of traditional evaluation criteria in qualitative research is questioned (i.e., *legitimation crisis*).
- There is a question of whether it is possible to affect change in society if we only write about it (i.e., a combination of both of the other two crises).

With this moment qualitative researchers struggle to best represent their participants and phenomena, be flexible in how they evaluate the rigor of qualitative design, and consider alternative methods beyond writing to disseminate their findings.

## Postexperimental Inquiry and Beyond

While our understanding of recent history is still evolving, Denzin and Lincoln (2011) identified eight historical moments and provided some major events and tasks yet to come. First, qualitative research continues to help break down discipline boundaries and introduce new traditions. Second, novel forms of writing, such as poetry, autobiography, art, and visual media, are becoming increasingly common. Third, efforts are being made to come to consensus on the several research paradigms and traditions available to conduct research. Put simply, there are so many choices yet little agreement on the definitions and practices of these choices. Finally, greater attention is being placed on Indigenous studies, non-Western approaches, studies with social purpose, and overall methodological sophistication.

## Indigenous Contributions

Qualitative research with Indigenous populations as well as the use of Indigenous methodologies have become more popular in education and social sciences disciplines within the past couple of decades (e.g., Denzin et al., 2008; Lavallée, 2009; Smith, 2012), creating an emerging historical moment. Indigenous research is described in more detail later in this chapter.

## Philosophies of Science

One of the essential features of qualitative research is articulating a research orientation as you consider a research topic to be investigated, beginning with a research paradigm and then selecting a research tradition (see Chapter 4). Prior to discussing qualitative research paradigms, we present five core philosophies.

Science is the systematic search for and observation, analysis, and presentation of knowledge. Across time, scientific philosophy became more complex, yielding new research paradigms and traditions. It is important that you reflect on how you view science across core **philosophies of science** to select the appropriate research paradigm(s) and tradition(s) for your study. These philosophies include ontology, epistemology, axiology, rhetoric, and methodology. Essentially, each philosophy category represents a continuum of thought that overlaps and builds upon the others (Creswell & Poth, 2017). Before reading these descriptions, complete Reflexive Activity 2.2. Upon reading the descriptions, review the statements that you endorsed in the activity. How do these endorsements align with the philosophies of science?

**Ontology** is the foundation of science, as it refers to how broadly we define reality or the "known." Thus, ontology is the degree to which a universal truth is sought about a particular construct or process in qualitative research. Is reality objective or subjective? Is it universal (*etic*) or contextual (*emic*)? Are there factors that influence the reality of a phenomenon, or is reality independent from any factors? Thus, reality can be thought of as a continuum with objective truth (capital "t" *Truth*) at one end and subjective or multiple truths at the other end (*truth*). Qualitative research in education and the social sciences generally involves examination of how "real" a phenomenon is through the subjective lenses of both researchers and participants (Ponterotto, 2005; Varpio & MacLeod, 2020). Your ontological perspective is characterized by the extent to which you believe that reality is limited or predetermined.

Truth ←————————————————→ truth

For example, let's consider the construct of family discord. Researchers who fall toward the left side of the continuum (*Truth*) would argue that there is a universal definition or reality

**REFLEXIVE ACTIVITY 2.2.** PHILOSOPHIES OF SCIENCE

Review the following statements and mark an "x" next to those you endorse.

_____ There is only one reality or truth for any phenomenon.

_____ Multiple truths for a phenomenon exist; however, some truths are more salient than others.

_____ Truth does not exist, as there are multiple, equally valid truths.

_____ There is a limit to what we can know about a construct.

_____ Knowledge acquisition is limitless.

_____ Knowledge changes as social interactions change.

_____ A researcher should not integrate personal and professional values in a research design.

_____ Participant values should be considered in research design.

_____ Researcher subjectivity can be an important asset to qualitative research.

_____ It is inappropriate to use the first-person voice in a research report.

_____ It is inappropriate to use the second-person voice in a research report.

_____ Presenting data as numbers is more valuable than presenting participant stories or narratives.

_____ Methodology drives research questions.

_____ Research questions drive methodology.

of what family discord looks like for families. With enough investigation, information about family discord may be known and thus applied universally to work with families. Alternatively, researchers who fall toward the right side of the continuum (*truth*) would assert that a complete, universal understanding of family discord is impossible since the construct must be understood for a particular context. That is, multiple notions or beliefs about what family discord is are equally valid and valued.

**Epistemology** refers to the process of knowing, or the degree to which knowledge is believed to be constructed by the research process in general and in the context of the researcher–participant relationship more specifically. In other words, what is the relationship between the knower (e.g., researcher, participant) and the known (i.e., ontology)? Epistemology relates to knowledge acquisition for the phenomenon of interest; it is "how we know what we know" (Denzin & Lincoln, 2011; Ponterotto, 2005; Varpio & MacLeod, 2020). Is knowledge limited? A majority of qualitative research views knowledge as being actively constructed within the context of the research relationship and essentially unlimited. That is, an epistemological perspective in qualitative inquiry typically refers to the notion that knowledge about a research topic is only limited by the quality of the interactions of those involved in the research process.

Limited knowledge ⟵⟶ Unlimited knowledge

Let's examine this philosophy of science for the construct of family discord. Researchers with the epistemological stance that knowledge is limited would argue that the research relationship content is likely irrelevant to knowledge acquisition. That is, how we know what we know about family discord comes from a more generic, finite research process. For those who believe that knowledge is unlimited, knowledge about family discord can be continually expanded with changes in research design as well as research relationships and dynamics.

**Axiology** relates to how values shape research (Varpio & MacLeod, 2020). It is the role of the researcher's values and assumptions in qualitative inquiry and how they influence research questions and research design. Additionally, it includes consideration of the values of participants and the research setting (Ponterotto, 2005). Concepts of axiology are related to researcher reflexivity, discussed in Chapter 1. What is the role of values in qualitative inquiry? Do you think values should be considered in research design? How are our scientific pursuits guided by what we as researchers value as knowledge and reality? Qualitative researchers are encouraged to reflect on what role, if any, their values play in the research process.

Objectivity ←——————————————→ Reflexivity

For the family discord example, objective researchers would attempt to minimize the role of values in research and thus try to maintain the research relationship as neutral, uninfluenced by the researchers' assumptions or experiences. Researchers would likely not disclose their perspective related to family discord in order to not "bias" participants. An axiological stance that valued the researcher as an instrument in the design would emphasize the importance of relating their experience and assumptions about family discord to the research–participant relationship. The research relationship would likely be a collaborative process of investigating family discord.

**Rhetoric** refers to qualitative data presentation and the type of voice used. As will be described in later chapters, data may be presented in various formats depending on the selected research paradigm, tradition, and general study design. How you present data involves decisions about the use of voice (i.e., first, second, or third person) of the researcher(s) and participants, terminology to present data collection and analytic methods, and the degree to which narratives, thematic categories, and/or numbers are presented as findings (Creswell & Poth, 2017; Ponterotto, 2005). Should data be presented in the form of narratives, numbers, or both? Generally, the more narratives allowed in qualitative inquiry, the more voice participants have in a report. However, the more a researcher takes the expert stance in report writing, the less participant voice may be present, no matter the use of voice.

Researcher Voice ←——————————————→ Participant Voice

This philosophy of science relates heavily to the role of voice, introduced in Chapter 1. Researchers who value a prominent researcher voice in data presentation would likely present more aggregated data related to family discord; this might involve statistics and/or minimal narratives and discussion of the findings using the third person (e.g., "The researcher found ...") with greater attention to researcher interpretation of the findings. Those who value participant voice in data presentation would likely provide participant quotes and narratives and attempt to represent data from participants' perspectives. When they provide interpretations, researchers use first- and second-person voice (e.g., "We interviewed 21 participants …").

**Methodology** as a philosophy of science involves the actual practice of qualitative inquiry, or the approach used to identify and/or develop knowledge about a phenomenon (Varpio & MacLeod, 2020). It is heavily influenced by other core philosophies of science. Our ideas about what constitutes truth and knowledge in the context of the values of those involved in the research process sets up how we design a qualitative study. Thus, methodology refers to decisions about aspects such as selection of research paradigms and traditions, research questions, and data collection methods (Creswell & Poth, 2017). Should data designs be qualitative, quantitative, or a combination of these (i.e., mixed methods; see Chapter 5)? Thus, a study of family discord could involve qualitative or quantitative data, or both.

Quantitative ◄─────────────────────► Qualitative

In summary, scientific pursuit involves an active and continual reflection on how the researcher envisions the intersection of perspective (ontology), knowledge construction (epistemology), values (axiology), and dissemination of findings (rhetoric). These overlap and influence research design decisions (methodology). Figure 2.2 illustrates these considerations, using a research problem as a guide.

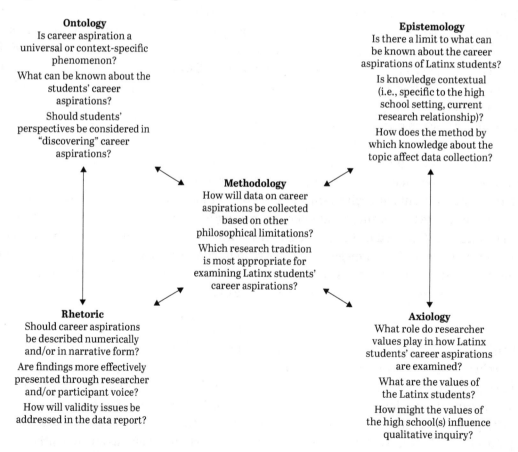

**FIGURE 2.2** *Career Aspirations of Latinx High School Students*

# Research Paradigms

Research paradigms may be thought of as belief systems based on the core philosophies of science (Creswell & Poth, 2017; Denzin & Lincoln, 2011; Hays & Wood, 2011). As noted earlier in the chapter, some research paradigms (e.g., positivism, postpositivism, constructivism) were introduced beginning in the colonial ethnography period of the 17th through 19th centuries. Others, such as critical theory and Indigenous research paradigms, were introduced in the 20th and 21st centuries, respectively. Table 2.3 illustrates the relationships among various

**TABLE 2.3** Research Paradigms and Philosophies of Science

| Paradigms and accompanying philosophies of science | Foci in qualitative inquiry |
|---|---|
| **POSITIVISM, POSTPOSITIVISM**<br><br>*Ontology:* There is a universal truth that can be known (positivism) or approximated (postpositivism), and the researchers' findings correspond to that truth at varying degrees.<br><br>*Epistemology:* Knowledge is obtained through measurable experience with participants and may be applied across a population. These experiences can be directly observed (positivism) or both directly and indirectly measured (postpositivism).<br><br>*Axiology:* Research relationships have minimal influence on the results, and researchers should remain emotionally neutral. Research may be value-free.<br><br>*Rhetoric:* "Neutral" report writing and third-person voice are used. *Methodology:* Structured methods and designs help control and manipulate conditions. Research is considered scientific if internal validity, external validity, reliability, and objectivity are addressed. | *Positivism:* What's really going on in the real world? How do the researcher's findings correspond to a truth shared within the scientific community?<br><br>*Postpositivism:* What can be known about a particular theory? To what degree can we accurately measure a phenomenon? What other explanations are possible for the research problem? |
| **CONSTRUCTIVISM**<br><br>*Ontology:* Multiple realities of a phenomenon exist.<br><br>*Epistemology:* Knowledge is co-constructed between researcher and participants.<br><br>*Axiology:* There is an emphasis on the values of the researcher, participants, and research setting.<br><br>*Rhetoric:* Data that are presented largely reflect the participants' voices and thoroughly describe the roles of the researcher and research setting in understanding the research problem.<br><br>*Methodology:* Decisions about what and how research problems are studied are largely determined collaboratively between researcher and participants. Research is considered scientific if it is contextually relevant and trustworthiness has been established. | How do participants conceptualize the research problem?<br><br>What contextual factors influence how participants and researchers construct, study, and report research findings? |

*(continued)*

**TABLE 2.3** Research Paradigms and Philosophies of Science *(Continued)*

| Paradigms and accompanying philosophies of science | Foci in qualitative inquiry |
|---|---|
| **CRITICAL RESEARCH PARADIGMS**<br><br>*Ontology:* Reality is subjective, and constructs tend to be defined by those with power in society, leaving out other ways of knowing. Participants' marginalized backgrounds are an integral component for understanding a construct from their perspective.<br><br>*Epistemology:* Knowledge is co-constructed between the researcher and participants. Cultural identities, in particular intersecting identities, are important organizing frameworks for generating ways of knowing.<br><br>*Axiology:* The researcher's values are instrumental in acknowledging social injustice and promoting change.<br><br>*Rhetoric:* Participants' voices are central to reporting findings.<br>*Methodology:* The research design seeks to minimize exploitive processes in qualitative inquiry by using appropriate data collection methods and considering how results may affect the social experiences of participants. | In what ways has the role of gender, race, and other cultural identities been ignored in qualitative inquiry?<br><br>What influences do forms of oppression (e.g., racism, classism, sexism, heterosexism) have on understanding the research problem?<br><br>How might qualitative inquiry create social and political change within and outside the research process? |
| **INDIGENOUS RESEARCH PARADIGMS**<br><br>*Ontology:* Available knowledge systems are a result of colonization of Indigenous populations in which some cultural aspects and their ways of knowing have been deleted and/or distorted.<br><br>*Epistemology:* Knowledge is continually constructed by Indigenous populations and can be more understood by the researcher as they share power and co-construct the research process with them.<br><br>*Axiology:* The researchers' values need to be critically examined, as they are influenced by research that has traditionally been colonizing to Indigenous populations. Participant values are a priority, and researcher values must be named explicitly.<br><br>*Rhetoric:* Participants' voices are central to reporting findings.<br>*Methodology:* The research design and decisions are shaped by the needs of Indigenous populations by which participants serve as coresearchers throughout the process. | What research questions does the Indigenous population want to explore?<br><br>How are current ways of knowing colonizing to the population? What knowledge systems from the population can be introduced in the research process as well as with the findings?<br><br>How can the research process allow an Indigenous population to reclaim or rewrite history and solidify community ways of knowing and identity? |

Sources: Chilisa (2020), Patton (2014), Ponterotto (2005), and Smith (2012)

research paradigms and philosophies of science discussed in the previous section, and Proposal Development Activity 2.1 at the end of this section provides an opportunity for you to consider which paradigm(s) may be aligned with your research topic. As we describe each research paradigm, we include a research example from education.

**PROPOSAL DEVELOPMENT ACTIVITY 2.1.** EXAMINING RESEARCH PARADIGMS

As you think about developing a research study, it is important to think about possible benefits and challenges for each of the research paradigms. To what degree do each of the research paradigms "fit" for your topic of interest? Write down on a separate piece of paper benefits and challenges for each paradigm.

## Positivism

**Positivism** is a paradigm focused on identifying and studying discrete, well-defined constructs. Founded in the early 19th century by Auguste Comte, it assumes that researchers may arrive at an objective, universal truth through direct observation and experience of phenomena. Thus, only verifiable claims should be considered genuine knowledge. Positivists are primarily concerned with empirically verifying existing theory through hypothesis testing with goals of operationally measuring constructs, replicating methods across disciplines, and generalizing knowledge to a population (Patton, 2014). In order to achieve these goals, positivist researchers seek to maintain objectivity in research design by establishing a clear boundary with research participants, avoiding a discussion of the values of those involved in the research, and using well-known statistical procedures to control contextual variables that impact a study. Positivism has dominated and characterized scientific pursuit for several centuries. However, given its characteristics, it is not generally used in qualitative research.

To illustrate positivism, consider the following research question: What is the effect of an online science education module on a fourth grader's reported academic self-concept? To address this question, a researcher would develop hypotheses and establish a research design using intervention and control groups and randomized sampling procedures, instructing the intervention group with a manualized science education module and operationally defining and objectively measuring academic self-concept. Through a controlled design, the researcher might demonstrate that the intervention group reported significantly higher academic self-concept after instruction than the control group.

## Postpositivism

By the early 20th century, philosophers such as Karl Popper asserted that all scientific observations are inherently subjective. Furthermore, many researchers believe that theory should be tested to be verified *and* falsified, leading to the development of **postpositivism**. Thus, theories should be falsified in order to strengthen them (Patton, 2014). While postpositivists hold similar beliefs about science as positivists, they assert that universal reality can never fully be realized, because you cannot say with complete certainty that a theory fully describes a phenomenon or construct. While postpositivists argue that reality or universal truths exist, they state that you cannot fully measure or understand it/them. With this paradigm, issues of validity, reliability, and alternative hypotheses are heavily emphasized.

Consider again the academic self-concept research example to further illustrate the use of this paradigm. Theories surround both academic self-concept and effective practices in science education instruction, yet the postpositivist would seek to find other practices that could be effective in increasing academic self-concept while exploring potential sources of error in measuring effectiveness of various forms of science education instruction. If a researcher is able to show that the online science education model is most effective for increasing academic self-concept, the theory is strengthened.

Postpositivism is used in conjunction with some qualitative research traditions (see Chapter 4). For example, qualitative researchers may be interested in identifying a set of best empirical practices for working with children with autism to develop social skills. Or they may want to identify what set of factors best lead to the effective treatment of phobias within an adult outpatient sample. These examples indicate a desire to identify universal findings that will apply to populations of interest but also a recognition that measurement error exists since qualitative researchers collect data from samples and identify findings to apply to the larger population.

## Constructivism

As scientific inquiry increased in education and the social sciences, many viewed the use of positivism and postpositivism as incongruent with characteristics of qualitative research. For instance, there was growing concern that findings were not applicable to all and minimized and marginalized various groups. Thus, the evolution and creation of research paradigms have been partly a result of changes in social movements (Saarinen, 1988). As such, several paradigms were introduced to attend to the context in which participants live and experience phenomena and involve participants' and researchers' subjective voices (Denzin & Lincoln, 2011).

**Constructivism** is a belief system that assumes that universal truth cannot exist, because there are multiple contextual perspectives and subjective voices that can label truth in scientific pursuit. This paradigm argues that reality about clinical and education phenomena should never be labeled as objective since the voices of the researchers and participants are biased and seated in different cultural experiences and identities. Constructivists seek to construct knowledge through social interactions as well as understand how individuals construct knowledge. Cultural, historical, and political events and processes influence these interactions. A collaborative dialogue among researchers and participants about defining and understanding the research problem as well as collecting and interpreting findings is highly valued (Patton, 2014; Ponterotto, 2005). Thus, those who identify primarily as constructivists enter a research setting with tentative questions versus a set of hypotheses to test. With constructivism, the notion of trustworthiness (discussed in Chapter 7) replaces the concepts of reliability and validity for establishing scientific rigor.

With the academic self-concept example, constructivists would conceptualize academic self-concept as a relative construct that can only be understood within the social context of the participants who may be experiencing it. Essentially, there is no universal definition of "academic self-concept." Thus, they would solicit information from participants about how they define the construct and how their conceptualization has been influenced by their schooling and other socialization experiences. Furthermore, constructivists would assert that various interventions (i.e., science education models) are contextual and that their effectiveness thus largely depends on the environment and situation in which they are implemented, attitudes of the researcher and participants related to a particular intervention and academic self-concept in general, and the interaction between the two.

## Critical Research Paradigms

In this section, we present three major critical research paradigms: feminism, critical race theory, and queer theory. With these paradigms, qualitative researchers not only seek to understand a phenomenon through various subjective lenses but also strive to create social and political changes to improve the lives of participants. Thus, they closely examine how social norms are manifested in both positive and negative ways in participants' lives. Followers of these paradigms view researcher objectivity as impossible and subjectivity as something that should be readily acknowledged and valued. Researchers intentionally reflect upon the role of cultural privilege and oppression, and their views around the role of culture in the research process as well as their and their participants' lives are often changed when employing these paradigms.

Critical research paradigms are tied to the philosophy of **poststructuralism**, or the critique that systemic structures (e.g., language) can be fixed in terms of their categories and interpretations. Poststructuralism was founded by French philosopher Jacques Derrida in the 1970s (Derrida, 1976, 1978, 1981), who noted that structures are not preestablished or binary, are constantly changing in society, and cannot be precisely defined or understood. The tendency for individuals to want to place constructs in discrete categories within fixed knowledge systems, poststructuralists would argue, perpetuates marginalization in society in general and scholarship more specifically. The objective of poststructuralism is the deconstruction and reconstruction of social structures.

### Feminism

**Feminism**, as a research paradigm, assumes that gender is an organizing principle in understanding and reporting research findings. These researchers argue that women have largely been excluded from scientific pursuit, or when women are included in research, they are often pathologized in some manner. The development of a feminist research paradigm is linked to the larger U.S. feminist movement, which tends to be characterized as occurring in four waves, although there is some variability in this characterization (Reger, 2017).

The first wave of feminism (late 19th–early 20th centuries) was focused on temperance and abolitionist movements, or attention to women's suffrage and their general participation in politics. This movement was largely led by White, middle-class, cisgender women. By the 1960s, the United States entered in a second wave of feminism that was in response to the anti–Vietnam War and civil rights movements. Within this wave, there was increasing solidarity with women of color to address socioeconomic issues as well as greater attention to gender as a social construct to develop a more culturally nuanced view of womanhood. A third wave began in the mid-1990s, informed in part by postmodernism. The crux of this wave was to continue to destabilize what is meant by "womanhood" and some reclaiming of traditionally objectified aspects of feminine beauty for themselves and not as externally defined by the patriarchy. In fact, third-wave feminists did not identify as a collective, unified group with universal concerns, even pushing back against the label of "feminist" itself (Reger, 2017). A present, fourth wave has emerged recently, welcoming women and men to destabilize traditional conceptions of gender and gender issues, articulate a broader umbrella or continuum of gender (e.g., transgender and gender-non-conforming individuals) and its intersections, and examine gender from a transnational perspective. Individuals within this wave largely reject the term "feminist" given its potentially radical and binary connotations.

As these waves indicate, feminism began with a focus on patriarchy and women's political advocacy and broadened to include a more nuanced, intersectional, and transnational view of gender. Applied to qualitative research, gender as an organizing system across cultures can be used to consider clinical and education constructs. Traditionally, knowledge of women has been filtered through relationships of power and subordination. How have clinical and educational constructs we study been shaped largely through a lens of masculinity and domination? How has a limited view of gender constricted scientific inquiry in general and advocacy within clinical and education settings more specifically? How has gender as a system served to make invisible the contributions of those who do not identify with a traditional binary view of gender? How can we be critical of gender as an organizing framework to develop and/or highlight alternative ways of knowing? These critical questions are prioritized within a feminist research paradigm.

Furthermore, qualitative researchers integrating a feminist research paradigm also emphasize the researcher–participant relationship in the research process. They seek to address and dismantle methods by which patriarchy may play into qualitative inquiry, often through liberatory experiences for women and those not characterized as cisgender men. For example, qualitative researchers can affirm participants as they share their stories and perspectives, using self-disclosure or highlighting how issues of gender or intersectional discrimination may shape the phenomenon under study. They are also sensitive to empowering participants to offer counternarratives and discuss examples of resilience and resistance to gender discrimination. Furthermore, they prioritize maximizing trust between themselves and participants throughout the research process, sharing information about the research process, identified themes, and general findings.

Unfortunately, feminism has been primarily focused on and developed by White, cisgender women, disregarding the gendered and intersectional experiences of most women and girls, thus negating valuable ontological and epistemological perspectives for clinical and educational settings (Collins, 2009; Kendall, 2020). As Kendall (2020) asserts, this omission of experience can result from oppressing women of color, LGBTQ+ women, differently abled women, and women of lower social classes and socioeconomic statuses, to name a few. In addition, the absence of feminist voice can result when women and men who are White and identify as feminists view struggles of women as universal because they do not readily attend to intersectional issues of oppression. As such, qualitative researchers must create space for collective standpoints, highlighting intersectional experiences, to broaden our understanding of constructs in clinical and educational settings. As discussed in the previous chapter, the feminist standpoint asserts that narratives stand on their own to offer alternative and affirmative images that foster individual and group empowerment and broader coalition-building.

A prominent and foundational figure of intersectional and standpoint feminism is Patricia Hill Collins. Collins (2009) identified several core themes of Black feminist thought for qualitative researchers to consider in framing their inquiry. These themes center around constructs of work, family, motherhood, relationships, sexuality, and others. She discusses each theme as a construct organized within intersecting oppressions of race, class, gender, sexual orientation, and nation for Black women—with White men and women creating and perpetuating stereotypes or controlling images of Black womanhood (and manhood). These controlling images serve to objectify and other Black women, limiting ways of knowing within clinical and educational settings about how Black women (and men) conceptualize work, family, relationships, and other constructs. Examples of these controlling images include "mammy," "welfare mother," "jezebel," "superstrong Black mother," and "angry Black lady" (Collins, 2009).

Importantly, Collins (2009) highlights the power of self-definition for Black women in response to these externally defined controlling images. She noted that intentional and active self-definition, constructed through their relationships within extended families, churches, literature, and Black community organizations, serve as a form of resistance and a means to identify and cultivate ways of being and knowing for Black individuals. Thus, it is important that qualitative researchers provide an opportunity for Black participants to express an individual voice within the collective context of family and community as a means of resilience and survival. In the research process itself, this could involve creating safe spaces for collective dialogue with other Black individuals and using data sources and methods that gather information from them regarding cultural ways of knowing and self-definition.

## Critical Race Theory

**Critical race theory (CRT)** began in the 1970s, when legal scholars increasingly noted significant stalls in the civil rights movement of the 1960s in terms of the dismantling of racism to foster racial equity and progress. CRT was built in part of the second wave of feminism. Along with others (e.g., Michel Foucault, Sojourner Truth, W. E. B. DuBois, Frederick Douglass, César Chavéz, and Martin Luther King Jr.), Derrick Bell, a legal scholar, is often cited as its principal founder, with the following individuals credited with furthering CRT and its strands: Alan Freeman, Richard Delgado, Kimberlé Crenshaw, Angela Harris, Patricia Williams, Neil Gotanda, Mitu Gulati, Jerry Kang, Ian Haney López, Kevin Johnson, Laura Gomez, Margaret Montoya, Juan Perea, and Francisco Valdes (Delgado & Stefancic, 2017).

Beginning in the mid 1990s, CRT splintered as scholars considered the unique needs of various marginalized people. These strands included Latino critical theory (LatCrit), Asian American critical legal studies, and queer critical legal studies. For example, LatCrit and Asian American critical scholars noted how subjectivity and "hunches" from judges were used to continually discriminate against individuals related to immigration and language. Their strategy, then, was to use the legal system as a method for social transformation and social justice locally, nationally, and globally (Delgado & Stefancic, 2017; Valdes, 2005). In addition to these strands, CRT extended to other disciplines such as education, beginning with Gloria Ladson-Billings and William Tate (1995). An example of some of the education issues explored from a CRT lens include school discipline, the school-to-prison pipeline, affirmative action, high-stakes testing, teacher preparation, racialized curricula, and alternative and charter schools.

For scholars of CRT and its strands, racial liberation is the central and most important method for advancing scholarship. Racial liberation involves a critical analysis of racism and White supremacy and its manifestation within scholarship as well as cultural, economic, educational, health, criminal justice, and political systems in general. In addition, it is the explicit valuing of race consciousness of BIPOC to shape new ways of knowing (Delgado & Stefancic, 2017; Dunbar, 2008; Salas, 2019; Valdes, 2005).

Scholars assume that power relationships—the economic, political, and sociocultural positionality of the researched and researcher—influence how research is collected and interpreted. Within CRT and its strands, scholarship and activism are inextricably linked. Qualitative researchers must engage in activism within and outside higher education, PK–12, and mental health institutions, working with communities to build and identify ways of knowing and producing scholarship. Furthermore, there is a focus on community- and coalition-building, both in their activism and how they approach conducting, critiquing, and employing scholarship.

The following assumptions about race, racism, White supremacy, and intersectionality are prevalent across critical theory paradigms:

- Racism is viewed as an ordinary part of societal functioning. It is an ongoing, multidimensional, and dynamic process inherent in the development and maintenance of an institutionalized, hierarchical racial classification system on individual, group, and system levels.
- Racism is upheld by a deeply entrenched set of assumptions and norms (i.e., White supremacy) that privilege the views of White people who have traditionally held the most power. Furthermore, White supremacy works in concert with and is sustained by other power systems, such as capitalism and patriarchy (hooks, 2000).
- Because racism benefits White people and those who approximate White, there is little interest for them to dismantle it (i.e., *interest convergence*). Beliefs and behaviors related to White privilege are deeply embedded and intertwined with culture, gender, Christianity, and capitalism to collectively promote racialized power. Such outcomes include the exploitive sharecropping labor systems and other forms of indentured servitude, residential redlining, housing segregation, the school-to-prison pipeline, health care disparities, voter suppression, and threats to reproductive freedom and upward career mobility for women and BIPOC (Hays & Shillingford-Butler, 2023).
- Race and its categories are social constructions, not biological distinctions, designed to justify continued exploitation of BIPOC. The use of racial classifications in all institutions of society (e.g., family, education, employment, government) results in the socialization of a racial worldview for all its members; this worldview is transmitted across generations.
- It is important to attend to how multiple cultural identities and experiences intersect with racism. Crenshaw (1991) noted three processes of intersectionality: (a) structural intersectionality (i.e., how location of intersecting cultural identities creates different

experiences for a phenomenon or construct based on different levels of power and status); (b) political intersectionality (i.e., how one social category is used politically to marginalize those who are disadvantaged in another category); and (c) representational intersectionality (i.e., how social categories that are culturally represented in media and other popular culture can disadvantage some at a particular location).

With these assumptions, qualitative researchers adhering to this paradigm prominently weave storytelling into their methodology. Storytelling, through construction of racialized narratives and counternarratives, afford BIPOC an opportunity to voice their lived experiences and perspectives. Through the process of reflection and telling, storytellers through narratives and counternarratives express their individual and collective cultural experiences, a historical and political process for participants. Narratives and counternarratives can foster race consciousness and new ways of knowing, create community among BIPOC, and challenge the dominant stories upheld within White supremacy. Critical scholars thus commit to making shared stories matter in both qualitative research and communities (Salas, 2019; Salinas et al., 2016; Solórzano & Yosso, 2002).

### Queer Theory

**Queer theory** is a critical research paradigm that was coined by feminist theorist Teresa de Lauretis in 1990 (Ramello, 2020) in response to gay identity politics that were prominent in the 1980s. It asserts that concepts of gender, sexuality, and body are social constructions that are fluid, plural, and continually negotiated. These concepts function as essentialized categories that either privilege or marginalize individuals within society, perpetuating heterosexism, sexism, and other intersecting oppressions. They assert that those identifying as White, heterosexual, young, and normatively sized and able-bodied are privileged and essentialized as norms. Thus, those who do not meet these norms are pushed to the margins.

As a research paradigm, queer theory involves "queering" how social norms are naturalized and reliant on binary categories (i.e., engaging in a critical analysis of how these categories are defined, performed, and valued in society). Queer theorists eschew identifying precise definitions of these constructs, as they view a reduction in how they are conceptualized as marginalizing. As concepts and labels (e.g., cisgender, trans, lesbian, sexually attractive) are deconstructed and reconstructed, queer theorists highlight their fluidity. Thus, queer theory both critically interrogates social norms and provides voice to those on the margins (Riggs & Treharne, 2017).

Judith Butler, a prominent feminist and queer theorist, constructed the concept of *performativity*, or the "doing" of gender and sexual identity within daily life. Bodies are performed in a manner that is either intelligible (i.e., approximating particular social norms) or unintelligible. Individuals are marginalized to the extent they do not perform gender, sexuality, and body in a normative manner. Butler (2004, 2011) argued that intelligibility polices possibility in terms of expression of gender, sexuality, and body.

O'Malley et al. (2018) identified shared assumptions within queer theory that have implications for qualitative researchers in clinical and education settings. First, experiences, ontologies, and epistemologies that center gender and sexuality are underrepresented in research. Second, this underrepresentation limits the ability to resist, reconstruct, and transform policies and practices. Third, unintelligible bodies are frequently and pervasively marginalized despite the explicit attention in disciplines on the constructs of gender and sexuality. Fourth, intersectional research designs are needed to examine how intersectional oppression uniquely shapes the educational and life experiences of those rendered unintelligible.

Let's consider the academic self-concept research example to illustrate critical theory paradigms. Findings might lead researchers to seek to understand the degree to which oppression linked to particular cultural variables (e.g., race/ethnicity, gender, sexual orientation) impact the understanding and presentation of academic self-concept. For example, qualitative researchers employing a feminist research paradigm might focus on the role of gender and sexism—and intersectional identities—on the instruction of science education as well as academic self-concept. Qualitative researchers employing CRT could examine the role of racism in colonizing science education and its impact on academic self-concept. And a study using queer theory might critically examine how research on gender differences in academic self-concept is limited given its assumption of a binary classification of gender. Adhering to a critical research paradigm, the research process itself could prioritize creating a safe space for participants to share narratives and counternarratives about their school experiences to reclaim a collective history and share new knowledge. Furthermore, critical research paradigms could be used in a qualitative study to solicit information about changes that need to be made in science education to support academic self-concept for marginalized populations and/or develop recommendations for new ways of conceptualizing academic self-concept.

## Indigenous Research Paradigms

Greater attention has been given in qualitative research to the contributions of Indigenous research methodologies derived from knowledge systems of Indigenous populations. Snow et al. (2016) defined **Indigenous populations** as individuals or groups belonging to developing or underdeveloped regions nationally or internationally as well as those who have been marginalized by Eurocentric values and/or research methodologies. At an international level, Indigenous populations often have histories of imperialism embedded within contemporary sociopolitical realities; at a national level, Indigenous populations experience subjugation resulting from current and historical instances of oppression (Chilisa, 2020; Smith, 2012). While different in scope and specific experience, these groups balance sense of community and empowerment with distrust of the dominant culture.

Individuals, groups, and communities of traditionally marginalized statuses possess an intangible *cultural heritage*, or shared practices, expressions, knowledge, skills, artifacts, and physical and metaphorical spaces. This heritage is transmitted across and reshaped within generations to provide them a sense of identity and continuity. Identifying and respecting this cultural heritage in the research process has increasingly become part of the conversation of research ethics (Battiste, 2016; Kowal, 2015; Smith, 2012).

Battiste (2016) used the term *cognitive imperialism* to describe the act in which a dominant group's knowledge, experience, culture, and language is viewed as universal. Qualitative researchers operating from this paradigm reflect on the following as they engage in the research process (Smith, 2012):

- Whose research is it?
- Who owns it?
- Whose interests does it serve?
- Who will benefit from it?
- Who has designed its questions and framed its scope?
- Who will carry it out?
- Who will write it up?
- How will its results be disseminated? (p. 10)

An Indigenous research paradigm is based on four Rs (Chilisa, 2020; Kirkness & Barnhardt, 1991; Smith, 2012):

- *relational accountability/responsibility:* Researchers are aware that ways of knowing are based on the relationships between all life forms. There is a sense of responsibility for the impact of research on individuals and communities.
- *respect:* Researchers are to be humble and generous in the co-creating research process, engaging in practices that report back findings and share knowledge. All involved in research become family.
- *reciprocity:* All research is considered a form of appropriation and requires adequate benefits to all involved. There is a shared give and take of power.
- *rights and regulations:* Researches develop and adhere to a research process that is collaborative, based on Indigenous protocols, goals, and ways of knowing. Free, prior, and informed consent of samples and communities is an essential element.

In addition to these four Rs that serve as a values framework for qualitative researchers, Indigenous research emphasizes critical immersion within an Indigenous population; shared power, reflexivity, and co-construction of the research process; methodological flexibility and novelty; and participation and accountability (Snow et al., 2016).

Qualitative researchers operating from this paradigm view Indigenous populations' cultural protocols, practices, and beliefs as integral and explicit parts to the research process. They recognize that academic writing in clinical and education settings presents what is considered knowledge but is based on constructs. Furthermore, they seek to deconstruct the research process, based often on Western values, and reclaim knowledge and rewrite history in order to center ways of knowing of Indigenous populations. That is, research about Indigenous populations has often been done by outsiders of those populations, resulting in their dehumanization and erasure. As Smith (2012) noted, little about research is defined by populations themselves. Similar to CRT, stories produced within this paradigm can highlight ways to reconnect, identify with cultural history, and share new ways of knowing.

Applied to the academic self-concept research example, qualitative researchers using Indigenous research paradigms would engage extensively with an Indigenous community, seeking from the community which research questions they were interested in addressing. Then, they would serve as coresearchers with the community, co-constructing the research process and integrating a holistic approach to evaluating the constructs of interest. Qualitative researchers would respect cultural protocols as data are collected, interpreted, and reported. Furthermore, they would facilitate a process by which participants could articulate how they have been colonized by educational systems and rewrite research to showcase points of resilience and resistance in terms of science education and academic self-concept.

## Contributions of Qualitative Research

The key characteristics of qualitative research presented earlier in the chapter reflect that it is a useful approach to explore basic human processes, develop and verify theory, and/or enact social change. Furthermore, qualitative and quantitative methods are both "tools" of science that allow us to answer research questions; these approaches should be considered a continuum of complementary approaches and when used together produce a comprehensive and useful picture. All research has quantitative and qualitative elements or dimensions—whether explicit or not. The distinction between objectivity and subjectivity is artificial and thus not useful, and most constructs clinical and educational researchers are interested in are based on subjective judgments. So both methodologies can contain characteristics of the other, can be subjective and objective, and are to be interpreted collectively to address research problems in clinical and educational settings. Activity 2.1 provides an opportunity for you to examine a quantitative study to consider whether qualitative research characteristics are present.

Ercikan and Roth (2006) made several significant points about how several aspects of quantitative research are qualitative in nature. First, in designs using statistics, many of the reported

**ACTIVITY 2.1.** QUALITATIVE RESEARCH CHARACTERISTICS WITHIN QUANTITATIVE RESEARCH

Select and review a recently published quantitative study in your discipline. As a class or in small groups, reflect on the following questions:

- To what extent are the following characteristics present in the study?
  - inductive and abductive analysis
  - naturalistic and experimental settings
  - the importance of context
  - the humanness of research
  - purposive sampling
  - thick description
  - an interactive, flexible research design
- Which of the characteristics are most appropriate to strengthen if the study were replicated? How could you strengthen them in the design?

statistics are descriptive and thus qualitative in nature. For example, I (Danica) conducted a survey of dating violence prevalence on a college campus. While the survey contained quantitative items and I computed such descriptive statistics as measures of central tendency and variability, the results were discussed both in terms of prevalence rates and how participants responded to particular survey items. Yes, it was important to discover that approximately one third of the sample experienced dating violence, but it was also important to outline specific dating violence experiences. Researchers consistently provide qualitative information about a data set in the discussion or conclusion section of any manuscript they develop.

Another example of how quantitative research has qualitative research findings is in the use of rubrics or scaling methods. When scorers use rubrics, no matter how objective the rubrics are, they are still subjective in their judgments (Ercikan & Roth, 2006). Let's take for example a study that involves clinical supervisors assessing supervisees' skills through observing particular behaviors in a video recording. As each supervisor uses the scale, they reflect on the following "qualitative" questions: What does each point mean? How might various supervisors have different thresholds for when a skill has been demonstrated? Am I assessing skill level based on how competent the supervisee should be at this level of training, or am I assessing skill level based on a counselor who is able to see clients independently?

The reverse is also true. Sometimes in qualitative studies, researchers rely on frequency counts to interpret and present findings (see Part III of this text). For example, in a program evaluation, a research team may count the number of times a particular need was mentioned in several focus groups. While these needs could be presented in narrative form, it may be more meaningful in some cases to present them in some order, with the most cited need presented first.

## Top 10 Points About Qualitative Research to Consider

We hope that this chapter has provided you some important foundational information as you begin to think about your qualitative projects. We present to you our Top 10 points about qualitative research that we hope you will keep in mind throughout your qualitative study.

1. *It's a journey, not a destination:* Qualitative research is a process and not simply a product in the form of a report or presentation. It is interactive and reflexive based on the context. So you cannot plan every detail of your study. Issues, problems, and revised research questions will occur as you conduct your study. Ambiguity comes with the territory.

2. *Begin with a strong foundation:* Although a qualitative study is reflexive and evolving, its rationale is often founded in theoretical and philosophical assumptions. You should articulate your perspective on the nature of reality ("truth") and knowledge acquisition. Think of the base of your research endeavor as the historical/philosophical assumptions, research paradigms, and personal and professional experiences that have led to your research design. In a cyclical fashion, research questions drive your research design,

which influences your choice of methods. If you have a strong foundation of knowledge of why you are asking the questions you are asking, you will be more open to changes in your research.

3. *Keep it as simple as possible:* Select a single idea and single research paradigm to begin. Go from particular to general. The more people and things you include, the more data will pile up and become more difficult to manage.

4. *Of course, the more people and things involved, the better:* The strength and rigor of qualitative research lies in the number of data sources and researchers. The only way we can achieve this as researchers is to immerse ourselves in our fieldwork. However, there is no magic number regarding how many people or things should be involved in the study. Be open to combining approaches and techniques.

5. *Let go of your defenses:* We are all biased researchers; we may just admit it more often in qualitative inquiry because researchers serve as instruments of data collection and analysis. You cannot change what you know and/or how you know phenomena. You cannot change who you are or your unique experiences. Strike a balance between knowing that you have biases and being open to the fact that others do too. So accept that a majority of qualitative inquiry deals with multiple realities and perspectives. Because researchers offer unique perspectives to studies and engage in collective data analysis, their theories and/or findings are tentative and qualifiable. We as researchers have to be open to change and criticism. Finally, you cannot claim to know everything about a phenomenon, nor can you apply your results to other populations. Generalizability is not the goal.

6. *It is not just about words:* Qualitative research is not easier than quantitative research. It is not about identifying keywords and themes. It is a complex effort of attempting to search for patterns in light of frequency of data occurring. It is about comprehensiveness for a particular group or context. It should go beyond description to build theory or apply directly to a discipline. Unfortunately, qualitative research never ends: You have to decide when to stop.

7. *Quantity is not always important, and quantitative research is not the enemy:* On the other hand, it is not just about numbers either. As discussed previously, one major critique of quantitative research is that statistical control (i.e., isolation and measurement of variables) and large samples may distort the meaning of process and outcome data and limit voices of participants. Thus, counting is not always helpful or necessary. Further, qualitative and quantitative research are legs in a race; it is a team effort. Team members and their order may look different depending on the research question(s). Each adds something essential and unique and can build upon one another. They are congruent in that research designs may combine or use both areas of inquiry at various points of a study.

8. *We are all studying and being studied:* Researchers and participants influence each other. We are all instruments of data collection. Our participants know more than us about a phenomenon, and we affect how much they tell us. Further, this mutual influence should not stop until data have been analyzed and changes have been implemented for

those involved in the research. Research should bring some change in awareness and/or action on the part of the researcher(s) and/or participant(s).

9. *Data collection and analysis occur somewhat simultaneously:* Qualitative research is typically an inductive process. Recursivity is an integral component of asking better questions. You should constantly compare and revise themes and codes as you gather data.

10. *Acknowledge your role as a researcher-practitioner and consider the role of your research in social change as you build a research agenda:* Assume the role of researcher-practitioner-advocate (RPA) in qualitative work. Because all research is political, remember the power you hold in these roles and consistently seek to share power with participants and understand their needs. Consider how your qualitative study fits within a larger research agenda.

## CHAPTER SUMMARY

This chapter began with several characteristics of qualitative research, including (a) inductive and abductive analysis; (b) naturalistic setting; (c) person in context; (d) the humanness of research; (e) purposive sampling; (f) thick description; and (g) an interactive, flexible research design. In essence, qualitative research attends to social interactions and context and honors collaboration and participant voices and perspectives. We also included perspectives of how qualitative characteristics are present in quantitative and mixed methods research.

Then we described the history of qualitative research, highlighting several scholars' conceptualizations of the key moments of this work. These span ethnographies from early colonizing efforts; to case studies of urban regions; to attention to cultural diversity and voice; to greater attention to context, method sophistication, and the interrelated nature of researcher, writing, fieldwork, and Indigenous ways of knowing. Specifically, these moments are classified as early ethnography, colonial ethnography, hermeneutics, the traditional period, phenomenology, pragmatism and the Chicago School, the modernist phase, blurred genres, crisis of interpretation, triple crisis, postexperimental inquiry and beyond, and Indigenous contributions. As qualitative inquiry moved more toward the present and in response to a changing and diversifying society, qualitative researchers have gained a multitude of methods, approaches, and traditions to use in their work. In present day work, we are increasingly focused on voice, representation, advocacy, and alternative and Indigenous ways of knowing to support our scholarship.

Historical movements in qualitative research have introduced and shaped how we view scientific inquiry and the research paradigms we use to develop the blueprint of a qualitative research study. We presented information on the five core philosophies of science (i.e., ontology, epistemology, axiology, rhetoric, and methodology). Then we introduced several research paradigms and how they align with qualitative research to inform a selected research tradition. These paradigms include positivism, postpositivism, social constructivism, feminism, CRT, queer theory, and Indigenous research paradigms. Finally, we concluded the chapter with a Top 10 list of key points for qualitative researchers to consider in their work.

## Review Questions

1. What are some of the key trends related to the history of qualitative research?
2. Compare and contrast early ethnographic work with later approaches, such as hermeneutics, phenomenology, and symbolic interactionism.
3. How would you ensure that study context is evident in a qualitative research design and report?
4. What are some of the similarities and differences among the three critical research paradigms presented?
5. What function does each research paradigm listed in this chapter serve to advance knowledge for any given construct?

## Recommended Readings

Chilisa, B. (2020). *Indigenous research methodologies* (2nd ed.). Sage.

Creswell, J. W., & Creswell, J. D. (2017). *Research design: Qualitative, quantitative, and mixed methods approaches* (4th ed.). Sage.

Delgado, R., & Stefancic, J. (2017). *Critical race theory: An introduction* (3rd ed.). New York University Press.

Denzin, N. K., & Lincoln, Y. S. (2011). Introduction: The discipline and practice of qualitative research. In N. K. Denzin & Y. S. Lincoln (Eds.), *The Sage handbook of qualitative research* (4th ed., pp. 1–19). Sage.

Maxwell, J. A. (2013). *Qualitative research design: An interactive approach* (3rd ed.). Sage.

Smith, L. T. (2012). *Decolonizing methodologies: Research and indigenous peoples* (2nd ed.). Zed Books.

## Image Credit

Fig. 2.1: Joseph A. Maxwell, "The Interactive Model of Qualitative Research Design," *Qualitative Research Design: An Interactive Approach*. Copyright © 2005 by SAGE Publications.

## CHAPTER 3

# Ethics and Qualitative Research

## CHAPTER PREVIEW

Research ethics is multilayered and ever evolving, particularly as researchers increasingly engage in qualitative research. Using select ethics codes from educational and social sciences disciplines, we present in this chapter several key ethical constructs, dilemmas, and considerations that apply to all aspects of the research process. The chapter begins with a brief history of ethics.

## A Brief History of Ethics

Debates about ethics have long predated the research ethical guidelines and regulatory bodies initially developed in the 1980s (Hammersley, 2018). Ethical philosophy has shifted across the centuries, reflecting societal changes in attitudes regarding morality, values, and reason. In this section, we provide a brief history of ethical philosophy with a primary focus on the ethics since the 20th century. It is important to note that European and American (i.e., White, male, Western) philosophy has been the dominant influence on research ethics today, pushing to the margins other forms of knowledge (e.g., Indigenous ethics, feminist ethics) from nondominant groups (e.g., women, racial/ethnic minority groups, tribal communities). In response to this, we highlight alternative ways of knowing toward the end of this section as well as throughout the chapter.

Despite the codification of research ethics beginning in the 1980s, there was a lack of explicit attention paid to the contributions to ethical thought and research epistemology by individuals, groups, and communities that are marginalized in society. Furthermore, there was a lack of direct naming of the impact of utilitarian ethics on those outside of the "rationale" majority. Thus, researchers today are encouraged to reflect on ethical tensions of current ethics codes and guidelines when working with marginalized populations, integrating other schools of thought, such as feminist standpoint ethics, feminist communitarianism, and Indigenous research ethics.

## Western Influences and Research Ethics

A great deal of what researchers traditionally understand as "ethical principles" can be traced to the Enlightenment period or "Age of Reason" of the 17th through 19th centuries in Europe. During this time, science and experimental reason as well as self-determination and individual freedom were privileged as real evidence, while morality, culture, and spirituality were eschewed as subjective and irrational. Thus, a Western researcher would prioritize neutrality, controlled research means or processes, and evidence through direct observation. Interpreting or applying research findings was avoided: The notion of developing practical or political outcomes from research was rejected as nonscientific (Hammersley, 2018).

John Stuart Mill (1806–1873) emphasized that neutrality was required for individual freedom or self-determination. Through inductive pursuit, he noted that information about human truth could be synthesized across history and thus be generalized and considered universal. Max Weber (1864–1920), another prominent figure, disputed Mill's claim that morality and culture could be divorced from reason in constructing knowledge. As such, *value-relevance* (i.e., the initial values researchers bring to scientific inquiry) could not be eliminated from initial scientific inquiry. However, he argued that the application of scientific findings must be value-free in its application and researchers should display an attitude of moral indifference (Christians, 2017). Weber advocated for *value freedom* or *value neutrality*, which is the pursuit of factual knowledge that is void of subjective evaluations or recommendations by the researcher.

### Individual Freedom, Context, and Power

Since the 20th century, variations of ethical thought from Western Europe based on Enlightenment principles have largely influenced U.S. research ethics. Schroeder (2004) identified four overlapping movements of ethics during the 20th century in Europe, beginning with (a) a primary focus on the individual, (b) a shift to a self in relation to context, an (c) ethics of personal transformation, and (d) Marxism. The first movement, *value realism*, is characterized through the works of Franz Brentano (1838–1917), Max Scheler (1874–1928), and Nicolai Hartmann (1882–1950). This movement focused on the intrinsic values and an analysis of emotions. Specifically, ethical courses of action are pursued based on the highest intrinsic values that could be obtained for a particular situation; sensory, intellectual, moral, and spiritual (i.e., Christian) values could be understood objectively. Philosophers of this movement noted how the logic of particular emotions (e.g., love, humility, shame, etc.) influence intrinsic values for ethical decision making.

The second movement, in which a relation to other people is its central feature, is reflected in the philosophies of Martin Buber (1878–1965), Emmanuel Levina (1906–1995), Karl Jaspers (1883–1969), and Luce Irigaray (1930–present). This tradition attends to the role of others in influencing an individual's reality and values. Through an effort toward reciprocity, the individual can achieve genuine presence; however, full reciprocity and synthesis with another is not viewed as possible.

A third movement, an ethics of personal transformation, is best characterized by the philosophies of Martin Heidegger (1889–1976), Jean-Paul Sartre (1905–1980), Simone de Beauvoir (1908–1986), Michel Foucault (1926–1984), and Gilles Deleuze (1925–1995); their works were influenced by Søren Kierkegaard (1813–1855) and Friedrich Nietzsche (1844–1900). The essential characteristic of this movement is that achieving an ethical ideal requires the individual to recognize that humanity is made both individually and socially: Individual freedom is not fully possible without communal freedom, and communal freedom is not possible without social, economic, and legal equality. For example, through critiquing historical knowledge systems and their focus on universal ethics, Foucault emphasized that knowledge is socially constructed and thus contextualized within each encounter (Jardine, 2005). Knowledge generation is connected to self-examination and participation with others. However, he and Deleuze noted that power dynamics have created a system of naming and evaluation in which some norms are institutionalized, considered "common sense" and part of scientific knowledge, and thus remain largely unexamined or critiqued (Morar, 2016).

A fourth movement is Marxism. Jürgen Habermas (1929–present) has taken up the torch for his predecessor Karl Marx (1818–1883), developing his work in the 20th century. For this movement, the focus is on the moral challenges of the effects of capitalism on culture and humanity. Thus, ethics is directly tied to the immorality of economic self-interest.

### Utilitarianism

Utilitarianism, based in these Western European movements, influenced professional codes of ethics that came into wide use in the 1980s in Europe and the United States and are still prominent today (Christians, 2017). **Utilitarianism** is based on a value of research utility: That which produces the greatest good for the greatest number of individuals is the right course of action for an individual and/or society in general. Utilitarianism assumes there is a universal set of rules of morality that determine what individuals ought to do; applied to research ethics, there is a primary focus on researcher expertise and compliance to ethical guidelines. John Rawls (1921–2002), one of the key philosophers of this movement, noted that fairness to one another is important and social arrangements are deemed fair if all "rational" people agree to them. However, determining who is considered rational to make these decisions was not discussed and can be inferred to relate primarily to those in the dominant group.

### Ethical Tensions and Malpractice

Based primarily on dominant Western group schools of ethical philosophy and practice, the history of research ethics reflects quite a bumpy road to the development and application of ethical codes, legal statutes, and research compliance. In fact, the evolution of ethical standards and legal protection largely resulted from reacting to atrocities against participants. Table 3.1 outlines some examples of ethical malpractice across disciplines.

**TABLE 3.1**    Select Research Studies Demonstrating Ethics Violations

| | |
|---|---|
| **Nazi medical experiments (1940s)** | Experiments conducted on Nazi prisoners involving exposure to high altitude, extreme cold, malaria, sterilization, sea water, poison, and mustard gas led to the eventual illness and death of thousands. These experiments were reportedly designed to assess physiological changes to various conditions; however, participants were never provided informed consent. |
| **Tuskegee syphilis experiment (1932–1972)** | With a purpose of understanding the natural course of syphilis in Black men and trying to justify treatment programs for them, the U.S. government intentionally withheld life-saving, well-accepted medical treatment (i.e., penicillin) as symptoms worsened. Participants had been told they would receive free medical treatment for their condition, although they were not informed of what that condition was and were deceived regarding the treatment they were receiving (i.e., a placebo). This case highlighted the improper use of deception in research. |
| **Guatemala syphilis experiment (1946–1948)** | Documents discovered in 2010 evidenced unethical research experiments on human subjects conducted by the U.S. government in Guatemala from 1946–1948. The research involved intentionally infecting over 1,300 subjects with syphilis to test the effectiveness of penicillin in preventing this disease. Only 700 subjects were given penicillin, and 83 died as a result of the study. Participants were never provided informed consent. |
| **HeLa stem cell research (1951–present)** | Henrietta Lacks, an African American woman, underwent treatment for cervical cancer at Johns Hopkins Hospital and died later that year. Researchers discovered that they were able to culture the cells from Lacks's tumor (named HeLa cells) and keep them alive, which was the first time that scientists had been able to grow a human cell line. HeLa cells were used in thousands of biomedical experiments as well as commercial use without her consent and without providing the family any compensation. In 2013, the NIH reached an agreement that gave Lacks's family control over access to the data and acknowledgment in scientific papers. |
| **Milgram blind obedience experiment (1960s)** | Stanley Milgram and his associates investigated participants' responses to demands from an authority in an effort to assess the construct of blind obedience. Most participants obeyed the researcher's request to deliver "shock treatment" for incorrect answers, resulting in severe distress for them. The researchers did not tell participants of the true research purpose, nor did they debrief them at the end of the study. |
| **Jewish chronic disease hospital study (1963)** | Patients of various health statuses were injected with live cancer cells so that researchers could evaluate the body's reaction to cancer cells based on the health status of the patient. Patients were never aware they were injected with these cells and thus did not give consent. |
| **Willowbrook hepatitis study (1960s)** | Using a school for children with mental disabilities as a controlled setting to examine the effects of hepatitis, researchers injected all admitted children with the virus. Informed consent was obtained from parents; however, there was no indication in the document that participation was voluntary and that a child's admittance was not based on the decision to participate or not. |

(continued)

**TABLE 3.1**   Select Research Studies Demonstrating Ethics Violations  (*Continued*)

| | |
|---|---|
| **Tearoom trade study (1970)** | Laud Humphreys researched the prevalence of male-male sexual activity in restrooms and then followed up with "participants" at their homes from contact information he obtained through license plate numbers. Although the intention of this dissertation was to better understand the lives of these men, Humphreys did not get his participants' consent. Participants were neither aware of the nature of the study nor were they debriefed after data were collected. |
| **Samoa HIV/ AIDS research (mid 1990s)** | Following leads provided by Samoan traditional healers, U.S. researchers studying HIV/AIDS isolated prostratin as the active component of the mamala plant of Samoa. U.S. researchers filed patents relating to prostratin without the ostensible approval of any Samoan authority. The case raised questions related to Indigenous research about informed consent concerning the use of plant samples and associated traditional knowledge by outsiders, intellectual property rights, and the fair allocation of benefits to eligible beneficiaries. |
| **Autism and vaccinations study (1998)** | Andrew Wakefield and colleagues falsely linked autism to the vaccine for measles, mumps, and rubella. A journalist found that Wakefield had not disclosed a significant financial interest and had not obtained ethics board approval for the study. Wakefield's research had been supported by a law firm that was suing vaccine manufacturers. A lawyer for the firm had helped Wakefield recruit patients. |
| **Cambodian sex worker study (2004)** | U.S. and Australian researchers planned a randomized trial to assess the safety and efficacy of the drug Tenofovir for HIV prevention. The plan was to recruit 960 HIV-negative female sex workers in Cambodia, but activists protested that the trial was unethical and the Cambodian prime minister closed the trial early. Violation claims were that there was limited discussion of ethical issues with the community, sex workers were given false and conflicting information, and there was a lack of guarantee for ongoing care for sex workers adversely affected by the trial. |
| **Children's environmental exposure research study (2004–2005)** | The Environmental Protection Agency (EPA) examined children's exposure to pesticides and other chemicals used in U.S. households. The study sample was located in Duval County, Florida, known for its high concentration of pesticides, and was disproportionately comprised of Black, low-income households. The EPA had received $2 million of its $9 million proposed budget from a national lobbying group for chemical companies. The study was shut down due to the concern that families may have been coerced to expose their children to pesticides for compensation. |

## Feminist and Indigenous Influences and Research Ethics

From the late 1980s to present, the value-free, linear perspective of utilitarian ethics has been increasingly challenged (Chilisa, 2020). Thus, ethical decisions in research were increasingly viewed as non-neutral. In response to Western influences on research ethics, several scholars began advocating for positions that intentionally considered the role of researcher and participant values and cultural factors within the research process. These approaches include feminist standpoint ethics, feminist communitarianism, and Indigenous ethics.

## Feminist Standpoint Ethics

**Feminist standpoint** refers to centering the voices of traditionally marginalized cultural groups in order to showcase their ways of knowing that are embedded within that group's values and ethics (Collins, 2009). Standpoint theory asserts that narratives "stand" on their own and take into account how gender, race, socioeconomic status, sexual orientation, and other identities intersect. Nancy Hartsock (1983) is largely credited as the originator of feminist standpoint theory. Hartsock noted that, while there are multiple cultural identities that influence women's lives, there are commonalities among women in Western societies. Sandra Harding (1991), another feminist standpoint theorist, notes the embeddedness of gender in scientific activity: Scientific knowledge is disproportionately representative of the cisgender male experience, and women's (and, we would argue, that trans or nonbinary individuals')

## WILD CARD 3.1. FEMINIST STANDPOINT ETHICS AND CONFIDENTIALITY

As discussed later in the chapter, ethics codes of professional organizations emphasize that—with a few exceptions related to a duty to warn and protect—practitioners and educators ensure that information collected during the research process remains confidential. Typical reasons for maintaining participant confidentiality are protecting participants from harm, respecting their privacy, and maximizing the accuracy and integrity of research by creating space for participants to speak more candidly. Feminist researchers note, however, that a potential downside to maintaining confidentiality is that naming is in itself an act of empowerment; thus, erasing parts of women's narratives can be disempowering and perpetuate unequal power relationships in research (Gordon, 2019).

Research that embeds feminist ethics within its approach seeks to center localized women's knowledge and apply that knowledge to social change. As Gordon (2019) asserts, "As feminist research requires us to place women at the centre [sic] of the research process, women's own opinions about ethical concepts should also be of utmost importance" (p. 543). Thus, as qualitative researchers in clinical and educational settings approach research with women, feminist ethics caution about strict adherence to ethics codes.

If you are considering providing an opportunity for participants to self-identify in the research report, carefully review the benefits and challenges of confidentiality in research. Further, be transparent about how the research will be used so that participants are fully informed prior to consenting to rejecting confidentiality protections. As an additional measure, have participants check narratives, contextual information, and quotations in qualitative reports to ensure you have represented their voices authentically.

social location in that knowledge is largely absent. Given this, it is important to consider alternative epistemologies that capture gender, race, and other intersectional identity influences on knowledge. In addition, through understanding alternative epistemologies, we also learn more deeply about the experience of White, cisgender men.

Collins (2009) serves as an important resource for standpoint theory, as she privileges the voices and historical experiences of Black women in the United States. As discussed in Chapter 4 of this text, Collins addresses in her text the core themes that shape Black feminist thought. Researchers are to familiarize themselves with these themes and integrate them into how they approach research with Black women to maximize the effective application of the aforementioned metaethical principles. In addition, Collins discusses an ethics of personal accountability, whereas Black feminist epistemology is developed through dialogue and women are accountable to their knowledge claims. Applying this form of ethics to qualitative research, researchers respect the value placed on knowledge claims regarding Black women: They codevelop ways of knowing with Black women through meaningful and intentional dialogue and are accountable to the claims they make in data reporting.

### Feminist Communitarianism

Traditionally, research ethics indicated that research was conducted for the benefit of society as whole (with assurance that the costs of conducting research did not outweigh its benefits). Rowan (2000) noted, "Most of the ethical codes which have been drawn up are based on the empirical paradigm, where the researcher is the one in charge, keeping his distance, and using the subjects for his convenience" (p. 103). Thus, decisions are to be made in terms of ever-changing human relationships and social structures. Carol Gilligan wrote of an *ethic of care*, whereas conflict resolution, in this case in terms of ethical dilemmas, involves fostering relationships and nurturance as opposed to simply avoiding harm and liability. Ethics is to be viewed as a more fluid process, without the assumptions of impartiality and formality (Christians, 2017).

**Feminist communitarianism**, a term coined by Norman Denzin (1941–present), critiques utilitarianism for ignoring the role of power and ideology on social and political institutions. In general, communitarianism is a social philosophy that emphasizes the need to balance individual rights and interests with those of the community (i.e., a greater focus on collectivistic goals). Individuals absorb social values in their own individual identities. When we assess benefit, then, we assess increasingly in terms of community benefit, and individual benefits and rights are minimized. There is a commitment to a core of shared values, norms, and meanings as well as collective history and identity (i.e., moral culture; Etzioni, 2009).

This philosophy rejects the melting pot theory and focuses on the politics of recognition and representation. Thus, it recenters humanity and research as a moral dilemma imbued in social and political crises. Furthermore, community morals are intrinsic to the community's identity and are to be embraced rather than evaluated upon an external set of norms. The mission of science should be for community transformation; research becomes a collaborative and participatory community endeavor. It challenges researchers to make building community among researchers and participants the mission of their research and involve participants in ethical decisions and research design. It emphasizes research process and outcome as well as community participation and includes the following characteristics (Christians, 2017):

- The community is the unit of identity.
- There is a focus on community strengths.
- Research is a collaborative process among academic researchers, community organizations, community members, and others.
- Participants have a voice in how and when research is conducted and determining whether findings are relevant and accurate.
- All partners work together as colearners.
- Researchers value empowerment, solidarity, community, and shared governance.
- Knowledge based in local and cultural experiences is disseminated to all partners since it benefits all.

It should be noted that feminist communitarianism is sometimes at odds with traditional perspectives of research ethics that use a biomedical model and focus on individual rights and institutional protection.

### Indigenous Ethics

The increasing attention paid to Indigenous populations provides a rich opportunity for researchers to expand their ways of conducting research ethically. **Indigenous ethics** recognize Indigenous communities' shared ways of knowing based on a reflection of and resistance to colonization in various realms. As noted in Chapter 2, researchers engaging in Indigenous research reflect on who owns, designs, interprets, reports, and ultimately benefits from the research process and products (Smith, 2012). Research then becomes a process of rewriting history. (See Case Example 3.1 for a study example involving teacher preparation and practices.)

As Indigenous ways of knowing and self-determination continue to permeate conversations within qualitative research, a greater scrutiny of common research ethics arises. Rather than a focus on inclusion of Western ethics, Indigenous ethics emphasize that Indigenous populations are to be protected from potential harmful effects of traditional research. Specifically, caring for the collective body of Indigenous people is a priority: This involves not only care of a physical body but also nurturance of Indigenous views and deferring to them to advance knowledge (Kowal, 2015). Indigenous peoples should control their own knowledge, decide whether they participate in research, and collaborate with and benefit from research outcomes produced from research conducted by educational institutions (Battiste, 2016). This "dual citizenship" of science and advocacy for the researcher is paramount (Kowal, 2015).

Herman (2018) identified nine guidelines for approaching research in Indigenous settings across three principles: integrity, responsibility, and reciprocity. *Integrity* refers to open consultation regarding all aspects of the research project that are negotiated with the community and its representatives and respect for Indigenous values and cultural protocols. *Responsibility*, which parallels common ethical values in Western ethics, refers to consent, confidentiality,

## Case Example 3.1. Indigenous Teacher Education in Idaho

Anthony-Stevens and colleagues (2020) explored the effects of the Indigenous Knowledge for Effective Education Program (IKEEP), an initiative that sought to effectively prepare teachers who identify as Indigenous. In the program design and evaluation, the authors attended to Indigenous research ethics components such as self-determination, sovereignty, and community-building between the University of Idaho and tribal nations. For example, the program goals were developed from collaboration with tribal nations in the northwestern United States and review of Indigenous teacher education programs; the goals included honoring and strengthening the knowledge and lived experiences of Indigenous teacher candidates and transforming educational leadership to affirm Indigenous students' desires to serve their communities, peoples, and lands. In addition, the researchers partnered with Indigenous teacher candidates and mentors to investigate the following research question: How does an Indigenous teacher education program at a rural, mainstream institution support the development and application of culturally responsive, self-determination-centered approaches to teaching and learning with Indigenous youth?

The research methodology for this longitudinal study anchored on the Indigenous research ethics (e.g., respect, relationality, reciprocity, responsibility); thus, researchers remained accountable to Indigenous populations as they navigated traditional academic practices. For example, researchers remained cognizant that research process and outcomes continue to shape Indigenous communities and narratives about these communities for multiple generations.

Anthony-Stevens et al. (2020) used multiple data sources (e.g., program activity fieldnotes, autoethnographic audio journals, and individual interviews with Indigenous scholars and teacher mentors) to identify five main categories: sovereignty and self-determination, education as service to community, relationship between community knowledge and academic knowledge, health and well-being of community over emphasis on individual achievement, and reciprocity to community, people, and land. From these categories, the researchers came to consensus with their coresearchers (i.e., Indigenous participants) regarding three major findings:

- nation-building orientation in administration: attending to university capacity building
- nation-building orientation in mentorship: grounded support systems with Indigenous teachers
- nation-building orientation among students: sustaining and revitalizing youth-teacher-community relationships.

In summary, IKEEP depicts an initiative whereby a higher education institution can be cultivated to prioritize self-determination and tribal sovereignty over mainstream assimilationist education approaches.

Source: Anthony-Stevens, V., Mahfouz, J., & Bisbee, Y. (2020). Indigenous teacher education is nation building: Reflections of capacity building and capacity strengthening in Idaho. *Journal of School Leadership, 30*, 541–564. https://doi.org/10.1177/1052684620951722

and protection. *Reciprocity* refers to partnership, review, and benefit-sharing. The guidelines are as follows:

- *open consultation:* All aspects of the research project (its aims, methodology, and sponsors) should be openly discussed and negotiated with the community or its representatives before the project begins.
- *values:* Research should be conducted within the values framework of the Indigenous peoples involved and should reflect and support those values rather than reframing them into a Western context.
- *respect:* Cultural protocols and traditions appropriate to the community, the local area, and the research participants should be respected.
- *consent:* Full and informed consent from those participating in the research or those affected by it must be secured. Depending on the context, such consent may be individual, collective, or both.
- *confidentiality:* Confidentiality, anonymity, and public recognition of participants are delicate if not dangerous matters for many Indigenous peoples and must be clearly and carefully negotiated before any project materials are made public.
- *protection:* Indigenous knowledge and the intellectual property of the holders of traditional knowledge and nations must be safeguarded within the bounds agreed to in negotiation with the community.
- *partnership:* Research partnerships with Indigenous individuals, communities, or organizations should be pursued, to the extent that they are desired. Collaborative work in full partnership with the community is often preferred.
- *review:* Research participants and community leaders should have the opportunity to review and revise drafts of the study and should receive copies of the final study. They should receive acknowledgment, fair return, and royalties where appropriate.
- *benefit-sharing:* Every effort must be made to ensure that benefits flow to Indigenous peoples from research and that potential impacts are minimized.

In addition, Indigenous organizations (e.g., Australian Institute of Aboriginal and Torres Strait Islander Studies, 2012) offer several best practices found across Indigenous research guidelines and protocols:

- *rights, respect, and recognition:* Recognize the diversity, priorities, self-determination, and ways of knowing of individuals and groups within communities in planning, carrying out, and reporting their research.
- *negotiation, consultation, agreement, and mutual understanding:* When relevant, develop a formal agreement where ownership and licensing of intellectual property is discussed. Understand relevant laws and policies for the protection and maintenance of intangible cultural heritage.
- *participation, collaboration, and partnership:* Identify the individuals, groups, and communities at the beginning of the project with rights and interests who are responsible for Indigenous knowledge and/or practices that may be involved or will facilitate involvement. Foster equal research participation throughout the research process.

- *benefits, outcomes, and giving back:* Provide fair and equal benefits to those who contribute traditional knowledge, practices, and innovations. Outcomes should include specific results that respond to the needs and interests of Indigenous people.
- *managing research use, storage, and access:* Report findings to individuals, groups, and communities before publication and/or discussion with media. Agree on the disposition and storage of results, including primary data.
- *reporting and compliance:* Regularly report research progress to a review board, and ensure it complies with guidelines. Advocate with institutional review boards as needed to maximize best practices in Indigenous research.

## A Case for Ethics in Qualitative Inquiry

**Ethics** is part of our human world and refers to a set of guidelines established within a professional discipline to guide thinking and behavior. Whether we are acting in the role of practitioner, educator, peer, researcher, or concerned citizen, ethical dilemmas and decisions surround us. When we are conducting qualitative inquiry, these roles often blur, and we are required to justify the benefits and costs of research for all involved. Also, the emergent nature of qualitative research creates unique ethical dilemmas—and often political choices. The feature (and sometimes "flaw") in qualitative research from an ethical perspective is the openness of the design, the changing views of what is important to ask, observe, collect, and report. Furthermore, selected methodologies are influenced by the selected research ethics (see Decision Points 3.1). Thus, ethics and methodology are inseparable (Shordike et al., 2017).

Ethics can be considered two-pronged: One prong is the **procedural ethics,** or the general protocol that is approved by review boards, and the other is the **ethics of practice**, or abiding by relevant, professional behaviors when addressing day-to-day ethical issues that occur during the conduction of research (Dawson et al., 2017). When qualitative researchers think about ethics, they generally are considering procedural ethics or compliance with institutional review boards (IRBs). IRBs, discussed below, tend to focus on what researchers intend to do rather than how they intend to be during a study. Given the dynamic nature of qualitative research and the necessity to adjust research design and process decisions, not all ethical considerations can be determined at the beginning of a research project (Carpenter, 2018).

It is ethically imperative that educators and practitioners conduct research and contribute to the knowledge base in a way that improves students' and clients' lives. As examples, the American Educational Research Association's (AERA, 2011) Code of Ethics notes:

> Education researchers are aware of their professional and scientific responsibility to the communities and societies in which they live and work. They apply and make public their knowledge in order to contribute to the public good. When undertaking research, they strive to advance scientific and scholarly knowledge and to serve the public good. (Section E)

**DECISION POINTS 3.1.** ETHICAL FRAMEWORKS AND QUALITATIVE RESEARCH PROCESSES

Bridges (2018) argues that ethical codes constrain researchers and that there can be tension between epistemological goals and ethical codes. Ethics is not just about adherence to established ethics codes but also attention to ownership of the research process and outcome. Specifically, the following have to be considered: identification of what research questions are asked, who the researchers are, whose voices are expressed, who has control of data and their interpretation, whose contributions are recognized and how, and how research engages with policy and practice. These factors have different considerations based on adherence to utilitarian, feminist standpoint, feminist communitarian, and Indigenous research ethics. As an example, let's consider how research questions are identified for a study:

- From a utilitarian lens, researchers are guided by professional codes of ethics, with the IRBs at their respective institutions based in Western ethical influences. Thus, IRBs are likely to expect that researchers identify research questions based on their expertise and assumed leadership in the study. These questions may not involve codevelopment with participants or focus on cultural aspects of the participants and/or communities.
- With a feminist standpoint lens, researchers would attend specifically to research questions that examine the situatedness of gender and power and how gender intersects with other cultural and social identities. Furthermore, researchers prioritize knowledge claims of their participants and would likely defer to them in research question development.
- A feminist communitarian lens would highly value researcher–participant relationships and collectivistic interests when identifying research questions while noting a necessary fluidity in the development process.
- An Indigenous research lens would highly prioritize naming and preserving intangible cultural heritage while developing research questions, avoiding imposing questions that would reinforce colonized ways of knowing for a clinical or educational topic. Similar to feminist lenses, Indigenous research would involve continual consultation with participants and their communities and remaining attuned to partnership and self-determination as questions are developed and refined as needed.

The Introduction of the American Counseling Association's (ACA, 2014), Code of Ethics reflects this value:

> Counselors who conduct research are encouraged to contribute to the knowledge base of the profession and promote a clearer understanding of the conditions that lead to a healthy and more just society. Counselors support the efforts of researchers by participating fully and willingly whenever possible. Counselors minimize bias and respect diversity in designing and implementing research. (Section G)

So, what is ethical research practice in general? As noted earlier, ethics can be considered a set of guidelines established within a professional discipline to guide thinking and behavior. These standards and principles are similar across disciplines, although certain subcomponents may be emphasized more so than others depending on the discipline. And professionals within the same discipline may interpret guidelines very differently! Thus, making sound ethical decisions involves understanding various ways to think about ethics and blending them as appropriate (see Activity 3.1).

 **ACTIVITY 3.1.** CONCEPTUALIZING ETHICS

Review the following research topic in dyads and respond to the questions that follow.
  You are required to develop a qualitative proposal for your qualitative research course. One topic that has intrigued you for quite some time is the role of sponsors in Alcoholics Anonymous (AA). You would like to conduct interviews with sponsors with varying durations of sobriety on their experience supporting individuals with addictions. Given the difficulty of obtaining participants, you consider approaching sponsors at several AA meetings and soliciting their participation.

- Based on the various ways to conceptualize ethics, develop an argument for how this plan for participant recruitment is *both* ethical and unethical.
  - utilitarian ethics
  - feminist standpoint ethics
  - feminist communitarianism
  - Indigenous research ethics
- What are some micro-level ethical considerations?
- What are some macro-level ethical considerations?
- Which way of conceptualizing ethics seems most comfortable for you?

Furthermore, ethics concerns decisions about the research design itself (**micro-level ethics**) as well as ethics of how knowledge is used (**macro-level ethics**). Thus, researchers are to attend to design issues such as data collection procedures, participant protections, researchers' roles, as well as how the knowledge produced will circulate in the wider culture and affect other individuals, groups, and communities (Brinkmann & Kvale, 2018). Questions of micro- and macro-level ethics in research might include:

- To what degree are participants protected during the research process (micro)?
- Are worthwhile societal goals being met (macro)?
- How does politics shape the way data are interpreted and presented for a sampling frame (micro) as well as the larger community of knowledge (macro)?

There can be behavior that is ethical at a micro level but unethical at a macro level, and vice versa. In fact, many experiments in Table 3.1 demonstrate this.

Values and virtues inform the process by which researchers determine what qualifies as ethical research practice. **Values** are defined as the principles that are used to evaluate outcomes and actions from research. Qualitative researchers make value judgments of those principles; thus, value conflicts are inevitable, and adherence to these principles will vary depending on the practical relevance and priorities across study contexts (Hammersley, 2018). The first epistemic value is *truth*, or the knowledge produced from research. Because of differences in research paradigms (see Chapter 4), qualitative researchers may conceptualize the "truth" of that knowledge in different ways. Another epistemic value is *justifiability*, or the strength of evidence that the pursuit itself of truth is warranted. A third epistemic value is *relevance*, or the importance of the research questions asked and findings produced. The final epistemic value is *feasibility*, or the ability to conduct research on a solvable problem (Hammersley, 2018).

In addition to the epistemic values researchers hold, **virtues** (i.e., desired personal dispositions for research) factor into the practice of ethical qualitative research. Personal virtues applied to the research process can include honesty in reporting, having courage (i.e., willingness to follow an argument wherever it leads), having humility (i.e., willingness to consider criticism of one's work by colleagues), and reflexivity (i.e., an inward critique of one's research or personal process as a researcher; Carpenter, 2018; Hammersley, 2018). As researchers develop, they are to be intentional about continually pursuing and building these personal virtues, aiming for moral excellence (Carpenter, 2018).

Thus, ethical decision making in qualitative research must weigh epistemic and ethical values and virtues. The outcome of this process is usually evaluated in two ways. The first mode is known as **consequentialism**, or determining what impact research actions are likely to have on those directly affected. The second mode is **deontologicalism**, which refers to whether an action—regardless of its actual consequences—is appropriate in itself (Hammersley, 2018).

## Institutional Review Boards

The **Nuremberg Code** was the first legal attempt to deal with controversies of research, specifically to those of the Nazi medical experiments. Established in 1947, it was an initial effort to put forth guidelines for social, medical, and behavioral research, with particular emphasis on informed consent. In response to continued ethical violations and a need for more comprehensive standards, the National Research Act of 1974 was passed and mandated that a commission be developed to identify the primary ethical principles that researchers should comply with to protect human subjects. The Commission for the Protection of Human Subjects in Biomedical and Behavioral Research was established in 1978 to develop the **Belmont Report**.

The Belmont Report indicated what were considered at the time the three moral standards of researchers: respect for persons, beneficence, and justice. Collectively, these principles indicate prominent ethical notions of autonomy, a thoughtful benefits-risks analysis for participants, and fairness in involving individuals of various groups and demographics (Christians, 2017). These principles, referred to as "metaethical principles," are discussed in greater detail later in the chapter.

The commission set forth regulations that helped to operationalize the Belmont Report. These regulations, known as 45 CFR 46, called for protection of human subjects for research that was federally funded in some manner (known as the Common Rule). As part of 45 CFR 46, **Institutional Review Boards (IRBs)** were created to review research applications and monitor federal compliance with aspects of the Belmont Report. In 1989, with the formation of the Commission on Research Integrity, IRBs also focused on data fabrication and plagiarism issues (Christians, 2017). Furthermore, the National Institutes of Health Revitalization Act of 1993 required women and people of color to be included in health research. Today, it is common practice to have all research involving human subjects reviewed by an IRB, even though it may not be a federally funded study.

What is an IRB? While IRBs help to protect an institution (e.g., university, hospital, federal agency) from liability, their primary function is to protect human subjects. An IRB is typically composed of five members of an institution; these members come from various disciplines and possess expertise in research, and there should also be a nonscientist and community member. Depending on whether a project crosses the minimal risk threshold (i.e., a study involves more than minimal risks for participants), a project can be exempt from review or need an expedited or full review from the board.

IRBs often carry a utilitarian agenda in terms of scope, procedures, and assumptions (i.e., research as value-free). Adhering to a communitarian ethics approach to evaluating qualitative research practice, Denzin and Giardina (2016) critiqued IRBs for their primary adoption of the Belmont Report and its general disallowance of collaborative and participatory research designs. That is, the current IRB model assumes that all research fits into the Belmont criteria of beneficence, respect, and justice. Some of Denzin and Giardina's (2016) arguments include the following:

- The current definition of "research" contends that a design is created to test a hypothesis. Researchers are value-neutral, and human participants are turned into research subjects, which removes the essence of what it means to be human.
- Research is seen as event based rather than process based.
- The IRB often fails to see humans (participants and researchers alike) as social and complex creatures that are not value-neutral, anonymous subjects.
- Beneficence is impossible to quantify; thus, it is difficult to determine what qualifies as minimal risk.
- Respect for persons goes beyond the informed consent and includes caring for, honoring, and treating the person with dignity.
- Justice extends beyond equal selection and benefits to society to include care, love, kindness, shared responsibility, honesty, balance, and truth.
- It is difficult or sometimes inappropriate to have participant anonymity given the goals of qualitative research.
- IRB staff reject or are unaware of several qualitative research traditions.
- IRBs do not typically address research with Indigenous people, espouse universal human rights, or regulate inappropriate conduct in the field, which includes a grievance process for participants.

With a more complex view of ethics (e.g., feminist standpoint, feminist communitarianism, Indigenous), qualitative researchers may come in conflict with what IRBs have traditionally viewed as ethical research. Scholars (e.g., Slovin & Semenec, 2019; Waldrop, 2004) expressed other concerns that IRBs might have about qualitative inquiry based on traditional criteria used:

- Emotional expression during data collection can create unexpected psychological harm for participants.
- The fluid nature of qualitative research may mean that individuals who select to participate feel coerced to continue participation, even when they perceive an intrusion of their privacy.
- The depth and thick description of data collection and analysis compromises participant confidentiality.
- There can never be any real guarantee of the depth and scope of the project, including specific data collection and analysis procedures.

Given these tensions, researchers engaged in qualitative research are to remind IRB members that traditional ethical principles must be reconsidered given the complexities of qualitative inquiry. This is particularly salient when you consider the conflict among ethics types (see Case Example 3.2).

**Case Example 3.2. The PHAT Project: Ethical Tensions in Community-Based Research**

The following description is of issues arising with an IRB for a participatory research project funded by the California Tobacco-Related Disease Research Program, the Protecting the Hood Against Tobacco (PHAT) project (Malone et al., 2006):

> The PHAT project was initiated in 2002 to address tobacco usage for two predominately African American neighborhoods in San Francisco, based on community survey data indicating that approximately half of residents were smokers with half who believed that health and illness was beyond their control. The researchers wanted to engage in a project whereas participants were considered community partners who could assist in reducing the limits of single-cigarette sales at convenience stores. (State law prohibited sales of single cigarettes, and the availability of single-cigarette sales in these communities served as an obstacle to smoking cessation.) (p. 1915)

The PHAT project began as exploratory focus groups among community members to assess their responses to tobacco industry marketing of cigarettes to African Americans. Based on their focus group participation, several African Americans agreed to be community partners and further assist in designing the project. Based on community surveys that confirmed the availability of single-cigarette sales and its connection to relapse, PHAT researchers and community partners were committed to assessing the proportion of convenience stores in their community that sold cigarettes in violation of state law.

IRB approval for an observational study was obtained; however, researchers and partners noted the impracticability of collecting data this way and resubmitted the proposal. The revised proposal outlined a procedure whereby the partners would approach a clerk to purchase a single cigarette. In the modified proposal, the researchers guaranteed clerk confidentiality would be maintained at all stages of the research process.

The IRB at the researchers' institution did not approve the application, citing that the research partners were not viewed as coresearchers and that they were placing store owners and managers in potential entrapment situations. In its appeal, the researchers defended the use of community partners and cited that store owners and clerks had a right to refuse sale of single cigarettes (an illegal activity). The appeal was reviewed by the university's risk management and legal departments, and the legal department stated it could not approve any university "involvement in illegal activity" (the researchers pointed out the sale, not the purchase, of single cigarettes was illegal, so the university was not liable). The legal department determined the IRB had final approval. A third request for IRB approval was denied even though the researchers argued, with support of the state attorney's written opinion, there was no risk of entrapment and that it was important for the university to respect the community's knowledge and skills in this type of research.

Interestingly, the community partners conducted the study without the assistance (and research expertise) of the university researchers. Unfortunately, the knowledge gained from the process could not be published or presented as an aspect of the PHAT project: IRB holds the power for dissemination of research related to this project.

Source: Malone, R. E., Yerger, V. B., McGruder, C., & Froelicher, E. (2006). "It's like Tuskegee in reverse": A case study of ethical tensions in institutional review board review of community-based participatory research. *American Journal of Public Health*, 96 (11), 1914–1919.

## Ethical Guidelines in Education and Social Sciences Disciplines

With the primary goal of promoting welfare of others, ethical codes serve three key roles: to establish ideal methods of practice and educate individuals within a discipline about sound ethical behavior; to serve as an apparatus for accountability in situations where an individual has deviated significantly from an agreed-upon standard of practice; and to guide improvements in practice (Corey et al., 2018). Even with the legislation, ethics codes, and IRB monitoring, ethical issues still occur, although to a lesser extent (Christians, 2017). As we increase qualitative inquiry, special challenges to the idea of utilitarian ethics are bound to occur.

There are many associations within clinical and educational settings, each having various specialty areas within that organization. With each division and subdivision of disciplines, codes for ethical practice abound. We will highlight six codes of ethical conduct in this chapter pertaining to counseling, psychology, social work, couples and family therapy, education, and higher education. In our discussion, we will focus particular attention to codes that focus specifically on research and publication issues; however, other areas will be mentioned as they relate to the practice of qualitative research.

While there are parallels across codes, it is important to review the codes and standards for your particular discipline if it is not covered here. In addition, examine specialty areas and their ethical guidelines in relation to a broader discipline (e.g., American School Counseling Association guidelines within the American Counseling Association). We also offer a few considerations as you review codes associated with your professional organizations. First, codes present very general and often vague guidance on key ethical issues. Researchers are to reflect upon epistemic and ethical values, metaethical principles, and virtues as they engage in ethical decision making. Second, many codes and standards present several interrelated issues, such as informed consent and confidentiality, as if they were independent issues that can be solved by simply "looking up rules" for a particular issue. Third, because ethical codes are largely based on utilitarian ethics, feminist and Indigenous research considerations are largely ignored. Finally, judgment of ethics is situation-specific, and thus, codes of practice in counseling and education only frame these discussions. At best, standards of ethical practices for effective research are a work in progress. Thus, we believe it is important to think critically about ethical issues and thoroughly review codes across sections (and specialty areas) to formulate a more ethical and effective response.

## American Association for Marriage and Family Therapy

The American Association for Marriage and Family Therapy's (AAMFT, 2015) Code of Ethics includes nine ethical standards: responsibility to clients; confidentiality; professional competence and integrity; responsibility to students and supervisees; research and publication; technology-assisted professional services; professional evaluations; financial arrangements; and advertising. The AAMFT Code of Ethics was first published in 1962 and has been revised more than 10 times.

## American Education Research Association

The American Education Research Association (AERA, 2011) put forth a code of ethics to guide the work of those conducting research in education settings, emphasizing the connection between research and education. The ethical standards of the AERA were first adopted in 1992, with its third and most recent revision in 2011. The code is divided into six sets of guiding standards. These include scientific, scholarly, and professional standards; competence; use and misuse of expertise; fabrication, falsification, and plagiarism; avoiding harm; nondiscrimination; nonexploitation; harassment; employment decisions; conflicts of interest; public communications; confidentiality; informed consent; research planning, implementation, and dissemination; authorship credit; publication process; responsibilities of reviewers; teaching, training, and administering education programs; mentoring; supervision; contractual and consulting services; and adherence to the ethical standards of the AERA.

## American Counseling Association

The American Counseling Association (ACA, 2014) first published its code in 1961. After six revisions the current version of the ACA Code of Ethics was published in 2014. The code is organized in this manner: preamble and purpose, followed by eight major sections (i.e., the counseling relationship; confidentiality and privacy; professional responsibility; relationships with other professionals; evaluation, assessment, and interpretation; supervision, training, and teaching; research and publication; distance counseling, technology, and social media; and resolving ethical issues).

## American Psychological Association

The American Psychological Association (APA, 2017) was the first to develop an ethical code. The first publication, *Ethical Standards of Psychologists*, was published in 1953, resulting from 15 years of committee discussions. The document has been revised nine times, with the most updated document, entitled *Ethical Principles of Psychologists and Code of Conduct*, revised in 2017. The 2017 code is outlined as follows: preamble, five general principles, and 10 general ethical standards (i.e., resolving ethical issues; competence; human relations; privacy and confidentiality; advertising and other public statements; record keeping and fees; education and training; research and publication; assessment; and therapy).

## American Sociological Association

The American Sociological Association's (ASA, 2018) Code of Ethics outlines six principles that are infused within the code: professional competence; integrity; professional and scientific responsibility; respect for people's rights, dignity, and diversity; social responsibility; and human rights. The code presents ethical guidelines across 18 areas: competence; representation and misuse of expertise; delegation and supervision; discrimination; exploitation; harassment; employment decisions; conflicts of interest and commitment; public communication; confidentiality; informed consent; research planning, implementation, and dissemination; plagiarism; authorship; publication process; responsibilities of reviewers; education, teaching, and training; and contractual and consulting services.

## Association for the Study of Higher Education

The Association for the Study of Higher Education (ASHE) formally adapted the AERA (2011) Code of Ethics for use in higher education. The code augments their 2003 *Principles of Ethical Conduct* document, which identifies 10 themes for ethical practice: integrity; responsibility; credit; honesty and accuracy; originality; respect; fairness; advancement; responsibility to clients and to the public interest; and conflicts of interest.

## National Association of Social Workers

Since its first published code in 1960, the National Association of Social Workers (NASW, 2017) has revised the code six times, with the most recent revision adopted in 2017. The Code of Ethics of the NASW is presently organized in this manner: preamble; six general principles (i.e., service, social justice, dignity and worth of a person, importance of human relationships, integrity, and competence); and six ethical standards. These ethical standards related to social workers' ethical responsibilities to clients, to colleagues, in practice settings, as professionals, to the social work profession, and to the broader society.

## Key Ethical Concepts in Qualitative Research

No matter the discipline, certain basic principles govern research with human subjects. In this section we will describe six **metaethical principles**. Metaethical principles lay the ground-work for several important components of ethical practice: informed consent, confidentiality, multiple relationships, and researcher competence. After reviewing the key concepts outlined in this section, see Case Example 3.3.

### Case Example 3.3. Case of Cora

Cora is considering a multiple case study of the experiences of families with children involved in special education in a local school district. She has been a school counselor in the school district for 12 years and has worked with several special education students in her current school. In working with these children and their families, she noted that parents and guardians seemed to not be involved in the classroom. Cora plans to conduct several interviews with the children and their family members to better understand their relationship with the school system. She hopes findings will provide insight into ways in which to increase family involvement.

- To what extent would you apply each of the six metaethical principles? How might they conflict with one another?
- What are some issues related to developing and securing informed consent?
- How might confidentiality be a concern?
- Does Cora have multiple roles? To what extent do any multiple relationships conflict with one another?
- What areas of competence are important for Cora to possess?
- How can Cora resist colonizing structures that seek to sustain an "us versus them" division in qualitative research?
- How do these areas of competence relate to taking up the roles of researcher, practitioner, and advocate we have discussed in earlier chapters of this text?

Scholars (e.g., Carpenter, 2018; Hammersley, 2018) discuss several ethical values that researchers are to weigh in the design and process of research. These include nonmaleficence, autonomy, beneficence, justice, fidelity, and veracity. Respect for persons (i.e., autonomy), benef-icence, and justice are directly linked to the Belmont Report; these principles are embedded within several Western ethical protocols (e.g., United States, United Kingdom). As you review these principles, you will likely believe it is important to apply them all equally. Unfortunately, though, when we start to apply them at the same level in research design, conflicts arise. Each principle has its own value assumptions; ethical dilemmas, it can be argued, result when there is conflict in trying to adhere to these principles in an equal manner. To complicate matters, ethical dilemmas (or conflict among these principles) arise in different ways depending on the topic, population, and setting. Thus, we believe that researchers are to weigh for themselves the degree to which each principle should be applied in research design and process, given contextual information and personal and professional values.

In addition to these principles, we ask you to be mindful in particular of equity, diversity, and inclusion and their implications for conducting, analyzing, and reporting qualitative research. In Chapter 1, we introduced the AERA (2011) principle of respect for people's rights, dignity, and diversity. Aligned with the metaethical principles, qualitative researchers are accountable to their participants in terms of taking an anti-oppression stance throughout the research process. This includes acting with intention to reduce the impact of researcher bias that may harm the research process and being critically conscious of the impact of discrimination on participants' and communities' lives and research experience in general. Furthermore, it can involve constantly disrupting colonizing efforts in qualitative research to maximize equity, diversity, and inclusion. Qualitative researchers are to consider how they can maximize these concepts within their application of the metaethical principles.

Bhattacharya (2016), through personal narratives, highlights the colonizing epistemologies that can exist in academic research: a division of "us" (i.e., those with authority over academic knowledge production and distribution and who are typically White scholars) and "them" (those with little or no power to shape knowledge or introduce alternative forms of knowledge and are often marginalized by what is produced). Bhattacharya (2016) writes about the dangers of not interrogating current research practices in academic institutions:

> Privileging work that is filtered through academic structures can re-inscribe colonization, especially when raw knowledge, street knowledge, and knowledge from other non-traditional sources are dismissed as "unscholarly" in academia. … I am advocating that we further interrogate the ways in which scholarly work is written up, exploring its intersections with various sources and its connections to the experiences we seek to understand and write about, with, and against. (p. 317)

## Nonmaleficence

Because removing all potential risk of harm in research is impossible, researchers value **nonmaleficence,** or minimizing harm. Researchers are to consider what potential or actual consequences are for participants, whether those consequences are beneficial or harmful, how likely harmful consequences are to occur, and whether harmful consequences are below a reasonable or acceptable level of risk in research (i.e., benefits outweigh the risks, and risks are not significantly harmful). The issue of deception of research relates here, and researchers should take care to design research as free from active deception as possible, without affecting the outcome of the study if the participant were fully informed of its purpose. Deception is discussed further below.

## Autonomy

The ethical value of respecting **autonomy** refers to showing consideration for the rights of individuals, groups, and communities. Through an informed consent process, participants are provided the agency to (a) decide whether they are a part of a study, (b) withhold data for any reason, and (b) withdraw from the study at any time. When qualitative researchers successfully respect participant autonomy, participants are not coerced and feel as if the research is being carried out *with* them instead of *on* them. Thus, respecting autonomy extends beyond promoting agency to emphasizing research as a collaborative process. To operate with full autonomy, a participant must also be completely informed of the research request (and understand the implications of the information and their decision).

Risks for harm are prominent in qualitative research: Researchers immerse themselves in individual, group, and community settings, invading their privacy and potentially inducing reactions such as anxiety, stress, or sadness. They ask much of their participants' time and energy. They analyze data and present findings that often only have been analyzed by a research team. Given the often intense relationship in qualitative research, it is important to constantly monitor participant reactions and not place unnecessary risks for the sake of research.

## Beneficence

**Beneficence** refers to the implementation of sound research that yields beneficial effects for the intended population. In essence, beneficence is "doing good" for others, engaging in work that gives back and works with participants as copartners. In qualitative inquiry, researchers are to maximize the benefits for individuals who participate in research. At the same time, qualitative researchers are to ensure that participants and possibly the community at large gain something valuable from the findings. Thus, researchers are continually accountable to participants' needs and respect their ways of interacting and knowing throughout the research process.

## Justice

Related to promoting good in research, **justice** as a metaethical principle relates to promoting good equally for individuals of various groups, circumstances, and statuses. In essence, it is an issue of voice and representativeness. Whose perspective do we privilege? What ways of knowing are we highlighting or appropriating?

Justice goes beyond simply maximizing benefits to include an intentional focus on the risk that certain individuals of certain backgrounds are being left out, or even objectified, by a research design. It also refers to ensuring individuals of dominant groups are not overrepresented in a research design (and do not benefit unsystematically from its findings). Additionally, justice involves ensuring that findings derived from a disproportionate or unfair sampling process are not misapplied to certain groups.

## Fidelity

**Fidelity** refers to being honest and trustworthy and having integrity with the individuals with whom we are working, whether in a practitioner or researcher role. It involves creating a trusting relationship. It is the extent to which we honor participants during research in a manner that maximizes trustworthiness (Haverkamp, 2005). Haverkamp (2005) stated, "We must consider how we, as researchers, assume a fiduciary role in reference to our research participants. A fiduciary relationship is one of trust, in which one party with greater power or influence accepts responsibility to act in the other's interest" (p. 151).

## Veracity

The final metaethical principle discussed here is veracity. **Veracity** involves being truthful to individuals we encounter, holding the relationship as a top priority. Veracity may be viewed as a precursor to fidelity: We cannot build a strong, trusting researcher–participant relationship if we are not truthful with participants.

## Informed Consent

Traditionally, **informed consent** has been viewed as a cornerstone of research whereby researchers seek permission from a participant to engage in research with them. In consideration of feminist and Indigenous ethics, researchers are to reflect upon who (e.g., individual, Elder, organization, community) provides informed consent and how securing informed consent is prioritized among the stakeholders.

In the discussion, the researcher describes the purpose of research, emphasizes the voluntariness of participation, and provides information about the researcher, the extent of participation, limits of confidentiality, and any foreseeable risks and benefits of participation and nonparticipation (see AAMFT Standard 5.3; AERA Standard 13; ACA Section G.2; APA Principle 8.02, 8.03, and 8.05; ASA Standard 11; NASW Section 5.02.e–g). Furthermore, researchers are to indicate in informed consent not only what data will be accessed and presented but also how it will be accessed and presented. Informed consent is an important ethical and legal concept that clearly identifies and outlines research activity and rights and responsibilities of all parties involved.

There are two elements of an effective informed consent process. The first is capacity and comprehension. *Capacity* refers to having the functional cognitive ability to acknowledge one's rights and responsibilities as a research participant and consider these as one makes and communicates choices to participate in a study, and *comprehension* refers to understanding content-specific information of the document. When a person is not capable of giving informed consent, researchers provide an appropriate explanation, obtain assent to the extent possible, and obtain informed consent from a legally authorized person.

The second element is collaboration. *Collaboration* refers to the ongoing process of informed consent wherein the research and participant partner to discuss and negotiate the research relationship and process. Aligned with feminist and Indigenous ethics, we encourage researchers to engage in **process consent**, which means viewing informed consent as an ongoing, mutually negotiated and developed activity (Sanjari et al., 2014). If researchers decide to use process consent, specific procedures need to be outlined at the outset of the research with participants and other relevant stakeholders.

There are several special considerations in qualitative inquiry related to the informed consent process. First, the research process is emergent, meaning the design unfolds and changes based on changing directions of the study purpose or other design reflections. In quantitative research, there is often an assumption that informed consent is obtained at the outset of a study and that the study is well-planned, with a definite conclusion. In qualitative inquiry, however, the beginning, end, and everything in between are nebulous at best. And the degree of involvement is often unknown and usually quite involved due to the interactive and emergent nature of qualitative inquiry. This can cause difficulty with presenting informed consent to participants as well as addressing it with review committees.

A second related issue is the potentially coercive nature of qualitative inquiry, given the often unknown course of the overall process of obtaining informed consent. No matter the type of research, the process of obtaining informed consent is inherently hierarchical. Consent must be reviewed throughout the research process, particularly for individuals of vulnerable and Indigenous populations. For example, it is common for individuals, groups, and communities of marginalized status to have a historical mistrust of the research process and fear of how research findings may be used to further oppress them. In other instances, they may have limited experience due to being underrepresented within research and may seek additional information throughout the research process.

*Covert research*, data collection without the knowledge of the participant, is a third concern related to the informed consent process. Covert research is likely an aspect of observational research, particularly in naturalistic settings. If we told participants we were watching for behavioral problems within the classroom or disclosed we were assessing the degree to which they discussed multicultural issues in an introductory counseling course, we would likely have very different and biased results. According to the federal regulation Protection of Human Subjects (2009), informed consent may be waived, or some aspects may be adapted or omitted if "the research could not practicably be carried out without the waiver or alteration" (§46.116, c).

A fourth consideration related to informed consent is the use of deception. Deception can range in activities, from omitting minor information about the purpose of a research study to failing to disclose that research is being conducted at all. Deception may be warranted if there are provisions in the informed consent that allow the researcher to withhold information, assuming that the benefits of the research outweigh participant risks. In general, participants should not be deceived about aspects of research that would significantly influence their decision to participate. Should you decide to deceive your participants for the benefits of research, you will need to discuss this as soon as possible and usually during debriefing procedures (e.g., ACA Section G.2.h; APA Section 8.08). Debriefing is especially important, as it provides participants an opportunity to withdraw data if they so choose. In covert research, the use of deception and debriefing is obviously trickier.

The final consideration relates to participant characteristics. Why do some agree to participate? Are there specific participant characteristics, and do these carry ethical concerns? Threats in participant selection are a concern no matter the research design; however, given the intensive nature of qualitative inquiry, you have to consider why someone would commit

**PROPOSAL DEVELOPMENT ACTIVITY 3.1** DEVELOPING INFORMED CONSENT

Construct an informed consent document for your proposal, using the Protection of Human Subjects (2009) guidelines. After completing a draft, reflect on the following items:

- Do I include all the necessary components of informed consent? If I have omitted certain elements, what is my rationale?
- To what degree are procedures for ongoing consent addressed?
- Is covert research a part of the proposed study? In what ways am I able to secure informed consent?
- To what degree is deception a part of my study? How do I, if at all, deal with debriefing procedures?
- Who is protected by the document or informed-consent process? Participants? The larger community? The institution?
- What issues of equity and advocacy can I identify in the overall process of developing informed consent?

to such involvement. Do they feel coerced? Do they want to put forth a certain agenda? Are they similar to others in the sampling frame?

Participant characteristics are also important relative to marginalized populations as well as those obtained through a gatekeeper or key informant. Marginalized populations may be less likely to give formal consent. In addition, written consent can jeopardize relationships. Who do we identify as key informants, and why? Are certain, more powerful, gatekeepers "volunteering" less powerful groups? Who is actually giving consent? Are gatekeepers excluding certain individuals?

## Confidentiality

**Confidentiality** is linked to the informed consent process and relates to the client's right to privacy in the research relationship. There are laws to safeguard confidential personal and medical records, and researchers are to keep this in mind as they conduct qualitative inquiry. For example, the **Privacy Rule** is a federal law that protects participants' health information and limits who can receive that information (U.S. Department of Health and Human Services, 2013).

The Protection of Human Subjects (2009) regulation indicates that the only record that can connect participant identity to a research study is the informed consent document and that great care must be taken to prevent a breach of confidentiality. To further protect the participants' confidentiality, instead of offering a consent form to be signed, researchers should review the form with participants, seek verbal consent, and note in the transcript that verbal permission was obtained. Then the researcher could provide them with a copy of the informed consent document.

When our role as practitioners blurs with our role as researchers, several constructs may be pertinent. Let's review some other terms related to safeguarding participant information:

- **privacy:** Privacy refers the basic human right of protecting an individual's worth, dignity, and self-determination. Individuals should not feel intruded upon by the research process. If a participant agrees to the research process, researchers are to ensure the participant feels safe and comfortable with the process. When working with groups and communities of marginalized status, it is important to consider privacy individually and collectively.

- **anonymity:** Research is only truly anonymous when participant identity is concealed from the researcher. Since researchers are primarily interviewing and observing participants directly, anonymity is seldom possible. And given the nature of qualitative reporting, true anonymity is indeed a difficult task due to the depth and detail of reports. Confidentiality is often confused with anonymity; confidentiality refers to protecting an individual's identifying information, and it must be maintained even if anonymity is not.

- **privileged communication**: Privileged communication is the notion that confidential communication is protected within a judicial system, unless that right is waived by the individual. Depending on the state, researchers may have judicial protection should details of a research study be subpoenaed.

Ethical codes of professional organizations typically assert that information obtained about research participants during the course of research is confidential; information should be safely stored. Some cited exceptions include when there is danger to self or others and court-ordered disclosure unless otherwise protected. Furthermore, it should also be clear to informants and participants that despite every effort made to preserve it, anonymity may be compromised.

Maintaining confidentiality in qualitative inquiry may be difficult in several instances. First, confidentiality becomes an ethical concern in qualitative data collection, management, and analysis. The nature of collecting detailed personal stories puts confidentiality at risk. As Waldrop (2004) reported, "Qualitative data are, however, 'live,' encompassing tapes and transcripts of interviews as well as the researcher's notebooks and journals, all filled with purposefully thick and rich descriptions. Coding does not always remove identifying information" (p. 244).

There are several additional potential breaches of confidentiality. First, on-site research methods, such as observations and interviews, often complicate protection of participant confidentiality since there are often just a few, quite visible individuals in a setting. Second, transcriptions provide another ethical concern when individuals external to the process are involved.

A second issue involves third parties. Examples of third parties might include counselors, teachers, administrators, parents, peers, gatekeepers, and key informants. Third parties in qualitative research are more likely to know that someone is participating in research given the intensive engagement involved. Qualitative researchers are charged with keeping information confidential, particularly from those whose interest conflict with participants or the group or community to which they belong. At the extreme, this may mean adapting the report to change particular site or demographic characteristics.

Third parties can also be harmed or have their privacy violated during data collection. When researchers interview participants, observe them in a setting, or even review documents and other unobtrusive methods, it is quite likely that others will be mentioned in some manner. At times individuals may mention in connection to sensitive issues identifiable information about a third party. And while researchers discuss participant confidentiality on consent forms, they seldom include third parties. Third parties mentioned in transcripts, involved in observations, and so on are least likely to have their confidentiality protected since they are not direct research participants. It is imperative that qualitative researchers remember to mask their identities, even though they have not provided formal consent.

A final consideration in qualitative research related to confidentiality relates to researchers' duty to warn and protect in research settings when child or elder abuse or neglect is occurring. **Duty to warn and protect** is the ethical and legal responsibility to warn identifiable victims and protect others from dangerous individuals or, in some instances, from harming themselves. All states have legal mandates for child abuse and neglect reporting, with several similar protections for elderly people (National Institutes of Health, 2019; Williams & Ellison, 2009). In instances where researchers are concurrently engaged in multiple roles, such as a counselor or educator, they are to follow state mandating laws as well as adhere to ethical standards and principles of their profession (e.g., AAMFT, AERA, ACA, APA, ASGW, ASHE) and observe relevant Indigenous protocols. While there are several articles that discuss duty to warn and protect in practice, there is minimal written about this in research settings. Additionally, there is nothing specifically addressed in major ethical standards about the duty to warn and protect in research settings.

## Multiple Relationships

Practitioners who engage in qualitative research often do so because they want to collaboratively explore a phenomenon or provide an opportunity for individuals who are typically not included or who are misrepresented in the research process. According to various codes of ethics, the term **multiple relationships** refers to having more than one role with the same individual, a role with an individual as well as someone who is closely associated to that individual, or a role with an individual with the intention of having a future role with that same individual or someone closely associated to that individual. Multiple relationships in research, then, involve blurring boundaries and roles to meet several goals: to improve practice, to better understand an individual, to expand knowledge, to empower an individual, to advocate and create political or institutional change, and the list goes on. The issue of multiple relationships is particularly important with culturally diverse and other Indigenous groups. No matter researchers' good intentions, though, there will be power issues related to possessing multiple roles and agendas that are to be continually monitored. For example, some researchers (e.g., Sanjari et al., 2014) have highlighted potential ethical issues when the researcher–participant relationship takes on characteristics of a therapeutic or clinical relationship.

In quantitative research, researchers are deemed ethical to the extent to which they protect participants by maintaining objectivity and clear boundaries and keeping researcher values out of the research process. In qualitative research, it is important to develop and maintain relationships that protect participants yet collaborate and engage with a participant. Thus, it is often appropriate to introduce features of feminist and Indigenous ethics in order to establish rapport and gather a thick description of a phenomenon. Researchers often cannot avoid multiple relationships in qualitative inquiry, nor would it be appropriate. They have to manage them well. We provide some strategies for managing multiple relationships in Table 3.2.

**TABLE 3.2**   Strategies for Managing Multiple Relationships in Qualitative Inquiry

- Discuss the nature of your personal and professional roles with participants and other relevant stakeholders during the informed consent process. Seek their input and negotiate roles as relevant.
- Document the reasons you believe multiple roles are beneficial to the research participant and the study itself. Continually reflect in a journal and as part of a research team on these benefits in the context of minimal risk issues.
- Anticipate potential consequences of the multiple relationships and brainstorm ways you will work to minimize and/or remediate those consequences.
- Consult with colleagues if you or a participant are concerned about negative consequences.
- Consider the short- and long-term impact of being an insider, or studying your own group, as applicable.
- Assess any alternatives to engaging in multiple relationships for your study.

## Researcher Competence

To be passionate about and take on a research idea is an exciting adventure. However, whether one is competent to address the topic or engage in qualitative research in general can be an ethical dilemma. **Competence** refers to having the necessary training, skills, professional experience, and education to work with a population of interest in some capacity. When conducting research, practitioners need to determine if they have taken into account any special issues of the population and necessary competencies, including general training and specialty training. Various professional codes of ethics speak to acknowledging and expanding boundaries of competence. Themes include practitioners and educators conducting research within the boundaries of education and experience, seeking additional education and supervision as needed, disclosing actual and potential conflicts of interest, and presenting findings accurately and fully.

At times, practitioners and educators may be harmed in some manner from the research process. Perhaps negative emotional reactions result from interacting with participants and hearing or observing their experiences. If so, it is important to reflect on this impairment and consider how it is impacting the research process and, ultimately, the participants, groups, and communities involved. Reflexive Activity 3.1 provides some questions for consideration.

**REFLEXIVE ACTIVITY 3.1.** DETERMINING YOUR RESEARCH COMPETENCE

Consider the following:

- In which areas of qualitative research do I feel most competent?
- In which areas of qualitative research do I feel least competent?
- What clinical or educational issues or phenomena do I have an interest in pursuing as a research agenda? To what degree do I feel competent to address that research topic?
- In what ways can I build my competence as a researcher for my research proposal?
- How can I verify my competence during the research process?
- How will I manage times when my competence may be impaired during the research process?

## Additional Ethical Considerations in Qualitative Inquiry

This section highlights some additional ethical issues related to the above ethical concepts in designing, implementing, and reporting a qualitative study. Specifically, we will address pertinent ethical issues in conceptualizing the study (e.g., research paradigms and traditions, research goals, and the role of the researcher), implementing the study (e.g., qualitative interviewing, online research, and working with vulnerable and marginalized populations), and reporting qualitative data. Further, other parts of this text introduce other aspects of qualitative inquiry with ethical and professional implications. Every task in qualitative inquiry, from planning the study, to entering the field, building relationships, and collecting and analyzing data, should be considered in the context of how it benefits individuals, groups, and communities at the micro and macro level.

### Conceptualizing the Qualitative Study

There are several foundational and design aspects of qualitative inquiry, and we will discuss research paradigms and traditions, research goals, and the research relationship here.

### Research Paradigms and Traditions

Participants should not be exposed to a design that is not sound, because the benefits of the information obtained will never likely outweigh the risks to participants. A sound design involves selecting research paradigms and traditions that are suitable for the research purpose. The reasoning is that if the design is not congruent with research goals, the design may not be working in the best interest of those involved, because participants may be placed at unnecessary risk during data collection and reporting.

There are ethical concerns when working within any research paradigm, and researchers are to consider how the assumptions inherent in a paradigm could harm participants. For example, any claim to know an objective truth creates issues about knowledge and power, with an assumption that any generated knowledge labeled as "universal" is oppressive for particular individuals, groups, and communities. When researchers fail to consider how educational or clinical phenomena were initially conceptualized and operationalized over time, how contextual factors and issues of power shaped those definitions, and how there may alternative ways of knowing and resisting those phenomena, they may inadvertently enable inequitable research practices.

In addition to concerns with selecting a research paradigm, qualitative researchers are to reflect upon how each research tradition and its assumptions create ethical dilemmas. Research traditions possess their own assumptions and privilege particular ways of data collection, analysis, and reporting. Researchers are to weigh the costs and benefits of each research tradition for their research goals.

## Research Goals

In Chapter 5 we present research goals and discuss their role in topic selection and developing a conceptual framework. Each goal has an agenda, and there are usually multiple goals in qualitative inquiry. Unfortunately, these goals relate to competing agendas among participants, researchers, funders, and communities. To the extent possible, researchers are to actively involve participants, groups, and communities and codevelop research goals. Although researchers make compromises to meet competing personal, scholarly, community, and funder goals, they are responsible for protecting participants. Hence, researchers may be faced with conflicting interests.

With respect to funding goals, in particular, researchers are also to consider the impact of funding on research ethics. With the increasing need for institutional and educational support, researches need to identify to what extent sponsors research content, approaches, and findings (Smeyers & Depaepe, 2018). There is a tendency for sponsors to have too much control of research output and design; researchers should advocate for their rights and obligations to place findings in the public domain and within reasonable reach of practitioners, policymakers, and community stakeholders (Bridges, 2018).

## The Role of the Researcher

Reflexivity, introduced in Chapter 1, is based in the intricate relationship between the researcher and the researched. We see two key ethical issues related to the researcher's role: (a) the researcher as an instrument and (b) developing and maintaining an appropriate researcher relationship relative to the research purpose. As Corbin and Strauss (2015) asserted, we cannot separate who we are from what we do in qualitative research. Thus, researchers' professional and personal identities (i.e., positionality) is an inescapable instrument of qualitative research (Stone, 2018). The researcher as instrument may have both positive and negative ethical implications for the qualitative inquiry that need to be considered when conceptualizing a research study.

In qualitative research the researcher relationship is the major conduit for collecting quality data as well as an understanding of the study context. From an ethical standpoint, this is both a feature and a flaw: The more we create connections and thus stronger relationships, the more likely power comes into play. Both researcher subjectivity and neutrality can create ethical dilemmas.

Researchers often observe and interpret data often from their own frames of reference. Thus, the researcher is to constantly evaluate why particular participants, topics, or methods were selected and how these might relate to personal interests. These reflections can indicate important data as well as work to avoid harming participants. Qualitative researchers are to constantly reflect on how they as a person influence the process and outcome of qualitative inquiry and how research relationships reflect their professional selves.

Power imbalances in research relationships are inevitable. As discussed earlier in this chapter, Indigenous ethics provides ways to acknowledge and dismantle power in the research relationship. Researchers are to monitor their presence within a group or community and the potential consequences of their presence. Furthermore, they must actively seek individual and/or community definitions of key terms and remain open to challenges of their views and actions for the inquiry itself, academia, or the research community as a whole (Stone, 2018). Through intentional and reflexive acts, researchers can fulfill their duty to represent the lives of relevant populations well.

## Implementing the Qualitative Study

In this section we will discuss ethical considerations related to participant recruitment, interviewing and observations, online research, and working with vulnerable and marginalized populations. Table 3.3 provides key strategies to deal with ethical considerations related to study implementation.

### Sampling

In participant recruitment, there is an inevitable process of including some and excluding others. It is important for researchers, however, to not prematurely limit the sampling pool through their research questions and sampling method as well as the manner in which they enter the field, determine inclusion and exclusion criteria, or develop recruitment materials. Who counts as a research sample is a political endeavor with substantial consequences (Dawson et al., 2017).

Successful sampling is closely linked to research goals that benefit the participant, group, and/or community. As Dawson et al. (2017) noted, "One of the key motivators for research participation is the hope of the research having a positive impact for the group concerned" (p. 258). In addition, researchers are to consider how any recruitment processes and materials maximize involvement. The manner in which researchers enter the field, build rapport with relevant stakeholders, and include affirmative language in recruitment materials can yield more ethical research practices, particularly for sensitive topics (Dawson et al., 2017).

**TABLE 3.3** Strategies for Minimizing Ethical Dilemmas in Qualitative Data Collection

- Maintain an ongoing informed consent process.
- Discuss a priori with members of the target group any issues that are sensitive and relevant to the consent process to minimize the hierarchical nature of providing informed consent.
- Spend time learning about the populations and settings you are studying, particularly when research involves vulnerable populations.
- Form partnerships with community organizations and share power positions in research design decisions.
- Anticipate and plan to the extent possible potential participant reactions to content and process during data collection. Have a list of community resources available to participants.
- Combine both online and offline data collection methods to allow for depth, privacy, and authenticity of data. For example, consider using social media and other online platforms to recruit participants.
- Whether using online or offline methods, create a process whenever possible in which participants can return data responses in an anonymous manner. Consider the use of pseudonyms.
- Use trustworthiness strategies to assist in managing ethical dilemmas (e.g., reflexive journaling, member checking, triangulation of investigators, peer debriefing).
- Strike a balance between personalizing and being distant from the research topic and setting.
- Remember to "give back" to participants; do not exploit the participant for personal gain of data or access.
- Provide adequate protections for participants and third parties with respect to confidentiality.
- Do not approach participants by presenting a study as a method for them to gain self-awareness of the injustices they face, as this may be taken as patronizing and damaging. This may leave them feeling more vulnerable.
- Be aware of any previous experiences participants have with researchers. Whether negative or positive, seek to understand and value their experiences.

## *Interviewing and Observations*

When does interviewing and accompanying observations become too intrusive? The interview process can involve processing intense and difficult experiences—and thus unforeseen emotional experiences—that may create psychological harm for participants. Researchers are to carefully screen potential participants as possible for specific vulnerabilities and be prepared to exclude those who might have significant difficulty with the interview process. In addition, they should prepare safeguards for addressing risks that may arise as sensitive topics are broached.

There are power imbalances inherent in interviewing, although interactive interviewing helps with this (see Chapter 8). Brinkmann and Kvale (2018) presented some additional ethical challenges in the qualitative interview related to power imbalances:

- There is an asymmetrical power relation of the interview. The qualitative researcher defines, initiates, and dictates the interview. There is a research agenda as well as research goals. Even when the goal is to hear participant voices, researchers still dictate that.

- Interviewing is not a bidirectional process. Interviewees do not typically ask questions.
- The interview is a means to an end. It is a tool to gather data according to a researcher's interests, not a goal in itself.
- It can be a manipulative dialogue, with hidden agendas on the part of the researcher or participant.
- The researcher is privileged as the interpreter and reporter.

Observational research can be overt or covert. As Chapter 8 of this text outlines, researchers engage in observation along a participant observation continuum. Earlier in the chapter, we discussed the issue of deception and covert observational research. In addition, when participants are aware of being observed, ethical issues may arise depending on the insider–outsider role of researchers, the duration and intensity or the observational period, and the nature of what is being observed. Researchers are to carefully weigh the data generated from observations with the protection of participant, group, and community rights and self-determination.

## Social Media and Other Online Research

Researchers are increasingly using social media and other online platforms to extract data as well as generate data collection opportunities (e.g., online forum, focus group, emails) so participants can generate data for specific research purposes. Data sources can include direct or mass tweets, Facebook messages, website content, LinkedIn profiles, direct messages, emails, and Instagram posts, to name a few. Many of these sources are publicly available, with unrestricted access, and thus researchers have even greater responsibility in how data are extracted, interpreted, and reported (Granholm & Svedmark, 2018).

With respect to social media–based online data, Beninger (2017) identified three platform users that have implications for how these ethical issues are addressed: (a) *creators,* or those who post original content; (b) *sharers,* or those who share or repost content from creators or other sharers; and (c) *observers,* or those who only read and view content. These types of users are not independent, as users can take on these roles at various points. However, the extraction of research data garnered from creators or third parties, such as sharers, can involve different ethical considerations.

Two key ethical issues related to social media and other online research involve (a) privacy, anonymity, and confidentiality as well as (b) informed consent. Depending on whether the researcher seeks previously available or new online data, these ethical issues may be addressed differently. Perspectives 3.1 highlights one study examining Facebook usage among undergraduate students with regard to their intimate relationship development.

The Association of Internet Researchers (2019) provides multidisciplinary and multinational (i.e., Western) ethical guidelines for researchers and ethical review board members who are interested in online research. In its third revision, the guidelines guide the reader through the research process to consider ethical considerations surrounding epistemic and ethical values mentioned earlier in the chapter. The guidelines infuse a discussion of culture in ethical decision making, highlighting how online researchers are to consider how the cultural values of individualism and collectivism influence the overall research design, including the informed consent process, data management, data ownership, and access rights.

## PERSPECTIVES 3.1. FACEBOOK USE AND INTIMATE RELATIONSHIP DEVELOPMENT

Sherrell and Lambie (2016) conducted a phenomenological study with 16 under-graduate students, exploring their experiences with Facebook use and the extent to which those experiences influenced their intimate relationship development. Data were collected in nine semistructured individual interviews and one semistructured focus group interview with seven undergraduate students who did not participate in individual interviewing.

When interviewed about the study, Sherrell identified several ethical considerations when interviewing participants about the topic of social media as well as when social media platforms serve as the data source. Specifically, researchers are to:

- Be aware of how social media use has changed the way individuals communicate aspects of themselves and how they communicate with one another.
- Be cognizant of how individuals may communicate differently with one another on social media platforms versus other methods (e.g., interviews, face-to-face conversations). Issues of social desirability and privacy can vary depending on the communication method.
- Have knowledge about the social media platforms in which they are investigating.
- Be aware that participants may look at researchers' social media sites and the content they post or share.
- Consider how they will handle friend requests or other types of connections with participants before, during, and after the study.
- Be aware that technology related to social media changes quickly and findings need to be distributed quickly so that data are relevant.
- When extracting and analyzing social media content, consider how the amount of content posted or shared may be limited by the platform and/or the participant themselves.
- For publicly available data where privacy settings are less restricted, consider whether participants understand how public their data actually are.
- Determine whether informed consent is obtained and from whom (e.g., participant, third parties).
- Determine how to select and manage data given the vast amount of data (e.g., original or shared content, original or shared photographs, responses to content and by whom, who or what is tagged in posts, creator and user behaviors on platforms, number of posts and by whom, etc.).
- Reflect on the ethical implications of extracting data from private versus public profiles and how data will be collected, analyzed, reported, and safeguarded in general.
- Identify as possible whose or what data are not included and why and how these factors may impact the study's rigor.

Sherrell (personal communication, June 5, 2020) highlighted several ethical dilemmas, particularly associated with using social media as a data source:

> Ethic[al dilemmas] come up particularly while using social media as the data source. … Let's say I [extract] something that you posted and I'm using your comments as my data. What about all the other people who commented [on the post] as well? … Who fills out the informed consent. … How do I keep [the participant's and/or third party's] data safe because I have their names and opinions about things. … We are just at the beginning of learning how to use social media as a data source appropriately and effectively.

Trustworthiness strategies are particularly helpful for social media research and managing associated ethical considerations. (These are discussed further in Chapter 8.) For example, Sherrell used multiple strategies in the study, such as reflexive journaling, triangulation of data sources and methods, use of an audit trail, peer debriefing, external auditor, and thick description.

Source: Sherrell, R. S., & Lambie, G. W. (2016). A qualitative investigation of college students' Facebook usage and romantic relationships: Implications for college counselors. *Journal of College Counseling, 19,* 138–153. https://doi.org/10.1002/jocc.12037

---

## Privacy, Anonymity, and Confidentiality

There are different perspectives on the extent to which online data are publicly available and thus exempt from human subjects protections. These perspectives can vary depending on the platform and the extent to which that platform is open to the public (i.e., no passwords or member restrictions). Account holders often sign data use agreements in order to use various platforms, and it can be assumed they are aware that a particular platform owns their data. However, they may be uncomfortable with their personal data being used for academic research purposes. To avoid reputational risk, researchers should uphold anonymity and confidentiality to the extent possible. To complicate matters, some platforms, such as Twitter, require acknowledgment of sources when tweets are extracted. Thus, researchers have to balance anonymity with platform requirements.

Despite the legal ownership of data by an online platform, researchers are to consider the moral ownership of data and be responsible with content derived from online sources. Account users may expect there is some degree of privacy for their content and/or may be concerned with how their content may impact their personal reputation or those of friends and family members. For those who understand that their content is not private, there may be some impression management of what they post or share. This management can be positive or negative, yet the result is the same for researchers: Online data is to be viewed as flawed and incomplete.

Although ethical codes outline the importance of maintaining participant anonymity and confidentiality, this can be problematic in an online environment. First, publicly available data are permanent records that can be easily traced back to account users. For example, direct participant quotes can easily be identified by including the quote in an online search engine.

Data cannot be deleted permanently, and content can easily be copied and shared in multiple ways without creators' or sharers' consent. Furthermore, researchers are to consider the rights of those who may be featured in online content (e.g., posts, photos) but are not the subject of research. When possible, researchers are to use alternative ways to present data to maximally protect the identity of others (Granholm & Svedmark, 2018). Finally, another consideration is that data generated from an online group may not be remain anonymous, as group members may be aware of others' identities.

## Informed Consent

Researchers must consider ways that they can obtain informed consent in some manner when using data collected online. This is particularly important when content is of a sensitive nature (e.g., political, religious, etc.). In addition, they are to reflect on the openness of the platform. When they seek to use data from more restricted sources (e.g., member-restricted groups, data from "friend of friends" of Facebook friends or Twitter followers, etc.), researchers are to take reasonable steps to notify potential participants of their intention to use data.

When recruiting participants for researcher-generated online content, researchers should aim to accommodate different types of users and be explicit regarding how their content will be used and for what purpose. Including security and privacy terms in recruitment materials is necessary. When possible—and in addition to typical informed consent—researchers should disclose to potential participants what personal information is or will be available, how that personal information will be used for research purposes, and the extent to which anonymity and confidentiality can be maintained in the research process and report (Beninger, 2017).

## *Vulnerable and Marginalized Populations*

In Chapter 2 we provide a brief history of qualitative research, highlighting several eras of history where qualitative researchers studied the "other" (i.e., those with less power and representation) and fit findings into a dominant schema. When researching vulnerable or marginalized populations, it might be easy to reinforce a power imbalance and repeat history. Vulnerable populations include minors, prisoners, pregnant women, and those with mental disabilities (Protection of Human Subjects, 2009). In addition, we identify populations of marginalized statuses (e.g., Indigenous populations) as potentially vulnerable, given the traditional manner in which research is conducted.

Voices of marginalized youth are underrepresented in research in general. It is important to not only engage in dialogue with this population for the sake of interactions but also to assume that minors are experts of their own experiences and thus have something of value to say to add to theory in education and social sciences.

Minors do not and cannot consent to research. Parents or guardians give proxy consent for children. However, an ethical dilemma arises when the parent's consent is not in the best interest of the child or the child cannot understand the implications of their participation (Ireland & Holloway, 1996). In regard to assent, an IRB will determine the methods for obtaining assent if it is determined that minors are capable of providing assent given developmental, psychological, and other factors (Protection of Human Subjects, 2009). In addition, researchers should be cognizant of avoiding penalty for minors who withdraw from educational or clinical research.

The content of data collected from minors may also place them at risk. Such content can include illegal drug use, unsafe sex practices, and criminal behavior, to name a few. It is imperative that qualitative researchers are careful to protect them by ensuring the data shared do not harm the participants. Sometimes, this may mean leaving out "great stories" that could reinforce negative stereotypes and/or jeopardize their confidentiality. When highly sensitive issues are considered in research, minors should have access to an advocate—particularly through the initial phases of the study (Sanjari et al., 2014). Scholars (e.g., Granholm & Svedmark, 2019; Nelson & Quintana, 2005; Sanjari et al., 2014) outline several key ethical issues related to researching minors:

- Children may be difficult to access.
- The research relationship is likely influenced by the context and setting surrounding the individual, which is largely outside the child's control.
- Children may feel powerless and consent to research regardless of not being comfortable with the process.
- Developmental issues, such as language development and attention span, can impact a child's power to be a part of the research.
- Developmental factors may inhibit the data collection process.
- The use of particular measures (interviewing, projective techniques, observations) can further intrude upon their privacy.
- It can be difficult, if not impossible, to verify the age of individuals developing blogs and social media content through individual and group platforms. Specifically, minors can create false profiles and identities.

## Transnational Research

As the global community increasingly engages with one another, opportunities to conduct qualitative research increase—as do possible ethical considerations. **Transnational research** can be defined as research typically conducted across multiple nations, societies, or territories that involves transnational research teams.

Common areas of ethical concerns relate to respect and understanding when researchers' cultural norms differ from the research participants. This also refers to the use of Western-developed and validated research protocols and definitions of phenomena and constructs in non-Western cultures and the appropriateness of ethical boards' requirements to other contexts (Shordike et al., 2017). The inclusion of individuals from the host area is imperative, whether as coresearchers or as key informants and gatekeepers.

Successful transnational research relies on strong research partnerships among the researchers and participants and their communities. Working within transnational teams, members are to outline expectations and their individual and collective understandings of research; how well suited the research design may be for different contexts; and the ability to have procedural equivalence in sampling (e.g., inclusion and exclusion criteria, recruitment plans, consent procedures, data collection processes). Furthermore, when ethical review boards or protocols do not formally exist, it is imperative the transnational partner provides guidance to the team (Shordike et al., 2017).

As possible, it may be useful to conduct within-culture data collection (i.e., researchers collect and analyze data for their respective home nations). The quantity and quality of verbal and nonverbal data garnered from data collection may differ based on cultural differences and practices as well as language differences. Following within-culture or insider data collection, researchers can come together to examine cross-cultural similarities and differences. As researchers collect and analyze data, they strive to honor emic knowledge as they explore conceptual equivalence across cultures (Shordike et al., 2017).

## Reporting Qualitative Data

There is power in the qualitative report: It speaks volumes as to what is most important and from whose perspective the research is conducted (Brinkmann & Kvale, 2018). Researchers ultimately control whose data are included and how data are presented and in what voice. Professional codes of ethics primarily focus on data authenticity in terms of avoiding fabricated, inaccurate, or misleading research claims. Data accuracy issues involve data fabrication, use of fraudulent materials, omissions, and either intentional or unintentional false interpretation and reporting of findings (Christians, 2017). There are a couple of clear ways qualitative researchers may interpret and report data falsely (intentionally or not). First, they risk misinterpretation when they do not check data or analyses with participants (i.e., member checking) or other investigators (i.e., triangulation; see Chapter 8). Second, they act unethically when they fail to report their process through an audit trail. Since a qualitative report is often limited in scope by journal restrictions, the audit trail is an ideal place to "show your work" to participants, peers, and others in the community.

There are other considerations in terms of representation and accuracy in terms of data reporting. Consider the following considerations and strategies:

- Inform participants at the outset of the study that their narratives, even if told from their perspective, will be presented at least in part through a researcher lens.
- Prior to reporting data in any format, engage in member checking or some other method of verifying the findings. As relevant, seek permission from groups and communities to share the findings with the public.
- When reports require substantial editing to meet publishing guidelines (e.g., academic journals, policy briefs), discuss the implications of this with participants. When possible, engage them in defining how and what findings are included.
- Consider multiple methods for reporting data to maximize public access to the findings.

The quality, content, and distribution of the findings may affect relationships with your participants as well as their communities. Furthermore, Christians (2017) recommended that researchers prioritize interpretative sufficiency. **Interpretative sufficiency** refers to sufficiently and authentically accounting for participants' narratives and experiences to represent multiple voices. Through careful attention to multiple interpretations and cultural complexity, social transformation can occur.

## CHAPTER SUMMARY

This chapter outlined several key ethical constructs and issues in qualitative inquiry. We began this chapter with a brief history of ethics, highlighting Western influences that shaped utilitarianism and then introducing feminist (i.e., feminist standpoint, feminist communitarianism) and Indigenous research ethics that serve to challenge utilitarianism concepts. We have defined "ethics" and outlined several ethical concepts, including metaethical principles, informed consent, confidentiality, multiple relationships, and researcher competence. Further, we have explored ethical dilemmas in conceptualizing, implementing, and reporting qualitative data.

We hope you will consider each of these areas and reflect on their interconnections in qualitative inquiry (see Proposal Development Activity 3.2). Ethical issues and salient concepts should not be considered from a top-down approach, where the qualitative researcher simply examines material in this chapter in a compartmentalized fashion. Rather, it should be experiential and inductive, where the researcher is constantly reflecting on ethical concerns relating to themselves, the research team, as well as with those being studied.

## Review Questions

1. How did Western influences on research ethics shape utilitarianism?
2. How do feminist standpoint, feminist communitarianism, and Indigenous research ethics compare and contrast with one another? Use a hypothetical study topic as you consider similarities and differences.
3. What are the benefits and challenges of institutional review boards?
4. The six metaethical principles presented in the chapter can create ethical dilemmas when researchers prioritize multiple principles within a study. What is an example of a potential ethical dilemma resulting from competing metaethical principles?
5. What are some ethical considerations unique to social media and other online research?
6. How are your answers to the above questions informed by your role in the researcher-practitioner-advocate (RPA) model? Why are the issues of equity and advocacy continuously emerging in ethics in qualitative research?

## Recommended Readings

Association of Internet Researchers. (2019). *Ethics guidelines for Internet research 3.0.* https://aoir.org/ethics/

Christians, C. (2017). Ethics and politics in qualitative research. In N. Denzin & Y. Lincoln (Eds.), *The Sage handbook of qualitative research* (5th ed., pp. 61-80). Sage.

Herman, R. D. K. (2018). Approaching research in Indigenous settings: Nine guidelines. In First Nations of Quebec and Labrador Health and Social Services Commission, Université du Quebec en Abitibi-Témiscamingue, & Université du Quebec en Outaouais (Eds.),

*Toolbox of research principles in an aboriginal context: ethics, restrict, fairness, reciprocity, collaboration and culture* (pp. 103–113). https://www.cssspnql.com/docs/default-source/centre-de-documentation/toolbox_research_principles_aboriginal_context_eng16C3D3AF-4B658E221564CE39.pdf

World Intellectual Property Organization. (n.d.). *Resources.* https://www.wipo.int/reference/en/

## PROPOSAL DEVELOPMENT ACTIVITY 3.2. CONSIDERING ETHICAL DILEMMAS FOR YOUR STUDY

Reflect on each ethical consideration in the first column for your study. How do you anticipate each will be addressed in your study? Next, consider how you think about and what you plan to do in your study in the context of the metaethical principles listed in the first row. Which are in conflict with one another? In what ways? Which areas of your project have the most potential for ethical dilemmas?

| | Autonomy | Nonma-leficence | Benefi-cence | Justice | Fidelity | Veracity | Equity, diversity, and inclusion |
|---|---|---|---|---|---|---|---|
| Informed consent | | | | | | | |
| Confidenti-ality | | | | | | | |
| Multiple rela-tionships | | | | | | | |
| Competence | | | | | | | |
| Conceptual-ization/ Establishing research agenda | | | | | | | |
| Implementa-tion | | | | | | | |
| Reporting data | | | | | | | |

## CHAPTER 4

# Qualitative Research Traditions

---

## CHAPTER PREVIEW

Choosing a research tradition creates a solid foundation for your research design. In this chapter, we outline several research traditions that are used in qualitative research. Data collection and analysis procedures are elaborated upon in later chapters. The research traditions are presented in clusters based on common characteristics across research traditions. Specifically, the clusters are as follows: (a) case study; (b) grounded theory, phenomenology, heuristic inquiry, and consensual qualitative research; (c) life history and narratology; (d) ethnography, ethnomethodology, and autoethnography; and (e) participatory action research and community-based participatory research. The research traditions included in this chapter are ones that are most prominent in education and social sciences research. Thus, they are not an exhaustive list of research traditions. Table 4.1 provides an overview of the clusters' characteristics and outlines how a research topic pertaining to dual-career families may be examined based on each research tradition.

## Philosophies of Science, Research Paradigms, and Research Traditions

In Chapter 2 we introduced the concepts of philosophies of science and research paradigms. Specifically, five core philosophies of science (i.e., ontology, epistemology, axiology, rhetoric, methodology), or approaches to scientific inquiry, influence the selection of a research paradigm (i.e., positivism, postpositivism, constructivism, critical research paradigms, Indigenous research paradigms). The research traditions presented in this chapter were developed and have evolved to reflect different research paradigms. Thus, research paradigms are belief systems based in researchers' approach to science, and these belief systems determine how **research traditions**, or methodological blueprints for the research process, are implemented.

**TABLE 4.1**    Qualitative Research Traditions

| | Cluster characteristics | Tradition characteristics | Study example |
|---|---|---|---|
| **Cluster 1: The Hybrid Tradition** | | | |
| **Case study** | | Describes a single or multiple case (e.g., phenomenon, event, situation, organization, individual, or group of individuals studied in naturalistic settings) within its surrounding context (bounded system) | Study of conflict among partners in dual-career families: With dual-career family as the case, the researcher examines the individuals, activities, events, and processes of several families (multiple case study) to describe ways that family and career are balanced within and across cases. The bounded system is dual-career families working within one university system. |
| **Cluster 2: Experience and Theory Formulation** | | | |
| **Grounded theory** | Discovery of local and/or grand theories, subjectivity, action or process oriented, descriptive or application of individual experience | Theory behind experience; theory generation, primarily inductive, theoretical sampling, saturation, constant comparison | Develop a local theory to describe and explain how conflict impacts dual-career families. The researcher uses an inductive approach and theoretical sampling to understand sequences, processes, causal and intervening conditions, and actions associated with the phenomenon. The researcher remains close to the data and seeks a core category or central idea that unites other constructs and accounts for variation in conflict outcomes. |
| **Phenom-enology** | | Emphasis on universal and divergent aspects of experience itself; participants' direct, immediate experience within their life-worlds | Explore the direct lived experiences of conflict through interviewing of dual-career families. Upon bracketing experiences and assumptions about the study topic, the researcher seeks to fully describe the collective and individual experiences of the phenomenon. |
| **Heuristic Inquiry** | | Interaction between experience and person; topic has personal significance for researcher; results primarily increase researcher's self-knowledge with some implications for general field. | Explore the direct lived experiences of conflict through interviewing of dual-career families. The researcher integrates their personal experience and data throughout the research process to better understand their own conflict experiences. |

(continued)

**TABLE 4.1**   Qualitative Research Traditions   *(Continued)*

| | Cluster characteristics | Tradition characteristics | Study example |
|---|---|---|---|
| CQR | | Experience and participants' perspectives useful in generating theory; emphasis on consensus, frequency counts, and shared power among researchers and participants | To understand how dual-career families negotiate whether both partners will work outside the home, the researcher collaborates closely with participants and team members to arrive at consensus of a local theory that includes general, typical, and variant themes regarding participant experiences of the phenomenon. |
| **Cluster 3: The Meaning of Symbol and Text** | | | |
| Life history | Language, symbols, story, identity, context | Individual narratives of social experience; personal meanings and context; may involve rewriting history or re-storying | Identify themes within a biographical study of a dual-career family with substantial conflict. The researcher conducts personal interviews with respective partners to gather data on their individual and collective career trajectories and concerns of work-life balance. |
| Narratology | | Plot structure, content, and purpose of narratives; exploration of communication methods and audiences of narrative | Study the interplay of narrator, audience, and context as each partner of a dual-career family recounts conflict they experience. |
| **Cluster 4: Cultural Expressions of Process and Experience** | | | |
| Ethnography | Cultural processes and experiences, prolonged engagement, participant observation, fieldwork | Social, behavioral, and linguistic group patterns and norms; global description of culture or cultural group | Explore the attitudes and practices of dual-career Black families living in a small community. The researcher builds a relationship over time, engaging in fieldwork that involves participant observation and interviews to understand the extent to which the community provides support and shapes norms regarding dual-career work. |
| Ethnomethodology | | Description of social patterns and rules; "everydayness" of behaviors | Examine shifts in social patterns after a sudden, nontraditional shift in breadwinner roles for a straight couple. |
| Autoethnography | | Researcher as group member with self in report; first-person account of cultural event of processes | Explore for a group of researchers as participants (collective autoethnography) their attitudes toward resources for themselves as partners within dual-career families. The researchers synthesize data to contextualize their experiences within a larger phenomenon. |

*(continued)*

**TABLE 4.1**   Qualitative Research Traditions   *(Continued)*

| | Cluster characteristics | Tradition characteristics | Study example |
|---|---|---|---|
| **Cluster 5: Research as a Change Agent** | | | |
| **PAR** | Advocacy and change of conditions, context, researcher, and participants; power analysis; action research | Individual-level advocacy and change | Conduct action research with a group of dual-career families who seek support for conflict. The researcher critically reflects on their power in the research relationship as well as ways they can equitably include participants in the research process to empower them to alleviate conflict. |
| **CBPR** | | Community- or group-level advocacy and change | Engage with family advocacy agency to advocate through research for dual-career families who need assistance with childcare policies, a noted source of conflict among dual-career families. The researcher works collaboratively with community stakeholders and the agency to collect data to enact policy changes. |

Note: CQR= Consensual Qualitative Research. PAR= Participatory Action Research. CBPR= Community-Based Participatory Research.

Collectively, core philosophies of science, research paradigms, and research traditions influence one another to share research orientation (see Figure 4.1).

## The Hybrid Tradition: Case Study

The case study tradition is often considered versatile, methodologically diverse, and under continual development (Harrison et al., 2017). It involves a comprehensive, in-depth study of a complex issue framed through a **case** (i.e., unit of analysis or object of study) within a *bounded system* (i.e., has distinctive boundaries of time, sampling frame, activity, and/or physical space or setting that frame and constrict the research focus). A case may be a phenomenon, event, situation, organization, individual, or group of individuals studied in naturalistic settings. Once the case is identified, qualitative researchers explore relationships among the case's individual characteristics, processes, and events (Starman, 2013). Typically, multiple data sources and collection methods are used via fieldwork to describe the case and its intersection with various contextual variables. Furthermore, qualitative researchers are to clearly define what a case and its bounded system are. When deciding the scope of the case study, they can investigate one case (i.e., **single case study**) or several cases (i.e., **multiple case study**).

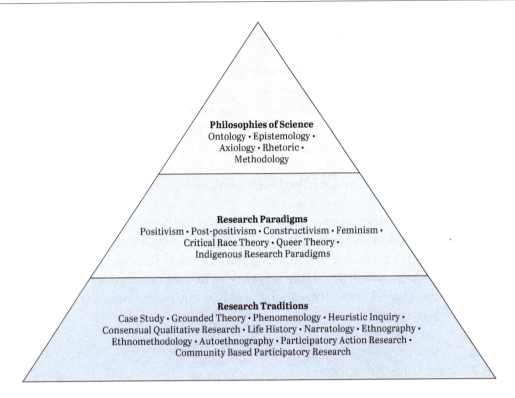

**FIGURE 4.1** The Foundations of a Qualitative Research Orientation

In general, a **case study** is the intensive exploration of a case and the interactions of the object of study within its surrounding context (i.e., bounded system). It can be descriptive or explanatory, include a case or cases with function or working parts, and indicate patterned behaviors such as sequence or coherence (Stake, 1995, 2006; Yin, 2017). Starman (2013) notes that case studies can be useful for theory development, given their utility and fluidity in linking causes and outcomes within a context, exploring case elements and their relationships, developing and testing hypothesized relationships, and understanding the sensitivity of case elements to the bounded system. Thus, the case study may be the optimal research tradition to utilize when educators, counselors, and other practitioners are seeking to answer "how" and "why" questions, when control over events is limited, and when a phenomenon is studied in its natural context.

Although most attention to developing the case study tradition in education and social science disciplines has been within the past 40 years, contemporary case study research has been significantly influenced by ethnographies conducted during the Traditional Ethnography and Pragmatism and the Chicago School period (i.e., early 1900s–1960s; see Chapter 2). Case studies have also been influenced by clinical case study methods, such as those of Piaget and Freud, which involved intensive interviewing to further develop psychological theory. Robert Yin and Robert Stake, prominent contributors to case study research theory from the social sciences and education research fields, respectively, emphasized in the 1970s and 1980s the use of case studies to describe and evaluate programs in clinical and education settings (Harrison et al., 2017).

We refer to the case study as a hybrid tradition, given its evolving and fluid development as an approach and its potential to employ multiple qualitative and/or quantitative methods as well as multiple sources of evidence. A case study attends to both the particular and the universal aspects of an object of study, moving back and forth between the two in description and/or theorization. Case study research may also be considered a hybrid tradition because it may be integrated with several of the research traditions described in the remainder of this chapter. Because most traditions listed in this chapter deal with cases, there is a natural blend of research traditions.

Qualitative researchers can approach case study research differently, depending on whether they adhere to postpositivism (see Yin, 2017) or constructivism (see Stake, 1995, 2006). Selection of the case study approach will depend on the study aim and best alignment with the qualitative researcher's worldview. Table 4.2 provides further detail about Yin's and Stake's approaches to case study. Perspectives 4.1 features how one researcher uses Yin's approach in her case study research.

**TABLE 4.2**  Case Study Approaches

|  | Yin | Stake |
|---|---|---|
| **Case study definition** | *How* or *why* the case is; the study of a contemporary phenomenon within its real-life context, especially when the boundaries between a phenomenon and context are not clear and the researcher has little control over the phenomenon and context; focused on case scope, process, and methodological characteristics | *What* or *when* the case is; "the study of the particularity and complexity of a single case, coming to understand its activity within important circumstances" (Stake, 1995, p. xi). |
| **Case study designs** | Decisions about case study design are made at the outset of the research process, with minimal changes once it begins. Types: **single holistic design**, single unit of analysis within a single case; **single embedded design**, multiple units of analysis within a single case; **multiple holistic design**, single unit of analysis across multiple cases; and **multiple embedded design**, multiple units of analysis across multiple cases | Decisions about case study remain flexible throughout the study, as knowledge is constructed between the researchers and participants. **Intrinsic case study**, where the researcher as an individual has an internally guided or intrinsic interest in a particular case; **instrumental case study**, where the researcher seeks out cases to assist in an understanding of a particular issue exterior to a specific case; and **collective case study**, where multiple cases are used to investigate more general or broad phenomenon or population |

(continued)

**TABLE 4.2** Case Study Approaches *(Continued)*

| | Yin | Stake |
|---|---|---|
| **Paradigmatic influence** | *Postpositivism:* Knowledge is discovered. Application of experimental design tenets to naturalistic inquiry. Focus on maximizing "objectivity" in methodology to maximize validity and reliability similarly to quantitative research. Researchers reach an objective truth or approximated truth about the case | *Constructivism:* Knowledge is constructed, and thus multiple versions of case description are likely. There exists multiple, equally valid realities derived from researcher perspective, participant perspective, and an interaction between the two parties. Researchers are aware that case study findings are tentative first impressions based on knowledge constructed at a particular time |
| **Case study goals** | Highlight cause and effect and develop and verify theory (via seeking rival explanations). Determine whether a theory's propositions are correct or whether some alternative set of explanations might be more relevant. More amenable to study events or processes as case | Conduct a holistic analysis and describe case. More amenable to study individuals, groups, or programs as case |
| **Case selection criteria** | Ensures case is typical, of high interest to others, and has the potential for replicability of similar or contrasting findings (**theoretical replication** or **literal replication**, respectively) | Allows discovery of meaning and understanding of experiences in content for a case of interest within itself. Look for texture to or multiple dimensions within a case that interacts with its environment in a complex way |
| **Data sources** | Quantitative and/or qualitative data sources through careful a priori planning | Qualitative data sources are selected as case study evolves and researcher reflexivity occurs |
| **Data analysis** | Development of theoretical propositions to guide data analysis; seek triangulation for developing and verifying theory | **Categorical aggregation**, or the examination of several occurrences for critical incidents, concerns, and issues; **direct interpretation,** or the focused analysis of the meaning of a singular critical incident; and **pattern identification,** or the focusing on broad categories within the case for their relationships and/or interactions |
| **Data reporting** | Detailed and structured description of methodological decisions and the role of theory in shaping the case study | Use of vignettes or narratives to thickly describe the case in part or whole; significant attention to researcher reflexivity |
| **Generalizability/ Transferability of findings** | Seek generalizability and replicability of findings, particularly for multiple case study designs | Through thick description of cases in similar contexts, researchers can maximize **naturalistic generalizability** |

Sources: Harrison et al. (2017), Stake (1995, 2006), Yazan (2015), and Yin (2017)

## PERSPECTIVES 4.1. POSITIVE BEHAVIORAL INTERVENTIONS AND SUPPORTS IN A MIDDLE SCHOOL

Emily Goodman-Scott, who identifies as a counselor educator, professional school counselor, and former special education teacher, often uses the case study tradition in her research within K–12 settings. One study involved investigating the implementation of positive behavioral interventions and supports (PBIS) for a middle school in an urban setting (Goodman-Scott et al., 2018).

Goodman-Scott initiated the case study after she attended a presentation given by a principal. In the presentation, the principal described significant positive outcomes at her middle school. Goodman-Scott (personal communication, June 18, 2020) recounted in an interview with me (Hays):

> [The middle school] had a reputation and incidents of violence … discipline referrals … there were so many challenges within the school. … The principal came in and then in five years she totally revamped the culture of the school and the outcomes of the school. Hearing this presentation … I talked to the principal and [asked] would you be willing for me to showcase this incredible work that you've done as an exemplary case study? … I interviewed her, the school counselor and the team who implemented PBIS. I also met with the assistant principal, and he provided me with a lot of data. … I had quantitative and qualitative data … it was a beautiful way to show what they were doing.

Aligned with Robert Yin's (2017) work, Goodman-Scott (personal communication, June 18, 2020) cites several characteristics of the case study tradition that make it optimal for her work. First, the study of a case within its natural setting allows the researcher to tell a story from the real world, bringing to life what is happening in the field and how that story can translate to the work of other researchers and practitioners. Furthermore, capturing the boundedness of the case (i.e., the context) through incorporating multiple and diverse data sources can yield a thick description of the setting. Second, through careful planning of the research design at the outset of the research process, the case study tradition allows for a systematic approach to inquiry that can use qualitative and quantitative data. The selection of type and quantity of data sources, she adds, is dependent on the depth and breadth of the story qualitative researchers want to tell. Third, she notes the sheer amounts of data that comes from conducting case study research. For the PBIS study, Goodman-Scott noted several data sources that included transcripts from interviews with the principal, professional school counselor, and other PBIS team members; discipline referrals; course schedules; media stories about the school; school expectation matrices; a school discipline flow chart; and positive reinforcement examples and incentives. Finally, she cites the role of flexibility for this tradition: Researchers have flexibility during phases of data collection and analysis and they must remain flexible when working in a complex, bounded system.

Source: Goodman-Scott, E. G., Hays, D. G., & Cholewa, B. (2018). "It takes a village": A case study of positive behavioral interventions and supports implementation in an exemplary urban middle school. *The Urban Review, 50*, 97–122. https://doi.org/10.1007/s11256-017-431-z

There are several ways case study research has been categorized within the literature, and Starman (2013) summarizes several types of single and multiple case studies. Importantly, the single case types listed below can be expanded to investigate multiple cases. Following a brief description of each type, we provide an example using a hypothetical research case study of elementary teacher candidates who completed an education module designed to improve STEM instructional practices. Throughout these examples, the case is identified as the preservice teachers, mentor teachers, school, or module itself. The theory referenced throughout refers to best practices in STEM instruction identified in the literature. After reviewing the examples, consider how you can apply each type to a study topic of interest (see Activity 4.1).

- *retrospective case study:* A case is examined for a particular historical period. Example: Evaluation of candidates' learning from a module completed for a 2-year historical period is conducted for one elementary school (single case study) or three elementary schools (multiple case study) within the same school district. Changes in instructional practices are also evaluated for the period.
- *snapshot case study:* A case is studied within a current period. Example: Throughout the module implementation, candidates' perceptions of various components are investigated at one elementary school (single case study) or three elementary schools (multiple case study) within the same school district.
- *diachronic case study:* A case is investigated for changes over time (i.e., longitudinal study). Example: Changes in instructional practices over 1 year for a teacher candidate (single case study) or 10 teacher candidates (multiple case study) within the same school.
- *atheoretical/configurative idiographic case study:* A case is explored for illustrative purposes only. Example: One (single case study) or five (multiple case study) teacher candidates' successful implementation of learning from the module within their student teaching (i.e., highly rated STEM instructional practices by mentor teachers) are examined within the same school district.
- *disciplined configurative case study:* Existing theory is used to explain a case. Example: Using best practices for elementary STEM instruction outlined within previous scholarship, a researcher describes teacher candidates' use of module learning in their student teaching at one elementary school (single case study) or three elementary schools (multiple case study) within the same school district.

 **ACTIVITY 4.1.** APPLYING THE CASE STUDY TRADITION

Select a topic of interest in your profession. Consider how the case study tradition might influence how you would study the research topic. How might you approach the topic from each of the single and multiple case study types Starman (2013) describes?

- *heuristic case study:* An outlier case is examined to identify unique theoretical considerations. Example: Using a sample of preservice teachers who received very high mentor teacher ratings of their STEM instruction, the researcher interviews mentor teachers at one elementary school (single case study) or three elementary schools (multiple case study) to understand their perceptions of what contributed to successful STEM instructional practices.
- *theory-testing case study:* A case is used to test or verify existing theory. Example: A researcher evaluates one teacher candidate (single case study) or five teacher candidates (multiple case study) on the implementation of module learning to STEM instructional practices.
- *"building block" case study:* Various elements of a case are studied, and findings are combined to contribute to a more comprehensive theory. Example: Teacher candidates who completed the module are interviewed about the extent to which various module components linked to their STEM instructional practices at one elementary school (single case study) or three elementary schools (multiple case study).
- *nested case study:* Multiple elements of a case or cases within the same bounded system are examined to comparing each case's elements with other cases in that system. Example: Grades 3, 4, and 5 teacher candidates within one elementary school (multiple case study) are observed and interviewed to determine differences in STEM instructional practices by grade level.
- *parallel case study:* Multiple cases are occurring and are investigated concurrently. Example: A research team explores teacher candidates' STEM instructional practices within 1 academic year at multiple elementary schools (multiple case study).
- *sequential case study:* These are based on the assumption that cases occurring consecutively are affected by the previous case and will affect future cases. Example: A researcher interviews cohorts of teacher candidates each year (multiple case study) to evaluate annual changes in module components across a 5-year period.

## Experience and Theory Formulation: Grounded Theory, Phenomenology, Heuristic Inquiry, and Consensual Qualitative Research

The second cluster is one of the more popular collections of research traditions. This cluster includes grounded theory, phenomenology, heuristic inquiry, and consensual qualitative research. It focuses on developing subjective local and/or grand theories regarding a phenomenon that outlines processes, direct experiences, and/or actions. After reading about these four traditions, complete Activity 4.2.

### Grounded Theory

**Grounded theory** is one of the most popular research traditions in clinical and education disciplines today. The purpose of a grounded theory approach is to generate theory that is grounded in data from participants' perspectives for a particular phenomenon. Depending

---

🔄 **ACTIVITY 4.2.** APPLYING THE EXPERIENCE AND THEORY
FORMULATION TRADITION

---

Suppose you are interested in studying the role of technology in your profession. Consider
how each of the traditions discussed in the Experience and Theory Formulation cluster
would influence how you might study the role of technology. Compare the traditions
and discuss benefits and challenges of each for your topic.

---

on the paradigmatic assumptions used with this tradition, the theory generated can either
be descriptive or explanatory. The theories that are generated often explain a process or
action surrounding an experience, describe a sequence of events pertaining to a particular
phenomenon, and provide implications for practice and policy based in the theory scope and
intended audience.

Grounded theory originates from sociology and has four key figures: Barney Glaser, Anselm
Strauss, Juliet Corbin, and Kathy Charmaz. Beginning in the late 1960s, grounded theory has
developed strands based in varying paradigms: positivism and postpositivism (Glaser, Strauss,
Corbin) and constructivism (Charmaz). In *The Discovery of Grounded Theory*, Glaser and Strauss
(1967) introduced the original tradition strand (classic or Glaserian grounded theory; CGGT)
after conducting research on terminal illness. Through interviews and participant observation, they were able to develop a theory that informed compassionate care with terminally
ill patients. CGGT asserts that an inductive approach to developing theory and informing
practice is as important as a deductive approach that tests existing theory. With a pure focus
on inductive methods, CGGT does not rely on existing literature or researcher experience to
develop research questions or inform theory. Thus, the theory generated is purely descriptive
and directly grounded in participant data.

While Glaser and Strauss agree with many of the general characteristics of this approach,
in the 1990s their ideas of how purely inductive grounded theory should be diverged (see
Glaser, 1992; Strauss & Corbin, 1990). In 1990, Strauss and Juliet Corbin published *The Basics
of Qualitative Research*, now in its fourth edition (see Corbin & Strauss, 2015). The Straussian
grounded theory (SGT) strand retained postpositivist assumptions from CGGT; SGT assumes
prior theory and researcher experiences (i.e., *theoretical sensitivity*) could inform developing
theory from present data. Furthermore, Strauss and Corbin (1990) formalized grounded theory
data analysis, introducing terms such as open coding, axial coding, and selective coding (see
Chapter 11). Thus, SGT moved away from CGGT's pure groundedness of the data to generate
theory and further systematized data analytic processes.

A third grounded theory strand, based in constructivist assumptions, was developed by
Kathy Charmaz (i.e., constructivist grounded theory; CGT). In her text *Constructing Grounded
Theory*, Charmaz (2006/2014) assumed that multiple, contextualized truths and several social
processes can explain a particular phenomenon. She acknowledged that the research process
and reports are mediated by the researcher's perspectives, and to this end, researchers are to

engage in reflexivity throughout the research process. With CGT, theory is very localized and co-constructed between the researcher and participant (Charmaz, 2014).

Although there are several grounded theory strands, there are some common characteristics. After reviewing these characteristics, read Case Example 4.1, which highlights these characteristics in a published study. The first common characteristic of grounded theory is its inductive approach. That is, qualitative researchers set aside preconceived notions when they approach a phenomenon to formulate a theory about that phenomenon, moving from simpler to complex and refined constructions or descriptions. In its purest form, as CGGT depicts, grounded theory is a process by which an underlying theory exists and can be discovered by remaining close to participant-generated data. With SGT and CGT, prior theory and/or assumptions may be introduced into the research process so that the approach is not purely inductive, as CGGT endorses. With these two strands, there is no single existing theory that is discovered but multiple theories that are shaped by the researcher–participant relationship; theories are constructed, not found (Charmaz, 2014; Strauss & Corbin, 2015).

Second, concurrent data collection and analysis (i.e., constant comparison) is integral to this approach, allowing evolving theory to inform how and what data are collected. With CGGT, data collection tends to be more unstructured, especially in the initial phases of research. Third, as theory is refined with further data collection and analysis, qualitative researchers select participants and/or refine data sources (e.g., interviews, participant observation) to focus in on theory components (i.e., theoretical sampling). Qualitative researchers move from participant data (e.g., transcripts, observation memos), to initial concepts, then to more refined theoretical constructs that have been revised over the process as new data are introduced. Although labels involved in data analysis vary by grounded theory strand, there are similar coding processes across them (see Chapter 11).

Fourth, qualitative researchers continue with data collection and analysis until they reach **saturation**, or the point at which no data are available to refute conclusions and the theory has been fully developed. That is, the model is saturated and no new categories or variations within categories have been identified for the sample and strand purpose. Finally, grounded theory seeks theory development, and the theory includes a core category and various action- or process-oriented domains and domains that link to that category. Saturation and "fit" within a theoretical model is evidenced when the domain audits of related subdomains are multifaceted and multilayered. For example, Bolin et al. (2021) conducted a grounded theory research of 20 counselor educators and practitioners to identify factors that facilitate research-practice partnerships (RPP). One of the identified domains was *resource capacity* (i.e., availability of committed resources to engage in and sustain RPP activities). They identified three subdomains: infrastructure, funding, and personnel. Data for each subdomain are represented on a continuum and include supporting participant quotes (i.e., inadequate to adequate infrastructure, funding, and personnel resources) to showcase their complexity.

It is important to note that the scope of theory and intended use of that theory will depend on the grounded theory strand selected. For example, CGGT seeks to generalize from participant data to explain and predict a larger phenomenon (Glaser, 1992; Glaser & Strauss, 1967). Theory would be more abstract in order to apply findings to more settings. SGT, however, considers

**Case Example 4.1 Transformative Learning Processes for Practicing Music Teachers Encountering Social Justice**

Salvador et al. (2020) conducted a CGT with 22 teacher candidates who had completed a philosophy of music education course. Using CGT strategies, they sought to develop an explanatory theory of transformative learning processes that occurred as part of the course. Thus, they viewed the research process as a collaborative endeavor between the researchers and participants by which the theory was co-constructed. Furthermore, the researchers engaged in researcher reflexivity throughout the study, beginning with writing positionality statements, then developing memos related to research team meetings as well as data collection and analysis, and finally member checking initial findings with participants.

- *inductive approach:* The researchers began with open coding interview transcripts independently and then through consensus. Open codes were then collapsed into themes that grew in complexity as more data were collected and analyzed.
- *constant comparison:* Each researcher first conducted a single semistructured interview with a different participant to review the interview process in general, then each researcher conducted a portion of the remaining interviews and met periodically during that 2-month period to analyze and collapse data. As they cycled in and out of data collection and analysis, they revisited transcripts, artifacts, and memos collected as part of the study.
- *theoretical sampling:* Based on the data collection and analysis of participants interviewed earlier in the research process, the researchers tailored the interview protocol to investigate more in-depth themes they had identified.
- *saturation:* Researcher memos reflected saturation of data before all 22 participants were interviewed, although the researchers wanted to honor participants' willingness to participate in the study. Through a peer review, the researchers were able to confirm their assessment that the data were saturated.
- *theory development:* The researchers co-constructed with participants a theory outlining transformative learning processes for music teachers encountering social justice. They identified four interdependent domains. Each domain included several submains or dimensions. After describing the theoretical model, the researchers provided implications for training, social change, ally identity development, and scholarship.

Source: Salvador, K., Paetz, A. M., & Tippetts, M. M. (2020). "We all have a little more homework to do": A constructivist grounded theory of transformative learning processes for practicing music teachers encountering social justice. *Journal of Research in Music Education, 68*(2), 193–215. https://doi.org/10.1177/0022429420920630

the interactive nature of data collection and analysis between researcher and participant to highlight contextual conditions that inform theory interpretation and application (Corbin & Strauss, 2015). Furthermore, CGT is less abstract and more localized, usually not moving beyond a local community in its theory construction and application (Charmaz, 2014).

Grounded theory has several benefits, including its high degree of structure, emphasis on collecting large amounts of data to generate theory, ability to fragment and analyze text, and focus on the researcher's role and acknowledgment of biases for SGT and CGT. Furthermore, given its focus on groundedness and context, grounded theory can be well aligned with culturally diverse populations and advocacy. For instance, Mosley and colleagues (2021) used CGT with a critical-ideological and Black feminist-womanist lens to develop a CGT of critical consciousness of anti-Black racism that produced a practical model for Black activists and organizers to prevent and resist racial trauma. Finally, other paradigms (e.g., feminist, critical race theory, queer theory, Indigenous) may be applied within this tradition.

These same strengths also create challenges for grounded theory studies because data collection and analyses often rely on researchers' skills and awareness of the role values play. Also, the large amount of data needed to generate theory is labor and time intensive. Finally, an additional challenge relates to determining the degree to which theories will transfer or apply to other settings.

Related to the last challenge, Hays and McKibben (2021) discussed the use of a **formal grounded theory**, or a metatheory, to maximize the generalizability of multiple substantive grounded theories (i.e., primary studies). In formal grounded theory, qualitative researchers identify a core category that serves as a "grab" for other conceptual categories across diverse primary studies using qualitative approaches. Researchers generate a formal theory with either studies within the substantive area or in other substantive areas. The goal of this formal theory is to expand the extent to which "universal" processes, sequences, actions, and consequences of a core category can be applied to practice within and across disciplines from its studies published on a particular phenomenon.

## Phenomenology

Along with grounded theory, phenomenology is one of the most popular research traditions used today. The purpose of **phenomenology** is to provide a rich description of concrete lived experiences of an individual or individuals who have direct experience with the phenomenon. The phenomenon of interest can be a process, relationship, or other experience, and researchers seek to understand unique individual experiences and their meanings and interactions with others in the environment. Then researchers analyze participant data across individuals to identify universal and divergent aspects of the experience of the phenomenon (Creswell & Poth, 2017; Hays & Wood, 2011).

Phenomenology grew from French and German philosophy and theology, shifting into psychiatry, psychology, education, and counseling. While phenomenology as a concept was introduced by Kant in the mid-1700s, Edmund Husserl is credited as the founder of phenomenology. He critiqued positivist approaches because he asserted that human experience cannot be studied without considering how it is shaped in context and within human interactions. Husserl primarily focused on the psychological processes, such as perception, awareness, and consciousness, highlighting that participants can consciously know their experiences to describe them. He coined the term **life-world** (*Lebenswelt*), or the structural whole of a lived experience that is socially and culturally shared yet individually experienced (Moran, 2005). Other key phenomenological concepts he introduced included:

* **epoche:** bracketing or the setting aside of researcher perspectives about a phenomenon to allow for empathic reflection on the participant's life-world
* **essence:** the delineation of essential features across participants about a lived experience to get at a phenomenological structure
* **intentionality:** actively describing the how and what of individuals acting on an experience and being conscious of the surrounding context of that experience (Creswell & Poth, 2017)

Martin Heidegger, a student of Husserl, extended his work and noted that complete bracketing of researcher perspectives may be too difficult to achieve. He also added that humans are inextricably tied to social, cultural, and political contexts (i.e., **situated freedom**) and that participants are not always fully aware of the meanings of their experiences (Crowell, 2001). That is, Heidegger focused on what humans experience rather than what they consciously know, and he believed that individuals are always embedded in their world (i.e., **being-in-the-world**). Furthermore, he coined the concept of **co-constitutionality**, or the notion that meanings that the researcher arrives at are a blend of the meanings articulated by both participants and the researcher (Reiners, 2012; Wertz et al., 2011).

Other philosophers that contributed to the theory of phenomenology as a research tradition include Jean-Paul Sartre, Maurice Merleau-Ponty, Paul Ricouer, Friedrich Schleimacher, and Hans-Georg Gadamer. In addition, several scholars contributed to the methods and analysis of phenomenology. They include Max van Manen, Amedeo Giorgi, Clark Moustakas, P. Colaizzi, Adrian Van Kaam, Jonathan Smith, Michael Larkin, and Paul Flowers. Collectively, these individuals, with Husserl and Heidegger, contributed to three strands that researchers can consider (Finlay, 2012): descriptive phenomenology, hermeneutic phenomenology, and idiography or interpretative phenomenological analysis (IPA). IPA is the most recent strand, developed in the 1990s in the United Kingdom by Jonathan Smith, a health psychologist. Table 4.3 introduces these strands, and other chapters within this text provide greater detail about data collection, analysis, and reporting procedures.

Across these phenomenological strands, there are some common characteristics. First, data are typically collected using individual interviews, and researchers ask questions using the five senses. Depending on the strand, interviews can be unstructured (descriptive phenomenology) or semistructured (hermeneutic phenomenology, IPA). Second, there is a focus on direct experience of a phenomenon. Descriptions and/or interpretations of experiences must be first-hand accounts from the participants. In addition, they are concrete and detailed, without significant generalizations made to a larger theory or phenomenon. There is an intentional focus on the relationship of person and environment. The third common characteristic is a use of **phenomenological reductions**. That is, researchers embrace a phenomenological attitude by which they enter research with curiosity about a topic to see "with fresh eyes." Researchers enter fully into the description and how the participant makes meaning to understand both the "what" and "how" of experience. Depending on the phenomenological strand, researcher

**TABLE 4.3** Strands of the Phenomenology Research Tradition

| | Descriptive phenomenology | Hermeneutic phenomenology | Idiography/ Interpretative phenomenological analysis |
|---|---|---|---|
| **Key contributors** | Husserl, Merleau-Ponty, Sartre, Giorgi, Coliazzi, Van Kaam, Moustakas | Heidegger, van Manen, Schleiermacher, Gadamer | Smith, Larkin, Flowers |
| **Description** | *Description as is*: Description of participant experience acting on a context. Description stands on its own. A generalized description is possible, and reality is considered objective and independent of history and context. | *Interpretation*: Description of the participant/researcher interpretation of participant experience. Make clear or interpret meaning or messages. There is continual review and analysis between the parts and the whole or meaning as well as continual revision of researcher understanding (i.e., hermeneutic circle). | *The particular*: Study of specifics versus the general for an experience of significance; person at the forefront of phenomenon; detailed analysis of experience from an individual or small sample; meaning of an experience of a particular participant or small group of experience |
| **Participant life-world** | *Essence*: universal | *Typology*: variants, highly general, bounded by contexts | *Idiography*: individual, incidental |
| **Researcher life-world** | *Suspension of researcher knowledge*: Researcher impact is constantly assessed and biases are neutralized via bracketing. Findings are a direct reflection of participant description. | *Inclusion of a priori knowledge*: Bracketing is difficult, and the researcher role is readily acknowledged in data interpretation. Findings are more co-constructed between participant and researcher. | *Inclusion of a priori knowledge*: Interpretation is grounded in the researcher meeting the text. Researcher considers participant accounts within a broader context/theory. Findings are most co-constructed between participant and researcher. |
| **Relationship of person and context** | Participant interacting on environment | Participant embedded within environment | Participant embedded within environment |

Sources: Creswell and Poth (2017), Reiners (2012), Smith et al. (2006), and Wertz et al. (2011).

perspectives can be suspended (descriptive phenomenology) or included (hermeneutic phenomenology, IPA) in the interpretation.

Phenomenology has several benefits to advance clinical and educational research. First, it supports a process in which researchers and participants can engage in deep description to generate greater reflection than a participant's previous understanding. Second, it prioritizes the direct participant experience, using the description and/or interpretation of that experience to expand understanding of the phenomenon in general. Third, attention to the role of context—particularly within the hermeneutic phenomenological and IPA strands—can lead to scholarship to attend to culturally diverse populations and their experiences within social, cultural, and political contexts.

There are some potential limitations of phenomenology that researchers should consider. First, phenomenology is not designed to develop theories or test hypotheses. While extraction of generalities can be made from individual narratives, it is not conducive to theoretical modeling or variable operationalization. Second, it does not include participant perspectives of what others' perspectives on a phenomenon are. Third, like other research traditions, researchers must balance depth versus breadth in terms of phenomenon description. Thus, they must make decisions about sample size and number and scope of interviews based on their research goals.

---

## PERSPECTIVES 4.2. INTERPRETATIVE PHENOMENOLOGICAL ANALYSIS, INTERSECTIONALITY, AND THE LGBTQ+ COMMUNITY

Christian Chan and Laura Boyd Farmer (a counselor educator and practicing counselor, respectively) conduct research related to intersectionality within the LGBTQ+ population. Their research interests evolved from their individual experiences. For Farmer, who identifies as a pan affectional cisgender woman, noted her interest in understanding the intersections of spirituality and sexual and affectional identity increased after her best friend came out to her in college and disclosed her struggles with navigating spirituality and sexual and affectional identity. Chan, who identifies as a queer Asian American man of color, experienced several critical incidents in his own life where he experienced a lack of support for queer men of color within the LGBTQ+ communities.

In an interview with me (Danica), they articulated the importance of intersectionality research. Farmer (personal communication, June 11, 2020) noted:

> The essence of intersectionality is about the complex and unique lived experiences and perspectives that we each have based on our multiple social and cultural identities. ... We're really missing the point if we make assumptions about someone based on one or even two of their visible identities, for example, and miss so much of the bigger picture and all the richness of who someone is and the perspective that they bring. ... We're multifaceted and multidimensional beings.

Chan (personal communication, June 11, 2020) added, "Sometimes we equate intersectionality only to multiple identities or diverse identities without recognizing that it's always linked to social structures ... and power." Furthermore, Farmer (personal communication, June 11, 2020) referred to IPA as a deeply personal methodology that provides an opportunity for "authentically connecting to participants in their experience and understanding them intersectionally."

In 2017, Chan and Farmer published a manuscript on the importance of using IPA to explore intersectionality within the LGBTQ+ communities. In this work, they highlight the ability of IPA to uncover the identity complexities of this population while producing counternarratives to the heteronormative research available about those who do not identify as straight. Furthermore, they cited the benefits of IPA in focusing on the particulars and intensity of participant experience, examining the existential meanings that result from a participant's interaction with their environment. Thus, IPA lends itself well to research with the LGBTQ+ communities, given its attention to participant voice, personal significance of a phenomenon, depth of data collection, and the role of power both in the research process and the phenomenon itself.

For this article, along with their independent research (e.g., Chan, 2018; Farmer & Byrd, 2015), Chan and Farmer (2017) highlight the importance of actively engaging in researcher reflexivity throughout the IPA study process. For example, Chan notes the importance of conceptualizing researcher reflexivity as an opportunity for self-interrogation, requiring vulnerability as a researcher and individual. Thus, researcher reflexivity extends beyond describing researcher identities and assumptions about the study topic. It is a constant and critical reflection on the ways in which the researcher may be shaping the study throughout data collection and analysis.

**Sources:**

Chan, C. D. (2018). The lived intersectional experiences of privilege and oppression of queer men of color in counselor education doctoral programs: An interpretative phenomenological analysis [Unpublished doctoral dissertation]. The George Washington University.

Chan, C. D., & Farmer, L. B. (2017). Making the case for interpretative phenomenological analysis with LGBTGEQ+ persons and communities. Journal of LGBT Issues in Counseling, 11(4), 285–300. https://doi.org/10.1080/15538605.2017.1380558

Farmer, L. B., & Byrd, R. (2015). Genderism in the LGBTQQIA community: An interpretative phenomenological analysis. Journal of LGBT Issues in Counseling, 9(4), 288–310. https:/doi.org/10.1080/15538605.2015.1103679

## Heuristic Inquiry

**Heuristic inquiry** can be consider closely related to phenomenology: Whereas phenomenology relates to *lived* experience, heuristic inquiry relates to *living* experience (Sultan, 2018). It has roots in humanistic psychology and was founded by Clark Moustakas, who also contributed to phenomenological data analysis steps (see Chapter 11). Moustakas, a humanistic psychologist, relied heavily on the humanist movement and its major scholars (e.g., Carl Rogers, Abraham Maslow) to develop a research tradition focused on subjective experience, autobiography, interpretation, and self-actualization (Sultan, 2018).

The term *heuristic* originates from the Greek word *heuriskein*, which means to discover or to find (Moustakas, 1994). Beginning with researchers' internal desire to understand a phenomenon in a personal, autobiographical way, heuristic inquiry evolves to include others' experiences of the phenomenon to identify the phenomenon's essence (Sultan, 2018). Heuristic inquiry as a tradition focuses on intense phenomena from the perspective of researchers with attention to how participants' experiences relate to researchers' increased self-awareness and knowledge. The researcher self is present throughout the study, beginning with selecting the topic and through to data reporting. Starting with their own experiences of the phenomenon of interest, researchers identify themes from their lived experiences and those of their participants, who are sometimes referred to as coresearchers. The goal of heuristic inquiry is for researchers to become more self-aware and transformed by new knowledge gained.

Moustakas's personal experience of loneliness associated with his daughter recovering from a serious illness prompted him to develop heuristic inquiry. Like Moustakas, researchers using a heuristic approach seek to understand moderately intense experiences of the human condition, such as grief, loss, love, anger, happiness, achievement, and mental illness. These phenomena have some personal significance to researchers involved in qualitative inquiry, and researchers have an openness to discovering knowledge about the phenomena. Through an openness to experience, they trust in their own self-awareness and understanding. Collaboration and a sense of connectedness among researchers and participants in discovering and describing the essence of shared experiences is significant.

Moustakas (1990, 1994) identified six phases of heuristic research design. First, researchers identify a phenomenon that is significant in their life (i.e., **initial engagement**). Typically, the central research question is "What is my experience of [phenomenon]?" (Sultan, 2018). In the next phase, **immersion,** researchers "live" the phenomenon and actively engage in self-reflection and interactions with others and artifacts in order to identify possible links between these experiences and the phenomenon. During immersion, researchers increase their knowledge of the phenomenon by examining their own experiences along with how the phenomenon manifests within their surroundings. In addition, they keep personal memos and collect artifacts. The third phase, **incubation**, occurs when researchers step back from the research study after the immersion phase. After an incubation period, researchers conduct interviews with participants and carefully study transcripts and experience "aha" moments (i.e., **illumination** phase). With illumination, there is new awareness or modification of previous knowledge associated with a phenomenon. At this time, researchers may collect data from participants. The fifth phase, **explication**, occurs when researchers translate new or modified awareness into identified themes. Moustakas noted two concepts key to explication: *focusing*, or targeting a significant idea relevant to personal transformation; and *indwelling*, or turning inward for an active self-dialogue to allow space for insight about the phenomenon from researcher and participant data. Researchers explicate *individual depictions* or singular narratives of experiences for each researcher and participant; *composite depictions*, or integrated narratives of the individual depictions; and *exemplary portraits*, or unique descriptions that bridge individual and composite depictions. **Creative synthesis**, the final phase, is the data reporting phase in which the presentation clearly reflects researchers' newfound understanding and personal transformation about the phenomenon.

Heuristic inquiry shares many of the benefits and challenges with phenomenology. In addition, it affords researchers an opportunity for deep personal transformation. Case Study 4.2 shows an example of a heuristic inquiry, reflecting the six phases of heuristic research design (Moustakas, 1990, 1994).

## Case Example 4.2. Spontaneous Transformation and Disordered Eating Recovery

Shelburne et al. (2020) conducted a heuristic inquiry to describe the direct experience of spontaneous transformation as a mechanism for change in the development of and recovery from disordered eating. The study participants included the first author (SS) and six coresearchers. The following research questions were addressed: How do adult women perceive and discuss their experiences of pivotal moments of change? How do these moments relate to the process of recovering from problematic eating?

Using Moustakas's (1990) heuristic research design phases, Shelburne et al. (2020) outline their inquiry:

- *initial engagement:* SS described recovery from disordered eating as a personal journey that was arduous. Furthermore, she identified moments of deep transformation adjacent to moments of near-miss crises that became an avenue for personal change.
- *immersion:* SS immersed herself fully in the topic through self-dialogue to uncover **tacit knowledge**, or internal self-knowledge that is potentially achievable but may not be able to be described or explained.
- *incubation:* SS stepped away from the topic to allow the topic to shift back into the unconscious.
- *illumination:* SS described how knowledge that was previously hidden (i.e., tacit knowledge) becomes apparent after a period of incubation. This new knowledge is integrated into the psyche with previous information, and SS conducted interviews with six coresearchers.
- *explication:* Through self-reflection and focused review of new information collected from coresearchers, SS identifies individual and collective depictions of the experience of spontaneous transformation as a mechanism of change.
- *creative synthesis:* SS provides a thick description of her personal understanding of disordered eating recovery along with the identified themes. Shelburne et al. (2020) identified six themes that were also reflected in the lived experience of SS: early messages from the environment of origin; moments of suffering as gateways of change; loss of control; implicit awareness resulting in transformation; physical expressions of expansion and constriction; and new definition of recovery. As themes are described, individual and collective depictions are shared to illuminate each theme.

Source: Shelburne, S., Curtis, D., & Rockwell, D. (2020). Spontaneous transformation and recovery from problematic eating: A heuristic inquiry. *Journal of Humanistic Psychology.* https://doi.org/10.1177/0022167820945803

## Consensual Qualitative Research

Introduced to the social sciences in 1997, **consensual qualitative research (CQR)** integrates phenomenological, grounded theory, and other approaches. Clara Hill and her colleagues (Hill, 2012; Hill et al., 1997, 2005) developed this approach to conduct qualitative inquiry that involves researchers selecting participants who are very knowledgeable about a topic and remaining close to data without major interpretation with some hopes of generalizing to a larger population. CQR varies slightly from other grounded theory and phenomenological approaches as researchers often reflect on their own experiences with a phenomenon when developing interview questions. Consensus is key to this approach, as qualitative researchers use rigorous methods to facilitate agreement in interpretations among themselves, participants, and a general audience.

Key components of CQR include (a) open-ended questions in semistructured interviews (see Chapter 8); (b) the use of judges for consensus building; (c) use of at least one auditor to evaluate the research (see Chapter 7); (d) and use of domains, core ideas, and cross-analyses in data analysis (see Chapter 11). Perspectives 4.3 and Case Example 4.3 illustrates these key components of CQR.

---

## PERSPECTIVES 4.3. DR. CLARA HILL ON CONSENSUAL QUALITATIVE RESEARCH

Dr. Clara Hill and her colleagues have been instrumental in introducing the CQR approach to helping professions. In her own words, she describes why CQR was developed and the strengths and challenges to the approach (Hill, personal communication, December 4, 2006):

> We wanted to do qualitative research and found that the existing methods were hard to understand and implement. So, after receiving extensive consultation from a qualitative expert and then trying out a number of different qualitative methods, we developed CQR and tried to write about it in a clear way so that others could easily use it. As we came to learn, however, qualitative methods are hard to learn and implement. It is probably always wise to work with a mentor on one's first study. In addition, I would add the CQR method is still evolving, and we continue to use it.
>
> The strengths are the use of consensus among judges, the use of auditors, and clear guidelines for communicating results. Another clear strength is that CQR is fun to do and it gets you close to the phenomenology of the topic. CQR is a very sociable way to do research, because researchers meet together and do everything as a team.
>
> The challenges are the length of time it takes to complete a CQR project, some difficulty in switching between doing the domains/core ideas and the cross-analysis because these require very different skills, and then making sense of the results. An additional challenge is that the method is best suited for interview data and less suited for other forms of data.
>
> CQR is very flexible and can easily be used in counseling and education research. Any topic that can be explored in an interview is appropriate for CQR. Interviewees do need to be aware of their experiences of the topic, of course, to provide good interviews.

---

## Case Example 4.3. Stay-at-Home Fathers, Depression, and Help-Seeking Behaviors

Using Hill et al.'s (1997) eight-step CQR analytic process, Caperton et al. (2020) examined the experiences of 12 stay-at-home fathers (SAHFs) with depression and their help-seeking behaviors.

1. The three researchers met to identify their assumptions about the study topic. Then the primary researcher conducted in-depth phone interviews with their participants (nine White, two Latinx, one Black) that were 45–75 minutes in duration. They used open-ended questions in order to not restrict the responses of participants on their experiences as SAHFs with depression and help-seeking behaviors.

2. Researchers then transcribed the interviews, and a subset of researchers reviewed the words of SAHFs in the transcripts that related to the phenomena of depression and help-seeking behaviors.

3. Two members of the research team served as coders and reviewed a small number of "cases" (participant interviews) to study in an intensive way related to the phenomena of depression and help-seeking behaviors as a SAHF.

4. The researchers used these cases to understand specific parts of the experience SAHFs had related to the phenomena of depression and help-seeking behaviors.

5. The researchers each inductively coded the transcripts and compared transcript coding to come to consensus in three areas the phenomena of depression and help-seeking behaviors as a SAHF: (a) *domain coding* to organize the data into core ideas to denote common content of the participant data, (b) *cross-analysis* to organize these core ideas into each domain and look across them to compare, and (c) *case comparison* to identify common themes. In this way, the researchers are following the structure within the data rather than testing a theory about the data or overlaying a structure already identified onto the data.

6. Throughout the process of data analysis, the researchers came to consensus on the phenomena of depression and help-seeking behaviors as a SAHF after exploring a wide variety of perspectives on the participant data. This included the assignment of frequencies to identify *general* (in all participant data), *typical* (in half of the participant data), *variant* (in less than half the participant data), or *no* (not in any participant data) codes related to the phenomena of depression and help-seeking behavior as a SAHF.

7. There was one auditor on the research team who reviewed the research team's processes for coming to *consensus* and ensuring there was no overlooked data or possibilities for consensus or divergent perspectives missed on the way to consensus about the phenomena of depression and help-seeking behaviors as a SAHF.

8. Throughout the analysis, the research team continued to revisit the original participant data transcripts to ensure the findings were reflective of the phenomena of depression and help-seeking behaviors as a SAHF.

Source: Caperton, W., Butler, M., Kaiser, D., Connelly, J., & Knox, S. (2020). Stay-at-home fathers, depression, and help-seeking: A consensual qualitative research study. *Psychology of Men and Masculinities,* 221, 235–250. https://doi.org/10.1037/men0000223

Goodrich and Luke (2019) used CQR to explore the experiences lesbian, gay, and bisexual (LGB) people had in counseling that addressed religion and spirituality. Using a primary team of interviewers or judges, the team members individually coded transcripts one at a time and met together afterward to share about their codes in each participant transcript. Then a second group of CQR judges coded the same transcripts, organizing the core ideas identified in the transcripts into larger categories. Once the categories were identified, an auditing process began in order to review the coding and accuracy of the larger themes identified. In another CQR example, Brattland et al. (2016) conducted a study examining therapists' reactions to receiving negative verbal feedback from clients. The researchers examined the descriptions of how they responded to negative client feedback and learned from this feedback to improve their future counseling. Four of the authors served as coders, and two served as auditors with the data. Each of the coders named their assumptions about the study topic at the beginning and throughout the data analysis. Then the researchers coded the data for core ideas and orga-nized the data within domains and categories that portrayed a common grouping of content in the data, including assigning frequencies to each of these to note general (in all participant data), typical (in half of the participant data), variant (in less than half the participant data), or none (not in any participant data). Findings indicated three major themes or domains that helped establish how the therapists learned from negative client feedback.

One feature of CQR is its focus on data consistency to inform theory to allow for greater applicability within a setting. Another unique aspect of CQR is its emphasis on power in all aspects of the research process: Researchers share power among each other with the use of research teams as well as with participants. Part of the rationale for sharing power in the research process deals with the notion that researcher bias, or assumptions and values about what data are collected and how they are interpreted, is inevitable in qualitative inquiry. Thus, sharing power allows various research team members to discuss how their personal and cultural identities and assumptions about the research topic influence data collection and analysis as well as appreciate the perspectives of participants for better practice. For instance, Kasturirangan and Williams (2003) interviewed nine Latino survivors of domestic violence to inform counseling practice. As a result of sharing power with participants, counseling researchers discovered from the participants how ethnicity, gender, and family interact with domestic violence interventions.

## The Meaning of Symbol and Text: Life History and Narratology

The third cluster predominately involves a meaningful "symbol" to us all: language. Further, researchers adhering to traditions in this cluster typically examine textual documents for the role of language in shaping attitudes and behaviors as well as relying on verbal and nonverbal communication as a process for learning about social symbols. Bhattacharya (2017) suggests there are six methods for studying narrative to identify the meaning of symbols and text. We discuss autoethnography as its own research tradition in the next cluster.

- *thematic narratives:* narratives that inquire how people's lives are stories with themes that reflect the meaning-making process of their lives

- *biographical study:* narrative inquiry that seeks to tell the story of a person living or deceased that often involves review of documents and other media to tell a narrative of this person around an event, time period, or other imposed discrete unit
- *autoethnography:* The researcher tells their own story surrounding a lived experience, telling the story of the cultural context and other "actors" in their experience of a specific phenomenon or series of phenomena.
- *life history:* Similar to biographical studies, life histories explore the stories of a person but include the entire life history of a person.
- *oral history:* narrative studies that center around a historical event or period of a person's life or community and how they experienced this event or period, which they share in their own words.
- *arts-based narratives:* involve performances in various media formats (e.g., dance, written, film)

After reading about these traditions, complete Activity 4.3 to apply them. Perspectives 4.4 provides an example of the use of narratology in examining parenting for child sexual abuse survivors.

**ACTIVITY 4.3.** APPLYING THE "MEANING OF SYMBOL AND TEXT" CLUSTER

Consider a study in your discipline focused on how children's literature has communicated information about gender roles. How might each of the traditions described in this cluster address this research topic?

## Life History

The **life history** tradition represents an account of a person's entire life couched in a broader social context; it is a research tradition that seeks to identify personal meanings individuals give to their social experiences (Bhattacharya, 2017). Oftentimes, life histories allow qualitative researchers to "rewrite history" and give voice to marginalized groups. The researcher will gather stories and explore meanings for an individual as well as how the stories fit into a broader social or historical context. While the term "life history" is used interchangeably with the terms "biography," "autobiography," and "oral history," Creswell and Poth (2017) defined each of these terms to highlight their differences:

- *biography:* life story of an individual from archival documents written by someone other than the individual
- *autobiographies:* life story written directly by an individual
- *life history:* presentation of an individual's life derived from interviews and personal conversations in which a researcher accounts the individual's life and how it relates to cultural, social and/or personal themes
- *oral history:* personal recollections of events and their impact on the individual taken from taped or written works of living or deceased individuals

## PERSPECTIVES 4.4. NAVIGATING PARENTHOOD AFTER SURVIVING CHILD SEXUAL ABUSE

Maria Haiyasoso, a counselor educator and counselor working in private practice, conducted a narratology with nine parents who survived child sexual abuse (CSA). In this work, Haiyasoso and Trepal (2019) sought to explore how adult female survivors of CSA discuss their parenthood experiences. They used a relational cultural framework (RCT; see Jordan, 2010), which focuses on connection based in healthy relationships that are authentic and mutually affirming, naturally occurring ruptures in connection (i.e., disconnection), and relational images, or the templates and patterns for engaging in relationships that are formed early in life. Haiyasoso and Trepal identified three themes from these mothers: negotiating a balance of protecting and letting go, using relational images as guideposts for parenting decisions, and exploring functioning in relational contexts.

Haiyasoso and Trepal (2019) found that the use of RCT tenets was an important tool in the research itself. Specifically, being intentional about facilitating connection within the researcher–participant relationship involved creating a nonjudgmental space for participants to share their stories and relational images. To maximize connection, Haiyasoso noted the importance of continually engaging in researcher reflexivity throughout the research process, taking breaks between interviews to ensure she was open and ready to hear their stories fully, and being aware of her positionality as a Mexican American mother as well as the position of power she may hold as a practitioner working with survivors of CSA.

Haiyasoso notes the power of narratology as a research tradition:

> [People] relate to the power of story. It's a tool to empower. ... Restorying helps de-center abuse. ... I think we can help de-center that primary story [of abuse] that they may be most identified by. We can recalibrate where that actually fits into their broader narrative of life.

Thus, narratology as an approach allows participants to restory their past as well as yield a narrative or counternarrative to the narrative that has been produced about them in some cases. Haiyasoso adds:

> Participants shared stories but did not always share them in a linear fashion. Sometimes they shared about outcomes without sharing the context or key features. And then sometimes that was reversed. But taking the totality of the narratives, making sense of my field notes and memoing and the member checks, helped me follow up and ask questions that naturally led to restorying [narratives] if they weren't doing that already.

Source: Haiyasoso, M., & Trepal, H. (2019). Survivors' stories: Navigating parenthood after surviving child sexual abuse. *Journal of Counseling & Development, 97*(3), 281–292. https://doi.org/10.1002/jcad.12268

Creswell and Poth's method of categorizing overlaps with Bhattacharya's (2017) types of narrative research described above. The understanding and conceptualization of the life history tradition—and narratology (described below)—is still evolving in education and the social sciences.

Many life history methods are categorized as case studies (Creswell & Poth, 2017). While there is great overlap, the distinction we see with life history methods as making meaning of symbol and text and as the hybrid tradition (case study) is the intention of the researcher: Are they using the method to describe a bounded system and plan to use various data sources to understand the context and activities of a case, or are they interested in using the method to reflect solely on the process of meaning-making of language or another symbol (e.g., social phenomena)?

Life history as a research tradition has been used in various disciplines, such as literature, anthropology, history, sociology, and psychology. It was first introduced in sociology by Thomas and Znaniecki (1927), who used personal letters and autobiographies to examine the relationship between Polish peasants' native culture and community disunion. Life histories gained significance in the 1930s with works of Chicago School researchers (e.g., Shaw, 1930, 1938; Shaw & Moore, 1931; Sutherland, 1937) that explored criminality via criminal careers and in the 1940s with works such as Allport et al.'s (1941) study of the life histories of refugees in Nazi Germany. Further research by theorists such as Levinson (1978) and Eriksen (1963) to understand developmental stages demonstrated that this method could be viable for understanding psychological processes. More recent examples of the life history method that could be applied to counseling and education include the works of Sommers and Baskin (2006), who collected life histories of 205 people who were addicted to methamphetamine to understand violent behavior, and Powell (2005), who interviewed 10 adults who repeated a grade in elementary school to examine factors related to grade retention.

Lanford et al. (2019) note that life history is a research tradition that not only examines the entire life of a person but also allows for an exploration of the individual's life and the historical context of the times in which they lived, which can bring forth important ethical issues as their relationships to people and their societal context are explored. For example, Spooner (2019) cites that life histories can "give voice" to help name systems that minoritize people and communities, as researchers study a person's entire life. Spooner also notes the value of using Indigenous methods in tandem with life histories in order to name essential questions of "place" (i.e., the land upon which a person's life history is gathered). Case Example 4.4 provides illustrates the life history tradition to explore the construct of "outsiderness" for two nontraditional undergraduate students.

## Narratology

Similar to the life history tradition, **narratology,** or narrative analysis, seeks to understand what stories or narratives reveal about an individual. With origins in social sciences and literature, it extends the hermeneutic approach by examining data sources such as interview transcripts, life history and other historical narratives, and creative nonfiction (Patton, 2014). Just as other approaches in this cluster, recorded data reveal cultural and personal information about an individual with potential applicability to a larger context. Individuals communicate their sense of their world through stories.

**Case Example 4.4. The Outsiderness of Nontraditional College Students**

Lanford (2019) presents the life histories of Demetrius and Christine, two nontraditional students at an institution in Florida, in order to understand outsiderness and its impact on undergraduate student success. Lanford defines *outsiderness* as feeling isolated within a college environment and having a dearth of knowledge about one's own college readiness and the instructors' expectations. The life history is based on a 1-year immersive study of the two students' first year of coursework, using interview transcripts, text messages, observations, memos, and artifacts as data sources.

Lanford (2019) begins the article with narrative, introducing the two students and offering a snapshot description of the interview process in a personally engaging way. Demetrius is a 28-year-old Black man who persevered through homelessness, and Christine is a 22-year-old White woman from a rural background and with a background of family turmoil and financial limitations. After introducing the students, Lanford cites previous literature on outsiderness, which he notes offers positive and negative attributes of the phenomenon.

Through the narrative, Lanford (2019) reflects parallels between the two students and frames these in three themes: early influences, life as education, and building relationships in college. Weaving in transcript excerpts, he presents these themes in the students' lives and then draws the parallels in a discussion section that follows. Despite their cultural differences, he noted the following commonalities between Demetrius and Christine:

- They displayed resilience and persistence throughout their life and educational experiences, despite financial and societal obstacles.
- They placed great value in the skills they cultivated through life experiences.
- They learned to become comfortable with themselves due to a certain degree of social isolation.

Through this life history, Lanford helps to reshape the narrative of nontraditional students that often portrays a deficit model of nontraditional student success. "Demetrius and Christin are not hampered by insufficient motivation, underdeveloped critical thinking abilities, or an inability to demonstrate measurable academic skills that are necessary for college-level work. If anything, they exhibit abundant positive qualities in these areas" (Lanford, 2019, p. 510). Lanford concludes the article with an epilogue section that updates the reader on where the two students are after the first year of coursework as well as their future career plans.

Source: Lanford, M. (2019). Making sense of "outsiderness": How life history informs the college experiences of "nontraditional" students. Qualitative Inquiry, 25(5), 500–512. https://doi.org/10.1177/1077800418817839

There are additional key assumptions of narratology. First, individuals speak in narrative form, connecting events over time through stories. In a sense, our stories are not random sentences but constructed in a personally and often culturally meaningful manner. Second, individual identities are shaped by the stories they recount and share with others. Finally, narratives change depending on the narrator, audience, and context. What is deemed important often depends on these three dimensions. A narrative thus is not just text but a sequential and causal account of events, people, and processes that expresses how individuals make sense of their worlds (Clandinin et al., 2018).

Within clinical and education settings, narratives can yield information about individuals' sense of identity, co-constructed between storyteller and audience and recounted in the context of social interactions. For instance, those who practice using a narrative therapy or story-telling approach to work with students and/or clients use these narrative approaches to allow clients to resolve or reframe emotional distress and actions and reconstruct personal identity to optimize mental health (Llewellyn-Beardsley et al., 2019). Whether narratives are generated in the therapeutic or research relationship, researchers can attend to how sequence, content, social power, and consequences of a client's story relate to the client's life context as well as to the therapeutic relationship (Clandinin et al., 2018).

The term "narrative" is often used synonymously with "story." However, the story represents only one component of a narrative: A narrative involves the dimensions and properties of a story (Llewellyn-Beardsley et al., 2019). These story properties can be viewed as extended personal accounts that develop over single and multiple interviews or educational and clinical sessions serving as discrete units of analysis. Researchers engaged in narrative inquiry are interested in several features of the story: study purpose; how and why events are storied; what the story contents are; temporal order of the story; for whom the story is constructed; changes in the story expression based on audience; story consequences; cultural or other macrosystem components present in the larger narrative or narratives; and any gaps and inconsistencies that may warrant alternative or counternarratives (Clandinin et al., 2018; Reissman & Speedy, 2012).

**Narrative synthesis**, also referred to as metanarrative, is the collective analysis of multiple narratives. The analysis of primary study narratives or metanarratives takes many forms; the focus is on how human interactions shape the construction, meaning, and reconstruction of narratives individuals express—and how those expressions differ depending on audience and perceived power. Thus, personal accounts or stories are framed and told within social interactions that are steeped in macrosystems (Clandinin et al., 2018; Reissmann & Speedy, 2012). As the expression of personal narrative can be therapeutically beneficial in educational or clinical practice, the analysis of collective narratives can either highlight predominant dimensions and properties of a phenomenon or can help to counter dominant cultural narratives that may hinder groups with less power and representation.

Examples of narratives of primary research studies could involve case examples that include student, client, or trainee stories; first-person author accounts; a life story; a poetic representation of the phenomenon in stanza form (Gee, 1991); or a direct scribe in which clients or participants dictate their self-narratives to the transcriber followed by reflections on the self-narratives that yield further transcripts (Martin, 1998). For a narrative synthesis, researchers discuss narrative themes across studies and then refer to specific aspects of a narrative or narratives (e.g., transcript excerpts) as well as macro-level cultural context of production to support the theme. As researchers develop metanarratives, they must caution against stripping primary narratives of sequence and consequences in an effort to synthesize primary studies (Reissmann & Speedy, 2012).

The following examples help to illustrate the use of narrative synthesis in clinical and educational disciplines. Llewellyn-Beardsley et al. (2019) conducted a narrative synthesis of 629 mental health recovery narratives found across 45 studies for an 18-year period. They identified a conceptual framework of mental health recovery that included nine dimensions present across the studies (e.g., positioning, emotional tone, trajectory, etc.), with each dimension containing two to six types. As each of the nine dimensions of the conceptual framework of mental health recovery are presented, reference to specific primary studies is made to help illustrate the whole dimension as well as define the types. Brooks et al. (2013) provide a second example; they analyzed multiple narratives (*N*= 19) of clinical patients to develop a grand narrative of the process of alcohol and drug recovery and relapse. In the report, the authors mapped the grand narrative to a stages of change model and a recovery model to further support the frameworks. Several transcript excerpts across participants were included in the report.

Previous education and social science scholarship also offers an opportunity to synthesize personal published narratives. For example, in 1999 the *Journal of Counseling & Development* published a series of personal narratives related to racism that could be synthesized to develop a metanarrative of how counseling scholars personally experience racism. Researchers would begin with reading and rereading each personal account, selecting segments or units for more analysis and comparing the whole account in relation to a part, paying particular attention to sequence and consequence within and across narratives. As they extracted data, they would retain the primary study authors' terminology used for narrative components to the extent that is was possible. In reporting, researchers would identify narrative themes related to racism and then refer to specific aspects of a narrative or narratives (e.g., transcript excerpts) as well as macro-level cultural context of production to support the theme. In addition, researchers would explicitly discuss their relationship to racism and how their personal narrative was negotiated as a result of conducting the narrative synthesis.

Narrative inquiry can take many forms, from reviewing documents and artifact to interviews and focus groups. Digital storytelling has recently been a part of the narrative inquiry research tradition, where educators and clinicians use digital media to portray participant findings in powerful visual interventions and social change efforts (Long & Hall, 2018). For instance, Adams-Santos (2020) used narrative inquiry to examine the coming-out stories queer Black women used on YouTube to note how their coming-out stories were different from those individuals of queer, White, middle-class stories of coming out. Anderson and Mack (2019) used digital storytelling to center the voices of Black adolescents telling their own stories about their identity development while living in neighborhoods where the occurrence of violence was high and financial and educational resources were low.

# Cultural Expressions of Process and Experience: Ethnography, Ethnomethodology, and Autoethnography

The fourth cluster, cultural expressions of process and experience, includes the essential feature of including a culture-sharing group. That is, examining social and cultural norms is a significant aspect of ethnography, ethnomethodology, and autoethnography. No matter the tradition in this cluster, researchers share the following in common: (a) knowledge and understanding of cultural anthropological terms and concepts; (b) prolonged engagement with the culture studied; (c) manuscripts that are narrative and literary in style about the cultural group; and (d) researchers face challenges in fieldwork (e.g., "going native" in which the researcher is unable to continue the study due to absorption by the culture studied or compromised data; Creswell & Poth, 2017). Ethnographic research also shares an acknowledgment that the research process is recursive, demanding flexibility on the part of the researcher and attention to the contextual realities involved in conducting fieldwork. Activity 2.6 provides an opportunity for you to apply these traditions to a research topic of your choice.

## Ethnography

**Ethnography** is a research paradigm in which the researcher describes and provides interpretations about the culture of a group or system (Creswell & Poth, 2017; Hays & Wood, 2011). A data collection method common to ethnography is **participant observation**, which involves **prolonged engagement** over a significant period of time with the group studied in order to describe the process and experience of its culture (Lincoln & Guba, 1995). As discussed in Chapter 2, ethnographic research has its intellectual roots in anthropology, a field in which researchers examine comparative cultures. These early scholars were dedicated to ethnographic research that provided a first-hand account of a group's culture, and their research was typically in the form of a monograph that resulted from long-term participant observation (see Chapter 2). Fieldwork is a critical aspect of ethnography in that the researcher becomes immersed in the context of the group (i.e., daily life activities of members) in order to understand the culture of the group.

Ethnographic research first emerged from the British and French social anthropologists in the 1920s and 1930s who studied "exotic" cultural groups who were typically under colonization regimes (see Chapter 2). These early researchers separated themselves from the more traditional research methods of anthropological sciences in that they were interested in studying the cultural norms (e.g., language, behavior, etc.) of various cultural groups. Soon after European ethnographic researchers began producing monographs and detailed texts of these cultural groups, ethnography was used in the United States by sociologists at the University of Chicago. Ethnographies are primarily utilized in clinical and educational settings as a way to examine socialization processes.

Ethnographic approaches are valuable to the counseling field, as counselors typically have prolonged engagement with cultural groups and systems as well as individuals. Ethnographic methods, such as fieldwork and prolonged engagement, are effective ways to gather, describe, interpret, and understand the cultural identities of informants. For example, in advocating for qualitative approaches such as ethnography, Quimby (2006) focused on clients who are women and of African heritage as a group that is typically invisible in large, quantitative research methods in mental health. Recognizing the ways in which African American women face challenges in receiving culturally appropriate treatment—in addition to being underrepresented and understudied in research—Quimby asserted that ethnography is a way to rectify their absence in the counseling literature and inform more effective practice. Ultimately, ethnographic research serves as an important research tradition for counseling researchers who seek to conceptualize, build hypotheses, and test outcome data for groups that are typically marginalized in society.

Bhattacharya (2017) describes four common forms of ethnography. *Realist approaches* to ethnography strive to offer "neutral" observations of a culture and context. For instance, Grigorovich and Kontos (2019) used a realist critical ethnographic method to study the vulnerability of staff in residential long-term care setting to sexual harassment and used extensive observations and interviews to identify the management strategies these staff used to navigate sexual harassment. In contrast, *critical ethnography* seeks to acknowledge the inequities that exist in society and provide descriptive, interpretive research about these inequities, incorporating the critical race theory (CRT) paradigm. Rodriguez (2020) conducted a multisite critical ethnography study with undocumented Latinx youth, seeking to disrupt the idea of who the actual researcher was in the study. *Virtual and digital ethnographic approaches* include the study of online culture and contexts., whether this is through chat rooms, social media, or other forms of online spaces. There is exploration of the social relations of a particular group, for instance, in social media (e.g., the study of how Asian/Pacific Islander (AAPI) community organizers in a Facebook group are developing strategies to address anti-AAPI hate in society). Finally, visual ethnography uses various forms of media (e.g., film, photographs, collages, etc.) to study the culture and context of a group. Case Example 4.5 describes in detail an example of critical ethnography with Black adolescents.

## Ethnomethodology

Introduced in Chapter 2 as a key historical moment in qualitative research, **ethnomethodology** is the exploration of what individuals do to accomplish taken-for-granted social orders and structures in everyday work and life. Thus, qualitative researchers using this tradition are interested in studying the everydayness of social behaviors, "to study the things that persons in particular situations do, the methods they use, to create the patterned orderliness of social life" (Garfinkle, 2002, p. 6). Using a family meal as an example, de Montigny (2020) illustrates the ethnomethodology of how family members interactively coproduce a sequence of actions: turn-taking in conversation, telling jokes, leading the conversation, formulating recollections, asking questions, passing food, and so forth. With each component of this social behavior, individuals abide by social rules to order activities that can be readily studied. Thus, any social setting has properties "of practical activities detectable, countable, recordable, reportable, tell-a-story-aboutable, analyzable—in short accountable" to its members (Garfinkle, 1967, p. 33). Qualitative researchers can then study the methods by which members within a social setting

**Case Example 4.5. Critical Race Ethnography of a Post-Civil Rights Leader**

Woodson (2019) used a critical race ethnographic study to explore how eight Black adolescents understood what a "civil rights leader" meant and explored the processes that led to their understanding. The researcher reviewed literature on civil rights leaders and how they were "taught" in education and noted that there were no criteria that would establish who and what would give a person this label. Woodson (2019) also noted that the literature did discuss the valorization of certain people and their activities that resulted in a "superficial and often ahistorical portrayals of the Black freedom struggle" (p. 29).

Over 18 months, Woodson (2019) engaged this ethnographic study using many data collection and analytic processes to gain a critical ethnographic understanding of how Black adolescents would define who and what activities denoted a civil rights leader—specifically looking at the racial code words that defined them as such. Much of this data was collected by the researcher in 3-hour seminars led on Tuesdays and Wednesdays for 10 weeks that explored Black journalism and its historical and contemporaneous components:

- Use of critical race theory (CRT) to guide the conceptualization of the study and study design and other activities.
- Entry into the field with 10 weeks of participant observation and field note observations.
- Audiorecorded, semistructured focus group interviews with participants that were transcribed.
- Audiorecorded and transcribed individual interviews with 4–6 participants who participated in three interviews each about their assumptions of what a "civil rights leader" meant and explored the processes that led to their understanding.
- Analysis of all data collection, including journal entries, research assignments, and performances that were related to Black journalism, race and racism, and exploring racial dialogue within the media.

Woodson (2019) described multiple findings, including the adolescents' assessment that those designated as civil rights leaders had to be acceptable to White people and thus had to internalize values of Whiteness in being able to perform their activities. For instance, the Black adolescent participants described that Black English would not be acceptable for those labeled as civil rights leaders, as Whiteness would have to be embedded in their used of English in communicating to White audiences. These processes and constraints of Whiteness led to young Black people in the study feeling "estranged" from who and what designated a civil rights leader, which Woodson points out also excludes them from being connected to the civil rights movement.

Source: Woodson, A. (2019). Racial code words, re-memberings and Black kids' civic imaginations: A critical race ethnography of a post-civil rights leader. Anthropology & Education Quarterly, 50, 26–47. https://doi.org/10.1111/aeq.12277

coproduce a behavior and what they use to demonstrate its order. Hence, a social behavior within a social setting comes to be produced turn by turn.

Ethnomethodology is similar to ethnography in that both are inductive approaches that examine and describe the lives of their participants in a structured manner while having a strong sense of respect for the informants in the group studied (de Montigny, 2020). The focus of study in ethnomethodology is on the participants' perspectives of social order, assessments, and explanations. For instance, Edwards (2017) used ethnomethodology to explore the educational and professional experiences of Black women leaders in their career path to becoming superintendents to describe the patterns of how the intersections of their gender and racial identities and the contexts of educational settings they were in shaped these patterns. Similar to ethnography, researchers are expected to remain close to participants as they gain details of their social and cultural lives.

In order to study "normal" everyday social activities, qualitative researchers in clinical and education settings may opt to "shake things up" and do something outside a cultural norm to assess how people respond to it and expect normality. For example, let's say a teacher decides to move to the back of the classroom—or maybe even sit among the students— instead of standing in front of the classroom to teach. An educator might observe and conduct interviews of students to better understand their perceptions of this change in classroom behavior and structure.

**Conversation analysis**, developed by Harvey Sacks (1995), is an outgrowth of ethnomethodology specific to personal conversations. Paul ten Have (2007) highlights four frames to consider in conversation analysis as segments of conversational text are sequentially reviewed to develop and revise a **summary formulation**. The formulation includes general observations as well as any atypical instances in the data and explicate their relationship with other regular patterns observed. The organizational frames include **turn-taking organization** (i.e., taking a turn in a specific way), **sequence organization** (i.e., initiating a conversation sequence), **repair organization** (i.e., forgoing taking up an issue within a conversation), and **organization of turn-design** (i.e., overall organizational structure of interactions).

Ethnomethodology, in its detailed focus on phenomenon at a micro level, allows understanding of larger social and cultural phenomena. As such, it provides an opportunity for qualitative researchers to account for larger cultural actions related to privilege and oppression and highlight their production in order to advocate for change in social behavior. Decision Points 4.1 presents some reflections on how qualitative researchers can use their work to inform larger conversations on social injustice and advocacy within clinical and education disciplines.

## Autoethnography

**Autoethnography** is a research tradition used to systematically explore the researcher or researchers' personal experience (*auto*) in relation to a larger sociocultural context (*ethno*) through reflexive and critical representation (*graphy*; Hughes & Pennington, 2017). Through reflecting upon and sharing personal experience, researchers can inform clinical and educational practice and scholarship. In autoethnography, a researcher or research team provides a first-person narrative of a phenomenon with the primary purpose of connecting to the reader (i.e., **evocative autoethnography**; Ellis et al., 2011). **Analytic autoethnography** extends the

**DECISION POINTS 4.1.** ETHNOMETHODOLOGY AS A TOOL FOR SOCIAL ADVOCACY

One of the primary research foci that ethnomethodology is well designed for determining "how things stand in the world and [...] the methodic practices that produce and sustain the social order" (Rapley, 2012, p. 183). Clients and students, particularly those of minoritized statuses, practitioners and educator work with often encounter social injustice as well as exhibit resilience and resistance.

For each research topic, ethnomethodology can be a useful tool to highlight social interactions imbued in power at the micro level and how power structures are sustained at micro and macro levels. Qualitative researchers can describe the way power is coproduced, yet they need to be cognizant of not further pathologizing or minoritizing participants in the process. As they engage in research with these participants, decision points may include:

- To what extent is the research topic influenced by issues of power, privilege, oppression, resistance, and resilience?
- How can research questions be framed to showcase the application of micro-level findings to larger cultural conversations?
- How does the role of the researcher influence how power issues are broached within the research process and the reporting of ethnomethodological findings?
- Where are opportunities to foster resilience and resistance of minoritized participants?

Consider a study example in which qualitative researchers seek to describe communication patterns between a transgender elementary school student and a professional school counselor. While analyzing transcripts of a counseling session, they can note interactions using ten Have's (2007) organizational frames, with particular attention to affirming language and actions related to conversation content, sequence, and overall voice. Then they can develop a summary formulation that can foster more affirmative practices in schools.

storytelling function of evocative autoethnography: It requires the researcher or research team to engage with the phenomenon through self-reflection as well as social interactions and subsequently apply the constructed account to theory and professional practice for the research report (Anderson, 2006). Furthermore, analytic autoethnographies may be synthesized within (i.e., **collective autoethnography**) and across (i.e., metaethnography of autoethnographies) studies (see Hays & McKibben, 2021). Perspectives 4.5 provides an example of a collective autoethnography of doctoral students' development as instructors.

Both autoethnography and heuristic inquiry may be considered self-as-subject research approaches; however, there are some distinctions. Autoethnography is the sole focus of self as the object of research (or selves in the case of when a research team is used). With heuristic inquiry, the use of self is only one component of research, and other participants are included in research to augment the researcher or researchers' autobiographical perspective. Furthermore,

## PERSPECTIVES 4.5. THE PEDAGOGICAL DEVELOPMENT OF SIX DOCTORAL STUDENTS

Elliott et al. (2019) conducted a collective autoethnography of six doctoral students' experiences in an instructional theory course intended to prepare them for teaching in counselor education programs. Anna Elliott and Lynn Bohecker, counselor educators who conducted the study as doctoral students with others in their cohort, noted in an interview with me (Danica) that their cohort was curious about the impact of an instructional theory course and concurrent coteaching experiences on their instructional development as a future counselor educator. Bohecker (personal communication, June 16, 2020) noted about the use of autoethnography for this research topic: "It really allowed us that individual experience and individual process, but then to contextualize it as a group. … The feedback we received [from each other] was wide rang[ing] and the varied perspectives were necessary."

The authors used multiple data collection methods to foster self-reflection and evoke data in different ways: weekly written reflections, weekly photography submissions, and two focus group interviews within one semester. Elliott and Bohecker shared that the research process began with weekly journal entries in which they selected and analyzed photographs the coresearchers selected. After committing some time for introspection with these methods, the coresearchers met for the first focus group interview, followed by additional journal entries and photographs, and concluding with a second focus group interview. Elliott (personal communication, June 16, 2020) recalled the benefit of using focus groups:

> We were acknowledging and allowing us to be impacted by one another. … This process allowed us the opportunity to be vulnerable with each other in a way that felt respectful and productive. … The focus group not only allowed us to co-construct meaning … also helped us learn how to talk to each other and to be real with each other about our [training] process.

With respect to the journal entries and photographs, Bohecker (personal communication, June 16, 2020) stated, "I really appreciated the ability to journal … and then having the photos really was beneficial because of the ability to demonstrate through a photograph an emotion that maybe I wasn't able to really figure out how to write."

Elliott et al. (2019) identified seven themes regarding the role and impact of their pedagogical training: four methods of coping (i.e., fear and self-doubt, intentional authenticity, openness with the struggle, navigating opposing forces) and three methods of reinforcing (i.e., impact of other, growth-producing experiences, light at the end of the tunnel). The authors conclude their analysis by examining the relationship among the themes and developing a model of pedagogical development.

In our conversation, Elliott and Bohecker spoke about the insider-outsider nature of collective autoethnography (i.e., being a participant and researcher). Because moving from participant to researcher roles can be complex, they noted it was beneficial that data analysis occurred the following semester after they were able to take a break from the data. Like adjusting a lens on a camera, Elliott (personal communication, June 16, 2020) discussed zooming in and out to study the phenomenon:

> I spoke to my experience. What was central about it for me? Now I'm going to zoom out. I'm going to take myself out of the role of the participant. As a researcher, look at all the different things that each of us are saying and figuring out where our common ground is. If your commitment is truly to speak into the essence of an experience of multiple people … you're not coming from an agenda of wanting your voice to be heard over someone else's, you're trying to figure out what's shared. And that made moving from the inside to outside easier.

Bohecker (personal communication, June 16, 2020) added:

> I was able to share my experience so that it [wasn't] inside of me trying to get out anymore. Now I can look at [the phenomenon] as a collective, as a whole, as a researcher … putting my researcher hat on and engaging in analysis.

Source: Elliott, A., Salazar, B. M., Dennis, B. L., Bohecker, L., Nielson, T., LaMantia, K., & Kleist, D. M. (2019). Pedagogical perspectives on counselor education: An autoethnographic experience of doctoral student development. *The Qualitative Report, 24(4),* 648–666.

---

one of the goals of using autoethnography is to apply knowledge gained of self within a cultural process or group; heuristic inquiry is specifically focused on the lived experience of the researcher(s) and participants without necessarily theorizing to others.

Anderson (2006) noted several key features of analytic autoethnography:

- The researcher is a complete member of the social world being researched (i.e., complete member researcher [CMR] status), with group membership commonly preceding the research process.
- There is greater attention to the researcher's impact on the research context—and vice versa—to allow for mutual understanding.
- The researcher is visible in the text, accounting for important data.
- The researcher is actively involved with others to ensure representation in findings.
- There is a focus on actively gathering empirical data to understand a broader social phenomenon than that provided by data themselves, connecting biography with social structure.

 **ACTIVITY 4.4.** APPLYING THE CULTURAL EXPRESSIONS OF THE "PROCESS AND EXPERIENCE" CLUSTER

Select a topic of interest in your profession. Consider how each of the traditions in this cluster would influence how you would study the research topic.

Autoethnography, particularly analytic autoethnography, includes several benefits (Anderson, 2006; Custer, 2014):

- The researcher is both an insider (i.e., participant) of the group under investigation as well as an outsider as someone in a researcher role.
- Links are made between the researcher's personal narrative and a larger context.
- The researcher's voice is highly visible in the data.
- Others' narratives are infused to help define the research in relation to others as part of analysis and the report.
- Findings can be applied to a phenomenon under investigation.
- The tradition allows for methodological flexibility, which can support culturally responsive research.

In autoethnography, it is useful to connect the findings to a theoretical framework and explain to the reader how the framework is personally and professionally relevant for applying to the phenomenon of interest. Direct quotes from others who have a connection to the researcher or research team can be used to confirm the assumptions and findings (O'Hara, 2018).

Autoethnography has its beginnings in the Chicago School, discussed in Chapter 2. Later generations of Chicago School researchers used more explicit self-reflexivity in reporting findings. While ethnography and ethnomethodology both face epistemological challenges in "getting close" to their informants, autoethnography resolves this challenge, as it is a first-person account of events, interactions, and relationships.

Autoethnographers use their own thoughts, feelings, documentation of fieldnotes, and other personal experiences they have in response to their ethnographic examination of a culture as data. There is an opportunity to switch between being a member and being a researcher, to have an engaged dialogue rather than a detached discovery. This benefit is also a potential drawback if not carefully monitored:

> There is the elevation of the autobiographical to such a degree that the ethnographer becomes more memorable than the ethnography, the self more absorbing than other social actors. … This in turn reflects a wider problem in that the methodological has been transposed onto the plane of personal experience, while the value of sociological or anthropological fieldwork has been translated into a quest for personal fulfillment on the part of the researcher. (Anderson, 2006, pp. 402–403)

Thus, qualitative researchers are cognizant of not using this tradition simply as a springboard for documenting personal information or simply providing an insider's perspective.

## Research as a Change Agent: Participatory Action Research and Community-Based Participatory Research

### Participatory Action Research

**Participatory action research (PAR)** is a research tradition that focuses on how the participants and researcher are changed in the process of the examination. Essentially, the goals of

PAR are emancipation and transformation, and the researcher is required to critically reflect on the power of research as a change agent. Further, participants and researchers share power, and participants are a part of planning research and implementing its findings (Nastasi et al., 2020; Nastasi & Hitchcock, 2015; Wood, 2019).

PAR emerged from the applied anthropological inquiry and is recursive in nature because it seeks to align research with both practice and theory in order to encourage change of a culture and society. Researchers in school psychology have a long tradition of utilizing action research, where the data collection and analysis process drives decisions about practice and intervention. PAR involves a collaborative approach to problem-solving between the researcher and other key stakeholders (e.g., parents, teachers, school administrators) to guide interventions and practice with one or more students (Nastasi et al., 2020; Nastasi & Hitchcock, 2015; Wood, 2019).

Theory, previous research, and collaborative interaction between the researchers and stakeholders provide the foundation for PAR inquiry and guide formulation of research questions. Nastasi and Hitchcock (2015) describe PAR as using this foundation to generate a culture- or context-specific theory that applies to the examination, which will then guide the development of the culture- or context-specific intervention or practice. Ongoing evaluation of the research process is a critical way in which the researcher adapts the intervention or practice in the course of the inquiry and ultimately provides the field with an additional theory that is both general and culture specific. Theoretical information that is generated in turn changes researcher and participants, thus continuing the recursive process of the examination.

Previous to initiating PAR, the researcher must engage in critical reflection. **Critical reflection** refers to Freire's (1972) work that provided a critical analysis of power holders as a way to generate social and systemic change. PAR integrates critical reflection previous to and throughout the research process as a validity check and as a way to ensure that the focus is not merely a discovery of knowledge but also a collaborative creation of knowledge that will promote systemic change (Wood, 2019). Thus, critical reflection is an active process that does not merely focus on the outcomes of change of PAR but rather concentrates its reflection on the research processes so that readers may learn how to initiate change in a similar manner.

Consider Varjas et al.'s (2006) study exploring bullying intervention methods of LGBT (lesbian, gay, bisexual, transgender) adolescents in schools. Varjas and her colleagues interviewed 16 community and school service providers to better understand how they respond to LGBT bullying as well as how they perceive school barriers, resources, and existing bullying interventions influence changes to meet the needs of these youth. For this study, critical reflection would not only involve the reflections of the researcher on the informants (third-person reflection) but would also incorporate an analysis of the researcher on themselves (first-person reflection) in addition to the researcher *and* the informants (second-person reflection). With this example, the critical reflection on all three levels provides a more authentic way to document and promote change during the research process because the reflection is not limited and situated in the researcher alone.

PAR is a useful research tradition to employ in the field of counseling, especially as the social justice movement in counseling continues to grow. Social justice has been named the fifth force in counseling, urging counselors to move from gaining multicultural awareness, knowledge, and skills and toward advocacy on behalf of clients based on multicultural concepts (Ratts et al., 2016). PAR is a research paradigm that has traditionally been utilized more in school psychology research. However, the recent focus on social justice in counseling may urge counseling scholars to consider using PAR as the inquiry of choice when seeking to promote change in a community through the research process.

Stoecker (2018) advises that researchers answer three questions when selecting participatory methods. First, he suggests that one asks who the community is. For instance, in a study of people experiencing homeless after being displaced by the 1996 Olympics in Atlanta, an organization called Project South used participatory research methods in order to collaboratively change the living situations of these individuals, including challenging government policies (Project South, 2008). In this study the community was identified to be the homeless individuals, the organization and members of Project South, government agencies, and the Atlanta community at large, and the community was the sources of data collection and analysis (e.g., interviews, archival data, community meetings). A second question to ask is whether conflict or cooperation is involved in the situation that the researcher is interested in examining. This is an especially important question since the researcher will want to be aware of how conflict or cooperation may shape the research process from collaborative research question design to evaluation. A third question to ask is how the PAR approach may be biased in terms of voices that are present and absent in the collaborative process of research. A subset of questions may include attention to the stakeholders and which groups hold more or less power in the focus of inquiry.

In the course of the PAR examination, traditional data collection methods are used, such as semistructured interviews, artifacts and archival data, focus groups, participant observation, among others (Lincoln & Guba, 1995; Stoecker, 2018). Nastasi and Hitchcock (2015) describe using PAR methods to initiate a mental health services plan for schools that meet certain required criteria. Six phases were used to create a collaborative and recursive research process: (a) existing theory, research, and practice (exploring personal theory); (b) learning the culture; (c) forming partnerships; (d) goal or problem identification; (e) formative research; and (f) culture-specific theory or model. They also used a similar approach to HIV/AIDS prevention with adolescents in Sri Lanka (Nastasi et al., 1998), where initial theories and existing information generated data about alcoholism as a stressor for the adolescents, and social stressors (e.g., intimate partner violence, cultural norms of shame) were revealed to impact the transmission of HIV/AIDS. This information was gathered through semistructured interviews with individuals in addition to community focus group interviews, which were also methods of building collaboration and stakeholder identification for the next stages of the PAR inquiry.

Collective memory work (CMW), based on theoretical work in the 1980s by several feminist researchers (see Haug, 2008), has increased in use in clinical and education settings over the past decade and is a form of PAR (Johnson, 2018), as it engages participants as direct researchers of their own experience with the goal of raising critical consciousness. CMW typically requires close collaboration with participants and community members surrounding a topic that is selected as an important site of inquiry. For example, Johnson et al. (2014) used CMW to examine the collective memories of transgender, queer, and questioning youth in high school. In this CMW study, participants were asked to write about one positive and one negative memory that they had about their gender and sexual orientation identity development processes during high school. These stories served as a first level of data collection and were written in the third person. These anonymized stories were then reviewed within a focus group of the participants who had written the stories (none of them knew who had specifically written a particular positive or negative narrative). A facilitator worked collaboratively with participants to analyze the stories as data and identify overarching themes.

In summary, PAR is a tradition that focuses on a specific setting in counseling and education to readily apply research findings to real-world problems. To apply these findings, researchers are charged with working actively with participants on solutions. Complete Activity 4.5 to practice applying the PAR tradition.

## ACTIVITY 4.5. APPLYING THE PAR TRADITION

Select a topic of interest in your profession. Consider how the PAR tradition would influence how you would study the research topic.

## Community-Based Participatory Research

Whereas PAR has components that are in collaboration with participants as coresearchers, **community-based participatory research (CBPR)** establishes research questions and processes that directly benefit the community (Jacquez et al., 2013). In this way, the goal of CBAR is to influence social change in a positive direction and entails social justice and liberatory components. For instance, Oscós-Sánchez and colleagues (2021) used a CBPR research tradition to collaborate with youth and their parents to design and enact two public health and education interventions: a violence prevention program and a positive youth development program. This was a critical research study that was an intervention in a community that was already experiencing high rates of community and youth violence as the COVID-19 pandemic unfolded. Working closely with communities in this way helps encourage community members at large to see their own identities and interests reflected in not only the research team but also in the research design and implementation of study activities that lead to real social change solutions that have immediate impact. It also takes time, energy, and intentional investment on the part of academic- and community-based researchers working together. Oscós-Sánchez et al. (2021) worked over 17 months in 19 community-based meetings to design the CBPR study and intervention. Therefore, the decision to embark on a CBPR process must not be one in name only, or distrust and harm can certainly unfold in the process, which can have negative influences on communities already experiencing vulnerability and/or oppressive environments.

As such, building community trust and legitimacy in the process of CBPR is paramount, and the people involved as coresearchers must be those the community sees as having an investment in their overall well-being, support, and success. Community Tool Box (n.d.-a) includes the following overarching recommendations when designing CBPR studies:

- Determine when it is best to carry out a CBPR study: Is there time to engage a long-term, community-based and driven, trust-building, and thorough CBPR study? What are the anticipated challenges and opportunities along the way you will need to consider? Do you have enough people and other resources to carry out a CBPR study?
- Recruit a community research team: How will you use accessible language to describe your study and get the attention of your intended audience? How will you embed culturally responsive messages and meet your audience where they live and work?
- Orient and train the research team: What are the best ways to introduce your research team to one another and gain essential information about the CBPR, and what resources (e.g., transportation, childcare, food) will be provided during the process? How will the research team give and receive feedback along the way?
- Determine the questions the research or evaluation is meant to answer: What is the most pressing question the community would like to ask and have answered? How will this question or these questions be connected with solutions and social change? Are the correct people at the table based on the answers to these questions?
- Plan and structure the research activity: This is the who, what, how, and why questions that will drive timelines for study activities from design to implementation—as well as how findings will be compiled and distributed to the community and what advocacy for solutions will ensue.
- Anticipate and prepare contingency plans for problems that might arise: Similar to orienting and training the research team, designing feedback processes for the overall research team is crucial to build ongoing trust.
- Implement the research plan: These are the steps that have been collaboratively designed above. Who will conduct the activities, and how will they be carried out in and with community members?
- Prepare and present the report and recommendations: What is the best format in which to distribute findings (e.g., community presentation, press release, conference, e-newsletter, newspaper article, academic journal etc.)?
- Take (or try to bring about) appropriate action on the issue or intervention: What were the anticipated plans for action for social change in the solution identified in the earlier planning processes, and how might those be changed or enhanced to drive effective change advocacy?

 **ACTIVITY 4.6.** QUALITATIVE ARTICLE REVIEW

Select an article in your specific profession. Determine what research paradigms and traditions the authors chose. To what degree did they discuss these? How are they reflected in the methodology and findings sections of the article?

**PROPOSAL DEVELOPMENT ACTIVITY 4.2.** SELECTING A RESEARCH TRADITION

Which research traditions(s) resonate(s) most with you, and why? Which seems least appropriate for you, and why? (Remember, your final choice for a research tradition will likely change once you select a proposal topic.)

## Researcher Role and Reflexivity Across the Traditions

As you have reviewed the research paradigms and traditions, you have seen that the role of the researcher in each of these is an important one and that there is reflexivity on the part of the researcher that is demanded throughout the research process. As we noted earlier in this text, the RPA model demands that we as researchers constantly self-reflect on our positionalities and subjectivities as we bring research, practice, and advocacy together in our work.

Chilisa (2020) notes in her review of Indigenous methods that researcher reflexivity can be inherently colonized and that rather than focusing on an individualized researcher role, as qualitative researchers we can expand our understandings of authenticity and positionality. She cites the discussion of critical subjectivity or self-reflexivity by Reinharz (1992), who encourages researchers to identify the three selves we bring into any study: historical selves, social selves, and personal selves. In our work, for instance, with trans and nonbinary phenomenological research, we would ask how our personal histories of gender were influencing our role and reflexivity in these studies; we would ask how our social selves performed gender and were socialized in gender norms and assumptions about our social roles with gender related to our study topic; and we would ask ourselves how our personal identities of our current genders were entering the study and constructing a lens through which we understood our data collection and analysis activities.

Prasad (2005) asserted that how we engage our role and reflexivity as qualitative researchers can vary depending on the type of research tradition. For instance, Prasad notes that critical theories examine power in different ways and thus would situate the researcher in different power positions. For instance, consider the critical paradigms of historical materialism (the Marxist tradition in qualitative research describing the interaction of power and class) and feminism (gender theories examining the power that is assigned by gender and influences the exploitation of physical bodies). The cultural location of power from these theories would drive the role and reflexivity activities of the researcher: social class and gender, respectively. In addition, Prasad also describes how the traditions of the "post," such as poststructuralism (which embeds suspicions of language and institutions that design "grand narratives" to situate and uphold power) and postcolonialism (which critiques the legacies of White European colonization and imperialistic practices that drive who holds power and who does not), can situate the researcher with unique frameworks in which to question, interrogate, and continuously reflect on the power you have as a researcher and how you use it. To further your learning, complete Activity 4.7 to explore your researcher role and reflexivity.

**ACTIVITY 4.7.** REFLECTING ON YOUR ROLE AND REFLEXIVITY AS A RESEARCHER BASED ON THE TRADITIONS

Select a research tradition reviewed earlier in this chapter. Select a topic of interest in your field.

- What is your role as a researcher using this research tradition to study your topic?
- How does this research tradition guide you in your research reflexivity as related to your study topic?
- Discuss how the three selves (historical, social, and personal) will influence your researcher role and reflexivity.
- Chilisa (2020) notes the researcher can assume various stances regarding those researched within indigenous populations: (a) knower or teacher, who shares their knowledge; (b) redeemer, who attempts to provide solutions; or (c) transformative healer, who works to decolonize research practices and promote shared power and restoration. For the selected research tradition, how does each stance (i.e., knower, redeemer, transformative healer) influence your researcher role and reflexivity?

## CHAPTER SUMMARY

Your research orientation is an important foundation in constructing a qualitative study. This orientation is developed through reflection on philosophies of science, research paradigms, and research traditions, considering how these components build upon each other. Selecting a qualitative research tradition helps solidify the foundation for your research inquiry.

This chapter presented five clusters of qualitative research traditions. These include (a) the hybrid tradition (case study); (b) experience and theory formulation (grounded theory, phenomenology, heuristic inquiry, and consensual qualitative research); (c) the meaning of symbol and text (narratology and life history); (d) cultural expressions of process and experience (ethnography, ethnomethodology, and autoethnography); and (e) research as a change agent (PAR and CBPR). For some qualitative research traditions (e.g., case study, grounded theory), there are identified strands based on specific paradigmatic influences.

For the hybrid tradition cluster, the research focus is on describing a case within a bounded system in a naturalistic setting using diverse methodological approaches. The researcher in the "experience and theory formulation" cluster identifies a process or action surrounding an experience to describe or explain a phenomenon inductively (grounded theory), investigates a direct lived experience with a phenomenon to examine the interaction between individual experience and others' meanings in an environment (phenomenology), examines direct lived experience of the researcher and participants (heuristic inquiry), and integrates description of lived experience and theory development through consensus building (CQR). For "the meaning of symbols and text" cluster, symbols within language are explored to understand the participant(s) within a social context to derive meaning (life history) and narratives or dimensions, and properties of stories are investigated to examine plot structure, content, and sequence (narratology).

In the "cultural expressions of process and experience" cluster, the qualitative researcher describes social processes of a cultural group of system (ethnography), identifies social order and patterns oftentimes through disrupting cultural norms (ethnomethodology), and becomes the participant with the intent to connect to the reader and/or engage with the phenomenon to apply to a larger theory (autoethnography). The last cluster, "research as a change agent," involves seeking transformation and emancipation through shared power to impact change at an individual (PAR) or community (CBPR) level.

## Review Questions

1. What is the relationship between qualitative research paradigms and traditions? Provide an example using one of the tradition clusters.
2. Which qualitative research traditions are most closely aligned with theory development?
3. Which qualitative research traditions allow for qualitative researchers to be engaged as direct participants? What are some benefits and challenges associated with qualitative researcher as a participant?
4. How can qualitative researchers use qualitative research traditions to frame their inquiry to enact social change through attention to equity and advocacy? Provide an example, using at least three qualitative research traditions.
5. How is reflexivity different across the qualitative research traditions?
6. How are your deepening your understanding of your roles in the researcher-practitioner-advocate (RPA) model?

## Recommended Readings

Charmaz, K. (2014). *Constructing grounded theory* (2nd ed.). Sage.

Clandinin, D. J., Caine, V., & Lessard, S. (2018). *The relational ethics of narrative inquiry*. Routledge.

Corbin, J., & Strauss, A. (2015). *Basics of qualitative research: Techniques and procedures for developing grounded theory* (4th ed.). Sage.

Creswell, J. W., & Poth, C. N. (2017). *Qualitative inquiry and research design: Choosing among five approaches* (4th ed.). Sage.

Wood, L. (2019). *Participatory action learning and action research: Theory, practice and process*. Routledge.

# PART II

# Qualitative Research Design

■ **CHAPTER 5**

# Selecting a Topic

---

## CHAPTER PREVIEW

Building on the discussion of research paradigms and traditions earlier in the text, this chapter addresses the many interdependent considerations of selecting a topic in qualitative research. These include (a) establishing research goals, (b) developing a conceptual framework, (c) writing a purpose statement, (d) determining a research question or questions, and (e) deciding if a mixed methods approach is more suitable (see Figure 5.1). Each consideration is addressed in major sections of this chapter. Topics such as case and unit of analysis, research purpose, literature review, and concept mapping are explored with respect to the five considerations.

## Selecting a Topic

Ideas or research topics are everywhere. Selecting a general research topic is as natural as considering why you chose the career path you have. There are experiences and interests we have that have led us to choose to become a counselor, an administrator, a special educator, and so forth. One student described choosing to become a high school administrator after, in his role as a high school teacher, noticing higher teacher attrition in predominantly urban schools. Thus, a natural research topic for him involved teacher retention. Thus, on a broad scale, your general topic can relate directly to your discipline itself. Good questions to ask are as follows:

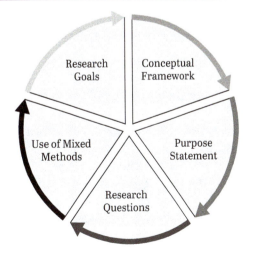

**FIGURE 5.1** Considerations in Research Topic Selection

What are you passionate about that led you to your profession? How will the research topics I am interested in be connected to social change? How will the RPA model influence my research topic?

Sometimes, it may be a combination of previous or current personal experiences that create general areas of interests. As humans, we have a natural curiosity to understand things more clearly, particularly if we have a personal connection to a topic. In Chapter 4, we introduced you to Maria Haiyasosa's work (see Perspectives 4.3). Haiyasosa became interested in child sexual abuse (CSA) based on her work as a forensic interviewer at a children's advocacy center. As she interviewed children, typically ages 3–18, about the circumstances surrounding their alleged sexual abuse experiences, she found herself interested in their resilience factors, perceived support, and coping skills. She also noted the intergenerational nature of CSA as she spoke with parents:

> They have experienced sexual abuse probably 9 out of 10 times. ... That parent that's bringing their child to see me has also been a survivor and has been subjected to those devastating experiences themselves. So, taking all of that together, it really led me to want to know more about adult survivors, relational health in general, but then specifically their parent-child experiences. (Haiyasosa, personal communication, June 5, 2020)

What may be obvious in selecting a general area of interest or research topic—whether personal or professional—is that selecting a topic is not a neutral process. There are likely personal and/or professional motivations we have for our interests, oftentimes based on social interactions we have had. We have assumptions about what the problem is and who might likely be influenced by it. It is important, then, to reflect on our interests and where they might come from. Ongoing analysis of a selected topic paves the way for a more rigorous qualitative research process. Perspectives 5.1 provides examples of how students selected their qualitative research topics.

## PERSPECTIVES 5.1. SELECTING A TOPIC: STUDENT PERSPECTIVES

I have been interested in LGBTQ [lesbian, gay, bisexual, transgender, and questioning] issues in adolescents in the school system for quite some time, particularly in how these students are being supported and counseled. In my master's program, I did work on this topic and wanted to expand my own knowledge while discovering new ideas and offering information to the field. Narrowing the topic to a research project that was doable was the major struggle. I decided to focus on schools in a particular area and on the perceptions of school counselors—as it was more feasible to discuss the topic with adults than minors in the school.

—*counseling student*

As a special educator, my interest lay in the area of teaching functional academic skills to students with severe and profound disabilities. As I began to conduct a preliminary literature review on that topic, I was able to locate dozens of quantitative studies, which documented progress and/or compared effective intervention strategies. However, I was unable to locate any research that conveyed the educator's views on teaching these students academic content. Therefore, I decided the best way to approach this subject would be to conduct a qualitative study. The research study would involve conducting a series of interviews with educators and administrators in order to ascertain their opinions regarding providing educational programming, based on an academic curriculum, to students with severe disabilities.

*—curriculum and instruction student*

I worked for 3 years in a university career center and provided career counseling to many international students. I noticed that they had different career needs than domestic students. For example, most international students are limited by their visa status as to where they can work, both during and after completing their education. I also noticed that international students' career development process was different than many domestic students. For example, for many international students did not go through a career exploration and decision-making process, but followed their family's expectations for their career. Because their experience of career development and needs were very different from domestic learners, career services did not seem to offer helpful/beneficial services to international students. I was tired of not being able to help this population when they come to my office. I selected a research topic of identifying vocational and psychological needs of U.S. international students from varying academic programs and student statuses. Some of the challenges of this inquiry include access to the population due to cultural barriers (e.g., language, unfamiliarity with social research or my research purpose in particular).

*—counseling student*

I had initially wanted to compare test scores for 7th grade students in schools in two adjacent cities whereas one city's students received comprehensive sex education and the other city's students received abstinence-only sex education. I became interested in the topic through my volunteerism with Planned Parenthood. I ended up having to switch topics though because a school district administrator who approves outside research would not give me approval. He said that the principals could speak to me if they wished but that the project would not have official approval. Yeah, right! When I called the principal in one of the cities to ask for an interview he said he "chose to forego this opportunity." It definitely taught me to check accessibility issues BEFORE committing to a project—especially in qualitative studies where you can't just download spreadsheets but really have to get in there and talk to people who are getting told NOT to talk to you! I believe it was political because of the controversial topic because another student in our class got the go ahead from the same administrator for another study she wanted to do for our class.

*—urban studies and public administration student*

I want to study the experiences, expectations, and reactions of the student in a graduate level multicultural class. I have been personally and professionally connected to the topic as a multiculturally aware counselor. I value studies that support the influence of culture and diversity in our counselor education as a significant competence for counselors. I sense that we are still finding our way in teaching multicultural competence and therefore this subject is important to me on those levels. I have faced many challenges: finding research that relates to the experiences of students in a classroom, arguing or defending why I think their voice is one we as educators should listen to as well as why I am approaching this study from a qualitative research approach rather than a traditional quantitative approach. I am currently struggling with trying to meet varied opinions on whose voice I should be focusing on: instructor, student, those of minority or majority statuses, one or several university settings, current students or alumni, doctoral or masters-level students, and so forth.

—*counseling student*

Once you have some idea of a general research topic, it is imperative that you refine your topic to make it more manageable. In other words, what aspect of a larger issue can you tackle effectively in one study? The following are some general strategies for refining a research topic:

- What do we already know about the topic? Reflect on what you already know *personally* about a general topic. We may have some personal connection to a topic that can direct us to more specific areas of inquiry.
- Additionally, think about what you already know *professionally* about a general topic. What does previous research tell us about the topic? Conducting a thorough literature review is important to uncover areas or perspectives that could and should be explored.
- Brainstorm potential research questions for your general topic and consider how each question will be answered. What specific audience's perspective might be most informative and relevant for the topic and for addressing the research question(s)?
- Creswell and Poth (2017) suggest drafting a brief or working title or, alternatively, developing a brief question for a study topic. Doing this early in the research process creates content that can serve as a road map for the research design process. We agree that this may be helpful as an initial step in determining research goals, conducting a literature review, and developing a sound conceptual framework.
- As you become more specific about your topic, consider whether the topic can be researched. For instance, do you have the necessary resources to investigate the refined topic? Qualitative researchers need to consider how time, financial, and social resources impact their topic. How much time is necessary to collect and analyze data? How much money is necessary to complete the research, considering things such as travel and supply expenses? To what degree does access to the research population influence the quality of obtained data?
- Consider if the research topic is feasible. Even if you have ample resources, there may be ethical or professional barriers that inhibit a specific investigation. What might be some ethical and professional considerations related to your specific topic?

These strategies are discussed more fully throughout this chapter and other sections of the text. Remember, whatever topic you select for qualitative inquiry will stay with you throughout the life of the study and beyond, so choose wisely! There is a significant time and energy (scholarly and otherwise) commitment to the selected topic. In the remainder of this chapter, we will discuss some key considerations in topic selection. These include (a) determining research goals; (b) developing a conceptual framework; and (c) outlining quality research questions. While these components are presented independently, they often occur in qualitative design concurrently, as decisions in one area often impact another.

## Research Goals

In Chapter 4, we provided 12 qualitative research traditions commonly used in education and social sciences. Even in collapsing them into five clusters, the decision of which tradition to use to frame your study can be cumbersome! To help with that decision, sometimes it is helpful to consider what the research goals are. A **research goal** is a broad plan for achieving a desired result that considers what data need to be obtained based on the needs of all those involved in the qualitative inquiry. Maxwell (2013) notes that there are three kinds of research goals: personal goals, practical goals, and scholarly goals. It is imperative to reflect on what motivates you personally to conduct a qualitative study (i.e., *personal goals*), what need or objective needs to be met (i.e., *practical goals*), and what intellectual understanding you want to obtain about a topic (i.e., *scholarly goals*). Your research topic can address any of these three goals, although the latter two are often deemed more justifiable in qualitative research and thus more germane to developing research questions (discussed later in this chapter). Maxwell (2013) notes five scholarly goals (Items 1–5) that can benefit three practical goals (Items 6–8):

1. Understanding the *meaning*, for participants in the study, of the events, situations, experiences, and actions they are involved with or engaged in.
2. Understanding the *contexts* within which the participants act and the influence that this context has on their actions.
3. Understanding the *process* by which events and actions take place.
4. Identifying *unanticipated phenomena and influences* and developing new "grounded" theories on the latter.
5. Developing *causal explanations*.
6. Generating *results and theories* that are understandable and experientially credible, both to the people you are studying and to others.
7. Conducting research that is intended to improve existing practices, programs, or policies, which is often called *formative evaluation*.
8. Engaging in *action, participatory, collaborative, or community-based research* with participants in the study. (see pp. 30–32)

With an understanding of the three primary goals for research goals, let's move on to additional aspects to consider in developing these goals. Some key questions in determining research goals are:

- What is the case to be investigated?
- What is the purpose of the inquiry?
- What type of information is sought?

## What Is the Case to Be Investigated?

In Chapter 4, we introduced the case study tradition in which qualitative researchers investigate a **case** (i.e., unit of analysis or object of study) within a bounded system (i.e., has distinctive boundaries of time, sampling frame, activity, and/or physical space or setting that frame and constrict the research focus). Cases can involve individuals, groups, settings, processes, or events studied in naturalistic settings. Applying these case types more broadly to establishing research goals, qualitative researchers consider what their primary unit of analysis is, or the case of which they are exploring in a study.

An *individual case* is specifically focused on one or a few informants with a distinct purpose of gaining information about them personally. An individual case may be a particular person, couple, or family, for instance. A *group case* would focus on individuals but at a collective level, attending to group characteristics or features. Example group cases might be a teacher's union, counseling organization, and university committee. A *setting case* would attend to characteristics of a site, such as an agency or a classroom, or a geographical region. A qualitative researcher may be interested in an individual or individuals within that setting to inform the study, yet the primary goal is to learn about that setting. Researchers exploring *process cases* are primarily interested in phenomena and the content and dynamics surrounding phenomena. Finally, there is often an event that may be viewed as significant by qualitative researchers in counseling and education disciplines. Thus, an *event case* would isolate an event and study it from multiple angles and perspectives. Individuals, settings, and processes inform our knowledge of the event. Table 5.1 provides examples of each of the five case types.

## What Is the Purpose of the Inquiry?

Now that you have an idea of what type of case you are interested in exploring, consider what type of information is most important to you. One of the first steps in the research process is getting clear about the research purpose. That is, in what types of outcomes are you most interested? Identifying the purpose of your inquiry early in a proposal will facilitate the development of meaningful research questions. There are four major types of research you can pursue, each with a different purpose. These four can be considered to fall on a continuum with theory development on one end and social action on the other. Most often, research will begin with more general findings and will be eventually applied to specific populations and problems.

**TABLE 5.1**  Case Examples in Qualitative Inquiry

| Case type | Study reference | Study description |
|---|---|---|
| Individual(s) | Vidourek, R. A., & Burbage, M. (2019). Positive mental health and mental health stigma: A qualitative study assessing student attitudes. *Mental Health & Prevention*, *13*, 1–6. https://doi.org/10.1016/j.mhp.2018.11.006 | The study investigated positive mental health and mental health stigma among college students (*N*=23). Identified themes were as follows: staying mentally healthy, awareness/education, compassion/understanding, and benefits and barriers to mental health treatment. Students reported that increasing education and awareness, linking students to resources, and being compassionate and understanding to those experiencing mental health problems were important to reduce stigma-related attitudes. |
| Group | Garcia, C. E. (2020). Belonging in a predominantly White institution: The role of membership in Latina/o sororities and fraternities. *Journal of Diversity in Higher Education*, *13*(2), 181–193. https://doi.org/10.1037/dhe0000126 | This qualitative, multiple case study explored the role of involvement in Latina/o sororities and fraternities in how Latina/o college students develop and make meaning of their sense of belonging within predominantly White institutions. Findings address ways Latina/o college students described their institutional sense of belonging in addition to a discussion of five primary characteristics of belonging: where I have a role or responsibility, where people look like me, where I am valued and cared for, where my racial identity and culture is recognized and valued, and where I share interests or values with others. |
| Setting | Carter, D. (2019). *Providing counseling in a rural setting: a new multicultural perspective* [Unpublished doctoral dissertation]. Northern Illinois University. | The author explored the phenomenological experiences of counselors working in rural communities. Benefits and limitations of working in rural environments were identified to recommend policy changes to repair potential deficits and better prepare clinicians to work in rural environments. |
| Process | Swensen, M. S. (2019). *Finding a job: A descriptive qualitative study of challenges of female refugees resettled in the United States* [Unpublished doctoral dissertation]. Grand Canyon University. | The author explored how resettled female refugees (*N*=12) perceive the challenges of seeking employment and securing self-sufficiency in a mountain west region of the United States. Eight themes were identified: education, language, family relationships, environmental changes and acculturation, work-related experiences, gender, connections, and self-sufficiency. |

*(continued)*

**TABLE 5.1**   Case Examples in Qualitative Inquiry   *(Continued)*

| Case type | Study reference | Study description |
|---|---|---|
| Event | Gallagher, R. J., Reagan, A. J., Danforth, C. M., & Dodds, P. S. (2018). Divergent discourse between protests and counter-protests: #BlackLivesMatter and #AllLivesMatter. *PloS One, 13*(4), e0195644. https://doi.org/10.1371/journal.pone.0195644 | Through a multilevel analysis of over 860,000 tweets, the authors studied how protests and counter-protests diverge. They found that #AllLivesMatter facilitates opposition between #BlackLivesMatter and hashtags such as #PoliceLivesMatter and #BlueLivesMatter in such a way that historically echoes the tension between Black protesters and law enforcement. |

The first type, **basic research**, serves to expand the scope and depth of knowledge of a case for the sake of contributing knowledge to a particular discipline. **Applied research** often builds upon collective findings of basic research and seeks specialized knowledge about a specific problem in order to intervene in the problem. For example, basic research endeavors may yield a clearer understanding of etiology of eating disorders, while applied research may use that knowledge as a foundation to study how to treat Black women with disordered eating. The third type, **evaluative research**, refers to assessing the effectiveness of a program or intervention throughout its course. Two common forms of evaluative research, *formative evaluation* and *summative evaluation*, involve the examining practices throughout a program or intervention to improve and shape it and assessing the outcomes at the end of the program or intervention, respectively. Using the disordered eating topic as an example, let's say that a 4-week psychoeducational program was employed in a school of predominately Black students to educate women about the prevalence and potential causes of disordered eating. Some examples of formative evaluations might include interviewing women after each week to explore their knowledge of the topic and administering screening tools to assess for the presence of correlates of eating disorders (e.g., depression, anxiety). Based on these weekly data, program effectiveness would be monitored and changes to the program would be made to address the needs of the students accordingly. A summative evaluation might be administering a posttest to assess knowledge, attitudes, and behaviors related to eating disorder symptoms.

The fourth type of research, **action research**, corresponds to the purpose of solving specific problems and engaging individuals in solving those problems. That is, the researcher focuses on a specific site, collaborates with individuals with a relationship to the topic, and works to resolve key issues to improve the lives of those at the site. As one can surmise, evaluative research could be an important component of action research, specifically if the evaluative methods are specifically geared to a particular site or problem. Table 5.2 highlights key points regarding each of the four research types.

**TABLE 5.2**  Four Purposes of Research

Basic research
- Gain knowledge for the sake of knowing.
- Build theory and test existing theory.
- Publish findings in scholarly journals and books.
- Attend to the rigor of the study (validity, accuracy, and integrity of the results).

Applied research
- Investigate the generalizability of the results.
- Apply knowledge gained to human/societal problems.
- Use knowledge to intervene.
- Share findings with policymakers, educational leaders, directors of human service organizations, and those working with the problem.
- Limit results to a specific time, setting, and condition/problem.

Evaluation research
- Evaluate the effectiveness of solutions and interventions to human/societal problems.
- In formative research, improve a specific program while it is in progress.
- In summative research, investigate the effectiveness of the program after it has been completed.

Action research
- Seek to solve specific community, program, or organizational problems.
- Investigate problems specific to a particular group, setting, and time.
- Focus on fostering change.
- Actively involve participants in research.
- Mirror researcher's social values in the design.

Sources: Haverkamp and Young (2007) and Patton (2014)

Some of the research traditions discussed in Chapter 4 correspond to particular research purposes. For example, if you are interested in action research, a participatory action research or community-based participatory tradition may be congruent for your research goals. Further, a grounded theory tradition may be suitable for basic research, while an ethnography or phenomenology tradition may be appropriate for applied research, and so on. As you decide on a tradition and related paradigms most suited to your research topic, be sure that they are congruent with your research goals, and vice versa.

Something that may be helpful in determining your research purpose may be reflecting on who your audience is, or who will be most impacted by your findings. So, what outcomes are you most interested in for whose benefit? Those who are most affected would be considered your *primary audience* (e.g., students, clients). In basic research the primary audience may be other professionals in your discipline, while in action research the primary audience may be individual clients, students, or teachers, to name a few. As we move along the continuum from theory to action, the primary audience tends to become more specific. If you are interested in theory development, you are more likely interested in a group rather than specific cases, such as in action research.

There may be others who hold interest in your study that need to be considered in selecting a research topic. These who are indirectly affected by specific findings would be considered a *secondary audience* (e.g., prospective students, family members of clients). Secondary audiences vary depending on the purpose of your research and need to be addressed in some manner in all aspects of the research process.

## What Type of Information Is Sought?

Another consideration in conjunction with the purpose of the research is this: What is the depth and scope of your research topic? Are you interested in studying a topic, such as eating disorders, intensely for a specific subpopulation (i.e., *depth*)? Or are you interested in studying the topic at a broader level, such as across various populations (i.e., *scope*)? Obviously, there is a trade-off of resources here. Qualitative researchers have to consider and make decisions about how they want to use their time and financial resources when studying a topic in more detail. The more you intend to study a topic in depth, the less likely you are to cover the scope or breadth of the topic. Therefore, it is important to consider how your interests and resources to complete a research study lean more toward depth or scope and what the limitations of that bias may be for the overall findings.

In this section, we have described three types of research goals along with three considerations when establishing them: What is the case to be investigated, what is the purpose of the inquiry, and what type of information is sought? Proposal Development Activity 5.1 provides an opportunity for you to select a topic for your qualitative research study.

### PROPOSAL DEVELOPMENT ACTIVITY 5.1. TOPIC SELECTION

- Write down 2–3 general research topics that you would be interested in investigating. Reflect upon why these are of interest to you.
- For each general topic, brainstorm subtopics that would be interesting. What do you already know about each subtopic personally and professionally?
- Consider each subtopic and its initial supporting evidence. (Note: You may find that your initial topic may be tweaked as you develop a conceptual framework, discussed below.) What research goals are intended to be addressed for each subtopic? What is the case to be investigated for each subtopic? What is the purpose of each subtopic? What outcomes are you most interested in and for whose benefit?
- Outline the benefits and challenges of each subtopic related to its feasibility. What are the necessary resources and participants needed to study each subtopic?
- Discuss your general research topic and subtopics with your peers.
- Decide on a tentative research topic for your study.

## Conceptual Framework

Once you have determined your research goals and selected a general research topic, the next step is developing a conceptual framework. A conceptual framework is also referred to as a *theoretical framework* or *idea context*. Establishing a detailed conceptual framework will assist you in refining your research topic and moving onto creating a clear purpose statement and sound research questions.

Maxwell (2013) describes a **conceptual framework** as a network of concepts, theories, personal and professional assumptions, exploratory studies, and alternative explanations that collectively inform your research topic. He identifies four major components of a conceptual framework:

- *experiential knowledge:* Experiential knowledge refers to the qualitative researchers' assumptions, expectations, and biases regarding the research topic in general and the interconnections among concepts more specifically. Experiential knowledge is also known as *researcher bias* (Maxwell, 2013; Patton, 2014), *critical subjectivity* (Reason, 1994), and *reflexivity* (Corbin & Strauss, 2015), which was discussed in Chapter 1. Further, Corbin and Strauss (2015) use the term *sensitivity* to refer to "having insight as well as being tuned in to and being able to pick up on relevant issues, events, and happenings during collection and analysis of the data" (p. 78). Sensitivity, then, is the skill of using our insight—informed by previous knowledge and experience—to become more in line with the data and arrive at an understanding of what the data are telling us. Background, knowledge, and experience not only enable us to be more sensitive to concepts in data but also enable us to see connections between concepts. In summary, experiential knowledge may be positive or negative and must be carefully reflected upon in developing and revising a conceptual framework.
- *prior theory and research:* This component typically makes up the preponderance of the conceptual framework and is also referred to as the *literature review*. When there is little theory or research available for a topic, this may be a very minor component of the conceptual framework. The literature review is described more fully in the following major section of this chapter.
- *pilot and exploratory studies:* In preparing a conceptual framework, there may be some concepts derived from pilot and exploratory studies you have conducted on the research topic. The purpose of these types of studies is to develop an understanding of the concepts and theories held by the individuals you are investigating, also referred to as **in vivo codes** (Corbin & Strauss, 2015). Pilot and exploratory (or open-ended) studies are a good idea in developing an accurate picture of the "middle range" theory of your research topic. A *middle range theory* refers to one that is firmly situated in the data rather than a *grand theory* that might purport an interpretation of the data that is universal. These concepts may be added to the initial conceptual framework. You may want to differentiate the concepts in pilot and exploratory studies from those of previous theory and research in your conceptual framework.

- *thought experiments, "waving the red flag," and the "flip-flop" technique:* Corbin and Strauss (2015) discuss using these techniques to develop theoretical sensitivity during grounded theory analysis. However, we believe these three techniques may be used to help you develop your conceptual framework as well. Thought experiments can be considered one of the final processes in developing an initial conceptual framework. After articulating their conceptual frameworks, it is imperative that qualitative researchers rely on research team members and/or colleagues outside the inquiry to critically analyze the developing framework. A *thought experiment* is a process in which others challenge you to consider alternative ways that concepts and assumptions tie together to describe your research topic. It is imperative to think of several possibilities that explain and relate concepts other than the initial conceptual framework or model. "Waving the red flag" refers to the process of identifying researcher biases and assumptions and how these influence interactions with the phenomenon of the research. Using this technique in developing a conceptual framework would translate to identifying how your research assumptions are shaping the framework of your study. Using the "flip-flop technique" as applied to developing a conceptual framework involves comparing opposites or extremes in order to identify salient aspects of the framework that may not be readily apparent.

As you can gather from this description, developing a conceptual framework goes beyond simply conducting a literature review, as doing so may leave invaluable personal and professional resources untouched. Qualitative researchers have several unique personal and professional experiences that provide assumptions and hunches about concepts that may be related to their overall topic. In addition, researchers often work in teams to strengthen the research process, and additional team members provide divergent views on the research topic.

It is important to note that a conceptual framework is tentative and may change throughout the process of data collection and analysis. That is, qualitative inquiry is by its very nature interactive and is influenced by changes in the research questions, access to specific data sources, selection of data collection methods, and views of various research team members and participants. Case Example 5.1 demonstrates a conceptual framework of a study examining factors of academic leadership development (Hays et al., 2021), introduced in Chapter 2 (see Case Example 2.1).

**Case Example 5.1. Conceptual Framework: Academic Leadership Development**

The following outlines important components that created a conceptual framework that led to assessing the following research question using a grounded theory tradition: What factors influence whether counselor educators engage in and sustain academic leadership positions?

### Experiential Knowledge

- The researchers were counselor educators, representing three academic ranks (assistant professor, associate professor, professor).

- The researchers had more than 2 decades of experience in academic leadership roles, including service as a program coordinator, clinic director, department chair, and executive associate dean.
- Some of the researchers' assumptions identified were as follows: (a) academic leadership opportunities are often pursued because it is someone's "turn" to serve; (b) counselor educators are not typically trained effectively or supported as academic leaders; and (c) counselor educators leave academic leadership because they are not able to engage in activities they enjoy as faculty members (e.g., scholarship, teaching).
- This component was continually reflected upon as researchers continuously monitored their expectations and assumptions through regularly scheduled research team meetings over a 22-month period.

## Prior Theory and Research

- This component was comprised of several areas of prior literature:
  - literature available on counseling leadership in practice settings and professional organizations
  - counseling leadership qualities and outcomes
  - availability of academic leadership training in higher education settings
  - attrition of academic leaders in higher education settings
  - benefits and challenges of academic leadership development and engagement
- The researchers noted that there was a lack of scholarship on how academic leadership development is experienced during training as well as in the workplace, what factors relate to entering academic leadership positions, and what outcomes occur for those who serve as academic leaders.

## Pilot and Exploratory Studies

- There were no pilot or exploratory studies conducted for this study. Thus, this component was not included in the conceptual framework.

## Thought Experiments

- The researchers analyzed the data and then met to discuss their independent findings. In these meetings team members presented alternative models to challenge the assumptions of the findings initially identified.
- Throughout this process the researchers identified biases and compared salient components of a theoretical model of academic leadership development.

Source: Hays, D. G., Crockett, S., & Michel, R. (2021). A grounded theory of counselor educators' academic leadership development. *Counselor Education & Supervision, 60*, 51–72. https://doi.org/10.1002/ceas.12196

## Literature Review

A **literature review** is the process of learning what is already known about a topic. It involves gathering, reading, and synthesizing literature on a particular topic (Hempel, 2020). It provides a snapshot of what studies in a general topic area have been found, summarizing key findings and highlighting major limitations or "holes" in the literature most related to your research topic. That is, a review of the literature sets the proposed research in context, frames it within what has already been done, and provides a rationale for the current investigation. There are some qualitative approaches (e.g., grounded theory) where an a priori literature review may not be necessary to conduct in advance of the study.

Wiersma and Jurs (2009) articulated the value of performing a literature review. Specifically, it

- limits and identifies the research problem and expectations of findings;
- informs the researcher about what has been done;
- provides possible research designs and methods;
- suggests possible modifications to avoid unanticipated results;
- identifies research gaps; and
- provides a backdrop for interpreting research results.

One diversion we take from Wiersma and Jurs's opinions is that there may not be a need in qualitative research to "avoid unanticipated results" since qualitative research findings will often offer the researcher unexpected results to integrate with identified themes. We view this as a natural part of qualitative inquiry.

Conducting a literature review also has two other main advantages. First, a sound literature review helps to justify the need for your specific study. Second, it can be a source of data that builds or tests theories related to your topic. Qualitative researchers should be cautious, though, in either relying too much on existing theory without critical analysis of it or not using existing theory enough to inform their topics. For example, Hays and colleagues (2021; see Case Example 5.1) conducted a thorough literature review of available empirical research on academic leadership development. In their review, they carefully analyzed each study's findings and noted methodological limitations in order to identify a theory of factors that influence academic leadership.

Qualitative inquiry poses unique considerations for conducting a literature review. First, due to the nature of qualitative research as exploratory and emphasizing missing voices in the literature, qualitative researchers may find that there are limited studies available on a particular topic. This may be quite different from quantitative approaches where several studies are available and are suited for hypothesis testing and more deductive approaches in general.

Second, there must be great thought given to the depth to which a literature review is to be done prior to conducting a qualitative inquiry. On one hand, conducting a comprehensive literature review allows us to identify more confidently the gaps in research as well as collective limitations of previous research. On the other hand, having this knowledge from a comprehensive literature review creates the risk of confounding the data analysis.

That is, the more we know about what has already been found, the more likely we are to "see" phenomena in a similar manner. We recommend that you begin with some review of previous research and consult the literature on an ongoing basis as you identify themes for your study.

Third, how a literature review is conducted is often influenced by the selected qualitative research tradition. For example, the more a tradition relies on experience and theory formulation (e.g., grounded theory, phenomenology), the less likely previous literature will guide the study. Because these traditions are primarily inductive and refer to generating theory for often unexplored topics, it makes sense that there may be little previous literature to frame the study. For those traditions that rely on symbols, text, or cultural context (e.g., narratology, ethnography), you will likely provide a more thorough literature review to help familiarize the reader with some background of a particular text or culture.

The qualitative research tradition also influences when previous literature is presented in a qualitative report or proposal. In preparing a qualitative report, Creswell and Poth (2017) identified three uses of a literature review. The first use of a literature involves relying on it to establish a rationale for a particular topic. Thus, available literature is presented in the beginning of a report with a primary emphasis on demonstrating why a topic needs to be investigated. The second use of literature is the traditional "review," or use of a separate section of the report to discuss in-depth the various factors or constructs associated with a research topic. This use is common in positivist or postpositivist approaches. The third use refers to presenting the literature at the end of a report to couch present qualitative findings. With this final method, the literature typically does not direct the qualitative inquiry, a characteristic common of more inductive approaches.

Moore and Murphy (2005) cite several questions you should be able to respond to:

- What knowledge does the current research contain, and who are the leading authors, recognized experts, and researchers in this area of study?
- What different definitions, concepts, and issues are relevant to this topic?
- What changes have been made in the subject's research over the past few years?
- What are the different and sometimes conflicting theories in this topic area?
- What are the key points of disagreement in the existing literature?
- What are the unanswered problems in the literature, and what attempts have been made to address them?
- Where is the future research on your topic headed?
- What is your own research's place in the field? (p. 120)

We have presented these questions to stimulate you to think broadly about your literature review—especially because we know that beginning qualitative researchers may or may not have acquired this learning. However, we also want to remind you as the reader that these are initial suggestions and that ultimately one must be flexible in determining the reliance you have on previous literature and the bodies of knowledge you select to review, which we discuss further below.

## Strategies for Conducting a Literature Review

There are two major steps of conducting a literature review: selecting specific pieces of literature to include in the review and the actual writing of the literature review. There are various strategies associated with these two steps, although the following list is not intended to be exhaustive. Perspectives 5.2 and Perspectives 5.3 offer additional strategies for conducting a literature review.

## PERSPECTIVES 5.2. NAVIGATING THE LITERATURE REVIEW PROCESS

Laura Decker, an English professor who instructs on writing literature reviews, offers several strategies on the literature review process. In an interview with me (Danica), she discussed (personal communication, June 24, 2020) her dissertation work (Decker, 2020), a qualitative study that examined identity formation and negotiation among university writing center tutors embedded in classrooms where they shared coteaching space with a faculty member.

- *beginning the literature review*: Decker describes the literature process as recursive and recommends that scholars engage in several rounds of reading previous literature. For each round, scholars might choose a keyword or phrase, search literature, read everything that is available, and annotate and organize that information. After conducting several rounds with different keywords or phrases, she suggests that scholars then begin writing draft sections of the literature review.

  Decker (personal communication, June 24, 2020) cites the importance of including scholarship that both supports and challenges our initial ideas. Likening the process to water running through a river bank, she notes:

  > We want to go find the sources that support what we want to say, but I would caution people to think about what the literature is telling you. Don't try to shape what it says and what it's going to look like until you've read everything you can. ... Disagreement is fine and actually adds to the complexity of your topic. ... Like water running through the river bank ... go where the literature is taking you and don't fight the river stones. You're going to have some bumps and you're going to come to an article that says something totally different or maybe add something. ... Keep it in the riverbed with you. And then when you start to put everything together, there's probably a place for all of that, that's going to help your project be even better.

- *annotating and organizing the literature*: To annotate and organize the literature, Decker highlights the use of a research matrix to capture bibliographic information and other important aspects of each source (e.g., study population, setting, methods). As the matrix is completed, it serves as a cover sheet that is stapled to a physical printout of an article, where she writes at the top of the article the name(s) of the author(s) and the article's main findings. These physical copies and accompanying matrices are helpful for quickly revisiting multiple literature sources.

- *refining the literature review*: Decker cites that seeking support and writing models throughout the writing process is imperative. She notes that reviewing published literature reviews can be helpful to note what works well as a reader and then modelling that in one's own writing. In addition, she suggests joining a writing group and/or seeking input on ideas and drafts is helpful for clarifying writing as well as checking that the evolving literature review is multidimensional and complete.

Decker's professional background as a poet is also helpful for refinement:

> I read all my work aloud repeatedly. I'm always listening for rhythmically what sounds right ... what sounds good, but also where I am being redundant ... where I can put [redundant sentences] together but also being really careful not to lose the meaning [of the studies' findings]. ... When we think about [the literature review] as a story, we're probably more prone to find places where we're being repetitive or where we combine ideas. ... We need a story that's quickly moving (personal communication, June 24, 2020)

Having a thorough literature review process can be validating as a scholar. She notes:

> When I started seeing threads from the literature review show up in my findings, I realized I was on the right track ... that identity negotiation is definitely an important part of moving from the writing center to classroom roles, [that] embedded writing tutors often form unique roles or identities once they were in the classroom and that there was tension between the faculty role and the tutor role ... that power was an important aspect. While I saw these threads coming through for my literature review, I was also able to add knowledge that hadn't been found before. That was really exciting. I am doing something in this conversation but I am also adding to this conversation. (personal communication, June 24, 2020)

- *incorporating the literature review in the report*: Decker (personal communication, June 24, 2020) envisions the literature review as a triangle whereby information is funneled. That is, the base or broad part of the triangle contains the corpus of available works for the study topic, and the point or narrow part of the triangle is more focused and concise:

> For publication, you are having a conversation with scholars in the field ... [starting with] the biggest part of what you are looking at and narrowing it to the most narrow parts. For publication, I would probably only include that really narrow part and maybe a sentence or two that captures the rest of [the broadest part].

Source: Decker, L. (2020). *The noise from the writing boundaries: Collaboration and tutor identity in writing intensive courses* [Unpublished doctoral dissertation]. University of Nevada, Las Vegas.

## PERSPECTIVES 5.3. WRITING THE LITERATURE REVIEW

Writing the literature review, and academic writing in general, is a process unique to each researcher. We offer our writing strategies here as just two examples for you to consider.

Having an organized reference system really helps me look at a snap-shot of each data source related to my research topic. With these snap-shots I collapse the literature into broad themes, setting literature aside that no longer seems relevant to my research topic. Then, I create a detailed outline of how the literature review will funnel into a sound ra-tionale for a study. Once I have this outline, I can set writing goals and deadlines.

I primarily write for a couple of hours per day, usually at the same time each day. My writing goals typically involve working on one section of my outline at a time. After completing an initial draft of my literature review, I create a literature map to assess visually how the literature flows from more broad concepts to a detailed rationale that frames my research questions and research paradigm and tradition. I then compare this litera-ture map with my evolving conceptual framework and integrate the two into a more final draft of the introduction of an article.

—D. G. H.

Once I have identified an area of research, such as resilience and child sexual abuse, I conduct a literature search and identify articles that will be necessary for my literature review. I spend a good amount of time reading each article and summarizing the authors' main points, in addi-tion to my own reactions to the article in terms of what I see as its unique contributions and/or limitations. I then create a literature map of introduc-tion of my study, which becomes a more solid outline for the manuscript. If I am working with a strict page limit, I may even include the number of pages I will allot to each section of my outline in order to keep the manu-script concisely written.

Similarly to Danica, I write regularly at the same time each day. I write best in the late morning, so I try my best to make sure I do not schedule meetings or other appointments during this time period. My mantra for writing is: "If I say 'yes' to this appointment, then I am saying 'no' to my writing!" This helps me set and maintain boundaries around my writing. Now, I look forward to my writing time—especially since I know it is a time, I have all to myself without distractions.

—A. A. S.

First, create a list of keywords for your general research topic. Use this list to help you narrow the scope of what you are researching. Specifically, what areas related to your research topic do you really want to address in the literature review? What are the considerations related to equity and advocacy that are important to you to include in this scholarship review?

Where do you go for information? Your library is an important resource for you in obtaining data sources, either in person or through virtual means. Most libraries provide orientation workshops and written materials describing their services as well as how a researcher could go about locating specific data sources. It is also important to know your library's online resources and how to gain access to them. Familiarize yourself with library databases. Search engines such as EBSCO Host, First Search, ProQuest, and Cambridge provide several electronic research databases with access to abstracts and often full-text articles, books, papers, and monographs. Table 5.3 includes a listing of some of the more common electronic databases used in clinical and education disciplines. This list can assist you in gaining some initial data sources related to your research topic. Also, it is important to expand your search beyond databases specific to your discipline. For example, Google Scholar can help locate resources that may not be indexed in databases. We just caution you *not* to start with Google Scholar: You will miss out on some very important and foundational studies that may not be included in a simple internet search.

Individuals in your discipline are also an invaluable resource for locating data sources. Make time to speak with your peers, colleagues, professors and others you trust to guide you to pertinent literature. As you are locating literature, they may also be helpful in guiding you in gathering data that may be most relevant to your research topic. Requesting references for books, papers, and articles within the past 5–7 years—as well as original, foundational works—will be most beneficial.

The internet can be an important resource, although you should use it with caution. Because there is a vast amount of information available, often from noncredible websites, you should carefully review the legitimacy of any online document and seek outside opinions. Your librarian, professor, or colleague can provide you with lists of important and credible websites related to your research topic. Some internet sources that we recommend, depending on your research topic, are listed in Table 5.4.

There may be useful data sources that do not immediately come to mind for you. For example, it may be helpful to begin with secondary sources when you are less familiar with a general topic. Examples of secondary sources include textbooks and encyclopedias. Secondary sources are invaluable for citing foundational articles or works, primary sources. Another data source is dissertations and theses. Graduate students write countless dissertations and theses to fulfill degree requirements yet may not publish these manuscripts in journals or other sources.

Organization is key as you collect pertinent literature. First, summarize individual empirical and conceptual works that relate to your topic in a detailed and organized manner. Then, develop an organized system for capturing the important information about each data source. This creates a reference system that can be used in the future to expand upon and refine your conceptual framework. It is natural to be overwhelmed a bit when you first dive into the

**TABLE 5.3**  Electronic Databases

| Academic Search Complete | 1887–present: Multidisciplinary database with selected full-text articles for approximately 1,000 journals |
|---|---|
| Dissertation Abstracts | 1861–present: Author, title, and subject guide information for most U.S. dissertations. Some information about theses since 1962 is available. |
| Dissertations and Theses | 1861–present: Comprehensive database for dissertations and theses with selected full-text sources |
| Education Research Complete | 1984–present: References for all levels of education and all educational specialties. Selected full-text sources are provided for over 900 journals and 100 books, monographs, and conference papers. |
| Education: A Sage Full-Text Collection | 1982–present: Although coverage varies by journal, it contains over 5000 articles in education, assessment, counseling, and school counseling published in SAGE journals. |
| ERIC | 1966–present: Internet-based digital library of educational research by the Institute of Education Sciences |
| Medline | 1965–present: Provides medical information for various health care disciplines. The database was created by the National Library of Medicine. |
| Mental Measurements Yearbook | 1985–present: Reviews English-language assessments covering educational skills, personality, career, psychology, and other-related areas |
| Psycarticles | 1894–present: Contains full-text articles from the American Psychological Association journals |
| Psychology: A Sage Full-Text Collection | 1982–present: Psychology-related articles from approximately 30 journals published by Sage publications |
| Psychology and Behavioral Sciences Collection | 1965–present: Selected full-text articles covering topics such as psychiatry and psychology, mental processes, anthropology, emotional and behavioral characteristics, and observational and experimental methods |
| PsycINFO | 1887–present: Selected full-text articles from psychology and other related disciplines |
| Social Sciences Citation Index | 1956–present: Indexes journals across and specific articles across social science disciplines |
| Social Services Abstracts | 1979–present: Provides abstracts of research in social work, human services, and related areas |
| Tests in Print | Current: Contains test information for commercially available tests in the English language |

**TABLE 5.4**   Internet Sources

| | |
|---|---|
| American Counseling Association | https://counseling.org |
| American Educational Research Association | https://aera.org |
| American Psychological Association | https://apa.org |
| American Sociological Association | https://asa.org |
| Bureau of Labor Statistics | https://bls.gov |
| Centers for Disease Control | https://cdc.gov |
| FedStats | https://fedstats.gov |
| Library of Congress | https://loc.gov |
| National Association of Social Workers | https://nasw.org |
| National Institutes of Health | https://nih.gov |
| Substance Abuse and Mental Health Services Administration | https://samhsa.gov |
| U.S. Bureau of the Census | https://census.gov |
| U.S. Department of Education | https://doe.gov |
| U.S. Department of Justice | https://usdoj.gov |

literature base. Your organization system can help you manage that anxiety and stay focused on the very next step: reading pertinent literature related to your topic.

For each data source that you include, be sure to write down a complete reference in addition to specific notes and significance of the study. This includes the title of the data source, author(s) name(s), publisher and publication date, page numbers, and journal title and volume and issue numbers if applicable. Software programs such as EndNote, RefManage and Refworks may be helpful in creating an electronic reference system. Table 5.5 provides an example of a reference system for a study exploring young women's intimate partner violence (IPV) victimization and disclosure process.

After you collect several data sources, Creswell and Poth (2017) recommend constructing a literature map. A **literature map** is a display (e.g., figure, table, flow chart, etc.) that visually organizes themes of prior literature. The primary purposes of the literature map are to help you remain organized and give you new ideas about the literature itself or future research directions. This graphic may be considered a variation of the concept map, discussed below. There are three proposed models for literature maps. The first model, a hierarchical structure, funnels prior literature from most general to most specific with a primary goal of a top-down presentation ending with a specific rationale and proposed study. Figure 5.2 presents an example of a hierarchical literature map of the study discussed in Table 5.5. The second model, a flow chart, might present prior literature along a timeline with more recent studies toward the right side of the chart. The third model, like a Venn diagram, displays areas of research

**TABLE 5.5**   Reference System for an Empirical Article

| | |
|---|---|
| Type of data source: | Empirical article (grounded theory) |
| Keywords: | Adolescents, dating violence, rape, life course theory, community college, help-seeking |
| Rationale: | To explore IPV victimization (physical, coercive control, and sexual) during young women's abusive relationships with their first partners, and the factors that shape their process of disclosure. |
| Method: | Derived from a larger mixed methods study of 148 young women ages 18–24 from a university, two-year college, and community sites, the authors conducted semistructured interviews with 21 participants who reported IPV experiences during their relationship with their first partner ($M$ age = 20.67, $SD$ = 2.15). Grounded theory analysis was conducted (i.e., open, axial, and selective coding) using constant comparison until saturation was achieved. |
| Results: | The authors identified four theoretical patterns in the data: factors that shaped the unfolding of IPV within these relationships (e.g., quasi-parent-child dynamics between participant and perpetrator) and the impact on disclosure, instances of severe IPV accompanied with minimization of abuse and no or limited disclosure, factors that distinguished participants who sought help, and the role of stigmatization in concert with situational factors in shaping disclosure. |
| Implications: | Early IPV experiences reveal disclosure as a complex process. Participants' social location, youth, prior victimization, family characteristics, and homelessness played critical roles in victimization and the disclosure process. Prevention programs should begin early and focus on family violence, gender norms, and sexual IPV. Practitioners working with young women should be educated about all types of IPV and actively support disclosure and problem-solving. |

Source: Kennedy, A. C., Meier, E., & Prock, K. A. (2021). A qualitative study of young women's abusive first relationships: What factors shape their process of disclosure? *Journal of Family Violence*, 36, 849–864. https://doi.org/10.1007/s10896-021-00258-5

represented by distinct circles. The circles might intersect, indicating future research directions. Figure 5.3 presents an example of this third model, using qualitative data from a study with First Nations people in Canada and their experiences with training in mental health first aid (Delaney et al., 2021).

In addition to the strategies for conducting the literature review, there are several general strategies associated with the actual writing of it. No matter what type of data sources you use when conducting a literature review, it is important to avoid plagiarism as well as limit the use of direct quotes. The *Publication Manual of the American Psychological Association* (APA, 2020) warns about these two issues explicitly. To balance these two strategies, consider if you can rephrase the article or book content in a unique way. If you are unable to paraphrase the content, be sure to limit the word count of direct quotes.

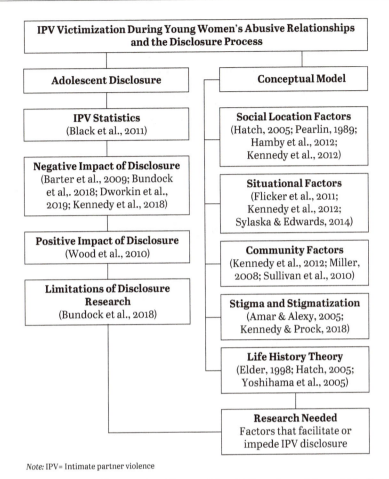

*Note:* IPV= Intimate partner violence

**FIGURE 5.2** Literature Map Example: Hierarchical Literature Map. This literature map depicts prior scholarship that informed Kennedy et al. (2021), a grounded theory that explored young women's abusive first relationships and their disclosure process.

## Concept Maps

Concept maps may be quite useful in displaying the components of a conceptual framework graphically. A **concept map** is a visual display of an evolving theory or at least assumptions about an area of inquiry. The idea is that they shape how you collect data and change as you analyze data. Concept maps are used in qualitative research because they are useful in displaying a large amount of information in a simpler way; they may be presented linearly or systemically. Researchers typically design concept maps to be read top-down. Qualitative researchers will often develop maps with different colors to differentiate among conceptual framework components.

In general, concept maps may be categorized as variance or process maps (Maxwell, 2013). *Variance maps* depict causal links or relationships between particular constructs or variables. *Process maps* are context specific and tell a story about specific events or situations rather

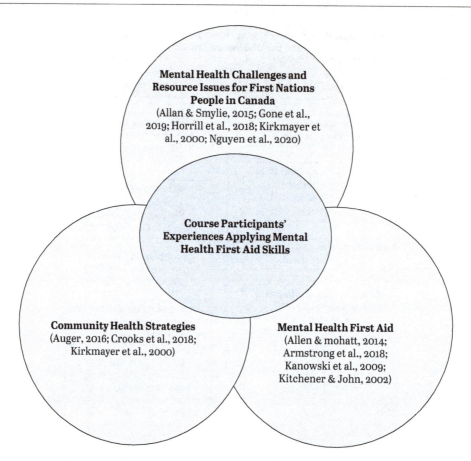

**FIGURE 5.3** Literature Map Example: Venn Diagram. This literature map is a Venn diagram of Delaney et al.'s (2021) qualitative follow-up on the mental health first aid training experiences of First Nations people in Canada. The research topic is in the center of the diagram.

than variables. In many cases the most important component of concept maps is the use and direction of arrows in a map. Arrows are typically used to connect nodes (or circles) to describe a process or sequence of a research topic.

Maxwell (2013) and Miles et al. (2020) described concept maps as representing any of the following: (a) an abstract framework; (b) a flowchart of events; (c) causal network of variables; (d) a treelike diagram; or (e) a Venn diagram presenting concepts as overlapping circles. An *abstract framework* is a graph that presents the relationship between concepts. Figure 5.4 presents an example of an abstract framework of the common components of assessment tools measuring IPV (see Hays & Emelianchik, 2009, for more information on this qualitative study).

A flowchart may be helpful to show sequence of events or processes in education and clinical settings. Figure 5.5 demonstrates a flowchart of how the contents of this textbook are presented.

**FIGURE 5.4**   Abstract Framework: Assessment Tools Measuring Intimate Partner Violence

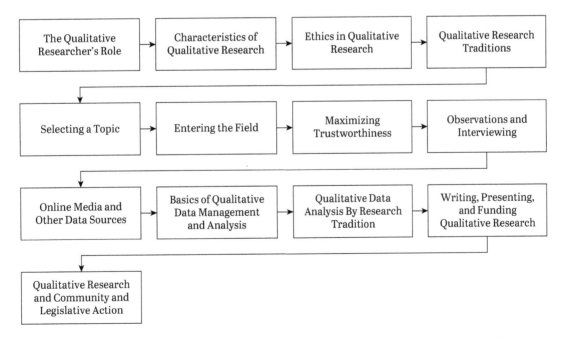

**FIGURE 5.5**   Flowchart: *Qualitative Research in Education and Social Sciences* Contents

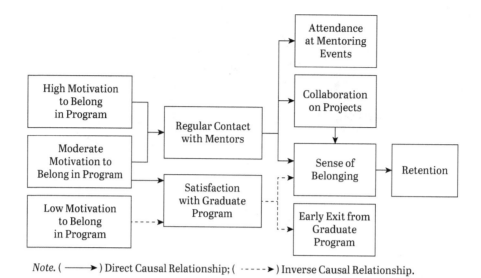

*Note.* ( ———▶ ) Direct Causal Relationship; ( ----▶ ) Inverse Causal Relationship.

**FIGURE 5.6**   Causal Network: Graduate Student Mentoring Program

Concept maps may also represent causal networks, or links among variables and influences. Figure 5.6 presents an example of a causal network of the program development and evaluation of a mentoring program for graduate students in education disciplines.

A tree diagram has a vertical display of nodes starting with a broad concept at the end with "branches" representing subconcepts. Figure 5.7 provides an example of a tree diagram. Additionally, the literature map in Figure 5.2 provides a variation of a tree diagram.

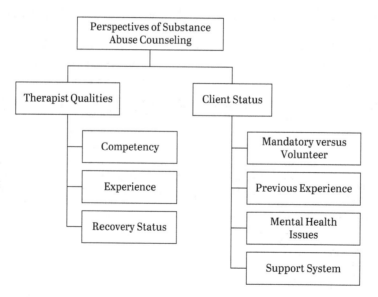

**FIGURE 5.7**   Tree Diagram of Factors Influencing
Substance Abuse Counseling Perspectives

Researchers create the final type of concept map, a Venn diagram, by using overlapping nodes or circles. The degree of overlap among the circles indicates the relative strength of the relationship among the concepts. Figure 5.3 presents an example of a Venn diagram.

Concepts maps have several advantages. First, they can structure your literature review such as in the case of literature maps described in the previous section. Second, they can help you make decisions about other aspects of your research design. That is, examining what existing literature along with previous literature and any exploratory studies have done in the way of research design can help you select data collection sources (e.g., interviews, documents) as well as assist with what type of sampling method and how many informants would be useful for your study. It can also provide some information about previous studies' limitations and validity issues, helping you make better decisions about your design. Third, concept maps help you visually see any assumptions you may have about the research topic in general. By including your experiential knowledge as a component of the conceptual framework and thus the concept map, you can see the proportion of your "theory" regarding a topic that is based on experience only and thus needs empirical support.

Finally, concept maps are very useful for depicting an emerging theory as data are collected. Many qualitative researchers will develop an initial concept map and further revise it as they collect more literature and gather more data. You may find that it is helpful to construct a concept map before data collection and analysis begins, develop independent concept maps based on independent informant perspectives, and then integrate informant perspectives and

**PROPOSAL DEVELOPMENT ACTIVITY 5.2.** DEVELOPING AN INITIAL CONCEPT MAP

This exercise has been adapted from Maxwell (2013).

- Write your preliminary research topic on a blank sheet of paper.
- What are the keywords related to this topic? This list of keywords may come from the literature, personal experiences, professional experiences, or all of these.
- For each keyword, brainstorm all the things that might be related to it. You may want to place an asterisk next to terms that are derived from experiences but perhaps not yet researched.
- Review your list of keywords and related terms. Are any of the terms overlapping and perhaps could be collapsed into one new term? What are some connections you see between the key words? What are some concrete examples of these connections?
- Draw a concept map, using different colors to represent which knowledge is from experiential knowledge.
- Examine how nodes (circles) are connected, such as the types of arrows that connect them.
- Have your peers review your initial concept map and challenge your connections (i.e., thought experiments).

the initial conceptual framework as one concept map. This final map would indicate a more defined theory related to your research topic.

## Purpose Statement

Once your research topic has been refined, it is time to develop a purpose statement for your qualitative inquiry. The intention of a **purpose statement** is to anchor the proposal or study; it is where the conceptual framework and research design meet. Creswell and Creswell (2017) note the purpose statement establishes the objectives, the intent, and the major idea of a proposal or a study. This idea is generated from the conceptual framework and is refined into specific research questions. Sometimes, beginning researchers confuse the purpose of research and research questions. A well-constructed purpose statement should situate your interest in the topic or phenomenon, whereas your research questions situate the actions you will take regarding your research purpose. Hopefully you can see that although your research purpose and research questions are separate concepts, both should complement and inform one another.

Although purpose statements vary in the literature, there are some common components and guidelines that frame them (see Creswell & Creswell, 2017). First, purpose statements are best displayed in a separate paragraph after the conceptual framework has been presented. Second, provide as much information about the selected research paradigms and traditions as possible. This will allow readers to better understand the values and assumptions you as the researcher relied upon to structure the research topic and overall research design. Some examples in which the terminology of the purpose statement corresponds to the research tradition are (a) to explore underlying processes (grounded theory); (b) to describe the lived experiences (phenomenology); (c) to uncover the plots within stories (narratology); (d) to describe beliefs, values, and practices of a group (ethnography); or (e) to learn about advocacy needs to empower participants. If you are using a mixed methods approach (discussed later in this chapter), be sure to identify if the design is sequential, concurrent, or transformative.

Third, focus on one phenomenon in your statement and keep the statement open, without suggestion of a particular outcome. For example, the following purpose statement would be neutral: "The purpose of this case study is to explore the expectations of third-grade mathematics teachers for students." Finally, operationalize words in the purpose statement based on those definitions derived from the literature. In the previous sentence, the concepts "expectations," "third-grade mathematic teachers," and "students" need to be operationalized. Case Example 5.2 provides an example of a former student's purpose statement and serves as a reminder that you should keep in mind the context in which purpose statements are written. For instance, if you were writing a qualitative research purpose statement for a grant committee, you would not use words such as "ontologically" or "epistemologically" as are used in the Case Example 5.2. Proposal Development Activity 5.3 provides an opportunity to practice developing a purpose statement for your study.

| Case Example 5.2.  Purpose Statement Example |

Review the following purpose statement:

The research will aim to develop understanding of the psychological factors, environmental factors, and relative differences of American and British culture that significantly influence expatriates' acculturation strategies. The study will employ a phenomenological research tradition to identify the essence of the lived experience of the phenomenon of acculturation by examining individual and collective meanings (Patton, 2014). The paradigm for the research will be social constructivism. Ontologically, it is assumed that culture exists only as an individually perceived phenomenon and therefore there is no objective reality or "truth" of acculturation and perception of American culture by participants. Epistemologically, it is assumed that the uniformly known meaning "out there" of one particular culture is socially constructed; therefore, the study's method of gaining knowledge will be through an iterative construction of meaning and experience by participant–researcher interaction.

The understanding and experience of acculturation is an extremely personal and reflexive phenomenon. As the axiology of social constructivism states that researcher values cannot be excluded and should not be excluded, sharing of participant and researcher values will be emphasized, for the purposes of developing a shared understanding. In this sense, the researcher will also be considered a participant. A primary reason for the appropriateness of the social constructivist paradigm is the assumption that the participants—including the researcher—will have a limited understanding of their own experiences with respect to the research questions. A key assumption underlying the social constructivist paradigm when it is employed in phenomenological research is that the participant cannot fully understand their individual lived experiences without engaging first in a dialogue about the experience.

Reflect on the following:

- What do you notice about this purpose statement?
- How does the student attend to research paradigms and traditions?
- To what degree is the purpose statement neutral?
- To what degree are the key terms defined in the statement?
- How would you approach this purpose statement differently?

## Research Questions

The research question acts as a compass for the research process (Neri de Souza et al., 2016). Thus, it connects the conceptual framework and theoretical orientation (i.e., research tradition and paradigm) to the methodology and the way findings are presented. In the qualitative proposal or study, a research question or research questions are located close to the purpose statement. Building on a purpose statement, qualitative researchers can specify a research question or questions at the outset of the study. According to Maxwell (2013), your research questions should consider your research goals, research paradigms and traditions, and the conceptual framework.

**PROPOSAL DEVELOPMENT ACTIVITY 5.3.** WRITING A PURPOSE STATEMENT

In 1–2 paragraphs, develop a purpose statement for your refined research topic. Attend to the following components:

- discussion of research paradigm(s) and related philosophical influences (i.e., ontology, epistemology, axiology, rhetoric, methodology)
- description of research tradition
- degree of neutrality
- operationalization of key terms
- attention to a single phenomenon

Review your purpose statement with a peer.

The interactive nature of qualitative research (Maxwell, 2013) means that data collection and analysis are iterative processes that happen simultaneously as the research progresses. This may require qualitative researchers to focus and specify their research questions as they sharpen their lenses (Korstjens & Moser, 2017). Because qualitative research is a nonlinear and emerging process—and data collection and analysis occur simultaneously—findings may suggest that the original research question be modified. Thus, qualitative research questions need to be designed to strike a balance between being refined enough to delimit the study and general enough to allow for an emerging design that is open to change as data are collected and analyzed.

Qualitative research questions differ from quantitative research questions. Quantitative research questions tend to be very specific in nature, are developed a priori to the quantitative research study, and tend to be deductive in nature. Qualitative research questions do not typically relate variables of compare groups, avoiding the use of words such as "influence," "effect," and "compare." Although comparative research questions could be specified before the qualitative inquiry begins, these questions usually emerge at some point during the study.

Readers are cautioned not to confuse research questions with interview questions: There may be a couple of broad research questions that help to frame the research design, while there are several questions tied to qualitative interviewing that serve to collect pertinent data to the research questions. Developing interview questions is discussed in Chapter 8.

## Developing Research Questions

One way to structure research questions is to have an overarching question followed by subquestions that are directly linked to specific components of the overarching question (Kross & Giust, 2018). Furthermore, questions tend to be broad and have an open-ended format to address questions typically with "what," "how," and "why." Researchers using qualitative research questions seek to discover, explore a process, or describe experiences. That is, they typically attempt to obtain insights into processes that exist within a specific context. It is important to have questions broad enough initially to allow in-depth description, exploration, or explanation of a phenomenon of interest. That is, they should be open enough to explore specific experiences, events, processes, or other concepts associated with the phenomenon. The broad nature of research questions should be flexible (i.e., without a preconceived answer) yet well-defined, measurable. Furthermore, research questions should also be relevant to the field of knowledge and ethical.

Qualitative researchers need to consider three broad areas when developing sound research questions: content, coherence, and structure. Wild Card 5.1 presents some cautions when writing research questions as these areas are considered. The first area, *content*, refers to the specific interest area of the research topic presented in a clear and concise manner. Related to the content component of research questions, qualitative research questions should be framed by the research goal components: case, research purpose, and type of information sought. Thus, information related to these components should be included either implicitly

## WILD CARD 5.1. PITFALLS IN DEVELOPING RESEARCH QUESTIONS

There are several pitfalls when writing research questions, and this list is not exhaustive by any means. Attention to pitfalls will minimize your risk of later realizing that your question is neither answerable nor feasible.

- Do not be concerned with the magnitude of effect of a construct. Research questions that include terms such as "best," "worst," or "most" should be avoided.
- Defined variables are not included in the question, only the intent to describe the variables during the inquiry. This may be intuitive since one of the key purposes of qualitative research is to explore an understudied phenomenon or construct.
- Although variables are not defined in the research question, a variable introduced in the research question should have been discussed to some degree in the literature review and rationale for the study. Thus, readers should not be surprised by a construct when they get to the research question section of a proposal or article.
- Avoid positivist terms in your research questions, such as "significant," "test," "universal," "predict," or "hypothesize." Consider using these nonpositive terms: "interpret," "explore," "construct," "describe," "view," or "perspective," to name a few.
- Do not be afraid to refine your research questions if your research design needs to be changed due to access or data collection issues.
- Debate sufficiently the merits of whether to review the literature before developing research questions or identify the research question after research is underway in order to potentially minimize researcher bias and/or give participants increased voice in the inquiry.

or explicitly in the research questions. With respect to a case, an individual, process, setting, or event should be mentioned in the research question(s). Some examples include:

- How do first-generation Filipino Americans experience government programs (individual)?
- What are the pedagogical practices of history teachers (process)?
- What are the benefits of an after-school program at Newbury Middle School (setting)?
- How did state budget cuts in 2009 impact educational planning (event)?

*Coherence*, the second area, involves clearly bringing together the philosophical and theoretical assumptions that underlie the study. Therefore, a good research question reflects the underlying research paradigm(s) and tradition(s) (Singh & Lukkarila, 2017). The next section provides examples of coherence, as research questions are congruent with their associated research traditions. Finally, *structure* refers to the notion that a research question contains sufficient information about the study topic, participants, context, time, and the way the study is conducted (Mantzoukas, 2008). That is, the structure of the research question should address the who, what, when, where, how, and why of the study. Qualitative researchers should also integrate the research purpose into their selected research questions. This involves shaping the research questions so that readers can ascertain the degree to which knowledge obtained from the study will be applied to a specific context (i.e., basic, applied, evaluative, or action research). Additionally, research questions should be framed in a manner that readers can determine who the primary audience is.

We offer two additional considerations for developing research questions in addition to these three board areas. First, qualitative researchers are to attend to the depth and scope when developing research questions. That is, how specific should attention to the case be? How broad should the research purpose be? Second, the four components of the qualitative researcher's role (i.e., equity and advocacy, participant voice, researcher reflexivity, researcher subjectivity; see Chapter 1) influence the selection of the research question or questions. In addition to providing space in the research design to allow for thick description and flexibility, qualitative researchers are to carefully consider each of these components of their role (see Proposal Development Activity 5.4).

## Research Questions and Research Tradition Clusters

Research questions need to be congruent with the selected research tradition, and vice versa. The following are sample research questions organized by cluster to help you design a research question in consideration of a selected research tradition or traditions.

### Cluster 1: The Hybrid Tradition

- case study: How did elementary school counselors respond before and after a school hostage incident?

### Cluster 2: Experience and Theory Formulation

- grounded theory: How does instructional leadership for special education occur in elementary schools?

## PROPOSAL DEVELOPMENT ACTIVITY 5.4. DEVELOPING YOUR RESEARCH QUESTIONS

Refer to your purpose statement and develop an initial draft of your research question(s). Use the following checklist as discussion points to determine if each of your research questions is suitable for your purpose.

- I have available necessary resources to address the research question(s) adequately (e.g., personal, equipment, supplies, travel).
- I have an adequate timeline for data collection and analysis.
- I can articulate needed participant resources.
- The research question(s) are interesting.
- The study is feasible given the depth, scope, and time frame associated with the research question(s).
- The research question(s) is/are worth pursuing.
- I have framed the research question(s) to allow for participant voice in the findings.
- I am considering various participants' and stakeholders' perspectives to maximize equity and advocacy.
- My question attends to content, coherence, and structure considerations.
- I have received input on my research question(s) to carefully consider researcher reflexivity and subjectivity.

- phenomenology: How do recent immigrants experience loss associated with acculturation?
- heuristic inquiry: What is the effect of conducting reflexive research on the development of the researcher?
- consensual qualitative research: What themes are present in college students' descriptions of their career decision making.

## Cluster 3: The Meaning of Symbol and Text
- life history: How do aspiring teachers relate to literacy and to older forms of technology once used for reading and writing?
- narratology: How is loss communicated in the plot and structure of 20th-century children's books?

## Cluster 4: Cultural Expressions of Process and Experience
- ethnography: How effective is a drop-in program for women experiencing homelessness in San Francisco's mission district?
- ethnomethodology: To what extent is death anxiety expressed differently across cultures?
- autoethnography: How do researchers experience work-life balance as assistant professors in high-research universities?

## Cluster 5: Research as a Change Agent

- participatory action research: What are the experiences of three undergraduate students who engaged in a project with a group of preadolescent Latina girls attending a public school in Boston?
- community-based participatory research: How can university-business partnerships support an after-school program serving refugees and immigrants?

**ACTIVITY 5.1.** MOVING FROM "FLAWED" TO "BETTER" RESEARCH QUESTIONS

A "bad" research question leads to a poor qualitative design. Before developing your research questions, consider the following bad research questions. After noting the limitations of each question, discuss how they be revised to "good" research questions. Also, articulate how each research question could be rephrased to fit within each research tradition cluster.

1. What is the most effective method for implementing preservice learning?
2. How can teachers strategize to improve children's social interactions?
3. How do people with substance addictions experience substance abuse treatment?
4. What are the latest interventions used with people with schizophrenia?
5. In what ways has technology harmed instruction?

## Is a Mixed Methods Approach Suitable?

A **mixed methods** approach is an important consideration when determining if your research question is "answerable." Typically, mixed methods approaches involve "mixing" qualitative and quantitative methods in one study (or among several studies) to best address a research question or questions. Using a mixed methods approach can enhance the trustworthiness of a study through increasing the integrity of findings and contextualizing findings while enhancing their transferability or generalizability.

As a researcher, if you decide to mix qualitative and quantitative methods, it is important that you have some conceptual knowledge of statistics and quantitative data analysis—even if this means hiring or consulting with a quantitative statistical expert to bolster your knowledge. Mixed method approaches also refer to pure qualitative designs, where the mixed methods that are used in research combine, for example, discourse analysis, interviewing, and direct participant observation. In this section, we will focus on the mixing of qualitative and quantitative methods.

Green et al. (1989) highlighted five purposes of mixing in mixed methods research:

- *triangulation:* convergence and corroboration of results from different methods
- *complementarity:* elaboration, enhancement, and clarification of the results from one method with the results of another method
- *development:* use of results from one method to help develop or inform those of another method, with development construed to include sampling, interpretation, and measurement decisions
- *initiation:* discovery of paradox and contradiction, new perspectives of frameworks, and the recasting of questions or results from one method to those of another method
- *expansion:* extension of the breadth or range of inquiry by using different methods for different inquiry components (p. 259)

Because research questions drive methods, a mixed methods approach may be more suitable for several reasons. First, this approach can offset some of the limitations of qualitative and quantitative methods. This allows expansion of the findings with a more comprehensive picture. Second, it may triangulate data from one method to another. Finally, this approach may confirm findings from a qualitative or quantitative investigation. Case Example 5.3 highlights an example of a mixed methods approach.

**Case Example 5.3. Sequential Explanatory Design: Changes in Music Use and Psychological Distress**

McFerran et al. (2018) employed a sequential explanatory design to determine whether participants involved in a brief music-based intervention reported decreased levels of distress and increased insight into music uses. A mixed methods approach was adopted, merging scores of distress and self-reported experience of the intervention to foster interpretation. Specifically, the following steps were taken:

1. Participants were recruited from three primary mental health service centers. Those who scored moderate to high on a psychological stress inventory at intake and who indicated an interest in music were eligible for the study.
2. The participants ($N = 23$) then engaged in two individual music therapy sessions with a trained and registered music therapist.
3. At the beginning of the first session and at the conclusion of the second session, 13 of the 23 participants completed a quantitative screening tool for anxiety and depression as well as a tool evaluating the intervention. Throughout the session, the music therapist asked prompts related to the session to promote participants' understanding of the relationship between music-use strategies and health outcomes. The music therapist then shared with each participant what they perceived to be some of the central ways in which the participant was using music and how these might relate to their mental health.

4.  The music therapist conducted a qualitative interview either at the conclusion of the second session or via a telephone interview with 12 participants. The interview protocol focused on participants' perception of their music use in relation to their mental health as well as how they experienced the intervention.
5.  The authors identified three themes: a sense of personal agency, changes in uses of music after sessions, and recommendations from young people.

Source: McFerran, K. S., Hense, C., Koike, A., & Rickwood, D. (2018). Intentional music use to reduce psychological distress in adolescents accessing primary mental health care. *Clinical Child Psychology and Psychiatry, 23*(4), 567–581. https://doi.org/10.1177/1359104518767231

Thoroughly defining and outlining various mixed methods approaches is beyond the scope of this text. However, the reader is encouraged to review some of the recommended readings at the end of the chapter.

There are several ways to determine how a mixed methods approach can be implemented depending on how and when each individual method takes precedence in a research design. Creswell and Plano Clark (2017) highlight four interdependent decisions that go into selecting a particular mixed methods strategy (see Figure 5.8).

First, researchers must decide on when each method is introduced into the research design, or the *implementation* procedure. Will you gather quantitative and qualitative data at the same time (concurrent) or at different phases of a research project (sequential)? In *concurrent designs,* qualitative and quantitative data collection processes are implemented at the same time. In *sequential designs,* researchers can collect either quantitative or qualitative data first depending on the research purpose and question(s). Researchers might collect qualitative data first to explore a topic from a small group's perspective and then survey a larger, more representative sample. When researchers employ qualitative strategies first, the design is referred to as an *exploratory design.* When they introduce a study with quantitative measures, the design is referred to as an *explanatory design.* Creswell and Plano Clark (2017) identified six mixed method strategies based on when qualitative and quantitative data are introduced in a research design (see Table 5.6).

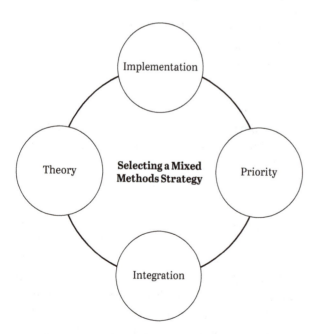

**FIGURE 5.8**  Factors in Selecting a Mixed Methods Approach

**TABLE 5.6** Mixed Methods Strategies

| Strategy | Description |
|---|---|
| **Sequential exploratory** | Qualitative data collection and analysis followed by quantitative data collection and analysis to explore an emerging phenomenon with a larger sample |
| **Sequential explanatory** | Quantitative data collection and analysis followed by qualitative data collection and analysis to interpret more thoroughly broader findings |
| **Sequential transformative** | Quantitative and qualitative data collection and analysis may occur first in a design, depending heavily on a guiding theoretical perspective and/or available resources to conduct the study. |
| **Concurrent triangulation** | The most common strategy whereby both methods are used simultaneously to confirm or converge findings in a single study |
| **Concurrent nested** | A similar strategy to the concurrent triangulation strategy, except that the less dominant method is nested within a more dominant method |
| **Concurrent transformative** | Simultaneous qualitative and quantitative data collection depending heavily on a guiding theoretical perspective and/or available resources to conduct the study; data collection may be triangulated or nested. |

A second decision when selecting a mixed methods strategy is how much priority each method has in a research design. One assumption is that the method that is more prioritized by the researcher carries more weight in a design and is thus introduced first and used more often. In concurrent designs, both methods tend to receive equal priority. In sequential designs, the method introduced first in the design tends to be more highly valued.

A third decision involves when each method will be integrated within a study. In concurrent studies, quantitative and qualitative data are integrated after a single data collection phase. In sequential studies, researchers may analyze data from each method independently (the order depends on whether it is an exploratory or explanatory design). Then findings from each method are integrated for a broader interpretation.

A final decision involves the theoretical perspective used in the mixed methods study. There are various ways that theories can guide research design. Depending on the degree to which theory guides a mixed method design (whether it is implicit or explicit in a study), a researcher may select a particular strategy over another. For example, if a researcher takes an advocacy stance regarding a research topic, emphasizing participant empowerment and highlighting missing voices or perspectives, they may make a theory more explicit in a design as well as prioritize qualitative approaches.

**ACTIVITY 5.2.** DISSECTING THE MIXED METHODS STRATEGIES

Review the six mixed methods strategies in Table 5.6 in small groups. How does each strategy relate to the four decisions proposed by Creswell and Plano Clark (2017)? Identify potential advantages and disadvantages of each. Brainstorm research examples of each.

## CHAPTER SUMMARY

This chapter reviewed the five major considerations or components of selecting a topic in qualitative research. Chapter 4 presented 12 qualitative research traditions that could also shape topic selection, although decisions about traditions should not be made in isolation. The considerations for selecting a topic include (a) establishing research goals, (b) developing a conceptual framework, (c) writing a purpose statement, (d) determining a research question or questions, and (e) deciding if a mixed methods approach is more suitable. While the components discussed in this chapter influence each other, they are presented separately to highlight some of the key aspects of each.

The first consideration, establishing research goals, refers to examining the unit of analysis of a case of interest. In addition, researchers need to consider the overall purpose of their research (i.e., basic, applied, evaluative, action) as well as the type of information sought (depth versus scope) and by whom (primary and secondary audiences). The second consideration, developing a conceptual framework, involves four components: experiential knowledge, prior theory and research (i.e., literature review), pilot and exploratory studies, and thought experiments. Guidelines for conducting a thorough literature review were discussed as well as the various types of concept maps.

The third and fourth considerations, writing a purpose statement and determining a research question or research questions, tend to form as a general research topic become more refined. The chapter offers suggestions and cautionary statements for writing both. Finally, since a research topic may be addressed by multiple research designs and can include quantitative features, mixed method strategies were discussed in this chapter.

## Review Questions

1. What are the scholarly and practical research goals that may be considered when selecting a topic? Remembering the researcher-practitioner-advocate (RPA) model, how might equity and advocacy influence your topic selection related to social change aims?

2. Using a hypothetical research topic, how would each of the four purposes of research discussed in this chapter be approached for that topic?

3. What are the four components of a conceptual framework discussed in this chapter, and what are the considerations for integrating each within a study?
4. What are key strategies outlined for conducting a quality literature review?
5. How do research questions and purpose statements relate to one another?
6. What are some considerations for conducting a mixed methods approach?

## Recommended Readings

Creswell, J. W., & Creswell, J. D. (2017). *Research design: Qualitative, quantitative, and mixed methods approaches* (4th ed.). Sage.

Creswell, J. W., & Plano Clark, V. L. (2017). *Designing and conducting mixed methods research* (3rd ed.). Sage.

Haverkamp, B. E., & Young, R. A. (2007). Paradigms, purpose, and the role of the literature: Formulating a rationale for qualitative investigations. *The Counseling Psychologist, 35,* 265–294.

Wiersma, W., & Jurs, S. G. (2009). *Research methods in education* (9th ed.). Pearson.

## Image Credits

Fig. 5.2: Based on Angie C. Kennedy, Elizabeth Meier, and Kristen A. Prock, "A Qualitative Study of Young Women's Abusive First Relationships: What Factors Shape their Process of Disclosure?," *Journal of Family Violence*, vol. 36, no. 7. Copyright © 2021 by Springer Nature.

Fig. 5.3: Based on Andrea Delaney, et al., "This Person Is Still Here with Us Today': A Qualitative Follow-up with Mental Health First Aid First Nations Training Participants," *Mental Health & Prevention*, vol. 22. Copyright © 2021 by Elsevier B.V.

■ **CHAPTER 6**

# Entering the Field

## CHAPTER PREVIEW

Once you have selected a topic in qualitative research, it becomes important to consider how you as a researcher will enter the field. Fieldwork can involve physical and/or online sites. Fieldwork considerations include choosing a sampling method; identifying sample size; selecting and entering a field site; building rapport with gatekeepers, stakeholders, and key informants in the field; and exiting the field. Figure 6.1 summarizes the main topics of this chapter. After reading the chapter, refer to the list of pitfalls to avoid in fieldwork (see Wild Card 6.1).

## Entering the Field

Entering the field is one of the most critical aspects of qualitative research. There are numerous ways to enter the field in terms of methods you use to gain access and the degree of interaction you as a researcher aim to have with participants. In this section, we introduce some of the common aspects of entering the field. Once you select a research tradition, we encourage you to delve into the literature within your discipline to consider additional aspects important to entering the field. While we will discuss some of the ethical issues involved with entering the field, please refer to Chapter 3 for additional information on ethical issues regarding entering the field.

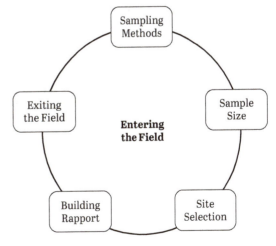

**FIGURE 6.1** Considerations When Entering the Field

**WILD CARD 6.1.** PITFALLS TO AVOID IN THE FIELD

Pitfalls abound when entering the field! From identifying a general, target, and accessible population; selecting a sampling method; thinking about sample size; selecting and entering site(s); working with gatekeepers, stakeholders, and key informants; and knowing when to conclude your sampling, pay attention to these reminders to enter the field in a strong, effective, and ethical manner.

- An unclear description of your population of interest will create difficulties in identifying the target and accessible populations. Once your sampling frame or accessible population is defined, critically examine how you will maximize participant voice, particularly for those who may have been underresearched and/or marginalized by previous scholarship.
- A solid sampling method is grounded in your research paradigm and tradition. Be able to deliver an "elevator speech" (i.e., 30 seconds or less) of how your research paradigm and tradition guide your sampling strategy.
- Do not select a sample simply because they are easy to access. You might miss participants who would best answer your research question(s). Additionally, you might miss identifying the people who might most benefit the most from your research.
- Do not limit your fieldwork to physical sites. Online environments can be invaluable sites for inquiry, especially for exploring sensitive topics across geographical areas.
- Do not select too few people for your study. A good practice is to consider a sample size larger than the actual number of people you think you will need. You do not want sample attrition to negatively influence your study. In addition, be open to changes in sample size needs.
- Follow the criteria you have established for your sampling. You spent extensive time and energy identifying why these criteria were important! At the same time, you do not want to find yourself in the middle of your study realizing that your sampling criteria has been too restrictive or too general to answer your research question. Stay flexible but have a good rationale for why you might alter your sampling criteria during your research process.
- Reflect on why you selected criteria for the sample you want to study. Ask yourself if these are the criteria that are critically important. If not, you could begin your study and realize you need other voices of participants to answer your research questions.
- Remember there is no one sampling method that is "better" than another. You are looking for the best fit for your research question(s). Sometimes, snowball sampling is the best way to go. Your sampling method may not be popular or "en vogue" at the time of your study. Still, it should be the most appropriate strategy for your study.
- Do not underestimate the importance of building trusting relationships with the gatekeepers, stakeholders, and key informants in your study. They can make or break your access to participants.
- Take access issues with your site seriously. Take time to plan how you will enter the site, conduct research, and exit the field.

- Do not forget to plan for the unexpected. You cannot anticipate everything in the field, but you can think wisely about the potential opportunities and challenges that may come your way.

Setting aside time and effort to intentionally consider how you as a researcher will enter the field is a necessary step after you have selected your topic of inquiry. Considering how you will enter the field is an important first step across all the research traditions because this is really the time in the process of your research where the "rubber meets the road." We use the word "field" to designate the context in which your study takes place. The field might be a social media platform if you are conducting qualitative research online. The field could also be a nonprofit agency where you have secured a confidential office space to interview participants for a study. The field may also involve several locations and/or be selected by participants. For instance, in one of our studies, we interviewed child sexual abuse (CSA) survivors in locations of their choice because we decided it was important for participants to be able to select the spaces in which they felt comfortable being interviewed. Thus, for this study, our field involved numerous locations, from participants' homes and office spaces to coffee shops and outdoor parks. The field is not, however, only a setting. The field you enter is populated by people and the relationships and interactions they have within the settings in which they work, in addition to the larger context that encapsulates those settings, people, relationships, and interactions. We encourage you to think about the field broadly as the spaces where your activities will take place in your study.

When you selected a topic, you spent a good deal of energy in identifying research goals, considering use of mixed methods, designing research question(s), developing a purpose statement, and identifying a conceptual framework. Now it is time to bring all your hard work to life in the real world. Because the real world—or the field—is often an unpredictable place, being deliberate and purposeful about how you enter this arena will help you anticipate potential challenges and capitalize on potential opportunities as your study unfolds.

Entering the field can often seem overwhelming, especially to those conducting their first qualitative study. To enter the field in an effective and ethical manner, we must actively assess ourselves as researchers. If we do not take the time to do this type of self-assessment, we may risk damaging our relationship with research participants and research sites. When we do take this time, we easily identify ways to build trusting relationships with our research participants and research sites. Thinking about both our interpersonal skills (i.e., how we relate to others) and our intrapersonal skills (i.e., how we relate to ourselves) is a good first step. So, it is important to consider even the most basic aspects of our personality as we assess our personal strengths and "growing edges" (i.e., areas where we could continue to learn skills) as researchers. Before we discuss the sampling methods most relevant for your study, take a moment to ask yourself the following questions as a self-assessment:

- What previous knowledge do you have of your sample?
- What knowledge do you need to acquire about your sample?

- What strengths in interpersonal/intrapersonal skills do you typically have in building relationships?
- What are your growing edges in interpersonal/intrapersonal skills in building relationships?

Below, I (Anneliese) note the importance of self-assessment when conducting research:

When I initiated a line of research with trans and nonbinary (TNB) people and the resilience strategies they developed in response to anti-TNB prejudice, I had developed previous awareness, knowledge, and skills with TNB communities through my own professional development, personal relationships, and community activism. This awareness, knowledge, and skills helped me know the importance of using accurate pronouns and correct names (chosen names as opposed to "dead-names" assigned at birth) and that my own exploration of my gender socialization was crucial to address in order to develop empathy and accountability as a research. I also had intimate knowledge of some of the struggles trans and nonbinary people experience through witnessing friends and community members experience anti-trans prejudice in their daily lives, from receiving poor health care to being discriminated against at work. However, I did not have personal or professional knowledge about other stressors trans and nonbinary people experience, such as career discrimination and health care concerns. Obtaining this knowledge prior to entering the field not only provided me with additional information about my topic of study, but also importantly allowed me to use this knowledge to build trusting relationships with trans and nonbinary people in my study. In terms of building relationships, I have often been told my strengths are having a warm and inviting personality that makes it relatively easy for people to relate to me (Danica says I will "speak to anyone": not true!). However, I have also received feedback that one of my growing edges can be that I talk really fast and sometimes it is hard to keep up with what I am saying. Reflecting on both my strengths and growing edges in building relationships gave me the tools I needed to create trusting relationships with trans and nonbinary participants in my study.

## The Field as an Online Environment

Over the past 2 decades, the use of online environments via computers and smartphones has grown exponentially. It is difficult to imagine qualitative researchers engaging in fieldwork without inclusion of these environments. We view the "field" in fieldwork as a physical or virtual platform on which social processes take place, which means fieldwork can be independent from geographical location. In the remaining sections of this chapter, we provide considerations for this broad definition of "field."

Every day, worldwide, individuals are using social networks, blogs, personal and community webpages, and other online channels to communicate their identity and share information as well as build knowledge, relationships, and collective practices (Addeo et al., 2020). Thus, online environments can become communities and cultures within themselves. Groups of online users are considered a community when they are interactive, have more than two communicators, there is a common public place where members can meet and interact, and there is sustained membership over time (Gruzd et al., 2011). However, with technological advancements and thus changing ways social media are used, qualitative researchers need to be flexible to the increasingly unbounded nature of sites or communities and thus how they are defined and determined discrete from one another.

Over the past few decades, qualitative researchers have sought ways to capture fieldwork and data sources linked with online environments. **Netnography** was developed by Robert Kozinets in the late 1990s in marketing and consumer research, drawing upon textual and visual data that are computer mediated or network based to understand online social experience or cultural phenomena. Kozinets (2019) identified four typologies of netnography:

- *autonetnography:* personal reflections on identity from researcher's own participation in social networks
- *symbolic netnography:* decoding individuals' characteristics and behaviors to explain practices, meanings, and values
- *digital netnography:* use of statistical techniques to determine patterns and construct cultural understandings from large data sets
- *humanistic netnography:* netnographic methods using a critical paradigm to address a social issue of great importance

Adopting ethnographic principles and techniques, netnography captures archival and emergent social and individual online interactions in a naturalistic setting. It is the study of online interaction and experience within a cultural context (Belk & Kozinetz, 2016). Qualitative researchers can observe and/or participate in an online format, immersing themselves in the virtual environment in which interactions are performed (Jong, 2017). Referred at times to as "virtual ethnography," netnography has found application in social sciences and education given the increasing presence of online activity worldwide (Addeo et al., 2020). The term "videography" is sometimes used for participant observation centered on audiovisual images (e.g., YouTube, Vimeo, TikTok). Case Example 6.1 provides an example of one researcher engaging in fieldwork while conducting a netnography.

In Chapter 3, we introduced ethical considerations in online research. As qualitative researchers select, enter, engage, and exit online site(s), they are to reflect upon those considerations carefully (Airoldi, 2018). Online communities can be open environments and/or include closed groups, which are characterized by different ethical quandaries. In open environments, qualitative researchers can assume covert access or lurking that allows them minimal to no interaction with community members. Lurking can be a useful way to gain knowledge about an online community and can be an initial step for the processes of developing research and interview questions or identifying relevant gatekeepers, stakeholders, and/or key informants. With closed groups, accessible only through user registration and site administrator/account holder approval, they are more likely to actively engage with the site and its participants. This participation can involve building rapport with gatekeepers, stakeholders, and/or key informants (Addeo et al., 2020).

## Case Example 6.1. Fieldwork in Online Fitness Communities

Jong (2017) engaged in a netnography to explore the way in which online communities contribute to young women's perspectives of health and how they may be barriers or facilitators to health-oriented behaviors among this online community.

- Jong selected online fitness communities through online bulletin boards, chat rooms, and social networking sites (e.g., Instagram, Facebook). Jong was an observer of these communities for 1 year prior to data collection to become familiar with the cultural meanings and languages, practices, and rituals of being involved in an online fitness community. Through this year of observation, she was able to consider which communities should be included in the study.
- Jong developed research questions after selecting the sites (i.e., online fitness communities).
- Upon IRB approval, Jong created alias accounts to have full access to Instagram and Facebook. She elected to have minimal one-to-one interaction with online fitness participants. In her profiles and engagements with participants, she disclosed that she was a doctoral student working on her dissertation research and provided information about the study.
- Using relevant hashtags that were made popular by the posts observed in the prior year (e.g., #fitfam, #fitness, #fitgirls), she searched through social networking sites for fitness accounts and pages. She followed relevant online fitness Facebook pages, and she observed posts with other members as a user in the fitness community. She followed women who used Instagram to communicate in fitness communities. Data collection occurred for 4 months.
- Given her limited participation role and the nature of the study, Jong did not build rapport with gatekeepers, stakeholders, and key informants.
- As she engaged with the online fitness communities, she kept researcher field notes using the several prompting questions (e.g., What is new? What is meaningful? What is absent from the findings that you expected to find? What do I not understand? What is it like to connect to the community members?).
- Thematic content analysis of the posts revealed the use of online fitness social networking sites as a comprehensive source of health information that impacts upon the health literacy of people participating in online fitness communities. Notable influences were made on the participant's health practices relating to diet and exercise from the knowledge gained through online fitness communities.

Source: Jong, S. T. (2017). Netnography: Researching online populations. In P. Liamputtong (Ed.), *Handbook of research methods in health social sciences (pp. 1321–1337)*. Springer.

Whether the field is physical and/or virtual, qualitative researchers engage in a series of iterative fieldwork activities aligned with their research goal(s) and question(s). As they select, enter, and engage with sites, sampling decisions are made and typically revised. The next three sections address general sampling considerations, identify purposive sampling methods, and present strategies for determining sample size.

## Sampling

There are many sampling methods from which to choose, and the best sampling methods in qualitative research are aligned closely with the aim of your research. In other words, what sampling methods will best help you answer your research question(s)? The good news and challenging news about selecting a sampling method is that there are no strict rules dictating these decisions. Although there are no "right" or "wrong" answers to these questions, it is important to critically consider which sampling method is most appropriate for your study.

A good starting point in sampling decisions is to consider the attributes most important to the focus of your study. Asking the following questions will guide you in the first step toward identifying your sampling method:

- *What is the unit of analysis in which you are most interested with your study?* In Chapter 4 we discussed four types of cases or units of analysis: individual, setting, process, and event. Additionally, Patton (2014) describes four units of analysis: (a) perspective/world-based (e.g., culture-sharing groups); (b) geography-focused (e.g., neighborhood, state, region); (c) activity-focused (e.g., critical event, period of time); and (d) time-based (e.g., season of the year, academic semester). He also notes that there may be overlap among the four categories.
- *Are there demographic factors important to your research question?* Examples of demographic factors that may be important to your study are gender, race/ethnicity, socioeconomic status, ability status, and religious/spiritual affiliation. Depending on the selected factor(s), you may have to use multiple sampling strategies to gain an adequate sample.
- *Are there institutional roles participants have that are essential to your study?* For instance, if you are studying bullying in schools, are you interested in students, teachers, counselors, and/or other school personnel?
- *Are you interested in a culturally diverse sample?* Having a culturally diverse sample in which participant voice from those of marginalized identities are centered is a necessary component of advancing knowledge within our respective disciplines. Including one woman in a qualitative study of chemical engineers does not necessarily attend to equity, diversity, and inclusion considerations. However, because sample sizes (which we will discuss shortly) are often small in qualitative work, it is also not necessary or realistic for you to include participants from every identity group. Most important is that you can answer the question of how you have attended to multicultural issues in your study. Even better is when you can link this answer to your research tradition(s) and research question(s).
- *What is your selected research tradition?* Some qualitative research traditions are more aligned with particular sampling methods. For example, research traditions such as phenomenology and autoethnography that seek to describe individual experience for a homogenous group may rely on methods that maximize participant description (e.g., criterion or homogenous sampling methods). Traditions that involve theory development

goals (e.g., grounded theory, consensual qualitative research) may rely on theoretical sampling. Furthermore, approaches that typically seek to maximize participant voice to enact change with those with marginalized identities (e.g., participatory action research, community-based participatory research) may use sampling methods such as extreme, politically important, or intensity sampling methods.

In addition to these considerations, qualitative researchers must clearly specify their population for readers to appraise the trustworthiness of the findings, a precursor to sampling (Asiamah et al., 2017). The *general population* is the largest group of potential participants of a qualitative study. However, the general population generally contains participants whose inclusion would be inappropriate given the research goals and assumptions. The *target population*, or sampling frame, is the group of participants with specific attributes or characteristics that are aligned with the research goals and can share experiences that provide a rich description and inform the phenomenon under investigation. Qualitative researchers draw from the target population using sampling method or methods described in the next section. However, not every member of the target population is willing, able, or needed to participate in the study. Thus, the *accessible population* is comprised of target population members who are willing and able to participate in the study. From the accessible population, qualitative researchers select sampling units based on the research goals and corresponding sampling method(s) (Asiamah et al., 2017).

These are some general reflections to get you thinking about sampling in qualitative research. Read about student perspectives on their approach to sampling methods depending on their stage of research in Perspectives 6.1.

-----------------------------------------------------------------------------------------------

## PERSPECTIVES 6.1. ENTERING THE FIELD: STUDENT PERSPECTIVES

I knew it was going to be tough to find the group I wanted to study. My first career was teaching sixth grade. I taught sixth grade in a suburban area, and the students were mostly White. I always noticed how bullying would start to go up in sixth grade. I saw these students struggle and not want to come to school. But there were some students who seemed to just deal with the bullying in a different way. When I started my PhD, I knew I wanted to study the perspectives of the students who seemed to cope better. Fortunately, I know what it's like in the school system! There are many gate-keepers I need on my side for this study—namely the principal, students, and parents. I am thinking about building a relationship with the school counselor at one suburban school because the school is known for having problems with bullying. I am hoping this relationship will help me establish a relationship then with the principal and a few teachers. Then, when I put my IRB [application] through for the county, the principal may be more likely to approve my study because she knows me.

*—early childhood education student*

I decided to study sexual identity development of female-to-male transgender people who identify as gay men. I attend a yearly transgender health conference, and I had an opportunity to complete an IRB [application] before I went to the conference. I didn't have a lot of time to think about sampling: It was a rare chance to have several transgender men in the same place who identified as gay men so I had to go for it! I used purposeful and convenience sampling: I had a booth set up to interview folks who walked by and saw the booth. I knew I would use snowball sampling too, because I asked participants to tell their friends and people in their community about the study. Only thing is when my research team started to take a look at the data from the interviews, it was difficult because there were so many other questions that came up I wanted to follow-up with participants about. But it was too late, because I had no way to contact many of the participants. They wanted to truly be anonymous and would only agree to be in the study if I interviewed them that one time. Although I would ideally go back and interviewed one person at a time, it wasn't realistic for this population. I used purposeful sampling. I think it was the best way to answer my research question: How do transgender men who identify as gay describe their sexual identity development? We got a lot of rich data in the end. I think this study will be a real contribution to the field.

*—counseling psychology student*

I study reading and multicultural education. Most recently I decided to use critical race theory to examine the counter-stories of struggling readers in middle school who are from families that are from rural, poor, and agricultural backgrounds. Counter-stories in critical race theory are the narratives from people who have been marginalized—and boy have these struggling readers been robbed of some important resources in their education. These kids get stigmatized early on in their education, but I have noticed these kids succeed in environments where they get to read about what goes on in their daily lives—like the places they live and see their parents work in so I have been most interested in what their "funds of knowledge are." So, I decided to use multiple sites in my study so I could access more students and get a larger sample size. I had a relationship with one of the schools. A teacher there introduced me to another teacher in a neighboring school, so I also used a convenience sampling method. I needed a larger sample size. I knew the larger size would help me use the data in talking with legislators about resources these kids need to succeed. I did classroom observations and focus groups with the kids and ended up with 50 participants at four different sites in three counties.

*—literacy education and reading student*

I want to understand how Indigenous practices of healing are addressed in counseling. There is a lot of information out there about what indigenous practices are, but we know so little about how these healing methods are used in the counseling office. I am not even sure if there has ever been a qualitative study on this before, because I have only seen conceptual work in the field. After I finish my literature review, I want to identify which indigenous group in the U.S. is most underrepresented in the literature. I have planned a year for my fieldwork—which I know is rare for a doc student—but I have good contacts in the southwestern U.S., mostly anthropologist friends who work in reservation settings. I want to use a phenomenological approach, so that means I won't predetermine a sample size, but will still aim for about 10–15 participants and interview them several times each. I have a place to live with friends during my study, so now I just need to identify what and whom I want to study. That will guide me to the site I go to: And because counseling centers on reservations are so rare, I am already preparing myself to think about using more than one site. I will not have a car, and public transportation is not so great on many reservations, so I definitely need to keep that in mind. I am excited to get started, but it will also be a bit stressful being so far away from my advisor who is on the east coast. I am planning monthly phone calls with her so I stay on track and focused. I am also thinking it might be hard to come back home after being in the field so long, but this is really what I want to do. I am interested in an academic position after I graduate and want to teach qualitative research, so my dissertation is not only of interest to me: It also will help me get a job later hopefully.

*—counseling student*

## Purposive Sampling Methods

Sampling involves the selection of data sources to address the research goals and questions. Data sources can include individuals, documents, blogs, and social media posts, to name a few. In the current field of clinical and educational research, purposive sampling has come to exemplify building rigor into your sampling strategy. **Purposive sampling**—sometimes called "purposeful sampling"—requires that you develop specific criteria for the sample of your study prior to entering the field (Patton, 2014). Both terms refer to establishing criteria to obtain information-rich cases of your phenomenon before you sample your population. This may sound like a simple—and commonsense—concept. However, many embark on qualitative studies without giving intentional thought to what the criteria are for their sample. This lack of deliberate planning never pays off in a solid (or ethical) qualitative study, so beware and pay close attention to this section. Using our previous example of sampling with South Asian American survivors of child sexual abuse (CSA), the purposive sampling of our study included the following criteria: above 18 years old, having an experience of sexual abuse between the ages of 5 and 18 years old, and being of South Asian American heritage.

Qualitative researchers cannot simply state sampling was purposive but must explain how. Thus, they are to devise a sampling plan. A **sampling plan** is a formal, broadly defined proposal outlining the sampling method(s), sample size, and recruitment procedures (Moser & Korstjens, 2018). Researches must provide a description and rationale for each choice. A plan is considered sufficient when the selected participants and settings are sufficient to provide the information needed for understanding the phenomenon (Moster & Korstjens, 2018). Furthermore, multiple sampling methods may be necessary to access vulnerable groups—and more time.

Miles et al. (2020) discuss 16 types of purposeful sampling methods. You can combine many of these sampling methods with one another, so we organize these 16 sampling strategies into three different clusters to help you think about the best fit for your study: (a) representativeness of sample, (b) description and presentation of the phenomenon, and (c) theory development and verification. See Table 6.1 for a list of purposive sampling methods within these three categories. Please note that you may select multiple methods within or across the clusters to meet your research goals. The most-used sampling strategies are criterion, theoretical, convenience, and snowball sampling (Moser & Korstjens, 2018).

**TABLE 6.1** Three Categories of Purposeful Sampling Methods

**Representativeness of sample**

> Convenience: relatively easy access to a sample; least representative
> Homogenous: participants who share many similarities to one another
> Maximum variation: participants who share many differences from one another
> Stratified purposeful: unique features of subgroups (or strata) of a phenomenon
> Purposeful random: randomly selecting from a purposeful sample to increase sample variation
> Comprehensive: selecting an entire group of people by established criteria; most representative

**Description/presentation of phenomenon**

> Typical case: average example of the focus of your study
> Intensity: cases that intensely demonstrate a phenomenon of inquiry
> Critical case: "benchmark" cases for other participants because of irregularity or richness
> Politically important: cases that draw political attention to the phenomenon
> Extreme or deviant: participants with the most positive or most negative experiences

**Theory development and verification**

> Snowball chain or network sampling: participants who "know" one another
> Opportunistic: appearance of new potential samples as research evolves
> Criterion: meet an important, predetermined criterion of the phenomenon
> Theoretical: evolving theory of data collection guides sampling strategy
> Confirming or disconfirming: similar participants that add depth to the study (confirming) as well as those to serve as exception cases (disconfirming)

## Representativeness of Sample

The first category of purposeful sampling methods is representativeness of sample. This refers to a sampling approach when the main goal guiding your selection of participants is representing individuals themselves. These methods can be particularly helpful when the focus of inquiry is at the individual level. We will discuss six subcategories of purposeful sampling: convenience, homogenous, maximum variation, stratified purposeful, purposeful random, and comprehensive.

Of these six subcategories, **convenience sampling** is the least representative sampling strategy. Convenience sampling is a method where the researcher has relatively easy access to a population. For instance, a counselor working in a community mental health center may decide to study the population using their mental health services; this is a convenient sample. The advantages of using convenience samples center on resources of the researcher. Convenience samples are easy to access because you use the sample available to you. If you, as a researcher, are short on money, time, or energy, this can be a helpful sampling approach. In our example of sampling South Asian American CSA survivors, convenience sampling translated to focusing on gaining access to participants within a South Asian nonprofit organization that served survivors of various types of violence.

However, carefully consider your decision to use convenience sampling because there are significant disadvantages to this method. Because convenience samples are so readily accessible, there are drawbacks to the type of information you can gather compared to if you used a more rigorous approach. Werle's (2004) study of the responses of eighth-grade students to the use of storytelling in violence prevention is a good example of when a researcher may choose to use a convenience sample. The author had convenient access to a health education class in a public middle school, so she studied the responses of 13 students to storytelling methods about aggression. This study generated important exploratory information about how this convenience sample responded to violence prevention techniques—namely, the positive engagement of students to storytelling tools of learning about aggression—and future research may build on these findings to use a more rigorous sampling approach. Because of this sacrifice of quality in the sampling process, many researchers will combine convenience sampling with another sampling approach.

When establishing criteria for your sample, you should consider whether you want to identify a homogeneous or heterogeneous sample (Miles et al., 2020). **Homogeneous sampling** involves including participants who share many similarities to one another. You would select a purposeful homogeneous sampling method if you were interested in gaining a depth of information about one specific subgroup. An example of homogeneous samples would be sampling a group of nontraditional Black college students over age 50 to understand their use of technology in mathematics courses. On the other hand, you may be more interested in a heterogeneous purposeful sampling strategy. Heterogeneity seeks to have maximum variation of characteristics within a sample. Using the previous example, an important aspect of your research question may be to understand generally the experience of nontraditional college students—not using race/ethnicity as a characteristic—and their use of technology in undergraduate mathematics courses. In this case, you are talking about a huge potential sample! The idea of maximum variation turns what could be challenging about this type of sample into strengths: The themes you identify across a group that has **maximum variation** of characteristics importantly illustrate the central aspects of your research topic (Patton, 2014). When you decide to use heterogeneous sampling, it is important that your data collection and analysis illustrate how this sampling technique impacts your findings. We will discuss maximum variation further in Part III of the text when we discuss data analysis and collection. With the example of sampling South Asian American survivors of CSA, we sampled a homogenous group culturally, yet we had variation within our sample in terms of the age the abuse occurred, age range, and in terms of the age they immigrated to the United States and/or being second- or third-generations immigrants.

Within purposive sampling, you may decide to use a random or stratified technique. You may decide to use **random purposeful sampling** to increase the variation of cases within your study. Random purposeful sampling literally means randomly selecting from a purposeful sample. For instance, in a study of coping resources of White women who are in recovery from alcoholism, you may decide your potential sample is too sizeable to manage realistically. In this case, random sampling helps you manage potentially large samples.

**Stratified purposeful sampling** allows qualitative researchers to demonstrate the distinguishing features of subgroups (i.e., strata) of a phenomenon in which you are interested. As a result, these unique features also allow a comparison of different subgroups if that is an important aspect of answering your research question. We return to the term "maximum variation" of a sample with stratification. Because your aim is to identify a broad range of unique qualities specific to certain subgroups, you may choose to compare subgroups to illustrate their differences. As an example of stratified purposeful sampling, suppose you are interested in instructional strategies at the high school level. Your strata could include the various instructional strategies where participants are selected that represent each stratum (i.e., teachers are selected based on their instructional strategy). With our example of South Asian American survivors of CSA, stratified purposeful sampling would have allowed us to examine the distinct meaning of their experiences according to the type of abuse and/or age when the abuse occurred. Because the focus of our study was on the resilience of CSA survivors and the meaning they made of their resilience and abuse experiences, we selected not to use purposive stratified sampling, as the focus of our study did not fit this sampling method.

Finally, the **comprehensive sampling** method is the most representative of the six in this category. In this sampling strategy, the researcher selects an entire group of people by an established set of criteria. An example would be if the focus of research is an examination of a multicultural counseling class to understand their experiences of racial identity development within the classroom. In this case, your sample is the entire group: students in a multicultural course. The main criterion for the participants in this study would simply be that they were a graduate student in a multicultural counseling course. Typically, comprehensive sampling methods are most appropriate when the population is small. To revisit our example of South Asian American survivors of CSA, if we had selected to study a support group geared to this population, we might have selected to use comprehensive sampling. Also, if we were studying a training group of counselors or educators seeking cultural competence in working with this group of people, we might have used a comprehensive sampling method for the study.

## Description/Presentation of the Phenomenon

For some qualitative studies, your sampling decisions are guided by the goals of describing or presenting the phenomenon of your investigation. For instance, in a study of a culture-sharing group, such as first-generation Korean American families, your focus of study is describing their experiences of acculturation processes. In this example, a presentation of their acculturative stressors would be critical, and you would want to use a sampling method that allows you to describe and present this focus. We group together five subcategories in this section: typical case, intensity, critical case, politically important, and extreme or deviant.

If you select a case study or life history research tradition, you may decide to use the first subcategory, typical case, as your sampling method. A **typical case sampling** strategy represents who an average example of the focus of your study is (Miles et al., 2020). Like convenience and snowball sampling, critiques of using a typical case rely on the lack of a heterogeneous sample. However, an advantage to using typical case sampling is that the researcher can study a complex phenomenon on a more individual basis. Sampling a typical case may also be helpful when a field of inquiry is relatively new and qualitative investigations are rare. In a study of play therapy, Snow et al. (2007) decided to examine a typical case sampling method to examine the therapeutic environment and play themes and behaviors of children over a period of 6 weeks. The researchers honed in on two typical cases for their study, acknowledging "[the case study] allows for the presentation of information which should never go unnoticed in a field of study as new and complex as that of child psychology" (p. 148). Focusing on typical cases for two 6-year-old children allowed the researchers to identify in-depth findings rich in information about the complex interactions within a play therapy context.

Whereas typical case is sampling the average case for a study, the second subcategory of **intensity sampling** refers to identifying cases that intensely demonstrate a phenomenon of inquiry. It is important to note that these are not cases that are extreme in nature; these types of cases would misrepresent the phenomenon and are not intense cases. An example of an intense case would be a qualitative examination of the grief and loss of parents who have lost a child. In this instance, every participant in your sample will likely be an intense case. But you would potentially decide to not interview parents who had lost multiple family members to avoid the potential distortion of the phenomenon.

In the third subcategory of **critical case sampling**, the researcher is looking for experiences that are particularly significant because of their intensity or irregularity to serve as a benchmark of the "cut-off score" for other participants ("If it happens here, it can happen anywhere"). The cases are selected because the researcher believes that they can be used to illustrate a point particularly well and gain the most knowledge about the phenomenon of interest. For example, consider a historical analysis of hate crimes against transgender individuals. A researcher may want to select a particular incident that was highly intense (e.g., murder and sexual assault of Brandon Teena, a female to male transgender individual) and analyze documents and interview participants who were associated with the event in some manner.

While the fourth subcategory of critical case sampling emphasizes significant experiences, a **politically important sampling** strategy is a type of critical case that draws political attention to the phenomenon. To understand this sampling strategy, think of typical news stories that "grab" your attention. There are usually several political components to this type of story, and you may have several political reactions to these components. A politically important case may be one that especially demonstrates a political issue, potentially motivating others to act as a result.

The final subcategory in this section is the **extreme or deviant case sampling**. The purpose of this form of sampling is to select participants whose experiences were the most positive or most negative, thereby helping researchers discover the "boundaries of differences within an experience" (Polkinghorne, 2005, p. 141). You can look at either or both extremes in the search for illuminative cases. For example, suppose that you want to evaluate a training seminar on counseling racial/ethnic minorities. You might seek out participants who rated the experience both high (i.e., seminar was extremely helpful) and low (i.e., seminar was not helpful at all) and interview them in depth to understand the boundaries of the experience. Unusual conditions or extreme outcomes can be relevant, particularly in program evaluations: From which cases can you learn the most? One weakness of this sampling approach is that it lacks generalizability (e.g., looking at outliers on a normal curve).

In each of the examples provided to illustrate these sampling strategies, it is important that the novice qualitative researcher pay particular attention to demonstrating empathy for participants. For instance, in extreme or deviant sampling, as a researcher you are literally on the outskirts of a sample, which likely will involve participants having intense experiences of a phenomena; therefore, researcher empathy will be a key component of this sampling strategy. Interactive interviewing—where the researcher provides opportunities for the participant to ask the researcher questions—can be a helpful aspect to integrate into these sampling strategies (see Chapter 8). In addition, researcher ethics and integrity are always important but especially so when your sampling strategy involves seeking to understand intense experiences of participants.

## Theory Development and Verification

This last section of purposeful sampling focuses on the development and verification of theory. We organize five subcategories in this section: snowball, opportunistic, criterion, theoretical, and confirming and disconfirming cases.

The first category, **snowball sampling** (also called "chain sampling" or "network sampling," is often a natural fit for a convenience sampling strategy. As the name implies, once you find a typical case for your study, you then ask if there are other individuals they know who are also typical cases. This sampling method goes on and on, having a "snowball" or "chain" effect because you are using people's relationships with one another to identify your sample. The main advantages are that this method can give you quick access to a population of study. Also, like convenience samples, if you are studying a vulnerable group of people (e.g., people who have survived violence), snowball sampling may be a desirable choice for your investigation. The researcher should address questions of whether a more diversified sample may have captured different information. Although it was previously thought that the main disadvantage of using snowball sampling in qualitative research is that you would not have a heterogeneous sample (or maximum variation, which we will discuss in the section on purposeful sampling), it is possible to use snowball sampling to sequentially build variation into your sample. For instance, you could use snowball sampling as a method to reach several distinct types of participants. In this case, rather than following the snowball sample within just one group, you would initiate the snowball sample within several groups of potential participants. With both convenience and snowball sampling, it is important that you select participants who represent information-rich cases, meaning that they exemplify the phenomenon in which you are interested.

The second subcategory, **opportunistic sampling** (sometimes called "emergent sampling"), is a sampling method that seeks to capitalize on the appearance of new potential samples as the research process evolves. This sampling method may seem to focus more on how to build advantages into your sampling strategy for your study. However, there is a deeper purpose of this sampling approach. Because so much of qualitative research involves aspects one cannot predict ahead of time, opportunistic sampling allows the researcher to address when both barriers and opportunities in the sampling process occur. This sampling strategy reminds researchers of the creativity inherent in qualitative inquiry.

The third subcategory, **criterion sampling**, refers to when researchers sample participants who are selected because they meet an important, predetermined criterion. The purpose is to review all cases that meet a criterion. For example, a researcher studying the experiences of racial identity development among counselor education students who have taken a multicultural counseling course would select only participants who had completed the course. Criterion sampling is typically used when program evaluation is an important aspect of your study.

Whereas purposeful sampling generally establishes criteria for finding your participants prior to beginning your study, the fourth subcategory, **theoretical sampling**, proposes the evolving theory of your data collection should guide your sampling strategy (Corbin & Strauss, 2015). Theoretical sampling is an obvious match for grounded theory designs because of the emphasis on having a systematic process through which you sample your population of inquiry. Theoretical sampling begins with criteria for the anticipated sample, like purposive sampling. For instance, if you are studying the impact of the achievement gap on Latinx students in elementary school, your sample in both purposive and theoretical sampling may begin with the following criteria: (a) identify as Latinx and (b) attend elementary school. As we discussed, the criteria purposive sampling would guide the selection of each of your participants. However, the process of theoretical sampling guides the researcher to systematically collect data in discrete steps, taking one step at a time. At the completion of one step, the researcher then revisits the previously collected data and analyzes saturation of the data that has occurred (discussed in the next section). It is important to be aware that unlike other sampling methods we discuss, theoretical sampling is often more linked to your data collection and analysis process than the initial participant selection.

One of the advantages of using a theoretical sampling method is that you will strengthen the rigor of your study if your aim is to generate a grounded theory of your phenomenon of inquiry. Another advantage is that the systematic method provides some structure to the process that may guide you through some of the challenges of the qualitative research process. Often during your sampling, you may ask yourself, "Have I collected enough data?" and "Am I missing important information for this study?" Theoretical sampling clearly links to a grounded theory research design and reminds you to use theory and your research questions to answer these challenges. The disadvantages of theoretical sampling are related to its inherent strengths: Your study's focus may not require as much structure throughout each step of the sampling process to answer your research question. For instance, if your research question is "What are the experiences of White, rural high school students with their school counselors as they prepare for college?" and you are most interested in the students' own perspectives, another purposive sampling method is a better fit for your line of inquiry. Because theoretical sampling demands a systematic process, it may require resources (e.g., time, money) that are beyond the reach of the investigator.

The final subcategory of this section is the **confirming or disconfirming sampling** method. This is a strategy that is often used as part of theoretical sampling. As patterns emerge, the researcher looks for confirming cases to add depth to the study and seeks disconfirming cases to look for "exceptions that prove the rule," or exceptions that disconfirm the pattern. An important reminder is that whereas theoretical sampling involves selecting cases in an exploratory, inductive manner as concepts emerge, confirming/disconfirming cases are selected to verify emerging theory.

Now that you have learned more about sampling methods, it is helpful to discuss the merits of the different sampling methods with qualitative scholars. See Activity 6.1 for guidelines in conducting an informational interview about sampling methods. Additionally, it is important to consider how your proposal might use the various sampling methods (see Proposal Development Activity 6.1).

## ACTIVITY 6.1. INTERVIEWING A QUALITATIVE RESEARCHER ABOUT SAMPLING METHODS

Before you enter the field and make decisions about the best sampling method to help you answer your research question, it is helpful to talk to other qualitative researchers about their experiences in this area. Set an appointment for an informational interview with one of the qualitative scholars in your department, college, or university. When you meet, start your informational interview with the following questions:

- How do you think about sampling methods in qualitative research?
- What are the typical challenges and successes you have faced when using sampling methods?
- In your most recent study, how did you choose a specific group to sample?
- How has your perspective on sampling methods changed since you first began conducting qualitative research?

Keep a journal during and after this interview to track your interviewee's responses. Make a list of insights about sampling for your study.

## Sample Size

In quantitative research, sample size is typically determined a priori via power analysis. With qualitative research, determining sample size is quite complex: Researchers can make tentative decisions based on the research scope and purpose; however, sample size is often

**PROPOSAL DEVELOPMENT ACTIVITY 6.1.** SELECTING A SAMPLING METHOD

After you have selected a topic for your qualitative proposal, it is time to weigh the various purposeful sampling methods to consider the most optimal way to address your research question(s). Address the following:

- What is your research topic?
- What are your research goals?
- What is (are) your research question(s)?
- What general category of purposeful sampling methods do you perceive as most appropriate for your study, and why?
- For each method within that category, consider what your sample would look like.
- Are there sampling methods outside your primary category that might be suitable to integrate in your sampling plan? If so, how would you do so?

adaptive and emergent due to the interactive design of qualitative research (Maxwell, 2013). It should be as representative of the population as possible, although it can be a tightly defined population (Boddy, 2016). Furthermore, there should be availability of enough in-depth data to show patterns, categories, and variety of the phenomenon (Moser & Korstjens, 2018). Sample size decisions should be based not only on the number of participants but also on the number of events, processes, and experiences that need to be represented or thickly described (Sandelowski, 1995).

Sampling decisions are made before data collection and/or after or in response to data collection (Moser & Korstjens, 2018; Sim et al., 2018). Thus, the sample composition and size can change during the study based on initial findings and new questions raised. Thus, inclusion and exclusion criteria may be altered, or sites may change (Moser & Korstjens, 2018). Across the many ways to sample, your sampling decisions will likely involve attention to the degree of depth and breadth in your sample. For instance, sampling strategies aiming for a smaller sampling typically desire more depth, whereas sampling strategies seeking larger sampling sizes tend to build more breadth into the sample.

Qualitative researchers can establish tentative a priori sample sizes by considering a multiple of factors. They should include a written justification for the selected sample size based on these factors, identifying both the a priori sample size selected and the final sample size. Furthermore, sample sizes can be too large, such as more than 12 focus groups or more than 30 in-depth individual interviews (Boddy, 2016). Students are often trained by instructors (who were trained by their instructors) to obtain "about 10 participants" for their study, particularly when they are conducting individual interviews. We are unsure where this "magic number" of 10 originated, but the magic number (or at least the initial sample size) derives from general guidelines of the research tradition and/or sampling method. Review the following factors as you make tentative sample size decisions:

- *scope of the study:* Studies investigating less explored and/or more complex constructs require larger sample sizes. Studies that seek to explain phenomena, as opposed to only description, also require larger sample sizes.
- *scope of the research question(s):* Larger sample sizes are needed for broader research question(s). In addition, the more research questions asked, the larger the sample sizes should typically be.
- *sample diversity:* For samples that seek greater homogeneity, samples of 10–12 participants may be adequate (Boddy, 2016; Sandelowski, 1995). For designs that seek to represent more diverse characteristics and experiences, larger sample sizes are needed (Sim et al., 2018).
- *desire for negative cases:* Qualitative researchers seeking to include data sources that strengthen findings by attempting to find disconfirming evidence (i.e., negative case analysis) require larger sample sizes.
- *accessibility of sample:* Samples that are more accessible tend to allow for larger sample sizes. Accessibility issues include setting characteristics (e.g., accessibility, time, vulnerability of participants, diverse types of stakeholders; Moser & Korstjens, 2018). Qualitative researchers are to critically examine accessibility issues and seek to include data sources that tend to be excluded in research or that have been inequitably represented in research.
- *degree of participant engagement:* Smaller sample sizes are more feasible when qualitative researchers spend greater amounts of time with each individual research participant. In cases of online research with data sources such as blogs or social media posts, it is expected that there may be less intensive engagement and thus greater amounts of data collected and analyzed.
- *qualitative research tradition:* Sampling size can vary by qualitative research tradition. Table 6.2 provides recommendations; however, these are simply recommendations, for a priori decisions may be revised during the research process. Furthermore, these recommendations are based on using the most employed data collection method: interviewing (see Chapter 8). Case Example 6.2 provides examples of how sample sizes were decided for two qualitative research traditions.
- *sample size for previous studies with similar designs:* Previous research using a particular research tradition can serve as numerical guidelines for sample size (Onwuegbuzie & Leech, 2007).
- *data collection period and amount of data collected per data source:* Smaller sample sizes would be appropriate for studies that extend for a substantial period of time and/or involve richer data collection (e.g., longer and/or multiple interviews, multiple artifact units per data source).

Decisions about sample sizes—even when samples are small—tend to be one of the strengths of qualitative research. As we discussed in Chapter 2, the goal of qualitative inquiry is to gain a depth of understanding about a topic area, rather than the breadth that is often the goal of quantitative research. Qualitative methodologists agree that the sample size should be

**TABLE 6.2**   Sample Size Guidelines by Qualitative Research Tradition

| Research tradition | Recommended sample size[a] |
|---|---|
| Case study | 25–50 units for single case study; 3–10 cases for multiple case study |
| Grounded theory | 20–30 |
| Phenomenology | 5–25, typically 12; 3–10 for IPA |
| Consensual qualitative research | 8–15 |
| Life history | 1–5 |
| Narratology | 3–10 |
| Ethnography | 10–20 |
| Ethnomethodology | 10–20 |
| Autoethnography | 3–8 |
| Participatory action research | 10–20 |
| Community-based participatory research | 10–20 |

Note. [a]Figures indicate number of units unless otherwise reflected. IPA= interpretative phenomenological analysis.

Sources: Bernard (2013), Charmaz (2014), Colaizzi (2009), Creswell and Poth (2017), Polkinghorne (1989), Smith et al. (2009), Stake (2006), and Yin (2017).

**Case Example 6.2. Two Rationales for Sample Size in Qualitative Design: Ethnography and Grounded Theory**

### Ethnography

Jones, S. (2006). *Girls, social class, and literacy: What teachers can do to make a difference.* Heinemann.

For me, the site was most important factor in my sampling decision. I wanted to be in a neighborhood and a school that was mostly a high-poverty context, but not with a majority-minority population. The site either needed to be either a racially diverse context with high poverty, or if a White context it to be high poverty. I ended up with a White and high poverty context, because where I was there were still significant enclaves of poverty from Appalachian areas where folks had migrated into the city, but were still poor. Particularly in education, there is a dearth of research about White, high poverty contexts—usually the field talks about African American students and recent immigrants.

Once I was at the site, I was introduced to a teacher who was willing to work with me. She said, "Sure, you can come in whenever you want during class." That's when participant selection started for my study: from a small elementary school class. In the beginning, I invited all students to participate and all their families agreed. So, I had a total sample of 18, with 9–10 girls and 8–9 boys. However, I soon realized across the first year of my 3-year ethnographic study that there were very different things working across the gender domains. I then decided, since this was my dissertation research, I could not focus on both girls and boys. I decided to go with focusing on the girls because I found more theoretical help in the international field of gender in education literature for my study. There just was not as much information on the boys: So I guess I decided to not be a pioneer in that area went with the paths that had been paved relatively well in the literature. I ended up with 8 focal participants and their families.

### Grounded Theory

Burnes, T. R. (2007). Opening the door of a bigger closet: An analysis of sexual orientation identity development for lesbian, bisexual, and queer college women of color. *Dissertation Abstracts International: Section B: The Sciences and Engineering, 67*(7-b), 41300.

I knew from the beginning of my dissertation process that I wanted to do a grounded theory design, so the biggest factor for me in terms of sample size was the saturation of the data. From my qualitative research classes, I had been exposed to several types of qualitative research designs. But for my study—understanding the sexual identity development of lesbian, bisexual, and queer college women of color—I thought grounded theory was the best fit for my study. I knew I would need to interview upwards of 25–30 people based on the literature. At the same time, I knew I would never finish my dissertation if I collected that much data! In the end, I decided to make my dissertation an exploratory study using grounded theory, so I sampled 15 people. Later, after I had graduated and when I was a first year as faculty, I decided to write a grant offered through my professional association that would support me with the time and resources I needed to interview 30 participants as a follow-up grounded theory study. That's the best part about qualitative research I think. The way you think about sample size doesn't have to be restricted to one certain number in one certain study. Who knows how many participants I will have by the time I finish this next project, but I do know I will be looking to the data to let me know when I have reached saturation. I am also thinking about conducting a similar study with gay and bisexual men of color.

consistent with the minimum number of participants you need to represent the phenomenon of inquiry, and this is guided by the study's purpose (Miles et al., 2020; Patton, 2014). A good example of determining sample size with a vulnerable population investigating a complex phenomenon is the study by Yeh et al. (2006) of the collectivistic coping strategies Asian American families used after losing a member of their family in 9/11 attack on the World Trade Center.

In this study, researchers used purposeful sampling to identify information-rich cases of the phenomenon. Initially, the researchers worked on outreach with multiple community organizations to identify 28 potential families who met the study's criteria; however, the sample size reduced to 16 actual interviews scheduled and resulted in a final sample size of 11 Asian American participants. The purposive sampling method (e.g., Asian American, loss of a family member during 9/11), combined with researcher intentions to capture as many participants as possible, yielded in-depth findings for the study and a strong rationale for their sample size of 11 participants.

## Saturation

For some qualitative researchers, saturation may be a threshold for determining the final sample size for a study (Sim et al., 2018). **Saturation**, a concept with origins in the grounded theory tradition, is often proposed as a litmus test for sample size (Saunders et al., 2018). It involves the development of no new concepts, no new properties of those concepts, and/or no new dimensions at an individual unit level. Thus, the present findings have information redundancy, richness, and conceptual depth. One view of saturation relates to **theoretical saturation**, or the determination that there are no new codes or themes identified from the data (i.e., the findings are described and elucidated enough to foster understanding and applicability as relevant). Saturation can also be identified at an early stage of the research process: Qualitative researchers might reach saturation for a particular model component and then adapt the design to seek different directions in sampling to learn about other model components (i.e., theoretical sampling). Glaser and Strauss (1967) defined theoretical saturation as follows:

> The criterion for judging when to stop sampling from different groups pertinent to a category is the category's theoretical saturation. Saturation means that no additional data are being found whereby the sociologist can develop properties of the category. As he sees similar instances over and over again, the researcher becomes empirically confident that a category is saturated. He goes out of his way to make certain that saturation is based on the widest possible range of data on the category. (p. 61)

Theoretical saturation may be further divided into two types: *code saturation*, or when no additional issues are identified, and *meaning saturation*, or when no further conceptual insights are gained (Hennink et al., 2017). Corbin and Strauss (2015) capture these two types within their definition of saturation: "the point in the research when all major categories are fully developed, show variation, and are integrated" (p. 135). Further, Charmaz (2014) adds to the saturation definition: "Your categories are robust because you have found no new properties of these categories and your established properties account for patterns in the data" (p. 213). Conceptual depth present in theoretical saturation may be reflected as the presence of a wide range of evidence to illustrate concepts, complex connections among concepts, resonance to previous literature, and applicability to those in the field of study (Corbin & Strauss, 2015).

A second view of saturation is **data saturation**, or the point of data collection whereby saturation is reached for an individual participant. As such, qualitative researchers have gained a sufficient understanding of the participant's perspective. This relies on saturation at the individual level for each participant engaged in the study. Data saturation can occur when using strategies such as prolonged engagement, persistent observation, and member checking (see Chapter 7).

Morse (2015) referred to theoretical saturation as being possible for all qualitative research and considered it the "gold standard" for determining sample size. However, others (e.g., Saunders et al., 2018) note that saturation is not necessary, depending on the importance of theory development within a tradition. For example, with narratology, life history, or interpretative phenomenological analysis, the focus on the individual level may mean that qualitative researchers are more interested in data saturation.

Saturation is matter of degree (Corbin & Strauss, 2015). A critical point of saturation is that achieving saturation does not mean that the qualitative researcher has fully developed or described a phenomenon or a participant, only that there is sufficient data to illustrate the complexity of the findings. Furthermore, data collection should discontinue when the process becomes counterproductive and when new data do not substantially contribute to the overall phenomenological description or explanation (Nelson, 2017; Saunders et al., 2018).

Qualitative methodologists discuss the ideas of theoretical sampling and saturation as integrally linked. This is a point where there are no new ideas identified in the newly collected data. At this point, as a researcher, you are recognizing all the new data's information as confirming what previous participants have shared. This saturation of the data is closely aligned with your research question: Is the new data giving the same "answer" to your research question that your previous sample has shared? The idea of saturation is the point at which theoretical sampling diverges from its common beginning with purposive sampling. Returning to the example of a research question about Latinx students at elementary schools and the achievement gap, to answer this question, you find that you also need to include the perspectives of teachers, parents, and other key informants because they can provide critical information on systemic barriers the students identified.

## Selecting and Entering a Site

Just as one selects a sampling method that is a good fit for their research question(s), selecting and entering a site should also be guided by the major focus of investigation and where you have access to potential participants who can provide the richest information (Moser & Korstjens, 2018). Site selection is a decision that should take some time and effort. Kozinets (2015) adds that for online fieldwork researchers should look for sites that offer a context that is directly relevant to the study's goals, has a high number of postings, offers many discrete message posters or users, is interactive and current, and provides detailed, rich, and conversational data.

You may immediately have a site that comes to mind. For instance, if you are conducting an ethnography of community-based organizations serving queer youth, you have an obvious site of study. However, the site for your study may not be as obvious. Perhaps, for this same example, you are interested in queer youth who live with depression. You may have greater success with a community-based organization that provides counseling services for queer youth.

Qualitative researchers may develop their research questions after spending time in the field (see Case Example 6.1). In other cases, sites may be selected based on research questions. In both scenarios, research questions may change due to the interactive nature of qualitative research design (Maxwell, 2013).

Furthermore, entering a site involves a continuum of participation. No matter the extent of observation, qualitative researchers are to reflexively and respectfully report individual and group experiences using personal stories and created artifacts and images (Jong, 2017). In Chapter 8, we discuss the participant observation continuum further.

Next, we discuss five steps of selecting and entering a site: (1) identify a site, (2) gain access to site, (3) plan site activities, (4) consider length of time at site, and (5) consider potential site pitfalls. See Figure 6.2 for a flowchart of these steps.

**FIGURE 6.2**  Flowchart for Selecting and Entering a Site

## Identify a Site

The first step, identifying a site, may be the most difficult step in the process. Several factors will guide your site selection, including your sampling method and accessibility of the site. An essential question to ask is, "Where will I find my targeted sample?" If you are studying children and adolescents, schools and other youth-oriented settings may be ideal sites. If you are investigating how urban policy around low-income housing impacts the lives of children and adolescents, community centers with after-school care may be a better fit for the sample for which you are looking. When discussing site selection, we often forget to also think about our comfort level with the site. However, this is an important factor, especially because you could be in the field for a significant period collecting data. Of course, we want to assess our "discomfort" level with potential sites as well. If we feel uncomfortable about a specific site, is that about researcher lack of skills, knowledge, and experience, and if so, how may you as the researcher plan to develop these skills? We also need to do a thorough review of how this discomfort may be related to issues of privilege and oppression. I (Anneliese) conducted many of my first qualitative and mixed method studies of LGBTQ+ bullying in middle schools. As a queer person myself, I consistently had to address fears that would come up from my own experiences of this sort in middle school settings. It was also true that I had power as a researcher when working with cisgender, straight, and LGBTQ+ middle school studies, and this power was important to address as well. So, make sure to slow down and do a self-assessment of related experiences of privilege and oppression that may influence your selection of and interactions within your site. All of these factors are important in selecting a site appropriate for your study. At this stage, you may also consider that to gain an adequate sample you need to work with multiple sites. If your research tradition guides you toward a large sample size, you may need to identify and work with several sites in your study.

## Gain Access to Your Site

The second step is gaining access to your site of interest. We will discuss this issue in further detail in the next section, as it relates to gatekeepers, stakeholders, and key informants. For this section, we discuss potential issues that may make accessing your site challenging. For instance, are there certain time periods when you have access to the site and other times when you do not have access to the site? How will this access impact data collection and analysis while you are in the field? Do you as a researcher have the resources you need (e.g., transportation, equipment, etc.) you will need to gain entry to the site? For example, one community mental health center we visited required two forms of photo identification and a security escort to access the area where counseling services took place. Once you have identified a site in the previous step, planning exactly how you will access the site paves the way for the third step: planning site activities.

## Plan Site Activities

By the time you are ready to plan site activities, you have already developed a general idea of what research components you would like to conduct at your site. Most likely, you identified these activities in your IRB application, but you also may have determined new site activities that are important to your study based on another review of the literature or your sampling method. Regardless, during this third step of selecting and entering a site, you methodically lay out the specific activities you will be conducting at a site. On one of Anneliese's recent studies on reducing bullying in a seventh-grade cohort in middle school, as soon as she identified the middle school she wanted to work with and gained access and permission to be at the site, she conducted a few site visits to ensure that her planned site activities "made sense" based on the physical building and classrooms of the school. For this study, she had art activities as part of the data collection, but on a site visit, she noticed the art classroom was on a different wing of the building than where she was granted permission to conduct the study. Between this site visit and the commencement of the study, she was able to gain permission to conduct the study in these areas. When planning site activities, make sure to also plan a site visit to cover all your bases so your research gets off to a smooth start.

## Consider Length of Time at Site

The fourth step you will take is to carefully consider the length of time you will be at the site. Sites in counseling and educational research tend to already carry immense demands on their time and resources. Preparing in advance of your study for how long you will be in at the site, from the length of the entire study to the length of your time needed with participants, will help you communicate with your site. In qualitative research, we know that plans for data collection may change while in the field. However, if you have previously planned the length of time for your study and communicate that information to your site, you build additional trust with the key players in the site. Then, if there are changes in the length of time that your study requires as it commences, the site may be more flexible in responding to your needs based on this trusting relationship.

## Identify Potential Site Pitfalls

Finally, identify the potential pitfalls of a site. These pitfalls can be small or large challenges that, if not addressed, can derail your study. When naming these pitfalls, brainstorm broadly! From people and time to resources and the site's unique strengths and challenges, make a list of these possible barriers at the site. Then address each barrier one by one to ensure that you are adequately prepared if you encounter one of these pitfalls. The authors of this text conducted a phenomenological study on the resilience of transgender people. The individual interviews went extremely well; however, site challenges arose when conducting the focus group. Anneliese had taken each of the steps systematically as she selected and entered the site (a community-based organization serving transgender people). However, on the night the final focus group was scheduled, 16 participants showed up to attend the focus group. We had expected and planned for 6–8 participants. So, why were so many participants in attendance? Hurricane Katrina had just broken the levees in New Orleans in 2005, and a group of transgender people from New Orleans had just evacuated from the city. Our study gave out gift cards as participant incentives, so the focus group was a mighty fine place to be from the perspectives of participants! Fortunately, we had brought more than enough informed consent forms, gift cards, and equipment to accommodate participants.

At the same time, there were serious issues of researcher ethics and integrity for us to address in this situation as well. How would participant incentives influence what participants shared? Well, we asked this question directly in the beginning and end of the focus group. Notice, we did not assume that there would be no influence. Instead, we worked with the assumption that participant incentives do provide an influence on participants, so our goal as researchers was to identify the "how" of this. If we had not asked these questions directly, the ramifications for our research might have been dire. For instance, participants might have felt they "had" to share certain things we as researchers "wanted to hear." An additional ramification might have been that only those participants who needed financial assistance came to the focus group. Our direct questions allowed us to identify these questions and influences right away, in addition to ensuring we as researchers reminded participants that the incentive did not mean that they had to share in a certain manner or about a certain topic. We took serious efforts to provide ongoing informed consent and remind participants that they could end their participation in the study at any time. In the end, we collected some wonderfully rich data, and the lesson of the story is that when it comes to working in the field, always plan for the unexpected and keep your researcher ethics and integrity "hats" on at all times.

Now that we have discussed sampling methods, issues of sample size, and selecting a site, answer the questions in Proposal Development Activity 6.2 to integrate what you have learned into your own study proposal. Perspectives 6.2 shares one researcher's process for engaging with Black women to gain understanding of how the Black church can both facilitate support and perhaps hinder or provide mixed messages about help-seeking outside the church.

**PROPOSAL DEVELOPMENT ACTIVITY 6.2.** DEVELOPING CRITERIA FOR SELECTING AND ENTERING YOUR SITE(S)

Write 1–2 paragraphs discussing guidelines and criteria for entering your site. Include the following components:

- What are the site(s) where you will find your participants?
- What sample size is appropriate per site?
- How will you gain access to your site? What permissions do you need?
- List the potential pitfalls you may encounter as you enter the site(s).
- What are your planned activities at the site(s)? Should you make a site visit?
- What is the length of time you will be at your site(s)?
- How will you prepare yourself as a researcher to relate to your participants?
- Who are the important gatekeepers, stakeholders, and key informants you will interact with at the site(s)?
- Describe how you will conclude your research at the site(s).
- Will you provide participant incentives? If so, how might these influence the sharing of your participants?
- Are there other considerations for entering your site(s)?

Share and review these criteria with a peer and/or a research team.

---

## PERSPECTIVES 6.2. THE BLACK CHURCH AS A FIELDWORK SITE

Janee Avent Harris, a counselor educator, often conducts scholarship with those in the Black church to identify their intersectional experiences with race, ethnicity, gender, spirituality, sexual orientation, and other cultural identities. Her research has informed how the Black church as a structure can inform mental health as well as help-seeking attitudes and behaviors.

In an interview with Danica (personal communication, June 11, 2020), she discussed several interrelated research design considerations for fieldwork to maximize the rigor and impact of qualitative research:

- *the role of the researcher*: Avent Harris noted the importance of navigating the insider and outsider roles that qualitative researchers play in the field as well as their own integration of personal and professional selves. She notes:

   I've come to a place where I'm comfortable not separating personal and professional. I think it's just kind of where I'm landing as a scholar and just as a human being. … I grew up in church. … I realized that if I can't separate myself, then I don't think [I] should expect our clients or our students to kind compartmentalize all parts of their identity. … I feel like the work has been more personal. … I do feel my identity [as a Black Christian woman] has gotten me in some rooms without having to do some of the leg work of building rapport. ... I am seen as someone who is a part of that community, but then in some ways it has worked against me. ... The Black church is still very much a patriarchal system. Sometimes when I am told no, or there's a block, I have to think to myself, "Oh, yes. I'm a young woman with a PhD and what does that mean for people who can't handle that?" I still navigate all those parts.

- *research goals*: Related to her role as a researcher, Avent Harris sees authenticity and intentionality as successful keys to partnering with communities, and growing scholarship while growing personally and professionally:

My grandma used to have this saying that "you start out the way you can hold out." Be intentional about starting out being authentically you ... to show up as you are. ... Be true to your scholarship because we need to hear that. ... When you approach communities, be honest about why you're there and don't make false promises. [Let them know] I'm here. I'm here to do this research. Here's why I care about this topic. Here's how I'm hoping you can partner.

This intentionality and authenticity also relate to having a critical lens toward and commitment to changing what is valued in the academy. She paraphrases a Twitter quote she once read to explain: "Don't fall in love with the academy. Fall in love with the people and the work that you do because the academy is a system that was never built for Black scholars." She goes on to remind us to take stock in who is at the table in informing scholarship in our disciplines:

We need to diversify the field. I think for White scholars, also be authentic in who you are. Partner with Black scholars. Amplify the voices of Black scholars. Be intentional in how you create research teams and what those teams will look like.

- *sampling*: When entering the field, Avent Harris expresses a desire to include participants who will provide diverse perspectives on a phenomenon, as she seeks to understand a collective experience in work that has been predominantly phenomenological. Furthermore, she highlights the value of snowball sampling (see Chapter 5) that allows her to include participant voice in her research that can counter some of the challenges of the insider–outsider role continuum while engaging traditionally marginalized communities in more trusting research experiences:

I'll interview one person and then they'll say, "Oh, I have somebody else who may want to participate," which has been really helpful because I'm a degree removed from them so they don't really know me. They may be more honest [in the interview]. That's been really helpful, particularly when you're studying communities that have historically kind of not trusted research because of the ways in which researchers take advantage. ... [Avoid] coming from a deficit [lens]. ... Even if communities have challenges, there is still resilience there. I think about Black communities all the time. There's this resilience, that through everything, we have still made it this far. ... What are some of those strengths that [researchers] can build on instead of just going in from, "This is what's wrong with you, and I'm here to save you"?

- *commitment to the community*: Avent Harris comments on her commitment to the Black church to avoid taking advantage of a site solely for one's own research and publication purposes:

    I'm always really particular about trying not to just go in a place, get what I need, and not give anything back. Part of what I give back ... is to do talks [on mental health topics] at churches for free ... so they know I'm not just trying to get something for me. ... I could write a journal article and that's great, but my biggest impact is when I go and speak to a church, because the people who I'm trying to reach don't even have access to these journals.

## Building Rapport with Gatekeepers, Stakeholders, and Key Informants

Before gaining access to the selected community, qualitative researchers become familiar with the community itself (e.g., rules, values, language, norms, members). For online communities, they also seek information about the most active participants, who the leaders are, which are the most popular topics, and any specialized language or activities shared by the community members (Addeo et al., 2020).

Thus, a study's success or failure can depend on how well you identify the important players in your field of inquiry. We call these critical connections the gatekeepers, stakeholders, and key informants. These are the people who can either help you access your sample or, in the worst-case scenarios, establish barriers so that you cannot access the sample you need for your study. One person may have some overlap in two or three roles. For instance, your gatekeeper may also have a stake in your study's outcome and be an important person to talk to in designing your study. In Indigenous research or studies that employ critical research paradigms (see Chapter 2), involvement of key players, such as Elders, community leaders, and advocates, can be especially important to maximize participant voice and be respectful of the site's community.

**Gatekeepers** are those people who hold access to participants and/or the site of study. For instance, if you are investigating how a prekindergarten program prepares students for learning, the gatekeepers would be the school administrators who oversee granting you access to your participants. **Stakeholders** are described as people or groups who have an investment—or "stake"—in the findings of your study. For example, stakeholders in an evaluation of a math tutoring program might include students, parents, teachers, and school administrators.

**Key informants** have some important distinctions from gatekeepers and stakeholders. However, we include a discussion of key informants here because we view all three groups as ones you will potential interact with in significant ways during your research process.

They include a wide range of people who are important contacts for your study and who often provide important information that may shape your study. Key informants hold specialized knowledge about the phenomenon and help to gain access to participants (Moser & Korstjens, 2018). The strengths of working with key informants is that they can potentially not only give you critical information but also can be participants in your study whose data elucidate the phenomenon you are studying. At the same time, there are challenges involved in the very nature of what a key informant represents: a one-person perspective that is inherently biased in one manner or another. Therefore, a good strategy in working with key informants is to keep both the strengths and challenges involved in their perspectives in mind as a researcher. In one of Anneliese's recent studies, a key informant was the security guard at the middle school in which she was conducting a study on bullying who would update Anneliese when participants were going to be late to focus groups.

Merely identifying these important players discussed above is often not sufficient. Building rapport with these players can sometimes make or break your study. In addition, there is often a brief time period that exists in which you meet with participants for the first time, but you also are negotiating the way that the participants experience you and the impression you leave with them (Pitts, 2007). In essence, building rapport is about building trust. We appreciate Pitts's (2007) study of 16 qualitative researchers and how each built rapport with their participants. The findings of this study identified five rapport-building patterns that we believe are useful to be aware of as a researcher (see Table 6.3).

**TABLE 6.3** Pitts's (2007) Stage Model of Participant–Researcher Relationships in Fieldwork

| Pattern | Question elucidating pattern |
|---|---|
| Other orientation | How can I help you feel comfortable participating in this research? |
| Self in relation to other | Who am I (as researcher) to you (as participant)? |
| Self and other linking | Who are we to each other? |
| Interpersonal connection | Where is the line between participating in research and friendship? |
| Partnership | How does our relationship enhance the research in which we are mutually invested? |

Adapted from Margaret J. Pitts and Michelle Miller-Day, "Upward Turning Points and Positive Rapport-Development Across Time in Researcher—Participant Relationships," *Qualitative Research*, vol. 7, no. 2, pp. 186–188. Copyright © 2007 by SAGE Publications.

It is also true that, depending on your study's focus and goals, the mere topic you are attempting to investigate may put you at odds with the goal of building rapport and trust with your participants. For instance, let's return to the example for when I (Anneliese) was researching gay bullying in middle school settings. I noticed challenges for trust and rapport-building. Often, participants—whether they be school counselors and teachers or students and parents—were hesitant to discuss their experiences of witnessing gay bullying behaviors or their own perpetration of such behaviors for fear of "getting in trouble" or what the findings may "say" about their school setting. In these instances, you may be unable to enact the exact rapport-building patterns discussed by Pitts (2007). However, we encourage you to attempt to build whatever trust you can with participants, even if that entails a simple acknowledgment of the difficulty participants may have in discussing a certain topic with you as the researcher. We also encourage you to always keep in mind the researcher-practitioner-advocate (RPA) model, which dictates that building trust and rapport with participants requires that you be a strong advocate as you study clinical and educational practices and environments.

Along with the importance of trust and rapport-building, there are also issues of access and cooperation when working with the important players to access your site and participants. Of course, you hope that you get good access to a site loaded with participants and then full cooperation from participants when you enter that site. However, remember there are important differences between these two terms (i.e., access and cooperation), and just because a gatekeeper grants access to a site does not translate to the full cooperation of participants at that site! There are subtle and not-so-subtle complexities involved in identifying gatekeepers. Therefore, we believe Wanat's (2008) questions are important to answer:

- Who grants access and cooperation?
- What are the differences between access and cooperation?
- How do perceived benefits or threats influence granting of access and cooperation?
- How do gatekeepers and participants withhold cooperation when access has been granted?

See Case Example 6.3 for information on how you might think about both the expected and unexpected issues in working with gatekeepers, stakeholders, and key informants in the field.

### Case Example 6.3. Working with Gatekeepers, Stakeholders, and Key Informants

Sheneka Williams's (2010) qualitative study examined adolescent cross-racial friendships within a desegregated school setting. She was interested in whether desegregation policy had reached the individual student level and used cross-racial friendships as a lens to examine policy implementation. Her investigation was a spin-off of her advisor's study: how Black parents made choices among magnate schools. So, the main gatekeepers were the parents because she was interested in how their children were interacting across racial lines within those schools. Sheneka shared with Anneliese:

> If the parents said I could not interview the child, then I would have lost that potential participant. My advisor was another gatekeeper in many ways—because she had the prior information for the parents and children. So, my advisor was really the main conduit for all of this to happen. During her own study, my advisor asked the participants she interviewed if I could later follow up with them and talk to their children. In many ways, this helped me have an established prior relationship with the parents on which to build rapport with them. Interestingly, my advisor had a book deal with a publisher for the study. The publisher has said that the only

way the book would get published was if we had the voices of the students. So, in a way, the publisher became a key stakeholder in the process as well.

So, for my study, there was a series of building relationships: first, with my advisor, then with the parents on my advisor's study, and then with the children. A lot of times you can get through the "gate" if some of the gatekeepers feel like they can trust you. This is true especially in the case of the parents and children I worked with. As long as they knew I wouldn't harm them or their children, I could get through the gate to them. Also, racial/ethnic identity became a gatekeeper of sorts—with the Black families especially. It was who I was as a person and how I presented myself that allowed me entry through the gate. I was just an African American student at Vanderbilt University, but to share these identities with the African American parents—that was golden. They wanted their children to see this African American doctoral student, which meant they wanted their children to see me. I represented something their children didn't see that often. So, the interviews would often go beyond the focus of my study. The parents and children would ask me about my career path and life experiences. Really, who I was in terms of my identities and all I represented to them gave me the package to get through the gate.

Source: Williams, S. M. (2010). Through the eyes of friends: An investigation of school context and cross-racial friendships in racially mixed schools. *Urban Education, 45*(4), 480–505. https://doi.org/10.1177/0042085910372350

## Using a Mind Map Strategy

It is helpful to use a mind map (Buzan, 2018; Crowe & Shephard, 2012) to brainstorm and identify who the gatekeepers, stakeholders, and key informants are in your study. **Mind maps** are visual diagrams that organize your thinking about this area, allow you to thing broadly about the important players in the field, and document potential challenges and opportunities while you are in the field. Mind maps are particularly useful if you are a more visual person who needs to "see" on paper what the brainstorming process of identifying important players in your study "looks like." In addition to utility, your research study might benefit from the use of a mind map if you are having difficulty identifying key players who can help you gain access to participants or if you want to ensure you have examined a multitude of potential people to contact for your study. Mind maps can be a fun way to free your mind to think more creatively about how you will enter the field and relate to people. They are easy to create, can be done alone or with others on your research team, and require simple tools: a large chalk board, a large piece of paper, or even your notebook.

To create a mind map, you start by placing your topic (e.g., your field site) in the middle of the page. You then brainstorm what the important considerations are that "branch" off this central idea. Each branch may lead to other important subbranches that also will require important consideration. For instance, if your research inquiry is investigating Black female students'

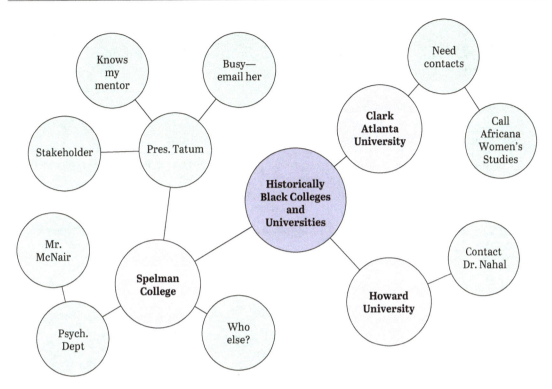

**FIGURE 6.3** Mind Map of Gatekeepers for a Study of Women's Experiences in Historically Black Colleges and Universities

experiences in historically Black colleges and universities and you intend to use purposive sampling of participants, the keyword in the middle of your mind map for entering the field might be "historically Black colleges and universities." As you brainstorm important considerations in identifying gatekeepers in these sites, the branches radiating out of the central idea may be certain people you know or need to identify through other relationships you have. Perhaps a branch represents a relationship you have with a president, dean, or faculty at one of these institutions. From this branch, there may be important considerations in working with these people, from her busy schedule to the best way to contact her and even other people she may know. See Figure 6.3 for an example of a mind map of this topic.

As you can see, mind maps "keep going" and only end when you can brainstorm no further! The most important approach to developing a mind map is that you commit to using the more creative aspects of yourself: Do not think too hard, access your intuitive abilities, and if you get stuck go to another part of the mind map. Mind maps also critically assist researchers in remembering important connections and considerations for their study. So, in many ways, mind maps help you identify new or previously untapped resources you may develop or have. By the time you complete your mind map, you will have a thorough picture of the important people and considerations involved in entering your research site. See Figure 6.3 for an example of a mind map related to gatekeepers. Next, see Reflexive Activity 6.1 to start a journal entry on how you see yourself entering the field for your study.

**REFLEXIVE ACTIVITY 6.1.** JOURNAL ENTRY ON ENTERING THE FIELD

Congratulations! You have spent a good deal of time learning about entering the field for qualitative research. Now it is time to reflect on some of what you have learned for your study. In your journal, write the answer to the following questions:

- What interpersonal and intrapersonal considerations/skills do you need to consider as you select and enter the site of your research?
- What are the potential challenges as you build trusting relationships with the participants in your study?
- Will you need multiple sites for your study? If so, how will you interact with these sites?
- What are the best ways for you to interact with the gatekeepers, stakeholders, and key informants in your study?
- How will you know you have "completed" your study?
- What steps do you plan to take as you exit the field?

If you have not selected a site, select a fictional site and respond to the above.

## Exiting the Field

You should put as much thought into exiting the field as you have put into how you entered your field of study! This is a step many beginning researchers forget, give little thought to, or, worse, ignore. There is a real lack of information about exiting the field in clinical and educational research, so we offer four points we believe are important to consider: review ethical practice, evaluate researcher and participant relationship, leave participants with research products, and conduct researcher self-assessment.

The first area, *review ethical practice*, refers to revisiting how you as a researcher managed the previous stages of entering the field: selecting a sample method, thinking about sample size, selecting a site, and working with gatekeepers, stakeholders, and key informants. Have you made any missteps in ethical practice along the way? If you have, the time to address this is before you exit the field. Obviously, no researcher plans on conducting an unethical practice. However, there are always challenges that appear along the research process that you should be assessing ethically along the way, and exiting the field is a suitable time to review your ethical standards of research. Especially in working with vulnerable populations, such as children, this is also a good time to review your informed consent forms, your relationships with key players in your study, and even your IRB approval to ensure you have followed the ethical research strategies you previously planned. Because there is no way to detail the unanticipated processes in qualitative inquiry, your IRB will probably seem woefully inadequate when looking back on how your study was conducted. Good ethics questions to ask as you exit the field are:

"How would I rewrite my IRB now that the study has concluded" and "What implications do these revisions have for the protection of my participants?"

A long-time critique by feminist qualitative researchers (e.g., Bhattacharya, 2017; Love, 2017; O'Shaughnessy & Krogman, 2017) has been that researchers rarely consider the impact on the researcher–participant relationship. This is the second key area of ethical reflection as you exit the field. Huisman (2008) examines the issues of reciprocity and positionality and how researchers may reflect on these areas to minimize exploitation of participants in qualitative research. *Reciprocity* is the idea that there is a relationship between researcher and participant where knowledge is shared and constructed and innovative ideas are formed. Positionality refers to the social locations of the researcher and participants: What are the identities and experiences of privilege and/or oppression (e.g., race/ethnicity, gender, sexual orientation, disability, educational and class background, immigrant status, linguistic oppression) of both? We believe it is important to discuss reciprocity and positionality in tandem with one another so the researcher can also reflect on how power is distributed in the researcher–participant relationship and recognize where there are power differentials (often with the researcher holding more power than the participant). In Huisman's (2008) qualitative inquiry with Bosnian Muslim refugees, she "outlines three tensions she experienced and addresses how these tensions were related to her shifting and sometimes contradictory positionality as a woman, a researcher, a friend, a graduate student, and as a person who was straddled between two classes" (p. 372). These tensions were (a) tensions with herself, (b) tensions with academia, and (c) tensions with the Bosnian community. We share this example to help you think about what tensions have existed when you were entering in the field and when you are now preparing to exit. Once you identify these tensions, there may be actions you want and/or need to take before you leave your site of study.

The third ethical question to ask yourself as you exit the field is to what degree you have left your participants with the products of your research. Have you made promises to share your research findings with individual participants, field sites, or both? Prior to leaving the field, establish a timeline and gather contact information so that you can follow through with distributing research findings. It is easy to skip over this step; however, it is important for two reasons. First, should you wish to return to the field to conduct research, you want to build on a strong previous relationship you have established. Doing what you said you would do in delivering the products of research will help strengthen those relationships. Second, providing those findings could not only positively impact the site and participants your worked with but also provide doorways to new research questions, interesting community conversations, and knowledge about using research in a multitude of manners (e.g., advocacy). Make sure you have conversations with gatekeepers, key informants, and stakeholders—in addition to the participants—about what format would be most beneficial for presenting your research. They may request a PowerPoint presentation to other stakeholders at the site, a brochure of your findings, or even a final copy of your study in a report or manuscript format. Leaving participants with the products of your research is typically most helpful when in a nonacademic, easily readable form.

A fourth ethical consideration as you exit the field is to conduct a self-assessment of yourself as the researcher. By the time you exit the field, you have spent a good deal of time designing your study, reviewing appropriate literature, relationship-building, interviewing participants, and a multitude of other tasks! You may even have been anxiously anticipating the end of your time in the field so you can move on to the latter stages of the research process: data analysis, interpretation, writing, and publication. However, you may also be surprised by some of your reactions as you prepare to leave the field. Take some time to reflect on what your anticipated reactions may be as you leave your field of inquiry. Reflect on the ideas, thoughts, and feelings that come up as you exit the field. See Case Example 6.4 for Corey Johnson's insights on what researchers themselves experience as they leave the field.

## Case Example 6.4. Exiting the Field

Corey Johnson, an education scholar, discussed (personal communication, June 8, 2010) with Anneliese their experience exiting the field after an ethnographic study:

> This was an ethnographic study focused specifically on how a gay male country western bar's clientele used dress (e.g., saddlebags) as a marker of hegemonic masculinity and how bar patrons changed their dress, and consequently their masculinity, as they migrated to other bars in the city. My selection of Saddlebags was no accident; I consciously selected it for a variety of reasons. What I didn't consider, however, was the impact the people I met in the bar would have on my feelings, perceptions, and actions. My connections to these individuals have made it particularly hard as I move on. Since my data collection ended in December 2001, I have frequently experienced Saddlebags-withdrawal. There is something to be said about the comfort of familiarity.
>
> For me, Saddlebags became familiar and I grew to care about the people and the bar as an institution. Even now, I want to know information about these men's everyday lives. And, the truth is that I can't stay away. I miss these men, and I know they miss me. But I also know that all good things come to an end, and I have spent some time grieving for the loss of community I am currently experiencing. In leaving the field, I also thought about how I would share my research in a consumable manner, instead of merely in academic form. I repackaged my dissertation in a readable form and the key informants placed it behind the bar: It lives there.

Source: Johnson, C. W. (2008). "Don't call him a cowboy": Masculinity, cowboy drag, and a costume change. *Journal of Leisure Research, 40*(3), 385–403.

## CHAPTER SUMMARY

The field, whether physical or virtual, involves several key considerations to ensure ethical and rigorous practice. This chapter reviewed important aspects of entering the field. First, after reviewing several sampling considerations that differentiate among general, target, and accessible populations, we discussed several types of purposeful sampling methods and both their advantages and disadvantages. Three categories of purposeful sampling methods were outlined and are categorized based on research purpose: representativeness of sample, description/presentation of phenomenon, and theory development and verification.

The second component of fieldwork, sample size, is typically established a priori to study implementation yet is expected to change as data are collected and analyzed. We discussed the opportunities and challenges that exist when thinking about the sample size for your study, including issues of one's research tradition and access to participants. Third, we reviewed the different steps in selecting a site—specifically, around issues of access, planning research activities, considering the length of time you will be at a site, and addressing potential pitfalls of being in the field. Fourth, we reviewed how to best work with gatekeepers, stakeholders, and key informants in the field, which is where we build trusting relationships and minimize our demands on their resources so we gain good access to our participants. Finally, we discussed how one should conclude research and exit the field in an ethical manner while considering the important researcher–participant relationship, leaving participants with research products, and conducting a researcher self-assessment of the research process.

## Review Questions

1. What self-assessment can you do prior to entering the site to ensure you are considering your awareness, knowledge, and skills related to the site you will work with in your study?

2. How does fieldwork in physical sites compare to virtual sites? What are some considerations for each?

3. What are the types of netnography, and how might these be carried out using social media platforms?

4. How would you differentiate the three categories of purposive sampling methods? What is a study example of how one from each category might be used?

5. What are typical benchmarks for determining sample size a priori? What are some considerations in research design that would require you to adjust your sample size?

6. When working with participants and communities who have experienced multiple and interlocking oppressions, what additional steps might you take when identifying and selecting a site, entering the site, building trust and rapport, and exiting a site?

## Recommended Readings

Boddy, C. R. (2016). Sample size for qualitative research. *Qualitative Market Research: An International Journal, 19(4),* 426–432. https://doi.org/10.1108/QMR-06-2016-0053.

Buzan, T. (2018). *Mind map mastery: The complete guide to learning and using the most powerful thinking tool in the universe.* Watkins Publishing.

Digital Methods Initiative. (n.d.). *DMI tools.* https://wiki.digitalmethods.net/Dmi/ToolDatabase. (This site lists several free social media data collection tools.)

Kozinets, R. V. (2019). *Netnography: The essential guide to qualitative social media research.* Sage.

Moser, A., & Korstjens, I. (2018). Series: Practical guidance to qualitative research. Part 3: Sampling, data collection and analysis. *European Journal of General Practice, 24(1),* 9–18. https://doi.org/10.1080/13814788.2017.1375091

# Maximizing Trustworthiness

## CHAPTER PREVIEW

How do we know whether qualitative research is rigorous? How are equity, advocacy, and social change related to this question? Determining the quality of qualitative research is one of the most debated topics today. In education and social sciences research, we seek to maximize trustworthiness in our studies guided by the researcher-practitioner-advocate (RPA) model. This chapter presents important aspects of trustworthiness to consider as you conduct, participate in, and review qualitative research. It begins with a review of three lenses for evaluating research in general and then moves on to specific features of evaluating qualitative research. Specifically, criteria and strategies for trustworthiness are presented. Finally, considerations for selecting criteria and strategies are discussed.

## What Is "Good" Research?

Many of you were likely exposed very early to the scientific method, most likely in elementary school. The **scientific method** describes, with experimental approaches, how researchers move from asking a research question, to formulating findings based on observation, experimentation, and hypotheses testing, to generalizing any findings to a population of interest. You were taught that this strategy is the only legitimate way of arriving at "truth" or "good science." As elementary school students, engaging in good science seemed so easy to do! All you had to do was identify a problem, formulate a research question, construct a hypothesis, test that hypothesis by doing an experiment, analyze data, draw conclusions, and report findings. This basic process, you were taught, was the path to the "holy trinity" of "good" research: validity, reliability, and generalizability (Brinkmann & Kvale, 2015). At the same time, you likely did not learn that the roots of what we have come to know as "science" actually originated in the continent of Africa (it makes sense that it did, as this is where humanity also originated; Assante, 2007).

The other shoe drops when you start to apply what you know from practice to research areas of interest and consider any related issues of advocacy and equity. As educators, practitioners, and social scientists, you quickly learn that you cannot conduct experiments all the time (e.g., randomly assigning participants to a certain classroom experience, mental illness, socioeconomic status, and so forth). The problem with the scientific method—you quickly surmise—is that there are very few instances where you can purely look at phenomena outside of the context in which it occurs. That is, the scientific method assumes a reality that *everyone* and *everything* experiences things similarly and objectively. Also, there are issues of systemic inequities to consider and how they may shape the phenomena we observe and study.

As qualitative inquiry becomes more prevalent and useful in education and social sciences, ideas of what counts as good science and thus good research are expanding. The discussion of this expansion somewhat parallels that of paradigms in Chapter 2. However, there are specific terminologies more closely relevant to these shifts in how we judge or evaluate research. Figure 7.1 illustrates the emerging continuum of evaluation criteria.

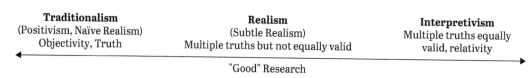

**FIGURE 7.1**  Three Lenses for Determining Good Research

**Traditionalism**, also known as *positivist realism* and *naïve realism*, represents a lens through which educators, practitioners, and social scientists verify a single truth for a phenomenon in science using the five physical senses (Angen, 2000; Denzin & Lincoln, 2018). Thus, if we cannot observe it or experience it directly, it does not exist. Through experimental methods and empirical verification, we look for rational, objective, and logical explanations to our research questions. Denzin and Lincoln (2018) describe this lens as viewing reality as real and apprehensible. The traditionalism lens best captures the "holy trinity." This lens for evaluating research is closely aligned with a positivist paradigm (see Chapter 2).

**Realism**, or *subtle realism* (Hammersley, 2004), as a lens pertains to the notion that we can only know reality from our own perspective. However, most realists argue that there is an underlying common reality. For instance, Silverman (1993) suggested that clinicians and educators should use inductive analysis *and* quantify qualitative data to the extent possible to arrive at an approximate understanding of a common reality for the phenomenon of interest. To this end, there are always limitations to how we understand reality based on personal perspectives. Subtle realists would assert that validity should be framed as confidence rather than certainty (as naïve realists would argue). Also known as a *modernism*, this lens for evaluating research is closely aligned with the postpositivist paradigm (see Chapter 2).

**Interpretivism**, viewed as the polar opposite of traditionalism, refers to the perspective that "everything is relative." Interpretivists believe that criteria for determining the value (or validness) of research are socially constructed, just like everything else (Angen, 2000). Polkinghorne (1989) labeled this lens "postmodernism." Interpretivists assert that validity should be reframed as validation since "what we know is always negotiated within the culturally informed relationships and experiences, the talk and text of our everyday lives ... [derived from] constant meaningful interactions with people and things" (Angen, 2000, pp. 384–385). This approach for evaluating research is most closely assigned with constructivist, critical, feminist, and queer theory paradigms (see Chapter 2).

These three lenses collectively present various ways of evaluating research. Each lens has an appropriate utility in research as a whole and can offer helpful criteria no matter the approach. As research paradigms and traditions emerge that value critical and participatory approaches, the interpretivism lens is growing in popularity.

## Validity and Qualitative Research

In quantitative research, **validity** has been defined as evidence of authentic, believable findings for a phenomenon that results from a strict adherence to methodological rules and standards. Validity is further categorized as internal and external validity. *Internal validity* refers to the likelihood that there is a causal relationship between two variables without interference from other variables or threats. *External validity* refers to the degree to which a study's sample, research design, and findings may be generalized to an outside population or setting. Both forms of validity are examples of the traditionalism lens for judging research.

Validity in qualitative research is known by many names: "truth value" and "credibility" (Lincoln & Guba, 1995), "trustworthiness" (Denzin & Lincoln, 2018; Eisner, 1991), "rigor," "authenticity" (Guba & Lincoln, 1989), and "goodness" (Emden & Sandelowski, 1998; Marshall, 1990), to name a few. (We will refer to validity primarily with the term "trustworthiness.") **Trustworthiness** refers to the degree to which a qualitative study genuinely reflects participant perspectives and the context under investigation through its design and report (Denzin & Lincoln, 2018). Trustworthiness poses the question, "Can the findings be trusted?" In essence, it is the truthfulness of your findings and conclusions based on allowing maximum opportunity to hear participant voices in a particular context.

In discussing the "truth value" (Lincoln & Guba, 1995) of the research process, it is imperative that clinicians and educators also think of establishing validity as demonstrating not only research strengths but also noting research limitations. Maxwell (2013) sums up the criteria and strategies for trustworthiness best by asking, "Why should we believe the results?" and "How might you be wrong?" Thus, it is imperative for establishing validity that educators, practitioners, and social scientists find the "holes" in their research designs and findings even while locating study strengths.

In considering all three potential lenses for evaluating good research, there are several options for determining rules and standards appropriate for establishing theoretical and methodological rigor in qualitative inquiry. Reviewing the four positions below, determining validity is based on the degree to which you think qualitative and quantitative research are similar as well as your desire to see qualitative research as being just as scientifically legitimate as quantitative research (Tobin & Begley, 2004). (After reviewing these four positions,

## ACTIVITY 7.1. POSITIONS DEBATE

What is the best method for evaluating qualitative research? Divide the class in four groups and assign each group one of the four positions mentioned in this section. Distribute a copy of an article of a qualitative study and have each group discuss evidence of rigor within the article based on their position. More specifically, address the following questions:

- How would your position view this study's rigor?
- What would your position argue are the limitations of other positions specific for this article?
- To what extent does your position allow for the study findings to be applied to practice?
- How could you strengthen the study's trustworthiness based on your position?

see Activity 7.1, Figure 7.2, Reflexive Activity 7.1, and Table 7.1 to further your learning.) The four primary positions are:

1. Use quantitative criteria such as validity, reliability, and generalizability.
2. Translate quantitative criteria to be more aligned with the goals of qualitative research.
3. Allow new evaluation criteria to emerge from qualitative inquiry. Evaluation should be framed as interactive and inclusive of quantitative criteria, as appropriate.
4. Disregard quantitative criteria altogether since "everything is relative." That is, the judgment is based on the researcher(s), participant(s), and reader(s) in a particular context; there are no set criteria through which qualitative research can be evaluated.

## The "Holy Trinity"

Research in education and social science settings has been historically determined by the extent to which three interdependent "gold standard" criteria of quantitative research are met: internal validity, reliability, and external validity (Hays & McKibben, 2021; Tobin & Begley, 2004). We refer to this position as the "holy trinity" given its prominence and early application to maximizing rigor in qualitative research. The first position is typically argued by the biggest critics of qualitative research. That is, qualitative research is

How four friends judge the quality of a piece of art:

1. Ms. Trinity: "It's awful! It's no Rembrandt!"
2. The Translator: "I like it. It has some resemblance to Picasso."
3. The Innovator: "This could be an exciting new art form!"
4. Mr. Relativity: "What *is* art?"

**FIGURE 7.2** Validity is in the eye of the beholder.

**REFLEXIVE ACTIVITY 7.1.** TRUSTWORTHINESS IN QUALITATIVE RESEARCH

How do you see trustworthiness as similar to the concepts of reliability and validity in quantitative research? How is it different?

**TABLE 7.1**   Sample Evidence of Rigor for the Four Positions

| | | |
|---|---|---|
| **The holy trinity** | Randomization, controlled designs, generalizability, reliability, validity | Using a representative, randomized group of individuals experiencing homelessness with established data collection methods |
| **Translation of quantitative methods** | Credibility, transferability, dependability, confirmability, authenticity | Including individuals experiencing homelessness in your study who represent information-rich cases and working with them and your research team to arrive at consensus to meet established qualitative criteria |
| **Emergence of qualitative criteria** | Validation versus validity, openness to new and different criteria | Following similar study design as Position 2 and using the translated methods as a guide yet being open to determining what rigor is as the context changes |
| **Criteria as relative and changing** | Establishing criteria as unnecessary since criteria are contextual and always evolving | Focusing primarily on interviewing individuals experiencing homelessness about their experiences and remaining open to criteria that fit for the participants and context. It may be determined that establishing criteria for rigor is unnecessary. |

"research" only to the extent that it looks like quantitative research. Part of this position rests on the notion that qualitative research is less familiar in education and social science settings, and for many conducting this form of research, there is often a lack of rigor in the design (Chwalisz et al., 2008). Further, quantitative research evaluation criteria remain the "language" of research rather than that of only one research approach.

## Translation of Quantitative Standards

Lincoln and Guba (1995) are major proponents of the second position. They identified four components of rigor in qualitative research by translating the quantitative concepts of validity and reliability to something more aligned with the goals of qualitative research. These components are credibility, transferability, dependability, and confirmability (see next section for further description). Authenticity, described later in this chapter, was a fifth component added to possible criteria as an attempt to move beyond methodological issues (Lincoln & Guba, 1989).

It is important to note that while this position is predominant in evaluating qualitative rigor, it can be considered problematic since it translates quantitative criteria and thus may not align with paradigmatic assumptions of qualitative research. Thus, translation of quantitative criteria to qualitative research may hinder the acceptance of qualitative findings as they are applied to general discipline knowledge. Thus, when taking this second position, it is imperative that we legitimize both qualitative and quantitative research as equally valid approaches.

## Emergence of Qualitative Criteria

The third stance for evaluating qualitative research involves honoring qualitative research as having its own universal set of criteria independent of quantitative research. Qualitative criteria can be thought of as having different evaluative components and processes given the nature of qualitative research. Thus, Angen (2000) proposes the term "validation" over validity to more accurately describe the process of establishing rigor in qualitative research. Validation, she argues, speaks to the interactive and contextual nature of qualitative research findings and less to the deterministic view of validity. Rolfe (2006) agrees that we must remain open to various standards of rigor: "The real issue is not whether a universal standard for judging the validity of qualitative research has or has not been argued, but rather, why so many different positions should remain not only viable but also fiercely contested" (p. 306).

## Criteria as Relative and Changing

The fourth position is that there should be no set criteria since every study is couched in its unique context. This last position is even more tentative when it comes to establishing trustworthiness. For example, Tobin and Begley (2004) raise the question, "Do we really need consensus of criteria or just simply increased acceptance that criteria are emerging?" Although this position is less popular overall among qualitative researchers, not working toward establishing criteria and strategies for trustworthiness could lead to qualitative research being even less valued and more thought of as "fiction writing."

## Who Determines What Quality Is?

In addition to the degree to which to consider quantitative criteria in evaluating qualitative inquiry, clinicians and educators are faced with two additional challenges. Specifically, what components of qualitative inquiry should be attended to when determining rigor? And who determines if a study is trustworthy? Very few have weighed in on these challenges.

Rolfe (2006) takes on a more outcome-based view of determining trustworthiness: You can only make judgments on what a researcher reports, and it is the reader who determines rigor. "Judgments can only be made about the way the research is presented to the reader rather than directly about the research itself. ... Such judgments are predominately aesthetic rather than epistemological" (Rolfe, 2006, p. 308). That is, the reader is inevitably the reviewer. S. Porter (2007) agreed with Rolfe but also argued that the process cannot be separated from the outcome or product of qualitative inquiry: The research design shapes how we report the findings. So, by determining the rigor based on the qualitative report, we are in some ways making judgments about the quality of the research itself.

However, Morse et al. (2002) asserted that the responsibility of establishing trustworthiness relies solely with the researcher(s) rather than the reader(s): "The lack of responsiveness of the investigator at all stages of the research process is the greatest hidden threat to validity and one that is poorly detected using post hoc criteria of trustworthiness" (p. 11). That is, educators, practitioners, and social scientists have an ethical and moral obligation to design, carry out, and report findings in a rigorous manner, no matter how much the reviewer or consumer ultimately sees.

Educators, practitioners, and social scientists tend to judge trustworthiness after the research has been conducted and presented. Thus, trustworthiness is largely determined by the degree to which readers/consumers have confidence in the findings (based on what is presented in the qualitative report and other tangible forms of evidence). We believe that there are three interrelated components of the research process that need to be examined when judging the quality of qualitative research: (a) the research design, including researcher characteristics that influence a study, conceptual framework, contextual factors, use of research paradigms and traditions, research goals, purposes, questions, and data sources and data collection methods; (b) data analysis and interpretation, which refers to the description of the coding process and collapsed themes in the context of the researcher's theoretical perspective and the context of the study; and (c) the qualitative report itself along with any related physical evidence (i.e., audit trail; see below for more information). Thus, quality judgments rest with the process *and* outcome of qualitative research. Additionally, the researcher, reader/consumer, and participant are responsible for determining rigor, with the researcher solely accountable to research design.

It is important to examine the interplay of five major components when considering how validity threats impact your research design. Peshkin (1988) and Bhattacharya (2017) used the term **procedural rigor** to describe how researcher subjectivity influences all components of the research design.

Case Example 7.1 provides an example of how these components may create validity threats. The components include:

1.  Goal(s): As discussed in Chapter 4, establishing study goals involves determining what the unit of analysis, research purpose, and type of information sought will be.
2.  Conceptual framework: A conceptual framework is made up of experiential knowledge, prior theory and research, pilot and exploratory studies, and thought experiments (see Chapter 5).
3.  Research question(s): Outlining research questions dovetails with the purpose statement and should contain content, coherence, and structure that are congruent with the case studied as well as the research tradition used (see Chapter 5).
4.  Role of researcher(s): As discussed in Chapter 1, this component refers to the various roles researchers play in the research study itself as well as the overall relationship we have with participants. These roles may also include those of insider and outsider. Proposal Development Activity 7.1 provides an opportunity to consider how you are both an insider and outsider to your study.
5.  Methods: The fifth component, discussed in Chapter 6 as well as in Chapters 8–11, involves activities such as entering the field, interviewing and observing participants, and managing and analyzing data.

The process of considering threats to trustworthiness through these components should begin early in proposal development.

**Proposal Topic: An Assessment of Generational Differences in Technology Comfort Level at a Public 2-Year Institution**

| Research design component | Study examples | Potential threats |
|---|---|---|
| Goal(s) | Examine the impact of generational status on students' comfort level with technology at a 2-year institution. | Is age the main influence?<br><br>Is this an appropriate setting for this study?<br><br>Am I missing any technologies? |
| Conceptual framework | Experiential knowledge: interaction with students as faculty member<br><br>Thought experiments: various models to explain technology comfort<br>Pilot study | Preconceptions based on own experiences, stereotypes<br><br>Four generations: Silent, Baby Boomer, Gen X, and Gen Y<br><br>Missing literature? |
| Research question(s) | How do students at a 2-year institution view technology?<br><br>How, if at all, does generational status impact technology comfort? | Assumes they think about technology.<br><br>Assumes age/generational status is a main factor. |
| Role of researcher(s) | Faculty member<br>Investigator | Involved with students on daily basis<br><br>Access issues<br><br>Grading issues<br><br>Power dynamics |
| Methods | Individual interviews<br>Focus group interviews<br>Chat room observations | Students know me, so they will act differently.<br><br>Social desirability<br><br>Hawthorne effect<br><br>Are interview questions leading? |

## The Role of the Qualitative Researcher and Trustworthiness

In Chapter 1, we explored how the researcher's role influences qualitative inquiry and the importance of attending to the four components of the role of the qualitative researcher: equity and advocacy, participant voice, researcher reflexivity, and researcher subjectivity. Furthermore, the evolution and identification of research paradigms (see Chapter 2) have increased the recognition of the role of the qualitative researcher as a necessary and inescapable force throughout the research process. Thus, the researcher's cultural and social background related to identities and experiences of privilege and/or oppression contain subjectivities in terms of values and assumptions that may influence data interpretation (Fusch et al., 2018).

**PROPOSAL DEVELOPMENT ACTIVITY 7.1.** BEING AN INSIDER AND OUTSIDER

Tinker and Armstrong (2008) introduced the concept of being both an insider and outsider as a researcher. For your research study, consider how you are both an insider and outsider to the study. In brainstorming, consider both personal and professional characteristics.

| | Insider | Outsider |
|---|---|---|
| Research topic | | |
| Research goal(s) | | |
| Research question(s) | | |
| Sample | | |
| Access to research site | | |
| Research team | | |

Now, review your characteristics with peers. What are their reactions? Do they have anything to add?

Qualitative researchers must reflexively engage and attend to their subjectivity in the research process by explicitly identifying and describing how their own beliefs, values, and subjective perceptions shape how they analyze data, including the findings they identify and the conclusions and implications they provide the reader (Varpio et al., 2016). Furthermore, they are to be mindful of maximizing equity, advocacy, and participant voice throughout the research process. By attending to the criteria and strategies of trustworthiness presented later in this chapter, qualitative researchers can strengthen their roles and the research relationship as they maximize rigor of the work they do. Perspectives 7.1 outlines ways in which we engage reflexively in the qualitative research process.

--------------------------------------------------------------------

 **PERSPECTIVES 7.1.** REFLEXIVITY IN ACTION!

Reflexivity is complicated, but it's simple at the same time. The first time I heard of reflexivity, I thought it meant I had to be transparent about my every thought and feeling with each participant, my research team, and my audience. As I have grown as a qualitative researcher, reflexivity is now just something I constantly do all the time: I don't have to think about it much. Right when I first begin thinking about a project, say the topic area is school counselors and social justice, I open up a Word document and title it "Reflexive Journal School Counselors and Social Justice." I always put the date and time of my entry, in addition to the "task" on which

I am reflecting (in this case it would be a brainstorming session). I allow myself to write whatever I am thinking and feeling at the moment.

I like having two approaches to maintaining a reflexive journal. First, a structured approach is making sure that I journal each time I interact with my data and/or participants. That means having my laptop available before and after I interview a participant or conduct a focus group since I keep my reflexive journals electronically. In a pinch, I will use a notepad and transcribe my notes into my electronic journal file later. The second approach I use is an unstructured one. If I am driving and a thought comes to me about the data or a focus group I just conducted, I will write that down in my reflexive journal as soon as I can. Then, my reflexive journal documents my process as a researcher throughout a study without me having to think too hard. There are all my thoughts and feelings about my study that then becomes important data to consider and acknowledge when it comes time to interpret the data.

—A. A. S.

Reflexivity begins for me in topic selection, when I challenge myself to think about how I am an "insider" to the research. What is it about a topic that intrigues me? Am I concerned with a topic for my own interests? What about others' interests? Even at the initial research design stages, I note feelings and thoughts I have about the literature I search as well as the scholarship I opt to not review. During data collection and analysis, I use a spiral notebook to jot down my attitudes about the participants I encounter, those which I do not have access to, the process of entering a site, as well as the fit between the data I am obtaining and the data I expected to find when I began the study.

Reflexivity reminds me of keeping a diary, except you have to be aware that anyone can and should access it at any time. Just as we want our participants to be authentic and collaborative in our studies, we have to be authentic to them as well. Reflexivity (and subjectivity for that matter) helps us remain more honest to our study as well as be more open to ourselves, participants, and readers.

—D. G. H.

The extent and quality of the research relationship has the potential to serve as a major threat in qualitative research. (Do not worry! The research relationship has plenty of benefits to combat this threat.) Because we are researchers *and* humans, our professional and personal selves are likely to intertwine in developing the research relationship. Table 7.2 highlights just a few of the potential researcher threats in qualitative inquiry, and Proposal Development Activity 7.2 provides an opportunity for you to consider these threats in your own research as you consider the components for procedural rigor discussed earlier in the chapter.

**TABLE 7.2**  Examples of Researcher Threats

- Developing inappropriate or unattainable study goals (e.g., focusing predominately on personal or funder goals)
- Selecting an inadequate sample (e.g., sample does not meet criteria, not enough participants to address research question, etc.)
- Conducting an insufficient literature search for your research tradition
- Disregarding researcher subjectivity (e.g., not bracketing your assumptions)
- Creating unanswerable research questions
- Describing data inaccurately (e.g., failing to check data with participants, not providing thick description, etc.)
- Failing to use multiple data sources (e.g., participants) and methods (e.g., interviews, photographs)
- Not noting patterns among data (e.g., limiting coding process; see Chapters 9 and 10)
- Selectively observing a setting to "see what we want to see" (e.g., observer subjectivity, confirmation bias)
- Creating a Hawthorne or novelty effect for participants
- Creating interview responses based on order and type of questions
- Creating a false consensus among a research team during data collection (e.g., engaging in "groupthink")

**PROPOSAL DEVELOPMENT ACTIVITY 7.2.** THREATS TO TRUSTWORTHINESS CONSIDERATIONS

This activity is intended to assist you in thinking about how various threats play a role in your proposed study. Create a grid similar to that in Case Example 7.1. In the first column, list the five components of goal(s), conceptual framework, research question(s), role of researcher(s), and methods. In the second column, briefly describe how each component relates to your study. In the third column, discuss how the components specifically may threaten your design.

Review your grid with a peer and/or your research team. Revise based on any feedback you receive. Remember, your grid is a work in progress, so revise as your research design emerges.

Miles et al. (2020) argue that the development and characteristics of the research relationship is influenced by both the effects of the researcher on participants as well as the effects of participants on the researcher. Maxwell (2013) labels the effects we have on participants in two ways: researcher subjectivity and reactivity (these labels link to the concept of researcher subjectivity discussed in Chapter 1). The effect of the participant, however, is another important component that affects the research relationship and thus may influence the research design in ways that are not accountable to participants. This involves participant personal characteristics, attitudes, and actions both within and outside the research design that change researchers in some manner. Perspectives 7.2 outlines an example of this effect from one of our research studies (Singh et al., 2010a).

**PERSPECTIVES 7.2.** THE PARTICIPANT EFFECT

In preparing to conduct a qualitative study (Singh et al., 2010a) examining child sexual abuse experiences for South Asian women and the resilience strategies they used to survive, we bracketed our assumptions and relationships with the topic and population. We could easily speak to our personal and professional experiences with the topic. We knew what to watch out for. Or, at least we thought. As we started reviewing their stories in the interview transcripts and analyzing the data, we were overcome with unexplained emotion. We weren't surprised by what they would say, but we were surprised by how it would impact us. Very early on in this research, we worked collaboratively on establishing self-care practices for the remainder of the study as well as having an open and honest discussion of how participants were affecting us.

—A. A. S. and D. G. H.

## Criteria of Trustworthiness

With an understanding of some of the divergent positions on trustworthiness and the role of the qualitative researcher within maximizing trustworthiness, we outline criteria of trustworthiness linked with the second position. Quality in qualitative research involves both theoretical and technical concerns; thus, criteria will address both research design and implementation.

This section will present several criteria for trustworthiness that involve various aspects of qualitative inquiry, such as the overall research process/design, data analysis, and the qualitative report. Five criteria of trustworthiness are discussed in this section: credibility, transferability, dependability, confirmability, and authenticity. Criteria of trustworthiness, which may be used across several positions of rigor described earlier in the chapter, are different from strategies of trustworthiness and additional strategies for procedural rigor; these strategies are discussed in the next section.

### Credibility

Lincoln and Guba (1995) refer to **credibility** as the "believability" of a study or the degree to which research outcomes seem accurate based on the research process. Credibility is somewhat analogous to internal validity in quantitative research, or the likelihood that there is a direct link between concepts. Thus, credibility is one of the major criteria qualitative researchers use to determine if conclusions make sense for a qualitative study.

Applying the forms of internal validity of quantitative research, qualitative researchers can maximize credibility in several ways. Like establishing internal validity in quantitative research, qualitative researchers are to expect that sampling and measurement errors will exist for their data sources and methods, respectively.

The first type of internal validity involves *construct validity*, or the extent to which a construct or concept is measured as it is intended to be measured. Translated to qualitative research, this would involve ensuring the extent possible that a phenomenon of interest is thoroughly investigated and data collection methods are appropriately developed and validated. For example, qualitative researchers would take great care to develop and revise an interview protocol to maximize its ability to measure the phenomenon and not another or additional phenomena. In addition, they are intentional about including data sources (e.g., participants, documents) that should be measured by a particular data collection method. Qualitative researchers are to thoroughly explain how they developed a particular data collection method and how they reflexively engaged with the development process to minimize researcher subjectivity and seek to support participant voice, equity, and advocacy. In addition, they describe any revisions they made to the data collection method(s).

The second type of internal validity, *content validity*, is the extent to which the data collection method measures all domains or components of a phenomenon that theoretically should be explored. Thus, the content of the data collection method should be inclusive of the "population" of content for the phenomenon of interest. The third type of internal validity, *criterion validity*, is the likelihood that findings for a particular data collection method used with data sources parallels other findings of studies measuring the same phenomenon. This second set of findings may be identified for a study occurring concurrently or in the future.

## Generalizability and Transferability

**Transferability** is like external validity in quantitative research (Lincoln & Guba, 1995), or the degree to which findings could generalize to a population. In quantitative research, generalizability is typically considered synonymous with statistical-probabilistic generalizability (Carminati, 2018). However, the application of this form of generalizability in qualitative research is problematic given that qualitative researchers typically do not randomly sample participants from a target population. Randomization assumes that sampling error is minimized or neutralized; however, there are always errors in sampling and measurement of that sample. Applied to qualitative research, researchers only have access to a subset of the target population due to time and personnel resources as well as reliance on participant willingness to engage in research. Second, researchers—at times with participants serving as coresearchers—select data collection methods and design protocols that are inherently biased in their selection and development. That is, they restrict the focus and method of their inquiry based on their subjectivity and skill set. Furthermore, "constructs related to human behavior and attitudes contain error throughout the research design, are contextualized, and thus change with time, space, and power and other relationship dynamics" (Hays & McKibben, 2021, p. 178).

Most studies note that generalizability is not a goal of qualitative research, yet findings generated through multiple and intense uses of trustworthiness strategies can apply to a broader population or setting. It is important, then, to conceptualize generalizability in a manner that aligns with the paradigmatic assumptions of qualitative research in order to extrapolate findings to advance knowledge within a respective discipline. Thus, qualitative researchers can conduct a metastudy or "analysis of the analysis" of multiple primary studies in order to more clearly understand a phenomenon for a broader population or setting and abstract a contextualized metatheory as relevant. In addition, they can examine multiple studies to review the degree to which study contexts are similar (i.e., *situational representation*) despite differences in samples (i.e., *demographic representation*; Hays & McKibben, 2021). We encourage you to review Hays and McKibben (2021), who outline four metastudy approaches useful for maximizing generalizability (e.g., formal grounded theory, autoethnography, content analysis, and metasynthesis).

Hays and McKibben (2021) identify four types of generalizability that can be useful in qualitative research. As you will note, transferability is only one type of generalizability for qualitative research. These types should be maximized within a single qualitative study or analysis of multiple studies (i.e., metastudy):

- **Naturalistic generalizability:** The transfer of findings situated in one study context to others of similar contexts (Stake, 2013). As readers review the qualitative report, they determine the extent to which the findings within a specific study context are related to their own personal and professional contexts. Does the context for which the findings are reported make sense to them personally or professionally? Does the context match or align with another context they want to study?
- **Inferential generalizability:** Most closely linked with Lincoln and Guba's (1995) concept of transferability, this is the requirement that qualitative researchers provide enough information to readers to determine the extent to which findings apply from one situation or context. Although similar to naturalistic generalizability, inferential generalizability refers to the "sending context" of the researcher, while naturalistic generalizability refers to the "receiving context" of the reader (Hellström, 2008).
- **Analytic generalizability:** The translation of findings to an established construct or theory, even when samples and contexts are different. Analytic generalizability involves the construction of new concepts or deconstruction of previous concepts and theories and applying or integrating them within research knowledge.
- **Intersectional generalizability:** The extent to which research is done in order to understand a community and its intersections (Polit & Beck, 2010). Intersectional generalizability requires qualitative researchers to be accountable and substantially engage and persistently observe samples and contexts to identify intersectional differences in social and cultural identities.

## Dependability

**Dependability** refers to the consistency of study results over time and across researchers (Lincoln & Guba, 1995). This is similar to the concept of reliability in quantitative research, although the way consistency is measured in quantitative research can diverge from how it is measured in qualitative research, given its focus on research team consensus and member checking. Dependability goes beyond credibility in that clinicians and educators are charged with engaging in strategies to show that the similar findings extend to similar studies, and research team members can reach consensus or agree with the study's findings.

In quantitative research, reliability is typically represented by four types: test-retest, inter-rater, parallel forms, and internal consistency (Campbell & Stanley, 1996). *Test-retest reliability* refers to consistency of findings over time. Translated to qualitative research, dependability may be evidenced by having the same researcher analyze data (e.g., interview transcript) from a data source (e.g., participant), identifying the same codes and findings. *Interrater reliability* in quantitative research refers to consistency of findings among multiple researchers; in qualitative research, this may be evidenced by comparing the way that two coders or research team members analyze data for a data collection method (e.g., comparing identified themes for an observation).

*Parallel forms reliability*, the third type of reliability, refers to the equivalence of multiple forms of a test in quantitative research. In qualitative research, dependability may be sought for this type of reliability by having research team members or others external to the process (e.g., peer debriefers, external auditors) examine the degree to which two interview protocols for two samples are similar. Finally, *internal consistency* refers to the alignment of individual items on a test in quantitative research. Translated to qualitative research, this may refer to addressing dependability by maximizing the likelihood that individual questions on an interview or observation protocol are aligned with one another to consistently measure the phenomenon of interest.

## Confirmability

**Confirmability** refers to the degree to which findings of a study are genuine reflections of the participants investigated (Lincoln & Guba, 1995). This concept is most similar to objectivity and neutrality in quantitative research. Achieving confirmability, then, means the degree to which interference from the researcher was prevented. To do this, clinicians and educators must "listen to data" and report it as directly as possible.

Although qualitative researchers eschew the notion of objectivity and neutrality because they are viewed as impossible traits to possess in qualitative research design, some qualitative scholars (based on the four positions we discussed earlier, those in Position 4 think the idea of subjectivity in qualitative research is misguided as they believe *everything* is subjective and to pretend otherwise is not helpful) do make efforts to minimize researcher subjectivity by engaging in researcher reflexivity. In Table 7.2, we present several potential researcher threats that can negatively impact the trustworthiness of qualitative research. Through researcher reflexivity, qualitative researchers can maximize the confirmability of the findings by selecting and employing data collection methods appropriately.

## Authenticity

**Authenticity** is similar to confirmability in that clinicians and educators strive to represent participant perspectives authentically (Guba & Lincoln, 1989). The subtle difference between these criteria is that confirmability refers to methodological criteria and authenticity refers to theoretical criteria.

# Strategies of Trustworthiness

There are several strategies available to maximize the above criteria for trustworthiness (see Table 7.3). It is important to use multiple strategies that address the research process, data interpretation, and report writing. However, the use of multiple strategies does not guarantee trustworthiness. That is, no matter how many strategies you use to maximize trustworthiness,

**TABLE 7.3**   Criteria and Strategies of Trustworthiness

| | Credibility | Transfer-ability | Dependability | Confirma-bility | Authenticity |
|---|---|---|---|---|---|
| **Primary strategies of trustworthiness** | | | | | |
| **Reflexive journals** | | | X | X | |
| **Field notes/memos** | X | | | X | X |
| **Member checking** | X | | X | X | X |
| **Prolonged engagement** | X | | X | X | X |
| **Persistent observation** | X | X | | X | |
| **Triangulation** | X | X | X | X | X |
| **Peer debriefing** | X | | X | | X |
| **Complexity of analysis** | X | | X | X | X |
| **Negative case analysis** | X | X | | X | X |
| **Thick description** | X | X | | X | X |
| **Audit trail** | X | X | X | X | |
| **Complexity of analysis** | X | | | X | X |
| **Sampling adequacy** | X | | | X | |
| **Referential adequacy** | X | | | X | |
| **Additional strategies of procedural rigor** | | | | | |
| **Quality introduction section** | X | X | | | |
| **Coherence** | X | X | X | X | X |
| **Use of appropriate citations** | X | X | | | |
| **Integration of findings** | X | X | X | X | |
| **Discussion of limitations and implications** | X | X | | X | |
| **Substantive validation** | X | | | X | X |
| **Ethical validation** | X | | | X | X |

Note. X= key strategies of trustworthiness per criterion.

you can never fully establish a study's rigor. Further, select strategies that are most congruent for establishing trustworthiness that makes sense for your research tradition(s). At the conclusion of this section, see Proposal Development Activity 7.3 and Reflexive Activity 7.2 to further your learning.

**PROPOSAL DEVELOPMENT ACTIVITY 7.3.** SELECTING STRATEGIES FOR TRUSTWORTHINESS

1. List the criteria for trustworthiness discussed in this chapter.
2. For each criterion, list associated strategies for trustworthiness.
3. Review the criteria and strategies and circle those that you feel most relate to your research proposal at this point.
4. Memo about why you feel these may be valuable to your study as well as how they might be implemented in your research design.

**REFLEXIVE ACTIVITY 7.2.** TRUSTWORTHINESS CRITERIA AND STRATEGIES

- Which criteria of trustworthiness seem more important to you? Why?
- What strategies do you think are most helpful overall in qualitative inquiry? How so?

In this section, we describe several strategies for maximizing trustworthiness. These are divided into primary trustworthiness strategies and additional strategies for procedural rigor. Given the role of researcher subjectivity, qualitative researchers must describe for the reader not only what strategies they used and why but also how they employed the strategies and interpreted and incorporated the outcomes of strategy use in the research process and presentation of findings. Thomas (2017) offers four reasons why trustworthiness strategies may be employed, and qualitative researchers may use one or more of these reasons when establishing rigor:

- *theory generalization:* to develop or verify theory
- *representation:* to represent participants' realities accurately and thoroughly
- *participation:* to collaborate with participants through multiple contacts throughout the research process
- *change:* to facilitate personal and social change, including "therapeutic" benefits as a result of engaging in the research process

The types of strategies employed to maximize trustworthiness vary study to study. And within those studies, scholars may list particular strategies of trustworthiness they employed yet fail to provide ample evidence for how those strategies were employed. In one 15-year review of published qualitative research within the counseling profession, Hays et al. (2016) found that scholars of published research tended on average to list they primarily used the strategies of reflexivity, member checking, and external audit in their report of triangulation, complexity of analysis, and prolonged engagement. Unfortunately, Hays et al. found that only approximately two-thirds of the articles provided evidence of the use of the main trustworthiness strategies within the described studies, independent of whether they noted in the report that a particular strategy was used. Thus, there is some disconnect between what authors state they applied versus what procedural evidence is described in the report. For studies employing at least one trustworthiness strategy, Hays et al. found that researchers are engaging in thick description, triangulation, and reflexivity. Strategies least used included peer debriefing, external audit, and substantive validation.

Strategies of trustworthiness can complement one another. Furthermore, certain strategies are more aligned with particular criteria of trustworthiness. In Table 7.3, we highlight how strategies and criteria of trustworthiness typically align in qualitative research. However, this is just a guide and is not intended to be prescriptive. To begin the discussion on employing strategies of trustworthiness, Perspectives 7.3 includes students' perspectives on strategies they have found most helpful in their first qualitative research study.

---

## PERSPECTIVES 7.3. ESTABLISHING TRUSTWORTHINESS: STUDENT PERSPECTIVES

Students completing their first qualitative proposals as part of an introductory qualitative research course were asked what they considered the most important strategy for maximizing trustworthiness was:

> Engaging with my research team on a weekly basis, sometimes more, was essential to maintaining the integrity of my study.
>
> —*counseling student*

> Triangulation is the most important because it gives a variety of ways to collect data. I used interviews, focus groups and an observation. Each gave me a different view of how my research questions could be interpreted.
>
> —*literacy leadership student*

> I used interviews as well as unobtrusive methods in my study. Data collected in multiple ways that still reflect common themes renders data more trustworthy and inspires the audience of trust in the researcher.
>
> —*curriculum and instruction student*

Triangulation from several sources recognizes researcher subjectivity because you have a certain amount of power, and if precautions are not put into place to prevent abuse of power, a researcher could lead a project in the direction of his or her choice.

*—occupational and technical studies student*

Since the data is collected from the participants, it is important to cross-check the results the researcher found with the participants. This helps with making interpretations and acknowledging researcher subjectivity.

*—counseling student*

Simultaneous data collection and analysis is very important to ensure accuracy of interpreting results. Waiting too long to analyze information can distort understanding and allow for misunderstanding. During data collection analyzing the results helped to shape my interview questions for the next data collection.

*—literacy leadership student*

Peer debriefing was most helpful for me because I had some blind spots in data analysis. It was difficult for me to see some of the discrepancies or some of the more negative aspects of what was said.

*—counseling student*

An audit trail: If you have a good audit trail, then it would include all of the evidence that you have been making a consistent effort to maintain trustworthiness.

*—educational leadership student*

## Primary Trustworthiness Strategies

In this section, we outline several trustworthiness strategies that we consider primary tools in qualitative research. These include reflexive journals, field notes, and memos; member checking; prolonged engagement; persistent observation; triangulation; peer debriefing; negative case analysis; thick description; external audits; complexity of analysis; sampling adequacy; and referential adequacy.

### Reflexive Journals, Field Notes, and Memos

Given that the role of the researcher is an integral part of qualitative inquiry, keeping adequate notes and reflections throughout the research process is imperative. The first method for doing so is keeping a reflexive journal. A **reflexive journal** includes thoughts of how the research process is impacting the researcher. The nature of qualitative inquiry creates several moments throughout the research process when researchers need to reflect upon how the participants, data collection, and data analysis are impacting them personally and professionally. Several types of entries may be kept in either an electronic or paper journal. These might include reactions to participants and settings involved in the research, thoughts about data collection and analysis procedures within a research team, hunches about potential findings, and descriptions of how data method, source, and analysis plans may need to change. It is important to keep this journal as part of your audit trail; notes about how data were collected and analyzed will be helpful reminders as to why you talked to various stakeholders and key informants, coded themes in a particular way, and so on.

Especially when first learning about reflexivity, it is easy to feel lost in how to "do" reflexivity since there are not many examples provided in the literature. For this reason, Watt (2007) wrote about her process of keeping a reflexive journal during her qualitative study on home education. Her reflexive process began in advance of the study, where she reflected on her motivations and interests in this line of inquiry. As a parent who home schooled her children, Watt had intimate experience of the phenomenon at hand. She wrote questions in her reflexive journal asking how these experiences would shape her expectations of participants and of the data in addition to how she would manage hearing information that contradicted her experiences. The journal was also a method of considering how she would react to more challenging aspects of qualitative research. Consider her following journal entry prior to a pilot interview with her first participants:

> Do I have the courage to be totally honest no matter what I might find? I know my participants and would never want to hurt them. However, it wouldn't matter who the participants were, I would not wish to paint anyone in a negative light. This issue has led me to question whether I am cut out to be a qualitative researcher. Why would anyone participate in a research project if they thought I might write something negative about them anyways? (Watt, 2007, November 1, 2003, journal entry, p. 87)

Interestingly, Watt's journal entries over a month's time are about similar concerns: How would she negotiate identifying data or writing about "negative" aspects of her participants or about her study? How would she manage the tensions of being both a researcher and a person who was intimately connected to her phenomenon of inquiry? Her journal entry a week later sheds some light on this tension:

> What will I do if my participants and I don't agree on some aspect of the "findings"? You certainly can't misrepresent your participants. At the same time, you are more familiar with the literature, and as a researcher have your own expertise/ perspectives. It is my research. These issues are complex, and frankly, more than a little scary. ... It seems that qualitative researchers are constantly engaged in a find balancing act on a number of levels. (Watt, 2007, November 7, 2003, journal entry, p. 88)

It is clear that Watt's reflexive journal becomes a strategy of accountability, honesty, and trust, which allows her to document her internal processes as a researcher and understand her influence on the research process itself.

Watt (2007) discusses several values of maintaining her reflexive journal in advance of her study, during the data collection and analysis, and after the study's completion: "If I had not kept a journal much would have been lost, both during and now after the project" (p. 98). She also notes the advantage of being able to understand the connections between the theory of qualitative research and the practice of it. Finally, Watt (2007) recognizes her reflexivity as being a goal without an end point: "Becoming a qualitative researcher is a never-ending process indeed" (p. 98). In this manner, Watt identifies her reflexive journal as being one of the key ingredients in her becoming a stronger qualitative researcher and actually *seeing* herself in this light as well.

**Field notes** and **memos** are other researcher records kept to describe and analyze findings as they develop throughout a study. These are typically associated with specific data collection methods, such as interviews, documents, and observations. For example, in a life history of 10 preservice teachers' ethics toward social justice teaching, Johnson (2007) constructed memos when analyzing interviews. One of the memos concerning an interviewed preservice teacher, Gretchen, reads as follows:

## Memo: Gretchen's Early Literacy Learning

Gretchen grew up in a suburban neighborhood that has all the classical markers of a middle-class community. Few of Gretchen's neighbors were from non-European American backgrounds, and most of her classmates came from English speaking families. Gretchen's parents engaged in typical middle class childrearing practices: They read nightly to their children, using materials often found in grocery store aisles: Dr. Seuss and Berenstain Bears' books. Her parents were both elementary school teachers and they played active and foundational roles in her literacy learning, providing Gretchen with the materials she needed to become literate and limiting her access to materials they saw as hindering her learning. Gretchen described how her parents hid some reading materials from her. … Gretchen also described how her parents provided her access to reading materials that she would eventually encounter in school, such as books written by Lois Lowry and Jerry Spinelli. Gretchen does not mention reading many books about families from diverse backgrounds. … Is this because her parents as teachers did not value such texts because they knew they were not yet being integrated into school instruction? (Johnson, 2007, p. 303)

Field notes and memos are discussed in more detail in Part III of the text.

### Member Checking

**Member checking** refers to the solicitation of input from participants to deepen, verify, and adjust study findings as needed to enhance what scholars (e.g., Koelsch, 2013) have termed "transactional validity." Thus, it is a process of consensus building among qualitative researchers and participants by which the accuracy of data and analysis is supported (Caretta &

Pérez, 2019). Member checking is also referred to by different names: *respondent validation, member validation, participant feedback, member validation, dependability checking* (see Thomas, 2017; Varpio et al., 2016). Depending on the qualitative researcher's goals for using the strategy, these alternate terms may be more appropriate to use in the report. After reviewing this section, read Wild Card 7.1 for arguments against using member checking in your study.

Member checking may be accomplished in multiple phases. The first phase may be within real time as the data are collected from participants, particularly during interviewing. This can involve using follow-up questions to gain clarification on the meaning of a participant's statement or asking for examples of attitudes, cognitions, behaviors, and/or feelings associated with the interview content shared by them. The second phase may involve participants being asked to review research products (e.g., interview transcripts, observation memos) to indicate whether the content match their intended meanings and/or behaviors. This phase may be accomplished by requesting that participants review and comment on a research product. During this second phase, member checking is not asking participants to confirm the technical accuracy of the research product. For example, in a review of the use of member checking, Thomas (2017) reported that qualitative researchers who had reported the use of member checking primarily described member checking as sending an interview transcript back to participants to check for typos.

The third phase is when participants are asked to review tentative findings, which can include a participant case summary or note, an initial model for a grounded theory, or a holistic description of a phenomenon across participants. Finally, the fourth phase is the review of the final report prior to publication and distribution. The most common procedures for member checking are sending interview transcripts or participant summaries for review (i.e., second and third phases). Qualitative researchers may discuss initial findings or follow up on a transcript during a follow-up interview (Thomas, 2017).

Selected research paradigms and traditions can help guide decisions about whether member checking is employed or the rationale for its use. For example, member checking can be particularly helpful for qualitative researchers engaged in more participatory research paradigms (e.g., feminism, critical race theory, Indigenous) and research traditions (participatory action research, community-based participatory research), as they are accountable to those with which they conduct research. Within these types of inquiry, data analysis is often co-constructed by researcher and participant. Thus, member checking becomes integral to co-construction of findings, and exclusion of participants from this process does not allow for sound methodology. When there are conflicts in interpretation and/or requests by a participant to not include specific data or their interpretation in the report, qualitative researchers will likely privilege these requests over their own interpretation (Caretta & Pérez, 2019; Varpio et al., 2016).

Member checking in program evaluation can be particularly useful for increasing stakeholder buy-in for the final report and thus the extent to which recommendations are implemented (Thomas, 2017). In addition, member checking during program evaluation can help navigate components of the report and how the data are presented. The following excerpt highlights an

**WILD CARD 7.1.** THE CASE AGAINST MEMBER CHECKING

The following are arguments for not using member checking in your work:

- Findings generated are typically designed for a wide audience and thus will differ from the individual participant account given the differences of roles in the research process. Should the researcher address specific concerns from an individual participant for a document that may represent the account of multiple participants and other data sources, this may cause the researcher to constrain the findings to a more low-level descriptive analysis that may not advance knowledge of the phenomenon at a broader level.

- In studies that seek to generate theory, technical inaccuracies or discrepancies noted by individual participants are unlikely to influence theory development. Individual feedback, thus, is likely unnecessary. Furthermore, when researchers are also interested in data saturation, member checks to obtain additional information are potentially less effective than increasing sample size.

- Depending on the timing of the data collection and the member checking, significant time lags can occur. Like history and maturation effects described in quantitative research (Campbell & Stanley, 1996), participants may not remember the context in which the first account was provided and/or their perspectives on the research topic may have changed. Thus, member checking may not be helpful or relevant in terms of converging or confirming participant perspectives of the initial data source.

- There are ethical challenges associated with engaging in member checking, especially for highly sensitive topics. For instance, participants may be reluctant to disagree with the researcher's interpretation given a view of the researcher as expert. Several questions are recommended to evaluate the potential ethical concerns during member checking: Were participants made aware, through an informed or process consent process, that member checking was a potential part of the process? Would a member check potentially coerce participants to prolong engagement with qualitative research? Are participants being asked to review potentially sensitive data again, and what might be the outcomes of this request? Would member checking disrupt relationships between the participant and researcher, among participants, and/or between the participant and their respective community?

- There may be limited to no utility of member checking in terms of an effect on findings, particularly considering the time and effort required of participants. Thomas (2017) reviewed 44 literature sources where authors reported information about member checking and found that response rates to member checks are commonly low. Low response rates can be indicative that participants are indifferent to the findings and/or resist further contact. In addition, when participant input is received and reported, there tends to be a "romanticized" account of the member checking process in the report whereby participants never disagree with the findings. Thus, interactions are often portrayed as being conflict free and of a "benevolent" researcher who shares the final work with the participants.

Sources: Caretta and Pérez (2019), Thomas (2017), and Varpio et al. (2016).

example of how member checking during program evaluation allowed specific stakeholders to consider what and how data were reported:

> A graduate student accepted an invitation to carry out an evaluation of services provided by short-stay residential facility for children with health problems. The evaluation was commissioned by the facility manager. During the data-gathering, frontline service staff were critical of the manager's lack of cultural competence when organising events at which families of children attended (most of the families were from a non-dominant ethnic group). Potentially the frontline staff could lose their jobs if the information they provided was included in the evaluation report to be sent to the manager. After discussions with university supervisors, the graduate student took the section of the text covering staff criticisms bad to the relevant staff. She asked them which comments they wished to have included (with an option being to include no comments at all) and if the comments were included, how they would like those comments expressed. In this way she handed control back to the frontline staff to make decisions about content of the evaluation report that was relevant to their work. After time to think about the content of the draft report, the staff decided their critical comments about the manager should be left in the final version of the report. (Thomas, 2017, pp. 31–32)

Unfortunately, when member checking is employed, it is seldom reported (or is reported minimally) in the report (Thomas, 2017). This is a lost opportunity to share with the reader as a trustworthiness strategy. Member checking is not enough, of course. When writing about the member checking process, qualitative researchers are to discuss why member checking was employed, including how it was congruent with their selected research paradigm and research tradition; how many participants were invited to member check and why; which participants were invited to member check and why; how many responded (i.e., provided member checking); and changes in data interpretations that resulted from the member checks. Furthermore, while member checking intends to co-create knowledge, it is not necessarily geared toward accuracy. Thus, after determining that a certain level of certainty of the findings is attained, qualitative researchers are to acknowledge this incongruity in their report. As relevant, researcher–participant disagreements during data analysis phases are also acknowledged as equally valid results (Caretta & Pérez, 2019).

## Prolonged Engagement

**Prolonged engagement** is another strategy of trustworthiness. It involves "staying in the field" to build and sustain relationships with participants and settings to be able to accurately describe a phenomenon of interest. Typically, the more time a practitioner or educator stays in a setting or engages with a participant, the more trustworthy the findings. However, the time researchers spend in the field may be too long and can cause ethical and professional challenges. Specifically, prolonged engagement may be viewed as intrusive to participants and their communities. In addition, when qualitative researchers have a more insider role in the research process or are embedded fully as a participant within the field, they may become too immersed in that they are no longer able to effectively collect and analyze data. Thus, prolonged engagement refers to sufficient interaction with a sample and/or community before, during, and after data collection.

While the time and energy necessary to establish prolonged engagement varies depending on a study's goals and research question(s), this strategy is usually met once qualitative researchers perceive they have established trust with participants and gained detailed, sufficient information about them, their culture, the setting, and the phenomenon of interest.

An example may illuminate the nature of prolonged engagement. Kourgiantakis et al. (2021) explored master's in social work (MSW) student perspectives on redesigned teaching approaches within a course. Prior to data collection, the researchers and research assistants in this study had been engaged in redesigning the course on social work practice in mental health and observing student learning over a 3-year period. Then they offered the course and conducted focus group and individual interviews over a 2-month time frame at the conclusion of the course. Another example is Hays et al. (2021), whereby researchers engaged in the setting and with participants for a 22-month period to identify factors linked with academic leadership development.

### Persistent Observation

**Persistent observation** refers to having depth in data. It is demonstrated through a more focused interaction and exposure to sample in a setting or context, through data collection methods. Evidence of prolonged engagement should also include a discussion in the report of how data collection method(s) was/were developed and revised over time.

Persistent observation is the intentional effort of seeking detail to various aspects of a phenomenon. As qualitative researchers laser in to their research process, research questions, interview protocols, and observation protocols may be refined as the phenomenon of interest is described and/or explained. Depth in data collection may occur by engaging in several data collections with a participant, refocusing the way data are mined to more clearly address a research question, soliciting theoretically opposing data as an attempt to disconfirm a theme, and so forth. While persistent observation may arise as a result of prolonged engagement, this is not always necessary or true. Similar to the first phase of member checking, clinicians and educators could establish persistent observation by simply asking increasingly refined and detailed questions or conducting more complex observations to better address a research question.

An example of persistent observation may be found in the work of Alaggia and Millington (2008). In this phenomenology the researchers investigated the lived experiences of 14 adult men who were sexually abused in childhood. They conducted in-depth interviews examining the men's experiences of sexual abuse in childhood, the process of retelling the trauma, the influence of the abuse as children and as adults, and the meaning attached to these three experiences. Implications for social workers were derived based on detailed interview data.

## *Triangulation*

**Triangulation** is a common strategy of trustworthiness that involves using multiple forms of evidence at various parts of qualitative inquiry to support and better describe findings. Triangulation was originally developed in geographical studies to determine a location by mapping its relation to multiple points of reference. The strategy has been used by qualitative researchers across disciplines, describing it as an approach in which multiple methods, theories, investigators, and/or types of data are used to enhance research rigor. Originally, qualitative researchers using triangulation assumed that multiple sources of information within and across the following categories converge upon a "truth" and thus provide evidence of trustworthiness. With the evolution of research paradigms, triangulation may serve the purpose of capturing the richness and diversity of perspectives. Triangulation is also referred to as "crystallization" given its more recent focus on enhancing research rigor through comprehensiveness rather than convergence (Varpio et al., 2016).

Types of triangulation include data triangulation, methodological triangulation, investigator triangulation, and theory triangulation. The more triangulation occurring within each type as well as the use of more types of triangulation can indicate greater rigor. Using a hypothetical study, Figure 7.3 reflects how these forms of triangulation may work together to increase the intensity of the strategy.

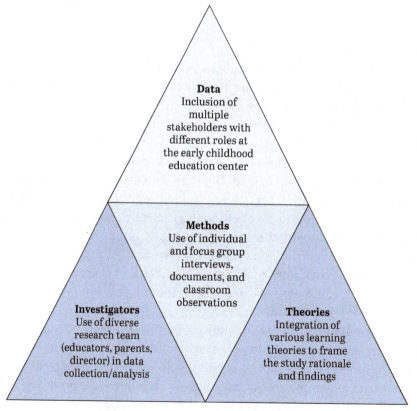

**FIGURE 7.3** Triangulation Within a Hypothetical Case Study of Learning Outcomes at an Early Childhood Education Center

### Data Triangulation

**Data triangulation** refers to using multiple sources of data (i.e., people, time, and space; Denzin, 2012). Each source represents different data of the same event and take place over time (e.g., days, weeks, months, years; Fusch et al., 2018). Data triangulation might involve several participants representing a similar perspective, having multiple roles within a setting, experiencing a phenomenon in various ways yet possessing similar characteristics, and so forth. When data are collected across time and/or settings, this is sometimes referred to as "environmental triangulation." For example, data triangulation can involve interviewing various participants across a study period. Participants can serve similar or different roles depending on the study goals.

### Methodological Triangulation

**Methodological triangulation** is the use of multiple data collection methods to obtain data pertaining to the same research question. Data collection methods can be qualitative (e.g., interviews, observations, social media, document analysis) or quantitative (i.e., mixed methods research). Methodological triangulation can serve to bolster research rigor in two interdependent ways that can appear contradictory at times. First, the use of multiple methods can converge upon a single conclusion to better support the conclusion than a single data collection method. Second, different data may be generated as a function of the method used; thus, multiple methods may show some converging findings, yet there may be diverging findings based on the type of data that are able to be produced by a respective method (Heesen et al., 2019). Having different findings by method does not necessarily evidence a lack of rigor, as there can be specific findings by method. However, there should be some convergence for some findings across the methods.

### Investigator Triangulation

**Investigator triangulation** refers to the use of multiple researchers or research teams to participate in data collection, analysis, and/or reporting. To determine who should be included in investigator triangulation, qualitative researchers are to select those who have the best skill sets and should be closest to the data (Fusch et al., 2018). Depending on the selected research paradigm or tradition, participants and other community members may be considered coresearchers. This strategy may appear many different ways, including (a) use of a single team or revolving teams during data collection only; (b) use of a single team or revolving teams during data analysis only; (c) use of a single team or revolving teams during both data collection and analysis; and (d) use of one team (or one investigator) for data collection and a separate team for data analysis. Having multiple researchers or research teams participate in more than one research component (e.g., study design, data collection, data analysis) signals more intense use of the strategy.

### Theory Triangulation

**Theory triangulation** refers to the use of multiple theories to analyze the findings. Thus, qualitative researchers view the data through a theoretical lens as well as contradictory theories in order to verify and strengthen the findings. This strategy illuminates the importance of conducting a literature review throughout qualitative inquiry, discussed in Chapter 4. Furthermore, Fusch et al. (2018) noted that multiple research traditions may be used in what they term a *blended design*. Examples of blended designs include phenomenological case studies and ethnographic narratives.

### Peer Debriefing

Consulting with a peer, or **peer debriefing** (Patton, 2014), allows for another check outside of a designated research team. Peers can be interested colleagues, classmates, or individuals within the community of which the phenomenon is investigated. Peers should play the devil's advocate in that, while they are supportive of the clinician's or educator's research efforts, they serve as an additional layer to challenge the findings.

Lincoln and Guba (1995) assert that peer debriefing can strengthen a qualitative study's credibility. The authors suggest that the researcher themselves is an "instrument" of any qualitative endeavor. Therefore, peer debriefing provides essential accountability to recognize and understand the influence of the research on the interpretation of the data. We agree with this view of the researcher as instrument, and we encourage you to identify ways you may incorporate this strategy throughout your study.

Spall (1998) explored the use of peer debriefing sessions by graduate students in education who used peer debriefing in their dissertation, finding three key ingredients to the peer debriefing process. First, the participants described trust as not only being an important aspect of selecting a peer debriefer but also as playing an important role in the interpersonal interactions involved in peer debriefing (e.g., trust that peer debriefing was a collaborative dialogue rather than a debate). Second, participants reported that both the researcher and the peer debriefer focused on the study's methodology in their peer debriefing sessions. For instance, if the peer debriefer was playing the role of devil's advocate to the researcher's interpretation of findings, both turned to the methodology of the study to guide them in the peer debriefing session (e.g., if a grounded theory study, considering the goals of the tradition as it related to the peer debriefing session). Third, the graduate students described peer debriefing as vital to further developing their research skills in the course of a study.

Because it can be challenging to understand how exactly to conduct peer debriefing, Spillett (2003) suggests the following prompts you as a researcher may use when serving as a peer debriefer:

- What do you mean by ...?
- What is important (or not) about this to you?
- Let's brainstorm some alternatives.
- Why do you think this is true?
- What were you thinking at that point?
- What would happen if ...?
- What are the benefits or risks of that approach?
- How does that relate to ...?
- What areas do you feel uncertain about?

As you reflect on these prompts and engage with peer debriefers, document your reflections and actions. What specifically was noted in the sessions? How did the sessions specifically alter and/or influence the decisions of the researcher(s) at critical points of the study, such as data collection and interpretation of findings?

## Negative Case Analysis

**Negative case analysis** involves refining a developing theme as additional information becomes available (Lincoln & Guba, 1995; Maxwell, 2013; Patton, 2014). The concept behind negative case analysis is constantly searching for data that goes against your current findings or searching for cases that may be represented by the same findings yet differ from the population of interest. When we search for evidence that refutes what we think we will find, we help to minimize researcher subjectivity and ultimately strengthen a study. In addition, negative case analysis can occur at the participant recruitment stage, whereas qualitative researchers intentionally seek those with divergent perspectives and experiences to help verify and strengthen the findings.

Negative case analysis can occur within a data source or across data sources and methods. When searching for disconfirming data in interviews for each participant, clinicians and educators will often design questions that address "what else could be going on." For example, when I (Danica) was conducting individual interviews to assess what training practitioners previously had with respect to promoting healthy relationships in school settings, I included in the interview protocol some questions that assessed how their training had addressed this issue. By including these probes, I was working to acknowledge my subjectivity that training had been inadequate by allowing an opportunity for participants to explain how training *was* adequate.

With respect to negative case analysis through use of different data sources and methods, let's say we are interested in career barriers among Native Americans. We develop a study using a sample of Native Americans: those living on reservations as well in those living in urban areas. There are three ways (among many others) we could engage in negative case analysis:

- Include cues that could help to examine career support for this community.
- Determine if there are discrepancies in career supports and barriers based on data collection method (e.g., individual interview versus document).
- Examine if similar career barriers are found for populations other than Native Americans.

## Thick Description

One of the easier strategies that you can implement to strengthen your study is to provide thick description of your findings (Maxwell, 2013). To understand thick description, we think it is important to understand what thin description is: *Thin description* refers to providing inadequate description that prevents the reader or other researchers from inferring meaning from that description. Conversely, **thick description** is a detailed account of your research process and outcome, usually evidenced in your qualitative report but may also be included in an audit trail (see below). The emphasis is on description and interpretation of aspects of the research context and all aspects of the research process that goes beyond simply reporting details of the study (Geertz, 1973). Given its importance as a tool, several scholars (Agar, 2006; Geertz, 1973;

Hammersley, 2008) note that thick description is more than a strategy of trustworthiness; it is a way of thinking about data interpretation and reporting.

It is important to note that thick description goes beyond providing details of participant accounts in several ways. Geertz (1973), who coined the term "thick description," suggested it is an account of the details of a study's form and process and the situational-specific reflections that build on the account of these details. That is, it goes beyond the basics of facts, feelings, observations, and occurrences to include inferences into the meaning of present data. Denzin (1989) noted four components of thick description: "(1) it gives context of an act; (2) it states the intentions and meanings that organize the action; (3) it traces the evolution and development of the act; [and] (4) it presents the action as a text that can then be interpreted" (p. 33). Further, Morse (1999) added that qualitative research must "add something more to the participants' words for it to be considered a research contribution, whether it be a synthesis, interpretation, or development of a concept, model, or theory" (p. 163). Components of your report that can be thickly described include:

- research paradigms and traditions and how and why they were selected
- research questions and purpose statement
- researcher subjectivity
- participant recruitment
- data collection procedures
- data methods used
- how sampling method matches research tradition
- data analysis steps
- coding challenges and how coding system developed
- verbatim participant quotes
- researcher notes
- professional, ethical, and cultural implications of findings
- trustworthiness strategies

### External Audits

**External audits** involve the use of an external auditor to review physical evidence of the research process. This evidence is usually in the form of an audit trail that is used to ensure that a study was properly carried out and the findings are authentic representations of the data. An **auditor** is an individual who reviews the audit trail to determine the extent to which the researcher or research team(s) completed a comprehensive and rigorous study. Selecting an auditor is similar to selecting members of your research team: They must have the expertise and interest in your study necessary to assist you in developing a trustworthy study (see Proposal Development Activity 7.2). However, an auditor differs in that they should be a disinterested party. That is, there is no conflict of interest pertaining to your study for the auditor (e.g., they have no authorship rights and thus can actively search for disconfirming evidence to refute overall themes). We believe that selecting someone to audit your research process is similar to having an IRS agent audit your tax report: This person should be objective, fair to the

**PROPOSAL DEVELOPMENT ACTIVITY 7.2.** SELECTING AN AUDITOR

Selecting an auditor involves considering many factors. Write a few sentences for each of the questions below as you finalize your selection:

1. What are the areas of expertise needed to review your qualitative inquiry? What type of content knowledge is needed with respect to the phenomenon of interest?
2. Who might best understand the participants proposed in your study? Who could ensure that their voices are most fairly represented? In what ways can they ensure this?
3. How can an auditor be most helpful to you during your proposal? Who would be willing to invest the time and energy needed to ensure a trustworthy study?
4. What, if any, are power dynamics among you and potential auditors? How might these impact the research process?

---

data and the individuals it represents, and detail oriented.

Maintaining an audit trail is a necessity in qualitative inquiry, particularly since published qualitative reports limit wordage. An **audit trail** is physical evidence of systematic data collection and analysis procedures. Typically, an audit trail may be kept in a binder or a locked file cabinet. Audit trails are kept because they provide a collection of evidence of the research process for an auditor or any other consumer to review. Just as with record keeping with our clients and students, we have an ethical and professional obligation to keep records of the research we conduct. Table 7.4 provides some examples of what might be included in an audit trail.

### Complexity of Analysis

Another strategy for trustworthiness involves ensuring the **complexity of analysis**. This can involve collecting and analyzing data simultaneously or in close

**TABLE 7.4** Sample Contents of an Audit Trail

- Timeline of research activities
- Participant contacts
- Informed consent forms
- Demographic sheets
- Data collections
- Observation rubrics
- Interview protocols
- Checklists
- Field notes
- Memos
- Reflexive journals
- All drafts of codebooks
- Data management tools (e.g., contact summary sheets, document summary forms, case displays)
- Research team meeting notes
- Reflexive journal
- Transcriptions
- Instrument development procedures
- Videotapes, DVDs, audiotapes
- Artwork
- Photographs
- Copies of internet blog entries
- Social media posts

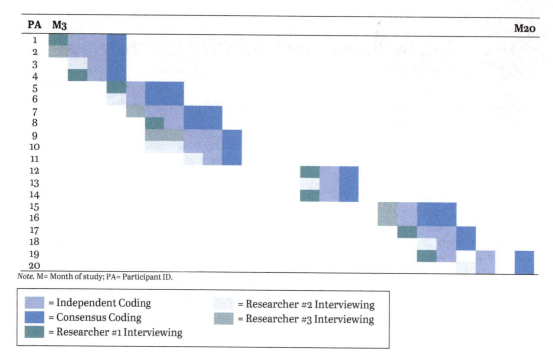

FIGURE 7.4 Simultaneous Data Collection and Analysis for a Grounded Theory of Academic Leadership Development

sequencing, which allows for immediate analysis of information from a data source and use of that analysis to guide collection of additional information from the same or other data sources. This can also be indicated by use of data management strategies (e.g., contact summary sheet, case displays; see Chapter 10).

Another method for engaging in complex analysis is to move beyond descriptive identification of themes to identifying relationships among those themes for description and/or theory development. Figure 7.4 highlights how Hays et al. (2021) engaged in simultaneous data collection and analysis to identify factors that influence academic leadership development and the relationships among those factors. Over time, consensus coding involved more complex analysis of the relationship among themes to develop theory. Grounded theory data analysis will be discussed further in Chapter 11.

Because qualitative inquiry is an emergent design (Maxwell, 2013), it is likely that your research questions and data sources and methods will change as you conduct a study. So, do not wait to analyze data until after all of your data are collected! You might miss out on important questions you should have asked, other participants that were more information rich, clarification opportunities for data already collected, and so forth.

## Sampling Adequacy

**Sampling adequacy** refers to using the appropriate sample composition and size based on the research question(s) and research tradition(s). In addition, it relates to comprehensive and extensive information collected from a sample. This refers to having a sampling method congruent with a research design, collecting data from enough participants to represent the sampling method, and including those who have specific knowledge of the research topic. Who and how many you involve in a qualitative study will depend on the overall nature of the study. Thus, determining sampling adequacy largely depends on the overall research design.

Sampling adequacy can be determined by the sample size and/or degree of information obtained from relevant participants. Saturation, a concept introduced in Chapter 6, is often used as a primary indicator of sampling adequacy. Furthermore, determining sample size was also discussed in Chapter 6.

### Referential Adequacy

**Referential adequacy** involves checking preliminary findings and interpretations against archived raw data, previous literature, and existing research to explore alternative explanations for findings as they emerge. This can also lead to searching for rival hypotheses or different interpretations of findings based on existing knowledge regarding the phenomenon at hand.

Hays et al. (2004) used referential adequacy as a strategy for trustworthiness in their grounded theory of White counselors' conceptualization of privilege and oppression issues. After a theoretical model was developed that outlines how privilege and oppression awareness changes over time, Hays and colleagues used archived data collected at varying points to test the model. In essence, the notion behind referential adequacy is that the data on which a theory is derived should be represented by that theory.

## Additional Strategies of Procedural Rigor

Earlier in the chapter, we described components that Kline (2008) identified to minimize researcher subjectivity across the research design (i.e., procedural rigor). In this section, we describe additional strategies related to maximizing the trustworthiness or rigor of the research report. Many of these strategies correspond to best practices in writing, yet there are some strategies with implications for the actions that we must take during the research process itself. Additional strategies in this section include maximizing the quality of the introduction section and study rationale, coherence, use of appropriate citations, integration of findings, discussion of limitations and implications, substantive validation, and ethical validation. Additional writing strategies are presented in Chapter 12.

### Quality Introduction Section

A quality introduction section of a qualitative proposal or article clearly addresses two questions: Why is the study important to conduct? Why now? A quality introduction section involves (a) providing a strong study rationale by highlighting a comprehensive and balanced literature review and showing research design gaps and (b) articulating a clear purpose statement and research question(s) relevant to the profession (see Chapter 5).

### Coherence

**Coherence** refers to the congruence between research approach; research purpose; research questions; and data collection, analysis, and presentation (Kline, 2008). Coherence is judged not only by the cohesiveness among research design components but also by the researchers' ability to document that cohesion. Furthermore, a strong rationale for methodological decisions is also apparent in the report.

Thus, coherence must clearly evidence appropriate use of a selected qualitative research paradigm and tradition. Kline (2008) defines coherence as the degree of consistency of an epistemological perspective throughout the research design—that is, how we and the research tradition(s) we select assume knowledge to be constructed in our study is to be addressed. Once an appropriate research tradition(s) is (are) selected, the researcher is responsible for infusing it throughout the research process and describing it thoroughly in the research report. Thus, there is a thread tying all aspects of a study together: the research question matches methodology, and the question and methodology align with data analysis and interpretation. Related checks for coherence include:

- Does the methodology fit the study purpose?
- Does the researcher use terminology to describe a design that is appropriate to a selected research tradition?
- How comprehensive are data collection and analysis procedures?
- Are conclusions consistent with other parts of the research design?

## Use of Appropriate Citations

The use of appropriate citations, particularly in the method section, is paramount to maximizing trustworthiness. This refers to using authoritative sources when discussing methodology, ensuring that citations are updated.

## Integration of Findings

Comparing and contrasting findings with previous literature in the discussion section of a research report helps to contextualize the present study's findings. Qualitative researchers are to reflect on the following questions: To what extent do the study findings extend previous knowledge? How has the present study served to address gaps in knowledge or limitations of research designs from previous scholarship? As they integrate current findings with previous research, they should avoid leaping to conclusions, or extending beyond the current data in their recommendations.

## Discussion of Limitations and Implications

The discussion of study limitations, along with future directions for practice and research, should be comprehensively presented at the conclusion of the qualitative research report. Although a common limitation cited for qualitative research is its inability to generalize (Hays & McKibben, 2021), we have discussed earlier how it can and does have the potential to produce transferable and generalizable findings. Future research for practice and training should be tailored toward various academic and community audiences and stakeholders.

## Substantive Validation

The last two criteria (i.e., substantive validation and ethical validation) are interdependent and relate to accurate and relevant application to client populations. **Substantive validation** refers to the degree to which findings are meaningful and beneficial to society, a particular community, and the profession (Angen, 2000). Thus, rigor and application are inextricably linked.

Substantive validation relates to the question, does the research report and other products have "substance" (Angen, 2000)? Qualitative research is substantive to the degree to which it significantly contributes to a profession. This form of validation is also known as *relevance criterion* (Mays & Pope, 2000), whereas research either adds new knowledge or supports existing information about a phenomenon.

No matter what research tradition you select—or which methodology you employ—the final products should be rich with evidence that both confirms and potentially disconfirms your conceptualization of a phenomenon. Is your work quality in that it strongly argues (with evidence) a perspective? That is, are claims relevant and appropriate, and is the process to those claims transparent and open to scrutiny?

## Ethical Validation

**Ethical validation** refers to treating all aspects of the qualitative research process, from designing a study to presenting findings, as a moral and ethical issue (Angen, 2000). That is, we should only engage in research that provides insights to practical and meaningful real-world problems. It is the extent to which inquiry addresses a real-world issue and transforms practitioner and educator actions. Thus, we need to evaluate the potential of a study and its actual relevance to current and future theory and practice. Further, clinicians and educators are charged with being sensitive to the nature of human, cultural, and social contexts in conducting and presenting qualitative research.

Participants and their respective communities are treated as more than just data points by emphasizing the voluntariness of research participation; the protection of vulnerable populations, such as minors and members of oppressed statuses; the exposure of participants to minimal risk throughout the study; and the fair distribution of risks and benefits to all stakeholders (Wester, 2011). Establishing rigor or research quality in qualitative research is an ethical issue because poorly designed studies may lead to misinterpretations that affect client treatment or risk harm to participants (Angen, 2000; Wester, 2011).

As Angen (2000) argues, we need to engage in research that informs practice, generates new ideas for the field, and transforms practitioners' actions: "We have a human moral obligation to take up topics of practical value, and we must do everything in our power to do them justice" (p. 391). S. Porter (2007) further asserts, "It is the relationship between knowledge and practice that provides the key to judging research" (p. 83). Whether individuals review the process or product of your work, they should get a sense that it truly contributes to the profession in some way and sparks new questions.

Ethical validation is also demonstrated by maintaining ethics (Drisko, 1997); using informed consent appropriately depending on tradition (Fossey et al., 2002); empowering and liberating individuals (Lather, 1986); and reporting findings that are useful in policy decisions (Onwueg-buzie & Leech, 2007).

## Postscript: Considerations in Maximizing Trustworthiness

While several criteria and strategies of trustworthiness have been provided to help maximize your study's rigor, there are several considerations before selecting them for your particular study. First, some strategies may be more relevant than others depending on the research tradition. Thus, how do we weigh criteria? Oftentimes, clinicians and educators will decide criteria and strategies to focus on based on the research tradition. "Criteria for evaluating qualitative research must fit within the philosophical/epistemological assumptions, purposes, and goals of the paradigm selected for the research" (Drisko, 1997, p. 6).

For example, for a grounded theory you may decide ethical validation, substantive valida-tion, and theory development are the more important trustworthiness criteria and sampling adequacy and keeping an audit trail are the more important strategies. Or let's say you are considering a phenomenological approach. You might decide that authenticity, prolonged engagement, persistent observation, and member checking are most important. In essence, selecting criteria and strategies of trustworthiness is a major decision that is based on your research design. This decision should not be done in isolation, so consult with peers, research team members, or auditors.

Relatedly, strategies for trustworthiness are not supported similarly for all paradigms and research traditions (Chowdhury, 2015; Whittemore et al., 2001). As we increase our under-standing of research traditions in mental health and education settings, there may be a need to consider new or at least more specific evaluation criteria. However, it is important to note that while there are some differences in evaluation criteria and strategies based on research approach, there are some universal ones (Horsburgh, 2003).

Finally, educators, practitioners, and social scientists need to remember that proposed criteria and strategies of trustworthiness have evolved as there has been a movement away from a traditionalist lens and thus a positivistic view of research. It might be natural to deduce that the more criteria and strategies you use in your study—and the more intensely you use them—the more rigorous the design. Angen (2000), among others, caution that having this assumption might lead us back to trying to get at a static truth (i.e., positivism) rather than honoring the contributions of qualitative inquiry.

# CHAPTER SUMMARY

This chapter illuminated the complexities of establishing rigor in qualitative research. It traced our assumptions of what determines good research to an early introduction to the scientific method and subsequently presented alternate lenses for evaluating research. When considering which lens and approach to use when judging the rigor of qualitative research, we are presented four primary positions. These include (a) using quantitative criteria such as validity, reliability, and generalizability; (b) translating quantitative criteria to be more aligned with the goals of qualitative research; (c) allowing new evaluation criteria to emerge from qualitative inquiry; and (d) disregarding quantitative criteria altogether since "everything is relative." That is, the judgment is based on the researcher, participant(s), and reader(s) in a particular context; there are no set criteria for which qualitative research can be evaluated. As with every step in qualitative research design and implementation, the RPA model helps us remember that our decisions about trustworthiness criteria and how we address our subjectivity are guided by our important roles as researchers, practitioners, and advocates.

Validity, a common term used in quantitative research, goes by many names in qualitative inquiry, including rigor, trustworthiness, credibility, and goodness, to name a few. Using trustworthiness as a primary reference label, we provided several criteria and strategies of trustworthiness. Criteria include credibility, transferability, dependability, confirmability, and authenticity. Strategies of trustworthiness include reflexive journals, field notes, memos, member checking, prolonged engagement, persistent observation, triangulation, peer debriefing, negative case analysis, thick description, external audits, complexity of analysis, sampling adequacy, and referential adequacy. Additional strategies of procedural rigor were also presented. They included a quality introduction section, coherence, use of appropriate citations, integration of findings, discussion of limitations and implications, substantive validation, and ethical validation. When selecting criteria and strategies of trustworthiness, it is important to consider the weight of each per research tradition as well as any risks they might pose to be viewed as promoting positivism.

## Review Questions

1. How does validity and reliability concepts in quantitative research compare to trustworthiness strategies used in qualitative research?
2. What are the similarities and differences across the four positions of qualitative research rigor? How might the strategies of trustworthiness be used with each position?
3. How can generalizability and transferability be maximized within qualitative research?
4. What are the types of triangulation and how might they be interdependent?
5. What are the benefits and challenges of employing member checking? How might these differ based on your selected research paradigm and tradition?

## Recommended Readings

Angen, M. J. (2000). Evaluating interpretive inquiry: Reviewing the validity debate and opening the dialogue. *Qualitative Health Research, 10*(3), 378–395.

Hays, D. G., & McKibben, W. B. (2021). Promoting rigorous research: Generalizability and qualitative research. *Journal of Counseling & Development, 99*(2), 178–188. https://doi.org/10.1002/jcad.12365

Kline, W. B. (2008). Developing and submitting credible qualitative manuscripts. *Counselor Education and Supervision, 47*(4), 210–217.

Morrow, S. L. (2005). Quality and trustworthiness in qualitative research in counseling psychology. *Journal of Counseling Psychology, 52*(2), 250–260. https//doi.org/10.1037/0022-0167.52.2.250

# PART III

# Data Collection and Analysis

# ■ CHAPTER 8

# Observations and Interviewing

---

## CHAPTER PREVIEW

Qualitative research offers several strategies for collecting data. Decisions about data collection are influenced by and influence aspects discussed in Parts I and II of the text as well as data analysis (see Figure 8.1). This chapter will review two primary forms of data collection: observations and interviews. In the discussion of each, information about the format, advantages and disadvantages, and strategies for successful data collection are presented. The chapter closes with additional data collection considerations, including data recording, initial data management, and data transcription.

## Linking Method to Research Design

As noted in Part II of the text, research designs can change, and thus qualitative researchers need to be open to variations in what and how data are collected. Several factors help determine the type and use of various data collection methods. These include (a) the nature of the study purpose (i.e., the more exploratory, the more open ended the method); (b) the extensiveness of existing scholarship for a study topic; (c) available resources, such as researchers' and participants' time and the number of cases to be investigated; and (d) relationships with all stakeholders, including participants, gatekeepers, and funders (Maxwell, 2013). In essence,

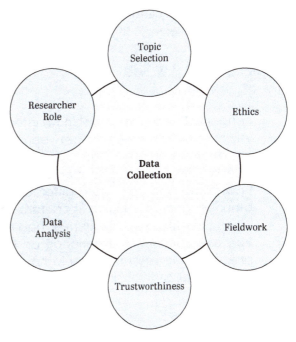

**FIGURE 8.1** Research Design Components Influencing Data Collection

planning about data collection methods involves all the things we have discussed thus far in the text: selecting a topic and research question, distinguishing which research paradigms and traditions fit your topic, considering ethics, identifying your role in the research design, deciding the extent to which you will be engaged in a research setting, and including methods to maximize trustworthiness.

Talking about data collection methods before developing a solid research question and supporting materials can set you up for failure: Without a proper foundation, what you did to collect (and analyze) data may not be trustworthy. Maxwell (2013) reminds us, however, that research questions are a guide for data collection methods. That said, research questions are not a direct translation into similar interview questions, observation protocols, or other methods: Methods require flexibility and particular attention to issues of trustworthiness, research relationships, and so forth. Thus, we have to be careful to not select methods that will get the "data we want" at whatever costs.

Further, qualitative data collection can serve as an intervention in itself for participants as well as the researcher. Be prepared to be changed by the research process as you uncover realities specific for participants and settings: Your attitudes and behaviors related to a particular phenomenon may shift as you learn from your participants. Also, your motivation to continue to speak for those with limited or no voice in research will likely be strengthened. If you have interacted with someone in your role as a practitioner or educator, you are probably familiar with this change process. The social nature of qualitative inquiry generates new knowledge and affective understanding of phenomena: You may start to think, feel, and respond in different ways as you become immersed in qualitative inquiry. Perspectives 8.1 offers some of our experiences with data collection as an intervention.

------------------------------------------------------------------------

## PERSPECTIVES 8.1. AUTHORS' PERSPECTIVES ON DATA COLLECTION AS AN INTERVENTION

I engaged as a participant in an interpretative phenomenological analysis of feminist mentorship between cisgender women mentors and cisgender men mentees. The process of being interviewed allowed me to deeply reflect on specific mentorship attitudes, behaviors, and skills that I possessed and how those differed in relation to mentoring men versus other genders. In addition, it crystallized my understanding of how my relationship with a specific mentee had evolved over a 5-year period. It was truly eye-opening to experience and consider how my knowledge and practice of feminist mentorship had been shaped by this specific mentee—as well as through the process of the interview itself.

—D. G. H.

At the outset of a study exploring the intersection of racial/ethnic and gender identities for transgender people of color that were survivors of trauma (Singh & McKleroy, 2011), I remember feeling really excited about the topic and working with participants. Then, as the interviews progressed, I heard numerous stories of severe victimization from participants. From severe beatings and hate crimes to intimate partner violence and child sexual abuse, these stories of violence all came back to transgender persons of color not being allowed to just grow, develop, and flourish in their identities. Fortunately, Danica and I had done a previous study with survivors of violence. From that experience, I remembered how we took care of ourselves as researchers and how we engaged in advocacy movements working to end violence.

—A. A. S.

Whichever methods you select for your design (and we recommend using multiple methods), each method decision needs to be explained and justified in your qualitative proposal or report. Maxwell (2013) highlighted that describing the context or setting can help the reader understand why certain decisions were made.

## Fieldwork

**Fieldwork** refers to research activities individuals engage in before, during, and/or after inquiry when in a particular setting —whether it is a classroom, a counseling agency, a focus group session, and so on. The purpose of fieldwork is to gather a thick description of the context and provide a deeper understanding of a particular phenomenon. As noted in Chapter 6, fieldwork considerations include choosing a sampling method; identifying sample size; selecting and entering a field site; building rapport with gatekeepers, stakeholders, and key informants in the field; and exiting the field. These interdependent considerations are integral to data collection and impact the quantity and quality of data gathered from various methods.

Qualitative researchers are trying to understand a research setting and participants and their behaviors and attitudes. So, if one is interested in the effectiveness of a grief group, conducting fieldwork would involve thickly describing a setting in objective and clear terms as well as providing information about participants in relation to that context. Immersion in the field (i.e., prolonged engagement), no matter the data collections that follow, is important to "know" how participants think, see, feel, and experience their realities. Thus, the setting is an important window into participant lives. To maximize trustworthiness, then, qualitative researchers might remain in an environment for an extended period of time, conducting observations, focus group interviews, individual interviews, and other methods.

Fieldwork is harder than it may seem. As Glesne (2014) notes, doing good fieldwork involves making the strange familiar and the familiar strange. Qualitative researchers are to remain open to new information that can test their taken-for-granted assumptions about a phenomenon. The notion of challenging all things familiar in a setting can be difficult: Imagine you are a therapist conducting research in the hospital in which you work. You would have to look at all the people, places, and things that you are used to seeing in a manner that has come to be so natural and thus no longer readily visible and reexamine them as if encountering them for the first time.

Now, pretend that you have been invited to a party where you know very few people. Initially, being at that party is quite anxiety provoking (especially for one of the authors of this text, who is quite the introvert!). You try to observe everything about the party site: what people at that party are like, how they are dressed, how they interact, what they talk about, and so forth. Initially, you try to take it all in and observe everything that is happening. Eventually, you become more selective and specific regarding your focus. You have likely been to parties before, so you have some ideas of what is normative or not. You constantly reflect on what you are experiencing and integrate it into the information you have about those you do know at the party, those you just met, and your experiences of parties in general. Observations are a bit like attending this kind of party: You are constantly making detailed notes, whether mental or otherwise, about what you see and experience and how you feel about it. The key to observing well, though, is to assume you always have something to learn about a setting and the individuals or artifacts that comprise it.

In Chapter 5 we discussed the importance of defining the case to be studied. In fieldwork, the case type will influence what aspects you attend to during data collection. Let's take the grief group effectiveness example just presented. An individual case might lead you to observe more closely particular individuals and thus could involve observing those individuals in settings other than the grief group. Your unit of analysis may be those grieving who do not attend a group. A setting case could involve also making observations at that agency outside of that group hour to learn about contextual dynamics that might relate to the effectiveness of that one group. The unit of analysis, for example, could be observing individualized interventions in that agency. A process case may focus more intently on group session dynamics, and an example unit of analysis may be remembrance and mourning. An event case could focus on something occurring within or outside the group—perhaps a group member's suicide attempt (i.e., unit of analysis)—and observe various angles and perspectives to capture how that event shapes group effectiveness.

The remainder of this chapter will present two primary data collection methods: observations and interviews. Toward the end of the chapter, data collection considerations are discussed.

## Observations

**Observations** are a primary source of qualitative data used to gather sensory information about a context or setting in whole or in part. Patton (2014) outlined several benefits to observational data:

- Observations allow the qualitative researcher to better capture and understand the context.
- Observations involve more present moments that allow a researcher to obtain setting details now rather than relying on others' conceptualizations of it.

- Participants may not be willing to discuss certain things in an interview, and the researcher can only obtain this by direct observation.
- Participants being interviewed may not be aware of particular dynamics or may have certain biases about a setting due to their subjective and active involvement.

Further, conducting observations involves ongoing and continual reflection of the setting, the participants, and your influence on the setting and participants that varies from interviewing or other forms of data collection.

Some study topics are more suitable to observations than others. As a rule of thumb, if you are more interested in what people do rather than what they say they do, observations are more appropriate. If your research tradition lends itself more to creating change (e.g., participatory action research, community-based participatory research) or understanding process to generate theory (e.g., grounded theory), observations are more suitable as compared to capturing meaning ascribed to an experience (e.g., phenomenology, autoethnography). Furthermore, they can stand alone as their own methods or supplement others. For example, if you are interested in triangulating whether what participants self-reported in individual interviews or personal blogs is accurate, observing their natural behaviors within a context can support the trustworthiness of the data.

On the surface, observing something seems simple. It is just watching something and taking mental notes, right? People do this all the time! Wrong. Try to describe this recent observation: You had dinner at a friend's home recently. What did the cookware and serving dishes look like? What was your friend wearing? What were the topics of conversation at dinner? Can you remember some important quotes? Can you summarize the conversation? How long were you at your friend's house? How long did it take you to eat? Who initiated the welcome and goodbye? These questions about this dinner interaction can be difficult to answer and highlight that witnessing and experiencing is not the same as *observing* something. Observing is so much more than watching or looking at something: It is training yourself to focus in on relevant participant and setting characteristics and behaviors and examining these things as you have never before.

Commonly referred to as *naturalistic observation*, this method has four guiding principles. First, there is typically noninterference on the part of the researcher. That is, one's impact should be as negligible as possible to not upset naturally occurring phenomena. A researcher can interact with participants yet in most cases should not intrude so much to change naturally occurring events. Second, the observation is to involve invariants, or naturally occurring behaviors. Some of these behaviors might include hyperactivity, teamwork, client disclosure, group process, or meeting agendas. Third, observations are to be used for exploratory purposes. Observations are quite beneficial when unexplored or underexplored phenomena are studied. Finally, observations are primarily descriptive. That is, a researcher is to provide a thick description of the setting so that an outsider can imagine sensory and behavioral aspects in order to fully experience it in detail.

## The Observation Continuum

For the most part, observations involve some degree of researcher participation. The observation continuum contains four points that range from little to no participant interaction to

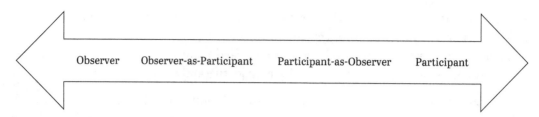

**FIGURE 8.2**  The Observation Continuum

full participant interaction (e.g., "going native"; see Figure 8.2). The **observer role** refers to having minimal or no interactions with participants. In these cases, participants are often not aware that they are being observed. A study on secretly observing hand-washing behaviors in a public restroom might be an example of the observer role. Examining individuals through a one-way mirror is another example. Non-participant data collection (i.e., observer role) can also involve video recording to collect data. If appropriately used, it can enhance the credibility of an observation study by capturing and making permanent records of nonverbal and verbal communication. This permanence allows opportunities for independent researchers to review the data repeatedly. However, we caution that video recording may make some participants even more unwilling to be observed, so care with the video recorder's "presence" is also an important consideration. In essence, the use of video recording needs to be justified as well as weighed against other forms of data collection, such as direct observation and audio recording.

The **observer-as-participant role** involves having a primary role as an observer with some interaction with study participants. An example of this role might be an education graduate student observing students from the back of a classroom with very few exchanges specific to the study. The **participant-as-observer role** can be considered the opposite of the observer-as-participant role: It involves becoming more a participant than an observer of others. Patton (2014) highlighted the paradox that although as researchers participate more in a setting, they become less objective with respect to the study, researchers also learn more as they participate more. Finally, the **participant role** refers to functioning both as a member of a community, classroom, or counseling agency under investigation and as an investigator. While going native is rare, it is most likely to occur with this role.

**Participant observation** refers to the researcher's active involvement in the setting and is best presented by the participant-as-observer and participant roles. Participant observation, however, is much more than points on one end of a continuum: It is often used in interviewing and other activities to negotiate tensions in a setting. It is a dance of participation, observation, and conversation that allows for deeper data collection, relationship-building, and often stronger designs. Patton (2014) reminds researchers that having an active role during data collection does not guarantee that you will be able to better understand participant experiences.

Where you begin on the observation continuum is influenced by many things, including the selected research tradition(s), the context of your study, and your theoretical perspective. Further, the degree of participation can change during qualitative research for several reasons. First, it can change based on research questions evolving or new ones emerging from data collection. As qualitative researchers collect observational data, it may be necessarily to collect data more actively (i.e., involve participants directly) to answer a more refined research question. Or observations may become more focused as you begin to search to confirm and disconfirm preliminary themes. Second, research relationships can dictate the qualitative researcher's involvement in observations. As relationships build, a researcher's participation in a setting may increase: Researchers communicate more with participants, engage in their daily activities, and observe them more intensely. Further, researcher participation will likely lessen as a research study comes to a close and researchers exit the field or site. Activity 8.1 provides an opportunity to consider the relevance and appropriateness of an observation for your study topic.

## ACTIVITY 8.1. ENGAGING IN OBSERVATIONS

Reflect on the following in dyads:

- How could observations be used in your study?
- What would you observe? How would you know you observed it?
- Using the observation continuum as a guide, how do you envision your role in an observation?
- What degree of involvement do you believe would be appropriate for data collection in your observations?
- How might your presence in a setting influence participants?

No matter the course of participation throughout qualitative inquiry, it is important to figure out ahead of time what you might find or expect to find in a setting. These ideas are likely to come from your conceptual framework and the setting itself. Before conducting observations as a sole data collection method or in conjunction with interviews, for example, it is prudent to jot down key behaviors or expressions that you expect to find. When studies are exploratory, enter the site with just these notes, if possible. At times, these "observation rubrics" become more focused (i.e., persistent observation) in cases where there is prolonged engagement in observing a setting or studying a phenomenon.

## Observation Protocol

An **observation protocol** includes instructions and rubrics for qualitative researchers to identify indicators of a phenomenon of interest. The protocol can be designed to observe a single or multiple target behaviors. Furthermore, it can be used to code behaviors by partic-ipant role. Data from observations may be narrative and/or numeric and can be reported in qualitative and/or quantitative form.

For example, qualitative researchers may be interested in exploring the extent to which the cultural identities of faculty members within one department are linked to department-meeting behaviors in an online environment. For this example, a qualitative researcher uses a sample of meeting recordings from a particular semester as the meetings are regularly recorded (i.e., observer role). Based on a thorough literature review related to meeting structure and interactions in higher education, the qualitative researcher identifies several cues that typically illuminate the phenomenon of interest. These cues could include quality and quantity of turn-taking, meeting content/topic, interruptions, bodily shifts (e.g., eye contact, turning camera off, eyebrow lift, smiling) related to meeting content, and so forth. Behaviors could be coded for each faculty member to explore cultural differences in meeting behaviors.

Qualitative researchers must carefully define concrete behavioral expressions of actions, thoughts, and feelings. If there are multiple observers, they are to establish agreement among how and when cues are coded, how data are reported on the protocol, and whether and how they will address any revisions to the protocol as new cues are identified. This agreement may be reached via consensus and/or calculated as interrater agreement. In the meeting example, how will turn-taking be coded as compared to interruptions? How will meeting topics be coded? Case Example 8.1 shows how one observation rubric, the Comprehensive Counseling Skills Rubric, was developed (Flynn & Hays, 2015).

## Case Example 8.1. Development of the Comprehensive Counseling Skills Rubric

Flynn and Hays (2015) developed the Comprehensive Counseling Skills Rubric (CCSR) as a tool that could allow for trainee self-assessment, a formative assessment of changes in a trainee's skill level after each counseling session, comparisons in a trainee's skill level with different clients or client issues, measurement of changes in skill level at various points in training, evaluation of the effectiveness of supervision interventions, and/or detection of professional impairment and programmatic training deficiencies. The following steps were taken to develop the CCSR:

- *initial item development:* They conducted a thorough review of empirical counseling skill classification systems and counseling skill preparation textbooks identified through multiple keyword searches. They then created an exhaustive list of all skills promoted within the literature and retained items that were frequently cited. Finally, they came to consensus on whether a skill was better accounted by a previously generated item. The initial CCSR was 28 items.
- *content validity:* Flynn and Hays used two panels to provide input on the CCSR items. The first panel consisted of seven counselor educators who had expertise in test development and experience in teaching a skill-based course. A second panel included 17 students in professional counseling or school psychology programs who had taken at least one counseling skills course during their respective programs.
- *initial interrater agreement:* Four counselor educators with comparable expertise as the seven expert panelists from the content validity step applied the CCSR for rating a digitally recorded mock counseling session to identify utility of the CCSR and to document agreed-upon skills present in the session.
- *additional interrater agreement:* Flynn and Hays recruited 63 counselor educators, counselor education doctoral students, and practicing professional counselors to review a mock counseling session and use the CCSR to assess the skills being utilized and the quality of skill execution.

- *final CCSR:* The final version of the CCSR is comprised of 30 items with five domains on a 6-point scale. They are as follows: *invitational skills* (nonverbal communication, encouragers, vocal tone, observation, and silence); *attending skills* (goal setting, open-ended questioning, closed-ended questioning, clarification, paraphrasing, summarizing, normalizing, and reflection of feelings); *influencing skills* (advocacy, immediacy, challenging and pointing out discrepancies, feedback, reflecting meaning and values, reframing, interpretation, self-disclosure, psychoeducation, homework, and directives); *phases of a counseling session* (opening phase, working phase, and closing phase); and *sessions of the counseling relationship* (intake, assessment, and termination).

Source: Flynn, S. V., & Hays, D. G. (2015). The development and validation of the Comprehensive Counseling Skills Rubric. *Counseling Outcome Research and Evaluation, 6*(2), 87–99. https://doi.org/10.1177/2150137815592216

Observation cues can be coded by frequency and/or intervals. *Frequency coding* is tabulating the number of actual occurrences of a behavior, and *interval coding* is marking whether a particular behavior was present within a specific interval. Intervals should be equal time frames. Figure 8.3 provides an example of an observation protocol for one target behavior (i.e., turn-taking) during a 1-hour meeting on the topic of promotion and tenure criteria for new faculty. The example includes opportunities for frequency and interval coding within a classroom. The counts can be interpreted quantitatively or qualitatively, alone or as part of multiple data sources (e.g., interviews with each faculty member).

In addition to designing an observation protocol whereby counts are recorded in some matter, qualitative researchers can include space for information about what occurred before, during, and after a target behavior. With the meeting example, the observer might develop

*Instructions:* Mark for each 10-minute interval the number of times each faculty member took a turn to contribute to the meeting topic discussion. Contributions are verbal utterances.

| **Faculty Member** | 9:01–9:10 | 9:11–9:20 | 9:21–9:30 | 9:31–9:40 | 9:41–9:50 | 9:51–10:00 |
|---|---|---|---|---|---|---|
| White Cisgender Man | 2 | 4 | 1 | 0 | 2 | 3 |
| Black Cisgender Man | 0 | 1 | 1 | 0 | 0 | 0 |
| Asian Transgender Woman | 0 | 1 | 0 | 0 | 0 | 1 |
| White Cisgender Woman | 1 | 3 | 2 | 1 | 1 | 2 |
| Latin Transgender Man | 1 | 0 | 0 | 2 | 1 | 1 |
| Black Cisgender Woman | 0 | 1 | 0 | 0 | 0 | 0 |

**FIGURE 8.3**  Observation Protocol for Turn-Taking in a Department Faculty Meeting

notes about what happened right before a faculty member took a turn to speak, the verbatim quote of what was stated during the turn, and what the consequence was for that faculty member or the other faculty members because of the respective faculty member taking a turn to contribute to the conversation.

Qualitative researchers may pilot an observation protocol, refining it as data collection progresses. Furthermore, they may develop one from field notes as they note commonly occurring behaviors and their cues (see the next section).

## Field Notes

**Field notes** are written records developed within an observational period (as possible) and continually expanded and revised after the observation has occurred. Sometimes referred to as *observational records*, the primary purpose of field notes is to create an accurate and thorough written record of field activities. Additionally, data collections (especially observation) are assumed to be a representation of purposeful behavior and actual expressions of feelings; thus, field notes are assumed to be important records of that information. They are an important data management and analysis tool that we think is important to address in this chapter of data collection methods due to their use in real-time data collection.

While we provide some examples of what to include as field notes and in what format, it is important that you develop a method that feels natural for you. Table 8.1 outlines some potential components of field notes. Figures 8.4 and 8.5 provide some field note templates you might consider adapting for your own use. These templates are useful to develop preliminary thick

**TABLE 8.1**   Field Notes Components

- Descriptions of physical setting (e.g., physical space, décor, signs/postings, ratio of people based on various categorizations and roles)
- Spatial or physical arrangement of people or things
- Participant information (e.g., dress, demographic information)
- Sensory impressions (what you see, smell, taste, hear, and feel)
- Daily routines and patterns of individuals and subgroups
- Transitions between activities
- Special events within a setting
- Important quotes
- Summaries and paraphrases of conversations
- Communication patterns (both verbal and nonverbal) and interactions among individuals based on various categorizations and roles
- Diagrams and sketches of physical setting
- Different participant perspectives
- Comments about potential key informants to provide additional data
- Unobtrusive data obtained during the data collection period
- Your thoughts, feelings, and reflections regarding the setting
- Notes about the participants' reactions and interactions with you
- Thoughts about what or whose voice might be missing from the setting
- New questions and ideas that impact the research design

**Field Note Template**

| Time | Cue | Behavior | Comments |
|------|-----|----------|----------|
|      |     |          |          |

**FIGURE 8.4** Field Note Template

description of your observation. They may be used in whatever format is most comfortable to you, whether it be a spiral notebook, index cards, a binder of loose-leaf papers, notepads, or as electronic files.

While they are quite useful with observations, field notes can also supplement other methods. For example, field notes during an interview session can serve as supplemental evidence to an audio recording.

Bogdan and Biklen (2016) described two types of field notes: descriptive and reflective. Both types of field notes are important because you want to record objective facts and details as well as your responses and reactions to them. **Descriptive field notes** capture details of what occurred in a setting. They provide behavioral descriptions of behaviors that are often abstract, such as teaching and clinical work. With descriptive field notes, qualitative researchers are

**Date:**
**Time of Observation:**
**Location:**
**Observer:**

| Facts and Details in the Field Site | Observer Comments |
|---|---|
| *[Insert verifiable sensory information in chronological order.]* | *[Insert reflections/subjective responses to the facts and details of the setting.]* |

**Reflective Summary:**
*[Insert the overall impressions of the observation as well as additional questions you have for future data collection.]*

**FIGURE 8.5** Field Note Template

to provide detailed depictions of participants and the physical setting, thick descriptions of specific events, and paraphrased, summarized, or verbatim quotes from participant conversations. Additionally, Bogdan and Biklen suggest that qualitative researchers should make field notes on their own dress, actions, and conversations with participants.

The second type of field notes is reflective field notes. **Reflective field notes** refer to the subjective aspects of data collection, including assumptions, impressions, attitudes, and ideas (Bogdan & Biklen, 2016). These brief notes should be infused throughout descriptive field notes. You are likely to initiate reflective field notes for a particular data collection before the data collection occurs. For example, these might include comments about your worldview and/or perspective on a research topic specific to that setting, your relationships with participants, thoughts about a particular setting, ideas about how the data collection method is timely and appropriate for the research question(s), cautions you may have about potential methodological problems, and potential ethical and professional considerations. Oftentimes, reflective field notes can help "end" field notes: You might reflect on how the new information is supplementing your knowledge of a particular phenomenon, what patterns or themes are being identified, and future points for clarification that relate to additional data collection sources, refined research questions, strategies for trustworthiness, and so forth. Case Example 8.2 is an example of including descriptive and reflective field notes.

## Case Example 8.2. Child with Autism and the Art Classroom

The following case, shared by Cheryl Shiflett, an art therapist and counselor educator, involves observing the interactions of a child with autism in an art classroom (reflective field notes are in italics):

The art classroom is located in a local school built in 2007. Classroom size is approximately 40'x35', is well-lit by natural and artificial light, and is decorated with art posters tacked onto the walls. The classroom has many amenities: two sinks, a kiln room, large areas for storage, and pottery wheels. Tables are adjustable for height. The chalkboard is covered with the directions for an apparent ongoing assignment and the American Sign Language Alphabet (ASL) is posted. Many art materials are spread out on tables and spilling out of storage containers. The sink tops are covered with paintbrushes and clay projects.

*There is a general sense of disorganization and messiness. The art teacher is visibly upset and distracted by a personal matter that she disclosed to me upon my arrival.*

My observation took place on the final day of art class for this group of students. The teacher did not have the materials ready for the students upon their arrival, and much of the class time was spent sorting through accumulated artwork that students needed for the day's assignment or work that needed to be returned before the summer break. Throughout the class, R.V. was distracted by this task.

For observation purposes, I sat near the teacher's desk. There were a few times when I became a participant; A student asked me for help with finding materials and I greeted the student with autism, as I have worked with him before in another setting.

*Observation 1: Art Classroom*

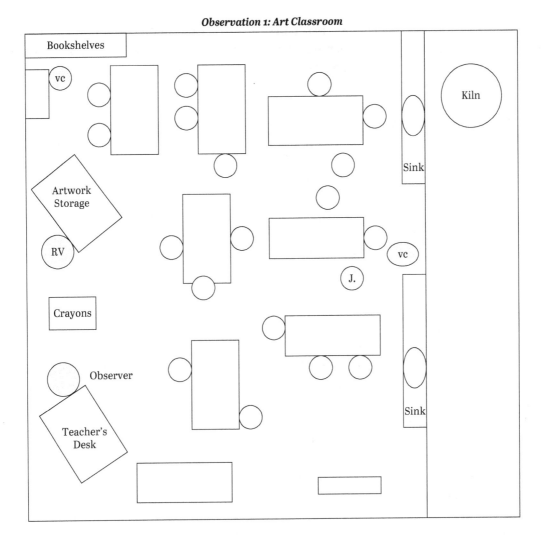

## 6/10/08 Observation One: Participants

R.V.: part-time, traditional art teacher in a local elementary school who has 30+ years of teaching experience. R.V. participated in an interview as well.

V.C.: a "floater" acting as J.'s assistant during art class. She is part of the self-contained special education classroom staff where J. is a student. A "floater" is a special education substitute who regularly fills in for special education staff who are absent

J. is a male, 9-year old student with Autism attending a self-contained classroom in a local elementary school where he has been mainstreamed into art for the 2007–2008 school year. He is in the fourth grade.

The class: traditional fourth graders

## 6/10/08, 8:15 A.M., Descriptive Notes from Observation One: Art Class Instruction with Student with Autism Included

Regularly scheduled class arrives, chatting and jockeying for seats. Teacher reconfigures seating choices by limiting three students to each table.

J. enters the classroom wearing a baseball cap, unaccompanied, three minutes after the other students and says, "Good morning!" brightly. *Where is his assistant? Why is he allowed to keep a baseball cap on when it is against school policy to wear one—Is this an accommodation for his autism?*

R.V. asks if his teacher is coming.

J. does not respond and, without hesitance, sits down at a table with two boys.

At 8:24 a.m. J.'s assistant arrives and picks up a chair and moves to a corner of the classroom where she can see J. but is out of physical and hearing proximity. *How can she physically assist or give verbal/gestural cues if necessary?*

J. engages in self-talk while his table mates talk to each other.

R.V. calls student names to come pick up their artwork. For J., R.V. specifically asks him to retrieve his paper. Not responding to the first request, R.V. repeats the direction to come get his art and, fidgeting with his hat, J. walks to the teacher to get his paper and sits back down at his table.

The assistant (V.C.) picks up her chair and moves closer to J. Apparently, she is realizing that she needs to be closer to J. in order to be effective.

The boys at J.'s table continue to talk to each other. There are no verbal exchanges or interactions between the two boys and J.

J. stands up and approaches R.V., who is next to the art supply trays, and inquires, "What about crayons?" Distracted, the teacher does not respond to his question and J. returns to the table. *I am impressed that J. does not take the crayons without the ok from his teacher.*

V.C. coaches J. to sit down.

R.V. says, "J. get your crayons." *Wow, doesn't this confuse J.? He requests something, is told to sit down, then is instructed to get up—a little "hokey pokey" ...*

J. walks to the art supply trays at the front of the classroom, picks up his crayons and returns to the table to sit down.

The boys are sorting through their own crayons and make joke about the brown crayon looking like chocolate milk. The boys laugh and J. laughs too. *It's difficult to determine whether J. gets the joke or is echolalic, however, perceptively, I don't believe he "got it."*

Laughing to himself, bouncing in his chair, and waving his arms intermittently, J. begins to color.

V.C. cues J. to put his arms down.

J. and one of his table mates have a brief verbal exchange. *This is the social interaction that is a primary goal for kids with autism.*

J. continues to talk to himself and color. Other students do not seem distracted by his behavior.

J. tosses his crayon up into the air, continues to rock in his chair and laughs. V.C. redirects J. to stop inappropriate behaviors. *Other students do not seem to notice this exchange.*

R.V. asks, "J. are you drawing some more stuff?" She reiterates the direction that J. should be using his crayons to create more images on his paper. *This is the first 1:1 interaction at the student's table.*

J. approaches the teacher's work area per her request. Two other students approach as well. R.V. irons J.'s paper image onto a piece of cloth.

R.V. asks J. to get a box of fabric markers.

J. appears unsure of what is being asked. Continuing to iron for other students, R.V. intermittently repeats the direction four times.

J. fiddles with the waistband of his pants and wanders around the classroom.

R.V. calls J. back to her and repeats the direction to use the fabric markers on the lightly faded image transfer to darken the cloth so that the image can be better seen.

J. states, "I don't want to draw." *J. seems resistant to using the markers on his drawing.*

V.C. redirects J. to go back to the table and encourages him to work on his "flag." *J.'s original drawing is a composition of neatly drawn animals. His transfer image is a faded copy of his original.*

J. diligently colors on the original drawing while his two table mates are talking to each other. One student is not working on anything.

J., engaging in self-talk, is asked about his work by V.C. J. does not respond.

J. continues to work on the original drawing rather than enhancing the cloth piece he was instructed to use. *J. is not following the teacher's direction. Is he expected to follow the direction? Does the teacher know he is not following her direction?*

V.C. walks around the class and chats with the other students about their artwork. Does this normalize her attendance to the class with J.? How does the teacher feel about this? Is it appropriate?

V.C. returns to J. and appears to recognize that he is not following the directions and encourages him to use the fabric markers on the material.

J. continues to color on the original drawing. Stubborn.

R.V., checking on what students have accomplished, stands in front of the classroom and asks J. to hold up his fabric flag.

J. says, "no," stomps his feet, groans, and continues to color on his paper.

V.C. encourages J. to hold up his fabric flag. J. has done no work on the fabric.

J. runs, stomping, to the front of the class, and shows R.V. his fabric. Without comment, J. runs and stomps back to the table. R.V. makes no comment that he has not followed the direction. V.C. does not discuss this with R.V. either.

R.V. says, "Lineup."

J. cleans up, gets his book, and groans as he leaves. J. has his planner with him to help with transitions, but he did not use it.

V.C. redirects his agitated behaviors as they leave the classroom at 8:55 a.m.

### 7/19/2008, Field Reflections from Observation One:

* *J. displayed behaviors typical of students with autism, self-talk, arm-waving, and fidgeting in his seat and pulling at his clothes. Although these behaviors could potentially be distracting to his classmates, most students did not appear to notice.*

- *The student's assistant (V.C.) did not enter the art room at the same time as J. I am uncertain whether this was to allow J. a bit of independence and part of a strategy or if V.C. should have been with J. at all times. Because the art teacher asked J. the whereabouts of his assistant, I suspect that V.C. should have been with J. Initially, V.C. seemed unsure of her role by taking a chair and moving to a corner of the classroom away from J's table. However, once directions were given to J., V.C. seemed to recognize that she would need to return within a closer proximity to J. She appeared very responsive to his needs by redirecting inappropriate behaviors (arm-waving, groans, running and stomping, etc.). She also encouraged him to follow the teacher's directions for completing the artwork.*

- *It did not appear that V.C. took any notes about J.'s time spent in art nor did she communicate with the art teacher before, during, or after class. Student's assistants are supposed to have a notebook for recording information. I'm uncertain whether the teacher or parents will be informed of J.'s participation successes and weaknesses.*

- *Although J. brought his communication planner, it did not appear that it was used to encourage following directions (i.e. "Show me what you are working for?") or to transition out of the classroom. Perhaps if his book, typically used for communicating needs, which includes a visual schedule, and incorporates a reinforcement tool for earning some privilege, had been utilized, some difficulties could have been ameliorated. For example, the planner could have been used to visually remind J. that in order for him to "earn" his privilege he would need to follow the direction. Also, perhaps, if J. had been encouraged to check his book, then the transition out of the class would have been easier.*

- *Although J. sat at a table with two boys, there were minimal verbal exchanges and few attempts at sharing supplies. The tablemates talked and joked with each other throughout the class time. J. spoke to one student briefly and laughed (most likely echolaliacally). If one of the goals is to encourage social interactions with the student with autism, then any exchange, it seems, is expected to occur naturally. Neither the art teacher nor the student's assistant intervened to promote interaction (i.e., limiting supplies for sharing).*

- *The art teacher did not seem to notice that J. did not follow the art directive. Rather than embellishing the cloth "flag," J. continued to color on the original drawing. She made no attempt to redirect him. I'm not sure if she knows whether or not she is responsible for encouraging him to follow directions. J. became agitated when his assistant redirected him to work on the fabric.*

- *J. worked diligently throughout the class while many of his classmates talked and joked loudly. J. genuinely appeared to enjoy creating the art.*

As you collect observational as well as other forms of data, you may be struck with more extensive thoughts or reflections and want to jot these down without disrupting the "flow" of a field note. These longer pieces are often referred to as **memos** (Corbin & Strauss, 2015) and are an important data collection *as well as* data management and analysis tools. We recommend that you keep memos in a reflexive journal, a strategy described in Chapter 7.

**ACTIVITY 8.2.** FIELD NOTE EXERCISE

Taking field notes involves recording descriptions of both subjective and objective data from observing an individual, group, context, or all three. Considering the components listed in Table 8.1, practice conducting field notes in triads. Take turns, with one person talking about their day for 5 minutes, one person asking follow-up questions, and the other person recording field notes. Switch roles. Discuss with each other your field notes and examine how you would expand them.

 **ACTIVITY 8.3.** OBSERVATIONAL EXERCISE

You and your coresearcher(s) are interested in communication patterns among university students with particular emphasis on the role of culture in communication patterns. Conduct a naturalistic inquiry in a setting of your choice in which you serve primarily in the observer or observer-as-participant role. Conduct fieldwork for no less than 20 minutes in your university and be sure to take field notes. While there may be multiple researchers working with you, you are to work alone on your field notes.

Come back to the class, review your field notes, and add to them as needed for a few minutes. What things did you attend to during the observation? Why do you think you focused on certain things in the setting? To what degree were you involved with individuals in the setting? What challenges about observations do you note?

Discuss your findings with your research team. How did your field notes compare?

Listen to other group's field notes from other sites within the university. How did your observations compare? What initial themes about communication patterns and culture can you derive from multiple observations from multiple researchers?

Go back to your observation setting. Try to observe for 15 minutes without taking notes. What was this process like for you this time?

## Strategies for Writing Field Notes

Imagine you have spent several hours observing a special education classroom to examine students' behavior toward a new student. Due to your role in the classroom as a teacher's assistant, you are only able to mentally note your observations. A couple of hours pass before you are alone with your thoughts about the data collection, and you begin to panic because your memory is failing you. All you can really remember is the conversations you had with the teacher about the observation! Actions and conversations among the students seem to be lost.

This scenario is common with observations: Researchers tend to be overconfident during the observation that they will remember enough of the details of a setting and events to write an elaborate field note about the observation later. Thus, we believe that there are several important strategies for writing field notes.

First, write quickly and as much as possible! Constructing a detailed field note involves allowing ample time and attention to the data source. This will be particularly important if you are unable to write notes during the observational period itself. For instance, you probably do not want to take notes while observing a religious ceremony. Focus initial writing on remembering scenes and contexts rather than the words to describe the scene; avoid editing and refining the document too soon.

Field notes can be recorded in many forms that may include mental notes, jotted notes, or full notes, representing a continuum of less to more detailed note-taking. There are several strategies for recalling what happened and expanding notes: Start in chronological order; begin with a salient moment or high point of an observational period and then consider other significant events and interactions; or focus more systematically on events that relate to topics of interest. We believe that constructing a record in chronological order is the most effective strategy.

As soon as you can, construct (initially in a chronological manner) what happened and when it happened. While you may want to organize your data source differently, such as by topic rather than time, we find it is easier to recall details if there is a systematic method for doing so. We believe that relying on topics to jog your memory is dangerous because there may be topics you "leave out" (intentionally or not) because you do not see them as salient.

Second, be committed to sufficiently documenting the data source. For every 30 minutes you spend observing a site, prepare to spend at least 3 times that amount of time adequately reconstructing the period. It is important to not leave anything out; you never know what might be important. Even when completing what you consider a thorough field note, we encourage you to go back and edit it. That is, read and reread your notes and continue to develop memos. We have found that after writing it, there are things that get added as our memories continue to construct additional details. Further, we have found that reflective field notes and memos become richer with a thorough review and revision. For example, if you were conducting the observation in the special education classroom, you would consider the perspectives of others in the room (e.g., new student, peers, teacher) and memo about these perspectives and how they might influence data collection and analysis. No matter your strategy for completing field notes, "writing field notes from jottings is not a straightforward remembering and filling in; rather, it is a much more active process of constructing relatively coherent sequences of action and evocations of scene and character" (Emerson et al., 1995, p. 51).

Third, be aware of your impact on the setting. Your influence on the setting and its participants will be important to include as reflective field notes and memos for your ongoing data collection and analysis. **Observer effect** refers to the unintentional effect you as an observer have on the research and participants. It is important in your notes to ascertain normal behavior from behavior changed because of the researcher's presence. **Observer bias** refers to the subjective way you as an observer selectively observe particular individuals, events, and activities within an observation period. There are several ways to minimize any negative impacts of observer effect and bias, including receiving adequate training, minimizing the time spent conducting each observation, videotaping participants, maintaining audit trails, writing thorough field notes, using multiple observers, observing phenomena in multiple settings and at multiple times, altering your degree of involvement within one setting over time within one observational period as well as across data collections, and so on.

Finally, do not discuss the observation with others until you have a chance to construct a quality field note. As indicated in the scenario above, you may forget large chunks of details about an observation. Alternatively, others can bias your personal impressions of the data source or, worse, minimize its importance overall to your study.

 **REFLEXIVE ACTIVITY 8.1.** CONDUCTING AN OBSERVATION

Consider the following questions before developing an observation protocol:

- What is the nature of your planned involvement at a site or sites?
- How much will be revealed to people in the setting about the study purpose?
- How much will be revealed about you personally and professionally?
- How intensively will you be present? Why?
- How might your personality characteristics (e.g., sense of humor, degree of introversion) impact your observation?
- How focused will participation be? Why?
- How long will you observe each time, and how frequently will you observe?
- How can you safeguard against any negative impacts of your presence in the site or sites?
- How does your participation relate to your research question(s)?
- What are some key components you might find in your site? From where do these components originate?
- Which is more appropriate to begin observing: a field note or an observation protocol?

We would like to close this discussion on observations with some steps in observational research:

1. Select setting or context to observe based on the case and research question(s).
2. Determine degree of participation (see observation continuum, Figure 8.2).
3. Create a list of things you might expect based on your conceptual framework and other knowledge specific to the site or context. (As observations increase, develop a more refined observation rubric or protocol.)
4. Use a field note template to develop preliminary thick description, outlining descriptive and reflective field notes as well as memos.
5. While what you observe will depend on your study, you may select to observe setting characteristics, participant characteristics, and/or events (see Table 8.1).
6. Observe for brief periods, taking time to further develop initial thick description from field notes before returning to the field. It may be important to observe multiple settings, one setting at various times, or one setting from various angles.

# Interviews

**Interviews** are the most popular data collection method in qualitative research, a method that has helped to create and advance research traditions such as ethnography, grounded theory, life history, and phenomenology (Brinkmann & Kvale, 2015). Interviews have guided much of early theory in education and mental health settings and continues to be a preferred option for unexplored and underexplored social phenomena. Whom to interview is based on the research question(s) and the accessible population. Interviews can involve one individual (*individual interviews*), a pair of informants (*dyadic interviews*), and couples, families, or groups (i.e., *focus group interviews*). In this section, we provide some general information and characteristics about interviewing.

The term "interview" originates from the 17th century, yet the practice of informal interviewing increased significantly in the social sciences in the 20th century. Brinkmann and Kvale (2015) cited four historically significant interview studies: (a) Sigmund Freud's therapeutic interviews with his patients to develop new psychological knowledge about personality, sexuality, and neuroses (e.g., Freud, 1899/2010, 1905/2000, 1940/1989); (b) Jean Piaget's interviews with children to develop a theory of child development (e.g., Piaget, 1964; Piaget & Inhelder, 1969); (c) Elton Mayo, Fritz Roethlisberger, and William Dickson's interviews of workers at the Hawthorne Chicago plant of the Western Electrical Company to investigate increases in production level based on illumination changes (Mayo et al., 1939); and (d) Ernest Dichter's interviewing study of design and advertisements of consumer products (e.g., Dichter, 1947, 1964). These key studies paved the way for understandings about human development and behaviors and influenced the continued use of interviewing across disciplines such as psychology, education, counseling, and business, to name a few.

Scholars (e.g., Brinkmann & Kvale, 2015; Sands et al., 2007) have identified several general characteristics of interviewing:

- *qualitative:* There is a nuanced understanding of participant knowledge but does not aim at quantification.
- *meaning:* The interview process extracts participant-held truths and seeks to understand the meaning or central themes of what is said and how it is said.
- *descriptive:* The interviewer and participant(s) articulate the many differences and variations of a phenomenon versus identifying fixed categories.
- *specificity:* Specific situations and actions are elicited in the interview process versus general opinions.
- *deliberate naiveté:* There is an openness to new and expected phenomena wherein the interviewer adopts the stance of learner.
- *focus:* The interviewer directs the discussion toward derived themes.
- *ambiguity:* The interviewer clarifies ambiguities and contradictory statements as needed.
- *change:* Because knowledge construction is contextual, there is a likelihood that descriptions and attitudes discussed by the participant(s) can change throughout the interview.

- *sensitivity:* The interviewer has an "ear" for the phenomenon in that there are varying levels of sensitivity toward, and knowledge about, the interview topic.
- *interpersonal:* Knowledge is co-constructed as an interaction between the interviewer and participant(s). Interview data involves the social and cultural production of knowledge.

Conducting a quality interview and analyzing interview data, then, involve careful attention on researcher subjectivity, participant background, interviewer interaction, and interview content (Brinkmann & Kvale, 2015). And no interview is the same, so expect variations in interview process and content given that the interviewer and participant each bring different identities and experiences to the interview (see Wild Card 8.1).

## WILD CARD 8.1. NO INTERVIEW IS THE SAME!

Interviewers and participants are *not* interchangeable. No matter which form of interviewing you use, do not assume that you will gather the same types of data no matter who the interviewers or participants are. Both bring unique experiences, personality dynamics, cultural characteristics and skills that make the interview process unique and thus the content variable. Interviewers have different ideas about the purpose of the interview: Are you trying gain information or share information and create new meanings?

I had a research team of 10 conducting individual interviews. Even though we used a semistructured interview format, transcripts varied greatly among the research team. Based on interviewer characteristics and abilities, as well as relationships with participants, some transcripts were more expansive than others. Some research team members asked the questions verbatim, others disclosed personal information to elicit responses, and others diverted from the protocol yet still provided relevant data.

—D. G. H.

I remember piloting a new structured interview protocol. We were asking questions about risky behavior: topics which typically included talking about sex, drugs, and needle use. I found that certain people were less comfortable with the topics, so they would skip over these questions or not ask follow-up probes when participants gave answers that involved risky behavior. Then, there were interviewers who were *more* than comfortable with these topics, and at times asked questions that were too personal for participants. Because it was a pilot interview, I was able to regroup with the team and talk more about our comfort levels with the topic of risky behavior. This helped interviewers ask all the questions in the interview protocol, but we still had variance in some of the in-depth probes.

—A. A. S.

## Types of Interviews

No matter the participant(s), there are three primary types of interviews that qualitative researchers can conduct. The first type of interview is the structured interview. The **structured interview** relies on a preestablished sequence and pace of questions that a researcher follows rigidly. Questions are asked exactly as written, and probes—if included—are also standardized. Qualitative researchers typically do not reveal anything personal about themselves and remain as neutral as possible. One advantage of this form of interview is it assures that the same information (depth and breadth) is covered with all participants. Structured interviews are more likely used in survey research or telephone interviews. Some researchers (e.g., Bogdan & Biklen, 2016) argue, however, that the more structured an interview becomes, the less "qualitative" the data are since the interview content and process are so controlled. That is, participant voice becomes limited and increasingly defined by what the qualitative researcher wants a participant to say.

The second type of interview is the semistructured interview. The **semistructured interview** typically has an interview protocol that serves as a guide and starting point for the interview experience. Once the interview begins, the participant has more say in the structure and process. Even though there is a protocol, not every interview question needs to be asked, the sequence and pace of interview questions may change, and additional interview questions may be included to create a unique interview catered to fully describing the participant's experience. Although this type of interview does not ensure consistency of the data collection experience across participants, it is advantageous in that it can be more inclusive of participant voice as well as allow for a more interactive research design (Maxwell, 2013).

The third type of interview is the unstructured interview. The **unstructured interview** is a nondirective data collection method that does not include preestablished interview questions; the participant structures the interview as it unfolds. The label "unstructured" is misleading, as no interview can be fully unstructured: Qualitative researchers usually enter the field with some guiding topics for discussion. That is, they query in a manner that steers toward a research topic of interest. Unstructured interviews focus a lot on the surrounding context at the time of the interview. For example, qualitative researchers will often observe and memo about the context while approaching select participants (i.e., key informants, typically) to confirm their observations. Advantages of unstructured interviews are that they are heavily interactive with the research setting and context and allow qualitative researchers an openness that allows greater participant engagement and voice. In some ways, participants are more likely to ask questions of the interviewer, and interviewers may disclose more than in other interview types. One disadvantage of this type of interview is that it may be difficult to compare and integrate data across unstructured interviews. Another disadvantage is that it may not be an ideal choice for focus group interviews given the presence of multiple participants and thus the unlikely outcome of the interviewer being able to follow where each participant takes the interview.

It is possible to use multiple interview types in the same study: As a qualitative researcher proceeds through the study, the interviews may become more focused to explore specific topics, to test preliminary findings, or to begin to look for commonalities and differences across participants. Thus, interviews can become more structured.

# Strategies for a "Good" Interview

It may be difficult to determine what a "good" interview looks like, but there are a few general indicators. In general, as qualitative researchers conduct an interview, they are to listen carefully to participants, show personal interest and encourage them, and ask open-ended questions that allow them to speak freely and comfortably. In this section, we highlight general strategies that can maximize the success of your interview protocol, discussed in the next section. At the end of this section, we present some lessons learned from "bad" interviews (see Wild Card 8.2).

## Create a Diverse Research Team

In earlier chapters, we discussed the importance of the research team in maximizing trustworthiness throughout the research process. Research teams for interviewing should be culturally diverse and involve members with familiarity with the topic and skills for conducting interviews. Furthermore, it may make sense to divide interviewing responsibilities among the research team members. For example, each member can interview a subsample of participants, or some members can conduct initial interviews while others engage in follow-up interviews and/or member-checking activities.

## Develop an Interviewing Plan

Developing an initial plan for interviewing involves ethical considerations (Chapter 3), research tradition alignment (Chapter 4), sampling decisions (Chapter 5), field work considerations (Chapter 6), and planning for maximizing trustworthiness (Chapter 7), including attending to researcher reflexivity before, during, and after interviewing (Chapter 1). Regarding the general interview plan, qualitative researchers outline (a) who will be interviewed and by what method (i.e., individual, dyadic, focus group) and in what sequence; (b) how community members and/or potential participants will guide interview question formulation; (c) what adjustments may need to be made throughout interviewing; and (d) how they will engage with key informants or trusted members of a cultural community to gain relevant access. Qualitative researchers are also to plan for later interviewing to clarify points, member checking, or follow-up if the period for the study is extended.

While we discuss the interview protocol in more detail later in the chapter, it is important to note that a good interview includes questions that are sufficiently specific so the participant can respond but do not convey in any way there is one right answer. There is also shared terminology between the interviewer and participant: The interviewer understands how the participant conceptualizes concepts discussed in the interview, and the interviewer uses terms or labels used by participants in their daily lives rather than research topics established by a discipline.

Questions are also sequenced in a manner that facilitates comfort and disclosure: Qualitative researchers begin with open-ended questions and use nonspecific terms until the participant begins to label things. Furthermore, they begin with easy-to-answer questions to build confidence and trust for harder or more sensitive questions later in the interview. Thus, it is important to adjust the timing and ordering of questions so that sensitive questions are asked later, as relevant. Over the course of interviewing, qualitative researchers may also

### WILD CARD 8.2. LESSONS LEARNED FROM A BAD INTERVIEW

We asked our students and colleagues to talk about lessons learned from unsuccessful interviews. Here they are, in no particular order:

- Do not turn the tape off after the interview. Wait until you are completely done interacting with a participant. Some of the richest data comes from conversations after the interview protocol is done.
- Avoid telephone interviews unless geographical location presents a problem. The face-to-face interactions are extremely important to obtain nonverbal cues during the interview.
- Practice your interview with someone. If not, your anxiety as an interviewer may cause you to rush through the interview and jump from topic to topic.
- Do not be afraid to steer away from an interview protocol. Expand on spontaneous conversations and note dynamics of the research relationship. Although it is hard to attend to both content and process during an interview, it is absolutely necessary.
- Conduct your interview in a natural setting but without distractions, as possible. This means no other people in the setting, no background noises, and no interruptions.
- Remind your participants of who you are and what the purpose of the interview is at the beginning of your interview. Sometimes, participants will be nervous and will go off topic, especially if you are working with a vulnerable group.
- Do not use "ten dollar" words (e.g., "resilience") in your interview when you can use a simpler word that conveys the same meaning (e.g., "bounce back"). Definitely do not step away from the power you have as a researcher, because your participants will see you as the "expert." But use this power to be in collaboration with your participant as opposed to holding power over them as an interviewer.
- Avoid becoming the participant. If it feels too much like a conversation and you are the only one disclosing, it is likely no longer an interview. Disclose to build rapport, but step back to hear their voice.
- Relatedly, each question you ask takes time and space "away" from the participant. Be conscious about not firing away question after question. You do not want your participants to feel like they are being interrogated.
- Research questions are not interview questions. When you start translating your research questions directly to interview questions, you are likely to just get the responses you want. Be creative and seek help when developing your interview protocol.
- Take care with your presentation. You should dress and conduct the interview in a way that does not make the interviewee guarded or resistant to being honest with you. More so than not, you will be leaving the suits at home

identify commonalities among participants and build upon them in subsequent interviews to facilitate comfort.

## Prepare for the Interview

Qualitative researchers are to learn as much as possible about participants prior to the interview. This can include background or demographic information on participants and the contexts in which they live and work, familiarity with the expressions and terms that they routinely use, local norms for the kinds of questions and topics that are typically asked of the community, culturally specific information for a community of interest, and culturally appropriate behaviors for the interviewer in the setting.

There are also logistical strategies for preparing for the interview. These can include ensuring that the interview location (physical or virtual) is convenient, safe, and comfortable for the participant. When possible, give participants a choice in how, when, and where the interview will be held. Qualitative researchers are to consider data management decisions as well, such as video or audio recording. Is the location selected appropriate for audible recordings? How will the interview be recorded? Finally, ample time should be planned for the interview to sufficiently process the interview question responses, with additional time allowed for establishing rapport. In general, interviews can last between 30 and 90 minutes depending on the interview type and method. However, the duration of interviews needs to consider the comfort of participants, respect their time, and minimize intrusion.

## Maximize Participant Voice

Because of the dynamic nature of interviews among individuals of varying cultural and personal characteristics, power issues can enter the interview process. Thus, fostering an interviewing relationship wherein participant voice is maximized is imperative. Qualitative researchers can encourage participant voice through the interview process as well as during data analysis. With respect to the interview process, qualitative researchers are to:

- Be clear from the outset what the purpose of the interview and study is, outlining for the participants the topics that will be covered to allow them time to express concerns about the topics and/or how the data will be used.
- Express that the interview is a two-way dialogue and invite questions and comments throughout the interview.
- Give participants opportunities to introduce their own topics and concerns into the discussion.
- Provide appropriate "wait time" after the question.
- Use basic helping skills (e.g., eye contact, body posture, nodding, active listening) to help the participant feel heard.
- Commit to being empathetic and approach the participant with an ethic of care.
- As applicable, ask how participants feel or if they have concerns about being interviewed by someone of a different cultural identity, or offer to have them interviewed by someone of similar background if possible.

- Balance power between the interviewer and participant through self-disclosure and dialogue.
- Invite the participant to question the dialogue and encourage counternarratives as appropriate to dismantle how power has shaped conceptualizations of constructs under exploration.
- Allow space for the participant to share experiences of discrimination, misconceptions, and oppression to allow for counternarratives.
- Communicate to the participant that their interview responses are helpful. This can be done directly, like saying, "This has been very helpful" to more indirectly, such as saying, "That is really interesting. I have never thought of it that way."

When analyzing interview data, qualitative researchers are to include participants and the community as relevant in the process. Findings reported through a lens of decolonization, transformation, mobilization, and healing can contribute to restorative justice for marginalized individuals and communities.

## Avoid Questions that Limit Participant Responses

Responses can be limited by various types of interview questions. For example, **dichotomous questions** (i.e., yes-or-no questions) or forced-choice responses have participants select a response to a question without an opportunity to elaborate on why they responded in a particular way (e.g., Do you believe that college students are drinking more than last decade? Have you noticed a change in the quality of students entering your graduate program?).

Second, **multiple questions** (or double-barreled questions) involve asking more than one question within one question. The problem you face with this is that participants may never answer all parts of the interview questions thoroughly or accurately. This makes it difficult to analyze interview responses. Consider this example: What are the benefits and challenges of integrating special education students in the general classroom. No matter how the participant responds, it will be difficult to determine which are descriptions of benefits and which are of challenges. Additionally, not having a singular focus or question of benefits, with an additional, separate focus on challenges, sends a message that independent attention to each is not warranted.

In addition, the number of questions included in the interview protocol can limit participant responses. If there are too many questions, participants may become weary from the interview process and thus not fully attend to the question or respond in a limited manner. If there are too few questions, participants may not have an opportunity to provide a comprehensive response to address the phenomenon of interest. Furthermore, adjust the number of questions based on the age and developmental level of participant(s).

## Do Not Attempt to Get the Participant "On Your Side"

Whether intentional or not, we as interviewers may let it be known to each participant what our thoughts and attitudes are regarding a phenomenon. To minimize this from happening nonverbally or through probes, avoid behaviors such as head nods and changes in facial expressions for particular responses (e.g., grimace, wider eyes) and verbal statements (e.g., "right," "uh huh," and "really"). Essentially, you show interest in what participants are saying but do not give away your opinions and recommendations in a manner that disempowers their voice in their research or sways their attitudes or behaviors. **Leading questions** can influence the direction of the respondent's response and thus can limit the openness of the response; they are more direct verbal statements that can be harmful to rigorous data collection as well as to the research relationship in general. These types of questions might begin with more overt stems, such as "Don't you agree that ..." and "Isn't it true that ..."; however, leading questions can be more subtle to use. For example, pretend you are interviewing 7th grade students about the effectiveness of a study skills program. Asking questions that only assume the program was effective rather than also including questions that uncover program challenges or other interventions altogether that have helped them improve their study skills would be an example of using leading questions.

## Avoid "Why" Questions

Like leading questions, we would like to caution against the use of "why" questions: Asking a participant why something occurred is likely to make that participant defensive. And a why question might make an participant feel that they should know why something happened or is the way it is. Almost any why question can be reworded without the word "why." For example, an interviewer can ask, "Why is there more vandalism occurring in your high school?" and potentially get a defensive administrator who will want to exit the interview as fast as possible. Alternatively, the same question can be rephrased to "Tell me about the amount of vandalism that has occurred in your school over the past several years."

## Read the Results

Qualitative researchers typically create a transcript of the interview, discussed later in this chapter. The transcript can give a good indication of the quality of the interview. In reviewing the write-up, the participant's words should be represented significantly more so than the researcher's. Further, qualitative researchers should encounter several details and examples given by participants, based on questions that allow for a deep exploration of a phenomenon or experience.

In reading a transcript, you are likely to find responses you want them to follow up on or phrases that need clarification. As a method of member checking (see Chapter 7), we encourage you to conduct multiple interviews with each participant. At the very least, in instances when you are unable to sit down with a participant again, we recommend that you have them review the transcript and insert comments to clarify any questions you have or to elaborate on points they made.

## The Interview Protocol

If you are conducting a structured or semistructured interview, you are encouraged to spend time carefully developing an interview protocol. An **interview protocol** is a written document that outlines the interview questions and what will be said before and after interview questions are asked (e.g., informed consent information). A well-written interview protocol, in which qualitative researchers have carefully developed and tested the potential interview questions, will increase the trustworthiness of the study. Proposal Development Activity 8.1 can serve as a guide for developing your interview protocol.

**PROPOSAL DEVELOPMENT ACTIVITY 8.1.** DEVELOPING AN INTERVIEW PROTOCOL

Like developing items for scales or surveys, developing an interview protocol involves multiple phases to maximize the trustworthiness of the interview questions.

*Step 1:* For this activity, develop no more than 10–12 questions (or less, depending on your research questions and traditions). We suggest using your conceptual framework (Chapter 5) to generate initial interview topic areas. Then apply information in this chapter about types of interview questions and strategies for a good interview. As your develop a draft of interview questions, consider the wording and ordering of questions; note where redundancy of questions may occur; ensure they are not vague, invasive, or culturally insensitive; and rehearse the interview protocol aloud with a peer.

*Step 2:* Discuss your interview protocol with your research team or a peer.

- Are the interview questions too limiting or leading? (Is it biased so that certain "answers" will be generated that may falsely support what you expect to find?)
- Are the questions too broad?
- Are they clear, concise, and precise questions?
- Is there evidence of cultural bias in your interview questions?
- If you do find the answer to your interview question, what is the purpose (the "so what" factor)?
- What are the strengths of your questions?
- Do your questions offer an opportunity to maximize voice?
- What are some suggestions for improving your protocol?

*Step 3:* Revise the interview protocol and document the process for your audit trail. As you collect and analyze data, be sure to continually evaluate your interview questions with your research team or peer, or perhaps participants and other stakeholders.

Scholars (e.g., Brinkmann & Kvale, 2015; Patton, 2014; Roulston, 2013) have outlined several types of interview questions that serve as useful templates when developing an interview protocol. These categories of questions are likely suitable as primary questions or probes for most research traditions and settings. Questions may be asked in the past, present, or future tense as appropriate. Questions can be open or closed, although we encourage you to use open-ended questions to elicit rich information from participants. As we define each category, we will illustrate them by providing examples of interview questions using a study involving mental health practitioners' experiences with the homeless population. As indicated, some interview questions may be formatted in the form of a statement.

## Demographic Questions

**Demographic questions** are foundational questions that the interviewer should ask about the participant, setting, or phenomenon during the interview itself or in some written form, such as a demographic questionnaire. If these are included in the interview itself, they should be kept to a minimum since responses to these types of questions are likely to be concrete and superficial. Examples include:

- For how many years have you identified as a mental health practitioner?
- State your gender.
- Provide your job title.
- Estimate the typical number of clients you have facing homelessness.

## Background Questions

**Background questions** are typically included earlier in an interview to allow the participant to describe in some detail information about themselves or a context related to the study topic. They are largely descriptive, open-ended questions that allow depth in understanding of the participant or the phenomenon of interest. Examples include:

- Describe your background in working with the homeless population.
- Tell me about the skills needed to successfully address mental health issues with the homeless population.
- What are available resources in your community for individuals dealing with homelessness?

## Behavior or Experience Questions

This category of questions solicits information about participants' actions and their reflections on those actions. **Behavior or experience questions** are the "what versus why" questions: As an interviewer you are concerned with gathering a thick description of what occurred by and for the participants rather than *why* things occurred. Thus, you may ask participants to describe some event or situation and follow up with questions about their actions and experiences. Examples include:

- Tell me about what services, if any, you provide to the homeless population.
- How do your services for a client who is homeless compare to one that is not homeless? Can you describe it to me? What happened?
- What did you do when your client could not find affordable housing?
- How did you experience the city's housing office?

## Opinion or Value Questions

These questions pertain to collective and individual beliefs about why things occur. **Opinion questions** seek participants' personal beliefs about a phenomenon. **Value questions** involve those about social norms in relation to individual beliefs. Examples include:

- How do you perceive the homeless population is treated in this city?

- What concerns, if any, do you have about a client who is homeless seeking mental health services?
- What do you think are the factors hindering housing security within your community?

## Knowledge Questions

**Knowledge questions** solicit responses from participants about the amount of information they possess about a phenomenon as well as where that knowledge originated. Examples include:

- Approximately what percentage of client who come to your agency identify as homeless?
- What common concerns do clients who identify as homeless express?
- What are the typical demographics of clients who identify as homeless?

## Feeling Questions

Departing from "what and why" interview questions, **feeling questions** are not interested in the validity of how participants respond or what they know. Instead, you are interested in how they feel about something. Examples include:

- What feelings arise for you when you are working with a client who identifies as homeless?
- What emotional responses do you have to those clients who are children?
- What emotions occur for you when you consider housing assistance in your community?

## Sensory and Simulation Questions

Using the five senses (i.e., sight, hear, taste, smell, touch) in developing questions for this category, interviewers asking **sensory questions** are typically seeking information from participants about their bodily experiences. While this may seem strange at first, the use of sensory questions is useful for completing a picture of the participant's experience that is untapped in cognitive and affective responses. Sensory questions may also be referred to as **simulation questions**, which request that the interview verbally observe a phenomenon for the interviewer. That is, the interviewer will ask the participant to place themselves in a situation. Examples include:

- Describe for me the sights and sounds of a recent group session that includes clients who identify as homeless.
- If I were to listen in on an intake session between you and your agency director about meeting the mental health needs of the homeless population in this community, what would I hear?
- If I were a potential client coming to your agency, what if anything would I expect in terms of gaining knowledge about housing assistance?

## Role-Playing Questions

One successful method for engaging the participant is by emphasizing them as an expert on a phenomenon. **Role-playing questions** allow the participant to discuss a topic from a particular role of authority. The question stem "what advice would you give" is an example of this type of question. Examples for the sample study include:

- What advice would you give to beginning mental health practitioners when working with the homeless population?
- If you were in charge of supporting individuals experiencing homelessness in your community, what would you do?
- What recommendations can you provide to training programs for preparing practitioners regarding homelessness issues and mental health?

## Probing Questions

Seldom written out ahead of time, **probing questions**, or probes, are the "who, what, when, where, and how" questions that help to expand an participant's responses. Probing questions can be verbal, such as elaboration and clarification questions, or can be nonverbal, such as head nods. In interviews with multiple participants, they can encourage a deeper interaction among participants that facilitates potentially divergent attitudes, beliefs, and experiences. No matter what probes you use, the idea is to get participants to provide a richer interview because their voices are important. Oftentimes, you can use the participant's own words in the probe. Probing questions can be closed ended and serve as a follow-up to check interviewer understanding. Examples of probing questions are:

- Can you give me an example?
- Tell me a little more about that.
- What happened next?
- How did that happen?
- What was that like for you?
- Where were you?
- Who else was there?
- Earlier you talked about. ... Tell me more.
- In your description, you used the word ___. What did you mean by that?
- You mentioned ___. Describe an example of that.

## Comparison Questions

**Comparison questions** can be used to have the participant link information presented in other parts of data collection. Furthermore, data from other participants can be used as a reference point to elicit information from a participant. Examples are:

- Some participants have noted that most of their clients are working full time yet cannot afford housing. How does that fit for you?
- How does the mental health needs of the homeless population in urban areas compare to that in rural areas in which you have worked?
- What, if any, differences in mental health concerns have you noticed between clients who have and have not experienced homelessness?

## Presupposition Questions

While it is generally preferred that qualitative researchers ask questions in an open-ended manner to avoid influencing or limiting participant responses, sometimes it might be relevant to assume some experience in a question to encourage participant elaboration. **Presupposition questions**, then, assume some information from the participant. Using the scenario of an individual who has been abusing substances with a high likelihood of comorbid disorders, examples of presupposition questions include: Can you tell me about the depression or anxiety symptoms you have been experiencing? How have your physical symptoms changed in severity since you began drinking? Related to the homelessness and mental health study, and example presupposition question might be: Tell me about a time where you felt personally challenged with working with this population. This probe assumes that the participant has experienced personal challenges, which—if correct—could encourage honest and rich responses.

## Transition Questions

As the interviewers moves to different topics within the interview or closes the interview session, **transition questions** can assist to elicit further information or check for understanding. Examples include:

- You told me that family factors such as trauma and intergenerational poverty are most predictive of homelessness. Is that accurate?
- Before we move on, is there anything else you would like to share about your experiences partnering with the city for client resources?
- Today we discussed several recommendations for facilitating training about clients experiencing homelessness. Before we conclude the interview, would you share any examples of current professional development opportunities available to practitioners in your community, if available?

## Summarizing Questions

**Summarizing questions** signal that the interview is ending, and the interviewer offers an opportunity for the participant to add final comments or thoughts. We suggest a couple of questions that should always end your interview: "Is there anything else important you would like to add?" and "What else should I have asked you?" These questions allow participants to close the interview on their time and have the final word. We believe that this encourages participant voice and provides closure to a strong interview. Examples related to the homelessness and mental health study include:

- Is there anything else you would have liked me to ask regarding mental health needs of this population?
- As we conclude this interview, are there other reflections you have had throughout this process?

## One-Shot Questions

A **one-shot question** is popular with opportunistic sampling (see Chapter 5). It refers to preparing one question to ask a key informant should you get the opportunity to do so. Because data collection opportunities can morph throughout a study, we believe it is a good idea to prepare for possible interactions with participants you initially thought you were unable to access. For example, let's say you were studying the impact of budget cuts on faculty morale. A one-shot question might be the following intended for the head of human resources should you be able to interview them: "I am aware that your office collected data regarding faculty retention and university budget cuts. Could you tell me a little bit about your findings?" An example for the homelessness study could involve getting an unexpected opportunity to speak with a client of an participant about their experiences. You might ask, "In what ways, if at all, have you noticed changes in your mental health since working with your counselor?"

## Illustrative Questions

At times, a planned interview question can fall flat, or the participant might struggle with how to respond to a particular question. This can occur if a question is difficult to grasp or explain or if the participant is hesitant to respond. **Illustrative questions** help to get across to that you "have heard it all." That is, you present response extremes to illustrate a range of potential responses. For example, when I (Danica) was interviewing supervisors-in-training about their perceptions of current practices in their training programs, I got very little information at first. So I illustrated potential responses like this to expand the discussion:

> Several students I have spoken with have discussed that there have been several challenges, like time constraints, problems establishing rapport with their supervisee, getting paperwork completed, and even wanting to leave the program for lack of support from faculty. Others have talked about how beneficial it has been to have several supervisees from various settings to practice supervision. I am wondering if any of you have experienced these things.

## Use of Commentary

An interview question does not have to be a question at all. You can obtain information from a participant by using a statement rather than an interview question. Unlike an interview question, a comment does not preestablish how an interviewer might respond or pressure a participant to respond. That is, they can opt to respond or not, which is particularly important if a participant feels that the comment has little to no relevance to their experience. Types of comments include the following:

- *puzzlement:* expression of ignorance (real or not) to demonstrate that the researcher is confused and needs assistance. For example: "I am having a hard time making sense of what was done to you."

- *humorous comments:* use of sarcasm in a spontaneous manner to explore a sensitive issue. In interviewing an instructor about his workload compensation: "I am sure you don't have that much to do anyway, right?"
- *the replay:* restatement or paraphrase immediately following a particular response or as a method of linking several responses to ensure clarification and elaboration. For example: "I am hearing you say that you are gaining a lot from the support group yet would like housing assistance." This is an important tool to ensure the researcher has heard the participant correctly.
- *descriptive comments:* articulation of the concrete details of an experience that demonstrates the researcher's image of what the participant is stating; often, the description is used to compare to other experiences. For example: "I am imagining several students talking out of turn and moving about frequently while you are trying to teach them. This seems similar to parents I have spoken with who have experienced disruptive behaviors at home."
- *outrageous comments:* an absurdity stated to induce a strong reaction from a participant when vague responses continue. For the workload compensation study mentioned above: "Maybe you should just work less since you will never make what you deserve."
- *altercasting comments:* casting a participant in a role or identity congruent with an interview purpose to gauge rapport and appropriateness of including a particular participant in the study. For example: "I bet you have had a lot of trouble getting what you need as a client from this agency."
- *evaluative comments:* solicitation of a participant's actual or suspected values, feelings, or opinions for a phenomenon. These comments can serve to compare how one should feel or think from how they do feel and think, illuminating social norms. For example: "I wonder how social justice fits in your counseling philosophy."

## Interviewing by Research Tradition

Research traditions can shape the content and process of the interview (Brinkmann & Kvale, 2015; Dixon, 2015; Roulston, 2013; Seidman, 2019). In this section, we highlight some of the interviewing approaches available that are aligned with specific qualitative research traditions. It is important to note that these are just suggested frameworks that qualitative researchers can use to guide their work; thus, they are not intended to be prescriptive approaches within selected research traditions. Activity 8.4 at the end of this section provides you an opportunity to consider how interviewing approaches may vary based on a selected qualitative tradition.

### Seidman's Phenomenological Interviewing

Interviewing using a phenomenological tradition typically involves an open-ended format with relatively few interview questions. Qualitative researchers seek to gather specific details about a direct lived experience with the use of probes and active listening. Seidman (2019) provides guidelines for phenomenological interviewing method that qualitative researchers can use to

**ACTIVITY 8.4.** INTERVIEWING BY RESEARCH TRADITION

You are a part of a research team (dyad) that is interested in interviewing participants about public school education in comparison to private school education. You may choose which individual(s) to interview (e.g., students, community officials, school administrators, school counselors, parents, teachers). Select one (or two) of the research traditions below and develop an interview protocol.

| | |
|---|---|
| Case study | Narratology |
| Grounded theory | Ethnography |
| Phenomenology | Ethnomethodology |
| Heuristic inquiry | Autoethnography |
| Consensual qualitative research | Participatory action research |
| Life history | Community-based participatory research |

After you have developed the interview protocol, switch partners and reflect on the following:

- What type of interview (i.e., structured, semistructured, unstructured) does your protocol represent? What are the advantages and advantages of this?
- To what extent is the interview protocol appropriate for the research tradition?
- How might the sample affect the interview protocol? How might it influence the interview process?
- How might the interview modality (i.e., individual, dyadic, focus group) affect the interview process?
- What personal characteristics do you possess that might affect interviewing about this topic? What about with this particular sample?
- To what degree do you feel your relationship and any self-disclosure with participants during the interview itself might be appropriate?
- After reflecting on the above questions, what changes should be made to the interview protocol?

describe the essence of an experience that several individuals possess. With this focus on the lived meanings of a phenomenon across individuals, this form of interview is conducted in three phases, with each phase having a central question with probes. Specifically, the first interview is focused on the life history around the experience, the second interview is focused on details about the experience, and the third interview allows participants to reflect on the meaning of the experience. Each interview is typically spaced 3 days to 1 week apart from each other.

The first phase is the focused life history, which involves gathering a comprehensive yet overall picture of a participant's involvement over time for a phenomenon. For example, let's pretend that you want to conduct a case study of a high school recently affected by a school shooting. A focused life history would involve interviewing students about their overall experience in that setting, leading up to and during the school shooting: "Tell me about your experience at this high school, including those surrounding the shooting."

The second phase of this interview is the details of an experience. Essentially, participants reconstruct the concrete details of the phenomenon. The use of critical incidents is very important in this phase. Using the school shooting example, this might be your central question: "What are the specific responses you had during the school shooting?"

The final phase of the interview is reflection of meaning (although participants will be reflecting on meaning the entire interview process). This third interview heavily focuses on meaning-making and connecting thoughts and feelings from the first two interviews. Participants are asked to reflect on the meaning their experiences hold for them. With the school shooting study, an example of a third-phase central question might be the following: "Given your overall thoughts and feelings surrounding your experiences in this high school and those specific to the school shooting, how do you understand that school shooting today?"

## Episodic Narrative Interviewing

Aligned with the life history and narratology traditions (see Chapter 4), Mueller (2020) developed the **episodic narrative interviewing** approach. This approach allows qualitative researchers to directly ask for stories and the participant can attempt to structure the different happenings into in-depth depictions and episodes of those stories. *Episodes* are situations or incidents that are bounded and thus can be isolated from other life events; they can be further contextualized as part of the participant's work life, home life, community life, and so on. For this interviewing approach to be most useful, a phenomenon of interest must lend itself to being nested within a series of stories; it also must be experienced by the participants within bounded circumstances. Thus, the intent is to help the participant vividly recollect an episode or bounded situation in which they were likely to have also experienced the phenomenon of interest.

Mueller (2020) identified six steps to prepare for and implement an episodic narrative interview. The first step involves the qualitative researcher identifying the specific phenomenon of interest for the study. In the second step, participants are provided with a summary of the episodic narrative interview structure and process. The episodic narrative interview begins at the third step, with an invitation for the participant to define, describe, or characterize the phenomenon of interest. Example prompts can include the following: "Can you tell me what the phrase _____ means to you?" and "How would you define _____?"

Next, as the fourth step, qualitative researchers request that the participant tell a story about an episode. This first story request serves to provide a broad context within which the participant can locate the story of their choosing and then convey the details in whatever way feels most important to them. As the participant brings the story of the episode to a close, qualitative researchers then request another story (fifth step), a story about their experience of the phenomenon within the context of the episode. This nested story, where a participant's retelling of their experience of the phenomenon is intentionally nested within an episode, increases the likelihood of a thick description of the phenomenon of interest. The final step involves qualitative researchers allowing a participant to add or amend any parts of the narrative that they shared (Mueller, 2020).

## Interactive Interviewing

As discussed in Chapter 4, autoethnography is an approach that allows qualitative researchers to immerse themselves as coparticipants to explore individual experiences and construct a collective narrative and/or apply experiences to theoretically inform practice (Hughes & Pennington, 2017). **Interactive interviewing**, introduced by Ellis and colleagues (1997), provides an interpretive process by which participants can share their experiences for joint meaning-making. Interactive interviewing is particularly helpful for emotionally charged and sensitive topics. As Ellis et al. (1997) note:

> An increasingly intimate and trusting context makes it possible to reveal more of ourselves and to probe deeper into another's feelings and thoughts; where listening to and asking questions about another's plight lead to greater understanding of one's own; and where the examination and comparison of experiences offer new insight into both lives. (p. 122)

Thus, through this interviewing method, each researcher's and participant's attitudes, feelings, and thoughts affect and are affected by an emerging, reciprocal relationship.

Although there is limited information written about the procedures of interactive interviewing, Ellis et al. (1997) provide some general guidelines. First, while aligned with autoethnography, interactive interviewing can be used with other research traditions as appropriate. They recommend that the research team already have a formed relationship or be willing to work to develop a strong affiliation. They should also have a personal relationship with the phenomenon of interest or at a minimum be willing to embrace the personal stories of others on the research team.

Second, during successive interviews among the research team, they should revisit previous discussions to probe what each was feeling and thinking earlier in the process as well as after the respective interview session. These reflections thus become part of future transcripts and the overall findings. Third, the narratives or other findings constructed from the process should be a blend of "telling the story" with personal reflection interspersed within the story. Qualitative researchers may want to italicize personal reflections about the narrative content and/or the writing process itself within the findings section to distinguish them from the main narrative. Fourth, the narrative should highlight the interactive nature of how the narrative was co-constructed, focusing on how the narrative was shaped by each researcher's perceptions and personal disclosures by going through the interview process. Finally, the final narrative can have multiple parts, with each participant voice highlighted as separate sections as well as a narrative written as one voice.

To illustrate this method, Ellis et al. (1997) describe a process by which three participants discussed the phenomenon of bulimia (two of the three researchers live with bulimia). They met every 3 weeks over 5 months for 2-hour sessions. They transcribed each session and constructed four narratives from the transcripts: one per researcher and a collective narrative. In the findings, they italicized personal reflections about the topic of bulimia as well as their thoughts and feelings about each other.

# Individual, Dyadic, and Focus Group Interviews

Interviewing is a versatile data collection method that allows for engagement of different sample sizes. Based on the number of participants, there are different interviewing considerations. In this section, we describe individual, dyadic, and focus group interviews. Table 8.2 depicts interviewing characteristics across these three modalities.

## Individual Interviews

**Individual interviews** involve soliciting data from one participant at a time. As discussed earlier in this chapter, interviewing as a data collection method originated as individual interviews as early as the 17th century. Today, individual interviewing remains the most popular interviewing method in which qualitative researchers collect data from one participant. The interview generally has 6–12 questions, with 2–3 probes and prompts for each question.

Most of the strategies of interviewing and types of interview questions presented earlier in the chapter work well for individual interviews. In addition, interviewing approaches such as Seidman's (2019) phenomenological interviewing and Mueller's (2020) episodic narrative interviewing are particularly effective when interviewing one participant at a time.

## Dyadic Interviews

**Dyadic interviews** involve interviewing two participants at a time, and it is an approach that falls between individual interviews and focus group interviews. While dyadic interviews have the benefits of generating interactive data similar to focus group interviews, they are not to be considered "miniature focus groups." Dyadic interviews are fairly new in education and social sciences, although some previous research with couples or other family pairs has been conducted using dyadic interviews (Morgan et al., 2013).

Dyadic interviews are typically relationship-based interviews that involve bringing together pairs of individuals based on some shared interest in a research topic. In addition, pairs could share some common characteristic(s) that help to facilitate conversation versus a group discussion. Pairs may include couples, family members, peers, and coworkers, to name a few examples (Morgan et al., 2013, 2016).

Dyadic interviewing as a method needs further development, yet it can be an invaluable approach given some of the limitations of individual and focus group interviews (see Table 8.2). Questions such as who the pairs should consist of and how to moderate dyadic interviews warrant further study (Morgan et al., 2016).

## Focus Group Interviews

**Focus group interviews** have been used in business and marketing disciplines (and briefly in sociology) since the 1940s. In education and social sciences, they may be used as part of a needs assessment, program evaluation, and exploratory research. They are unique methods for generating data from interactions among participants that share a common experience or are homogenous in some manner. This method often serves as a catalyst for participant disclosure, connecting with others, and expanding on or challenging perspectives in a synergistic

**TABLE 8.2** Characteristics of Individual, Dyadic, and Focus Group Interviewing

| | Individual | Dyadic | Focus group |
|---|---|---|---|
| **Establishment of the interview** | There is more ease in selecting and scheduling participants for an interview time and format that works well. This approach tends to have low to no financial cost. | There may be some scheduling difficulty in scheduling two participants, although there can be flexibility in how the pairs are selected. This approach tends to have low to no financial cost. | Selection and scheduling of participants becomes more complex with larger samples as well as research with naturally forming groups. There may be some financial cost, although minimal compared to other methods. It may be difficult to form these groups depending on the topic. |
| **Quality of participant disclosure** | Participants can share information they may have withheld publicly. The participant has more control of what is shared, although they may not provide rich responses without other participants present. They may also have a desire to impress the interviewer with responses. | This interview type can mimic typical interactions found in conversation, snowballing responses as the pair exchange responses. One participant may be hesitant to share some information depending on who the other participant is. | Depending on the homogeneity of the group, interactions may help stimulate individual ideas about a phenomenon that were not previously recognized or remembered. Disclosure may be minimal, however, depending on the sensitivity of the topic. |
| **Participant rapport and trust** | The interviewer is to demonstrate facilitation skills and self-disclose as needed to foster rapport and trust. | When there are common interests between the pair, the participants will have greater rapport with and trust of one another. | Depending on the homogeneity of the group, participants will have varying levels of trust with one another. The interviewer is to link participants to maximize rapport and trust and empower individual members as needed. For sensitive topics, larger groups can hinder rapport and trust. |
| **Participant confidentiality** | Confidentiality can be maintained in the interview by the interviewer. | Confidentiality cannot be guaranteed in this interview. | Confidentiality cannot be guaranteed in this interview. |

(continued)

**TABLE 8.2**  Characteristics of Individual, Dyadic, and Focus Group Interviewing  (Continued)

| | Individual | Dyadic | Focus group |
|---|---|---|---|
| **Role of the interviewer** | The interviewer actively participates in the interview. They may have more control of presence in sharing the interview process. | The interviewer is an active listener between the pair, moderating the conversation as needed. The conversation flow between the pair will influence the amount of control or presence the interviewer has in shaping the interview process. | The interviewer serves primarily as a moderator, with some active listening to foster interaction. The group discussion with more members will limit the amount of control or presence the interviewer has in shaping the interview process. |
| **Interview duration and depth** | There is more time available for participant responses, and more interview questions can be included in the process. | Time within the interview is divided between the pairs, and the interviewer may ask fewer questions to allow equal response depth from the pairs per question. | The interviewer can only ask a few questions to allow participants to respond equally to the question. Less response depth may result when groups have more members, as the interviewer is less likely to facilitate detailed responses. |
| **Interviewer skill set** | The interviewer is to be skilled in probing questions to ensure that the participants are interpreting questions the way they are intended. Skills in establishing rapport and trust in a culturally responsive manner are heavily reliant solely on the interviewer. | The interviewer is to be skilled in group facilitation, attending to content and process. This skill set includes interpersonal, time management, cultural competency, and organizational skills. | The interviewer is to be skilled in group facilitation, attending to content and process. This skill set includes interpersonal, time management, cultural competency, and organizational skills. |
| **Data analysis** | In-depth interview responses can add to the richness of analysis of the interview, individualizing the experience per interview. However, the interviewer may have some difficulty analyzing the data across interviews. | The interviewer may find it easier to notice and bridge gaps in responses with pairs as compared to individuals across interviews or members within a focus group interview. | Identification of similarities and differences among multiple members can complicate data analysis yet can add complexity and credibility to the findings. |

Sources: Brinkmann and Kvale (2015), Hall (2020), Morgan et al. (2013), Roulston (2013), and Siedman (2019)

manner. While focus group interview data can provide insight on the attitudes, beliefs, and experiences of individual participants, it is the interactive nature of this data collection method that produces data that cannot be obtained from individual interviews. That is, focus groups are intended to produce data from individuals based in their interpersonal interactions, not simply of individuals in a "group interview" format. The focus group discussion should flow naturally with few interjections overall from the facilitators. That is, participants should do most of the talking and interact with one another, not with the facilitators.

Generally, focus group interviews involve 6–12 individuals with one or two facilitators; smaller groups may work better for more sensitive topics. They typically include 3–8 interview questions, with probes to facilitate interaction. Focus group interviews tend to have at least two facilitators to solicit participant responses and concurrently take note of group dynamics.

When establishing a focus group, qualitative researchers should weigh these factors as they select participants to maximize interaction quality: degree of commonality among participants; position or status among them; nature and format of intended discussions; and the extent that facilitator(s) and participants are familiar with each other personally. When gauging homogeneity of the focus group, however, qualitative researchers are to be aware that participants who occupy a same social or cultural location may not view themselves the way researchers do. Furthermore, it is not always possible to select participants for a focus group interview. Groups form naturally in our everyday worlds, without prescreening and outside a qualitative researcher's control. Common groups in which participant preselection is likely impossible might include online chat rooms, students in a classroom, employees at a counseling agency, and so forth.

The initial stages of a focus group interview may seem parallel to securing informed consent in clinical settings, reviewing a syllabus or course outline in a classroom, or setting an agenda for a meeting among educators or administrators. At the beginning of a focus group interview, facilitators are to:

- Explain the purpose of the qualitative study as well as the purpose of the focus group interview as a component of that research design.
- Set the agenda for what the focus group interview will look like (e.g., approximate number of questions, duration of interview).
- Describe the roles of focus group members and facilitator(s).
- Discuss participant rights and responsibilities.
- Develop ground rules for appropriate and inappropriate behaviors during the interview session (e.g., one person speaks at a time, there are no right or wrong answers, no side conversations).

**Talking circles** is an Indigenous research method that can be used as an alternative to focus group interviews. Based in African tradition, talking circles occur when individuals form a circle and are given an opportunity to speak uninterrupted. A common practice in talking circles is to share a sacred object, which is passed around from individual to individual as they speak. According to Chilisa (2020), this sacred object symbolizes the co-construction of knowledge and the relationship among the talking-circle members. Typically, talking circles comprise four rounds.

To use this method, qualitative researchers can work with individuals participating in the talking circle to identify a sacred object to be used during the interview. Qualitative researchers can then ask an interview question, "passing the baton" or sacred object to an individual who self-identifies as ready to share or respond to the respective question. Then they pass the object to another member. We recommend that researchers dedicate some time at the beginning of a talking circle for members to introduce themselves to the group, using an object of personal meaning to them to foster disclosure and further connection among the members. At the conclusion of the interview, qualitative researchers are to spend some time asking members to share their thoughts on the group process as well as some of the themes they identified as they co-constructed knowledge.

## Managing Interview Data

While we have provided some general information about the structure, advantages and disadvantages, as well as strategies for observations and interviews, there are several other data collection considerations. Here are just a few of the more salient ones; others will be introduced throughout the remainder of the text.

### Recording Interview Data

Interviews can be recorded in many ways. The most common way to record interview data is using a digital audio recorder, although there are various ways to record data. Some of these methods include videorecording, typing, or handwriting verbatim or abbreviated interview responses. If you are using a recorder, be sure to bring extra batteries. If you are using a smart phone, be sure it is fully charged or bring a charger with you. We like to use two recorders during each data collection just in case one does not operate correctly at the last minute. If you are conducting an interview in an online environment, record the interview if possible through a videoconferencing platform.

Audio and video recorders can make participants nervous, so take this into account before beginning an interview. We suggest turning the recorder on about 5–10 minutes before beginning an interview. Eventually, most participants will get used to having the recorder present and will interact more naturally with the researcher.

### Managing the Data, Initially

While we discuss many other data management tools in Chapter 10, is it important to note that contact summary sheets are important tools in data collection, as they need to be created shortly after each data collection. A **contact summary sheet** is usually a cover sheet summarizing a single contact with a case. For each interview or observation that occurs in fieldwork, a contact sheet helps qualitative researchers capture their own reflections about the data, outline initial salient themes based on the interview process, and jot down additional questions to be asked of a participant or setting. Thus, contact summary sheets serve as the first step to qualitative data analysis, discussed in Chapters 10 and 11. Contact summary sheets should be completed within a couple of days after the data collection to best capture a researcher's impressions.

Miles et al. (2020) presented several things that could be included in a contact summary sheet:

- identifying information about the contact (e.g., date, setting, method of contact, who or what was the subject of the contact, when the contact was made, when was contact summary sheet completed)
- important issues and themes of the data collection
- individuals, events, settings, and processes involved in this contact
- brief responses to interview questions
- observation rubrics
- new or additional questions to be considered for the next contact

While we provide an example of a contact summary sheet (see Figure 8.6), we encourage you to review Miles et al. (2020) for additional formats.

The following represents a contact summary sheet for an individual interview from a study examining counselors and counselor trainees' understanding of healthy relationships.

---

**Contact Summary Sheet**

**Interviewer: SC**                                     **Interviewee: T007**

**Contract Date: 1/15/09**                          **Today's Date: 1/16/09**

**1. What were the main issues or themes that stuck out for you in this contract?**

- Good communication, respect, and valuing each other are components of healthy relationships. Control, power struggles, secrets, and dishonesty are components of an unhealthy relationship.
- Seemed to have difficulty conceptualizing what types of clients would be easier to work with, but immediately knew types of clients that she would not have trouble working with.
- Bases knowledge of unhealthy/healthy relationships and relationship violence on her own personal experiences with it (i.e., her relationships and her daughters).
- A lot of anger against clients that are violent in relationships (i.e., abhor violence, those kind of people).
- Had difficulty expressing how to work with a client involved in a violent relationship.
- What seemed to be most important in working with individuals in unhealthy relationships was the processing of her own baggage related to her own personal experiences in unhealthy relationships.
- Took a course in couples counseling during master's program.
- Felt that practical experience was the most valuable in learning how to work with clients who have relationship issues.

**2. What discrepancies, if any, did you note in the interviewee's response?**

- Knew how she would respond to those involved in violent relationships, but really unsure about her strengths for helping those in violent relationships. Seemed to indicate low self-efficacy rather than a lack of knowledge.

**3. Anything else that stuck out as salient, interesting, or important in this contact?**

- Absence of physical violence from interview when discussing relationship violence and unhealthy relationships.
- Focus on emotional/psychological pieces of violent relationships (i.e., anger, control, lowered self-esteem), but not on the physical aspects of it.
- Personal experiences, unresolved personal issues with relationship violence were seen as the main challenge to working with individuals in violent relationships.

**4. How does this compare to other data collections?**

- Not applicable, This was my first data collection for this study.

---

**FIGURE 8.6**  *Contact Summary Sheet Example*

## Transcribing Interview Data

Transcripts are the main data for interview data sources and involve the typed responses of recorded interview data. They are used as not only physical evidence of collected data but also as important data management and analysis tools. Transcribing is quite time consuming, and we have found that for every 15 minutes of recorded data, we spend about an hour transcribing the data. Before transcribing data, listen to the recording carefully and write down some preliminary thoughts about the content and process. What themes or patterns are you hearing and/or seeing? Were there stumbles or repairs in the participant or interviewer responses?

The following factors can impact the characteristics and quality of the final transcript:

- whether interview data were audio and/or videorecorded
- interview duration and setting
- how the transcript is formatted
- the extent to which verbal cues, pitch, volume, utterances, pacing of speech, length of silence, and intonation are noted in the transcript
- the extent to which nonverbal cues (e.g., facial expressions, eye contact, body movements) are integrated in the transcript
- the influence of language differences between interviewer and participant
- intended audience of transcript
- degree of editing of transcript (e.g., removing swear words, utterances, fixing grammar)

We strongly believe that interview data should be transcribed verbatim as relevant. At times, it may be more convenient to save time by transcribing only participant responses to interview questions. However, a good interview is likely to have allowed participants to expand on the research questions, empowering them to speak freely and honestly. Thus, there may be invaluable nonverbal or extra data that becomes important in data analysis. Responses such as "Okay," "Yeah," "Um," and "Ah" may be insightful information about the conversational content and flow. Whether you transcribe verbatim or not, it is important to reflect on how you transcribe. The amount of detail of a transcription can be a result of your personal preferences, time and other constraints, or the research question(s). See Decision Points 8.1 to consider some of the issues and decisions related to transcribing data.

### DECISION POINTS 8.1. CONSIDERATIONS IN DATA TRANSCRIPTION

Reviewing a transcript, you might take the written record at face value as an accurate representation of the interactions of an audio- or videorecording. However, qualitative researchers have a large role in the rigor of the transcript and make choices about whether to transcribe, what to transcribe, and how to represent the record in text. The quality of transcripts may be adversely affected by researcher alterations and other decisions, whether intentional or not. Thus, the final transcript is far from a neutral, comprehensive, and directly transferable indicator or what occurred in data collection.

We offer the following considerations:

- *sentence content* (e.g., problems with sentence structure, the use of quotation marks, omissions, and confusing phrases or words for others): Because people speak in run-on sentences or fragments, it is important that transcribers attend to where they place things like commas, periods, or other punctuation marks since doing so can easily change the meaning of responses. Poland (1995) outlines several sentence content issues:

  - *sentence structure*: A period or comma is inserted in the wrong place and changes the sentence meaning: "I hate it, you know. I do." versus "I hate it. You know I do."
  - *use of quotation marks*: The transcriber fails to identify when an participant is quoting, mimicking, or paraphrasing someone else: "She was 'mortified' about the way teachers were 'fired'" versus "She was mortified about the way teachers were let go."
  - *omissions*: A transcriber wants to "tidy up" a transcript and leaves out several meaningful utterances and side conversations, or they mistakenly leave out a word ("I lost a very close friend of mine to cancer" instead of "I lost a very close friend of mine to lung cancer" in a transcript for a smoking cessation study).
  - *confusing words or phrases for others*: A digital recording is unclear: "Consultation" gets transcribed as "confrontation."

- *involuntary utterances* (e.g., coughs, cries, laughs, and sneezes): These can be meaningful or misleading if included. When I (Danica) was interviewing individuals about university climate around multicultural issues, there were times where it was very relevant to note when participants laughed, as it often indicated sarcasm or discomfort with an interview question.

- *participant language*: How participant language is transcribed is an important issue, and qualitative researchers are encouraged to carefully consider how translation might impact their and the audience's data interpretation. Language factors can include the use of slang, accent considerations, grammatical issues, and diction, to name a few. In addition, direct translation of specific words or labels may not be possible or require "translation" if these words or labels have different meanings in various contexts or if there is no direct translation in the case of second-language factors. Poor transcribing decisions can lead to disempowering participants, especially those of marginalized backgrounds. Reflect on the following before you decide how to transcribe an interview:

  - How do you ensure that the meanings of slang or euphemisms are properly conveyed to the reader?
  - Should words (particularly when English is not the primary language) be transcribed as spoken, or should you "translate" them for the reader?
  - What do you transcribe when words are mispronounced?
  - How do you deal with grammatical errors for you and the participant?

Even if you have the budget to hire a transcriptionist, we *adamantly* believe you should transcribe your own interviews. Since you conducted the interviews, you can include nonverbal aspects of the interview process that no transcriptionist can. Additionally, in cases where there is more than one participant (i.e., focus group interviews), you are likely able to identify "who said what," potentially enriching data analysis. If you hire a transcriptionist, we encourage you to work closely with them to ensure the accuracy and thoroughness of the transcript. It is important to immediately review the transcript to add pertinent information (e.g., nonverbal communication such as fidgeting, pointing, and hand gestures) or correct any misplaced punctuation or missed utterances (e.g., sighs, laughter, voice inflections). Table 8.3 provides some common transcription instructions you may find useful as you transcribe data. Additionally, in Figure 8.7 we present some additional pointers for formatting the transcript page.

**TABLE 8.3** Transcriber Instructions

| | |
|---|---|
| **Pauses** | Denote short pauses during talking with an ellipses (...). Denote longer pauses by the word "pause" in parentheses (pause) for 2–3 second breaks and "(long pause)" for pauses longer than 4 seconds. |
| **Laughing** | Indicate in parentheses: (laughing) or (laughter). |
| **Coughing, sneezing, etc.** | Indicate in parentheses: (coughs), (sigh), or (sneeze), for example. |
| **Interruptions** | Use a hyphen (-) to show when someone's speech is broken midsentence (e.g., "What do you -") |
| **Overlapping speech** | Use a hyphen (-) to indicate when someone interrupts one speaker, include the speech of the other with "overlapping" in parentheses, then return to the original speaker:<br><br>R: He said it was impos-<br>I: (overlapping) Who, Bob?<br>R: No, Larry. |
| **Garbled speech** | Flag unclear words with square brackets and a question mark. For example, "At that, Harry just [doubled? Glossed?] over."<br><br>Use "x" to denote undecipherable passages, with the number of x's denoting the approximate unclear words. For example, "Gina went xxxxx xxxxx xxxxx xxxxx and then [came? went?] home." |
| **Emphasis** | Use caps to denote strong emphasis: "He did WHAT?" |
| **Held sounds** | Repeat the sounds that are held, separated by hyphens. If they are emphasized, then capitalize as well: "No-o-o-o, not exactly" or "I was VER-r-r-y-y-y happy." |
| **Paraphrasing others** | When it is assumed that a participant is parodying what someone else said or an inner voice in their heads, use quotation marks and/or indicate mimicking voice. For example:<br><br>R: Then you know what he came out with? He said (mimicking voice) "I'll be damned if I'm going to let YOU push ME around." And I thought to myself: "I'll show you." |

Adapted from Blake D. Poland, "Transcription Quality as an Aspect of Rigor in Qualitative Research," *Qualitative Inquiry*, vol. 1, no. 3, pp. 302–303. Copyright © 1995 by SAGE Publications.

**Participant P001 Interview 1, Duration 24:20 minutes (1.18.09, Transcribed by DGH)**

**DGH: Thank you for agreeing to participate in this study. As a practitioner your responses will be helpful in training others about working with those having relationship difficulties. I would like to begin learning a little bit about your training. Can you tell me about your training around relationship issues?**

PA: Do you mean academically or could be professional training in the community?

**DGH: Anything that seems relevant for you.**

PA: When I first started working with trauma and domestic violence, and that's where I started right after graduation, I went through a domestic violence training. They called it an institute but it was kind of like a conference where we had of 4–5 days of training with police officers, it was with the Commonwealth's attorney.

**DGH: So it was all for these different disciplines?**

PA: Just different types of providers, right. It was open to anyone, and I think it was at [University name]. It was really good. We got a lot of different areas input. Dispatchers came and talked I wouldn't say it really taught us how to do things, but it made it more aware of what out there and systems we could use. I would say the most training I got was I was on a domestic violence taskforce in [Virginia city], and there was a lady there [female's name] just gave us a lot of hands-on experience.

**DGH: So what was the task force for?**

PA: To change laws, to help the people. She was all about education police officers and working with the shelters. She was really a real activist.

**DGH: And how long did you do that for?**

PA: I was on that team for about a year and a half, and then I moved to juvenile detention and shifted my focus to juvenile offenders.

**FIGURE 8.7** Excerpt from an Interview Transcript

On the first couple of lines, include information about who was interviewed (using codes), who interviewed and transcribed, the date and duration of the interview.

We like to use PA to represent the participant in individual interviews, with PA1, PA2 and so forth used in focus group interviews (when individuals can be identified by the transcriber)

Create ample margins for later data analysis. We usually leave at least 1.5" margins for memoing.

Include line numbers (continuous) on your document to make referencing easier during data

## CHAPTER SUMMARY

In this chapter we have provided information about primary data collection methods: observations and interviews. While these are often used together in qualitative research, we presented information about their formats and characteristics and gave strategies to maximize success using each method. In deciding which methods are appropriate, it is important that qualitative researchers consider which are most congruent with their research questions.

Observations are at the core of fieldwork in qualitative inquiry. There are various degrees of researcher participation that fall on a continuum: acting as an observer, observer-as-participant, participant-as-observer, and full participant. No matter your degree of participation as a researcher, creating a thick description of the setting (field notes) is important, and we have provided strategies for doing so.

In this chapter we have outlined various types of questions to include in your protocol as well as strategies for conducting a good interview. It is important to remember, however, that the questions in your interview protocol will be guided by your research tradition(s).

Individual interviews are the most common data collection tool in qualitative research. There are three types of interviews: structured, semistructured, and unstructured, with unstructured interviews being the most used. Dyadic interviews involve pairs of participants with a common interest in the research topic and/or shared characteristics. The aim of dyadic interviews is to foster a conversation about the phenomenon of interest. Focus group interviews are unique in that they highlight data from the interaction among more than two participants, something that cannot be captured by individual or dyadic interviews. This chapter presents unique considerations of these three types of interviews.

Finally, additional considerations were presented. These involve recording interviewing data, managing data using contact summary sheets, and transcribing interview data.

## Review Questions

1.  Describe the participant observation continuum. How do varying levels of participation impact qualitative research design components?
2.  What are key strategies of developing field notes? What cautions are provided in this chapter?
3.  What are best practices for developing an interview protocol?
4.  What are the distinctions among individual, dyadic, and focus group interviews? What are the benefits and challenges of each type?
5.  What are some of the key issues and considerations of transcribing interview data?

## Recommended Readings

Brinkmann, S., & Kvale, S. (2018). *Doing interviews* (Vol. 2). Sage.

Hall, J. (2020). *Focus groups: Culturally responsive approaches for qualitative inquiry and program evaluation.* Myers Education Press.

Poland, B. D. (1995). Transcription quality as an aspect of rigor in qualitative research. *Qualitative Inquiry, 1*(3), 290–210.

Roulston, K. (2013). *Reflective interviewing: A guide to theory & practice.* Sage.

Siedman, I. (2019). *Interviewing as qualitative research: A guide for researchers in education and the social sciences* (5th ed.). Teachers College Press.

## CHAPTER 9

# Online Media and Other Data Sources

### CHAPTER PREVIEW

In the last chapter, we discussed observation and interviewing data collection methods for qualitative research. However, often in education and social sciences, your topic demands that you supplement these traditional qualitative data collection methods (i.e., interviews and observations) with data from various online media and other data sources. Remembering the researcher-practitioner-advocate (RPA) model—especially the role of advocate—can guide you in the selection of the online media and other sources of data collection methods you use. In the first half of this chapter, we outline various forms of online media that include social media, virtual and augmented reality sources, blogs, vlogs, online focus groups, discussion boards, and chat rooms. Then we discuss additional data sources, such as audiovisual media (e.g., art, film, music) and documents and artifacts. Throughout the chapter, we discuss the benefits and challenges of using each of these data collection methods.

## Online Media

The number of online field sites is always increasing, with dramatic upticks in users (Addeo et al., 2020). Specifically, globalization and advancement of technology, data transmission and processing, and popularization of internet use serve as the catalysts for their use in qualitative research across disciplines (Morais et al., 2020). Data created by online communities are vast and can be created by an individual or group. Data sources can include textual and visual data, sound files, audiovisual productions, websites, vlogs and blogs, and podcasts, to name a few (Jong, 2017). In the first part of this chapter, we discuss several forms of **online media**, including social media; blogs and vlogs; online focus groups, discussion boards, and chat rooms; and audiovisual media. Although these are presented as separate sections, online media sources can be described using multiple labels. For example, Facebook is a social media platform and a microblog (a form of blog).

Online research allows researchers to examine cultures and social relationships and activities of those communities and development of cultures, providing insight into people's online behaviors and an understanding of how people negotiate their internet activities (Jong, 2017). See Perspectives 9.1 to read first-person accounts of using online media. Then use the questions listed in Activity 9.1 to explore how using online media for data collection may be beneficial for your study.

## PERSPECTIVES 9.1. RESEARCHERS' PERSPECTIVES ON USING ONLINE MEDIA METHODS

I have used the internet for qualitative research—specifically using it to conduct interviews online via Instant Messages for a study examining online experiences of men who have sex with men. I used America Online because at the time I could create a profile. I would go into a chat room and people could look at my profile in the chat room. There was a link to my informed consent on the profile. I interviewed the participants using Instant Messaging technology. Basically, I cut and pasted the interview questions I had from a previously prepared word processing document into the Instant Messaging "window." There were some technological problems because sometimes I would get disconnected from the Instant Messaging technology while I was interviewing a participant and it could be really hard to find that person again to complete the interview. Some participants I interviewed were pretty skeptical about whether I was for "real" as a researcher conducting a qualitative study online. Some folks were skeptical and were afraid I was from an evangelical Christian perspective and would try to "convert" them. One person called the IRB to complain that I was in a chat room invading his privacy: Nothing came of that because I had previous IRB approval. Because I was online, there was no way for me as well to confirm that the participants were really who they said they were. I could have been interviewing someone underage or someone who wasn't the sex or gender they said they were. On the other hand, because of the participants' anonymity, they were definitely more open with what they shared with me. A lot of people were excited about the topic of what I was studying. It was also pretty easy to recruit participants, because I could just go online and find them. I didn't have to go into the community to find participants; they were readily available online. And I was able to get a diverse participant pool. I am proud of this study because I did it as a predissertation study as a graduate student in 2003. At that time, there were no studies out there talking about doing qualitative interviews online.

—*Michael Chaney, PhD*

My field is applied linguistics and teacher education. I have become interested in practice-oriented research using the internet due to some of my teaching experiences online. I am using WebCT Blackboard to put my entire course online. The students in my course are all around the world. So, it is a live classroom where I can actually talk and type with students with a live session. I upload my presentation and ruminations, and students interact with one another in chat rooms to discuss class materials. The one assignment that I have them do is to read a nontheoretical book with 3–4 options. I set up literature circles where students meet together and talk about their book. In the past, I have only done that in WebCT Blackboard. I find this platform clumsy, and group work is somewhat clumsy for student-student interactions. There are some technical glitches and students don't have as much group interaction. Now, I am experimenting with a Wiki classroom, and the student feedback I am getting it is superior to using Blackboard to facilitate group work. I am just now starting to collect data on this first group of 25 students. I am also interested in qualitative interviews online on the topic of professional identity development—but doing this with people who live in France, China, and around the world. The internet makes this type of interviewing more possible than ever before. The trick is that I am in linguistics, so I won't be able to "see" their nonverbals as well—even if I am using a web camera. So, I as I design this study, I will need to account for how this might shape data collection and interpretation.

*—Katherine Kiss, PhD*

I have supervised student research using email interviewing, but I think chat rooms can be better because you can have synchronous interactions. One study examined the experiences of classroom interactions of Chinese immigrant students in the U.S.—specifically, what contextual factors may be inhibiting their talking in class. A huge advantage of these chat rooms is that when you are working with participants where English is a second language, there is less pressure for the researcher and participants to reflect you can pause the interaction in a chat room. It doesn't have to be rapid-fire questions and answers, which can help people feel less pressured. The other big advantage is that is there is no transcription: It's done when you are done with the interview! However, I know when I transcribe my interviews, I get a lot out of doing the transcription. So, I am interested in what a researcher might lose in not doing a transcription. Email interviewing in that manner might be more analogous to having someone else do your transcript. You will have to re-read it to get that prolonged immersion in the data. The other disadvantage is don't have body language and intonation of participants, so you lose what you might have picked up with your other senses. One of the things I would encourage researchers to talk to participants about when collecting data online is to not worry about the spelling when they are communicating. A lot of participants will worry about that, so I tell them don't let that impede what it is you are thinking that spell check is for! One other thing is in using these types of technologies, it is important to find a technology that the participants feel comfortable with it and not impose a technology on them because it can create more anxiety for participants. And don't just think about internet technology as an age-related thing: big mistake! Using the internet to collect data is a comfort thing for participants. For instance, there are probably some 19 to 20-year-olds who haven't used all the features of Skype because they are texting and Facebooking more; yet there may be lots of 40- and 60-year-old professionals who use Skype quite a bit. Use caution in the stereotypes you might have about using technology in your data collection: You might think that the younger your participants are they more they will know how to use it—not true!

—Janette Hill, PhD

 **ACTIVITY 9.1.** USING ONLINE MEDIA FOR YOUR STUDY

Reflect on the following in your research teams:

- How could the internet be used in your study?
- Would the internet increase the availability of participants who have experienced the phenomenon you are studying?
- Are there challenges and/or benefits to participant confidentiality if you integrated the internet into your study's design?
- Would the benefits of using the internet for data collection outweigh the challenges?
- How will using the internet to collect data influence researcher bias?
- Are there any ethical issues that would encourage you to use the internet or preclude you from using the internet for data collection?
- If you have already used the internet for data collection, how might your discussion within your research team guide you to revisit and refine your data collection methods?
- What issues does the RPA model—especially your role as advocate—guide you to identify when to use online media for data collection?

Use the answers to these questions to identify how you will or will not use online media for collecting data.

## Social Media

**Social media** are a collection of internet-based applications that allow creation, co-creation, and exchange of user-generated content based in social interactions. Thus, they increase individuals', organizations', and communities' ability to share and interact with one another.

In Chapter 3, we discussed some of the ethical considerations of using social media as a data collection method. These considerations are important to monitor as you design your study using social media and analyze and report data. In this section, we illustrate various data collection methods using social media platforms. Types of social media platforms are as follows (McKenna et al., 2017):

- collaborative projects (e.g., Wikipedia)
- blogs and microblogs (e.g., Twitter)
- social news networking sites (e.g., Digg)
- content communities (e.g., YouTube, Pinterest)
- social networking sites (e.g., Facebook, Instagram, TikTok)
- virtual game worlds (e.g., World of Warcraft)
- virtual social worlds (e.g., Second Life)

No matter the social media platform, the study of social media from a qualitative research perspective can be conducted from multiple perspectives:

- *Who* uses social media? What are the demographic characteristics of those who use particular social media platforms? Who interacts with various social media content? What are the demographic shifts in social media usage?
- *What* is the content displayed on social media? Is the content synchronous or asynchronous? What are themes within social media content with respect to a particular research question?
- *Why* do individuals engage in social media content? Why does their activity with particular social media platforms or content change? What are their attitudes regarding social media platforms and/or particular content?
- *How* does social media usage impact individuals? Are the outcomes of social media usage beneficial or harmful? Do the outcomes vary by social media platform, participant demographics, or time frame?

In addition to how qualitative researchers approach social media, there are three types of data collection typically involved with social media (Belk & Kozinetz, 2016; Jong, 2017). First, researchers may use *archival data*, or the saved social networking site interactions back through time. Examples from research include attitudes regarding the COVID-19 vaccine on Twitter for a 3-month period (Liu & Liu, 2021) and the content of Facebook's announcements on tackling online disinformation, misinformation, false news, and fake news over a 3-year period (Iosifidis & Nicoli, 2020). Second, researchers may analyze *elicited or co-created data*, or data created through researcher and participant interaction. For example, Richards (2013) used a researcher-generated YouTube channel as a method for improving parental involvement within a middle school. Third, *field note data*, or researcher observations, can be analyzed. For example, Subrahmanyam et al. (2004) identified themes regarding adolescent sexuality and identity from their observations of an online teen chat room for 1 month. In addition to these examples, Perspectives 9.2 provides student experiences in using instant messenger and social networking sites.

## PERSPECTIVES 9.2. STUDENT RESEARCHERS AND ONLINE DATA COLLECTION

My dissertation study is about Anime fans who role play people from Anime in online games, using Instant Messengers and Livejournal as their platform for their role plays. Therefore, the data that I collected pertained to these platforms. I collected instant messenger logs of gameplay, as well as Livejournal posts and unofficial Livejournal interviews. I liked that this data collection was naturalistic, more or less: I was collecting data in the environment that I was studying, using their means for interaction in a natural way. It wasn't artificial, or imposing online methodology onto an offline stud. I used a theoretical frame of Pop Culture Studies out of the Media field and my methodology was case study with ethnographic data collection techniques. The only challenge was with my ability to keep up with it all! It was actually tremendously easy to collect data because it's all generated and stored electronically, so there's no need for in-person interviews, transcription, scheduling—just some asynchronous collection, and some synchronous data collection. It all flowed really well. For others doing an online ethnographic study, my main advice is "know thy participants." If they are night people, do not attempt to collect synchronous data in the morning! If they use certain kinds of messengers and bulletin boards/blogs, go to them. Do not make them step out of their comfort zones.

—*Achariya Rezak*

I used Myspace and Facebook to send messages to participants and ask follow-up questions from face-to-face interviews. I conducted a series of interviews in with 8th grade students on the perceptions of reading by struggling 8th-grade readers. During transcription, my research partner and I had some additional follow-up questions to ask of some of the students. However, school was out and the students were very busy in their summer schedules. So I used Myspace and Facebook to connect with the students. I messaged the student with the questions and they responded to the questions, much like I am answering your questions through email. Also, we were able to see how these students represented themselves on the social networking sites. The challenge was short answers. The students typed a short answer to most questions. When I ask for more, they wrote a little more. I know that they would have verbalized more if they had been sitting with me in an interview session, but they didn't want to take the time to type it out. The benefits were easy access. These students didn't drive and were scattered across the country due to summer break and traveling vacations, but they stay connected to their friends through social networking sites. I was able to connect with them wherever they were and ask our questions. It depends on the research questions and the

participants. My participants were students who were labeled as struggling readers and writers by the school. This label may have played into
reluctance to write long answers. So, my advice is know your participants.
I knew mine were on Facebook and Myspace, which allowed me to finish
up a study, but I would rather have talked to them in person.

*—Emily Pendergrass*

As qualitative researchers collect social media content, it is important to identify and eliminate spammers, as possible, as well as determine which posts are meaningful to be included
in the sample. Kearney's (n.d.) TweetBotOrNot tool can be used to determine the probability
that a particular user is a bot or fake social media account. Furthermore, to eliminate potential users from analysis, you may want to consider the following metrics: What is the level of
interaction for the user with others (e.g., some users post more than 1,000 tweets to a hashtag
but had received zero retweets)? Are there users that share a substantial number of hyperlinks
without original content (e.g., some users use hyperlinks only in 100% of their posts)?

## Blogs and Vlogs

One of the most readily available sources of data collection on the internet can be in the exponentially increasing number of blogs and vlogs (Raby et al., 2017). Blogs include microblogs,
or brief content from various social media platforms. The reach of these media is global and
connects people with lived experiences of various topics far and wide. Furthermore, blog
and vlog technologies offer opportunities for educators, practitioners, and social scientists to
collaborate beyond their local setting to national and international settings. Thus, they play
a key role in facilitating personal and/or professional connections and interactions among
geographically dispersed individuals with common interests and needs.

### Blogs

A **blog** (or weblog) is a type of journal that is either publicly or privately written online (Wilson
et al., 2015). Blogs allow for individuals and communities to express everything from one-
time, sporadic, or ongoing thoughts on a topic that are often private or "taboo" to share (e.g.,
disordered eating, the experiences trans and nonbinary people have of social and/or medical
transition, etc.) to ongoing public communication with a particular audience (e.g., engaging
in mental and physical health practices, living with an emerging health disability, exploring a
new areas of clinical or teaching practices, etc.) and private explorations that mirror a traditional diary and for personal use only that are under password lock. On a fun note, there are
multiple blogs about qualitative research you can follow as well (Lim, 2016).

Like email interviewing, blogs leverage the inexpensive, publicly available, and unobtrusive
aspects of data collection. Without the boundaries—and potential barriers—of digital recorders
and face-to-face interviews, blogs truly are a way to collect naturalistic data. In this manner,

blogs provide a peek into the very private lives of participants that happen to be communicated in a very public way. Because blogs are an increasingly popular way for individuals and groups to communicate with others, there is a huge variety of blogs that exist.

A first step for a researcher who is considering using blogs for data collection is to consider whether the researcher wants to sample existing participant blogs and/or ask participants to blog about a certain topic. For instance, Prescott et al. (2015) used a blog to collect the lived experiences young people between the ages of 11 and 19 years old have of juvenile arthritis. The researchers created a website exploring this topic, and participants who were in a pediatric hospital were invited to write blog topics that were meaningful to them using sentence stems and structure prompts. The researchers included participatory components of the study, such as collaborating with young people on the website design and visual presentation as well as the blog categories.

The researchers then studied the frequency and length of visits to the website as well as the themes in the content across the 187 blog entries. While this was an innovative study in this area where participants were directly involved in creating their content and how they consumed other blogs, the authors noted some technical challenges in the study (e.g., firewall restrictions on desktops and laptops in school and work environments, including the pediatric hospital).

If you would like to study preexisting blogs, explore the current and various blog content management systems (e.g., Blogster, LiveJournal, Xanga, Blogger). For instance, a researcher may be interested in certain demographics of the bloggers they would like to sample—say Latinx men living with depression or first-generation college students living away from home for the first time. The type of search engine on the blog may lead a researcher to select or avoid a certain blog content management system because the search engine may or may not allow the researcher to locate the participant samples they need for their study.

Once a researcher have decided which blogs to study (new or preexisting blogs), the researcher should consider if and how they should establish a researcher presence online. This may entail initiating a blog account for the researcher, which then facilitates researcher entry and allows for participant sampling and data collection. However, you may be more passively studying existing blog content, doing a content analysis of themes in existing blogs (such as young adults experiences of living with schizophrenia).

Ultimately, the use of blogs in qualitative research is no longer a new method of data collection but rather one that is continuously being used and expanded. For instance, Campillo-Ferrer et al. (2021) explored how academic blogging impacted students' motivation and perceived learning of social science skills and competencies in preparation for being future social science teachers. The authors gathered digital skills learning from participants cultivated through their blogging experiences using a pre-post approach and explored their self-motivation and social and civic competencies. Interestingly, the authors found that participants' blogging had impacts on increasing their collaborative social skills with their peers as well as increasing their understanding and perception of perspectives different from their own. Qualitative studies using blogs may also examine the impact of reading blogs on social identity. For instance, Evans et al. (2017) explored how trans youth and their caregivers used online resources related to young trans and nonbinary people.

**Microblogs** are concise blog posts that can have images, GIFs, links, infographics, videos, and audio clips. Various social media platforms, such as Twitter, Facebook, and Instagram, may be considered microblogs. *Hashtags* are digital devices for categorizing and collating posts for a specific topic. Users rely on hashtags to create conversation threads around a common topic and they can help posts reach beyond their existing follower–followee networks. This network expansion can be particularly powerful for qualitative research that seeks extensive reach on a topic. Case Study 9.1 in the next section provides an example of how Twitter content was analyzed to examine educators' professional activity regarding 16 education-related Twitter hashtags.

## Case Example 9.1. Educators' Professional Activities and Twitter

Carpenter et al. (2020) examined 16 education-related Twitter hashtags over a 13-month period to examine teacher professional learning and development in a digital era. Research questions were (a) "What trends existed among all 16 education-related Twitter hashtags combined during the 13-month window?" and (b) "What were the similarities and differences between the 16 education-related hashtags during the 13-month window?"

The authors used purposeful sampling to select 16 education-related Twitter hashtags that represented a variety of content, geographic regions, audiences, and purposes. They considered three major criteria in hashtag selection: variety in content/purpose, presence of a synchronous chat for the hashtag, and a minimum threshold of activity. After removing data from prolific spammers, they employed descriptive statistics to present monthly counts of original tweets (OTs), retweets (RTs), and hyperlinks shared across 15 of the hashtags during asynchronous and synchronous chats between September 2016 and September 2017. During the 13-month data collection window, 1,078,666 OTs (40.4%) and 1,590,270 RTs (59.6%) were sent that included one of the 16 hashtags of interest, resulting in a data set of 2,668,936 total tweets.

There was an overall 5.25% decrease in OTs and an 79.27% increase in RTs, yielding an overall 36.41% increase in total traffic (TT) during the data collection window. OTs, RTs, and TT varied substantially by month during the data collection window. With respect to hyperlinks in tweets, 39.8% of the OTs included hyperlinks, while 29.4% of the RTs did (i.e., 33.6% of the TT included a hyperlink). During the data collection window, there was an overall 10.4% decrease in hyperlink sharing, with a 17.3% decrease in OTs including links and a 4.3% decrease in RTs doing so.

Comparing the hashtags with 13 months of data, 12 hashtags saw a decrease in total link sharing over the 13-month data collection window. Trends in link sharing did not necessarily mirror trends in the quantity of tweets sent to the hashtags. Hashtags differed in terms of what percentage of OTs, RTs, and TT occurred during synchronous chats. Hashtags thus varied quite dramatically in terms of how much their associated synchronous chats appeared to define their traffic. Although synchronous chats featured less retweeting than was common during asynchronous use, this varied by hashtag.

Carpenter et al.'s (2020) analysis concurred with findings from prior research that indicate some educators regularly use more than one education-related hashtag. If different hashtags meet different needs and/or have different cultures, then educators may choose to access various hashtags at different times and participate in different ways (e.g., posting OTs and replying in some and lurking or posting RTs in others) to create a larger ecology of professional development that spans more than a single affinity space. Furthermore, they may move in and out of affinity spaces as they see fit, and they may combine their use of Twitter with other social media, such as Instagram and Pinterest.

*Source*: Carpenter, J., Tani, T., Morrison, S., & Keane, J. (2020). Exploring the landscape of educator professional activity on Twitter: An analysis of 16 education-related Twitter hashtags. *Professional Development in Education*, 1–22. https://doi.org/10.1080/19415257.2020.1752287

## Vlogs

A **vlog** (or "videoblog") is the next generation of blogs (Parnell, 2017) that uses video to integrate the diary-like component of blogs—and is also either in the public or private internet domain. The use of vlogs has exploded recently, creating new ethical questions and considerations (see Chapter 3). When you think about what vlogs are, they have become everyday parts of our lives. Vlogs are an increasing part of social media (e.g., TikTok, YouTube, etc.), are part of what we may send from our phones to connect with others (e.g., a quick video saying "I love you" to family members and friends), and are an ongoing part of websites and communication materials to share information, evoke emotions and reactions, and inspire action and change.

Vlogs are increasingly a source of social change and, as you think about the RPA model we discuss in this book, might become a critical part of how you design your study, collect data, and distribute your findings and relevant implications of your study. Research has shown that vlogs can help shape consumer's lifestyle choices and purchases (e.g., travel destinations, health behaviors) and promote positive information-sharing about topics that are rarely discussed openly in larger society and explore social justice issues (e.g., Standing Rock Indigenous water protectors vlogging, Black Lives Matter rally and march organizers), but they can also influence people in more negative ways (e.g., negative impacts on body image and health; Parnell, 2017).

Like blogs, vlogs can be used in a wide variety of education, practice, and social science contexts. For instance, Snelson (2013) engaged a mixed methods study with an online ethnographic purposive component that examined 120 vlogs on YouTube about school over a 3-month period. This study's findings can help you consider the various components of vlogs you will want to consider when you use them in your data collection. For instance, Snelson found five areas that were key to student vlogging about school:

- characteristics: who was vlogging and who was viewing
- context: the location of the vlog
- content: information shared
- culture: patterns and themes
- motivations: what moved students to vlog about schools

If you are studying the experiences of international study abroad vlogs, for example, you can use these five areas during your study design to guide your research implementation strategy.

As you consider including vlogs as a source of data collection in your study and dive into the research in this area, you will quickly see that much of the research in this area has been in the communications industry, driving product purchasing and engagement of users (Hill et al., 2020; Ladhari et al., 2020). This body of research can help you think about communication styles, attitudes, values, and expertise of a vlog you create for your research study or dimensions of study for existing vlogs; however, it is important to be aware that vlog studies in these disciplines can also obfuscate issues of social justice and sustain oppressive systems of inequities (Garcia & Vemuri, 2017). For example, Garcia and Vemuri (2017) used YouTube to explore how girls and young women resist rape culture. The researchers selected vlogs created by girls and young women (13–30 years old) exploring rape culture and consent. The researchers first encountered the challenge of how to identify relevant videos amongst an internet search (using terms such as "rape culture," "vlog," and "consent") that yielded approximately 1,000 results. The next challenge the researchers faced included the "ethics of representation" (citing Caron et al., 2016) to address how they as researchers analyzed vlogs where there was not permission from the vlog producers. To help them face these ethical challenges, the researchers used feminist and poststructural theories to guide them in their decision making, selected pseudonyms for vloggers (whom they called "video producers"), and developed clear criteria for vlog inclusion related to rape culture and topics of informed consent. The researchers also were mindful to share information in a table about the 10 vlogs ultimately selected and the following categories: year created, length, views, comments enabled or disabled, description.

## Online Focus Groups, Discussion Boards, and Chat Rooms

Researchers can artificially create **online focus groups**—similar to offline focus groups—where the researcher recruits and organizes an online meeting of several participants who share an experience of a phenomenon. An example would be a study investigating the coping resources of parents who have children living with autism. In this example, a researcher might recruit participants through web postings and/or email announcements to offline and online support groups focusing on this topic. Especially with the unfolding of the COVID-19 pandemic, many researchers pivoted to using online focus groups to address social distancing barriers that precluded in-person gatherings at various points during the pandemic. An advantage of online focus groups is that larger numbers of participants may be accommodated than with their offline counterparts (Lobe et al., 2020). Additionally, online focus groups may provide in-depth explorations that do not feel as accessible when focus groups are held in person due to the physical separation that exists in virtual focus groups (Archibald et al., 2019).

Once participants are contacted for the online focus group, the researcher may organize an internet space such as a chat room to conduct the focus group. **Chat rooms** are bound online spaces that are preestablished either by online users or internet providers (Allen, 2017). Users also spontaneously create chat rooms as they interact with one another around a common topic. Online focus groups are most effective when the social group is naturally occurring on the internet. In these cases, the researcher does not plan the online focus group in advance.

An example is a **discussion board**, where participants could post their thoughts, read the thoughts of others, and access the discussion board content at any time (Allen, 2017). Discussion boards and chat rooms both provide the advantage of having ready-made transcripts so there is an ease to data collection. Often, as you read in Perspectives 9.1, researchers just have to copy, cut, and paste participants' sharing into a word-processing document—rather than transcribing data—so it is ready for data interpretation.

A critical role to consider for the researcher is how to manage or moderate online discussions in focus group or chat room formats. The role of the moderator may range from being more active in an online setting where participant-to-participant interaction is slow-moving to a more passive role where these interactions are happening spontaneously and quickly (Golonka et al., 2017). Another moderator role may be to actively respond to those who may be distrustful of the researcher's intention and/or purpose of the study. Because online spaces are often unmoderated—especially when a researcher is joining a ready-made online focus group, discussion board, or chat room—it is important to be prepared for those who feel the presence of a researcher is an invasion of their "privacy" online.

Another moderator role is being prepared to manage the technical challenges of conducting research online: Internet technology can fail or disconnect during important researcher–participant exchanges (Carter et al., 2021). It can also be challenging to track the participants who are sharing in an online format due to large numbers of participants or use of participant pseudonyms that may be similar to one another or unfamiliar to the researcher. These challenges contribute to the overall disorientation researchers can feel when conducting online research (Golonka et al., 2017). However, as with the primary data collection methods reviewed in Chapter 8, researchers must weigh the pros and cons of using each approach.

## Audiovisual Media

**Audiovisual media** is media that contains auditory and/or visual aspects. Audiovisual media sources you may draw from for data collection might include photography, drawing and painting, film and video, sculpture, collage, murals, printmaking, craft-making, mixed media, and multimedia. The main advantage of using audiovisual media as a data collection strategy is that it includes a wide variety of data collection sources. For this chapter, we will focus on visual arts-based media, such as photography and drawing or painting. See Table 9.1 for tips on how to think about incorporating visual-based data collection methods in your study.

Whereas one of the disadvantages of using the internet to collect data is that your study can become limited to those with convenient and consistent internet access through home or school computers, one of the advantages of using audiovisual methods for data collection is that you as a researcher can literally put a tool of research in their hands. Visual methods in general provide participants the opportunity to express themselves in a nonverbal manner that may access deeper aspects of their understanding and/or experience of a phenomenon.

Moon (2019) states that visually based (i.e., arts-based) qualitative research can be transformative, aim toward social justice, and provide flexibility necessary to work with diverse

**TABLE 9.1**   Tips for Including Visual Media in Your Study

- Use an arts form that is easily used by your participants. Making art does not always appeal to every age group and/or participant. Some may even have negative experiences associated with art. Consider the comfort level of your participants with the arts-based data collection method you select.
- Plan for anticipated and unanticipated challenges in using art to collect data. For instance, what if a participant's camera does not work? How many supplies will you need for each of the participants?
- Question yourself. Are you using arts-based data collection strategies because they fit your research tradition and theoretical framework?
- Anticipate questions your participants may have about the art medium you are using. Consider having a prepared list of instructions for participants, especially if participants will be engaged in the art outside of the researcher's presence.
- Consult with an expert in the area of the arts-based medium you will use. Their expertise can save you time, money, and frustration and help you focus your study.
- Speaking of money, ensure you have enough funds for the art medium you would like participants to use. You do not want to run out of necessary supplies for your participants.
- Revisit your arts-based data collection methods often. How might they need to be refined?
- How does the RPA model guide you in making decisions about using arts-based data collection in your study?

communities. These data collection methods can be complex and challenging to describe because of the many varied forms art can take. Cole and Knowles (2008) assert that arts-based data collection methods can truly assist participants in translating the meaning and value of their experiences of a phenomenon into a visual format. In one of their studies that examined the life histories of teacher educators, the authors noticed their participants tended to use metaphorical and pictorial language in describing their histories. This type of participant sharing inspired the use of art as a result of their research. Other times, arts methods are used to represent the data collected to communicate the narratives of participants more powerfully.

One of the most powerful ways to use arts-based data collection in research is to explore social identity. For instance, Allen (2019) used an arts-based journal to explore a social identity of disability—especially in relation to identity development moving from experiencing (and being taught) disability as a "deficit" to a more positive view of disability as an important identity in their life. Participants included pictures of art they generated to represent their disability identity.

## Photography

Qualitative researchers select photography for data collection typically to supplement the primary collection methods discussed in Chapter 8. Photographs may be "found" or may be taken as instructed by a researcher. This data collection strategy is often used with children or other groups where words alone may not capture the depth of participants' experiences of a phenomenon. There are many ways you might consider incorporating photography into data collection in your project. You can send participants into their communities with a camera to document a phenomenon, such as stressors or sources of resilience in their lives. You could also hold a focus group with participants around a certain topic, such as inviting middle school students to photograph school factors that increase their sense of belonging in school.

We "photograph" things in our settings as practitioners all the time, and taking photographs allows for permanence and thus potentially more intense data analysis, whether for formal research processes or not. For example, a doctoral-supervisor-in-training of mine (Danica) began a master's level clinical supervision group one semester and asked his supervisees to take pictures of their office environments. The supervisees were instructed to not take pictures of actual clients or students, just the physical setting. They brought the photographs to group supervision the following week when my student (the great clinical-supervisor-in-training that he was!) discussed how the environment might affect those deciding to seek counseling services and how the trainees could make the environment more inviting to them.

**Photovoice** (Wang & Burris, 1994) is a well-known qualitative data collection strategy using photography as a way to document visual information. As with other data collection strategies, your theoretical and research traditions should guide your selection of this strategy. For instance, in a photovoice study of counseling students and their internship journeys, Wells and Hunt (2020) used photovoice as a way to help participants reflect and make meaning of their internship journeys in nonverbal, creative, and participatory ways. In a metasynthesis of photovoice studies with people living on the autism spectrum, Do et al. (2021) looked across multiple studies, finding that photovoice as a data collection tool facilitated more active and holistic engagement with participants living with autism. In a study of survivors of suicide, Mayton and Wester (2019) used photovoice to examine the grief and loss that can follow suicide of a loved one. The researchers selected photovoice to explore the nonverbal aspects of grief and the meaning-making that happens over time for survivors of suicide.

The use of photography as a supplemental data collection method can be especially useful with ethnographic, case study, and phenomenological designs that seek an in-depth understanding of a phenomenon. We will discuss how existing photographs may be used as archival data collection methods later in this chapter. Regardless of how photography is used as a media source, there is an empowerment approach embedded in this data collection strategy because the participants are valued for the images they themselves create.

Other advantages of this media include the potential for participatory action and social change during and after the research process, such as Vision Zero Photovoice in Denver, which sought to reduce the number of deaths for people walking and using bicycles, and BRITE Prevention's photovoice project gathering community voices to explore racial inequities in their community. Disadvantages of using photography can be the cost involved if researchers provide cameras for participants and the expense of developing the photographs. However, given that many individuals have smartphones with built-in camera, the costs may be minimal. Other challenges include ensuring participants understand the purpose of using the photographs. One way to address this challenge is to print an instruction sheet or provide a digital version with guiding questions about the study's focus that participants may take with them as they take photographs.

Liedenberg (2018) urges qualitative researchers to think critically about the use of photovoice, especially in the aim of empowerment and social change. She encourages researchers to use photovoice in thoughtful ways where researchers are not just using photovoice because it seems interesting to collect photographs but rather consider the powerful components of social change photovoice can offer. She also cautions those using photovoice as a data collection tool to only call it a method of participatory action research if the aim of the study itself is connected to social change.

Other studies have specifically used visual ethnography to document a phenomenon. **Visual ethnography** is the use of images, such as photographs or paintings, to understand a culture-sharing group (see Chapter 4). Previous to data collection in visual ethnography, it remains important to consider the role of research reflexivity and the context in which the visual data is collected and then interpreted. For instance, Pink (2013) discusses context in terms of the external and internal narrative an image has. The external narrative serves as the context for the image, whereas the internal narrative is the interpretation of the image by those who view it.

Visual images may stand on their own as a data collection method. After they are collected, these images are then interpreted for themes. Visual images may also be used in tandem with other data collection methods in seeking to understand a phenomenon. Lennette and Boddy (2013) used a visual ethnographic method to seek to understand the lived experiences of women with refugee status in Brisbane, Australia. In their study, photographs and digital movies were used as source data to provide meaningful and nuanced explorations of sensitive themes, allowing richer themes to be identified rather than focusing on conversations alone. Researchers shared how nascent the scholarship was exploring refugee women's lived experiences and that the use of visual methods as a data collection allowed them to be respectful of the levels of trauma and other mental health challenges participants had and thus identify four key findings: (a) a sense of achievement, pride, and accomplishment; (b) a sense of health and well-being; (c) a sense of ownership; and (d) a sense of burden. One photograph from this study demonstrated the first theme, where women discussed their cooking skills as intergenerational skills passed on through the generations to sustain their families and communities pre- and postmigration.

## Participant Artwork

Participant artwork is another data source that allows visual documentation of behaviors and contexts that are often unconscious, giving researchers access to participant subjectivity. Artwork not only expresses a particular moment but can also suggest why and how it was obtained, what it represents about the participant, and socially constructed meanings participants and researchers may communicate at various times. Finally, it often generates interview data that is typically triangulated with interviews or other data methods (Glaw et al., 2017). Being able to present findings in both visual and verbal data allows for a thicker description of participants' experience.

As part of a dating violence prevention program, Hays et al. (2009a) explored how adolescent girls conceptualized healthy and unhealthy dating relationships. Based on the developmental level of participants, developing artwork to express ideas about dating relationships was beneficial to understand how they define them and from where these definitions originated. During focus group interviews, the participants created artwork to represent these concepts and then shared their work with other focus group participants and the researchers cofacilitating the focus group interview. One powerful artwork example was a drawing from a 14-year-old, who drew a picture of a woman lying in blood on a bed. She included the words "you have been raped and murdered" on the drawing. During processing of the artwork in the focus group interview, she shared a story of a family friend who was victimized within her intimate partner relationship as a young woman.

## Additional Audiovisual Media

In addition to these arts-based data collection methods, there are other forms of art you may select to incorporate in your study to collect data. The focus of your study should drive the type of art you use. Whether you select music, film, expressive writing, sculpture, poetic writing, or other forms of art, it is best to identify which arts-based data collection strategies you will use in advance of your study. It is also important to keep a keen eye on the needs of your participants in "telling their story." See Perspectives 9.3 to read how a researcher integrated music into a qualitative study.

---

## PERSPECTIVES 9.3. USING MUSIC IN A QUALITATIVE INQUIRY

I initially became interested in using music in research when writing about Tupac Shakur for an undergraduate project. I had been thinking about Tupac's lyrics as important to analyze, because the lyrics discussed racism and sexism explicitly. I had the students analyze his music in terms of masculinity, hyper-masculinity, racism, and sexism. That's when I decided to start using music in qualitative research. The biggest challenge in using music in qualitative research is that is a lot harder to analyze because there is so much context to music, and in many ways a lot more subjective. Also, I definitely had to be aware from the beginning as a researcher of my own personal bias with regard to his lyrics. I think the most useful part of using music in qualitative research is that as a researcher you can dive deeper into significant themes: You can even build theory and through identifying the aspects of your participants' experience of music. For instance, what exactly are the mechanism and thoughts that go on in terms of how people use and experience music? This is exceptionally hard to capture if you are using quantitative measures.

The advice I would give to others is that you must have a solid qualitative paradigm: You need a good methodology. Creswell was my mentor. I used a phenomenology as a paradigm: It describes the essence of the meaning of the phenomenon I wanted to study in rap music. So, phenomenology guided my research question. I would say just because you are using music, does not mean you should throw out your theory and research tradition! Be open to all the types of creative aspects you can use in music as well—such as how music may be an outlet for clients. I would love to study that too. I have used music as a way to have a common ground to bond with my participants around a topic as well. Music helps participants express their feelings more because they are talking about themselves through the music. Especially when you are exploring sensitive topics, music can be easier outlet to talk about racism and sexism if just talking about the music instead of a more upfront question, like "What have been your experiences of racism?" I have used this type of approach with music and research in a youth development center and it has been a powerful way to collect data.

*—Derek Iwamoto, PhD*

## Additional Data Collection Methods

Written materials can be an important source of data collection. Similar to interviews and focus groups, written materials can provide insight into your participants' experience of a phenomenon. However, written materials are distinct from interviews and focus groups because they offer a less invasive manner to collect data. This may be important if you are researching a sensitive topic because writing can give participants the opportunity to express themselves in a more private manner and/or have more time to reflect on a phenomenon. Your research focus can also benefit from collecting written materials when they provide source information critical to understanding a phenomenon. For instance, if you are studying the intergenerational experiences of educational attainment of White students in rural Georgia, participants' grade reports, diplomas, and other educational materials have the potential to elucidate understanding about this phenomenon. There is a vast array of written materials you may select for data collection, some of which may include participant journals or diaries, notes, lists, records, reports, and many more. After reviewing this section, see Activity 9.2.

### Journals and Diaries

For some studies, you may select to have participants write or journal as a way to collect data. Often, this can be an unobtrusive way to supplement your data collection. Especially for phenomenological, life history, and case study examinations, participants' written material can help you more fully understand the phenomenon you are studying. You may be specifically studying writing, such as Grove's (2021) examination of the lived experiences of international students that used diaries as a way to explore their everyday routines.

More often, written materials are used as supplemental data collection. Lestari (2020) studied the emotional experiences preservice teachers had in a school-based practicum and perceived program benefits. The primary data collection strategy was the semistructured

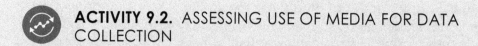

**ACTIVITY 9.2.** ASSESSING USE OF MEDIA FOR DATA COLLECTION

Select 2–3 media (e.g., internet, photography, drawing, music, written materials, etc.). Answer the following question for each of the media you selected:

- How would you use this type of media in data collection for your research topic?
- What information will this media allow you to collect?
- What information will be more challenging to collect using this media method?
- If you have already used media data collection methods, how might your answers to the previous questions guide you to revisit and refine your methods?

interview, which was then supplemented with samples of the participant writings (i.e., reflective journals). Using participants' written material can invite a participatory component into your study. Cullen (2009) integrated participants' writings into a participatory action research project for student affairs professionals' development of an antiracist professional identity. The project included group meetings where participants discussed becoming an antiracist as a White person in student affairs. In addition to semistructured interviews before pre- and postgroup experience, the participants keep written journals after each group session. These written reflections helped the researcher document the various schemas in White identity development that otherwise might not have been as fully captured.

In counseling, Mackrill (2009) encourages the use of participant diaries in qualitative research. He points to the use of client diaries in the work of many famous psychotherapists, such as Carl Rogers and Irwin Yalom. He discusses the advantages of using this data collection strategy, including the ability to show change over a period of time and to showcase the context of participants' lived experiences. Mackrill points out that diaries may be solicited as a form of qualitative data collection or unsolicited (i.e., a personal document that may be used as a source of data collection that we will discuss in the next section).

Additional strengths of using diaries for qualitative data collection are that they can reveal what participants might not feel comfortable sharing because they are "taboo" and they can help researchers understand the differences between participants' experience of a phenomenon. Mackrill (2009) also identifies some of the challenges in using participant diaries—namely, the presumption that participants have the skills and feel comfortable writing and the participants' motivation to write within the structure (e.g., time, duration, frequency) prescribed by the researcher. Woodbridge and O'Beirne (2017) describe in their findings section the use of journaling by counseling trainees to facilitate reflective thinking:

> Participants reported some costs to sharing their reflections, which for most resulted in some level of self-censorship: "I think [having an external audience] does take away from how personal you can be with it. ... I guess it's like how much

can you trust other people or even yourself when you're writing it out" (Participant Three). Participant Four shared: "I wanted to make sure it was my thoughts, but it was still graduate-level writing. And that's probably what prevented me from writing down my, you know, my initial gibberish." However, self-censorship was not universal, as Participant One expressed: "[The journal] gave me a place to express my feelings unfiltered. ... Writing, I always feel like I'm able to just spit it out. And I didn't filter or buffer anything I was thinking at the time."

## Personal and Public Documents

Personal and public documents can be rich sources of secondary data collection. **Personal documents** are typically solicited to help understand the culture and context of participants' experiences of a phenomenon. Personal documents have a naturalistic and ethnographic value, for they emerge from participants' own environments (Roulston, 2019). Examples of personal documents include letters, books, health care records, diaries or journals, financial records, report cards or grading sheets, homework assignments, legal documents, and any other artifact that may help elucidate the phenomenon you are studying. For instance, artifacts such as family documents handed down through generations may provide insight into your participants' lived experiences. In another example, say you are conducting a study on the intergenerational transmission of trauma. You might elect to explore personal artifacts within a participant's family that the participant states are important to review in order to understand the history of trauma in their family. This might entail family records surrounding a family's experience of trauma, which could include photographs, medical records, and other documents involving major stressors within or outside of the family. Often in school counseling research, evaluations of group interventions will involve use of secondary personal documents such as school attendance and tardiness records, grade reports, and teacher assessments of classroom performance.

Like personal documents, **public documents** can also be from a wide variety of sources. Official records, newspapers, newsletters, magazines, reports, tax records, legal reports, and other public data may serve as public documents. These documents might also include wills, health care documents, and yearly or other reports from nonprofit, government, and/or corporate organizations and can be found on paper or on the internet. This should give you an idea of the numerous available public documents you may select to use in your study. When examining archival data, keep in mind that your focus of study could be on a small sample of text in a document or a macroscopic focus, such as collecting documents that cover a lengthy period.

## Genealogy

**Genealogy**, also called "family history," is commonly known as tracing one's family lineage: an endeavor that is shaped and complicated by sociopolitical experiences of oppression and privilege (e.g., enslavement, forced migration, migration by choice, assimilation; Hart, 2018). Hershovitz (2016) reminds us that people have long searched for the roots of their existence but that the tracing of genealogies have varied widely across cultures and continents in terms of what is culturally valued about passing on lineages. For example, oral traditions of some cultures are the method of passing on genealogies rather than written documents. Hershowitz further notes that some qualitative researchers make a distinction between genealogy (tracing of established family relationships between people) and family history (researching deeply the stories of the people in these relationships). Foucault (1984) used the term "genealogy" to represent studying a collection of texts in the domains of power, knowledge, and norms in, for example, an academic discipline. Christensen (2014) used a genealogical approach derived from Foucault to study education texts in Denmark, exploring

> current trends, which were analysed [sic] for norms (anticipations, expectations to the subject, rules for behaviour [sic]), knowledge (application of scientific arguments) and power (subjectivation, practice). In order to identify the discursive sediments, ruptures and transformations, the "traits" were traced back to the beginning of the twentieth century. The trends are not evaluated according to whether they are "good" or "bad," but only in relation to which possibilities for subjectification they constitute. (pp. 8–9)

## Archival Data

**Archival data** is ready-to-use data that is typically collected by government and other institutional research organizations. This data has been described as "raw" data waiting to be used by a researcher. Archival data can be a helpful supplement to primary data collection because it can provide an enhanced understanding of your study's focus. For instance, you may be studying the mental health of recent immigrants from Ethiopia to the southeastern United States. Looking to U.S. Census Bureau and other government agencies tracking the migration of Ethiopian residents to the United States can help you as the researcher understand the larger contextual factors influencing the individuals you are studying.

Archival data can be of any format (e.g., written materials, statistics, etc.) and are maintained by a variety of organizations. Recently, there has been an increase in maintaining qualitative archival data. For instance, the Inter-university Consortium for Political and Social Research in Michigan and the United Kingdom Data Archive digitally store qualitative data for research. These data collection storehouses are excellent resources for researchers and facilitate both national and international collaborations in qualitative work.

Managing archival data analysis can be overwhelming, but it may make sense to include in your study. Gladstone and Volpe (2008) discussed five types of archival data analysis one may use. First is *supra analysis*, which is secondary qualitative analysis that goes beyond the initial focus and explores new research questions. The second type is *supplementary analysis*, involving a more microscopic examination of the initial data that was outside of the first study's focus. With the third type, *reanalysis*, the researcher revisits the original data collection and examines the congruence of the initial analysis. In the fourth type, *amplified analysis*, qualitative data from several studies are analyzed to increase the sample size with a research topic. Finally, the fifth type is *assorted analysis*, where the researcher uses a combination of data that is naturalistic or initial data collection with analysis of an archival data set.

Singh et al. (under review) conducted a supra-analysis of an original qualitative study they had conducted with 90 trans and nonbinary people exploring their risk, resilience, and identity development with participants across three sites: Atlanta, New York, and San Francisco. In this supra-analysis, researchers revisited this archival data set and asked a new question of the portion of the data from 20 Black trans and nonbinary participants across the three sites. The authors outline several challenges in using archival data in this manner—namely, how one using archival data will ensure the quality, context, and ethics of reexamining this data.

In addition, the authors used a theory, critical race theory (CRT), in the supra-analysis that was added to the theoretical frameworks of gender, resilience, and intersectionality theories that guided the original qualitative data collection. The use of this CRT allowed for new research questions of the secondary analysis. Whereas the original research question was "What are the experiences of risk, resilience, and identity development for trans and nonbinary people?" the supra-analytic study asked, "What are the experiences of resilience and resistance to racism, trans-prejudice, and other intersectional oppressions that Black trans and nonbinary people have?" Also important for establishing quality is the degree of availability of the initial qualitative data products: Are there items available or not available, and how will this influence the way the data "speak" after the initial analysis? Finally, in terms of ethics, the authors cite IRB challenges, including whether reexamining the data is covered within the informed consent participants signed. Researchers should also consider the ease with which they may access previous participants and, if this is feasible, the appropriateness of contacting these participants if necessary for a secondary analysis. See Table 9.2 for considerations when using documents as a method of secondary data collection.

**TABLE 9.2** Considerations in Using Documents as Data

You should be able to answer the following questions when incorporating documents into your study for data collection:

- What are the benefits or challenges of using documents in your study?
- What is your rationale and what are the ethics for using documents as data collection in your study?
- What is the context of when the documents were created? You may even want to know the sociopolitical and cultural environment of the documents, including if there were original theoretical frameworks or other perspectives that guided their creation.
- Who were the authors of the documents? What is their expertise?
- What is the credibility and trustworthiness of the documents?
- If you do not use the documents as data, will there be an integral aspect of your study left undiscovered?

We have reviewed many types of secondary data collection in this chapter. However, there are instances where there may not be secondary data collection methods available to you as you conduct your research. See Activity 9.3 to brainstorm ways you may address this situation in your study. Then see Wild Card 9.1 for some general tips to help you think about data collection in your study.

**ACTIVITY 9.3.** WHEN THERE ARE NO SECONDARY DATA

Brainstorm professional issues in which there are no secondary data collection methods available. Discuss the following in your research groups:

- Think of 2–3 examples of research topics in your field where the topic would preclude secondary data collection methods.
- How would you handle when there are no available records, documents, archival data, or media tools that verify the existence of a phenomenon?

 **WILD CARD 9.1.** TIPS TO KEEP IN MIND AS YOU USE MEDIA

It is challenging just to think about traditional data collection methods in your study, much less to be open to using media and other secondary data collection tools in your study. Use the following tips to keep your mind open to various data collection strategies:

- Let your research focus, research tradition, and theoretical framework guide your use of secondary data collection strategies. It may sound innovative to use social networking sites to gather data for a case study on families with a child who has autism, but it might not be the best fit for your study's design. Remember your roles within the RPA model, and let the intersection of research, practice, and advocacy guide you in your decision making.
- Embrace the ambiguity that media data collection can provide! You may not have as much researcher "control" as in traditional data collection, but you may open the door to more fully understanding your participants.
- This may seem contradictory to the second bullet, but have a plan for data collection. Using media and embracing ambiguity should *not* translate into "anything goes" in your data collection. You should have a plan to manage the solicitation of data and the potentially rapid responses (especially if you are online) of participants.
- Always wear your ethical hat. Remember entering the world of data collection via the internet and other arts-based data collection strategies can be disorienting. This does not mean you should not use similar ethical guidelines in interacting with participants. For example, is it smart to accept a Facebook request from a participant? What if your blog research suggests you portray your participants in a less favorable light? There are no quick and easy answers to these questions. However, you can use your good sense of personal and professional ethics, consultation with research methods, and good knowledge of your research area to guide you.
- Use long-standing principles of qualitative data collection and apply them to innovative data collection methods. For instance, if you are asking

participants to vlog about their experiences of living with social anxiety, be sure to have discussions about how, when, where, and why this data collection will take place.

- Expand your ideas of data collection—but not too much! Have conversations with your peers and research mentors about which data collection methods might be "too much" or "too little" for your project. You do not want to over-collect data and drain or burden your participants. You also do not want to miss out on a creative way to collect data that might be less obtrusive for participants and/or help you understand their experiences more fully. It is like that overused mantra you hear often about life: "It's all about balance!"
- Consistently revisit your data collection methods, assess how they are going, and refine the components that need to be adjusted accordingly so your data collection methods are of the highest integrity and quality.

## CHAPTER SUMMARY

We have discussed in this chapter the many ways secondary data collection may be conducted in qualitative research. Similar to the primary data collection strategies discussed in Chapter 8, the researcher should be guided by the research tradition and theoretical framework for the study. When using secondary data collection methods, there is a wide variety of media one may use. From the expansive reach of the internet to the hands-on visual methods of photography and artwork, these secondary data collection strategies can enhance the researcher's understanding of a particular phenomenon. Additionally, there may be documents that are personal and public documents or involve archival data that researchers may use as secondary data sources. No matter what secondary data collection strategy one selects, there should be a thorough understanding of their impact on participants. A more sensitive research topic, for instance, may require secondary data collection methods that are less obtrusive to best meet the needs of participants. On the other hand, a topic that requires participants who are difficult to access may require the use of the internet to case a wider reach. Regardless, consider your use of secondary data collection as carefully as you would primary data collection methods in order to gain the best understanding of your phenomenon.

## Review Questions

1. Consider a hypothetical study of U.S. protests against anti-Black racism after the year 2000. What would be potential sources of online media data collection?
2. How would your roles in the RPA model shape your decision making in which media sources are best for your study?

3. If this was a retrospective study with Black activists and protest leaders, what would be the advantages and disadvantages of using vlogs, blogs, or diary entries to understand the phenomenon?

4. If you collected data on this topic using chat rooms, what considerations would you need to keep in mind in terms of building trust with participants? What would you need to consider if participants ask you to join in their activist and protest work?

5. What personal and professional documents might you consider using in this study?

6. How will your identities related to privilege, oppression, and their intersections (and related systems of privilege and oppression) shape your role within the RPA model?

## Recommended Readings

Christensen, G. (2014). Genealogy and education research. *International Journal of Qualitative Studies in Education, 29*(6), 763–776. https://doi.org/10.1080/09518398.2016.1162871

Moon, S. (2019). *Three approaches to qualitative research through the Arts: Narratives of teaching for social justice and community.* Brill.

Pink, S. (2013). *Doing visual ethnography* (3rd ed.). Sage.

Salmons, J. E. (2015). *Doing qualitative research online.* Sage.

Wilson, E., Kenny, A., & Dickson-Swift, V. (2015). Using blogs as a qualitative health research tool: A scoping review. *International Journal of Qualitative Methods, 14*(5), 1–12. https://doi.org/10.1177/1609406915618049

## CHAPTER 10

# Basics of Qualitative Data Management and Analysis

---

### CHAPTER PREVIEW

Greater attention to the components and processes associated with qualitative data management and analysis is needed in qualitative research studies today. In this and the next chapter, you will hopefully find some helpful information to guide qualitative data management and analysis. In this chapter we provide some basics for qualitative data management and analysis that we consider as more typical steps and components regardless of your selected research traditions. In Chapter 11, we will discuss qualitative data analysis more specific to different research traditions. First, we present some foundational information as you embark on your present qualitative research proposal and beyond. Qualitative data management, a process of both data collection and analysis, will be discussed later in the chapter. Figure 10.1 depicts the key components and sequencing of qualitative data management and analysis.

## Qualitative Data Management and Analysis

---

Qualitative data analysis is a challenging and time-consuming yet creative and fun process! Trustworthy qualitative data analysis relies on the researcher as an individual as well as a skilled professional. Patton (2014) described the complexities of qualitative data analysis:

> [It] involves us not just making sense of the world but also in making sense of our relationship to the world and therefore in discovering things about ourselves even as we discover things about some phenomenon of interest. ... Because qualitative inquiry depends, at every stage, on the skills, training, insights, and capabilities of the inquirer, qualitative analysis ultimately depends on the analytical intellect and style of the analyst. The human factor is a great strength and the fundamental weakness of qualitative inquiry and analysis—a scientific two-edged sword. (pp. 432–433)

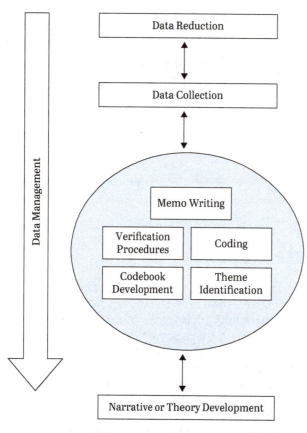

**FIGURE 10.1** Qualitative Data Management and Analysis Process

Although we present data collection and data analysis as separate processes, they should occur concurrently to maximize trustworthiness of the study (see Chapter 7). Unfortunately, many qualitative researchers fail to interweave these processes due to lack of time, interest, or knowledge of the power of simultaneous data collection and analysis (see Wild Card 10.1). We believe that it is not possible to have a rigorous research design without beginning qualitative data analysis with the first data source—if not before—and continuing throughout data collection: There is no way to speak to the trustworthiness of the study, and there are ethical considerations. If one waits until all data are collected, how do you investigate emerging research questions? How do you follow up with participants? If, as we describe as a distinguishing characteristic of qualitative inquiry, providing dialogue

 **WILD CARD 10.1.** THE "QUICK" QUALITATIVE STUDY

We have seen several published studies, as you probably have, that have simply conducted several data sources (often, interviews) and then presented themes of these sources. In essence, the design was so rigid that there were no built-in opportunities to revise data collection as data analysis occurred. Participants were not offered a chance to verify the findings. New data sources to better address the research questions were not made available, nor were revisions in data collection methods allowed.

Remember, ethically and socially responsible data analysis is more likely to occur throughout data collection if your study design is "looser" initially. The tighter your design, the more rigid your questions, and the less open you are to make changes as you start collecting data. Never, ever sacrifice your research design to simply save time for you. Leave enough room in your plan to change your data collection plan. Otherwise, you may complete a study quickly, but practitioners in counseling and education will likely not trust the findings.

opportunities with often silenced participants is important, how do we do that in a responsible way if we are "waiting to hear" them at the end of a study? Thus, the major fallacy of postponing data analysis can be summed up with a trite expression: If only I had known then what I know now. Since there are few opportunities to gather a thick description of participant perspectives as well as contextual information, it is a professional and ethical imperative that we think of qualitative data analysis as something that continually influences research design from the very beginning of the study.

## Key Concepts of Qualitative Data Management and Analysis

Before we dive into the steps of qualitative data analysis and strategies for qualitative data management, we want to familiarize you with a few terms that are used along the way. The bolded terms relate to general approaches to qualitative data analysis. Briefly define various forms of coding as well as qualitative data management.

In Chapter 2, we noted that qualitative research was characterized by inductive and abductive analysis; with qualitative data analysis, some deductive analysis may also be involved. Integrating these three approaches allows for a more organized and rigorous qualitative study (Bingham & Witkowsky, 2022). Inductive analysis involves a bottom-up approach where qualitative researchers read through or view the data source to identify codes as well as collapse or chunk codes to identify themes and patterns as analysis becomes more complex. Qualitative data analysis is not purely inductive: Our choices about research paradigms and traditions, research questions, topics, participant and site selection, researcher role considerations, and conceptual framework development (among many others) are affected by what data we expect to find. While these expectations may, unfortunately, be guided at times by what we need or want to find, oftentimes they are guided by preexisting "codes" in our everyday lives. Thus, no matter how open and inductive we strive to be, there are often predetermined ideas about a phenomenon that guide what codes we select. Qualitative researchers should consider their research questions as working assumptions that are able to be changed as data are collected and analyzed.

As noted in Chapter 2, abductive analysis is the temporary detachment from an evolving narrative or theory about the data; this moving away from the data allows time and space for hunches or new conceptualizations to take shape and helps qualitative researchers rethink and reorganize the data. Deductive analysis is when qualitative researchers apply predetermined codes to the data; these predetermined codes may originate from the literature, research questions, or their experiences. Thus, we seek to verify what we are finding. Verification involves seeking out cases to disconfirm present codes and themes in order to strengthen emerging models, and this component is a presented in Figure 10.1 as a part of analysis. In essence, initial data collection may be somewhat inductive, with later data collection, as a result of ongoing data analysis, becomes more deductive. The process by which qualitative data analysis moves from exploratory to confirmatory methods is known as **analytic induction.**

Throughout this chapter and the next, we will discuss codes and coding. A **code** is defined as a word or short phrase that creates a salient or summative attribute to a segment of qualitative data. *Coding*, then, is a useful and important way to manage, sort, and bring structure to unstructured data. It is the "systematic identification of topics, issues similarities and differences in data researchers consider relevant. This relevance connects to the researchers' a priori questions and the theoretical perspectives they choose to support the inquiry" (Richards, 2022, p. 156).

Analyzing qualitative data requires qualitative researchers to engage with data sources multiple times, as the process is iterative and cyclical; coding data is an integral part of the overall data analysis process. Saldaña (2016) identified two general categories of coding. First, *descriptive coding* is used to identify common elements of a data source to allow for initial comparisons of codes across data sources. It allows for basic coding procedures to identify frequency of individual codes as well as cooccurrences of codes. The second coding category, which builds on descriptive coding, is interpretive coding. *Interpretive coding* involves the reanalysis of initial codes, collapsing them to identify "deeper" codes. These codes may be labels derived from the literature or participants themselves (i.e., *in vivo codes*) or latent constructs determined with more complex analysis.

There are many ways to approach descriptive and interpretive coding, as these are not sequenced processes. For example, Bingham et al. (2018) proposed the processes of macro-coding and micro-coding. **Macrocoding** is a deductive process by which data are first sorted into broad categories, then inductive analysis is performed within each category to identify further codes, themes, and patterns (i.e., **microcoding**).

Related to coding, we often see the description in published studies of codes "emerging" from the data; this is a problematic way of describing the coding process. The concept that codes and themes (i.e., collapsed or chunked codes) "emerge" originates from Glaser and Strauss's (1967) postpositivist notions that there is a single, external truth that awaits discovery. Given this assumption, it is reasonable to see how qualitative researchers describe themes as emerging, that they unearth truth untouched by researcher subjectivity. Despite the rise of other paradigms (e.g., constructivism, critical paradigms) that recognize the inherent role of researcher subjectivity in the data process, the language of thematic emergence is still used widely today:

> The language of emergence implies that the themes reside in the data and somehow life themselves off the page, fully formed, and present themselves to the researcher. ... neither data nor themes possess agency per se, rather, it is the researchers' interactions with the data, and with one another, that bring forth thematic identification and description. (Varpio et al., 2016, p. 43)

The last concept we want to introduce will be discussed at length toward the end of the chapter: **qualitative data management**. As you begin a qualitative research study, it is imperative that you develop a system that will assist with tracking data collection and analysis. The system should begin with a clear plan of who will be collecting and analyzing data and a timeline for completing respective tasks (e.g., data collection, independent analysis, consensus coding; Turner, 2022). The system is to be well documented and serve as part of your audit trail; we recommend the system be electronic for ease of retrieval, and you might find that using qualitative software is helpful for developing this system (discussed later in the chapter). Furthermore, the system should be accessible to any research team members who may be involved in data collection and analysis.

System components typically include a timeline of data collection and analysis procedures; data source materials (e.g., transcripts, social media posts, artwork); various versions of codebooks; case displays; research team meeting notes; researcher memos; and so on. A qualitative data management system typically also includes a table or spreadsheet of data sources that captures key features of that data collection method. For example, with interviews, each participant is included as a row where basic demographics (e.g., gender, race/ethnicity, work experience, role type) are included as well as other potentially helpful information (e.g., interview setting and duration).

Qualitative researchers are to assign a source label or attributes to codes so that it is easier to examine whether codes or themes are systematically tied to a data source or to participant demographics. For example, in a school district study involving multiple data collection methods (e.g., interviews, personal documents), you could attach these source and attribute labels to an interview of the third participant with "P03, Interview 1: Black male teacher." For the documents tied to this participant, you could label them as "P03, Performance Evaluation 1: Black male teacher."

## Steps of Qualitative Data Analysis

Miles et al. (2020) view qualitative data analysis as a cyclical process of the following components: reduce data, display data, make conclusions, and verify. In this section, we outline eight steps of qualitative data analysis that capture these components. Using these steps, qualitative researchers assemble, disassemble, and reassemble information to address the research question(s) while applying various data management strategies discussed later in this chapter. The steps are approached in different ways based on the selected qualitative research tradition. In Chapter 11, we discuss qualitative data analysis by research tradition. What you will likely surmise after reading Chapters 10 and 11 is that there is an underlying basic process to analysis; however, various research traditions label it differently. Although we present these steps linearly, it is important to note that they are cyclical and recursive as you collect and manage data.

We will use data from one qualitative study to illustrate these steps. The study by Hays et al. (2009b) is a grounded theory that explored aspects of diagnostic variance in the clinical decision-making process for 41 counselors and counselor trainees. As you will see as we move through the steps, analysis moved from a priori data reduction, to several iterations of analysis, to data management as a tool in collection and analysis, to presentation of findings of how counselors vary in their clinical decision making.

## Step 1: Reduce Data

Referring to Figure 10.1, you will notice that data analysis begins before data collection. Thus, data reduction (i.e., the process of organizing, segmenting, and analyzing text) really begins even before data collection begins. How is this possible? What you decide to investigate, why, and with whom are all data reduction strategies. That is, you narrow your focus of analysis because it is necessary to do so. You cannot study everything, so you limit data analysis (and collection) options. Your selected topic, research questions, subjectivity, conceptual framework, access to participants and settings, and plans for establishing trustworthiness initially guide what you are likely to consider important concepts. Once initial "data" are reduced, you can make decisions about data collection. Proposal Development Activity 10.1 may assist you with the initial step.

---

**PROPOSAL DEVELOPMENT ACTIVITY 10.1.** DATA REDUCTION

Revisit your evolving audit trail and responses from earlier Proposal Development activities. Create an initial list of keywords related to each of the following areas. That is, what information or terms do you associate with each of these data reduction techniques?

Topic: _____

_____

Research question(s): _____

_____

Your role and assumptions about the study: _____

_____

Previous literature and pilot data: _____

_____

Access to participants and setting: _____

_____

Trustworthiness strategies: _____

_____

---

## Step 2: Collect Data

Data collection methods were discussed in Chapters 8 and 9, so we will just briefly mention them here. Data collection methods include observations; individual, dyadic, and focus group interviews; social media; artwork; and documents; to name a few. Decisions on these methods are largely based on your research questions and access to a population. Data are collected concurrently with data analysis, and qualitative researchers are to carefully document how they sequenced data collection and analysis, including how data collection continually shapes data analysis. For the diagnosis study (Hays et al., 2009b), the data collection method consisted of individual interviews.

## Step 3: Write a Memo

Recall from Chapter 8 that memo writing, or jotting field notes, immediately following data collection, is an important part of data collection. Memo writing is also an important component of data analysis, as this is often the immediate initial analysis that occurs with new data. Milhas (2022) noted that memo writing moves qualitative researchers closer to knowledge production wherein they discover the voice of their participant(s) as well as their own. As such, qualitative researchers should ask themselves, "What does the data source (e.g., transcript, observation, chat room discussion thread) teach me about my research question(s)?" Thus, memos preserve and develop qualitative researchers' ideas about the data as data collection and analysis occur. As memos are constructed, they are to remain grounded to maximize participant voice while engaging deeply in researcher reflexivity and advocacy.

Milhas (2022) identified three functions of memos: as a precursor, companion, or a follow up to coding. As a *precursor* to coding, early memos can be constructed by documenting reflections and understandings of the data immediately after the data source is generated as an initial review. Early memos can be used to mine for initial codes as well as be used for materials written later to reflect on how your conceptualization of the data has changed over time. Noting these shifts in understanding and construction in writing can serve as an indicator of rigor and may be included in your audit trail. As a *companion* to coding, memo writing during the coding process provides space for qualitative researchers to begin thinking more complexly about the data, deriving meaning, and sustaining inquiry within a data source. As a *follow-up* to coding, memo writing is a method for comparing codes across data sources to search for conceptual overlaps and patterns.

There are several types of memos that can be used individually or collectively as part of qualitative data analysis: document reflection, key quotation, parts-whole, and comparison memos. **Document reflection memos** are developed by examining the data source holistically for meaning, gleaning through repetitive content and initial patterns. For example, qualitative researchers may note overall impressions of participant artwork or themes within a blog or focus group interview. These impressions can be reoccurring ideas, labels, or features of the data source content, researcher reflections about the data source, and researcher reflections about the extent to which the data source shapes the research design, to name a few examples.

**Key quotation memos** focus on an illustrative or evocative quotation or quotations within a data source—what Milhas (2022) terms as a narrative's "fuse box." Qualitative researchers describe the quotation(s) and often reflect on the quotation(s). Reflections can involve what a quotation means for the research question(s), how it affects the overall study design, and/or how the researchers are affected personally or professionally. When qualitative researchers include multiple quotations in a memo from a data source, they have an opportunity to process how the excerpts compare in terms of meaning. Qualitative researchers can ask themselves, "How do these separate quotations inform each other? What do they reveal together that may not be otherwise evident?" (Milhas, 2022, p. 251).

For those interested in using both memo types in their research, a **parts-whole memo** allows examination of parts of a data source compared to its whole. Essentially, this involves combining the document reflection and key quotation memo functions. Thus, qualitative researchers reflect upon and document the extent to which a particular quotation mirrors or contradicts the holistic message of the data source.

Finally, **comparison memos** are written after coding is complete. Qualitative researchers extract quotations across data sources for a particular code, then illustrate a code's complexity and "stretchiness" by highlighting how different quotations may indicate various dimensions of that code: How do the quotations collectively demonstrate the code? How do they diverge to reflect its complexity? (Milhas, 2022).

Whether memos are developed as a precursor, companion, or follow up to coding, they can be compared across data sources to identify and synthesize patterns. With respect to memos linked with interviews, Milhas (2022) noted that memos can help qualitative researchers to identify a *typology*, or an identifiable cluster of participants based on shared behaviors, perspectives, or values. Qualitative researchers can reflect across memos about the following: Is there an identifiable pattern across memos, and do particular participants cluster together in some manner?

For the diagnosis study (Hays et al., 2009b), the authors and research assistants noted their impressions of potential findings directly following an interview and then again after the interview text had been organized (i.e., transcribed). After interviewing a 28-year-old, White, female school counselor about the process she used to diagnose a 32-year-old Latina woman, a research assistant created the following memo:

> I was struck with how this school counselor assumed that the client was in denial about her symptoms, and how quick she was to assume that this person had a personality disorder! She seemed to note a lot of symptoms for this client, yet focused in on such a pathologizing diagnosis, even though she became even more uncertain with her decision as we talked. She did mention that ethnicity and gender played a role in symptoms, but I do not think she talked about it when she presented the diagnosis. … I wonder if this participant's clinical decision-making is partly a result of the notion that she is a school counselor and does not work with 32-year-old clients.

Other memos (e.g., parts-whole memos) from the diagnosis study included more detailed information about the interviewer and the participant, clinical decision-making process, cultural factors, treatment recommendations noted, perceived prognosis, and so forth.

## Step 4: Organize Text and Audiovisual Data

"Organizing the text" usually refers to transcribing textual data, organizing audiovisual data, converting and expanding upon field notes, and creating data management tools such as contact summary sheets and document summary forms. You may refer to Chapters 8 and 9 for examples of data management tools. Figure 10.2 presents an excerpt of an interview from the diagnosis study (Hays et al., 2009b), with some initial codes (Step 5).

Interview transcribed by CRB: Interviewee ID # 016D     05/14/07, Duration: 36:58

Include information about the date and length of the interview when you organize text.

CRB: What diagnosis or diagnoses would you give this client?

PA: With this individual I think I would diagnose her with major depressive disorder and a personality disorder, probably borderline personality disorder.

Major Depressive Disorder
Borderline Personality Disorder

Gender

Availability-Broad

CRB: How would you summarize the symptoms used to arrive at your diagnosis?

PA: Well this individual has multiple symptoms prior, she has a couple of episodes of rage, she mentions crying almost daily within the last month, the attempted suicide, she is eating more lately, she has gained weight poor concentration, difficulty getting out of bed, she is doing impulsive things, she spent like $10,000 in a short period of time.

CRB: Are there other diagnoses that could explain the client's symptoms?

PA: Yeah, I think there might be some as well. Um, possibly, I don't think she has schizophrenia, but she has schizophrenia like symptoms, but not full blown schizophrenia, possibly bipolar, but I don't know if she's that extreme to be bipolar. There are some things here and there, but I don't know if I would diagnose her with, but I think it is a good possibility because she has such a variation of symptoms.

Uncertainty

Diagnosis rule-out (bipolar and schizophrenia)

Availability-Academic

CRB: What aspects of the case did you use to arrive at your diagnosis?

PA: OK, the multiple symptoms that she has, the weight gain, the eating, her lack of interest in doing things, her problems at work, she thinks the people that she works with are watching her, she has trouble getting out of bed, she worries and a lot of these things have happened with in the last 2–3 months. Very rapidly. She spent over $10,000, she has used her credit card a lot lately, and she is hearing voices. I have learned at [University X] that these symptoms tend to relate to a mood disorder.

Vividness criterion

CRB: Were there any particular salient criteria for you?

PA: Definitely. The extreme shifts in mood stand out to me.

Gender

Race/Ethnicity

[Transcript break]

CRB: What cultural characteristics, if any, are important to this client's presenting problem?

PA: Um, well, [long pause] I guess the fact that she is female, and as far as her changing her mood, I think that would be, well as far as her weight gain, that's really not that uncommon, but the fact that she is female, and she is Latin American, but I think there is a huge variation that she is having that is alarming.

Race/Ethnicity
Uncertainty about cultural "norms"
Race/Ethnicity

CRB: What cultural characteristics if any, are important to your diagnostic decision? How so?

PA: (long pause) Well I think the fact that she is Latin; we can look at her culture, because she is isolated and doesn't want to interact with others. I think it would be important to look at her culture and see if that is something Latin Americans like to do, they may not like to be very social. That may be very common for her culture. It also talks about her stress and it could be that there are some things here and there that is appropriate for her culture and you know she may not be doing anything out of the ordinary for her culture.

Needing treatment

[Transcript break]

CRB: How would you describe this client's level of functioning?

PA: She definitely needs some sort of treatment and I think I mentioned before that she does have a variation in her symptoms and they are pretty extreme as far as she has had a lot to the symptoms with in the last 2–3 months and that is pretty alarming. Right now I think her level of functioning I think she is able to function on one level, but she certainly needs some sort of continuous treatment. I wouldn't with this patient, she has had out patient treatment for um, pain killers, so I would be weary to prescribe medication. It may be something that she needs, but I would be weary of doing that.

"Alarming" symptoms [emic code]

Cautious about future medication

Client "Resistance"

[Transcript break]

CRB: And what might make it difficult to get the information for diagnosing this client?

**FIGURE 10.2**  Interview Excerpt for Diagnosis Study (Hays et al., 2009b)

## Step 5: Code

A *code* is a label or tag, "chunks" of various sizes based on the defined case. Codes may be descriptive or interpretive and specifically labeled by participants themselves (*emic codes* or in-vivo codes) and/or by qualitative researchers (*etic codes*). Codes can originate from predetermined categories or from the data. Complete Activity 10.1 to become more familiar with the coding process.

### ACTIVITY 10.1. CODING EXERCISE

Let's practice coding! In small groups, review annual Top 100 music lists for the past 5 years. (The Billboard annual Top 100 lists are good ones; visit https://billboard.com). The purpose of this "research study" is to investigate popular music according to a ranking system. Your group decides what categories are important to attend to as you develop a codebook, or coding system. First, create individual coding lists for your five documents. How might you categorize list entries? Then come to consensus with group members about your classification system. Develop a list of codes based on your coding system for approximately 15 minutes.

Discuss your coding system with the entire class. What were similarities and differences in coding systems? How might the way data were reduced influence this coding system? What other forms of data could be used to investigate popular music? How might this affect your current coding system?

Prior to reviewing any data source in depth for codes, we recommend that you engage in **attributional coding**, or the process of assigning data by source (e.g., interview, observation, social media; Miles et al., 2020). With multiple data methods and sources, this can be an invaluable process. For example, for a study involving classroom observations, interviews, and journal entries of a special education teacher in a prekindergarten classroom, data sources might be coded as Interview 1, Interview 2, Observation 1, Observation 2, Journal Entry 1, Journal Entry 2, and so on.

As you code, focus primarily on thickly describing the code before trying to shorten it. A code should be described thoroughly, using examples to illustrate it, so that another researcher could readily identify codes for a data source based on your detailed, operational definition of it. Miles et al. (2020) conceptualized codes as the abbreviations rather than words; however, we believe that phrases should be abbreviated later rather than earlier in the coding process to avoid confusion.

So, what do you code? How do you begin? Earlier steps have mentioned data organization strategies so that you can more easily see what information you have in front of you. First, code before you collect data as appropriate (see Step 1): Examine your conceptual framework and jot down several key phrases from previous literature, researcher assumptions, pilot findings, and so forth. This framework provides insights into possible codes and, in turn, will likely be revised as data are collected. Place these "codes" aside. Table 10.1 presents some codes for Step 1 for the diagnosis study (Hays et al., 2009b).

**TABLE 10.1** Codes Noted in Literature on Diagnostic Variance

| | Description | Example(s) |
|---|---|---|
| **Representativeness** | Likelihood that a criterion belongs to a specific diagnosis that we expect to see (and subsequently confirm) for certain disorders for certain populations. | Depression expected for women; crying spells a salient criterion for depression |
| **Availability** | Certain events or criteria are more available to us because they are salient and relate closely to a disorder, we are more familiar with criteria, or they are easier to retrieve. | Someone with a lot of experience with particular disorders will have those cues more available and will naturally lean toward certain diagnostic decisions. Certain symptoms may be personal for us. |
| **Vividness criterion** | Some criteria are more intense in their presentation and heavily influence our decisions. | Withdrawal symptoms as evidence of dependence |
| **Anchoring** | Earlier clinical data hold more weight in final decisions. There is a propensity to focus on later data that supports it (or later data not viewed as salient). | Mental status examination shows thought disorder symptoms more likely to find psychotic symptoms in intake to support diagnosis |
| **Locus of attribution (dispositional vs. situational)** | What caused the problem: Is it biological or external? | Irritability is a result of chemical imbalance or a maladaptive way of coping with an overwhelming situation. |
| **Confirmation bias** | We look for clinical evidence to support our diagnosis versus looking for symptoms that would lead us to select another diagnosis (this tool overlaps with some of the others). | |
| **Gender** | Gender stereotypes (overdiagnosis) | More severe diagnoses for women; women overrepresented with personality disorder diagnoses |
| **Race/ethnicity** | Racial and ethnic stereotypes (overdiagnosis) | More severe diagnoses for racial/ethnic minorities; more negative symptoms noted for racial/ethnic minorities, even when they receive the same diagnoses as majority group members |
| **Underdiagnosis** | When symptoms (a) do not fit an existing category, (b) are congruent with gender roles, (c) are more prominent for an oppressed group (then dominant group avoids the diagnosis), and (d) are viewed as happening to them versus because of them (locus of attribution issue). Also, the more resources we perceive the client to have (this can be connected to awareness of oppression issues), the more we will underdiagnose or avoid more severe diagnoses. | |

Second, take the organized text and/or audiovisual data and consider them in the context of your research purpose. Some researchers argue that coding should be guided strictly by the research question(s) since there are so many data sources, while others assert it is better to remain more "open" and code using various methods. Table 10.2 presents ideas for some potential sources to code. Finally, with written text, you have to decide if you will code by word, phrase, sentence, or paragraph. We find, while it may be related to your research purpose, the unit of analysis you code is a matter of personal preference.

**TABLE 10.2**   Coding Sources

- Research questions
- Interview questions
- Observation rubrics
- Other researchers
- Literature review
- Pilot studies
- Personal experiences
- Professional experiences
- Who, what, when, where, how, why questions
- Participant actions
- Participant activities
- Participant meanings
- Discrepancies (e.g., use of terms like "never," "always," and "should")
- Silences and other nonverbal communication
- Relationships among participants
- Setting information
- Absence of codes
- What participants label as codes
- What theory and practice determine are codes

Once a certain number of codes are identified (e.g., several dozen), it may be helpful to begin to manage and group codes into categories (i.e., *categorization*), collapse categories into themes, and examine whether there are relationships among themes. However, it is important to not collapse codes too early, or you can risk forming connections among individual codes prematurely. The process of collapsing categories into themes is discussed further in the next step. Richards (2022) noted the following considerations as qualitative researchers engage in the coding and categorization process:

- Do my codes relate to the meaning of the text they mark?
- Did I maintain meaning despite condensing data when I moved from codes to categories?
- Do all units under a specific code or category belong in that grouping?
- Did I make sure no two categories are too similar?
- Does this coding system make sense given my questions and assumptions, or do I need to go in a new direction? (p. 157)

A few other coding considerations are important to note. First, qualitative researchers should code specific data sources as soon as possible after data are collected. Second, if a code is used a lot, then create subcodes, even early in data analysis. (For example, in Figure 10.2, you will notice that the code "availability" has two subcodes: *Broad* refers to indicating a broad range of symptoms, and *academic* refers to the notion that a diagnosis is made based on academic training.) Third, continue to develop memos. You will find that additional impressions about your overall research design, including future data collection and analysis, occur as you code. Be sure to add memos about codes and add to your codebook. Fourth, you can code manually (e.g., writing directly on organized text, creating index cards of codes) or electronically (e.g., use of computer software). We actually prefer to manually code after organizing text with word processing or PDF documents; however, this may quickly become cumbersome as data accumulate. Remember, software does not analyze data; it facilitates data storage, coding, retrieval, comparing, and linking. Qualitative data analysis software is discussed later in this chapter. Finally, working across cultures and languages requires consideration of culturally and linguistically constructed realities and what this means for coding. Thus, idioms, dialects, colloquialisms, and so forth may not be easily understood by someone culturally different from the participant. When conducting qualitative research with participants and/or materials that are culturally or linguistically unfamiliar, seek consultation from the respective community, research team members, or others (e.g., external auditor, peer debriefer).

## Step 6: Identify Themes and Patterns

"Themes and patterns" refers to higher order codes (*pattern codes*), or codes or categories that have been chunked together to describe a phenomenon more fully (McLeod, 2011). Miles et al. (2020) assert that themes and patterns are *metacodes*, or codes of codes of the previous step. They appear as themes, causes, or explanations; relationships among people; more theoretical constructs; and so forth. Maxwell (2013) described this step as implementing connecting strategies to identify relationships among codes.

Like factor analysis in quantitative research, developing patterns involves examining codes and brainstorming ways in which the codes "chunk together," often to form a latent or complex construct. Two of the themes (with sample codes or subthemes following in parentheses) from the diagnosis study (Hays et al., 2009b) include (a) forms of diagnostic variance (information variance, observation variance, criterion variance); and (b) use of cognitive tools (representativeness, availability bias, vividness criterion, anchoring, and locus of attribution). *Forms of diagnostic variance* refers to the variability in information available or how it is interpreted in clinical decision making, and *use of cognitive tools* refers to the specific strategies that clinicians engage in that lead to misdiagnosis of mental health issues.

LeCompte and Schensul (2012) noted that patterns can be developed from several things:

- *declaration:* The participant explicitly identifies as a pattern during the data process of being interviewed, writing a blog, developing artwork, journaling, and so on.
- *frequency of omissions:* During the process of collapsing codes, this is when the researcher and/or participant notes something is missing. Thus, what is absent from the textual or audiovisual data may be important.

- *similarity:* The researcher notes a cluster of codes that have similar characteristics. For example, in the academic leadership study mentioned in other parts of this text, Hays et al. (2021) identified four similar codes (i.e., external leadership socialization, university leadership education, leadership by professional engagement, and internal leadership socialization) and clustered those as a more complex code for the model (leadership preparation).
- *cooccurrence of codes:* The researcher sees a pattern where particular codes characterize a typology. For example, the codes of "work-life balance" and "glass ceiling" may be found among women participants of a study examining experiences of faculty in community college settings.
- *triangulation:* Qualitative researchers conducting consensus coding note a particular pattern, which was not identified during independent coding and memo writing. For example, Hays et al. (2021) identified three codes that were chunked as "academic leadership outcomes": generativity, making a difference, and relational satisfaction.
- *sequence of items or events:* Codes may be temporal in terms of how they show up in the data source and/or how participants identify situations and events that are reflected by the codes. The diagnosis study (Hays et al., 2009b) example in the next section reflects this pattern identification strategy.

## Comparative Pattern Analysis

Identifying themes and patterns should not stop there. Patton (2014) termed a more elaborate process known as **comparative pattern analysis**. This involves researchers moving back and forth through chunked data to understand how the categories are alike and how they are different. Considering participant and contextual (e.g., time, setting, cultural) factors, how might text coded similarly be coded (i.e., metacodes)? More specifically, Patton described this as making sense of *convergence* (internal homogeneity) and *divergence* (external homogeneity) within a data source as well as across data sources. In his text, he used an apple-versus-orange metaphor to illustrate comparative pattern analysis: Although apples and oranges are types of fruit with other similar characteristics, there are ways in which they diverge or vary (e.g., texture of external layer, color, shelf-life). It is important to note that comparative pattern analysis identifies the metacodes that are not likely visible from directly reviewing data: It involves looking at the processing and sequencing of data and attending to where, how, why, and by whom that data occurred and was collected. And researchers seek and examine sequences and changes across time while triangulating data sources. Activity 10.2 may be a useful tool for understanding comparative pattern analysis.

An example from the diagnosis research might clarify what comparative pattern analysis looks like. After carefully coding, chunking data, and developing themes for the 41 interviews, Hays et al. (2009b) noted that participants become more uncertain (and less confident) about their diagnostic decisions as they were interviewed. Further, the research team found that many would defer to a professional they perceived was more competent (e.g., psychiatrist, psychologist) for a final decision. This led to an important training implication: Educators in

**ACTIVITY 10.2.** CODING EXERCISE, REVISITED

Return to your small groups and review your coding system for the Top 100 music lists from Activity 10.1. What patterns might be visible as you apply a more revised coding system to your five data sources? How do these patterns relate to "participants" (e.g., music artists, audience) and context (e.g., time, sequence)? What are the metacodes?

mental health professions need to discuss attitudes associated with diagnosis and the important role of counselors having the competency in their own right to diagnose. Thus, comparative pattern analysis led to two of many important metacodes included in the codebook: regressive uncertainty and perceived incompetence.

Noting patterns, particularly through comparative pattern analysis, can be a fun and creative endeavor. However, we caution that you should not create pattern codes too soon. Also, not every code will be chunked into a larger pattern or theme: Sometimes, we can code something initially and it "goes nowhere" as far as explaining a more complex aspect of a phenomenon. Finally, when you have developed patterns, check these codes in future data collection.

## Step 7: Create a Codebook

As qualitative researchers engage in coding, they will develop codebooks to capture information about the codes and categories. After more complex coding is completed, qualitative researchers are to reanalyze the data with the final codebook.

A **codebook** is a document with a listing of codes, subcodes, and patterns. A codebook can also contain a definition or description of each code, examples from data, and direct quotes or references to aspects of visual data. Although we list the codebook as Step 7, this step really starts once you begin coding and gets revised as you code more data and reach consensus. Figure 10.3 presents an abbreviated version of the codebook from the diagnosis study (Hays et al., 2009b).

**Constant comparison**, introduced earlier in the text, is an important component of developing a strong codebook. It refers to the continuous process of using earlier coding systems to code future data sources (Lincoln & Guba, 1995). Constant comparison works like this:

1. Use codes from your evolving codebook to label new data sources.
2. Add new codes to your codebook when existing codes do not readily fit data.
3. Reach consensus about all codebook edits.
4. Make decisions about collapsing codes in codebook after all data are analyzed (but not before!).
5. Go back and recode data sources with the more final codebook.

| | |
|---|---|
| **REPRESENTATIVENESS_CRITERIA** | Likelihood that a criterion belongs to a certain diagnosis (alludes to rigid adherence to DSM criteria), understanding of differential diagnosis (e.g., knowing that a criterion does not solely belong to a certain diagnosis) |
| **REPRESENTATIVENESS_CULTURE** | Likelihood that certain disorders belong to certain cultural groups (e.g., depression in females) |
| **ANCHORING** | Earlier clinical data hold more weight in final decisions, propensity to focus on later data that supports it (or later data not viewed as important) (e.g., MSE shows thought disorder symptoms and thus likely to find psychotic symptoms in intake to support diagnosis) |
| **AVAILABILITY_EXPERIENCE** | Diagnosis made based on clinical/personal experience, certain symptoms/disorders as available/familiar due to experience |
| **AVAILABILITY_ACADEMIC** | Diagnosis made based on general cluster of symptoms learned in academic training, certain symptoms/disorders as available/familiar due to classroom learning |
| **AVAILABILITY_CONTEXT** | Diagnosis made based on general cluster of symptoms made on environmental factors (usually indicative of giving a less severe diagnosis), symptoms familiar or common for certain environmental stressors |
| **AVAILABILITY_BROAD** | Integrates a broad range of Symptoms as identifies symptoms |
| **VIVIDNESS** | Some criteria are more intense in their presentation and heavily influence diagnostic decisions (e.g., withdrawal symptoms as evidence of dependence) |
| **NO VIVIDNESS** | No criteria were salient in the diagnostic decision |
| **DXCHANGE_SEVERE** | Transitioned from a less severe to more severe diagnosis as made the final diagnosis (e.g., MDD to bipolar; bipolar to schizophrenia) |
| **DXCHANGE_LESS_SEVERE** | Transitioned from a more severe to a less severe diagnosis as made the final diagnosis (e.g., schizophrenia to MDD) |
| **DX_RULEOUT** | Discussed a rule out diagnosis |
| **DX_CONSIDERATION** | Listed possible diagnoses considered but not advanced thought processes to rule out |
| **DX_DEFER** | Deferring a more severe diagnosis to avoid unnecessary labeling |
| **SITUATIONAL** | Locus of attribution that focuses on external factors causing the problem or presenting symptoms |
| **DISPOSITIONAL** | Locus of attribution that focuses on internal/biological factors causing the problem or presenting symptoms |
| **INFORMATION_VARIANCE** | Limitations of self-report in diagnosis, clients may not present all information about what is really going on (unintentionally); amount of type of data collected is limited by how much clients report as well as how much counselors seek |
| **OBSERVATION_VARIANCE** | There is variability in how the same data are interpreted among different counselors |
| **OBV_PERCEIVED_INCOMPETENCE** | Subcode of OBSERVATION_VARIANCE: information is interpreted differently based on experience level; Participant reports incompetence as compared to other professionals (e.g., perceives not able to give more severe diagnosis because not an MD, psychologist) |
| **CRITERION_VARIANCE** | Use of different criteria to diagnose; similar criteria can fit multiple diagnoses- alludes to the ambiguity/subjective nature of diagnosing; has insight into cognitive error/tools i.e., confirmation bias |
| **UNCERTAIN_INFO** | Participant reports uncertainty for the diagnosis given due to information presented in the case |
| **UNCERTAIN_EXPERIENCE** | Participant reports uncertainty for the diagnosis given due to his/her clinical or personal experience |
| **CERTAIN_INFO** | Participant reports certainty for the diagnosis given due to information presented in the case |
| **CERTAIN_EXPERIENCE** | Participant reports certainty for the diagnosis given due to his/her clinical or personal experience |
| **REGRESSIVE_UNCERTAINTY** | Participant initially comfortable or certain about diagnosis yet regresses in decision-making throughout interview to a lesser degree of certainty with the diagnosis given |
| **PROGRESSIVE_CERTAINTY** | Perticipant becomes more comfortable with the diagnosis given throughout the interview |
| **DXATTITUDE_POSITIVE** | Likes to diagnose; sees diagnosing as helpful |

**FIGURE 10.3** Diagnostic Variance Codebook (Hays et al., 2009b)

Now, let us turn to your data. Activity 10.3 will assist you in beginning the coding process. All you need is a single data source to get started. Case Example 10.1 provides an example of visual data to consider how the eight steps might be used for this data source.

## ACTIVITY 10.3. BEGINNING THE CODING PROCESS

Using a data source, like an interview transcript or some other form of textual data, review for codes and labels. Code by phrase, sentence, line, or paragraph. You can code for various reasons (see Table 10.2). Note whether each code is etic or emic and descriptive or interpretive. Feel free to memo on the data source itself. Then revisit code and develop themes as possible. Create a codebook for this data source, perhaps a listing of codes with some basic definitions.

Present your codes in dyads and discuss the features and challenges of the coding process. How was this coding experience for you? What might you do differently next time?

### Create Multiple Codebooks

One major issue that we have seen (and encountered) is creating only one codebook for all data sources and methods. You would have one reference guide to code all sources with similar labels. Initially, this might seem to make intuitive sense: This codebook streamlines the process of developing a main narrative or theory (Step 8). However, it really defeats the purpose of triangulating data collection methods. That is, if qualitative researchers are triangulating data to confirm (and try to disconfirm) findings, they need to assess them independently and note which codes are similar and dissimilar across data methods, and why. We strongly recommend that you create a codebook for *each* data collection method you use in a study. Then examine each "final" codebook for parallel findings. One thing we have found by doing this is that oftentimes more advanced pattern codes, through comparative pattern analysis, are evident when you examine the code by method.

## Step 8: Develop a Main Narrative or Theory

The final step of qualitative data analysis is bringing together patterns from multiple data sources and methods and examining how categories or concepts relate back to research questions and also how they relate to each other. Oftentimes, this step is analogous to report writing and data presentation, discussed in Part IV of the text. However, Step 8 may lead back to Steps 2–7 as you review the larger findings and discover that more data collection and analysis needs to occur.

The main narrative or theory will be presented differently for each qualitative report, depending on your research tradition, audience, and personal preference. Table 10.3 provides some ideas to consider for developing a main narrative.

## Case Example 10.1. Coding Visual Data

Use the eight qualitative data analysis steps to analyze the following political cartoon. In addition, reflect on the following questions:

IMG. 10.1

- At first glance, what would you say are the content and context of the image?
- This is a cartoon featured in an article on classroom discipline. How does knowing this affect your coding of the cartoon?
- What additional information might be useful to interpret the image?
- How does the cartoon relate to other experiences you may have with the phenomenon of classroom discipline?
- What are some cultural and advocacy considerations that might be important for analysis?
- Compare your findings in dyads. Discuss how data analysis differs from each other.

**TABLE 10.3**   Developing a Main Narrative

- Use research questions to structure the narrative.
- Create vignettes (e.g., normative depiction of phenomenon, typical day for participants, dramatic account to get reader's attention, use of critical events/stories).
- Provide a historical account of phenomenon.
- Describe a social process.
- Create summaries of interview results or individual profiles.
- Create a conceptual framework or other display (e.g., contrast table, event lists, matrices, scatterplots, conceptual diagrams, tree diagrams, pie charts, Venn diagrams, flow charts, sociograms).
- Develop a metaphor (or central meaning).
- Describe functions or organizational structure of group (i.e., basic components, operations, interconnections/relationships).
- Write up critical events in chronological order.

Source: LeCompte and Schensul (2012)

# Coding Considerations

With some basic coding methods presented, let's now move on to additional coding considerations that impact some of the steps. These include consensus coding and reliability, frequency counting, use of multiple classifications, taking a vacation from data, and member checking.

## Consensus Coding and Reliability

Recall from Chapter 7 that triangulation of multiple investigators is a strategy for establishing trustworthiness. Use of multiple researchers is particularly important for **consensus coding.** We recommend that you independently code a data source and then reach agreement on a code with your research team, discussing and agreeing on an operational definition of a code. Later in qualitative data analysis, qualitative researchers engage in independent coding then consensus coding on themes and patterns as well as the overall narrative or theory regarding a phenomenon of interest.

Consensus coding is one of the most important aspects of qualitative data analysis: By discussing and arriving at a shared operational definition of each code, researchers are co-creating new knowledge about the phenomenon at hand. Consensus coding is best accomplished through somewhat structured consensus meetings. Adapted from Miles et al. (2020), Figure 10.4 provides a template of a consensus meeting form that can be used to discuss each independently coded case. This form is analogous to a contact summary sheet presented in Chapter 8: It is a cover sheet for a consensus meeting. Prior to beginning the consensus meeting, the research team should pick a recorder to take notes on the form.

Computing interrater or intercoder reliability (also referred to as *reproducibility reliability*; see Weber, 1990) is another method for determining consistency or agreement among research team members. **Interrater reliability** is a ratio between research team members about the

Project ID:_____

Consensus Meeting Form

Date:_____          Case or Cases Discussed:_____

Research Team Members Present:

_____

_____

New Codes and Definitions:

Main Themes:

Salient Quotes/Key Phrases:

Primary Reflections:

> Reflections refer to member impressions for the case, and can be impressions held by the majority (primary) or those held by a minority (rival).

Rival Reflections:

Case Narrative:

Next Steps:

> Future directions for qualitative data collection are written here.

Codebook Revisions:

**FIGURE 10.4** Consensus Meeting Form

appropriateness for use of each code or pattern in textual or visual data. Miles et al. (2020) determine reliability with the following formula (see Figure 10.5):

$$\text{reliability} = \frac{\#\ \text{agreements}}{\text{total}\ \#\ \text{agreements} + \text{disagreements}}$$

**FIGURE 10.5** Calculating Interrater Reliability

Reliabilities will likely vary by level of coding, with words and phrases typically having higher reliabilities than coding at the sentence, paragraph, or document level. Regardless of selected coding level, Miles et al. (2020) established .70 as an acceptable cutoff for intercoder reliability, which we believe is adequate.

If you decide to compute interrater agreement, be sure that you and research team members agree about the definitions and labels of codes. There are several benefits and challenges to using consensus coding or interrater reliability (or both), and you have to determine what is most useful for your qualitative study as well as what your personal preference is (see Reflexive Activity 10.1).

**REFLEXIVE ACTIVITY 10.1.** CONSENSUS CODING VERSUS INTERRATER RELIABILITY

Journal about the benefits and challenges of using both consensus coding and interrater reliability. Should you use both in establishing triangulation of investigators? Why or why not?

One last form of reliability we would like to encourage is computing stability reliability. **Stability reliability**, analogous to test-retest reliability in quantitative research, refers to the extent that the same researcher codes text the same way more than once (Weber, 1990). To compute stability reliability, a researcher may want to identify codes in a transcript and then later recode that transcript similarly. Another way to compute it would be to examine how data of similar characteristics within the same data source is coded: If a keyword is used repeatedly to indicate similar data, then the data source may have stability reliability. It is important to note, however, that the longer duration between recoding, the more likely codes or keywords might change simply because of the fact that codebooks get revised. When interpreting stability reliability, the qualitative researcher needs to consider the tension for time elapses between recoding a data source and potential changes in research design and data analysis.

We have presented two methods that can be used to determine agreement when triangulating investigators. Complete Proposal Development Activity 10.2 with one or both triangulation strategies.

**PROPOSAL DEVELOPMENT ACTIVITY 10.2.** REACHING AGREEMENT IN THE CODING PROCESS

Using a data source that you and a research team member have independently coded, meet to reach agreement on codes and any patterns for that data source. You may decide to code for consensus, computer interrater reliability, or both. What was this process like for you? How might you reach agreement differently in the future?

## Frequency Counting

The issue of frequency counts is a tough one, and it is quite a debated topic! **Frequency counting** refers to tallying the number of times a code occurs for a data source. After a data source has been developed into an electronic record and the text and/or images have been analyzed, qualitative researchers review the records and count the frequency of each code related to the research purpose and then rank order codes by frequency. Some argue that counting the number of times things occur (or fail to occur) can denote an important theme or pattern that can be used to address a research question. So, the more a code appears, the more salient it is assumed to be. We see frequency counting as potentially valuable in observations of human behavior and needs assessments of new or existing educational or clinical programs. In seeking grants for various programs, for example, having numbers tied to qualitative data can "legitimize" a need.

However, we believe more times than not frequency counting is not necessary or helpful. The key assumption of frequency counting (i.e., that more is better) easily goes against the spirit of qualitative inquiry. How so? Well, let's say you are conducting several focus group interviews with parents and guardians of children with special needs and you are interested in their experiences in a local school system. After interviewing 20 parents, you decide to rank order their experiences for each identified group with which they interacted:

| Contact group | Theme | Frequency |
|---|---|---|
| Teachers | Provides extra attention | 45 |
| | Ignores child | 15 |
| | Meets regularly with parents | 15 |
| | Shows concern for special need | 13 |
| Teacher assistants | Shows concern for special need | 36 |
| | Provides extra attention | 30 |
| | Collaborates with school personnel | 5 |
| | Meets regularly with parents | 1 |
| School counselors | Meets regularly with parents | 5 |
| | Meets regularly with child | 5 |
| | Ignores child | 2 |
| Principals | Ignores parents | 55 |
| | Ignores child | 50 |
| | Collaborates with school personnel | 3 |
| Other parents | Ignores parents | 2 |
| | Meets regularly with parents | 1 |
| Child's peers | Ignores child | 1 |
| | Shows concern for special need | 1 |

You might make certain conclusions about this data. The most salient themes were that parents perceived principals ignored them and their children and that they perceived teachers provided the most extra attention for their children. You might also conclude that other parents and peers were not involved in parents' experiences with the school system. Examining further, you might guess that parents perceive that teachers are more willing to meet with them than teacher assistants, school counselors, or others in a particular school. From this interpretation you might want to examine training opportunities with school personnel of all levels on more effective interactions with parents of children with special needs. But wait: What if we let you know that most of the interview questions involved teachers' roles in working with their children? Also, what if in one of the parents in the focus group interview sessions spent most of the time discussing their principals, while in another focus group there was no mention of principals?

This example should show you two concerns we have about frequency counting. First, frequency counts must be considered in context. By the very nature of talking about one topic for a significant period of time, more codes about that topic are likely to appear. So, if an interviewer is probing an interview question regarding experiences with principals, it is likely parents will talk more about principals. If an interviewer runs out of time in most of the focus groups and cannot discuss the role of other parents and peers, it is likely that parents will not discuss these two groups. One can easily see that what information is solicited, the degree to which researchers and participants attend to a topic, and the notion that certain topics may not be covered well create a complicated picture for interpreting frequency counts. Based on these issues, we caution strongly to not "count too soon" and to ensure maximum opportunities to cover topics as adequately as possible.

Second, themes with low frequency counts (e.g., 1 or 2) may be just as meaningful as those with high frequency counts (e.g., 50 or 55). One of the key characteristics of qualitative inquiry that we mention throughout the text is that this research approach is designed to give voice to various perspectives and groups. So, with the parent focus group example, let's assume that there were plenty of opportunities in each group to look at parents' experiences within the school system and that parents report only 2 counts of other parents ignoring them. Should researchers ignore this theme since it has a low count? We believe absolutely not! Perhaps the parent that brought this issue up felt silenced in the focus group. Perhaps that participant "represents" many others with that opinion who happen to not be able to participate in the focus groups. Thus, there are so many challenges with frequency counting that we caution against solely relying on it. We highlight some of our views on frequency counting in Perspectives 10.1 with study examples.

- - - - - - - - - - - - - - - - - - - - - - - - - - - - - - - - - - - - - - - - - - - - - - - - - - - - - - - - - - - - - - - - -

## PERSPECTIVES 10.1. AUTHORS' PERSPECTIVES ON THE PROS AND CONS OF FREQUENCY COUNTING

I can share two experiences from qualitative studies I completed recently, one where I used frequency counts and another where I decided it was a bad idea. The first study involved examining counselors' attitudes toward and actions related to social justice advocacy in their work with clients wherein I assessed responses from 206 counselors. In this study, I computed frequency counts for each of the responses. Since there were so many participants in this study (and thus so much data!) and they were fairly representative of various demographic variables, work settings, and discipline, I felt it would be me more helpful to the reader to present the findings in counts to illustrate the frequency of various social advocacy attitudes and actions. In essence, the findings served as a needs assessment for working with practitioners and training students to remove barriers to social advocacy in their communities.

For the second study, I could not imagine conducting frequency counts. I worked with a group of adolescents aged 12–14 and discussed their conceptualizations of healthy dating relationships and experiences with dating violence. Given that there were a small group of participants (*n* = 7) with very diverse experiences and feelings toward unhealthy relationships (dating and otherwise), I felt it was important to portray their stories rather than count the most frequent responses. Thus, I felt that no one's experiences (no matter how common it was) were more valuable to presenting the findings.

—D. G. H.

I also have two stories that readily come to mind when frequency counting. In a mixed method study of social justice advocacy of counseling psychology trainees on internship (Singh et al., 2010b), we solicited quantitative and qualitative data through an online survey. Our research team went back and forth about the pros and cons of using frequency counting with the qualitative responses. After an initial look at the data, we found large domains and subcategories that were consistent throughout the qualitative responses. In the end, we decided to not use frequency counting because of our small sample size (*n* = 40) and in order to stay true to our participants' voices.

In other phenomenological examinations I have conducted of resilience of historically marginalized groups (Singh et al., 2010a; Singh et al., 2011), I would not say I used the traditional definition of frequency counting. However, I did count the number of participant responses that may not have been shared by all participants, but were shared by a majority of participants. Because both of these studies examined new areas of inquiry—South Asian American survivors of sexual abuse and transgender people—I wanted to make sure we communicated as much information as we could to our "audience" about their experiences in the hopes that future research will examine these topics in more depth.

—A. A. S.

## Single Versus Multiple Classifications

No matter what you decide your level of coding should be, you will collapse or chunk codes into larger categories, typically themes or patterns. Insch et al. (1997) noted that qualitative researchers have the options of single classification (i.e., codes assigned to one category, the category of "best fit") and multiple classification (i.e., placing codes in more than one category). Weber (1990) asserted that while single classification maximizes validity (because only codes directly applicable to one category get included), there is the potential that important code interactactions across categories may be missed. Insch et al. (1997) remind us that for codes in multiple categories, they may not be considered independent concepts. To minimize challenges during interpretation of these categories, we recommend that you consider creating a category that describes the overlap itself.

## Take a Vacation

Earlier in the chapter, we introduced the concept of abductive analysis. Take time off from your data. That's right! You have probably realized by this point that qualitative data collection and analysis (and we have not even gotten to data management yet) are time-consuming and require a lot of reflection. With any complex research project, you can start to lose your focus and thus may not be able to thoughtfully arrive at patterns and themes, brainstorm about future data collection methods, or revise your conceptual framework and/or theory. Taking time off from data does not necessarily have to mean not focusing on some aspect of the project: For example, you may want to take some time off and read some new literature on the topic or develop stronger relationships with participants and settings. We all have unique work styles, so the amount of time needed will vary by individual.

## Member Checking, Revisited

We come back to member checking, as we have in our discussion of data collection methods, to remind you of the importance of including participant voices in qualitative analysis. There are several opportunities for participants to help during qualitative analysis steps, including having them review initial codes and patterns individually or in groups or reviewing the findings section of the final report. As a qualitative researcher, it is a professional and ethical responsibility to be transparent with participants about how we arrived at a particular coding system and to have them provide judgments on that to the extent relevant. In summary, we encourage continued dialogue with participants from initial data collection to the final qualitative report.

# Additional Strategies of Qualitative Data Analysis

In the final section on qualitative data analysis, we discuss two other labels for the qualitative data analysis process we have encountered in the education and social sciences literature. Specific data analysis processes and strategies for various research traditions will be presented in Chapter 11. We do not claim that the two strategies we cover are exhaustive; however, we have seen them applied to a variety of research traditions. These include content analysis and attributional coding.

## Content Analysis

**Content analysis** involves unitizing, sampling, recording, and reducing data using qualitative and/or quantitative methods (Krippendorff, 2018). **Unitizing** refers to identifying the proportion of a data source that will count as one unit of analysis (e.g., social media posts, advertisements, journal entries, videos), which should align with the research questions and purpose of the overall study. **Sampling** refers to where and how the units of analysis are located: What is the sampling frame from which data sources will be drawn? Does the sampling process allow for transferring the findings from the sample to a broader population? **Recording** refers to how data are recorded in a way that they can be read by multiple coders. If the unit of analysis is a journal article, for example, then the data would be recorded as written text. Recording also involves specifying categories to be coded in the data and developing a codebook and coding sheet to guide the coding process. **Reducing**, or coding, of data can be done deductively (quantitative), inductively (qualitative), and/or abductively. It involves multiple researchers engaged in coding, a pretest to solidify the coding procedures, a process for tracking interrater reliability, and a consensus process by which the coding team resolves any discrepancies (see Krippendorff, 2018).

In addition to Krippendorff's (2018) steps, Insch et al. (1997) identified 11 cyclical steps for conducting a content analysis. We will highlight them in Table 10.4, incorporating information from other sources. You will likely note that many of these steps parallel those of our general data analysis steps. However, there are some minor differences. First, the developers emphasize the importance of creating a strong coding scheme with pilot data before more extensive data collection is conducted. Second, there is greater attention to reliability and validity. Perspectives 10.2 provides an example of how a researcher has used content analysis in his work.

Insch and colleagues (1997) note several benefits of content analysis. These include (a) potential for high reliability; (b) use of qualitative and quantitative approaches; (c) typically unobtrusive, which minimizes participant reactivity bias; and (d) use of a priori codes. Some challenges, however, have been noted. First, researcher bias, similar to other data analysis strategies, occurs in the type and form of data selected for analysis, and coding schemes (codebooks) are biased in that there is no want to confirm the universality of codes or themes. The second major cluster of challenges relates to what to code once data are selected. Specifically, these involve (a) assigning weight to codes (i.e., deciding whether codes carry equal values in a codebook); (b) assessing the value of missing data; and (c) inattention to nonverbal cues and insufficient attention to other contextual information.

## Attributional Coding

**Attributional coding** involves analyzing public attributions individuals make during spoken or written discourse that represent their understanding of the causes of various events of interest (Silvester, 1998). There are five major stages of attributional coding. Stage 1 is identifying source of attributions. Typically derived from transcripts of dialogues or written documents, public exchanges are identified based on the relevance to a research question. Stage 2 refers to extracting attributions, or a speaker's statements about causes and their consequences. The speaker is defined as the participant of interest. Stage 3 involves identifying agents and targets. *Agent-target coding*, which is initial coding in attributional coding, means that a

**TABLE 10.4** Content Analysis Steps

| Steps | Characteristics |
|---|---|
| **Identify research questions and constructs.** | Review the literature to articulate research questions and important concept or words to be counted. |
| **Identify texts to be examined.** | Determine which texts or data sources are appropriate for the phenomenon of interest (i.e., source validity). |
| **Specify the unit of analysis.** | The unit of analysis may be a word, phrase, sentence, paragraph, or entire document. Selection is to be based in consideration of the study purpose. |
| **Specify the categories.** | Chunk codes into categories. Categories are to be considered along three dimensions: single versus multiple classifications; assumed (a priori) versus identified categories from the data; and use of existing content analysis dictionaries. |
| **Generate sample coding scheme.** | Consider the face validity of the category definitions (i.e., researchers' definitions of concepts and the definitions of categories used to evaluate them). |
| **Collect data (pretest).** | Pretest the coding scheme. |
| **Purify the coding scheme.** | Examine pilot/pretest results and ensure that those familiar with the words in each category (themes) agree that they have similar meanings or relate to a category similarly (i.e., *semantic validity*). |
| **Collect data.** | Refer back to Step 2 and collect additional data. Be sure to make adjustments to coding protocol based on text type (e.g., local newsletter article may be coded differently from major newspaper article). |
| **Assess reliability.** | Inadequate reliability may be indicative of an inappropriate coding scheme or codebook. |
| **Assess construct validity.** | Examine how well themes represent underlying constructs. |
| **Analyze data.** | Begin data analysis and consider both qualitative and quantitative analysis techniques. |

Sources: Insch et al. (1997), Schreier (2012), and Weber (1990)

---

## PERSPECTIVES 10.2. MAXIMIZING THE SUCCESS OF CONTENT ANALYSIS

Bradley McKibben, a counselor educator with expertise in content analysis, has conducted multiple studies on the topics of clinical supervision, leadership, and mentorship. Example studies include a 40-year period of counseling leadership scholarship published in journals and books (i.e., McKibben et al., 2017), a study of 136 professional organization chapters and leaders' skill building efforts with their respective organization's members (i.e., Wahesh et al., 2018), and an analysis of Facebook pages to explore how professional counseling organizations utilize social media to engage with online followers (i.e., McKibben & Logan-McKibben, 2021), to name a few. In several of his studies, McKibben uses Krippendorff's (2018) four steps of content analysis (i.e., unitizing, sampling, recording, reducing).

In an interview with me (Danica), McKibben (personal communication, July 9, 2021) conceptualizes content analysis as the study of communication within a bounded context, or the communication patterns or themes of what is being communicated among individuals and groups through a well-defined set of documents, interviews, online media, and other data methods. He notes the hybrid nature of content analysis, taking on qualitative and/or quantitative components in data analysis:

> The coding process and using an auditor have a qualitative feel to them. And, there is a deductive approach that you can take with coding, where it is very descriptive and you're coding numbers and creating categorical variables [to count]. There is also interrater reliability and calculating that … [and] there is a goal built into content analysis that the themes you find … [are] hopefully generalizable to other contexts of communication.

McKibben notes several strategies that can be used in content analysis to maximize rigor. These include

- clear definition of the scope of sampling units
- an organized coding sheet for data management
- use of multiple coders and an auditor
- pretesting of about a 10% random sampling of the units to evaluate and refining coding procedures and the codebook
- attainment of at least 80% interrater agreement

McKibben highlights some of the greatest strengths of content analysis are its flexibility as an analytic method along with the creativity that can be used to decide what data sources can be studied. However, he cautions:

> A good content analysis is a simple content analysis. … The more [data] you are trying to pull out of a [sampling unit] and the communication that you're looking at, the more fatigued you're going to get, the more errors you're going to have. You can really get down the rabbit hole.

Sources:

McKibben, W. B., & Logan-McKibben, S. (2021). A content analysis of counseling organizations' social media usage. *Journal of Technology in Counselor Education and Supervision, 1*(1). https://doi.org/10.22371/tces/0001.

McKibben, W. B., Umstead, L. K., & Borders, L. D. (2017). Identifying dynamics of counseling leadership: A content analysis study. *Journal of Counseling & Development, 95*(2), 192–202. https://doi.org/10.1002/jcad.12131

Wahesh, E., Fulton, C. L., Shannonhouse, L. R., McKibben, W. B., & Kennedy, S. D. (2018). A content analysis of CSI chapter efforts to promote counselor leadership development. *Journal of Counselor Leadership and Advocacy, 5*(1), 82–94. https://doi.org/10.1080/2326716X.2017.1422997

researcher analyzes what the speaker states is causing something to happen (agent) and what the impact is (target). *Agent-target pairings* generally refers to individuals, groups, or entities. Stage 4 is coding attributions on causal dimensions. These dimensions or continua include stable/unstable (permanence of cause of an attribution); global/specific (degree of importance of cause); internal/external (whether a cause of an attributions originates within or outside the speaker); personal/universal (extent that a cause is individual or culturally specific); and controllable/uncontrollable (degree of control a speaker notes there is over the cause). The last stage, Stage 5, is analyzing data. Readers are encouraged to review Silvester (1998) for additional information on attributional coding.

## Qualitative Data Management

Recall in Chapters 8 and 9 that we began discussing qualitative data management with data collection. Some forms of qualitative data management, such as contact summary sheets, memos, and document summary forms, are performed immediately as data are collected. As we move forward, you will quickly see that data management is a job in itself, as data will pile up rather quickly! We strongly advise that you develop a data management system early and revise it as necessary as you go.

### Storing Data

While you are likely to develop a data management system that works for you, we would like to provide a few tips. First, we recommend that you format data similarly. Particularly for textual data, structure transcripts, contact sheets, memos, and so on, we recommend using a template for each. This is especially important if you are working with multiple research team members, and it makes it easier for an external auditor to review your audit trail. In summary, each data source should look as similar as possible, as if only one researcher formatted them.

Second, convert all data (to the extent possible) to electronic format using word processors and scanners and retain the hard copies (or originals) of data. Use binders and tabs for physical copies and an organized computer system for electronic formats. In essence, divide and label your audit trail carefully. (We discussed the contents of an audit trail in Chapter 7.)

Third, you will need a well-organized and secure physical space for storage. Keep physical data—removed to the extent possible from participant identifying information—in a locked file cabinet. Ensure that electronic data are password protected. We recommend that you keep data for at least 5–7 years upon completion of a project.

Our final tip relates to managing data during the coding process. As you create codebooks, you may find that you need to cross-reference data sources, even as you keep them separate initially for data analysis. Cross-referencing will be extremely helpful as you make sense of multiple codebooks to develop a main narrative or theory (Step 8). We like to keep a journal or log with memos about the data sources themselves, particularly to jot notes about potential codes that seem to overlap for data sources. Additionally, cross-reference the data sources themselves. For example, it may be important to cross-reference a meeting agenda that a participant mentions during an individual interview.

## Case Displays

A **case display**, a graphic depiction of reduced (and chunked) data, is one of the most valuable data management tools out there. We cannot imagine conducting a qualitative study without case displays as part of our initial thoughts about research design and throughout data collection and analysis. Case displays are initially created for each individual case (*within-case display*) and then are later consolidated to examine concepts and variables across cases (*cross-case display*) for increased understanding of themes and patterns and thus enhance generalizability (Miles et al., 2020).

Let's provide an example of how case displays are a useful approach. Let's say you want to complete a study on the impact of student activities organizations on the retention of first year students in a particular university. You interview 15 first-year students, five student organization leaders, and three university administrators. Because the amount of data for these 23 participants will likely become overwhelming, you want to create snapshots of each (i.e., within-group display), identifying variables such as the role and actions associated with participating in student organizations and activities, personal characteristics of participants (e.g., demographics, academic needs, and experience with the university), and the reported satisfaction with student organizations and activities as well as other academic and extra-curricular components, to name a few. Upon completion of individual profiles, you may want to group participants with common characteristics (e.g., role, time, and duration of participation by gender, major, etc.) and look at data collectively (i.e., cross-case display) to address the research question. By individualizing data management, analyzing each data source, and then collapsing this process to examine themes and codes across data sources, you are more likely to have an organized, easily accessible, and more comprehensive picture of your findings.

Case displays serve four basic yet interconnected purposes: They assist qualitative researchers to explore, describe, explain, and predict phenomena. By reducing data sources into one display per unit of analysis (e.g., integrating and graphically presenting findings from an individual interview and multiple observations for one participant), qualitative researchers have data and analysis in one place and can likely draw more valid conclusions. Other benefits of data displays are that researchers can absorb large amounts of information quickly, compare different data sets, and yield direct use of results in qualitative reports (Miles et al., 2020).

Case displays are formatted using matrices or networks. A **matrix** format involves using rows and columns to portray major concepts or variables. A **network** format refers to points or nodes with links between them. Oftentimes, the purpose of a network display is to show causal links or chronology among variables. Your choice of display format will be driven by your research question as well as emerging codes.

You will likely address your research question(s) one case at a time, moving to a more complex answer to your question(s) as you integrate your findings across cases in a cross-case display or displays. With cross-case displays, data usually are oriented by case or variable, although we recommend that you combine these strategies. These orientations may be presented using matrices or networks. Case-oriented displays focus on either structuring individual cases similarly to see is they match previous ones (Yin, 2017); analyzing each case for essential components and presenting these components in a particular order in a larger display (Denzin & Lincoln, 2018); or clustering cases that are similar and can be considered to be a "family" of cases and presenting by cluster (Lofland et al., 2005). Variable-oriented cross-case displays involve looking for themes that cut across cases (Miles et al., 2020). Like Yin's (2017) strategy with case-oriented displays, the goal is to synthesize similar components.

Miles et al. (2020) wrote extensively about the use of case displays as an analysis tool. We will highlight some basic information about various types and purposes of case displays; however, we encourage you to review their text for a more thorough review of the displays. Table 10.5 includes some general strategies for developing and interpreting case displays, and Table 10.6 shows common approaches to case displays.

**TABLE 10.5** Case Display Tips

*Designing displays*
- Be clear about the purpose of your case display: Are you trying to describe a phenomenon or explain one?
- Choose whether you want to display data for an individual case or multiple cases.
- Decide if order or placement of variables in a display matter. For example, you may find that strength or intensity of themes is important to show.
- Does time play a significant role in your research question(s)? If the ordering of variables is related to time, investigate time-ordered displays to allow for analysis of sequence, flow, causes, and effects.
- Determine how many dimensions your display has. We have found that most projects are two dimensional, yet your study may be better suited to use a three-dimensional (or more) display.
- Limit to four or five rows for matrices.
- Use both variable- and case-oriented cross-case displays.
- Write down decision rules or criteria for selecting and removing data from displays.

*Entering data*
- Be clear about the amount and level of data you want to enter in any display. (When in doubt, enter more!)
- Include any of the following in cells or nodes: codes, quotes, summaries, researcher reflection, ratings, or any of these combined.
- Note in matrix or network when data are missing or unclear.
- Use a coding system to locate important material in original data sources.
- Include a detailed reference to salient quotes as appropriate.
- Understand each case individually before lumping them.
- Write a narrative for individual case displays as possible.
- Look for typologies or case families, or those that cluster easily together due to similar characteristics.

*Interpreting data*
- Be aware that your display will likely change design as you interpret data.
- Cluster themes.
- Note patterns among themes.
- Investigate further into "deviant" cases (i.e., individual cases that vary from those that are easily synthesized and replicated).

Sources: Mishler (1986) and Miles et al. (2020)

**TABLE 10.6**  Case Displays

|  | Within-case displays | Cross-case displays |
|---|---|---|
| **Explore and describe** | | |
| **Partially ordered** | Context chart<br>Checklist matrix | Partially ordered meta-matrix |
| **Time ordered** | Event listing<br>Critical incident chart<br>Activity record<br>Decision modeling | Scatterplot over time |
| **Role ordered** | Role x time matrix | Contrast table<br>Scatterplot |
| **Conceptually ordered** | Thematic conceptual matrix<br>Conceptual map<br>Folk taxonomy | Content analytic summary table<br>Decision tree modeling |
| **Explain and predict** | | |
| **Effects matrices** | Explanatory effects matrix<br>Case dynamics matrix | Case-ordered effects matrix<br>Case-ordered predictor-outcome matrix<br>Variable-by-variable network |
| **Causal networks** | Causal network | Cross-case causal network |

Source: Miles et al. (2020)

## Exploring and Describing Data Using Case Displays

Whether you are interested in developing a within-case or cross-case display, there are some basic types of displays used for exploring and describing data. These include partially ordered, time-ordered, role-ordered, and conceptually ordered displays. For each of these displays, it is important to construct a narrative to "tell the story" for a case or across cases. This narrative will help in future data analysis as well as report writing.

### Partially Ordered Displays

**Partially ordered displays** are quite useful in the initial stages of data analysis, as qualitative researchers can attend to a variable of interest and its subcomponents as well as look at the various roles of those involved in a particular setting. There are two types of within-case and one type of cross-case partially ordered displays we would like to mention briefly here. The within-case partially ordered displays are the context chart and the checklist matrix. A *context chart* is a network that depicts the interrelationships among those in a particular setting, related to a behavior of interest. Context charts help to identify an underlying meaning of a behavior as the individual associations are mapped out for a particular context (the case). A *checklist matrix* can outline a major variable of interest and compare data from all key respondents. For this display, the case can be considered the variable of interest. A cross-case partially ordered display is the *partially ordered meta-matrix*. This display can be thought of as a "master chart" of descriptive data across all cases. To create this display, cluster all relevant data into major categories, then sort for each cluster, and, finally, examine the display for cross-category clustering.

To illustrate these forms of partially ordered displays, consider a study involving counselors and counselor trainees' degree of preparedness for working with clients involved in unhealthy relationships. Figures 10.6, 10.7, and 10.8 are useful for describing the phenomenon of preparedness. Figure 10.6 represents a context chart of the coding process for data of 10 trainees (represented by "T" followed by an identification number) by 10 researchers (represented by "R" followed by an identification number), all graduate students at University X, with relationships to the responsible project investigator. Figure 10.7 depicts various training components

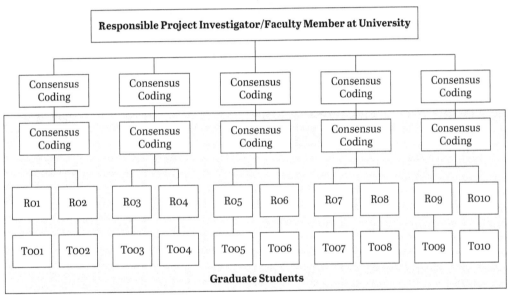

*Note:* R - Researcher; T - Trainee

**FIGURE 10.6**  Context Chart of Researchers and Participants at University X

| Training Experiences for Intervening in Unhealthy Relationships | | | | | | |
|---|---|---|---|---|---|---|
| | T01 | T02 | T03 | T04 | T05 | T06 |
| Workshops | Yes | No | No | No | No | Yes |
| Couples Counseling Course | Yes | Yes | Yes | No | No | No |
| Families Course | Yes | Yes | Yes | No | No | Yes |
| Child/Adolescent Course | No | No | Yes | No | No | No |
| Internship | No | No | No | Yes | Yes | No |
| Journals | Yes | Yes | Yes | Yes | Yes | Yes |
| Books and Online Resources | No | No | Yes | Yes | Yes | Yes |

**FIGURE 10.7**  Checklist Matrix of Training Experiences of Six Counselor Trainees

| Trainee | Knowledge | Abuse Victim | Forms of Abue | Consequences | Client Influences | Participant Influences |
|---|---|---|---|---|---|---|
| T001 | Defines as making someone feel unworthy, having limited communication, being at an impasse in relationship | Female or Male | Physical and emotional | Physical: Isolation Psychological: delayed awareness of situation, depression/suicidal, decreased self-esteem, self-blame | Media (television, movies) | Has never been in a violent relationship before, but sees them "all around" her |
| T002 | Defines as having feelings of not being loved, being unhappy, having negative affect | Female or Male | Physical | Physical: bruises, high blood pressure, chest pains Psychological: loss of focus, stress | None noted | Witnessed domestic violence at age 7 or 8 Parents model healthy relationships |
| T003 | Refer to as being taken advantage of, not supported, manipulated or controlled, having a loss of identity, and being someone "not strong enough" to leave a bad relationship | Female or Male | Physical and emotional | Psychological: lowered self-esteem (may have already been low), denial, dependency Physical: isolation | How they were raised, media, and Something in their lives making them more vulnerable/more accepting of relationship problems | Parents as model- it was "never an option," trying to emulate their healthy relationship in her own marriage, media (television) |
| T004 | Defines as degradation, putting someone down, having a selfish partner, limiting communication, not valuing, lacking trust and safety, both partners likely have a history of abuse | Female | Physical, emotional, and sexual | Psychological: lowered self-esteem | Previous history of trauma, their parents' relationship, culture | Own parents' relationship (they divorced and then entered healthy marriages) "shaped what I wanted," marriage and family development course taught her about gender differences in communication, watched sister in an unhealthy relationship |
| T005 | Refers to as abusing one another, being obsessive, and lacking trust | Female or Male | Physical, emotional, and sexual | Physical Consequences Psychological: Emotional harm, low self-esteem, feelings of worthlessness, suicidality, depression, inadequate feelings, incapable | Media (television/movies), friends who have been in a bad relationship | Coursework, Own abusive relationship |
| T006 | Involves not being valued, having a power struggle, limiting communication | Female | Physical, and emotional | Psychological: dependency, lowered self-esteem, less personal value, degradation or person, personality changes | Family/peer socialization/upbringing, media, cultural acceptance of violence, coping/resilience, personal factors | Personal and family experiences with violence most salient, "I know in my own life I have a hard time dealing with those types of people," coursework |

**FIGURE 10.8** Partially Ordered Metamatrix of Conceptualization of Unhealthy Relationships

that six key participants have received regarding intervening in unhealthy relationships. (The case or unit of analysis is training experience.) Finally, Figure 10.8 refers to participants' conceptualizations of unhealthy relationships.

### Time-Ordered Displays

A **time-ordered display** depicts a sequence or flow of events or processes of a phenomenon of interest. Essentially, it orders data by time and sequence. We will highlight four within-case and one cross-case time-ordered display. The first type of within-case time-ordered display we find helpful is the event listing. An *event listing* organizes a series of events or actions by time periods, sorted into categories. This display shows how events are connected to each other. The second type, a *critical incident chart*, is similar to an event listing yet limits the display to those events that are particularly salient for each period. Thus, the event listing can be considered more comprehensive overall, and the critical incident chart might hit the key points for a particular period. The third type is an activity record. An *activity record* displays a specific activity from the beginning to final phases or steps, making explicit each detailed step of each phase. The final type of within-case time-ordered display that we will highlight is a decision model. *Decision modeling* can be considered a "decision tree" of yes-or-no responses of the thoughts and actions associated with an activity record. Figure 10.9 is an event listing that outlines one school psychologist's participation at three schools.

| School | Aug–Dec 2020 | Jan–Apr 2021 |
|---|---|---|
| Craigen Elementary | • 3 evaluations<br>• 2 students referred to special education classes (7-year-old White girl; 9-year-old Latinx boy) | • 8 evaluations<br>• No referrals made |
| Parks Elementary | • 12 evaluations<br>• Consulted with parents for 2 students (8-year-old White boy; 8-year-old Black girl) regarding remediation<br>• Recommended further psychological testing for 4 students (5-year-old White boy; 5-year-old Asian girl; 10-year-old Black boy; 10-year-old multiracial boy) | • 1 evaluation<br>• Continued work with IEP (pending disposition) |
| Varner Middle School | • 2 evaluations<br>• 1 student pulled into a general classroom (13-year-old multiracial girl) | • No evaluations conducted |

**FIGURE 10.9** Event Listing for a School Psychologist in School District A

We have found one cross-case time-ordered display that is particularly helpful in data management and analysis: the *scatterplot over time*. This display provides a picture of a similar variable or concept over two or more time periods. In Figure 10.10, the school psychologist was interested in the relationship between number of psychological and educational evaluations for schools in School District A and degree of support for 2 academic years.

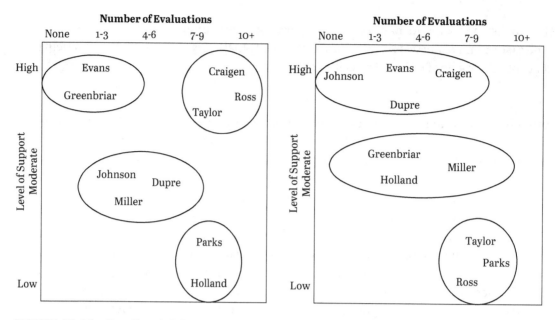

**FIGURE 10.10**   Scatterplot Over Time: School Evaluations (2019–2020 Versus 2020–2021)

## Role Ordered Case Displays

A **role-ordered case display** depicts social interactions for a setting or variable of interest; it provides a "role occupant" view for each key participant (Miles et al., 2020). Thus, it is the organizing principle for this participant role. We will highlight one within-case and two cross-case role-ordered displays that we particularly like, using a study exploring university administrators' perceptions of the financial aid profession. First, a *role X time matrix* is a within-case role-ordered display that is useful in cases where *when* something is done is just as important as *who* is doing it. Typically, roles will be listed in rows, and time periods will be listed in columns, or vice versa. Figure 10.11 depicts the administrators' views of the degree to which financial aid officers at University Z met job expectations.

| | 2016–17 | 2017–18 | 2018–19 | 2019–20 | 2020–21 |
|---|---|---|---|---|---|
| Provost | Moderate | High | High | Moderate | High |
| President | Low | Low | Moderate | Moderate | High |
| Faculty | Low | Moderate | Moderate | Moderate | Not reported. |
| Graduate Students | Moderate | Moderate | Low | Moderate | High |
| Undergraduate Students | Low | Low | Low | Moderate | Moderate |

**FIGURE 10.11**   Role X Time Matrix of Financial Aid Officer Job Expectations

The two cross-case displays are contrast table and scatterplot. A *contrast table* shows two variables of interest. Figure 10.12 depicts a contrast table of examining financial aid officers' job responsibilities and the perceptions from administrators of several colleges and universities. A *scatterplot* displays data from all cases on two or more dimensions that you conceptualize as related to each other. Figure 10.13 portrays data for job satisfaction and job ratings regarding 10 financial aid officers.

| | Berry University President | Lane College Dept. Chair | Belle College Provost | Hardy University Dean |
|---|---|---|---|---|
| Analyze financial information from applicants | Exceeds Expectations | Satisfactory | Satisfactory | Unsatisfactory |
| Develop financial aid policies | Exceeds Expectations | Satisfactory | Satisfactory | Unsatisfactory |
| Coordinate a work-study program | Satisfactory | Unsatisfactory | Satisfactory | Unsatisfactory |
| Manage financial loan programs | Satisfactory | Unsatisfactory | Exceeds Expectations | Unsatisfactory |
| Prepare detailed financial reports | Unsatisfactory | Unsatisfactory | Exceeds Expectations | Unsatisfactory |

**FIGURE 10.12**  Contrast Table Example of Financial Aid Officers' Job Ratings

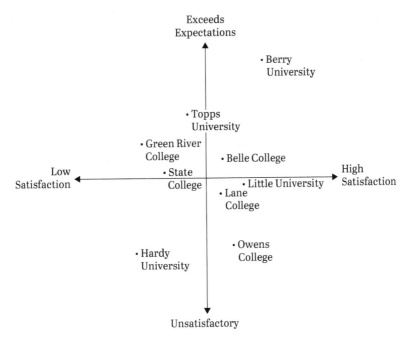

**FIGURE 10.13**  Scatterplot of Job Ratings and Financial Aid Officer Job Satisfaction

## Conceptually Ordered Case Displays

A **conceptually ordered case display** is helpful when the concept itself is the organizing principle rather than time periods or roles (Miles et al., 2020). While any display can look like a conceptually ordered display, it must be organized by a concept or variable to be considered one. We have already presented a conceptually ordered display in Chapter 5: the conceptual framework. As you may recall, this network portrayed the major nodes of a conceptual framework, including previous literature, personal experience, thought experiments, and pilot or exploratory data.

We will highlight three within-case and two cross-case conceptually ordered displays. The within-case displays include a thematic conceptual matrix, cognitive map, and folk taxonomy. A *thematic conceptual matrix* involves portraying data by themes rather than individuals or roles. You have already created an example of the second type, the *cognitive map*. Chapter 5 discussed developing components of the conceptual framework, and a conceptual framework (open to revisions as your study progresses) is essentially your thoughts of the important elements that organize your study. Thus, the conceptual framework is an example of a cognitive map. Finally, a *folk taxonomy* is analogous to a hierarchical tree diagram. Miles et al. (2020) suggest that a folk taxonomy may be created initially through the creating a batch of cards (each card has a key code or theme on it). Then cards are sorted. Figures 10.14 and 10.15 display a thematic conceptual framework and folk taxonomy for a study examining agency sexual assault counselors' experience with vicarious traumatization and self-care (Forman, 2010).

| Theoretical Aspects | Vicarious Traumatization | Burnout | Self-Care | Work Environment |
|---|---|---|---|---|
| Components | Intimacy, trust, control | None noted | None noted | None noted |
| Agency | Frequency of agency discussion—twice per month | Frequency of agency discussion-rarely | Addressed twice per week | Funding concerns, client load high, low salary, supervision inadequate, underlying politics Involvement of family |
| Others | Frequency of school's acknowledgment—once per year | Frequency of state's acknowledgement—trainings at state and school level | Acknowledgment by others: Not addressed at all—had to learn for herself | |
| Experiences | Dreams, memory, safety changes at work, home, world, travel | Supervisee boundary issues, staff support, too many clients and paperwork | See Coping Strategies | Mention of protection measures—safety concerns |
| Coping Strategies | None noted | None noted | Education (learning Spanish), reading, and media); use of humor; leisure activities; and volunteer work; processing with colleagues; receiving support | Informal and formal training; therapy for counselor |

**FIGURE 10.14** Thematic Conceptual Matrix for a Sexual Assault Counselor's Experiences

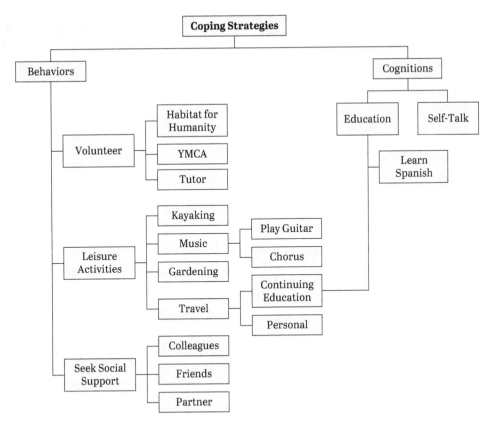

**FIGURE 10.15**   Folk Taxonomy of a Sexual Assault Counselor's Self-Care Strategies

The two cross-case displays are the content-analytic summary table and the decision tree model. A *content-analytic summary table* portrays the common elements or factors underlying a phenomenon of interest more so than each case. (In fact, you might not even mention from which cases the content originated.) First, you must determine how many cases share similar characteristics. Then sort each major characteristic and identify how prevalent that characteristic (or subcharacteristic) appears in a case. *Decision tree modeling* is used to depict a model or theory of "how something works" by piecing together individual decision trees to show the basic process across several cases. This can be conceptualized as a cross-case decision modeling described earlier in this section. Figure 10.16 depicts a content-analytic summary table of 15 sexual assault counselors' coping strategies. You will note that this is the same type of content presented by the folk taxonomy in Figure 10.15. (The number in parentheses indicates how many participants reported a particular strategy.)

## Explaining and Predicting Data Using Case Displays

Case displays can also play a significant role in theory building or model building, a goal of many research traditions and research questions. Displays that are suitable for explanation and prediction often move beyond those that are used for exploring and describing and toward

| Volunteer | Leisure | Social Support | Cognitive Strategies |
|---|---|---|---|
| Habitat for Humanity (3) <br> Food Bank (1) <br> YMCA (7) <br> Local schools (6) <br> Tutoring (1) | Kayaking (1) <br> Gardening (2) <br> Traveling to conferences (1) <br> Traveling to other trainings (7) <br> Personal travel (9) <br> Reading (9) <br> Playing guitar (1) <br> Singing (2) <br> Listening to music (12) <br> Exercise (1) <br> None (2) | Colleagues (11) <br> Partner (10) <br> Friends (2) <br> None (3) | Learn Spanish (1) <br> Workshops (8) <br> Self-talk (13) |

**FIGURE 10.16**   Content-Analytic Summary Table of Sexual Assault Counselors' Coping Strategies

**PROPOSAL DEVELOPMENT ACTIVITY 10.3.** CREATING CASE DISPLAYS

Based on your research purpose and available data, select two of the case displays used for exploration and description presented here (preferably within-case displays).

- Use your evolving codebook to develop a case display. Memo about your displays.
- Work with your research team members and review each "final" display. What are some recommendations made to alter the display? How, if at all, has the display solidified future data collection? How is this useful for data analysis?
- Now compare the two displays. What are some advantages and disadvantages of each? Are there other displays that might be helpful for your study? Why or why not?
- Continue to develop with pilot data within-case and cross-case displays to describe and explore your findings. Add these displays to your audit trail.

making "causal" statements and predictions about descriptive components. *Explaining data* refers to supporting a claim and making causal statements, and *predicting data* involves using explanatory statements to estimate what is likely to happen in the future involving what factors for a phenomenon of interest (Miles et al., 2020). Case displays that are used for explanation and prediction will likely include reference to antecedents, short-term and long-term consequences, and/or predictor and outcome variables. This second form of case display may be categorized as effects matrices and causal networks.

## Effects Matrices

We will highlight two within-case displays and three cross-case displays that are considered effects matrices. The two within-case displays are explanatory effects matrix and case dynamics matrix. An *explanatory effects matrix* depicts short- and long-term outcomes for a particular variable of interest with a primary purpose of explaining those outcomes. In fact, there is often a column used to note researcher explanations of outcomes. A *case dynamics matrix* traces consequences of outcomes for particularly salient or dynamic issues. In essence, the display will depict the process used to arrive at a particular outcome or outcomes for a particular "dynamic" issue.

To illustrate these effects matrices, consider a program evaluation of a social work program that addressed several initiatives to recruit and retain racial and ethnic minority students. This program has been active for 3 years. As you can see from Figure 10.17, future programming can be easily inferred from the effects and outcomes of important issues.

The three cross-case effects matrices are case-ordered effects matrix, case-ordered predictor-outcome matrix and variable-by-variable matrix. A *case-ordered effects matrix* is used when an important "cause" has a variety of results. (This is different from a causal model, discussed in the next section, which highlights a variety of causes for an important outcome.) The focus of this matrix is on the outcomes that may present themselves as a function of the cases. Cases are sorted for a major cause by intensity, with more intense or strong cases typically presented toward the top of the matrix. Figure 10.19 provides an example of the case-ordered effects matrix.

A *case-ordered predictor-outcome matrix* orders cases on a main outcome or criterion variable and provides data for each case on the antecedents for that outcome. Cases are sorted and ordered in the matrix by variable. A *variable-by-variable matrix* has two main variables in its rows and columns, and cell entries are case names. Figure 10.20 depicts a variable-by-variable matrix using the social work program evaluation, highlighting responses from 12 students of color.

## Causal Networks

A **causal network** is a display of the most important variables, showing directions and sequences rather than relationships (such as the case with displays used to explore and describe). In essence, it is a network of variables or factors with causal connections between them for theory building. Causality is a workable concept network that usually has three variations: Concept A, then Concept B; when Concept A, always Concept B; and another concept links Concepts A and B (Miles et al., 2020).

To create a causal network, Miles et al. (2020) recommend the following steps:

1.  Start with what factors influence each other (typically, those that appear together).
2.  Determine which variables happen first, later, and so on.
3.  Rate the importance of each variable in explaining and predicting (e.g., high, moderate, low).
4.  Determine antecedent variables, mediating variables, and outcomes.
5.  Construct a narrative.
6.  Refer back to existing theory and research about connections among variables.
7.  Solicit feedback from participants, research team members, and auditors.

| Initiative | Details | Short-Term Effects | Long-Term Consequences | Researcher's Explanation |
|---|---|---|---|---|
| Increase professional development mentorship | Create a diversity interest network. | The number of racial and ethnic minority students involved in program activities increased. Approximately half of students participate in independent research projects. | Students if color report increased stress and state they are having difficulty academically. White student perceive there is not as profes-sionally supported. | Faculty not ensuring self-care for students? Students may feel pressure to participate, or afraid to ask for help? |
| | Provide targeted research funding | | | |
| | Recruit racial and ethnic minorities for student leadership positions | | | |
| Create a supportive environment | Address diversity issues in social work curriculum | Several White students become more resistant to curriculum. Teacher evaluations decrease. | Cultural tensions develop in the program during the first year. Students of color report increased program satisfaction and a sense of belonging. | Need to address cultural resistance throughout the coursework? Targeted prejudice prevention? |
| | Invite students to contribute their perspectives in written program materials | | | |
| Increase communication | Present faculty and student expectations regarding diversity issues at monthly meetings | Diversity issues are discussed orally and in writing. | Students of color collaborate with faculty and work with student organizations at a high rate. | Greater communication, greater safety? |
| | Develop a monthly column in program newsletter that communicates diversity-related issues | | | |
| Conduct ongoing assessment of students' needs. | Conduct interviews with students at the end of their first semester and again at clinical internship. | Students of color report feelings of limited mentorship and feeling invisible. They report being gracious for the space to present their voices. | Assessment data reveal that feelings of belonging continue to increase. | The more voice given to participants, the greater sense of belonging. |
| | Assess faculty and administrators' views annually on recruitment and retention issues | | | |
| Build relationships with other social work-related programs | Develop database on undergraduate and graduate programs for marketing purposes | Over 100 programs are contacted and presented with marketing materials. | Students of color from national undergraduate programs select the social work graduate program. | Continued networking and creative communication |

**FIGURE 10.17** An Explanatory Effects Matrix of a Social Work Program Evaluation

| Effects | Causes | | |
|---------|--------|--------|--------|
| | *Intense* ⟵ | *Moderate* ⟶ | *Low* |
| Academic Difficulty | Student's fear to solicit assistance | Lack of self-care education | Psychological concerns |
| Funding Disparities | Perceived threats by Whites | Limited funding | Less White students are seeking funding |
| Increased Prejudice | Lack of prejudice prevention education | Recent racialized event in program | Limited communication among students and faculty |

**FIGURE 10.18**  A Case-Ordered Effects Matrix of Recruitment and Retention Initiatives

| Initiatives | Strategies | Enrollment | Curriculum | Climate | Professional Development Activities |
|---|---|---|---|---|---|
| Professional Development Opportunities | Diversity interest network Funding | Elle | Mary Charlotte Rebecca | Claudine Reginald | Rebecca Maya |
| Support | Curriculum changes Student voice in materials | Cynthia James | Maya | Martin | Jamal Elle |
| Assessment | Interviews Faculty surveys | Reginald | Amos | | Amos |

**FIGURE 10.19**  A Variable-by-Variable Matrix of Changes Resulting from Program

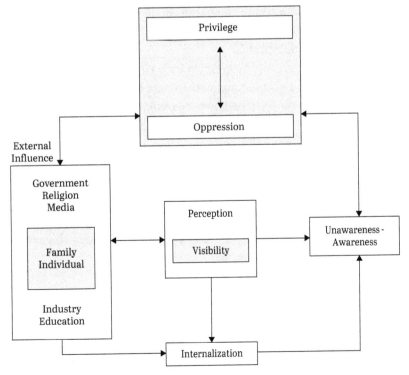

**FIGURE 10.20**  Causal Network of Developing Privilege and Oppression Awareness

Figure 10.20 presents a causal network for a cross-case display. This display is from a student exploring privilege and oppression awareness of counselor trainees (see Hays et al., 2004). This causal model depicts which variables create changes in levels of awareness of individuals.

A variation of the causal network for cross-case displays is the *cross-case causal network*. This display allows for a comparative analysis of individual cases, using the most influential variables accounting for a particular outcome as the organizing principle. This display rates antecedents found across cases and links variables and processes.

## ACTIVITY 10.4. REVIEWING CASE DISPLAYS

There are a lot of case displays to select from when managing and analyzing qualitative data, many more than we had space to cover in this chapter! In small groups, review the various types of case displays and compare them. What are their respective purposes? What are advantages and disadvantages to each?

## Postscript: Developing a "Theory"

How do you know when you have constructed an ideal display that is useful for explaining and predicting a phenomenon of interest? That is, how do you judge if you have a good theory or model in front of you? When do you stop analyzing and presenting data for within a source and across sources? When have you addressed your research question(s) sufficiently? Is a "final" framework, model, or theory acceptable?

First, a "good theory" in qualitative inquiry may be defined as one that can be applied to several cases (Glaser, 1992). As you construct within-case displays and integrate them to create cross-case displays, you may notice that the core explanation of what is going on is almost universal across individuals. While there may be variations in how codes and themes are expressed, all cases typically will possess common categories. Second, a sound theory will seem to connect "disorderly data," where carefully labeled codes and placement and sequencing of those codes seem to glue the data together to explain and predict data for a research question. In essence, a theory references two requisite causality components: time and sequence. Finally, a sound theory is open to change and is modifiable (Glaser, 1992). Since qualitative findings are contextual and involve a particular set of data, a theory should be developed to represent the fluid nature of a phenomenon of interest.

So, create a theory but understand the limitations of that theory. Your model or theory may be strengthened by conducting similar investigations across different contexts as you work to disconfirm a present theory. Recall from Chapter 7 that some strategies of trustworthiness involve negative case analysis and triangulation of multiple researchers, data sources, data methods, and theories to investigate a phenomenon. These strategies are quite useful when presenting your model or theory. We caution, however, even with methodological rigor and good intentions, a theory is undoubtedly open to scrutiny (see Wild Card 10.2).

**WILD CARD 10.2.** POTENTIAL CHALLENGES IN THEORY DEVELOPMENT

In our own as well as our students' and colleagues' qualitative investigations over the past several years, we have noticed that there are some common challenges that seriously impact a study's rigor. We present some of them here and hope that you will solicit outside feedback (e.g., peer debriefer, research team, auditor, existing theories and scholarship) before preparing and developing a theory for a particular research question.

- Attempting theory development when our research tradition(s) and research question(s) do not support it as a goal
- Use of data that are not adequate or sufficient to explain or predict
- Failure to return to the literature to confirm that there are no existing theories or models that already explain the developing theory
- Too much attention to ambiguous data
- Construction of a scenario or narrative to force a sequence or order to the present data and codebook
- Assignment of causal explanations to random events
- Failure to consult others who do not have a vested interest in the study being published

## Qualitative Software

Since the 1970s qualitative software has continued to evolve from single-text file coding and retrieval programs to more elaborate multiple text and media files for theory building and "quasicoding" programs (Grbich, 2012). Qualitative software is not a coding system; it is a tool that can be used to code, annotate, retrieve, and explore qualitative data. There are several options available, and the choice will come down to availability, personal preference, and/or whether the tool meets personally specific desired ways of working with data.

Further, software to assist you transcribe data is available. Finally, we cannot forget about the software right at our desks, the word-processing program. Word-processing software accommodates everything from data management and storage (e.g., creating displays, developing transcripts) to initial coding (e.g., inserting comments in margins, using "Find" option to search for word frequencies, etc.).

Below we present software related to various phases of the qualitative research process. Although this is not an exhaustive list, you may find it difficult to select the appropriate software for your proposal. Miles et al. (2020) highlighted some key questions that may be useful in selecting qualitative software (see pp. 313–315 in their text). These include:

- What kind of computer user are you? Are you new to computers or able to manage complex software?

- What kind of database and project is it? How many data sources and cases are you working with?
- What kind of analysis is anticipated? Are you exploring or confirming phenomena, using single or multiple classification, intending to display findings, and wanting to blend quantitative data into findings?

Upon reflecting on these questions, you may find qualitative software is not for you, and that is okay! We just ask that you educate yourself about the functions and types of qualitative software before making that decision. Table 10.7 presents some of the common functions of qualitative software. We highlight the types of software in the remainder of this section, and we encourage you to explore the features of each to identify the right software for your needs.

**TABLE 10.7**  Functions of Qualitative Software

- Composing field notes and memos
- Transcribing interviews or other data sources
- Developing contact summary sheets, document summary forms, or other data collection templates
- Storing text
- Coding key words, phrases, or sentences
- Searching and retrieving codes and key phrases
- Linking data across files
- Displaying data in matrices, charts, graphs, or networks
- Counting frequencies of codes
- Building theory
- Preparing proposals and writing reports

## Types of Qualitative Software

Transcription software can be an invaluable resource for you, particularly if you have several interviews to transcribe or memos and field notes to develop. Here is a sample of available transcription software:

- Dragon (https://nuance.com)
- Otter.ai (https://get.otter.ai)
- OTranscribe (https://otranscribe.com/)
- Express Scribe (https://www.nch.com.au/scribe/index.html)

There are so many coding software options available, and several of these can transcribe textual data. If you want to simply tag codes and categories in a text document and do more of the coding process online, you can do so with coding and retrieval programs. If you want to compare several different documents and files at the same time and use the programs to generate theory and/or conceptual networks as well as address some issues of validity and reliability, you can select theory generation programs. Finally, if you are interested strictly in computing word and category frequencies for textual documents, a content analysis program might be right for you.

- Atlas.ti (https://atlasti.com)
- DeDoose (https://www.dedoose.com/)
- Ethnograph (https://qualisresearch.com)
- HyperRESEARCH (https://researchware.com)
- MaxQDA (https://www.maxqda.com/)
- NVIVO (https://qsr.com)
- QDA Miner (https://provalisresearch.com/products/qualitative-data-analysis-software/)
- Taguette (https://www.taguette.org/)
- Tansama (https://www.transana.com/)
- WeftQDA (http://www.pressure.to/qda/)
- WordStat (https://provalisresearch.com/products/content-analysis-software/)

## Challenges of Qualitative Software

If you investigate qualitative computer software options, try it, and do not fall in love with it, you are not alone. In fact, several challenges have been documented related to the use of software (see Grbich, 2012). First, the notion of software for qualitative research implies increased control and manipulation. This increased structure may create a scenario where a computer program is influencing our understanding of the phenomenon of interest as we decontextualize data for software compliance purposes. As Grbich (2012) noted:

> In creating computer tools for the management of data, we cannot avoid shaping both the outcomes of our data interpretation and our perceptions of the outcomes. Each tool creates artifacts and metaphors (frames) which are not neutral in effect and which change our ways of thinking and seeking. "Reality" has to be segmented, truncated and textured to prepare data to "fit" a particular form of programming. (p. 230)

Relatedly, a second challenge is that as we rely on software to assist with qualitative inquiry, we decrease the interactive nature of research design proposed by Maxwell (2013; see Part II of this text). Using various framing processes mandates segmenting text at very early stages of data analysis, creating a very linear coding process for the steps described earlier in this chapter. Thus, it is harder to go back and recode and examine pattern codes when the data may be stripped so early from its context.

A third challenge is that qualitative software—particularly programs that assist in theory generation and concept networking—minimize the gap between quantitative and qualitative research. In essence, many qualitative software programs interface with quantitative software programs to allow for statistical analyses. On the surface, this may seem to help legitimize the value of qualitative research. However, there are significant conceptual differences between these two research approaches that impact sampling techniques, sample size, and degree of variable control that do not create parallel data. So, using qualitative data for quantitative interpretation can create a scenario where qualitative findings appear statistically insignificant and thus to some critics not as important as quantitative findings.

Grbich (2012) notes another challenge: Qualitative software programs that allow computer-to-computer or person-to-computer communication are not analogous to face-to-face consensus coding. Reviewing data in person is a spontaneous and interactive process that develops findings in a very different way than the structured and (often time-delayed) consensus process through computer use.

A final challenge we will attend to is the reputation and increased visibility of qualitative computer software. Software companies highlight features of new and/or updated software that can handle massive amounts of data, compute frequencies across multiple data files, interface with quantitative methods, and so forth. The message is clear to us: Qualitative research can be quick and easy to do, and more and more data can be considered. However, we believe that more technology is not necessarily good news if it is used to quickly analyze data.

## CHAPTER SUMMARY

Qualitative data analysis is an integral component of qualitative research in education, practice, and other social sciences settings constantly linked to qualitative data collection. We introduced qualitative data management strategies beginning in Chapter 8 and continue the discussion here to show the value of case displays in qualitative data analysis.

While various research traditions present their own analysis methods, we present eight steps of qualitative data analysis that seem to be found across research traditions (even though they may be labeled differently for the research tradition). The steps include: (1) reduce data; (2) collect data; (3) write a memo; (4) organize text and audiovisual data; (5) code; (6) identify themes and patterns; (7) create a codebook; and (8) develop a main narrative or theory. These steps are appropriate for textual and audiovisual data sources.

Several coding considerations were also presented, including a description of consensus coding and establishing reliability; debates around whether to use frequency counts; single versus multiple codes or classifications; and the importance of taking a break from data as well as using member checking during data analysis steps. Finally, related to data analysis, content analysis and attributional coding were discussed as two additional forms of qualitative data analysis.

Case displays are data management tools that allow for exploring, describing, explaining, and predicting phenomena. This chapter presented multiple examples of case displays as well as several tips for developing them.

The chapter ended with a brief presentation of qualitative software. There are several functions of software, and different software do various things with your data. We presented some common examples of transcription and coding software as well as general challenges to qualitative software to help you make an informed decision regarding what (if any) software is appropriate to use for your study.

## Review Questions

1. How do qualitative data collection, management, and analysis work together to maximize the trustworthiness of a study?
2. How can data be reduced throughout the qualitative research process?
3. What are the various forms of memos that qualitative researchers can use, and what are some strategies for writing memos throughout the qualitative research process?
4. How can the eight steps of qualitative data analysis apply to audiovisual data?
5. What are the general categories of within-case and cross-case displays, and in what ways are they each helpful in a qualitative study?

## Recommended Readings

Grbich, C. (2012). *Qualitative data analysis: An introduction* (2nd ed.). Sage.

Miles, M. B., Huberman, A. M., & Saldaña, J. (2020). *Qualitative data analysis: A methods sourcebook* (4th ed.). Sage.

Saldaña, J. (2016). *The coding manual for qualitative researchers* (3rd ed.). Sage.

Schreier, M. (2012). *Qualitative content analysis in practice*. Sage.

Vanover, C., Miles, P., & Saldaña, J. (Eds.). (2022). *Analyzing and interpreting qualitative research: After the interview*. Sage.

## Image Credits

IMG 10.1: Copyright © 2016 Depositphotos/andrewgenn.

Fig. 10.4: Adapted from Matthew B. Miles and A. Michael Huberman, *Qualitative Data Analysis: An Expanded Sourcebook*. Copyright © 1994 by SAGE Publications.

Fig. 10.14: Adapted from Julia M. Forman, "The Influence of Rape Empathy and Demographic Variables on Counselor Rape Myth Acceptance." Copyright © 2010 by Julia M. Forman.

Fig. 10.15: Adapted from Julia M. Forman, "The Influence of Rape Empathy and Demographic Variables on Counselor Rape Myth Acceptance." Copyright © 2010 by Julia M. Forman.

Fig. 10.16: Adapted from Julia M. Forman, "The Influence of Rape Empathy and Demographic Variables on Counselor Rape Myth Acceptance." Copyright © 2010 by Julia M. Forman.

Fig. 10.20: Danica G. Hays, Catherine Y. Chang, and Jennifer K. Dean, "White Counselors' Conceptualization of Privilege and Oppression: Implications for Counselor Training," *Counselor Education and Supervision*, vol. 43, no. 4. Copyright © 2004 by American Counseling Association.

## CHAPTER 11

# Qualitative Data Analysis by Research Tradition

## CHAPTER PREVIEW

In this chapter, we review the approach each qualitative research tradition has to data analysis. We begin the chapter with some general thoughts about data analysis across the research traditions. Then we examine qualitative data analysis across the five research tradition clusters discussed in Chapter 4 (see Figure 11.1). We begin our review with the hybrid tradition in qualitative designs: the case study. The four remaining clusters involve traditions that address experience and theory formulation (Cluster 2), those that investigate the meaning of symbol and text (Cluster 3), approaches that explore cultural expressions of process and experience (Cluster 4), and those that view research as a change agent (Cluster 5). With each tradition, we highlight the similarities and differences among data analysis approaches. We also include several case examples to bring to life what data analysis "looks like" for each research tradition. We refer to researcher reflexivity in data analysis across the clusters, and you may want to return to our in-depth discussion of researcher reflexivity in Chapter 1. At the end of the chapter, Table 11.7 summarizes data analytic approaches across the research traditions.

## Qualitative Data Analysis Across Research Traditions

As you collect and immerse yourself within the data, you are hopefully concurrently engaged in the data analysis. As Chapter 10 indicated, there are some typical steps to data analysis, and these are applied in different ways depending on the selected research tradition. As you get started on data analysis, review the Top 10 list in Table 11.1, with many of the presented tips serving as reminders of material presented earlier in the text.

Another general thought on data analysis is that you should have a data analysis plan. You can call it a "strategy": It might even feel like a "battle plan" at times (although we think it is always best to not position yourself as a researcher "opposite" of your data but find ways to work *with* your data). Establish your data analysis plan ahead of time and closely align your

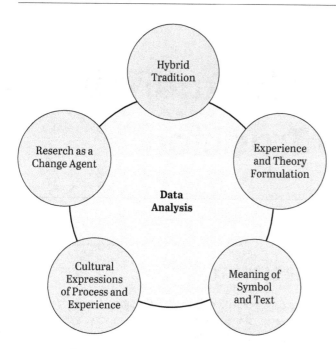

**FIGURE 11.1**   Qualitative Data Analysis by Research Tradition

data analysis activities with this plan. Often, this plan includes developing a codebook of some kind (introduced in Chapter 10), where you track the large domains and categories of data in addition to the subcategories and subdomains of your data.

Also, remember to not lose sight of how your selected research paradigm and tradition are lenses through which to view your data as you engage in analysis. For example, in our phenomenological study of the resilience of child sexual abuse survivors, we employed feminist and critical theory paradigms (Singh et al., 2010a). So, we had a solid data analysis plan. However, as we conducted data analysis, we continually invited our research paradigms into this analysis. The question we asked ourselves was "How true are we being to our theoretical framework?" In this study, this question translated to the extent to which our data analysis focused on themes of empowerment and acknowledgment of contextual factors and privilege and/or oppression experiences—exactly what our theories demanded we do in our data analysis.

We will discuss data analysis across many traditions. Before we delve into the distinct methods of analysis within each tradition, we emphasize the typical steps of qualitative data analysis presented in Chapter 10. Additionally, Miles et al. (2020) provide a list of common features of qualitative data analysis among the research traditions:

- Assigning codes or themes to a set of field notes, interview transcripts, or documents
- Sorting and sifting through these coded materials to identify similar phrases, relationships between variables, patterns, themes, categories, distinct differences between subgroups, and common sequences
- Isolating these patterns and processes, and commonalities and differences, and taking them out to the field in the next wave of data collection
- Noting reflections or other remarks in jottings, journals, and analytic memos
- Gradually elaborating a small set of assertions, propositions, and generalizations that cover the consistencies discerned in the database
- Comparing those generalizations with a formalized body of knowledge in the form of constructs or theories (p. 10)

You will notice similar processes that are described with different terms in the different research traditions. Honestly, this used to frustrate us! Now, we actually see it as a

**TABLE 11.1** Top 10 List for Qualitative Data Analysis

1. Findings do not "emerge." We are researchers who "identify" findings. Acknowledge your researcher role and how your biases and assumptions influence how you analyze data.

2. The point above is actually a good thing. We are researchers for a reason: We have and bring expertise to the data analysis, and we have the goal of involving our participants and relevant communities in this process. As you analyze data, continually consider how to best communicate the findings postanalysis and to what audience(s).

3. It is not always possible to form a research team, but remember they increase the quality of your data analysis. Try not to go solo on data analysis.

4. Multiple sources of data require multiple ways to analyze it. We will discuss many of these methods. However, the qualitative field evolves and grows constantly. Read this book and consider any new ways of analyzing data based on your field.

5. Think about how you "think" best and talk about how this is in common, or not, with your research team and participants. You do not want differences in style to be a barrier to your data analysis process.

6. Remember it is best to try to disprove and "argue" with your data along the way to ensure you are doing the best data analysis you can.

7. Be creative. Sometimes, you will have more questions than answers about how to proceed with data analysis. This can actually be useful as long as you are not just making things up to make it easy or take a shortcut and are not straying incredibly far away from your theory and research tradition (which both guide you in your data analysis).

8. Take a vacation from your data analysis. As we mentioned this in Chapter 10, it is a good thing and you will often come back "fresh" to see your data in a new light.

9. When you get stuck, revisit your data again and again … and again. Your participants' voices will often point to your path out of the quicksand.

10. Be familiar and have some facility with the range of data analysis techniques across research traditions. You may be borrowing from a few different traditions. Again, this should not just happen because you do not know what else to do but rather because you have a solid rationale for doing so and it helps you understand, interpret, and communicate your findings most effectively.

comfort. Each research tradition is undergirded with a particular philosophical bent, and this does and *should* be evident in how data analysis is described within each one. We think the best way to learn the most about the research tradition that is best for your research project is to get to know all of the differences and similarities across the various research traditions. A helpful way to learn them is to take your research topic and situate it in each of the research traditions. We have several activities where you can apply data analysis in research traditions and get a true feel for the ways each distinctly approaches analyzing data. Let's get started!

## Qualitative Data Analysis with the Hybrid Tradition: The Case Study

We discussed in Chapter 4 the unique position the case study has in qualitative research as the hybrid tradition given its versatility and methodological diversity. It involves a comprehensive, in-depth study of a complex issue framed through a case and within the context of a bounded system. Although case studies can include quantitative data collection and analysis, we limit our discussion in this text to qualitative data and encourage you to review Yin (2017) in further detail.

As discussed further in Chapter 4, a case may be a phenomenon, event, situation, organization, individual, or group of individuals studied in naturalistic settings. And a case study may involve a single or multiple case studies. Given the flexibility of this research tradition, including the various ways a case may be defined, data analysis can be challenging and involve multiple decisions. These multiple decisions, however, should be guided by the case itself.

A first step of case study analysis often involves a bounding of the data to include the case and pertinent contextual information: What is the case and its bounded system? Is this a single or multiple case study? We believe case study analysis should strive for a balance of presenting the major facts of a case with a complexity of findings and interpretation that will illuminate prior misunderstandings and/or lack of information about a case and delineate the case from the context in which it resides. As you immerse yourself in multiple sources of data you have collected, be sure to come up for air occasionally as you conduct a general analysis of all these sources. It is okay to trust in yourself and your own expertise to guide qualitative data analysis. Just make sure you are answering our "gut check" questions along the way! See Activity 11.1 to put some of these questions into action with case study data analysis.

 **ACTIVITY 11.1.** GUT CHECK QUESTIONS FOR CASE STUDY DATA ANALYSIS

In your research team, take your research topic (whether it is a case study design or not) and consider it within a case study design. You are looking at the data you have collected and analyzed. Answer the following questions with regard to your data analysis:

1. What data have I ignored and/or neglected to analyze that might contribute to the understanding of this case(s)?
2. What in my analysis of this case(s) is indicating a finding that appears to go against major identified findings?
3. Does my analysis reflect the most important findings I have identified in the case?
4. Where am I leaving my expertise as a researcher out of the data analysis?
5. How might my research tradition guide me to return to my data collection and analysis and shift the lens through which I analyze my data?

The tendency in case study data analysis can be to identify the major findings that help an audience understand the phenomenon, its boundaries, and its context more fully but leave out some of the important details. If you take that approach, it is challenging to "paint a full picture" of the case. So describe the case: How would you tell the story of your data based on your analysis? Remember, this should not be a "magazine" story of your case. Rather, it should include the most salient facts and details of the case. Let's say we are interested in a case study of a Chicana woman in treatment for bulimia; the case study report will likely include the following: The details and facts will probably include her diagnosis, her presenting issues, the duration of and type of treatment interventions, the major "players" in her treatment, in addition to demographic details, such as her age, socioeconomic status, and so forth.

A good way to stay on track with data analysis is to remember what led you to study the case in the first place. The case study strategy is

> preferred when the inquirer seeks answers to how or why questions, when the inquirer seeks answers to how or why questions, when the inquirer has little control over events being studied, when the object of study is a contemporary phenomenon in a real-life context, when boundaries between the phenomenon and the context are not clear, and when it is desirable to use multiple sources of evidence. (Schwandt, 2001, p. 23)

So, if you are examining a single case of an immigrant Chicana woman living with bulimia and her treatment outcomes in a residential treatment center, there will be numerous "pulls" on you as a researcher to examine the variables influencing the case (e.g., the family or the media) rather than the case itself. This does not mean you should refrain or limit analysis of numerous data sources. For instance, you may have interviews with the participant herself, the family, and her treatment team of counselors and physicians, among others. However, when you begin analyzing data in these interviews that take you away from the case itself, be sure to come back to the research question guiding your case study.

In Chapter 4, we presented two researchers' approaches to case study research: Yin's (2017) and Stake's (1995, 2006). Yin prioritized theory development and verification as the outcome of case study research, while Stake prioritized thick description of the case itself. As such, each scholar presents varying strategies regarding case study analysis. Yazan (2015) noted that Yin's approach involved highly structured analytic guidelines and principles to explore case-effect relationships and/or theoretical propositions, while Stake's approach emphasizes holistic analysis, case description, and researcher reflexivity.

## Yin's Case Study Analysis

Yin (2017) outlines four principles to guide researchers in case study analysis. First, the researcher should ensure that all data relevant to the case(s) has been the subject of analysis. A good gut check with this principle is to ask yourself, "What data have I ignored and/or neglected to analyze that might contribute to the understanding of this case(s)?" Second, Yin asserts that researchers conducting rigorous case study analysis should maintain not just the findings that are congruent with one another but also search out what we have discussed before as "negative case analysis." The gut check question here is "What in my analysis of this case(s) is indicating a finding that appears to go against major identified findings?"

Third, Yin (2017) gives the researcher permission to highlight the most significant, meaningful findings of the case study in the process of analysis. This aligns with our previous caution to "stay on course" with understanding your case, as opposed to veering down interesting (but perhaps not as important) roads in data analysis that take you further away from understanding the boundaries of your case. The gut check question for the researcher here is "Does my analysis reflect the most important findings I have identified in the case?" Finally, Yin advises the researcher must rely on and use their previous knowledge, which could be considered expertise, about the case to drive the analysis forward. This might be the most complex of his principles for case study data analysis. It is not enough to just observe the various data of a case study. The researcher brings themselves to the data analysis and should embrace, own, and consider how to use this perspective to produce the highest quality of analysis possible. The gut check question here is "Where am I leaving my expertise as a researcher out of the data analysis?"

Yin (2017) also provides four general strategies for tackling case study analysis:

- *relying on theoretical propositions*: Use preexisting theory (and your conceptual framework) that guided you to your case study in the first place and shaped your research questions. Theoretical propositions help to organize the entire analysis, pointing to relevant conditions to be described as well as explanations to be examined.
- *working your data from the "ground up"*: Contrasting the first strategy, this strategy uses an inductive approach whereby the qualitative researcher interacts with the data and begins to identify patterns that yield insights for the analytic path to take.
- *developing a case description*: This is the prioritization of case description to later evolve in some cases to theory development. This strategy can be particularly helpful if you are experiencing challenges with the first two strategies (i.e., having a lot of data without an initial set of propositions or research questions or being unable to surface any useful concepts from the data).
- *examining plausible rival explanations*: This involves testing rival explanations against an identified theory originating before and/or during case study analysis. Rival explanations can be *craft rivals*, or quantitative methodological considerations such as a null hypothesis and validity threats. They also include *real-world rivals* (Yin, 2000):
  - *direct rival:* An intervention other than the target intervention accounts for the outcome.
  - *commingled rival:* Other interventions and the target intervention both contributed to the outcome.
  - *implementation rival:* The implementation process, not the substantive intervention itself, accounts for the outcome.
  - *rival theory:* A theory different from the original theory explains the outcome better.
  - *super rival:* A force larger than but including the intervention accounts for the outcome.
  - *societal rival:* Social trends, not any particular force or intervention, accounts for the outcome.

With these general principles and strategies in mind, we highlight next five analytic techniques that may be used, according to Yin (2017). As we present these, we use the previously mentioned single case study of an immigrant Chicana woman living with bulimia. The first technique is **pattern matching**, or the comparison of the identified theory or pattern from your data to a preexisting theory or theories. Yin refers to the degree of alignment between the current and previous theories as an indicator of internal validity (also credibility; see Chapter 7 of this text). This alignment involves identifying similarities in patterns as expected and not identifying that alternative patterns or theories are plausible. With the bulimia example, let's say that your conceptual framework posits that particular eating disorder interventions at the residential treatment center (e.g., couples counseling, art therapy, and feminist-based individual counseling) are effective in addressing a client's bulimia. Pattern matching would be comparing the actual case findings with this conceptual framework, considering how the case findings highlight other effective interventions as well as seeking to disconfirm expected effective interventions.

The second technique is **explanation building**, a specific form of pattern matching in which the goal is to analyze the case study data by building an explanation of the case. Explaining a case involves describing in narrative form how or why something happened. Yin (2017) noted that the general steps for explanation building involve

1. making an initial theoretical statement or proposition;
2. comparing the findings of the initial case against the statement or proposition;
3. revising the statement or proposition;
4. comparing other details of the case against the revision;
5. comparing the revision of the findings from a second, third, or more cases;
6. and repeating this process as needed.

Applied to the bulimia case, the three initially identified treatment interventions identified as effective are compared to the findings, yet the qualitative researcher then goes back to the case for further analysis, includes other cases to check against the findings of the initial case study analysis, and repeats this process until the final theoretical statement or proposition is descriptive of the most effective interventions for bulimia treatment for the case and similar cases.

**Time series analysis**, the third technique, is used to examine "some relevant 'how' and 'why' questions about the relationship of events over time, not merely to observe the time trends alone" (Yin, 2017, p. 154). A simple time series involves one variable over time, or an intervention in the bulimia case study: multiple data points about bulimia symptoms occurring before an intervention (baseline) are explored in comparison to those after an intervention is introduced. With complex time series designs, multiple variables, or bulimia interventions, are examined across multiple data points. The more complex the design, the stronger the analysis or narrative can be.

**Logic models** is the fourth technique and is particularly useful in program evaluation and in studying theories of change. Logic models can be applied at the individual, organization, or program levels. This technique consists of matching outcomes of a particular case study against an initial theoretical statement or proposition, yet delineates immediate, intermediate, and long-term or ultimate outcomes. Furthermore, activities and contextual conditions of the case are also described and/or explained in the narrative. According to Yin (2017), qualitative case study analysis would begin with first comparing the consistency between the observed and initial theoretical framework, affirming or disconfirming the original sequence or model. Then, additional qualitative data collection and analysis would occur to explaining what the modeling sequence and outcomes were affirmed or disconfirmed. Applied to the bulimia case study example, a qualitative researcher would develop an initial logic model that includes interventions, contextual conditions, and anticipated outcomes based on a conceptual framework. As data are collected and analyzed, the qualitative researcher revisits the initial logic model to compare actual and predicted findings and then develops a final logic model of bulimia interventions, contextual conditions, and various levels of outcomes, highlighting how that model converges and diverges with the conceptual framework.

Yin's (2017) fifth analytic technique, **cross-case synthesis**, is specific to multiple case study designs. A cross-case synthesis can involve single cases within one study or can consolidate findings across multiple studies. In some instances, the outcome of cross-case synthesis is to extend case analysis to a higher level, to identify a broader or larger case beyond the single cases. As an example, let's say a qualitative researcher was examining the components or activities within a couples counseling intervention and their effectiveness for addressing bulimia for Chicano women. A cross-case synthesis could example multiple women (cases) narratives and how they compare for specific components or activities of the intervention.

## Stake's Case Study Analysis

Stake (1995, 2006) discusses four major forms of data analysis with case study designs. We see these forms as ways to approach, for example, building a jigsaw puzzle of the city of New Orleans, in which the puzzle is the case description and the individual pieces are components of the case, such as critical incidents, demographics, and other contextual factors. Thus, these forms are ways in which you might approach completing the puzzle in whole or in part. The first form of data analysis is **categorical aggregation**, where you as the researcher will examine several occurrences for critical incidents, concerns, and issues within the data you have collected. This may be likened to categorizing puzzle pieces into piles of similar pieces to provide a general description by category. For example, puzzle piece piles might be those that will form an image of Jackson Square, another the image of a jazz funeral procession, and another of a steamboat on the Mississippi River, for example. These piles, then, are analogous to case components and are described as sections of the puzzle (or dimensions of the case). For our bulimia case study example, the qualitative researcher may create broad categories of influences on the Chicana woman that have meaning for the case itself. For instance, in interviews with treatment team members, the client, and her partner, you may identify broad categories of media influence, peer relationships, religious influences, family dynamics, cultural factors, and negative self-concept.

The second form of case study data analysis, **direct interpretation,** is very distinct from the first, as it involves the qualitative researcher directly interpreting the meaning of singular critical incidents, concerns, and issues within the data (Stake, 1995, 2006). This process is like taking a single puzzle piece or meaningful cluster of pieces and carefully analyzing this data for meaning before interpreting it within the whole case (or puzzle) for its meaning. For our example study, this could mean taking an influence on the case or a chronological event (e.g., the couple's decision to participate in counseling as part of the woman's treatment plan) and separating that critical incident from the case itself to examine its meaning, then replacing this meaning within the context of the meaning it lends to the case as a whole.

The third form of data analysis is **pattern identification**, where the qualitative researcher examines broad categories within the case for their relationships or interactions (Stake, 1995, 2006). As the puzzle is built, we look for how each category of the puzzle relates to the overall "story" of the city of New Orleans. Returning to our example study, say the researcher has used direct interpretation regarding the couple's decision to participate in couples counseling as part of the woman's overall treatment plan. With pattern identification, the qualitative researcher also has examined art therapy experiences and outcomes for the client (i.e., another cluster of puzzle pieces). The qualitative researcher can then examine points of convergence and divergence in these categories to identify nuances and relationships among the interventions to inform the case description.

The fourth form of case study data analysis is **naturalistic generalization**, where the qualitative researcher actively interprets the data with an eye toward the ways an audience would be able to transfer or apply the broad categories or findings from the case study to another case(s). Thus, it is how the puzzle constructor describes the overall puzzle to a native and a nonnative of New Orleans, for example. In Chapter 7, we further described the concept of naturalistic generalizability as a potential indicator of transferability of findings; naturalistic generalization is also a data analysis process. For the bulimia example, naturalistic generalization may include identifying influences on healing and recovery from disordered eating that are common treatment elements across interventions, experiences reported by the woman by element or intervention, observations made by treatment team member by element or intervention, and so on depending on the audience to which the case is being described.

In addition to the gut check questions in Activity 11.1, we would like to offer the following tips for qualitative data analysis for a case study tradition:

* Your data analysis should be guided by the case(s) itself, not the factors that influence the case. For instance, in a case study of an urban college counseling center partnership with a local school, you may analyze data from staff members. However, the analysis should focus on how this data elucidates the case itself. Aim to stay on course with your analysis. Write your research question on an index card and keep it near you during data analysis, or post your research question on your codebook to help you stay on track.
* Construct a strategy for your data analysis. Is it based on the chronological sequence of events or other boundaries of the case? Use this strategy consistently throughout your analysis.

- Consider the benefits and drawbacks of using each of Yin's (2017) and Stake's (1995, 2006) approaches to case study data analysis. Which seem most relevant to your data analysis plan and case study purpose?
- Quality data analysis and reporting of case studies should be able to ward off the "so what" question, meaning that the reader of a study should not have this question come to mind at all if the data analysis has been well-thought-out and guided by the case study itself.

Case Example 11.1 offers an example of qualitative data analysis for the case study tradition.

## Case Example 11.1. Teacher Community in an Early Childhood Education Center

In this case study, Blank (2009) investigated the extent to which an early childhood education center included a focus on teacher community. She defined "teacher community" as entailing connections between teachers and students, emphasis on professional development, sources of innovation in teaching, reflective practice, and entailing a culture of its own, among other factors. Blank's data included participant observations of classrooms and participant development opportunities in addition to interviews with key school personnel (e.g., principal, teachers).

Blank's initial analysis involved immersing himself in the data through multiple readings of the participant observations and interview transcripts. This first analysis was general, and she began to identify large codes to set the stage for comparing data to one another. She used Stake's (1995) categorical aggregation and pattern identification to guide this process. The following quote illustrates some of the ins and outs of her data analysis:

> I utilized memoing, ... contact summary reports, and periodic interim reports as tools for grouping codes, to show that they are instances of a general concept or theme. The results of the study are grouped below according to two themes pertaining to teachers' views on community that were constructed through analysis: (a) shifting priorities, and (b) preference for privacy. Teachers' values, school acknowledge, external interests, and changes in leadership are examples of codes used to construct understandings of the teachers' shifting priorities. Interaction contexts, teacher feedback, and recognition of good teaching are examples of codes that were categorized as teachers' preference for privacy. (Blank, 2009, p. 376)

Here is a visual portrayal of Blank's case study data analysis plan:

**IMG 11.1**   Source: Blank, J. (2009). Life in the village: Teacher community and autonomy in an early childhood education center. *Early Childhood Education Journal, 36,* 373–380.

# Qualitative Data Analysis in Experience and Theory Formulation: Grounded Theory, Phenomenology, Heuristic Inquiry, and Consensual Qualitative Research

In this section, we discuss data analysis for the research traditions of Cluster 2 (see Chapter 4): grounded theory, phenomenology, heuristic inquiry, and consensual qualitative research. We discuss each individually, and you will notice some overlap in concepts because data analysis in all four traditions seeks to understand an experience and/or generate a theory. We will distinguish where some of these overlapping data analysis strategies use similar analytic techniques

## ACTIVITY 11.2. EXPERIENCE AND THEORY FORMULATION

Within your research groups, answer the following questions:

1. What are the unique differences and similarities between grounded theory and CQR data analysis?
2. With your research topic, what would be your data analysis steps if you used a grounded theory approach versus a phenomenological one?
3. What are the unique differences and similarities between data analysis with phenomenology and heuristic inquiry?
4. Take the four data analysis approaches with experience and theory formulation we have discussed in this section. Which approach do you naturally gravitate toward? Which approach do you find challenging?
5. If you have already collected and analyzed your data from an experience and theory formulation research tradition, how might you return to your analysis and refine it based on your discussion within your group?

yet have different names in the four traditions. We also interweave case examples to bring data analysis to life for each tradition. After reviewing the four traditions, see Activity 11.2.

## Grounded Theory

Grounded theory, as we have discussed previously, generates theory that is grounded in data from participants' perspectives for a particular phenomenon. Grounded theory data analysis "simultaneously employs techniques of induction, deduction, and verification to develop theory" (Schwandt, 2001, p. 110). In Chapter 4, we described three strands of grounded theory: classic or Glaserian grounded theory (CGGT; Glaser & Strauss, 1967), Straussian grounded theory (SGT; Corbin & Strauss, 2015; Strauss & Corbin, 1990), and constructivist grounded theory

(CGT; Charmaz, 2014). Because these strands are based in varying paradigmatic assumptions, there are some slight variations in data analysis.

No matter the grounded theory strand, qualitative researchers begin coding by identifying concepts that ultimately yield categories and identified patterns among those categories to develop theory. Thus, coding in the grounded theory tradition is iterative, building from initial keyword or image searches in a data source to linking complex constructs together to explain a phenomenon. Within coding complexity, qualitative researchers can identify similarities and differences for each concept, identify differences within a category and develop subcategories (i.e., building up categories to break them down), and move from descriptive to analytical tactics as they develop theoretical sensitivity. Throughout the coding process, grounded theorists particularly engage in the trustworthiness strategies of memo writing, constant comparison, negative case analysis, and referential adequacy (see Chapter 7).

There are several types of coding identified within one or more of the three grounded theory strands. First, **open coding** (used in CGGT and SGT) or **initial coding** (used in CGT) is a type of wide review of the data answering the question "What large general domains or concepts am I seeing in the data?" This might involve keywords or phrases provided by the participants (i.e., in-vivo codes) or developed by the researchers. Thus, it is a low-level description of the data. Charmaz (2014) identified the following initial coding processes for textual data: word-by-word coding, line-by-line coding, and incident-by-incident coding; these processes can be combined as needed, or one approach may be more appropriate depending on the complexity of the data collected.

As an example of open coding, in the aforementioned grounded theory study of academic leadership development (Hays et al., 2021; see Figure 11.2), one of the open codes was "visibility." This code was noted for all 20 participants, although the code had "stretchiness" and complexity and referred to negative and positive aspects (i.e., a context in which academic leaders are seen, valued, and respected within their institution, or the notion that academic leaders struggled being in the spotlight, feeling undervalued or disrespected within their institution).

The second form of coding, **focused coding** (used in CGT), can be considered a way to manage large amounts of open codes within and across data courses. Charmaz (2014) defined focused coding as identifying the more significant and/or frequently occurring initial codes to sift through large amounts of data. Thus, focused codes become "bins" in which qualitative researchers can organize data prior to more complex data analysis. In the academic leadership development study (Hays et al., 2021), some of the open codes related to academic leadership activities were placed into bins that helped the researchers to consider different levels of academic engagement as the study progressed.

The third form of coding, **axial coding** (used in SGT), is a process that begins to refine the open or initial coding and focused coding, as applicable, and examines relationships among them. Charmaz (2014) noted that "initial coding fractures data into separate pieces and distinct codes. Axial coding is [the] strategy for bringing data back together" (p. 60). Axial coding, thus, is a second-tier process by which open codes are collapsed into broader categories or codes. As codes are chunked or collapsed, sometimes some open codes are subsumed under another identified open code label, and other times multiple open codes are collapsed into a new code

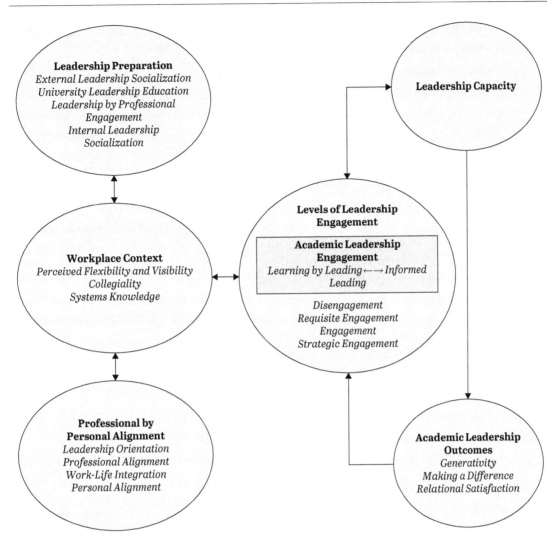

**FIGURE 11.2** A Model of Academic Leadership Engagement

label. The axial coding process is integral to understanding more in depth what the data are revealing regarding theory building.

For the academic leadership development study (Hays et al., 2021), "perceived flexibility and visibility" was the generated axial code that folded into it the previous open code of visibility. This new axial code referred to the degree of a university's commitment to identifying and sustaining academic leaders, evidenced by a context in which academic leaders are valued and provided flexibility in how they can serve as leaders within their institution. The following are examples of quotes that illustrate this axial code:

- "I felt valued. ... I was invited to participate at a higher level. I was invited to come into the dean's office and share my perspective" (PA 05).
- "I think at the dean level ... you are sort of held accountable for everything, but you don't have a lot of authority over certain elements, so I think it can be a lot of double binds" (PA 08).

- "There's just more flexibility when you're not in leadership. Your comings and goings, and the minute you're chair or associate dean you're so visible" (PA 14).

Glaser (1978) and Charmaz (2014) identified a coding type that overlaps with the functions of axial coding and selective coding: theoretical coding. In fact, the term preceded axial coding as the grounded theory tradition developed. **Theoretical coding** is a process by which qualitative researchers collapse or link focused codes to generate categories and subcategories like axial coding procedures and, later, theoretical relationships parallel to selective coding (described next). Thus, the smaller bins (i.e., focused codes) become larger bins that get linked to describe and explain theory.

The last form of grounded theory coding, **selective coding** (used in SGT), is the process of choosing one category to be the core category, or core selective code; further refining and collapsing axial codes into other selective codes, and identify links among the selective codes. The essential idea is to develop a single storyline to "anchor" data analysis and focus in data reporting, usually in the form of a theoretical model (like Figure 11.2 or Figure 10.20). Selective coding is truly the step that begins to "look like" a grounded theory of your phenomenon.

In selective coding, Corbin and Strauss (2015) emphasize two tasks: identifying the central or core category and integrating variation into data analysis. Corbin and Strauss (2015) discuss the core category as having "analytic power" (p. 189) that is kind of like a black hole: It is a central category that brings all the other selective codes together. When identifying a core category, they cite Strauss's (1987) criteria:

- It must be sufficiently abstract so that it can be used as the overarching explanatory concept typing all the other categories together.
- It must appear frequently in the data. This means that within all, or almost all, cases there are indicators that point to that concept.
- It must be logical and consistent with the data. There should be no forcing.
- It should be sufficiently abstract so that it can be used to do further research leading to the development of general theory.
- It should grow in depth and explanatory power as each of the other categories is related to it through statements of relationships.
- The central idea should also be capable of accounting for variation—or varying explanations—of the phenomenon. (p. 36)

As one example of a selective code, workplace context, noted in Figure 11.2 includes three axial codes: perceived flexibility and visibility, collegiality, and systems knowledge. Workplace context influences whether individuals engage in or sustain academic leadership and includes three elements: perceived flexibility and visibility ($n = 20$), collegiality ($n = 19$), and systems knowledge ($n = 16$). Of the 20 participants, 15 reported that all three elements—and five reported that two of the three elements—informed their academic leadership experiences. Furthermore, Hays et al. (2021) note through the model that workplace context is linked to the three selective codes of leadership preparation, professional by personal alignment, and levels of leadership engagement.

Selective coding is the most complex coding process in grounded theory wherein patterns, processes, and sequences are identified among axial codes to generate a theory about a phenomenon. Selective codes are the highest level codes in the generated theory: Their descriptions capture those of axial codes chunked within them, the processes and actions found across axial codes, as well as the processes and actions they possess with other selective codes in the model. CGGT and CGT strands identify typical bins that serve to capture selective codes:

- ***causal conditions:*** events or variables that lead to the occurrence or development of the phenomenon. This type of selective code is parallel to moderating variables in statistical modeling.
- ***context:*** "background" variables influencing an action strategy and/or causal condition
- ***intervening conditions:*** "mediating" variables of the phenomenon that influence the relationship between causal conditions and action strategies and the core category
- ***action strategies:*** purposeful, goal-oriented activities performed in response to the phenomenon and intervening conditions
- ***consequences:*** results of the action strategies, intended and unintended

For the academic leadership development study (Hays et al., 2021; see Figure 11.2), the core category for the model is academic leadership engagement. The core category was informed by leadership preparation (causal condition), professional by personal alignment (intervening condition), and workplace context (context). Furthermore, there are four levels of leadership engagement (action strategies) that yield various academic leadership outcomes (consequences); leadership capacity serves as an intervening condition or intermediate outcome of academic leadership engagement.

Case Example 11.2 presents examples and additional information about grounded theory analysis for a study examining advocacy strategies among school counselors (Singh et al., 2010b). Perspectives 11.1 highlights research team reflections on grounded theory data analysis with respect to this study.

**Case Example 11.2. School Counselor Advocates' Strategies for Social Justice Change**

Singh et al. (2010b) conducted a grounded theory exploring school counselor advocates' strategies for social justice change. Here is a raw transcript excerpt from one participant. (The underlined portions became an exemplar of an open code we defined as "relationship building.")

> You really have to, especially in the position that I am speaking from now the administrators at local schools are really, is really the key, that you really need to be able to work with. Number one, I think that they will be immediately available to listen to the data that you gather as a school counselor, and any social justice issues that you will have to raise. <u>Forming good relationships with them and making sure they know your job is to be an advocate for students</u>—having them understand that you're there for students, you care, you do a good job—that is key if you want to make change.

As my colleagues and I (Anneliese) delved into the axial coding process and revisited transcripts in our research meetings, we identified in the data that the broad open code of "relationship building" involved an action about their role for participants. We had identified a selective code that became "educating others about school counselors' roles as advocates." Toward the end of the data analysis, selective coding involved identifying relationships among the selective codes, which we decided to portray in a visual model that signified the close relationships among them. Here is an excerpt from the study:

Researchers built recursivity into each stage of the research process so that simultaneous data collection and analysis continuously informed each other and, in turn, the emerging grounded theory After the first two interviews were transcribed, four research team members individually reviewed and coded the transcripts using an open coding process. Open coding involved analyzing each line or paragraph of the transcripts for codes reflecting each participant's experiences. More specifically, each discrete idea, event, or experience was given a name (e.g., "courage," "dialoguing," "student empowerment"). To create a codebook for the remaining interviews, researchers used constant comparison with their discrete codes to identify categories that related to a common overarching concept and to discern any discrepancies between their discrete codes.

After each interview was conducted, transcribed, and coded using this codebook, axial coding was utilized to examine the relationship between each of the preestablished categories. During this stage, the research team created higher level categories based on the data (e.g., "methods of consciousness raising"), thereby contributing to the initial development of a grounded theory of the phenomenon under study. Finally, selective coding was used to refine the theoretical model based on the identification of an overarching core category that accounted for most of the variation in the previously identified categories (e.g., "school counselors' strategies for systemic change"). Researchers reviewed each participant's transcript using the codebook until saturation of findings was attained at participant sixteen, where no new data were identified.

Verification standards and procedures were built into each stage of the research process. Member checking of transcripts, researcher reflexive journals, routine team meetings, the use of multiple data analysts, and peer debriefing were utilized to maximize trustworthiness of findings. Researchers identified thick descriptions of the phenomena to demonstrate credibility of findings. The researchers' immersion in the data for a year, during which time the team continually reviewed and coded data as data were collected and analyzed, further strengthened the credibility of findings. Throughout the research process, a school counselor served as an internal auditor by attending research meetings regularly and reviewing the data for accuracy of the coding and theory-building process. An external auditor reviewed the products of the study (i.e., transcripts, research team notes, emergent model) for accuracy. Finally, the research team searched for evidence to disconfirm the emerging theory and modified the theory when necessary to ensure accurate representation of the data. (Singh et al., 2010b, p. 13)

Here is the visual portrayal of this grounded theory study.

**IMG 11.2** Singh, A. A., Urbano, A., Haston, M., & McMahon, E. (2010b). School counselors' social justice strategies used in school settings: A qualitative inquiry. Professional School Counseling, 13, 135–145.

-------------------------------------------------------------------------------

## PERSPECTIVES 11.1. GROUNDED THEORY RESEARCH TEAM MEMBERS LOOK BACK ON DATA ANALYSIS

The perspectives below are from three research team members working on the Singh et al. (2010b) grounded theory study. Read their perspectives to get a sense of what working on a grounded theory research team "feels" like in the data analysis stage:

> The grounded theory data analysis process allowed me to get very close to the experiences and voices of our participants through our data. We became heavily immersed in their collective perspectives, and where these perspectives overlapped in concrete, meaningful ways. The chal-

lenges were that the process is messy. It often seemed that we had a swirling, nebulous, mass of data that somehow we needed to bring order and structure to. This can be overwhelming and it takes a lot of conceptual work to develop this structure. I think you have to get comfortable with the constant shifting of structures and rearranging of your model as the theory emerges from your data. I enjoyed the collaborative, and intellectually engaged nature of the process. The constant conceptualization and reconceptualization of what you are seeing develop from your data is challenging, exciting, and fun. This is a very active process, and hashing out with your team what your data means and how it fits in the larger context of your emergent theory is a wonderful experience. I learned tremendously from the perspectives of my colleagues as we wrestled with our data. Because grounded theory data analysis is such a collaborative and interactive process I think it is important to have a great research team. It's also important to set the tenor of the analysis process as an open, collegial, communicative process, where all voices and perspectives are valued: those of the participants and also those of the researchers in analyzing the data.

—*Eleanor McMahon, MS*

Prior to becoming part of this research team, most of my research experience had involved quantitative data. Hearing our participants speak to their experiences, and then working to develop a model that honored these voices, was thus new territory for me. Connecting with the participants during the interviews made the data analysis process feel all the more significant to me: Having heard the participants' stories in person, having been granted the privilege of documenting their experiences, made it seem all the more crucial that we develop a model that was truly reflective of their collective message. One of the elements of the data analysis process that seemed most challenging was that the sheer amount of data: The ideas, themes, and concepts that emerged made it difficult to select those themes that were most significant and that were threaded throughout each of the participants' stories. In addition, it was also striking to me how I, as a researcher, approached the data that I collected personally, and the data that I didn't collect personally. More specifically, there are themes that emerge clearly on the page as you read the transcripts, and then there are feelings, ideas, "senses" that you get when you speak to someone in person. I, and we as a team, had to challenge ourselves always to come back to the data, to the words on the page. To be sure that the themes that were emerging were truly grounded in the written word, and not just in our own interpretations or the feelings we got when we spoke to the participants. To anyone interested in working with qualitative data, I would advise that patience is key. The process of working in the grounded theory paradigm is a long one, and can feel unclear at times. It is so important for all members of the team to trust the process: to know that if the team is committed to the data, and to the voices of the participants, the themes and the model that emerge will indeed be a grounded theory.

—Meg Haston, MS

The data analysis process for our grounded theory study was a complicated and rewarding one. We collected about 400 pages of rich data, which was initially overwhelming to sort through. We relied on each other—our research team members—to keep us grounded as we initially sorted through the volume of data during the open coding stage. Our team was passionate about the topic of social justice and became progressively more excited about the emerging theory as we moved from the open coding stage to the axial and selective coding stages. We used our analytic, creative, visual, and comedic selves throughout the analysis process and experienced a shared sense of excitement when our theory eventually reached its final form. One of the greatest opportunities of completing a grounded theory study is the chance to work collaboratively with a group of individuals who share a common interest. Another unique opportunity is the inevitable intimacy of the data analysis process, both among the researchers and with the participants (through their transcribed voices). By the end of the data analysis process, I felt empowered by and connected to sixteen social justice advocates (our participants) and three inspirational colleagues (the research team): quite an incredible experience!

For me, the greatest challenge of the data analysis process involved sorting through the huge volume of data, which was a circuitous process rather than a linear one. The real challenge here was accepting that the process was not going to be tidy, organized, and straight. I think I would give two pieces of advice for anyone embarking on the data analysis process of a qualitative study. First, select a supportive team that shares a passion or interest for the topic at hand. Second, accept before you even begin analyzing the data that it will be a circuitous process rather than a linear one.

—Alessandra Urbano, PhD

## Phenomenology

Phenomenology focuses on understanding the depth and meaning of direct lived experiences (Creswell & Poth, 2017; Hays & Wood, 2011; Moustakas, 1994) rather than to generate a theory. Three strands of phenomenology (i.e., descriptive, hermeneutic, idiographic; see Chapter 4) result in some variations in the interplay of researcher and participant lifeworlds throughout phenomenological data analysis. That is, qualitative researchers can analyze and report experience across participants as an essence, typologies, or ideographically, addressing researcher subjectivity in different ways depending on the phenomenological strand (i.e., fusion of *horizons*, or perspectives). Researcher subjectivity involves the degree to which bracketing or bridling is used in analysis, the timing and amount of infusing researcher prior knowledge and interpretation, and the depth and breadth of data reporting (see Table 4.3 in this text).

Moustakas (1994) is probably most influential is revisiting phenomenological data analysis techniques, summarizing and expanding the steps for analysis. We include two reviews: his modification of van Kaam's (1959, 1966) phenomenological data analysis, which includes seven steps in Table 11.2, and his proposal of the Stevick-Colaizzi-Keen method of phenomenological data analysis in Table 11.3. Creswell and Creswell (2018) assert that the Stevick-Colaizzi-Keen approach is used more often recently. We believe both modifications provide helpful ways to analyze phenomenological data. See Table 11.2 and Table 11.3 for helpful guides through the intricacies of phenomenological data analysis. Specifically, in Table 11.2 we have reproduced Moustakas's (1994) guidelines for phenomenological analysis.

There are several key constructs of phenomenological data analysis.

At the outset of phenomenological data analysis, the researcher immerses themselves in the data. A critical pre-data-analysis step is the **bracketing** of researcher biases and assumptions about the study's focus. Bracketing, or setting aside researcher subjectivity, is often referred to as "bridling."

Clark Moustakas is one of the more prominent scholars who has defined analytic constructs. Phenomenological data analysis begins with large domains, or categories of text. The term used to describe this process is **horizontalization**. As discussed in Table 11.3, the research team begins to identify nonrepetitive, nonoverlapping statements in participants' transcripts. This process yields clusters of meaning, invariant meaning units, or **horizons**. This is an important first step in not only analyzing the data but also managing the data in a way that is efficient.

The **textural description** is similar to the grounded theory process of beginning to refine the data into new categories. However, the real distinction here is that the textural description always strives to understand the meaning and depth of the essence or invariant structure of the experience.

Depending on how the researcher chooses to manage the phenomenological data analysis, the researcher may have a list or visual model that represents not a theory but the experiences of participants that are a result of refining horizons into a textural description of the phenomenon's essence. Then a **structural description** is identified that searches out multiple potential meanings within the textural description in addition to variation among these meanings (i.e., what is identified as "opposites" or as "tensions" in the data). You can think of structural description as similar to grounded theory's structural coding, where relationships are identified and where the complexity of these relationships is sought to be understood.

Because the goal of phenomenological data analysis is to deeply understand a phenomenon's essence, we advise that you be familiar with Moustakas's modifications in Tables 11.3 and 11.4. However, we also encourage you to invite into your data analysis any techniques you think are necessary to best understand the essence of your study. Often, this entails creating a case

**TABLE 11.2** Moustakas's (1994) Modification of van Kaam's (1959, 1966) Phenomeno-logical Data Analysis

Using the complete transcription of each research participant:

1. *Listing and preliminary grouping*

   List every expression relevant to the experience (horizontalization).

2. *Reduction and elimination:* To determine the invariant constituents:

   Test each expression for two requirements:

   a. Does it contain a moment of the experience that is a necessary and sufficient constituent for understanding it?

   b. Is it possible to abstract and label it? If so, it is a horizon of the experience. Expressions not meeting the above requirements are eliminated. Overlapping, repetitive, and vague expressions are also eliminated or presented in more exact descriptive terms. The horizons that remain are the invariant constituents of the experience.

3. *Clustering and thematizing the invariant constituents:*

   Cluster the invariant constituents of the experience that are related into a thematic label. The clustered and labeled constituents are the core themes of the experience.

4. *Final identification of the invariant constituents and themes by application:* validation

   Check the invariant constituents and their accompanying themes against the complete record of the research participant.

   a. Are they expressed explicitly in the complete transcription?

   b. Are they compatible if not explicitly expressed?

   c. If they are not explicit or compatible, they are not relevant to the coresearcher's experience and should be deleted.

5. Using the relevant, validated invariant constituents and themes, construct for each coresearcher an individual textural description of the experience. Include verbatim examples from the transcribed interview.

6. Construct for each coresearcher an individual structural description of the experience based on the individual textural description and imaginative variation.

7. Construct for each research participant a textural-structural description of the meanings and essences of the experience, incorporating the invariant constituents and themes.

From the individual textural-structural descriptions, develop a composite description of the meanings and essences of the experience, representing the group as a whole.

**TABLE 11.3** Moustakas's (1994) Modification of the Stevick-Colaizzi-Keen Method of Phenomenological Data Analysis

1. Using a phenomenological approach, obtain a full description of your own experience of the phenomenon.

2. From the verbatim transcript of your experience, complete the following steps:

    a. Consider each statement with respect to significance for description of the experience.

    b. Record all relevant statements.

    c. List each nonrepetitive, nonoverlapping statement. These are the invariant horizons, or meaning units of the experience.

    d. Relate and cluster the invariant meaning units into themes.

    e. Synthesize the invariant meaning units and themes into a description of the textures of the experience. Include verbatim examples.

    f. Reflect on your own textural description. Through imaginative variation, construct a description of the structures of your experience.

    g. Construct a textural-structural description of the meanings and essences of your experience.

3. From the verbatim transcript of the experience of each of the other coresearchers, complete the above steps (a–g).

4. From the individual textural-structural descriptions of all coresearchers' experiences, construct a composite textural-structural description of the meanings and essences of the experience integrating all individual textural-structural description into a universal description of the experience representing the group as a whole.

Clark Moustakas, Excerpt from "Phenomenological Research: Analyses and Examples," *Phenomenological Research Methods*, p. 122. Copyright © 1994 by SAGE Publications. Reprinted with permission.

display or writing the essence of the phenomenon for each participant and then combining these individual essences into one composite essence. Case Example 11.3 provides an example of analysis for a phenomenological study. See Perspectives 11.2 for the authors' descriptions of the frustrations and joys of phenomenological data analysis.

### Case Example 11.3. Wellness within Counselor Education Programs

Gleason and Hays (2019) explored doctoral-level counselor trainees' (*N* = 12) perceptions of wellness promotion in their respective programs.

- They used descriptive phenomenological methods (Colaizzi, 1978; Moustakas, 1994) to analyze data and provide a thick description of the findings. Prior to data collection, the researchers bracketed their assumptions about wellness and self-care practices.

- The research team independently read and demarcated invariant meaning units via horizontalization. Horizontalization involved identifying words and phrases that seemed related to describing a participant's lived experiences with wellness and self-care practices.
- The research team clustered invariant meaning units to develop a textural description of the phenomenon. Textural themes were as follows: coping self, creative self, essential self, physical self, ecowellness, and holistic wellness.
- They identified a structural description that yielded a comprehensive description (i.e., phenomenological essence). The structural themes included (a) components of wellness, (b) program culture, and (c) recommendations.

Source: Gleason, B. K., & Hays, D. G. (2019). A phenomenological investigation of wellness within counselor education programs. *Counselor Education and Supervision, 58*(3), 177–194. https://doi.org/ 10.1002/ceas.12149

## PERSPECTIVES 11.2. THE ESSENCE OF PHENOMENOLOGICAL DATA ANALYSIS

In our phenomenological study of the resilience strategies of South Asian American child sexual abuse survivors, I remember that Danica and I often found ourselves musing about when we would arrive at the "essence" of the phenomenon we sought. We had case displays. We had long debates, discussions, and meetings about each participant's experience of resilience and child sexual abuse. We bracketed our own assumptions and biases consistently. We talked about horizontalization, structural and textural description, and kept sifting through an immense amount of data. And then one research meeting, it hit us. The essence of participants' experience was speaking to us through the data. It felt like a moment out of that movie *The Matrix*, where the "grid" comes to light! It felt like a magical moment. But the truth was that we spent many long weeks laboring over the data, digging deep into participants' descriptions of the phenomenon. I probably could have recited Moustakas's modifications of phenomenological data analysis in my sleep! In the end, we had a rich, complex visual model of participants' experiences that captured their essence indeed.

—A. A. S.

One of the many challenges of phenomenological studies for me has been to honor and illuminate their great contribution, providing the essence of a lived experience of a phenomenon, stripped of my experiences for that phenomenon. Thus, being able to bracket and refrain from theory generation is a valuable skill to hone. Bracketing is difficult at times because it takes practice to "set aside" our own experiences and judgments of those experiences. Saying to myself, "This, what I know and have experienced, has to be placed outside the study so that I can provide space for what my participants contribute. There is no need to try to take their experience and apply it to others. This only limits others' descriptions of *their* essence of the same phenomenon."

No matter the degree I have experienced a phenomenon, it is not as "valuable" to the study as those participants with which I am interacting. Further, their essence is does not necessarily apply to others outside the study. (There is a reason you wanted to tell their story in the first place!) Saturation, common in other traditions, is irrelevant. The greatest joy of phenomenology and phenomenological analysis is to be present for your participants and give justice descriptively to *their* story.

—D. G. H.

## Heuristic Inquiry

In Chapter 4, we noted that heuristic inquiry refers to the exploration of direct lived experiences of both the researcher(s) and participants (Sultan, 2020). There are many overlaps between heuristic inquiry and phenomenological data analysis because they both "seek to understand the wholeness and the unique patterns of human experiences in a scientifically organized and disciplined way ... requiring the researcher to dwell intensely with subjective descriptions and to search for underlying themes or essences that illuminate the meaning of the phenomenon" (Casterline, 2009, p. 2). Moustakas (1994) noted that heuristic inquiry is different from phenomenology in terms of the role of the researcher. The role of the researcher is to not separate oneself from the phenomenon studied. Often, the researcher has an experience of the phenomenon and thus brings not only researcher expertise to the data analysis but also experience that must be analyzed.

Moustakas (1990) and Sultan (2018) outline important steps of data analysis for heuristic inquiry. First, **initial engagement** refers to connecting to the topic of interest or research question. Next, qualitative researchers engage in **immersion,** or committing to living the topic of question fully on a personal level. **Incubation** involves temporarily withdrawing from research. After reengaging in the research, **illumination** is the process of qualitative researchers becoming aware of information previously unknown. **Explication** is then performed, which is the quest of the researcher to identify categories, themes, and patterns of the phenomenon within the data. In this quest, the researcher begins to recognize the depth and meaning the phenomenon has (i.e., *focusing*), and the researcher uses self-reflection to further analyze the structural and textural descriptions that were described in the previous section on phenomenological data analysis (i.e., *indwelling*). Moustakas then describes the final task of data analysis in heuristic inquiry as **creative synthesis.** Similar to the final stage of phenomenological data analysis, the researcher seeks the best way to portray the findings as a composite whole. The key difference between this final stage is, again, the role and experience the researcher has of the phenomenon.

Eger (2008) conducted a heuristic inquiry to examine a teacher's feelings of disempowerment when advocating for change within a gifted program in an urban school district. During the illumination phase, she identified large domains of common themes across interview data she had collected of key informants within the school and from the research literature in gifted education. In the explication stage, Eger self-reflected on her personal experiences as a researcher and on her shared experiences with the phenomenon. The final data analysis in her study involved creative synthesis where she visually portrayed her findings to depict the essence of the feelings she experienced and the context in which she experienced them.

## Consensual Qualitative Research

Consensual qualitative research (CQR) blends many of the characteristics of grounded theory and phenomenology, attending both to individual experience and theory development. There are five main data analysis components in CQR (Hill, 2012; Hill et al., 1997, 2005). First, a primary research team conducts the **domain development and coding**. In this step, each research team member immerses themselves in all of the data, reading each participant transcript. As they read this data, their analysis begins by identifying a list of large domains, categories, or themes they see in the data. Then the research team meets as a collective group to present their identified domains to one another. The research team argues, debates, and comes to consensus on one group of large domains. Then the individual members revisit the data through a second analysis using these large domains to code.

Second, the research team abstracts core ideas within domains (i.e., **domain abstraction**). As the research team reimmerses themselves in the data, they keep an eye out for core ideas that illuminate aspects of domains they have previously selected to examine. Third, members of the research team meet and attempt to research consensus on these core ideas through a process of **cross-analysis**. In cross-analysis, categories are developed by team members through a consensus-building process. In this process, the research team members are examining each category for evidence across all, some, and/or none of the participants. Once the list of categories is finalized, the research team members then return to the data and code all participant interviews within these categories. This cross-analysis should result in a separate document that includes a list of domains and within-domains categories common to all participants and any participant data that was not common across participant and/or was not included in another domain or subdomain.

The fourth key component of CQR is the use of an **external audit**. In this process, a secondary research team comes in to assess the accuracy of the cross-analysis and creation of domains and subdomains common to all participants. The auditors also examine the data and categories listed as not common to all participants and/or placed in an "other" category. The auditors then communicate their audit to the primary research team, suggesting alterations, revisions, and/or data that were not addressed by the original abstracting of core ideas and cross-analysis. You can see how this process of using what might be termed a "primary research team" and a "secondary research team" can be complex—and perhaps even burdensome. However, this is the heart of the rigor of CQR, so it is a critical interaction between these two research teams.

Finally, the fifth data analysis step with CQR involves **frequency analysis**. Now, we have already discussed in Chapter 10 how we feel about frequency and the benefits and the challenges of frequency counts. Regardless of the epistemological challenges we believe are inherent in "counting" responses in qualitative research, this is a critical aspect of the way Hill and colleagues (Hill, 2012; Hill et al., 1997, 2005) constructed CQR data analysis. In this final step, research team members categorize domains into one of four categories: general, typical, variant, and rare. Frequency labels include the following: general (all or all but one case), typical (more than half of the cases up to the cutoff for general), variant (at least two cases up to the cutoff of typical), and rare (up to 3 cases; this category is used for sample sizes greater than 15). See Table 11.4 to see what CQR findings "look like" at the end of the five steps of data analysis.

Okubo et al. (2007) used CQR to examine the career decision-making processes of eight Chinese immigrant adolescents. The authors developed and coded the data from transcripts into large domains and subdomains for an initial list, or codebook. Then the research team

**TABLE 11.4**  An Example of Data Analysis in Consensual Qualitative Research Data

| Domain/category | Illustrative core idea | Frequency |
|---|---|---|
| 1. The homeless experience | | |
| a. Negative feelings about being homeless | Depression, shame, frustration, injustice, helplessness | Typical |
| b. Greater empathy for the homeless | Changed attitudes, greater sympathy | Typical |
| c. Homeless person's struggle with substance use, mental illness, and physical illness | Alcohol, drugs, mental and physical illness | Typical |
| d. Dichotomy of homelessness | There are two different types of homeless individuals: those who choose to be homeless and individuals who are not homeless by choice. | Typical |
| 2. Perceptions of men and masculinity | | |
| a. Man as the "breadwinner" | Breadwinner, provider, worker | General |
| b. No changes in masculinity since becoming homeless | A succinct "no" when asked if they viewed their masculinity differently since becoming homeless | Typical |
| c. Others perceive homeless men negatively | Viewed as drunk, looked down upon, outcast | Typical |
| 3. Changing social status | | |
| a. Aspirations for upward mobility | Desires to change to a higher social class, including not being homeless anymore and discussion of home, family, and job. | Typical |
| b. Barriers to change identified | "Myself," financial situation, substance abuse, and/or health | Typical |

Adapted from W. M. Liu, R. Stinson, J. Hernandez, S. Shepard, and S. Haang, "A Qualitative Examination of Masculinity, Homelessness, and Social Class Among Men in a Transitional Shelter," *Psychology of Men and Masculinity*, vol. 10, no. 2, p. 137. Copyright © 2009 by John Wiley & Sons, Inc.

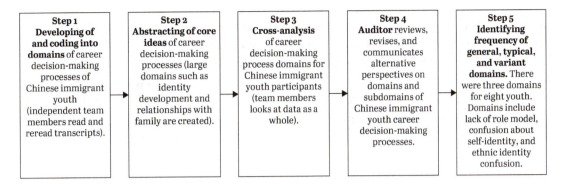

| Step 1 | Step 2 | Step 3 | Step 4 | Step 5 |
|---|---|---|---|---|
| **Developing of and coding into domains** of career decision-making processes of Chinese immigrant youth (independent team members read and reread transcripts). | **Abstracting of core ideas** of career decision-making processes (large domains such as identity development and relationships with family are created). | **Cross-analysis** of career decision-making process domains for Chinese immigrant youth participants (team members looks at data as a whole). | **Auditor** reviews, revises, and communicates alternative perspectives on domains and subdomains of Chinese immigrant youth career decision-making processes. | **Identifying frequency of general, typical, and variant domains.** There were three domains for eight youth. Domains include lack of role model, confusion about self-identity, and ethnic identity confusion. |

**FIGURE 11.3**  Steps in Okuba et al.'s (2007) CQR Data Analysis

members revisited the data, rereading each transcript using the codebook and domains and subdomains in the data. They invited recursivity into their data analysis by revising the codebook at several stages of data analysis based on what they were "seeing" in the data. When abstracting core ideas within domains, the research team members "constructed core ideas individually and then came to consensus" (Okubo et al., 2007, p. 442). Next, the cross-analysis of data included "bringing all the transcripts together" (Okubo et al., 2007, p. 442), utilizing an auditor to assess the accuracy of the data analysis thus far. Finally, the research team addressed frequency issues and categorized their domains as general, typical, or variant and then counted each of these and portrayed them in a table because CQR asserts that "representativeness can be plotted on [a] table to clearly show the results" (Okubo et al., 2007, p. 443).

At the end of Okuba et al.'s (2007) CQR data analysis, the research team had 10 domains they identified in participants' transcripts. They identified between three and eight subdomains per domain. Interestingly, for their study, all the subdomains were either typical or variant in their frequency. See Figure 11.3 for a visual portrayal of the CQR data analysis steps Okuba et al. used in their study.

## Qualitative Data Analysis with Symbols and Text: Life History and Narratology

In this section, we review the analytic strategies with narratology and life history. Especially with analysis of symbols and text within these traditions, we encourage you to immerse yourself in the literature of your field related to these approaches, as there are many creative and innovative analytic strategies continually being developed. After reviewing data analysis for these two traditions, complete Activity 11.4.

### Life History
The life history tradition describes an individual's entire life within a broader social context, identifying personal meanings individuals give to their social experiences (Bhattacharya, 2017). Data analysis with biography focuses on the life events and experiences of participants.

Creswell and Poth (2017) outline six steps for analysis of the data within this tradition. We will use an example of a life history of an expert in trauma in order to bring these steps to life. In the first step, they encourage the researcher to *organize data files* into a framework that will facilitate coding. For our example, we may have a series of interviews with the expert themselves in addition to interviews with their peers, clients, and trainees. A natural organizing strategy might be to organize the interview transcripts according to the type of person being interviewed (i.e., peer, client, or trainee). In the second step of data analysis, the qualitative researchers comb through the transcripts to *identify broad codes or domains* identified. For the biography of a trauma expert, we might have identified broad codes in the interviews with their clients as including empowerment interventions, attention to interpersonal skills, and cultivation of hope.

For the third step of data analysis, Creswell and Poth (2017) discuss the importance of *description*. This description should focus on the chronology of the participant's experiences in life. With our example, this might entail describing the critical incidents the participant identified as pivotal in the development of their interest in trauma, such as witnessing a traumatic event within her family and/or surviving a traumatic event themselves. The fourth step involves pinpointing the stories, or **epiphanies**, and any contextual materials of the participant's life. For our trauma expert, this could mean identifying stories they tell about their own trauma practice with clients. We might also describe epiphanies they have had in the development of their trauma experience, such as a particular mentoring or training experience. Then we could explore the contextual materials of these stories and epiphanies that have shaped them (e.g., influential texts they read or cultural artifacts in their life).

In the fifth step, Creswell and Poth (2017) encourage the researcher to *work toward a theory—* or a framework—that serves as an organizing structure containing the patterns and meanings the researcher has identified in the data analysis. In our example, we might have identified patterns and meanings of "rebirth" after tragic circumstances or resilience in the face of adversity. Thus, an organizing structure of resilience might be the framework or theory we propose in which we are able to describe the many subthemes within the biography. Finally, in the sixth step, the researcher expands the theory or framework in the fifth step to highlight both the distinct and more ordinary *aspects of the participant's life*. Back to our example, the biography of our trauma expert might describe both the everyday and extraordinary experiences of resilience within their life.

## Narratology

Narratology, or narrative analysis, seeks to understand what stories or narratives reveal about an individual, as the ways in which stories are told—and to whom—communicates critical information about the individual (Clandinin et al., 2018). Narrative data analysis, thus, is the process of identifying explicit and latent themes within narratives or stories.

We highlight Avdi and Georgaca's (2007) review of narrative data analysis techniques used in examining psychotherapy because of the specificity of the steps of data analysis in their review. The authors note five types of analytic approaches that have been used to examine details of client narratives. These five types are distinct in terms of the focus of their data analysis.

First is an approach involving general analysis of themes in the client narrative, or **thematic analysis**. This is a method where the researcher identifies central themes and their subthemes and tracks their development across counseling sessions. Avdi and Georgaca (2007) discuss studies that use this analytic technique to note a larger storyline in which these themes and subthemes are subsumed. Other approaches might include analyzing critical incidents within therapy sessions or examining the data for interpersonal and interpersonal processes within various modalities of psychotherapy.

The second approach entails investigations into the typology of clients' narratives, or **typological analysis**. *Typology* refers to a type of presenting issue clients may bring in to psychotherapy. They cite Dimaggio and Semerari's (2001) distinguishment between "effective" and "ineffective" narratives that are categorized based on the level of organization, integration, and assessment of meaning, coherence, and continuity of clients' narratives. In this type of analysis, Avdi and Georgaca (2007) note the focus is on the individual client narrative more than the interaction within psychotherapy or the content.

The third type the authors discuss is less common: data analysis that takes a dialogical approach of a client narrative, or **dialogical analysis**. They cite Lysaker et al.'s (2003) study of narratives of clients living with schizophrenia. Their focus was on where the dialogue failed within psychotherapy and was evidence of a lack of organization of the narrative or lack of interaction. Avid and Georgaca (2007) see this type of narrative data analysis as promising for noticing positive change in psychotherapy and suggest a focus on the psychotherapist's role in the discourse as well.

Fourth, Avdi and Georgaca (2007) review studies that emphasize the processes within the client narratives themselves, termed the **narrative process coding system** (NPCS; Angus et al., 1999). There are three analytic techniques within NPCS. The first is *external narrative sequences*, which describe events. The second is *internal narrative sequences*, which build on a description of clients' subjective experiences (e.g., thoughts and emotions) and expand these descriptions. The third are *reflexive narrative sequences*, which analyze the meaning of client narratives. These three analytic techniques enable "the researcher to track shifts both in the topics discussed and in the types of narrative processes involved in a client narrative, within and across sessions" (Avdi & Georgaca, 2007, p. 413).

Fifth, Avdi and Georgaca (2007) review a diverse group of studies whose focus of the narrative data analysis is on the whole client narrative, or **whole client narrative analysis**. The authors assert these studies are similar to case study data analysis, where the emphasis is on analysis that illuminates the entire "case" of the narrative rather than its diverse parts. They cite McLeod and Lynch's (2000) study of a female client's narrative of the satisfaction she experiences with her life as she copes with depression. The analysis focuses not only on the client's narratives and perspective but also on those of the psychotherapist—and how both intersect with one another to build a "whole" client narrative.

Kelly and Howie (2007) also outline steps for narrative data analysis in a study they conducted with psychiatric nurses and Gestalt therapy training. Their data analysis entailed eight steps:

1. connecting with the participant's story
2. attention to Dollard's (1946) life history
3. chronological ordering of events and experiences
4. core story creation
5. verification of core stories
6. examination of plots and subplots to identify a theme that discloses their significance
7. examination of plot structure
8. emplotted whole narratives (Kelly & Howie, 2007, pp. 139–141)

Some of the above steps for analysis will sound familiar to you from other analytic techniques we have reviewed. In Step 1 Kelly and Howie (2007) immersed themselves in the data through reading and rereading the transcripts and listening to original audiotapes to become immersed in the data. Step 2 involved examining the data through the lens of Dollard's (1946) life history analytic techniques to identify the narrative development of cultural context, character values, key players, actions and decisions of character, plotlines, history, and the beginning, middle, and end of the narrative. Step 3 involves using the chronology of the narrative to analyze the narrative. The authors color coded sections of the transcripts according to events during, before, and after the Gestalt therapy training. Step 4 involved the core story creation, which included identifying thematic fragments and subplots of four stories. In Step 5 the authors share the four identified core stories with their participants to determine the accuracy of the data analysis within the narratives. In Step 6 they investigated the plots and subplots to determine the meaning and significance of the narratives. Step 7 focused in on the plot structure, returning to the core stories in a microscopic manner. The authors used diagrams to break down each core story and identify major influences on the plot. Finally, Step 8 involved restructuring the four core stories they identified in order to create an entire whole narrative that subsumed them all. In the final version of their manuscript, the authors provided an example of a core story—the story of Mary—as a whole narrative example.

We have presented two strategies for narrative data analysis. Let's turn to Activity 11.3 to practice analyzing narrative data.

## ACTIVITY 11.3. NARRATIVE DATA ANALYSIS

Select a popular children's book and analyze the narrative using one or both of the narrative data analysis strategies discussed in this chapter. (Decide as a class what a possible research question could be to guide the analysis.) Work in small groups to discuss some of the benefits and challenges of narrative data analysis. Discuss your analysis as a class. How might it be useful for a research topic in counseling or education?

**ACTIVITY 11.4.** DATA ANALYSIS WITH SYMBOLS AND TEXT

In your research teams, answer the following questions:

1. What are the strengths and challenges of life history and narrative data analysis for your research topic?
2. What type of research team would you want to build for each of these two traditions? Would your research team differ or be the same in each tradition?
3. What are the similarities and differences you see across life history and narrative data analysis?
4. If you have already collected and analyzed your data from a symbols and text research tradition, how might you return to your analysis and refine it based on your discussion within your group?

## Qualitative Data Analysis of Cultural Expressions of Process and Experience: Ethnography, Ethnomethodology, and Autoethnography

As noted in Chapter 4, examining norms within a culture-sharing group is a key feature of this cluster. In this section, we explore data analysis with ethnography, ethnomethodology, and autoethnography. There are several similarities in the philosophies of the three traditions because they are each seeking to understand cultural aspects. Let's review the distinctions in data analysis in each. See Table 11.5 for tips on data analysis with culture-sharing groups in ethnography, ethnomethodology, and autoethnography.

**TABLE 11.5**  Tips for the Data Analysis Road with Culture-Sharing Groups

- Address the context of the culture-sharing group. If you select not to do so, have a strong rationale for this decision.
- Keep the purpose of your study at the forefront of your mind. What are you seeking to describe, and why?
- Select an order or framework for describing the culture-sharing group and/or your relationship to it. Note how chronology, sequence of events, critical incidents, and so forth will structure your description.
- Triangulate data sources (e.g., transcripts, records, artifacts) in your analysis.
- Look for variation within your description. Where are the "tensions" or inconsistencies within the culture-sharing group?
- Use general coding techniques throughout your analysis to stay organized.
- Do not forget to analyze and code your own researcher reflexivity. Reflect on your degree of cultural competency as you make sense of the data.

## Ethnography

Like other research traditions, ethnographic data analysis—at its best—should have recursivity built into the data collection and analysis. Therefore, the ethnographer begins data analysis immediately. Immersing oneself in the data, the ethnographer then *identifies broad patterns*, or categories that exemplify the culture-sharing group. As these categories and patterns are identified, the ethnographer then refines them by *seeking exemplar data* that "tell the story" of a culture-sharing group. Ethnographic data collection—much like case study data collection—may entail a variety of data sources, from interviews, participant observations, and focus groups to public and personal documents and other artifacts relevant to understanding the culture.

Creswell and Poth (2017) identify three data analysis techniques as important for ethnographic design: description, analysis, and interpretation of a culture-sharing group. First, the ethnographer uses *description* by using a chronological, sequential, or some other type of "order" to describe a culture-sharing group. This might remind you of some of the techniques used in case study data analysis. It should because the approaches share a similar goal: to describe the main events, occurrences, interactions, perspectives, key players, storylines, and so on of a culture-sharing group. Say you are conducting an ethnography of graduate students in a qualitative course. (You might have already wondered about conducting a similar study of your own class experience—we sure did!) The order could be framed by the syllabus, progression of topics introduced, themes in class discussions, group dynamics (e.g., who speaks when, how class participation occurs), and/or on other frameworks that would help you the most as an ethnographer to understand the culture of that graduate qualitative class.

Once you have decided on the most appropriate order in which to describe the data, you will begin **analysis,** which is a sorting procedure that involves highlighting specific material introduced in the descriptive phase or displaying findings through tables, charts, diagrams, and figures. This is a stage of data analysis where you might find yourself using more general qualitative data analytic tools, such as identifying patterns in the data (Creswell & Poth, 2017). It can be important to identify these patterns not just within the culture-sharing group, such as within our qualitative research class example above, but also in terms of comparing the cultural group to others, evaluating the group in terms of standards, and drawing connections and distinctions between the culture-sharing group and larger theoretical frameworks.

Applying this analysis to our example (i.e., an ethnography of a graduate qualitative course) might build on the description of the phenomenon and examine what patterns the ethnographer notes across data sources. You might use some of the data management techniques discussed in Chapter 10, such as case displays or concept mapping, to track these patterns. Examining the patterns in your reflexive journal, comparing the course to another very similar or opposite course, and identifying connections within the patterns might be important to elucidate the culture-sharing group. As the analysis continues to build the description of the culture-sharing group, there may also be patterns and/or themes you notice as an ethnographer that demand future study or suggest a restructuring of an ethnography of this group. For instance, maybe you notice the culture of this qualitative class is influenced by fatigue due to it being held in a shortened semester, and you note a longer semester might allow more of the culture-sharing group to be studied. Really, when you are conducting ethnography, it is the content and process of the culture-sharing group you are analyzing—in addition to your role as a researcher.

How will you analyze your role and influence in the research process when conducting an ethnography? This brings us to the idea of the "insider" versus "outsider" discussion regarding ethnography. Dwyer and Buckle (2009) assert the discussion of whether researchers should share "insider" status with their participants is not a dichotomous question. We agree, so if you are conducting ethnographic analysis, be sure to analyze your perspective and the space you occupy as a researcher along the insider–outsider continuum. It is typically not an either-or situation. Dyer and Buckle (2009) share:

> There are complexities inherent in occupying the space between. Perhaps, as researchers we can only ever occupy the space between. We may be closer to the insider position or closer to the outsider position, but because our perspective is shaped by our position or closer to our position as a researcher (which includes having read much literature on the research topic), we cannot fully occupy one or the other of those positions. (p. 67)

Hammersley and Atkinson (2007) assert ethnographic analysis should also seek to examine the situated meanings of a culture-sharing group. **Situated meanings** refers to the ways that a local culture experiences and makes meaning of the events within their group. The authors also note triangulation of data sources (i.e., comparing data from different chronological stages of data collection and various settings within the culture-sharing group) is important.

We also encourage you to consider Agar's (2006) discussion of the five parameters of an ethnography that we think can help guide your data analysis. First, he discusses *control*. This refers to whether you as a researcher have more of a tendency to "take charge" or "go with the flow" (Agar, 2006, p. 7) in your approach to data analysis. Second, he discusses the *focus* of your ethnographic study. Staying on course with that focus during your data analysis is critical. Third, he discusses the *scale* of your ethnography. Are you interested in an in-depth examination of a particular phenomenon (e.g., individual experiences) or are you seeking a more global or broad understanding of your topic? Fourth, the *events* of your ethnography can guide your data analysis. Are you examining one event in one setting or multiple settings and multiple people interacting in those settings? Finally, Agar discusses *event links*, which involves the recognition that events are particularly situated in time and can be influenced both backwards and forwards in time and space. How might this be important for analyzing your data? Case Example 11.4 illustrates ethnographic data analysis.

## Case Example 11.4. School Counseling in Barbados

Griffin and Bryan (2021) conducted an ethnography of five school counselors' roles, practices, challenges, and demands in Barbados. Through multiple interviews with and observations of each participant, they triangulated data methods and sources and immersed themselves at each school counseling site for 10–15 days. They identified the following themes: roles, responsibilities, and requirements; problematizing the policies, politics, and culture; and schoolfamilycommunity contexts.

Ethnographic analysis involved the following, moving from seeking exemplar data, to description and analysis, to telling a story about school counseling in Barbados. Specifically, they noted the following analysis steps:

- taking time to know the data well by repeated reading of the data, searching for patterns and meaning
- generating initial codes, coding the data inclusively for as many themes/patterns as possible
- finding themes, sorting and combining codes into larger themes and subthemes
- reviewing and refining the themes
- defining and labeling the themes, creating the thematic map and description of each theme
- creating this report after member checking, weaving together theme definitions, and selecting illustrative data elements into an analytic narrative (Griffin & Bryan, 2021, p. 6)

Source: Griffin, D. M., & Bryan, J. (2021). A qualitative study of school counseling in Barbados: A focused ethnography. *International Journal for the Advancement of Counselling, 43,* 424–445. https://doi.org/10.1007/s10447-021-09445-x

## Ethnomethodology

Ethnomethodology is the study of the "everydayness" of social activities, including conversations and speech patterns (de Montigny, 2020). In ethnomethodological analysis, qualitative researchers prioritize conversation text in analysis (i.e., *conversation analysis*; Sacks, 1995) rather than the interpretation of context surrounding the text in order to stay close to the details of the text. As such, they identify critical sequential events and meaningful interactions, asking questions of the text to fine-tune data analysis. Thus, questions may be asked of the data during analysis to fine-tune ways the data can "answer" these questions to illuminate the phenomenon studied. Review the following excerpt from de Kok's (2008) study in Malawai with women and men on the issue of infertility:

Recordings of interviews were transcribe verbatim, according to a simplified version of the standard [conversation analysis] transcription notation. ... In order to be able to examine the sequential organization of talk and the co-construction of meaning, I obtained translations of the interactions between interpreters and respondents (displayed in the extracts in italics). After reading and re-reading the transcripts, I coded the interviews provisionally, based on content, utterance design (i.e., kids of words, phrases or examples used), or actions performed (e.g., "discarding responsibility").

Preliminary analysis of the data drew my attention to recurrent reference to the cultural content. I therefore selected extracts in which explicit references to the cultural context. I therefore selected extracts in which explicit reference was made to "culture," "tradition," "society" or "community" for more detailed analysis, leaving out extracts in which the interviewer explicitly asked about cultural or traditional issues.

I used several "tools" in the analysis. First, I asked certain questions of the data, such as "what is the participant doing in this turn?" ... and "why this (utterance/ phrase/action) now?" ... Second, I made use of findings regarding discursive devices and their functions as reported in the discourse analysis and conversation analysis literature. Third, I paid attention to deviant cases; if a particular extract did not fit in with an analytic claim, I adjusted the claim in order to account for the anomaly, unless certain features in the extracts made them recognizably different from the "average" extract. ... Throughout the analysis I adhered to the principle that claims should be based on the participants' orientations and interpretations as displayed in their utterances. (p. 891)

In Chapter 4, we highlighted four frames to consider in conversation analysis (ten Have, 2007). To illustrate these four frames, we use a hypothetical study examining seventh graders' conversations during a group project in a science classroom. The use of any of these frames is referred to by ten Have (2007) as **summary formulation**: segments of conversational text that were transcribed verbatim to identify and describe a summary formulation. In the study example, the formulation can include general observations of interactions and patterns as each group worked together on the science project, citing atypical patterns or interactions to detail typical group interaction patterns.

- *turn-taking organization*: Conversations are observed to attend specifically to how turn-taking occurs within the group interactions. What are the points in which conversations about the group project shift to new speakers, and why? Who is taking turns to speak and lead the group project?
- *sequence organization:* attention to who initiates a new conversation and how conversation topics are introduced and in what order. How are topics about the group project sequenced? What are the demographics of those who initiate new conversation topics?
- *repair organization:* forgoing taking up an issue within a conversation. Are there instances where leadership conflicts are avoided during the group project? Is there evidence of groupthink during the collaboration?
- *organization of turn design:* examination of the overall organizational structure of interactions. As a whole conversation, how do speakers and listeners move through their work on the group project?

## Autoethnography

Autoethnography may typically be thought of as solely the autobiography of the ethnographer, an approach that systematically explores the researcher's or researchers' personal experience (*auto*) in relation to a larger sociocultural context (*ethno*) through reflexive and critical representation (*graphy*; Hughes & Pennington, 2017).

The data analysis techniques used in ethnography apply to autoethnography. The difference is that the aim of autoethnographic data analysis is to produce a descriptive narrative about the relationship of the ethnographer to the phenomenon. Because autoethnography can range in its focus—from a more "objective" (entailing attention to the details and facts) stance of the researcher to a more "subjective" description of the relationships between researcher and phenomenon (entailing attention to feelings)—the focus of data analysis will necessarily be distinct depending on the researcher focus (Anderson, 2006). Duncan (2004) urges, however, autoethnographers to not give over to feelings in autoethnography but rather to have authenticity about one's motivations to conduct an autoethnography and to locate the researcher's experience within a theoretical framework to increase the quality of data analysis. Wall (2008) notes the challenges in data analysis of autoethnography, including the degree of honesty and authenticity, or what she terms as "acceptability," both within academia and with her own self with regard to her autoethnography.

Hughes and Pennington's (2007) investigation of using autoethnography as a technique used with White preservice teachers in elementary schools working with students of color is a wonderful example of addressing some of the challenges mentioned above. She used critical race theory as a theoretical framework to analyze her own racism in the classroom and her experiences as both an educator and a researcher. She used her theoretical framework, critical race theory, to situate explorations of counternarratives of racism. Pennington also uses her own researcher reflexivity to describe her relationship to the topic: racism and preservice elementary school teachers. Guided by her theory and research tradition, she stays on course with her topic through self-analysis and description of the interaction between her own culture and the culture-sharing group of students and teachers. She writes, "I used myself to understand my participants. I used the similarities we shared, our skin color, our background as White women, and our placement in a school and community of color to provoke and process the discussions about race" (Pennington, 2007, p. 107).

## Qualitative Data Analysis When Research Is a Change Agent: Participatory Action Research and Community-Based Participatory Research

Although social change and empowerment can characterize research traditions discussed in the four clusters above, this cluster's tradition explicitly seeks to create and/or empower participant and community change. See Activity 11.5 to reflect on design decisions and Table 11.6 for a list of tips for data analysis steps for the participatory action research and community-based participatory research traditions.

### Participatory Action Research

Participatory action research (PAR) has three common elements: an emphasis on utility, use of diverse methods, and focus on collaboration (Stoecker, 2018). Like case study analysis, the management and analysis of data is often immense and comes from a variety of sources.

**ACTIVITY 11.5.** BUILDING ACTION COMPONENTS INTO YOUR RESEARCH DESIGN

IIn your research groups, answer the following questions:

1. How would your research topic change (or not) with a PAR or CBPR design?
2. Are there action components you could add into your study based on what you have learned about the purpose, focus, and outcome of PAR or CBPR?
3. What do you think are the challenges to PAR in terms of managing your influence and power as a researcher using PAR or CBPR techniques?
4. "Empowerment" is a word that is often misunderstood. We do not believe you empower people but rather create spaces where participants empower themselves. How might your research—whether a PAR or CBPR design or not—create spaces with the potential for empowerment and change?
5. If you have already collected and analyzed your data using a PAR or CBPR tradition, how might you return to your analysis and refine it based on your discussion within your group?

Just as a case study must endeavor to stay true to the case and not veer off course to data analysis that might be interesting, PAR data analysis must not lose its focus on its action, community and/or stakeholder involvement, and change. For instance, in a PAR study seeking to increase advocacy for a group of people with intellectual disabilities, participants were invited to be important players in each step of the data analysis, identify sites of change in the systems in which they were involved during data analysis, and take action steps during the process of data analysis. In this manner, developing your data analysis strategy in a PAR study must build in some flexibility so you can build in numerous places for you to collaboratively analyze data with your participants.

Another aspect of PAR data analysis is **critical reflection**, described in Chapter 4. Critical reflection, in which qualitative researchers turn inward to consider their positionality and researcher subjectivity (Wood, 2019). In addition to maximizing researcher reflexivity during a PAR study, critical reflection done before, during, and after the research process can create spaces in the research design to further empower participants and communities to enact change. Essentially, it helps qualitative researchers limit influence on the study that can hinder development and evaluation of various action steps. Therefore, a guiding force of data analysis includes ensuring there are periods of time where reflection is recursively built into the data collection, action, and analysis process. See Figure 11.4 for Riel's (2007) visual portrayal of progressive problem-solving with action research.

Like many other qualitative research traditions, data collection and analysis should be recursive. We believe it is best to have key informants from the community you are working with on your research team. However, this is not always possible. If it is not, a key initial decision in your data analysis will be to identify how you will integrate participant voices into the data analysis process. Often, the dialogue or reflection session is used to create a space where

**TABLE 11.6**  Tips for the Road of Data Analysis in PAR and CBPR Designs

- Your participants should be guiding your data analysis, optimally in person as an integral member of the research team. If this is not possible, collaboratively identify with your participants and/or community how you will integrate their voices into the data analysis.
- Strongly consider a dialogue or reflection meeting where an exchange of knowledge is conducted. Bring your expertise and ideas for the study and present various potential ways to collect and analyze data. Then be quiet and listen to your participants and/or community partners as they discuss their ideas and needs for social change. Let this discussion guide your data analysis plan.
- Be flexible. Once you collaboratively identify the best data analysis plan for your PAR or CBPR study, the subsequent actions and research involved may demand changes. Flexibility does not mean throwing all your plans out the window. Being flexible means you should collaboratively identify ways you and your participants will identify how to address challenges—both expected and unexpected—along the way.
- Analyze the process, not just the outcome, of your PAR or CBPR study. If you focus on an end "result," you may not only be disappointed but also likely miss out on opportunities to use data analysis of the process to inform the subsequent actions needed to produce social change.
- Collaboratively identify local cultural/contextual variables of the setting the change will be located in, for these variables may provide a more structured framework for data analysis.
- Use the following questions to guide your data analysis: How is this PAR or CBPR producing change? What are the opportunities for change based on individual or community needs and how is this occurring in the study? What are the barriers and facilitators for change in the study?
- Determine early in the process how you will collaboratively decide when the data analysis will end. Have a specific discussion about this with your stakeholders. You do not have to have a magic ball to do this; just brainstorm with them indicators that the data analysis will be complete.
- Are there analytic strategies that make more sense for the social change the PAR or CBPR study is seeking to affect?
- Be sure to bring all your organizing skills to a study. You may be the person with the best ability to ensure the products and processes of the data collection and analysis are brought to research meetings, dialogue and reflection sessions, and other aspects of the action research.

participants speak with one another and the researcher about the actions they are planning and/or implementing and the experiences they are having in the process.

These sessions can also be spaces where data analysis is simultaneously conducted within the session itself. For instance, if your PAR study is a peer-led intervention in middle schools on decreasing bullying and violence in school, your reflection and dialogue sessions may entail planning, identifying sites of change, and reporting on activities from participants and researchers. Within this meeting, the researcher can also present data—whether they are broad domains the researcher and/or research team is identifying about the change process within the school or analysis of the participation levels of each individual in the PAR sessions—and invite analysis in that moment.

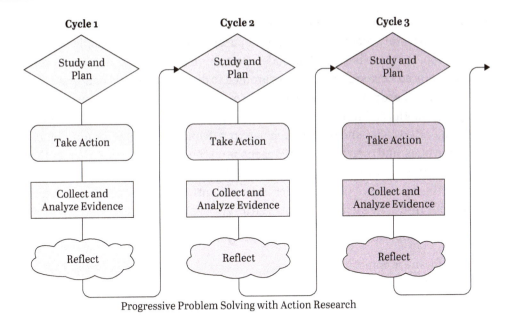

**Cycle 1**       **Cycle 2**       **Cycle 3**

Study and Plan

Take Action

Collect and Analyze Evidence

Reflect

Progressive Problem Solving with Action Research

**FIGURE 11.4** Riel's (2007) Visual Portrayal of Progressive Problem Solving with Action Research

Because of the level of involvement of the researcher *and* participants in PAR designs, the researcher must be well-organized and track how the collaborative partnership is analyzing data because the participants may already be overtaxed by the systems in which they are working. Whereas in other research traditions, the researcher decides when the data analysis ends (e.g., reaching saturation in grounded theory approaches or illuminating the boundaries of a case study), best practices in PAR should really follow the will and experiences of the participants and/or community in deciding when data analysis should end. Kidd and Kral (2005) remind those engaging in PAR that "the interaction of PAR with local culture can itself be a source of study along with the more specific course and outcome of groups' efforts" (p. 188).

Nastasi et al. (2000) note that these *cultural/contextual variables* specific to this local culture should drive the data collection and analysis. Therefore, collaboratively identifying these variables can be an important way to frame PAR data analysis. We would like to add that data analysis with PAR may borrow analytic strategies from other traditions when it makes sense for the goal of PAR's aim toward social change. See Case Example 11.5 for an excerpt from a PAR manuscript describing its approach to data analysis.

## Case Example 11.5. Family-School Participatory Action Research

As a first step toward organizing the data, three members of the research team analyzed the responses independently. Each survey that had a written response was counted as one response. This step of the process involved each member reading over the comments several times while keeping a separate running list of major ideas. A primitive step of the process involved each member reading over the comments several times while keeping a separate running list of major ideas. As a second step, the three independent coders compared their lists, and the numerous codes generated were systematically examined to discern emerging patterns. They transformed these patterns into categories or themes based on inductive content analysis guidelines. This process involved the coders first sharing and discussing their generated codes and the frequency, extensiveness, intensity, or uniqueness of certain ones, and then obtaining consensus on the most important themes that emerged from this discussion. For the third step, these themes were used for the final sorting of comments; each coder independently sorted the comments based on the four mutually identified themes. (Ho, 2002, p. 109)

The four themes identified in this PAR data analysis were:

- requests for more communication
- requests for information on ways to help their children
- expressed satisfaction with school
- requests for special parental consideration (p. 111)

These themes were organized with other data by the school psychologist in the study and shared with the community. The research team met with stakeholders to identify action steps for family-school partnerships, which included:

1. Develop mechanisms for decreasing language, cultural, and overall communication barriers to improve parents' involvement with the school.
2. Increase efforts to help parents become involved in reading and learning activities at home.
3. Increase opportunities for communication with parents about their individual child's educational progress and needs, and to provide families with resources. (p. 111)

Source: Ho, B. S. (2002). Application of participatory action research to family-school intervention. *School Psychology Review, 31*(1), 106–121.

## Community-Based Participatory Research

Community-based participatory research (CBPR) attends to the colonizing aspects of research, seeking to recalibrate relationships between academicians and local communities (Jacquez et al., 2013). Thus, data analysis using this tradition prioritizes collaboration and transformative healing and ensures research is relevant and responds to community priorities.

Indigenous research methods can be a useful framework for CBPR analysis. As Smith (2012) notes, researchers are "to get the story right and tell the story well" (p. 217). The story is at the community level, and qualitative researchers work with community members to tell a story that has not been told or told well and collaborate with community members on concerns or areas where change is needed to empower the community and co-create space for the community to thrive.

**WILD CARD 11.1.** CAUTIONS FOR THE DATA ANALYSIS "ROAD"

Here are a few general tips for you across the research traditions for data analysis:

1. Stay on course with your research tradition: How is it guiding your data analysis?
2. Balance your expertise and your power of interpretation with listening to the voices of your participants and data.
3. Ask different questions of your data. It is not a bad thing if your data has different—and even diverging—evidence within it. Variation is a good thing in data analysis: It helps you more fully represent your data.
4. Do not be haphazard in selecting data analysis approaches. Know why an approach is the best fit for your topic. This may mean a blend across traditions, but have a strong rationale for doing this!
5. Do not rely on one qualitative text (even ours!) to teach you about data analysis. Use this book to get your repertoire of data analysis techniques down. Then read, read, and read some more about how data analysis is conducted within your field and across disciplines, not just with your topic but also with your research tradition.
6. Do not throw in the towel during data analysis! This is a time to persevere, endeavor to do your best quality work, and challenge yourself. If your study is a marathon, the data analysis might feel like the point you "hit the wall" and your roll might begin to slow. Get reenergized and pour that energy into your analysis.
7. Be creative. Despite all the data analysis techniques we have discussed, there might not be a specific answer or guide in how to analyze a particular piece of data. Consider the general analytic techniques (e.g., coding, identifying themes, triangulation, etc.). You may have to supplement these with a creative approach that makes sense for your data.
8. Be open to pausing your active data analysis to return to data collection if your data is requiring this. Repeat after us: Recursivity! Recursivity! Recursivity!
9. Do not get overwhelmed by all the different terms used for data analysis techniques across the research traditions. Turn that anxiety into energy and get to know the similarities and differences in data analysis in each. You will not only will learn more about the tradition you are using but also become a better qualitative researcher!
10. Do not forget to analyze your own researcher reflexivity. Yes, we know you have already acknowledged your biases and assumptions at the beginning of your study. But good analysis demands we analyze how and why we are examining certain aspects of data and not others; it matters in terms of where our analysis ends up!

Chilisa (2020) identified these key considerations within CBPR:

- Community members are involved regarding the interpretation of the findings within the local social and cultural context.
- Because data interpretations between qualitative researchers and community members likely differ, negotiation in data analysis and reporting will likely occur.
- Indigenous analytical frameworks are to be used during data analysis.
- Identified themes and patterns should reflect Indigenous ways of knowing, limiting the tendency to have the researched speak through concepts and language of traditional theories.

In addition to these considerations, we invite you to revisit the discussion of Indigenous research paradigms and ethics in Chapters 2 and 3, respectively.

## Postscript: A Final Note on Qualitative Data Analysis

We have spent a good deal of time reviewing the tools each research traditions uses for analysis. Corbin and Strauss (2015) discuss the importance of embracing the researcher's role in the interpretation of one's data analysis. They acknowledge beginning qualitative researchers can shy away from the power of interpretation, feeling nervous about being "off" in their analysis of the data. Corbin and Strauss agree data analysis will range in regard to quality of standards. However, they encourage researchers to "push forward with analysis. With [analysis], we have more to gain than we have to lose" (Corbin & Strauss, 2015, p. 49). We wholeheartedly agree. Make sure you are an ethical researcher, staying close and true to the data you have collected as you interpret.

There will be also come a time when you must "abandon" your interpretation by deciding your analysis is at a stopping point. Notice we did not say you will reach a point where you will be "done" with your analysis. The process of data analysis and interpretation is a process that actually has no endpoint. And so it will feel like you are abandoning your data. And you are. However, you as the researcher should be abandoning with full disclosure of when, how, and why your decisions are the right ones for your study and are guided (you should be able to predict what we will say next!) by your research tradition, theoretical framework, knowledge of your data, and analytical skills. That is when your interpretation ends ... for now.

## CHAPTER SUMMARY

In this chapter, we have traveled the long road of data analysis, identifying the unique similarities and differences in approaches to handling data across the research traditions. Each of the research traditions has some version of categorizing data and "cooking" them down into a description or portrayal that illuminates a phenomenon. However, it is the philosophy of each of the traditions that becomes evident in *how* that categorization occurs. So, we have provided numerous examples from studies using the analytic techniques so you can get a picture of what the data analysis may look like for your study.

We began this chapter discussing data analysis strategies for the hybrid tradition: the case study. With the case study, we emphasized the importance of having the case itself lead the data analysis and cautioned against veering off into analytic directions that might be interesting influences on the case but that do not elucidate the case itself. Then we reviewed analytic strategies used in experience and theory formulation. Data analytic strategies for grounded theory, phenomenology, heuristic inquiry, and CQR focus on using a variety of coding methods designed to identify a theory of or the essence and meaning of a phenomenon for participants. Next, we reviewed data analysis with symbols and text. These analytic approaches also used coding strategies as well but typically had a focus on narrative analysis, building a structure for analysis (whether by chronology of events, time, etc.), and/or using the generic coding methods discussed in Chapter 10. We explored cultural expressions of process and experience with ethnography, ethnomethodology, and autoethnography and identified the unique analytic approaches between the three involving the role and perspective of the researcher and the analysis of contextual or cultural influences. Finally, we discussed data analysis used as a change agent in PAR and CBPR designs, where the process of analysis is guided by social action and, ideally, analytic collaboration with key stakeholders.

**TABLE 11.7**  Qualitative Data Analysis Steps by Research Tradition

| Research tradition | Central principle | Step 5: Code | Step 6: Identify themes and patterns | Step 7: Create a codebook | Step 8: Develop a main narrative or theory |
|---|---|---|---|---|---|
| Case study | Case description (how or why the case is or what or when the case is) | Pattern matching (Yin, 2017); categorical aggregation and direct interpretation (Stake, 1995, 2006) | Explanation building, logic models, and cross-case synthesis (Yin, 2017); pattern identification and naturalistic generalization (Stake, 1995, 2006) | Identify case components. | Theory development and verification (Yin, 2017); holistic case description (Stake, 1995, 2006) |
| Grounded theory | Theory development | Open coding (Strauss & Corbin, 2015); initial coding (Charmaz, 2014) | Axial coding and selective coding (Strauss & Corbin, 2015); focused coding (Charmaz, 2014); theoretical coding (Charmaz, 2014; Glaser, 1978) | Constant comparison and saturation | Theoretical modeling describing a core idea, causal and intervening conditions, context, action strategies, and consequences |
| Phenomenology | Essence of participant's direct experience of phenomenon | Invariant meaning units (Giorgi, 1985); horizontalization (Moustakas, 1994); descriptive, linguistic, and conceptual comments (Smith et al., 2012) | Textural and structural description (Moustakas, 1994); charting/mapping, abstraction, subsumption, and polarization (Smith et al., 2012) | Clustered meaning units | Develop an invariant structure or composite description of the experience (Moustakas, 1994); develop narrative and infuse researcher voice as patterns across narratives are reported. |

**TABLE 11.7** Qualitative Data Analysis Steps by Research Tradition (continue)

| Research tradition | Central principle | Step 5: Code | Step 6: Identify themes and patterns | Step 7: Create a codebook | Step 8: Develop a main narrative or theory |
|---|---|---|---|---|---|
| **Heuristic inquiry** | Integration of researcher's and participants' lived experience | Immersion, incubation, and illumination (Moustakas, 1990; Sultan, 2018) | Explication (Moustakas, 1990) | Identifying and organizing explications (Moustakas, 1990; Sultan, 2018) | Creative synthesis (Moustakas, 1990) |
| **Consensual qualitative research** | Consensus on experience | Development and coding of domains and researcher consensus (Hill, 2012; Hill et al., 1997, 2005) | Abstraction of core ideas of domains, cross-analysis, and external audit (Hill, 2012; Hill et al., 1997, 2005) | Noting frequencies of categories (general, typical, variant, rare; Hill, 2012; Hill et al., 1997, 2005) | Presentation of phenomenon |
| **Life history** | Participant story within social context | Identifying broad codes and domains (Creswell & Poth, 2017) | Description of chronology epiphanies (Creswell & Poth, 2017) | Create organization structure (Creswell & Poth, 2017). | Expand theory or participant story (Creswell & Poth, 2017). |
| **Narratology** | Narrative plots | Thematic analysis, typological analysis, dialogical analysis, narrative process coding system, and whole client narrative analysis (Avdi & Georgaca, 2007); connect with story and attend to Dollard's (1946) life history (Kelly & Howie, 2007). | Chronological ordering of events and experiences (Kelly & Howie, 2007) | Core story creation, verification of core stories, examination of plots and subplots, and examination of plot structure (Kelly & Howie, 2007) | Emplotted whole narratives (Kelly & Howie, 2007) |

(continue)

**TABLE 11.7** Qualitative Data Analysis Steps by Research Tradition (continue)

| Research tradition | Central principle | Step 5: Code | Step 6: Identify themes and patterns | Step 7: Create a codebook | Step 8: Develop a main narrative or theory |
|---|---|---|---|---|---|
| **Ethnography** | Culture-sharing group | Immersion and seeking exemplar data | Description and analysis through fieldwork and identifying broad patterns | Situated meaning of a culture-sharing group (Hammersley & Atkinson, 2007) | Describe cultural-sharing group. |
| **Ethnomethodology** | Everydayness of social interactions | Immersion in conversation text or interactions observed | Conversation analysis (Sacks, 1995) | Note content and process of interactions (Sacks, 1995). | Develop summary formulation of conversation text (ten Have, 2007). |
| **Autoethnography** | Autobiography of ethnographer(s) | Immersion and seeking exemplar data | Description and analysis through fieldwork and identifying broad patterns | Situated meaning of a culture-sharing group (Hammersley & Atkinson, 2007) | Describe cultural-sharing group. |
| **Participatory action research** | Participant-level change | Critical reflection | Identify themes and reflect on previous actions to create action steps. | Identify cultural/contextual variables. | Act or empower participant to take action and present data to create change for participants. |
| **Community-based participatory research** | Community-level change | Critical reflection and application of Indigenous methods | Identify themes and reflect on previous actions to create action steps. | Identify cultural/contextual variables in consultation with community. | Empower communities for healing and transformation. |

Note. Steps 1–4, discussed in Chapter 10, are excluded because they are similar across research traditions.

## Review Questions

1. Consider a hypothetical study of college students' study abroad experiences in Chile. What outcome for data presentation (i.e., Step 8) might each tradition prioritize?
2. Which research traditions are most likely to have seeking to develop theory as a goal?
3. What similar and distinct features do heuristic inquiry and autoethnography possess?
4. How can qualitative researchers infuse Indigenous research methods and principles in data analysis across the research traditions?
5. What are some of the key cautions regarding qualitative data analysis presented in this chapter?

## Recommended Readings

Corbin, J., & Strauss, A. (2015). Basics of qualitative research: *Techniques and procedures for developing grounded theory* (4th ed.). Sage.

Creswell, J. W., & Poth, C. N. (2017). *Qualitative inquiry and research design: Choosing among five approaches* (4th ed.). Sage.

Hill, C. E. (2012). *Consensual qualitative research: A practical resource for investigating social science phenomena.* American Psychological Association.

Moustakas, C. (1994). *Phenomenological research methods.* Sage.

Smith, L. T. (2012). *Decolonizing methodologies: Research and indigenous peoples* (2nd ed.). Zed Books.

Sultan, N. (2020). Heuristic inquiry: Bridging humanistic research and counseling practice. *Journal of Humanistic Counseling, 59,* 158–172. https://doi.org/10.1002/johc.12142

## Image Credits

# The Qualitative Research Proposal and Report

## CHAPTER 12

# Writing, Presenting, and Funding Qualitative Research

---

## CHAPTER PREVIEW

In this chapter we discuss the fundamentals of writing, presenting, and funding qualitative research. First, we describe foundational writing techniques you will need to convey your study from beginning to end. Next, we explore guidelines for submitting, publishing, and presenting qualitative studies. Finally, we discuss grant-writing strategies to help fund your qualitative research. Throughout the chapter, exercises guide you to assess the quality and basic components in writing, presenting, and funding your research study. Additionally, see Appendix for sample qualitative proposals.

## Writing Qualitative Research

Whether you are developing a research proposal or writing a research report to communicate findings of a qualitative study, it is important to consider your research goals, research questions, and your selected research tradition and paradigm as you approach writing. As discussed in Chapter 5, Maxwell (2013) outlined several research goals that guide our work and involve extricating participant/community meaning and contexts, processes associated with phenomena, descriptive and/or explanatory theories grounded in data, and community-embedded participatory research that can illuminate less explored research areas or center the voices of those typically underserved or even marginalized by previous research. Furthermore, qualitative research questions allow in-depth description, exploration, or explanation of a phenomenon of interest.

Research goals and questions inform and are informed by the selected research tradition and paradigm. With respect to research paradigms, the writer's beliefs regarding the nature of reality (ontology), the extent to which knowledge is constructed and limitless (epistemology), the role of values and the quality of the researcher–participant relationship (axiology), the use of participant versus researcher voice (rhetoric), and the overall methodology link to a variety of research paradigms that impact how the report is constructed (i.e., positivism, postpositivism, social constructivism, feminism, critical race, queer, and Indigenous theory; see Chapter 2). In Chapter 4, we presented several clusters of research traditions. Depending on the selected tradition and paradigm, the qualitative proposal or report may target different audiences (e.g., academic, legislative, general community), center participant and researcher voice differently, and vary in what aspects of the study are thickly described (e.g., in-depth participant experience versus theory development across multiple data sources). Furthermore, manuscripts may be longer than quantitative reports to allow thick description of the methodology and findings.

## Rhetorical Distinctions of Qualitative Research

Later in this chapter, we will discuss available reporting standards for qualitative research (American Psychological Association [APA], 2020b) to guide your qualitative writing. First, there are some features or distinctions that can guide qualitative research. Levitt et al. (2018) highlight three rhetorical distinctions of qualitative research that have implications for the research proposal or report: representation of process rather than standardized section demarcation, an ethic of transparency, and contextualization.

### Process Versus Section Demarcation

Qualitative researchers can present data as a narrative or story, organize data by themes, describe chronological events and processes in the report, use first-person or second-person voice, and so on. To align with your research goals and data and description to maximize trustworthiness, the use of traditional sections of a research proposal or report (e.g., method, findings, discussion) can vary. Furthermore, having fidelity to the study topic and achieving research goals, which can influence how information is best presented to the reader, should be prioritized. While we include writing recommendations and considerations within sections of a report or proposal, keep in mind that these are only guidelines and your final writing product can appear differently.

The way that authors select writing techniques depends on which of the positions they hold about "truth" in qualitative research (see Chapter 7). Do you hold Position 1, the *holy trinity position*, which asserts qualitative research is only a valid approach to the extent it looks like quantitative approaches? From this position, you should select a writing philosophy that seeks to be more similar to typical quantitative proposal writing. You might title your findings section "results," as quantitative writing would use, rather than using a word such as "findings." The latter is a more tentative word implying a discovery-oriented approach as opposed to results, which implies a finality of the research process. If you are more aligned with Position 2, the *translation approach*, your writing will seek to establish the "gold standard" of qualitative research (i.e., credibility, transferability, dependability, and confirmability; Lincoln & Guba, 1995). This gold standard is translated from the quantitative standards of validity and reliability. You might conceptualize this writing approach as helping the reader understand that there are rigorous criteria for evaluating qualitative research, and your proposal will reflect these criteria. For instance, you would provide a definition of "confirmability" and the other gold-standard components. Then you would seek to convey how you accounted for the subjective nature of qualitative research throughout your proposal writing using these components.

Position 2 guides you to use more tentative language than used in Position 1. However, you are still asserting the expertise of the researcher in describing the details of the research process.

Position 3, the *emergence of qualitative criteria position*, asserts qualitative research should have its own emergent definitions of what truth is according to one's individual study. Therefore, proposal writing from this perspective should use language exploring the topic of inquiry from an approach that recognizes that there are many ways to understand—and therefore write—about the phenomenon. For those who identify more with Position 4, which defines "qualitative truth" as relative and changing, one does not look to established criteria for one's writing approach. Position 4 asserts there should be *no consensus of criteria* for qualitative "truth" but rather increased acceptance that these criteria are constantly emerging. We encourage you to carefully consider the four positions and how they might guide your overall approach to your writing. However, we do not encourage to select one approach over another: You might blend these positions in your writing. Ultimately, being aware of your philosophical approach to representing the truth in your writing will be a helpful place to come back to anytime you feel stuck in what language to use to convey your study to your audience.

### Ethic of Transparency

Throughout the text, we have emphasized the importance of thickly describing the role of the qualitative researcher within the research process. This value of *transparency*, or how the researcher influences the data collection and analysis, is communicated in the research proposal and report (Levitt et al., 2018). How did researcher assumptions and their relationship to the topic, participants, and community change throughout the study? Was there a point where you collected data and realized your research question needed to recursively change in its focus? This would be an opportunity to convey this process in detail, using descriptive language to narrate this recursive process to help your audience understand its relevance for your phenomenon of inquiry.

The greater the extent the researcher can describe their role along with how research design changes as a study unfolds, the more trustworthiness is maximized and thus allows the reader to understand the process, findings, and the transferability and applicability of the process and findings. Kline (2008) noted the necessity of articulating

> researchers' prior experiences with and assumptions about the topic being researched, the rationale for the specific qualitative approach used as it relates to the research questions, and the presentation of sampling and data collection methods. In addition, researchers have the responsibility of describing how their biases influenced data analysis and how their relationships with participants affected their interpretation of data and findings. Finally, a rigorously presented manuscript includes implications that findings have for professional practice. (p. 211)

### Contextualization

The context of qualitative research matters, and a quality research proposal or report will highlight the researcher's relationship to the study topic, their relationship with their participants and their community, and the context of the study itself. Thus, *contextualization* refers to describing the phenomena, data sources, and researchers in terms of social location, time, and other characteristics (Levitt et al., 2018). Later in the chapter, we discuss more specifically how to contextualize the qualitative researcher and study setting(s) in the qualitative research proposal or report.

## Procedural Rigor

In Chapter 7, we introduced the term *procedural rigor* to describe how researcher subjectivity influences all components of the research design (Bhattacharya, 2017; Peshkin, 1988). Procedural rigor in the qualitative research proposal and report includes infusing the strategies of trustworthiness and additional strategies outlined in Chapter 7. As part of establishing procedural rigor, there are some additional strategies for writing a quality research proposal or report. These include telling a good story of your study, using researcher and participant voice, and citing relevant scholars. Perspectives 12.1 and Professional Development Activity 12.1 provide reflections and strategies for maximizing procedural rigor in your qualitative research proposal or report.

------------------------------------------------------------------

## PERSPECTIVES 12.1. WRITERS WHO HAVE INFLUENCED OUR QUALITATIVE WORK

I remember clearly when I found that "one" article that inspired me. It actually wasn't a qualitative article. It was a conceptual article on traumatology by Burstow (2003). Because my research agenda was looking at trauma in South Asian communities from a feminist perspective, I had difficulty finding relevant articles that had a resilience perspective. Burstow inspired me with every word she wrote: She was basically calling the entire trauma field to take an empowerment perspective, which was perfect for my literature review and for a good dose of inspiration. For qualitative writers, the two members of my writing group—Stephanie Jones and Corey Johnson—consistently push me to think differently, creatively, and with imagination about the use of words in writing. Reading their work on a regular basis has naturally influenced my writing. Stephanie is in early childhood education and Corey is in recreation and leisure studies, so the added bonus is getting to read across disciplines. I have learned new theories and different writing techniques along the way.

—A. A. S.

There are so many scholars that contribute to how I write up qualitative research! First, the works of Creswell, Miles, Huberman, Lincoln, Guba, Denzin, Lather, and others sprinkled throughout the text indicate that these are some of the major contributors that influence how I conceptualize and participate in qualitative inquiry. Second, Dr. Joel Meyers, one of the scholars we dedicate this book to, serves as a foundational model for me. He is an ethnographer and advocate for educational issues, whose writing not only captures rigorous aspects of a qualitative report, but has findings that directly translate to educational practice. Finally, I cannot forget the importance of promising and budding scholars with which I have the privilege to interact: students in counseling, higher education, and curriculum and instruction. No matter if I am instructing their course and witnessing them develop qualitative projects, or if I am working alongside them on research projects, they remind me of the importance of collaboration, interdisciplinary research, and thinking outside the box in qualitative inquiry. I truly am inspired by them.

—D. G. H.

### Tell a Good "Story" of Your Study

Telling the story of your study, or a cogent and compelling narrative of your findings, is integral to increasing the impact of qualitative research within local and academic communities. If you think of the great storytellers in your life, you can sense that this ability is both a skill and a gift. The gift of telling the story of your study through your writing is either there or it is not. However, fortunately, it is also a skill, especially when it comes to crafting a story through your writing.

This skill may well be among the most important criteria of qualitative writing because it has many implications. A good story should have a beginning, middle, and end. Furthermore, Golden-Biddle and Locke (2007) describe the importance of deciding about the "authorial character" of the researcher. In other words, you as a researcher are a character in your story. So, what authorial decisions will you make as you write to convey yourself as a character/storyteller? The authors discuss the tension that exists and the choices you will have to make along the way as you write. You can be the "character of the institutional scientist, carrying the marks of the Academy" (one end of the continuum) or you may recognize that "personal human depictions are equally crafted as the human scientist" (Golden-Biddle & Locke, 2007, pp. 78–79). Or will you write somewhere in the middle of that continuum?

Wolcott (2008) adds that telling the story of your study includes addressing the problem of focus. He shares that there is indeed a challenge if you are struggling with writing, for instance, a purpose statement. He does encourage people to seek outside support in talking through the focus of the story you will tell about your study. However, we really appreciate that he refers the researcher back to the written word. Rather than seeking to come up with solutions prior to writing, Wolcott sends us back to the paper to use our storytelling to resolve the problem of focus; writing, then, is not framed as the source of the problem in telling the story of your study.

In her discussion of writing the focus of qualitative research, Sandelowski (1993) takes a different approach, emphasizing that one must determine the point of the story. She asserts that quality writing about the story of your research will not happen until you are able to state the story of your study in one sentence. Her rationale is that if you cannot tell the story of your research in one sentence, then you are still unclear on the point of your study. Hmm. We do not think this means you are back to the drawing board if you cannot achieve the story-in-one-sentence task. However, we do think it is a useful organizing tool to ensure the "point" of your study is always in your mind to support the continued (and what Golden-Biddle and Locke [2007] call "theorized") story of your research.

## Researcher and Participant Voice

We discussed the issue of participant voice in qualitative research in Chapter 1 as part of the components of the role of the qualitative researcher. Now, let's revisit that issue so you understand how to write about voice: of yourself as the researcher and of your participants. Prior to writing, you should have decided on the degree to which your voice or the voice of your participants will be presented. As Sandelowski (1998) noted, "This decision involves thorny issues concerning authorial presence and power" (p. 377). It is a serious issue in your writing, however, so own that in making the decision, you are holding power. How does holding this power influence the way you write, what you write about, and the basics of whether you will write in first or third person?

Sandelowski (1998) asserted that qualitative researchers often write that their participants' voices will hold prevalence in the report but fail to deliver, with the researcher's voice still predominating and/or participants' voices being boiled down to one voice. Furthermore, Richardson and Adams St. Pierre (2018) encourage writing a *polyvocal text*, where the writer integrates several points of voice within the report. A polyvocal approach echoes the idea of a "layered text" we discussed previously. Essentially, you want your writing to incorporate the voice of yourself as the researcher and your participants in a format that contrasts the multiple perspectives rather than writing in a singular (e.g., participant voices while neglecting to write your own voice as a researcher) or dichotomous (e.g., delineating sections where you write in your voice from sections where you write participants' voices into your report) manner. We will briefly touch on the politics of publishing in the last section of this chapter, but we do want to acknowledge Sandelowski's implication that writing from a polyvocal stance may be challenging to more traditional journals that still view qualitative research from Position 1 (the holy trinity) or Position 2 (translation of methods). We encourage you to have your decisions in writing about voice in your report be guided by what your conceptual framework and research questions demand of you. For now, engage in Proposal Development Activity 12.1 to explore how the issue of voice will influence your report writing.

 **PROPOSAL DEVELOPMENT ACTIVITY 12.1.** EXPLORING THE USE OF VOICE IN YOUR REPORT

Develop an outline for a research report or proposal that is specific to your selected research tradition(s) and paradigm(s). What type of voice will you use in your write-up? To what degree do you feel that you could thickly describe your findings?

## Citing Relevant Scholars

A significant aspect of telling a good story about your study is having some reference point for your writing. Reference points should include instrumental writers in qualitative research as well as experts in the study topic. Consider scholars within a variety of disciplines and spaces, centering the work of those from marginalized communities.

Let's take this a step further and say that this reference point is an author (or authors) who inspires you. Pratt (2009) explicitly describes this as "modeling someone whose style you like or who consistently publishes qualitative work" (p. 861). He asserts that as the number of strong qualitative studies increases, there are more opportunities to find a diverse array of authors with whom you may resonate in terms of writing style. We would add that this number has increased across disciplines as well, so the typical advantages of reading deeply in the literature across disciplines (e.g., finding similarities and/or differences in how different fields discuss a topic of inquiry) are maximized further when you find a model that inspires you. Pratt cautions that an additional goal of looking for your exemplar writers across disciplines is that journals themselves—because of their individual review processes and related editorial approaches to identifying criteria for evaluating strong qualitative studies—will differ. Later in the chapter, we will share an example of one journal's criteria for qualitative writing. See Perspectives 12.1 for our listing of just some of the writers who have influenced our approach to qualitative writing.

## WILD CARD 12.1. CAUTIONS TO TAKE WHEN WRITING

A large component of writing a quality research proposal or report is making sure you know what *not* to include in your writing. Pratt (2009) called this "wandering down dangerous paths" (p. 857). Here are some cautions to avoid "dangerous paths" in qualitative writing related to casual or dramatic language as well as the use of "ten-dollar words."

In general, avoid using casual or dramatic language—or even using ten-dollar words. Examples of casual writing are "The researcher *wishes* to convey ..." and "The researcher *hopes* to convey ..." You could easily revise these two sentence stems to academic writing: "The researcher *aims* to convey ..." and "The researcher *seeks* to convey ..." As you can see, you really do not have to use ten-dollar words to rewrite casual writing into academic writing. It is a simple—but important—shift in your use of language.

Be cautious in using dramatic language, as it detracts the reader from your content. This might be tough, as it is likely you are passionate about your topic, which might draw you toward more dramatic language. Also, as you build your rationale for studying a phenomenon, you want to invite your audience to see how necessary understanding the phenomenon is for your field. It is fine to write so that you are building the reader's understanding of the need to study a phenomenon. However, as you build your case, you do not want your writing to be so dramatic that, when the audience reads the details of your actual study, they are so distracted that they miss the important components. Using words like "alarming," "frightening," "distressing," or "shocking" are good examples of dramatic language not to use. Instead, more academic writing—if you were describing the prevalence of a problem—might include "increasing," "concerning," or "rising. Even the word "escalating" would be a good compromise word here because it has a hint of the dramatic but would not overshadow the words that come next. Take a look at the difference below and notice what part of the sentence you are drawn to the most. You want your reader's eye to primarily be drawn to the focus of your topic:

> There is a frightening increase in the rates of children who are living in poverty.

versus

> There is an escalating increase in the rates of children who are living in poverty.

Pay attention to where your eye goes as a reader. Ideally, you want to aim for your reader's eye to go to the focus of your topic:

> The representational nature of grounded theory designs mimic episte-mological complications where the interface between researcher and subject are maximized.

Wow! Could you even keep up with the number of ten-dollar words in that sentence? Hopefully, you can see that writing in this manner creates a significant barrier between the author and the audience in terms of understanding *and* that the meaning of the sentence is somewhat lost amidst the verbiage. Next, we revise the above sentence to use more academic language while simultaneously inviting the reader to understand the author's focus:

> The goal of grounded theory designs is to seek the "truth" of what par-ticipants describe as their daily lived experiences of living in poverty. The role of the researcher and the participants is clearly defined in grounded theory studies and requires a collaborative relationship.

As you write, keep in mind Pratt's (2009) five writing paths you do not want to wander down. He discusses two main "perilous paths" that can lead you as a writer down the wrong road (Pratt, 2009, p. 857). First, Pratt describes what he sees often in weak qualitative writing as lacking a balance between theory and data. Pratt's reference to "balance between theory and data" refers to keeping an eye on this balance within the entire qualitative research report. He encourages writers to have a balance between writing about the findings of a study and showing the data to the reader. Additionally, Pratt urges writers not to overly focus on showcasing the data for the reader without using theory to interpret the data.

Richardson and Adams St. Pierre (2018) similarly discuss writing a "layered text" as a way to achieve this balance in your writing and integrate the researcher's voice, your findings, and your conceptual framework throughout your qualitative report. A good way to double-check that you have a balance in your writing between theory and data is to do an actual word count on how often you are talking about both: There should be a rough equivalence (although not exact) between the two. If you are not the type to like this approach, you can also read through your paper (or ask a peer or mentor to do so) while actively holding the questions of "How am I maintaining this balance between theory and data?" and "Where are the instances in my report where I am not maintaining this balance between theory and data?" And, of course, you do not want to merely hold these two questions. You want to identify the answers and make revisions accordingly.

## Form a Writing Group

In Chapter 1, we recommended developing a research team. Forming a writing group independent of a research team can give you structure when you are struggling to stay on track. There is nothing like the accountability that comes when you are given a deadline for writing that is set by a group rather than just yourself. Writing groups can, in this manner, increase your productivity and the quality of your work. If writer's block is something you experience, a writer's group can make the block not feel as gigantic and impossible to bust through as when you are writing alone. In addition, you might have discovered this in the route to pursuing a doctorate or seeking advancement as a faculty member: The journey is an individual one, ultimately, and research and the act of writing can be isolating for some. Being a member of a writing group not only combats that isolation but can also leave you with specific steps to take and inspiration to feel that may be difficult to generate when working alone. We list some helpful considerations to guide you in forming a writing group in Table 12.1.

**TABLE 12.1**   How to Start a Writing Group

1. Consider the focus of the group you would like to form: Is it to complete your qualitative report? Is it to give and exchange writing feedback? Is it a place to simply check in on the status of your report and brainstorm with your writing group members?

2. Keep it small: In our experience, a writing group of three people is the ideal. It is not so small that meetings and feedback become routinized and stale. Yet it is also not so large that the meetings feel stressful, especially if you are committed to reading one another's writing before the writing group meets.

3. Create some clear structure: How long will each meeting last? Where will you meet? Over what period of time will you meet? Any structure you agree upon in advance will help you through the inevitable challenges (e.g., busy schedules, emergencies) that will arise.

4. Set individual and group goals: One member might want to improve their writing in the discussion section. Another might struggle with the introduction section and literature review while another might just have trouble knowing where to begin writing or how to approach academic writing at all. Knowing one another's goals can help you check in on one another. Having a shared group goal, which might be general or specific, can help as well.

5. Commit to attending and supporting one another: If one of you misses the group or cannot make a previously scheduled meeting, talk in advance about whether you will reschedule so everyone can be present.

6. Protect your writing group time: This goes back to Number 3, but a critical aspect of your writing group is to support you in writing more and with better quality. So, if the time is not protected ... well, you can probably figure that one out.

7. Celebrate your accomplishments along the way: Each member has hopefully set individual goals, which do not happen overnight but rather step by step. Celebrate these individual steps and soon you will have behaviorally reinforced yourself that the act of writing is good and an important act in qualitative research.

# Writing Components of Qualitative Research

Now that you know the basics of conducting qualitative research that is meticulous and rigorous in its methods, it is time to understand how to convey your hard work to an audience. It may seem overwhelming to compile the steps of your research process into an integrative document. However, the key to not being overwhelmed is remembering that, in writing and presenting your qualitative study, your main goal is to be true to your participants. This goal can be achieved by understanding your philosophy about academic writing. This philosophy will guide your entire approach to composing your qualitative report.

In this section, we will use the American Psychological Association's (APA, 2020b) journal article reporting standards for qualitative inquiry (JARS-Qual) guidelines as a framework for providing recommendations for various writing components of a qualitative research proposal and report. JARS-Qual provides information and what should be included in a report to enable readers' evaluation of its rigor. While developing a research proposal, some of these components will not be applicable. Nevertheless, you should start thinking about these components and discuss in the proposal how each will be addressed in the final report. The JARS-Qual includes suggested report section headings; however, the final section headings and report structure will depend on your audience as well as your selected research paradigm and tradition.

Table 12.2 provides a summary of the JARS-Qual components; we encourage you to review Levitt et al. (2018) and APA (2020b) for additional detail. Table 12.3 is provided as a suggested structure or an overall visual of your report, suggesting parameters in terms of page length and organization for a 25- to 30-page qualitative report. It is incredibly challenging to condense a rigorous qualitative report that includes rich, thick descriptions of participants' voices. The suggested outline is not a one-size-fits-all approach but is rather a tool for you to reflect on a comprehensive picture of your report.

## Your Introductory Sentences

You want your introductory sentences to have three functions. First, your introductory sentences should immediately contain the topic of your qualitative inquiry. Both authors have reviewed several qualitative manuscripts for publications that waited too long to tell the reader exactly what was being studied. The writing may be good, but it is also a waste of time for your audience and—worse—can confuse your reader as to the topic of your manuscript. So, immediately dive into that first sentence with your topic. If you have conducted a case study of school reform, discuss school reform in the first sentence. Second, you want to give some type of pressing rationale for why the topic is important. Using school reform as an example, you might discuss that school reform is traditionally understood in terms of policies, but there is little known from the policymakers' point of view about how policymakers engage in the school-reform process. You might even decide to define the constructs early on in your introductory sentences if the topic is poorly understood in general, drawing on previous literature. Finally, you want your introductory sentences to "pop." Remember, we are avoiding using dramatic language, but we also do not want to bore the reader to death. We provide an

**TABLE 12.2**   Journal Article Reporting Standards for Qualitative Research

| Section or element | Description |
|---|---|
| **Introduction** | |
| Research question(s) | Contextualize and describe the research problem or question(s). Synthesize and critique applicable literature to clarify knowledge gaps. |
| Research goals | State the research goals as well as the target audience as applicable. Show an alignment with the research design. |
| **Method** | |
| Research design | Thickly describe and provide a rationale for the research tradition and paradigm. |
| Data sources | Describe the researchers' experience with the topic and qualitative methodology. Discuss the number and characteristics of the data sources. |
| Participant recruitment | Describe the recruitment process, eligibility criteria, sampling method(s), and the initial and final sample sizes and how each were determined. Describe ethical and recruitment protocols followed. |
| Data collection | Thickly describe the initial and final data collection methods used. |
| **Analysis** | |
| Data-analytic strategies | Describe the methods and procedures used and for what purpose. Identify the case and units of analysis. |
| Methodological integrity | Articulate how researcher reflexivity influenced analysis. Provide contextual information and a coherent and thick description of the findings aligned with the research design. Discuss strategies of trustworthiness used. |
| **Findings/results** | |
| Findings/results subsections | Describe research findings in a way that is compatible with the research design. Use synthesizing illustrations (e.g., diagrams, models, tables) as needed. |
| **Discussion** | |
| Discussion subsections | Describe the contributions of the findings, comparing to prior scholarship on the topic. Identify the study's strengths and limitations and implications for future research, policy, and practice. |

[a] Review the seventh edition of the Publication Manual of the American Psychological Association (APA, 2020a) for guidance on the title page, abstract, references, and other manuscript sections not listed here.

Adapted from: American Psychological Association. (2020b). *Journal article reporting standards: Qualitative research design (JARS-Qual)*. https://apastyle.apa.org/jars/qualitative

**TABLE 12.3**   A Structured Approach to Qualitative Report Writing

| Components of a qualitative report | Sample page length |
|---|---|
| *Introduction/rationale*<br>• Introductory sentence stating the topic<br>• Include relevant background information (e.g., statistics, important gaps in the research literature). | 3–4 pages |
| *Literature review*<br>• Review most relevant and recent (within 5–10 years) literature related to topic.<br>• Include older research (more than 10 years) only when seminal theory and research is related to topic.<br>• Include purpose statement.<br>• Introduce research tradition if used in a novel or innovative manner.<br>• See Chapter 5 for more information on writing a literature review. | 5–6 pages |
| *Method*<br>• Describe research tradition (if not introduced in previous section).<br>• Participant<br>• Demographics<br>• Procedure for study<br>• Describe research bias and research team.<br>• Describe instruments (e.g., semistructured interviews, researcher as instrument).<br>• Data collection<br>• Data analysis<br>• Standards for and strategies of trustworthiness | 5–6 pages |
| *Findings*<br>• Introductory sentences describing overall findings<br>• Provide thick description in describing findings. | 7–8 pages |
| *Discussion*<br>• Summary sentences of findings<br>• Describe relationship of findings to previous literature review.<br>• Identify implications of study.<br>• Discuss limitations of the study. | 5–6 pages |
| *Conclusion*<br>• Restatement of the study purpose and its connection to gaps in previous research<br>• Brief mention of major contributions of study findings to literature | 1–2 paragraphs |

example here from student Kim Molee's study on school reform entitled *School Reform from a Legislator's Point of View*:

> The nature of a republic requires the general population to elect our representatives, who then create policies that affect all our lives. An example of such a policy is the public school reform movement, and its impact on students, teachers and the public school system. There are many professionals, within different disciplines, such as social science scholars, policy makers and education practitioners making efforts to improve and reform our education system. Yet often these people work for similar goals and do not collaborate. Given this assumption, there is a need for more information about school reform to improve collaboration among scholars, policy makers and education practitioners. Finally, this information can be of value to the general public as well, if we are to be informed, participatory citizens.

You can see that Kim does something a little different with her introductory sentence. Its "pop factor" is present in that she paints with a broad stroke the implications of policymaking for all people's lives. Then she drills down on the specific topic of her study: educational reform. Kim's study specifically focuses on how collaboration occurs within educational reform policymaking, which she states within her first few introductory sentences. Our only suggestion to strengthen her introductory sentences might be to add statistical information or other specific information to help the reader define the construct of policy reform. However, since that information can also come in the second paragraph, we think Kim actually did a nice job of using her writing to invite her readers to care about her topic. That is what we call success in answering the "so what" question about your study. Case Example 12.1 provides another excellent model of introductory sentences.

**Case Example 12.1. Participant Selection in Your Report**

### The Experience of Success for Adolescents Diagnosed with Attention Deficit Hyperactivity Disorder by Anne M. P. Michalek

> ADHD is one of the most frequently cited medical/behavioral conditions and the most common childhood disorder (Barkley, 1997). Barkley (1997) describes ADHD as a developmental disorder affecting a child's ability to regulate behavior, control behavior, or keep future goals and consequences in mind. These deficits are manifested and demonstrated through a variety of behaviors, including an inability to sustain attention, effectively regulate levels of activity according to the situation, and effectively plan and complete tasks.

## Conceptual Framework

When writing your research proposal, an initial consideration across traditions is your conceptual framework. We discussed the development of your conceptual framework in detail in Chapter 5. As a reminder, the conceptual framework develops from experience, pilot and exploratory findings, available literature, and thought experiments (Maxwell, 2013). In essence, your conceptual framework is comprised of your literature review, research tradition, and any selected personal and professional theories that act as a lens through which to understand your research approach. As you write about your conceptual framework, the components should be fully defined within the research proposal. However, these components should additionally be defined in relationship to the interrelationships among them. For example, if you are using a feminist theory and a phenomenological research tradition (in addition to your literature review), you can begin with defining the feminist theory. Because feminist theory has numerous branches (e.g., liberal, radical, social) and subbranches (e.g., womanist, intersectionality), defining the particular feminist theory in appropriate detail is important. We like to think of providing appropriate detail as akin to whether your uncle who works in computer technology (about as far away as you can get from qualitative inquiry!) could understand the theoretical perspective for your study. We will call this the "uncle test" as one method of accountability you can use as you write any aspect of your research proposal. Then you do the same for your research tradition. Tell the reader why it is a critical method for understanding your phenomenon. In both your theory and research tradition, we encourage you to revisit the original sources for both so that you are clearly articulating their aims.

Once you have described your theory and research tradition in detail, you should next clearly explain to your audience what the interrelationships are among them and how they are appropriate for your study. In our previous example, a phenomenological tradition (Moustakas, 1994) and feminist theory (Collins, 2009; hooks, 2000) might share three major interrelationships that are critical, for instance, in writing up a qualitative study of children who live in poverty and their educational experiences. First, both emphasize the importance of honoring participant voices in understanding their truth. Second, there is attention to the role of researcher bias within feminist theory and phenomenological designs. Third, both of these value the role of contextual factors on the lives of participants: with feminism, through recognizing the impact of oppression; with phenomenology, through the valuing of daily lived experiences of participants.

To give you an example of how you might describe your conceptual framework in your qualitative report, we highlight a student paper from education of how to articulate a conceptual framework. In Michelle Espino's study of Latina professionals and their journeys in obtaining their doctoral degrees, she used critical race theory (CRT) from a Latino perspective (LatCrit; Solorzano & Delgado Bernal, 2001) and social constructionism (Berger & Luckman, 1966) to ground her qualitative study and examine the complex relationship between marginalized communities and the dominant culture in reproducing and resisting what she termed *master narratives*. We will highlight Espino's discussion of theory related to her conceptual framework.

In discussing how she has undergirded her study of 33 Latina doctoral-level professionals in higher education, Espino initially defines and contextualizes CRT:

> Although the critical race theory (CRT) movement began with legal scholars, educational researchers noted its applicability to analyzing the experiences of students of color, discussing critical pedagogy, uncovering racial microaggressions, and

developing best practices (Parker & Stovall, 2004; Solórzano, 1998; Solórzano et al., 2000). CRT offered an opportunity to design studies that would "identify, analyze, and transform those structural, cultural, and interpersonal aspects of education that maintain the subordination of [students] of color" (Solórzano, 1998, p. 123).

After she has defined and contextualized the use of CRT in her conceptual framework, Espino's writing moves to share her research positionality as it relates to her topic. Recalling Kline's (2008) standards of presentational rigor, her writing of her own positionality as it relates to her theory builds trustworthiness with her audience:

> Believing that research should lead to transformation and that CRT, as a framework, could illuminate new stories not yet shared in the literature, I devised a study of the life narratives of 33 Mexican American Ph.D.s. I was intrigued by the way participants told stories about their families and educational experiences because embedded within the stories were responses to societal messages about their communities. Consistent with challenging the dominant ideology, one of five main tenets in CRT, my goal was to deconstruct ideologies that blame Mexican American communities for low levels of educational attainment.

It becomes clear to her audience what the centrality of her role is as a researcher and her related assumptions. Rather than defining all of the tenets of CRT, Espino defines the specific component of the theory she is using to frame her qualitative inquiry. Then she cites an article the reader can reference for further details on additional CRT tenets. In addition to building trustworthiness, Espino has additionally set the writing stage for her to highlight forthcoming methodological and analytic rigor and to showcase the complexity of her findings. Her researcher positionality continues to invite complexity as she narratively describes the "surprises" entailed in her research process:

> However, I found that calling attention to these ideologies or master narratives led to more complicated, perhaps controversial considerations about power and oppression within U.S. society. (Re)presenting the findings from my study not only meant uncovering master narratives and counter-narratives, but also addressing the reproduction of master narratives within Mexican American communities themselves.

Our only critique of Espino's description of the position of her theory in her research is that we bet it could be revised slightly to pass the uncle test. For instance, the uncle test might guide her to define terms such as "master narratives" and "oppression." Overall, however, we believe Espino hits the mark in her writing, as she clearly communicates to the reader exactly how theory is a critical component in understanding her study. See Figure 12.1 for a pictorial description of all the components within her conceptual framework.

You can additionally think of writing your conceptual framework as answering the questions of what, who, how, and why. See Table 12.4 for a listing of these questions and related considerations related to our earlier example of studying educational attainment of children who live in poverty.

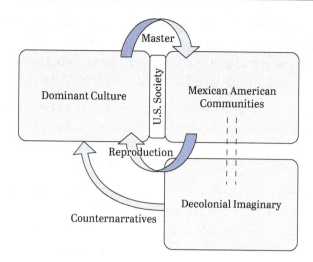

**FIGURE 12.1**   Conceptual Framework of the Relationship Between the Dominant Culture and Mexican American Communities, Master Narratives and Counternarratives, and the Location of Decolonial Imagery

## The Purpose Statement

Numerous qualitative scholars have discussed the importance of writing a strong purpose statement in the qualitative report. Writing a strong purpose statement is critical, as it transitions your writing from the rationale for and introduction of the study and related literature to a specific statement of the study's purpose (sometimes called the "problem statement"). In other words, your writing guides the reader from your curiosity and exploration about your topic to a problem that can be addressed through research. Your purpose statement should have several important components within it. Take a look at Sesha Joi Moon's purpose statement in her student paper for her study entitled *The Subsistence and Impact of Tokenism on the Doctoral Experiences of African American Females*:

> The purpose of this study is to investigate the subsistence of tokenism in higher education and its perceived impact on the doctoral experience by African American females at Traditionally White Institutions.

You can see that Sesha clearly states her study's problem in her purpose statement. Her writing avoids extraneous words and language that is uninviting, obtrusive, or unclear to her audience. Writing a purpose statement can vary across traditions in that these different research traditions, as we discussed in Chapter 4, require different research problems to be answered. See Table 12.5 for Creswell and Poth's (2017) template for a strong purpose statement across the research approaches. We especially like the formulaic approach for beginning writers of qualitative studies because learning this structure at first can help you later become more creative in crafting your purpose statement.

Another advantage of using this template for the purpose statement is that it clearly showcases that the purpose statement punctuates the qualitative report in its function of transitioning your report to the method section. However, before you move on to writing the method section,

**TABLE 12.4**  Sample Questions and Considerations for Writing About Your Conceptual Framework

Let's say you are studying the educational attainment of children who live in poverty and you are using phenomenology as your research tradition and feminism as your theory. In the left column are the questions you want to ask yourself about your conceptual framework. In the right column are considerations you want to keep in mind as you seek to answer these questions (the considerations in italics are the ones applied directly to our example of the educational attainment of children who live in poverty):

| Question | Considerations |
|---|---|
| **What?** | What are the relevant tenets of your theory and research tradition? *Phenomenology assisted the researcher to understand the essence and meaning regarding the educational attainment of children who live in poverty.*<br><br>*Feminist theory guided the researcher to explore the contextual influences of poverty (e.g., classism) on children's educational attainment and value their responses as the truth of their experiences.*<br><br>What are the critical constructs within your theory and research tradition? *Phenomenological designs allowed the researcher to seek an in-depth understanding of participants' daily lived experiences.*<br><br>*Important constructs within feminist theory as used in qualitative traditions are the development of a collaborative relationship between the researcher and participants in addition to seeking to understand participants' experiences of empowerment despite oppressive systems in society.* |
| **Who?** | Who are the major players within your theory and research tradition? *The researcher will use the tenets of phenomenology described by Moustakas (1994).*<br><br>*There are many strands of feminist theory. The researcher used the Chicana feminist theory articulated by Gloria Anzaldua (1987/2012)—specifically, her approach to exploring the "borderlands" where divergent cultures meet and intersect.* |
| **How?** | How will the combination of your research tradition and theory/theories influence your study? *The combination of phenomenology and Anzaldua's Chicana feminism guide the researcher to specifically seek to understand the essence and meaning of how Latina children who live in poverty engage educational systems at the borderlands where their race/ethnicity and social class meet.* |
| **Why?** | Why not pick another research tradition and/or theory/theories? *Although quantitative inquiries of Latina children's educational attainment have been conducted, there is not an in-depth exploration from the children's perspective about their daily lived experiences. The researcher considered a grounded theory design. However, the goal of the research was not to build a theory of Latina children's experiences but rather to understand the essence and meaning of their educational attainment.* |

**TABLE 12.5**  Creswell and Poth's (2017) Formula for a Purpose Statement

The purpose of this _____ (narrative, phenomenological, grounded theory, ethnographic, case) study is (Was? Will be?) to _____ (understand? Describe? Develop? Discover?) the _____ (central phenomenon of the study) for _____ (the participant) at _____ (the site). At this stage in this research, the _____ (central phenomenon) will be generally defined as _____ (a general definition of the central concept). (p. 132)

we suggest you briefly write 2–4 additional sentences to "unpack" your purpose statement and link it back to the focus of your study. To illustrate this, let's return to Sesha's purpose statement and how she links this purpose statement to her research tradition and important constructs in her study's examination:

> The purpose of this study is to investigate the subsistence of tokenism in higher education and its perceived impact on the doctoral experience by African American females at Traditionally White Institutions. A qualitative methodological approach was used to report the findings from a series of interviews with one (1) participant that intends to reveal the respondent's life history experience. Tokenism is operationalized as a person that is assigned to a group as a result of their auxiliary differentiations from the dominant group (Kanter, 1977; Blalock, 1967). Race and gender classifications are defined according to the participant's self-identification as African American and female.

Sesha did a beautiful job in her writing of moving from a clearly articulated purpose statement to her rationale for her use of life history as her research tradition. Next she described tokenism and race and gender classifications for participants in a manner that is accessible to the reader. She intentionally used words like "defined" and "operationalized" to guide the reader to more fully understand the context of her purpose statement.

## The Research Tradition

As we have discussed this throughout this text, your research tradition is a key component of your conceptual framework. So, you want to make certain that you convey its importance through your writing. We will talk about the politics of publication of qualitative research later in the chapter where you might be asked by a journal editor to shorten your description of your research tradition. However, we believe the best qualitative proposal writing aims to clearly articulate the research tradition as a way to contextualize the study. We lead you through what we consider an example of strong writing on the rationale for a research tradition from Okech and Kline's (2004) article: a grounded theory of group coleader relationships. Their writing begins with their reason for selecting grounded theory.

> This research used the grounded theory approach because of its ability to describe patterns and complex relationships between data and its sensitivity to process. Grounded theory uses systematic analysis (e.g., open, axial, and selective coding)

and analytic tools (e.g., constant comparison, asking questions, etc.) to build theory. During the data collection and analytic processes, researchers continuously compare data provided by participants with their emerging theoretical concepts, thus developing a theory consistent with participants' perceptions of the phenomenon under study. (Okech & Kline, 2004, p. 175)

You can see that the authors defined the research tradition themselves in three sentences. You could possibly need more, but we advise not much more, because you have much more to write! Plus, rather than simply defining your research tradition in your own words, you might want your writing to also showcase that you know something about the original texts upon which the tradition is based. Okech and Kline (2004) then cite Strauss and Corbin's (1998) as they describe the grounded theory tradition.

Next, Okech and Kline (2004) write in a manner that directly links their tradition to their phenomenon of inquiry: group coleader relationships. Again, their writing is simple to understand but not simplified beyond holding meaning for the reader:

Grounded theory, therefore, offered a structure for the conceptualization of the social and psychological processes of participants based on their experiences and perceptions. It did this not only by incorporating the perspectives and voices of the participants (Denzin & Lincoln, 1998) but also by involving the 'verification' of the collected data with the participants. (Okech & Kline, 2004, p. 175)

As you can see, in two sentences the authors are able to foreground their coming discussion of their data collection and analysis process. However, this foregrounding involved just a hint at this point—not a full discussion—to help the reader move from the definition of the research tradition and building a rationale for why it is an appropriate research tradition for their topic to a brief statement on what grounded theory techniques "looked" like within their study. As the authors wrap up writing about their research tradition, they explicitly restate the relevance of the research tradition. You might notice, their language is not repetitive but does have some aspects of the initial definition. The authors are assisting their audience—who might be reading about grounded theory designs for the first time—to understand the tradition's utility with their topic. They are also garnering respect from their readers who know a good deal about grounded theory, as they are further defining the theory and identifying the rationale for its use:

Grounded theory methodology is a scientific method that features the systematic analysis of data gathered through interviews with the participants under study to build a theory of their experiences (Strauss & Corbin, 1998). The emerging theory, because it grounds its concepts in data provided by the participants, is consistent with the phenomenon under study (Strauss & Corbin). Therefore, the used of grounded theory methodology was essential to the goals of the study. (Okech & Kline, 2004, p. 175)

## Participant and Procedures

Depending on how you organize your research proposal or report, you might have information about study participants and procedures presented in one or multiple sections. Any data that you collected (or will collect, in the case of a research proposal) about participants' demographics should be shared in this section. We suggest that you consider including the major identity categories of demographics listed below that are relevant to your phenomenon of inquiry:

- gender identity
- race/ethnicity
- socioeconomic status or social class
- sexual or affectional orientation
- ability identity
- religious/spiritual affiliation
- national origin
- geographic region

Of course, you may not include all of these demographics (or decide to add other categories), but try to interrogate yourself when you decide not to include a certain demographic component of your participants. What might the reader miss in understanding your study as a result of not having access to this demographic information? For instance, when Michelle Espino presents on her study of the pursuit of higher education by Latinx women, she often discusses how at the time of the study she was focused on the race/ethnicity and gender of her participants and missed the salience of sexual orientation for several of her participants who identified as queer—or even as heterosexual. That type of interrogation of your own work as you write not only builds trustworthiness with your audience but also gives your writing the freedom and permission to become more complex and interesting without becoming stilted in the process.

In addition, a good question to ask yourself is what the demographic components are that must be included or whether there will be inadequate information to understand your study. Also, be sure to write about the way you sampled your participants. This is a good place to, again, invite complexity into your writing. Tell the audience what the sampling approach was and how it was used in addition to its appropriateness for your phenomenon of interest. See Case Example 12.2 for a student example of a good beginning of the participant section. In this example, the student is writing a proposal for whom she *will* sample for her study.

| Case Example 12.2. Participant Selection in Your Report |

### Exploring Teacher Candidates' Reflections of Instructor Picture Book Usage in Teacher Education Programs by Julie F. Byers

Stratified purposeful sampling was used to select participants. Participant selection was criterion based and thus come from a pool of students whom had taken an education course in which a professor used a picture book in the college classroom. It was intended to gather participants with similar picture book experiences from various instructors. However, convenience sampling was the most logical choice due to the fact that the researcher utilizes picture books in her college classroom. From those chosen from the initial pool, an anticipated 6 to 10 participants were then be selected in a way that was be most representative of the demographics of the students currently in the education program at Old Dominion University. This was determined by analyzing the current statistics of enrollment of education courses. Selection will include sampling representativeness in terms of age, race, and sex of participant. Age was included due to the variety of age in current programs. Age differences between traditional and nontraditional students added a more rich range of lived experiences in regard to this study.

When your audience reads the procedure section of your report, it should be 100% clear to them what the procedural steps of your study are or will be. You should write about the setting and context of your study. The overall steps and approach to data collection should also be included, such as the type of instruments used for data collection (e.g., semistructured interviews, artwork, journals). Sometimes, the instruments of a section can be a subheading of your procedure section if you need to define them further. This is especially important if you are using an innovative instrument of which a general audience might not be aware. Other times, the overall description of your instruments will be sufficient as you detail the steps of your study in the Procedure section. We include a good example of the beginning of a procedure section in Case Example 12.3.

**Case Example 12.3. Emily C. Bouck's (2008)** *Exploring the Enactment of Functional Curriculum in Self-Contained Cross-Categorical Programs: A Case Study*

Data from the case study was collected through multiple means in an effort to triangulate (Stake, 1995). At each site data was collected through full school day classroom observations for two days a week for three months (Bogdan & Biklen, 2003). A total of 85 hours was spent at Harborville and 70 hours spent at River Bend. During classroom observations, the researcher took fieldnotes and observed the events within the classroom. Decisions about what to observe and when were based on purposeful sampling (Patton, 1980), such that observations were selected to present the greatest opportunity to understand and gain insight into the case (i.e., each program). In addition, document reviews were conducted. Students' CA-60 files were analyzed and data was gathered on students' IQ, achievement test scores, disability classification, years in special education, age, and other pertinent information. Prior to any data collection, the researcher collected student assent and parental consent for the collection of all data. (Bouck, 2008, p. 500)

As you can see, Bouck (2008) included the basic information and steps of how she secured the informed consent and assent of participants. This is a very important component of this section that we often see qualitative report writers omit. Do not make that same mistake!

## Researcher Reflexivity

We have emphasized throughout this book how critical it is to be able to clearly identify your researcher positionality. We discussed researcher reflexivity in Chapter 1 extensively and have referred to its importance throughout this book. When writing about your researcher positionality, we encourage you to use the concept of "getting real" with your audience. Throughout your data collection and analysis, you know how your researcher positionality has influenced your writing. Ideally, you have documented your positionality, interrogated it, and sought to identify how it influenced the findings and understanding of your topic. Do not leave all that work behind! Write about this process. There may have been times in the data collection and analysis where your positionality took an unexpected turn—or remained steady. Write about that process as well.

In our experience in reading both student qualitative reports and the manuscripts of more established qualitative researchers, we see folks touch lightly on their positionality. In the case of journal publication, some of this is because of the limits of journal page space. To the extent possible, however, do not skimp on this section. Although we will be transparent in that we ideally would love to read thick description on researcher positionality in every qualitative report, we can be realistic as well. Take a look at Case Example 12.4 so you can see how much researcher positionality you can pack into a brief two paragraphs when you get real in writing reflexivity for your audience.

## Case Example 12.4. Reflexive Statement/Research Positionality

### Experiences of Sexual Minority Greek Students by Joseph W. Davis

In relation to qualitative research, the issue of bias must be addressed to promote the ideal of trustworthiness. For the proposed study, the primary researcher is a 25-year-old White man who is working towards a doctorate in Counselor Education. The researcher identifies as gay and is actively involved in a Greek letter organization at his academic institution. He is at a level of complete disclosure within his organization in regards to his sexual orientation. The researcher has been involved with the interest area of sexual minority students in Greek letter organizations for five years and has brought a national speaker to his academic institution to present on the subject material.

The researcher holds the belief that Greek letter organizations have the potential to be beacons of acceptance for LGBQ individuals. However, this belief exists in that the potential for acceptance has rarely been met. He has experienced homophobic insults and derogatory jokes from within his own fraternity as well as others at his academic institution. These experiences have led to the occasional belief that the Greek system does not represent itself in an acceptable manner to incoming sexual minority students. Along with what he has witnessed, the researcher also recognizes the acceptance he has gained from the majority of the other people in his respective organization.

## Data Collection and Analysis

We do believe that every section of your qualitative report is incredibly important. And there is something about your data collection and analysis section that we think demands critical attention to detail. For those of you who love structure, this section should be fairly straight-forward to write. However, for those of you who are more fluid writers, this section might cause quite a bit of frustration. Essentially, your data collection and analysis sections should not only showcase your most concise writing but also requires you to metaphorically hold your reader's hand and walk them step by step through what you did with your data.

The key word here is "step." We actually advise you to use linear words like "step," "phase," "stage," and so on. We are not encouraging you to eliminate any recursivity that occurred in your data collection and analysis: quite the opposite. We are asking you to write in detail, step by step, about each component of your data collection and analysis. We include an excerpt from the beginning of a data collection and analysis section by Frankel and Levitt (2009) as an example of how detailed you want your writing to be in your data collection and analysis section:

> The transcribed data collected in the interviews was divided into meaning units (MUs). MUs are segments of texts that each contain one main idea (Giorgi, 1970). In the initial stages of the analysis, the MUs were labeled in a manner that remained very close to the language used by the participants. The MUs were compared with each other and organized according to their similarities, creating descriptive categories. MUs could be assigned to more than one category, as dictated by the meanings contained therein. Once the initial descriptive categories into higher order categories based on their commonalities. This process was repeated and, in this way a hierarchy of categories was developed. At the top of the hierarchy one core category was formed that represented the central interpretation drawn from the analysis. (p. 175)

Frankel and Levitt (2009) have begun discussing their analytic steps. We like that they did not talk about the data analysis process using words such as "emerged." Rather, they used action verbs, such as "developed," to acknowledge the power they had as researchers to identify patterns in the data. Next, (as grounded theory designs require) the authors discuss the recursivity of data collection and analysis:

> The process of collected data continued until the categories became "saturated," that is new descriptive categories did not appear to be present in additional interviews. This analysis became saturated at the sixth interview—meaning that the last three interviews did not add any new categories and that the analysis appeared to be comprehensive. (Frankel & Levitt, 2009, p. 175)

Our only critique of their writing in this section is their use of the word "appeared" in their writing. Whereas in their previous paragraph they were acknowledging their researcher power in the data analysis, they slip back into a passive voice with this word. A better word to strengthen their writing here would be to use a word such as "identified" or even the word "developed," which they used in the previous paragraph. However, they move into a strong section of writing in discussing their role as a researcher in the data collection and analysis as they wrap up this section:

> A detailed record of the researcher's intuitions, suspicions, feelings and thoughts about the interviews and analysis was maintained throughout the study. But noting these assumptions via memoing, an attempt was made to minimize any biasing effect they might have on the interviewing and analytic process, in order to keep the conceptualization of the phenomenon closely tied to the data and to keep a careful record of the procedures and theoretical developments of the analysis. (Frankel & Levitt, 2009, p. 175)

Again, we think the authors' writing is concise, detailed, and helpful for the reader to understand their steps. Our only suggestion here would be to give even more detail about the specific steps of *how* they addressed the "biasing effect" they reference. Without that information, although the writing is concise, it lacks some clarity as to what actually happened during those steps of acknowledging their biases.

There may be other components of your data collection and analysis that you want to include in your writing so that the audience can understand the scope of your study. Although you cannot share your entire set of data management tools you might have used with your audience in your qualitative report, we do encourage you to share your codebook with your audience (either as an appendix or table). See Table 12.6 for a student example by Ann Wendle Barnes of her codebook from her qualitative report.

## Findings

When you write your findings section, you should demonstrate alignment with your research tradition. In other words, if you are writing a grounded theory study, do not switch to a phenomenological portrayal of your findings or vice versa. In addition, there are several ways you can portray your findings. You might decide to use a table to summarize your findings or some type of visual portrayal of your model. However, again, keep in mind the ideas of coherence and congruence. If you are doing a grounded theory, your reader will expect to see some type of visual model that portrays your findings that might be transferable to other groups. However, you might also use a visual model to portray phenomenological findings. You just want to be careful to clearly state that this is not a model you expect readers to transfer to other groups but is representative of the group of participants involved in your study. Although an extensive exploration of writing up your findings is beyond the scope of this chapter, we refer you to Table 12.7, which reproduces Chenail's (1995) suggestions for presenting data both within the qualitative report and to professional audiences.

**TABLE 12.6** A Sample Codebook by a Student (Ann Wendle Barnes) for a Study on Lived Experiences of a Few Who Forged Women's Programming

| Term | Meaning |
|---|---|
| **Alone** | Cut off, disconnected, invisible, isolated, nothing, scattered, starved |
| **Barriers** | Traditions, prohibit, block, different, differences, difficulty, discouragement, shut down, threatening atmosphere, overcome by environment, old, not welcome, not allowed, feeling guilty |
| **Beginning** | Start of change, paving the way, infant stages, infancy, didn't happen overnight |
| **Change** | Community movement, student involvement, consciousness, funding |
| **Climate** | Negative, tolerated, understood, change in the room, across the board, institutionalized |
| **Control** | Funding, traditions, assistance refusal, acknowledgment refusal, work credit refusal, recognition refusal, domestic, elitist, unacceptable female course study |
| **Discrimination** | Anti-equal rights, discriminated against, disparate treatment, disrespect, intentionally embarrassed, irrational treatment by others, shouted down, sneered at, thrown out, thrown away, automatic "F" |
| **Harassment** | Blatant, appalling, eyeing, innuendo, looking a female up and down, mockery, sexual comments, wouldn't look at completed female student work, wouldn't give female students explicit directions, resentment of female students, demeaning word "dear-y," degrading |
| **Minority** | Not necessarily population number, could be race other than White, gender other than male, religion other than Christian, nationality other than American |
| **Strength** | Brave, confident, hard work, independent, rise above, sacrifice, struggle, stubborn, work twice as hard |
| **Support** | Community, accomplishments, achieve, assisted, connected, encouraged, encouragement, sameness, secure, security, sense of connection, support, supported, supportive, uplifting, strong, warm, welcome, opportunity |

## Discussion

Ah, you have made it to the discussion section! It is quite a feat to have made it to this point. And by now, you are likely tired—maybe tired of your topic in general or tired in terms of the work you have already put into things. Heppner et al. (2015) discussed three challenges they see students experience by the time they get to the actual writing of the discussion section. First, they discuss you might feel like you have run out of ideas and/or momentum at this point. We both have experienced this challenge quite a bit in our own qualitative manuscript writing.

**TABLE 12.7**   Suggested Formats for Presenting Your Qualitative Report

| | |
|---|---|
| **Natural** | The data are presented in a shape that resembles the phenomenon being studied. For instance, if the data are excerpts from a therapy session, present them in a sequential order or in an order that represents the flow of the session itself. |
| **Most simple to most complex** | For sake of understanding, start the presentation of data with the simplest example you have found. As the complexity of each example or exemplar presented increases, the reader will have a better chance of following the presentation. |
| **First discovered/ constructed to last discovered/ constructed** | The data are presented in a chronicle-like fashion, showing the course of the researcher's personal journey in the study. This style is reminiscent of an archeological style of presentation: What was the first "relic" excavated, then the second, and so forth? |
| **Quantitative informed** | In this scheme data are presented according to strategies commonly found in quantitative or statistical studies. Data are arranged along lines of central tendencies and ranges, clusters, and frequencies. |
| **Theory guided** | Data arrangement is governed by the researcher's theory or theories regarding the phenomenon being represented in the study. For instance, a Marxist-informed researcher might present data from a doctor–patient interview in terms of talk that shows who controls the means for producing information in the interaction, talk that illustrates who is being marginalized, and so forth. In clinical qualitative research, this approach is quite prevalent as clinicians organize the data in terms of their understandings of doctor–patient, nurse–patient, and therapist–client interactions. |
| **Narrative logic** | Data are arranged with an eye for storytelling. Researchers plot out the data in a fashion that allows them to transition from one exemplar to another, just as narrators arrange details to best relate the particulars of the story. |
| **Most important to least important or from major to minor** | Like the journalistic style of the inverted pyramid, the most important "findings" are presented first and the minor "discoveries" come last. |
| **Dramatic presentation** | This one is the opposite of the inverted pyramid style. With the dramatic arrangement scheme, researchers order their data presentation so as to save the surprises and unforeseen discoveries for last. |
| **No particular order** | As it sounds, data are arranged with no particular pattern in mind, or the researcher fails to explain how or why the data are displayed the way they are. |

We have found it helpful to grab some time with one another or other colleagues who "get" our topic and are willing to lend a listening ear. Sometimes, when addressing this challenge, one of us will actually become a notetaker for the other. So, the one who is having some trouble writing their discussion section will do some brainstorming of ideas out loud while the other one takes notes.

The second challenge Heppner et al. (2015) discuss is feeling some insecurity or doubt about the relevance of one's research. If you are a novice researcher, this feeling is to be expected. A good way to combat these feelings of doubt is to return to why you decided to study this topic in the first place. You can also reread some of your participant transcripts to remember the importance of their voices. Sometimes, this approach can backfire though. Your participants, remember, are *real* people. And so are you. You definitely want to seek to represent their voices in the most truthful, accurate way you can. However, do not let perfectionism in seeking to do so get you stuck. We have a feeling your participants would want you to do the best job you could, not the perfect job.

The third challenge Heppner et al. (2015) address is a researcher's hesitance or even fear of getting their work in front of an audience. If this happens to you, the authors suggest recognizing that making one's research public is actually a significant component of the research process. Once you have put all of that work into your study, it is now time to share it with others to receive feedback, stimulate the literature, and come out of the more solitary actions of being a researcher to interacting with the public about your findings.

Now that we have discussed some of the challenges you might experience, let's look at some specific steps you want to take in your discussion section. Below is a potential draft outline you could follow to get the "bones" of your discussion section in place:

1. Restate research problem.
2. Interpret each of your findings from your conceptual framework.
3. Describe any intersections amongst your findings that were unexpected or expected.
4. Explore the implications for your findings both within and outside of your field.
5. Write about the future research directions regarding your topic based on your findings.
6. Discuss the limitations of your study.
7. Write a brief conclusion summarizing your entire study.

## Presenting Qualitative Research

Presenting your qualitative research can involve presenting in formal or informal settings to various audiences using multiple formats (see Activity 12.1). Some of the audiences and settings include peers within a qualitative research course or at a professional conference or stakeholders within a community setting. Based on the audience, setting, and purpose of presenting the research, the format and content may appear differently. For example, while a slide presentation or poster may be appropriate in some circumstances, a video or talking circle may be more suitable in other settings. As you consider presenting your work, reflect

## ACTIVITY 12.1. PRESENTING QUALITATIVE RESEARCH

Select a topic of research. What are the journals and conferences (local, regional, national, international) that are most suited to presenting your research? How should your research be shared with and to communities and participants?

upon to whom it is most relevant to present the findings and their implications: researchers, participants, other community members, or a combination of these.

By the time you are thinking about presenting your qualitative research, you have already sorted through immense amounts of literature, theory, research paradigms, data collection and analytic tools, and data management techniques, just to name a few! So, where do you even begin in thinking about presenting your data? The simplest answer and approach we have found may sound a bit, well, simple: Start at the beginning. Why did you decide to conduct your qualitative study in the first place? There is probably a personal and a professional rationale; we encourage you to share both. The personal reason invites your audience to care about your study, while the professional reasons begin to build your credibility with your audience. After you have established your rationale, begin to inform your audience of the important constructs in your study. Define these constructs and make certain you are grounding these definitions in the previous literature. This something we often see writers omit. It might seem obvious what a construct like "self-esteem" is. You might even have a great definition of your own for self-esteem. However, your audience may have their own ideas of what self-esteem is, and those ideas may be drastically different from yours. Plus—and we know this is not a fun thing to think about—your definition is probably not an original one. It is more likely that a construct like "self-esteem" has been defined repeatedly in the literature, possibly for a long period of time. Cite these previous definitions, especially any incongruence and debates amongst scholars in how these scholars have defined the constructs you aim to understand in your study.

Take the same approach for your literature review. Depending on the time you have in presenting your findings, you may not have the luxury of elegantly articulating all the gaps in knowledge existing within the literature. Give your audience the most important basics though so they can understand the major underpinnings of your study. Next, be sure to let them know about your research paradigm and the essential demographics of your participants, procedure for your study, and details of your data collection and analysis. You may not be able to share all of the findings in your study. Again, select participant quotes that are thick and rich in description of the phenomenon you have studied. Do not forget to present your discussion section: the link back to earlier literature and your interpretation of your findings. This should include exploring the implications and limitations of your study.

We provide an outline for organizing your presentation in Table 12.8 that you can refer to as an example. Also, take a look at the student exemplar (Ann Wendle Barnes) for a class presentation of findings in Appendix B. Finally, no matter how much time you have to present, try to

**TABLE 12.8.** Sample Outline for a Slideshow Presentation of Your Findings

In this table we provide a sample outline for presenting your study in a 1-hour format. You can think of each section listed in the left column as the "title" that can be listed at the top of each of your slides.

| Slide and number of slides | Description |
|---|---|
| **Title** (1 slide) | Include your study's title, your name and credentials related to your field, and the date and place of your presentation. |
| **Rationale** (1–2 slides) | Ground this in statistics and any other important information related to the "why" of your study's topic. |
| **Literature Review** (2–3 slides) | Showcase the gaps in the literature. Define the constructs in your study and any consistencies and inconsistencies important for your audience to be aware of in understanding your study. |
| **Method** (2–5 slides) | Include the most significant aspects of your conceptual framework in this section. Identify research paradigm and tradition(s). Discuss your participant demographics, the study's procedure, and data collection and analysis techniques used according to your tradition. |
| **Findings** (5–9 slides) | This is the bulk of your presentation if you are presenting an entire study. Consider using some type of visual portrayal of your findings either before or after you present them to help the audience understand their importance. Make certain to include thick, rich description from participants in the form of direct quotes from participants and key observations you have because of analyzing how your researcher biases influenced your interpretation of your data. |
| **Discussion** (3–5 slides) | Summarize your findings and refer to your earlier literature review in terms of how your findings either aligned or did not align with your topic. Discuss the implications of your study for your field and possibly other disciplines. Detail your study's limitations and possible ways future research might address these. |
| **References** (1–2 slides) | You might not include your entire reference list for the audience. You can highlight the most salient references or refer your audience to your email so they may email you for your reference list. |

balance your time so you can do justice to each section you have planned to present. Common challenges we have observed in qualitative study presentations are:

- skipping over construct definition
- neglecting to state researcher positionality
- neglecting data analytic techniques to account for researcher bias
- overlooking details of the research paradigm and tradition(s)

- passing too quickly over identified findings
- making assumptions about participants that are not grounded in the data
- running out of time to discuss the implications and limitations of the study

The main thing you want to keep in mind when you present your findings is that, just like writing up your qualitative report, you are taking the role of storyteller. So, remember to make sure you have a beginning, middle, and end of your presentation. Invite your audience to give you feedback. Be comfortable with saying, "I do not know" if you really are stumped by a question (and then say that you will find out and get back to them!). Do whatever stress management techniques you need to do ahead of time and during your presentation so you do not distract your audience with too many "ums" or excessive movements of your hands. We have found that even taking a few deep belly breaths before you present can calm your nerves, activate your parasympathetic relaxation system, and set you up for a successful presentation. And finally, try to enjoy the moment. You have accomplished a good deal to get to the stage of presenting your findings. Congratulations!

One format that you may consider using is a poster presentation of your qualitative study. This type of presentation is often called a *poster session*, where many researchers present their work simultaneously within the same time slot while attendees walk through the poster session. The word "poster" indicates that your work may be compiled in a slide or other format that is then printed on a large poster-size sheet, which is then displayed on a large stand-alone bulletin board or a tri-fold poster board. No matter what the specific setup may be, posters are often arranged in rows so that attendees may walk through a poster session and either glance at your study's findings from afar or choose to approach you to hear more about your study.

The most helpful aspect of poster sessions is that you are informally presenting to a potential mix of your peers and other, more senior researchers and practitioners in your field. Many people are initially confused about how a poster session "works," but it really is an informal presentation where you may select to tailor your "presentation" to those who visit your poster. Some attendees may only be interested in your topic and pick up handouts that you should prepare that summarize your study. Other attendees will stop and want to discuss particular aspects of your study (e.g., your findings or the methodology you selected for your study). We believe poster presentations are an ideal vehicle to also gather feedback from others about your research study at various stages (e.g., literature review, method, findings) of the project or at its completion. These informal discussions and feedback can help you view your study from different perspectives and ultimately strengthen your overall study.

**ACTIVITY 12.2.** PRESENTING YOUR QUALITATIVE PROPOSAL

Conduct a 20-minute presentation in small groups of your research proposal and any initial findings. Evaluate your group members using criteria developed in earlier chapters.

## Publishing Qualitative Research

In addition to presenting findings orally, you might be considering finding a publication outlet such as academic journals for your work. In Chapter 13, we discuss ways in which qualitative researchers can communicate their findings through research briefs, policy papers, or other community outlets.

We suggest that qualitative researchers find journals that are appropriate for their topic and type of research and those that are of high quality. A good way to begin identifying appropriate journals is to ask your colleagues and to pay attention to where qualitative articles you like have been published.

You want to identify at least five journals you might consider submitting to within your field. Some of these journals you may have never read before. Once you have identified a list within your field, take your search even wider than your field to identify additional journals that fit the scope of your topic. Table 12.9 provides a list of select academic journals that specifically publish

**TABLE 12.9** Select Qualitative Research Journals

Action Research
Anthropology and Education Quarterly
Cultural Studies/Critical Methodologies
Ethnographic Encounters
Ethnography
Ethnography and Education
Field Methods
Forum: Qualitative Social Research
Grounded Theory Review
International Journal of Qualitative Methods
International Journal of Qualitative Studies in Education
Journal of Autoethnography
Journal of Contemporary Ethnography
Journal of Ethnographic & Qualitative Research
Narrative Inquiry
Oral History Review
Phenomenology & Practice
Qualitative Health Research
Qualitative Inquiry
Qualitative Psychology
Qualitative Report
Qualitative Research
Qualitative Research in Psychology
Qualitative Social Work: Research and Practice
Qualitative Sociology
Qualitative Sociology Review
Research in Phenomenology
Studies in Qualitative Methodology
Studies in Symbolic Interaction
Symbolic Interaction
Visual Ethnography

qualitative research. We encourage you to also review top-tier journals within your discipline to determine their receptivity and previous publishing patterns in terms of qualitative research.

Take some time to examine the typical manuscripts they publish. Often, you will stumble upon a journal that has issued a call for manuscript or proposal submissions for a special issue for which your study might be a good match. An example of this from my own (Anneliese) publications was the call for a special issue on LGBTQ issues and trauma for the *International Journal of Traumatology*. When I read the call, I knew little about the journal's quality and typical submissions. So, I first looked at some of their past issues. I saw that the journal published qualitative work—not often, but the ones they did publish were of good quality. The bonus was that I had just wrapped up a phenomenological study of the resilience strategies of transgender people of color who had survived traumatic life events.

Once you select a journal to submit your work to, carefully review manuscript submission guidelines, which are generally available online at the journal publisher website. In addition to components of the manuscript, we encourage you to develop a strong cover letter to attract the editor and reviewers to your manuscript. We recommend the following strategies as you compose your cover letter:

- Because the cover letter is a formal letter, use formal language that upholds the respect of the academic review process.
- Include the title of your manuscript in the first sentence of your cover letter.
- Describe anything that is unique about your study: *briefly*. For instance, is it the first qualitative study on a topic? Try not to be too editorial in this letter. Avoid saying you are studying a "serious" issue, for example.
- Identify the section within the journal that your qualitative manuscript would fall under (often a research section).
- Refer to the ethical codes and guidelines you adhered to while conducting and writing up the research study.
- Identify up front any ways that you may not be in accordance with their submission guidelines. Did you go over their suggested page limit (an easy thing to do with a qualitative manuscript!)? If so, say so. Own it, build a rationale for doing so, and explicitly give concrete details (e.g., number of words or pages over the page limit for manuscripts) to the editor.
- Be brief and limit the cover letter to 3–4 paragraphs.
- Thank the editor for their time in the review process. It is a real, live person who is the journal's editor. And chances are that they have been working hard to ensure each submission is handled in a timely, ethical, and respectful manner. Convey appreciation.

We provide a sample cover letter to bring these tips for writing a good submission cover letter to life (see Table 12.10). If have done a good job in preparing your manuscript for the review process, you will hopefully get a favorable decision from the editor. The range of editorial decisions can be (a) reject, with no invitation to revise and resubmit; (b) revise and resubmit; (c) accept, with major revisions; (d) accept, with minor revisions; and (e) accept, with no revisions (this is very rare). At times, manuscripts are desk-rejected, or immediately rejected by an

**TABLE 12.10** Writing a Cover Letter to the Journal Editor When Submitting Your Manuscript

Dear Dr. Auger,

Attached please find the manuscript *School Counselors' Strategies for Social Justice Change: A Grounded Theory of What Works in the Real World* for publication review in the research section of the Professional School Counseling (PSC) journal. This is the first grounded theory inquiry into the interventions school counselors who identify as successful social justice advocates use within their school to achieve success in improving their school settings. In preparing this manuscript for submission to PSC, we followed the standards for research set by the ethics codes of the American Counseling Association (ACA) and the American School Counselor Association (ASCA).

We would like to thank you in advance for the time and energy involved in the review of this manuscript. We look forward to your review. Please do not hesitate to contact us if you have any questions or concerns at asingh@tulane.edu.

Sincerely,
Anneliese Singh, PhD, LPC

editor because the manuscript is simply not aligned with the mission and scope of the journal. Other times, a rejection occurs because of methodological and/or conceptual concerns with the manuscript. We encourage you to carefully review the JARS-Qual standards (APA, 2020b) shared earlier in this chapter (Table 12.2) to maximize the chances that your manuscript will be reviewed by an editorial board.

If you receive a "revise and resubmit" decision, we suggest you strengthen your manuscript based on these revisions and delineate in the resubmission cover letter the ways in which you addressed the recommendations. Occasionally, you can get reviewer feedback that is confusing, brief, and/or actually conflicting. It is fine to contact the editor with specific questions, just do not overdo this contact. You do not want the editor to feel like they should be an additional author on your manuscript because of the amount of feedback and time they have poured into your manuscript. Plus, your manuscript—believe it or not—is not the only one they are managing, so be mindful and appreciative of their time. A critical last step (or really an ongoing one as you are revising your manuscript) is to detail how you responded to each of the reviewer comments and any feedback offered by the editor. We like to include this as a bulleted list at the end of the cover letter you will send when you resubmit your article.

The last steps of the publication process (and we are still continually surprised by this) involve a dramatic process of … waiting. You wait and then wait some more. Then you possibly even wait some more. The publication process in academic journals is rarely a quick-footed beast. Rather, it operates more at a turtle's pace, and do not think of the story of the turtle and the hare, where there is a fantastic ending replete with meaning. You usually just wait and wait. Eventually, you get proofs of your manuscript (exciting!) to review and ensure your citations are all in your reference list and vice versa and to double-check things like the spelling of your

**REFLEXIVE ACTIVITY 12.1.** EXPLORING PRESENTING AND PUBLISHING YOUR FINDINGS

In your journal, explore your answers to the following questions:

- What are the strengths and challenges you may face in presenting and publishing your findings?
- What resources will you need to bring your study to completion and to publish your findings?

name and your organizational affiliation. At some point, usually many years later, you get a journal with an article with your name right beside a fantastic study you have conducted with writing that has much improved as a result of the review process. We suggest celebrating every step along the road to publication, including the waiting.

Throughout this chapter, we have discussed various writing tips. We summarize some of these in Wild Card 12.2 as a reminder for you as you seek to make your writing "sing" off the page and draw the audience into your qualitative study.

## Funding Qualitative Research

We conclude this chapter with a critical component of the career of the qualitative researcher (whether that career is in academia or organization and practice settings): funding your research. The landscape of education and social sciences requires educators, practitioners, and other social scientists to identify the needs of those served and advocate for resources to address those needs. These needs can require program development or revision, program sustainability, materials and supplies, or the expansion of existing services and initiatives in terms of scope and/or the number of participants. Within education settings, for example, federal and state funding continues to dwindle, requiring school personnel to look for external funding opportunities.

Funding qualitative research can involve seeking and obtaining grants, attracting private donations, and advocating successfully for funds appropriated through the legislative process. External funding, especially through grants, can provide necessary financial resources to support research and programmatic activities. In this section, we focus on the grant-writing process.

Given the characteristics and uses of qualitative research, educators, practitioners, and other social scientists can employ qualitative methodology as part of their work to seek external funding. For example, constructs such as student achievement, opportunity gaps, school or workplace climate and culture, school safety, clinical outcomes, finance reform, and mental health access are complex and require an evaluation plan that can identify its dimensions well. Through funded programs that incorporate qualitative methodology, many positive outcomes

**WILD CARD 12.2.** CAUTIONS FOR THE WRITING ROAD

1. Refuse to give in to writer's block! If you are not writing, identify the reasons why and address them so you do not suffer in silence.
2. Do not write in the passive voice.
3. Use simple language that is accessible, inviting, and clear for your readers.
4. Vary it up! Do a word search for any words or phrases that you use too many times or are somewhat "stale."
5. Take your writing one section of the report at a time, especially if thinking about the entire manuscript overwhelms you. Sometimes, just taking it one sentence at a time helps us when we feel stuck.
6. Watch out for editorializing your participants' thick description (Wolcott, 2008)! Do not let your writing assume that you know more about participants' experiences than they do.
7. Be clear in your writing about your researcher interpretation. It is perfectly fine to say things like, "From the researcher's perspective ..." or "The researcher interprets this as ..." That way, you are transparent about where you participants "end" and your researcher perspective begins.
8. Keep your exemplars of qualitative writing you admire close by while you are writing. That way, when you are confused about how to transition to a new section or are unsure about how to write about a section, you have an example of good writing nearby.
9. Be open and actively seek feedback on your writing. We know not everyone may be keen on a writing group, and if that is the case, do not avoid getting commentary on your writing, because it will be to your detriment to not do so in the end. Writing can feel like a vulnerable act, and we feel less vulnerable and more open to feedback on our writing when we practice receiving (and giving) feedback.
10. Remember the uncle test at every stage of your writing.

can occur: First, the practitioner can implement a higher quality, better-resourced program with stakeholders to address their needs and improve clinical and/or educational outcomes. Second, the funded program or initiative can identify stakeholder needs as well as innovative and culturally responsive approaches and interventions that would not have been identified without funding. Third, the reputation of education and social sciences in general can be strengthened as educators, practitioners, and/or other social scientists share findings from funded programs or initiatives. For example, providing more evidence-based work within these disciplines can propel the discipline itself (Delaney, 2016). Fourth, clinicians and educators are in a unique position to provide leadership for systemic change: The roles of advocate and change agent are bolstered for those who successfully seek and obtain funding to improve the lives of those served.

While it is beyond the scope of this text to discuss in depth the external-funding process, we list below some of the key strategies of grant writing. In addition, we recommend that you review the resources listed at the end of this chapter.

## Identify Funding Needs

An initial strategy for funding qualitative research is to determine and identify why funding is needed in the first place. Grant funding is awarded to those organizations, agencies, or researchers who seek to address service gaps and provide unique solutions to societal concerns and scientific questions (Delaney, 2016). Thus, scholarly and/or service gaps should be clearly understood and documented.

Having a solid foundation for a needed program or initiative is critical for successful funding. What are your community needs in terms of mental health and education? Would a needs assessment be valuable to address these concerns in a more focused and effective way? What resources are needed to implement innovation to advance positive outcomes within a program or community? How would qualitative research help to address these needs?

Qualitative researchers, whether working in higher education, PK–12 education, or clinical settings, should determine project goals and develop a basic vision for their program or initiative.

At times, having some flexibility in what and how program needs could be addressed by external funding can be driven by what funding sources are available. Thus, you may discern there are multiple areas of intervention that would help individuals and communities. In reviewing available funding opportunities, these areas can become more refined so that a funding proposal aligns with funding priorities.

## Seek Critical Partners

Critical partners involve those who can guide you through the funding process at different stages. For example, you can identify peers who have had funding success and who can mentor you as you begin the grant-writing process. Reviewing successful proposals and receiving tips from mentors can assist to minimize some of the challenges of grant writing and facilitate successful funding outcomes.

Community and academic partners are also critical in ensuring the proposal and implementation process are strong. Thus, it is important to take the time to establish strong, mutually beneficial partnerships before any grant submission. For example, if you are interested in seeking funding for a program or initiative in high schools, having relationships and shared goals with specific school district personnel and high schools demonstrates collaboration and a strong foundation for your proposal to a funder. Thus, qualitative researchers are to familiarize themselves with local programs, agencies, organizations, and school or individuals; what each offers, or has the capacity to offer, in terms of addressing needs; and how those partners and their activities and goals might align with grant opportunities. As these partnerships grow, build a communication network so that each can share funding opportunities, partnering where possible. Having a well-established team or network of partners helps to demonstrate to potential funders that the proposer has the capacity to engage in a project immediately and successfully (Delaney, 2016; Gitlin et al., 2021).

Grant writing is best done using a team approach, and identified partners can and should assist as appropriate with the grant proposal and implementation if funding is received. As such, qualitative researchers collaborate early to identify a timeline for writing, divide responsibility and establish deadlines, and assign a lead to be responsible for the overall management of the grant proposal. Furthermore, they are to discuss with partners who will be involved in grant management components if the initiative is funded.

## Select a Grant-Funding Source

There are several types of funding sources of which clinicians and education professionals can seek to support their work. Federal, state, foundation, and corporate funders are excellent grant-funding sources. Federal agencies, such as the National Institutes of Health, National Science Foundation, U.S. Department of Education, and the Substance Abuse and Mental Health Services Administration, receive funding from legislative appropriations. These agencies tend to be the most competitive, provide substantial funding, support complex, multiyear initiatives, and require lengthy proposals. Federal funding opportunities are compiled at a clearinghouse (i.e., https://grants.gov). State and local government grants are another funding source derived from federal pass-through monies and are localized appropriations. These types of grants are attractive in that they tend to be location specific and/or geographically bound and thus may align better with a proposed initiative (Delaney, 2016).

Foundations and corporations can be independent, community, or company-sponsored initiatives and typically support educational or social causes, usually within a specific geographic region. Foundations can be funded by individuals, families, community organizations, or corporations. A promising resource to find information about foundation and corporation grants is the Foundation Center (https://foundationcenter.org; Delaney, 2016).

Once a funding source is selected, qualitative researchers learn about the organization providing the grant and determine whether their proposal fits within their goals and objectives. They are to review the mission and funding scope carefully for the selected funder. It is also helpful to examine recently funded projects: Are there particular areas or themes related to what has been previously funded (e.g., program types, stakeholder needs and types) and at what amount (Delaney, 2016; Gitlin et al., 2021)?

## Articulate Project Need

Successful grant proposals include a comprehensive assessment of a particular population's needs and whether the proposed project can feasibly address that need. R. Porter (2007) distinguished that content in a grant proposal looks very different from traditional academic writing and that proposals should draw in the reader quickly to an urgent need to address. He noted that successful grant writing uses direct, concise, and jargon-free sentences; provides graphs and tables to illustrate concepts and plans; provides a strong design and rationale for what will be done to address a need; and states how the grant writer can accomplish what the funder wants to accomplish.

Thus, qualitative researchers are to paint an easily understood picture of context, needs, and creative solutions to be exercised if funded. They include a thorough review of the current literature, which includes the most current research and best practices available and an outline of which strategies and interventions have shown to be effective. Thus, the proposal should extend the current literature with a unique solution or idea. Furthermore, they clarify what is known about the current population and available resources for that population.

## Format the Proposal Properly

A grant proposal can be outright rejected if formatting requirements are not met as outlined in a request for proposals (RFP). Thus, qualitative researchers note the details of the formatting requirements, such as pagination, font size and type, character limits, formatting, and sequencing. Related to proposal structure, we encourage you to understand the common components of a grant proposal as you begin to think about grant writing (see Table 12.11).

**TABLE 12.11**   Common Elements of a Grant Proposal

Although the RFP from funders may vary slightly, there are some common elements of a grant proposal:

- *cover letter:* Often viewed as the gatekeeper to the proposal, the cover letter typically includes the contact information for the applicant(s) and their respective institution or organization, RFP title and project title, and a brief description of the goals and objectives of the project.
- *abstract:* Typically limited to one page, the abstract is the "commercial" or "sales pitch" for your project. It should include the most relevant information and data about the program or initiative need and background, the research question(s), an overview of the methodology or work plan, and an outline of the goals, objectives, and broader impacts of the project.
- *project narrative:* The project narrative components are typically outlined in the RFP and should be followed closely. Typically, the description or narrative will include an introduction section, concise research questions, clear and measurable research goals and objectives, relevant literature review, and a detailed work plan or methodology.
- *key personnel:* An RFP will often include a key personnel or management plan section in which you outline the organizational chart of the project and provide details about key personnel and their backgrounds and roles in the project.
- *evaluation plan:* Designed to highlight that the stated project goals and objectives can be met, the evaluation plan provides an opportunity to discuss who is conducting the evaluation, what their qualifications are, what data sources and methods will be used, and how data are collected and analyzed.
- *sustainability plan:* The sustainability plan includes detailed information about how the results and findings will be shared with stakeholders and the public. Depending on the project, communication outlets can include academic articles, conference presentations, community forums, and policy documents. Furthermore, the sustainability plan should discuss as relevant how services can continue to be provided once grant funding has ended.
- *budget and budget justification:* A detailed budget plan should evidence that there is good planning and effective use of resources from the funder. The plan should outline the needs of the project, usually through an accompanying spreadsheet.

Sources: Delaney (2016) and Gitlin et al. (2021)

## Provide Relevant Budget Information

Understanding budget guidelines and communicating a clear budget plan is a critical part of developing an effective grant proposal. An RFP from a funder will outline allowable expenses that can be requested in a project budget. Typical project budget items can include personnel and fringe, supplies, equipment, travel, participant incentives, consultants, evaluation costs, and indirect costs or overhead. You should also note any budget restrictions from a specific funder. For example, furniture, office supplies, or salary caps for personnel may be articulated. Furthermore, the funder may require that a minimum amount of the budget be directed as incentives for participants and stakeholders benefitting from the project. Finally, follow project budget guidelines directly and do not go above budget limits.

---

## CHAPTER SUMMARY

In this chapter, we discussed the essential components of writing, presenting, and funding qualitative research. Given the characteristics of qualitative research, there are distinct opportunities when communicating its findings to multiple academic and community audiences.

We discussed several writing rhetorical distinctions of qualitative research, which centers the interactive nature of qualitative research design (Maxwell, 2013): process versus section demarcation, an ethic of transparency, and contextualization (Levitt et al., 2018). Furthermore, we discussed the JARS-Qual (APA, 2020b), which provides flexible yet critical guidance for the qualitative proposal and report, and we discussed strategies for maximizing procedural rigor and forming a writing group. Then we delineated considerations and components of various sections of the qualitative research proposal and report.

Presenting qualitative research can be accomplished orally and/or in writing to multiple audiences. The chapter includes strategies for preparing slide and poster presentations for professional and community audiences. As possible, we encourage you to involve participants or other stakeholders as you present findings. Publishing qualitative research, one form of presenting your findings, can be done in outlets such as academic journals. We presented a list of qualitative research journal outlets as well as strategies for successful publishing.

We concluded the chapter by discussing the role of funding in qualitative research, centering the discussion in this chapter to grant funding from federal, state and local, community, and foundation and corporate funders. Several strategies were introduced, including identifying funding needs, seeking critical partners, selecting and reviewing a grant-funding source, articulating the project need and budget to the funder, and formatting the proposal effectively.

---

## Review Questions

1. How is qualitative research writing distinct from quantitative research writing?
2. In this chapter we discuss the importance of writing groups as well as partnership for external funding. What are key strategies for effective teams in writing and funding qualitative research?

3. What are some ways that participants and other stakeholders can be involved in presenting qualitative research findings?

4. What are the major types of grant-funding sources, and how would you determine which source is most aligned with your project?

## Recommended Readings

American Psychological Association. (2020b). *Journal article reporting standards: Qualitative research design (JARS-Qual).* https://apastyle.apa.org/jars/qualitative

Delaney, M. E. (2016). Grant writing for the counseling professional. *Journal of Counselor Preparation and Supervision, 8*(3). http://dx.doi.org/10.7729.83.1135

Gitlin, L. N., Kolanowski, A., & Lyons, K. J. (2021). *Successful grant writing: Strategies for health and human services professionals* (5th ed.). Springer.

Singh, A. A., & Lukkarila, L. (2017). *Successful academic writing: A complete guide for social and behavioral scientists.* Guilford Press.

Wolcott, H. F. (2008). *Writing up qualitative research* (3rd ed.). Sage.

## Image Credit

## CHAPTER 13

# Qualitative Research and Community and Legislative Action

## CHAPTER PREVIEW

Attention to action in social, professional, and political settings is embedded in the work that qualitative researchers do throughout the research process. In this chapter, we provide a rationale for why qualitative researchers are "called to action" within their communities. Then we outline several competency guidelines and policy documents within professional organizations that may be applied to qualitative research for the purposes of community and legislative action. The remainder of the chapter explains social advocacy and legislative advocacy, and we outline key strategies, steps, and examples for each as they apply to qualitative research.

## A Call to Action

As we conclude this text, we return to one of the components of the qualitative researcher's role: equity and advocacy. As educators, practitioners, and social scientists engage with others in qualitative research, we encounter and explore phenomena that need to be understood in terms of how the phenomena are influenced by and influence equity-related considerations in education and social sciences. To this end, qualitative researchers have the opportunity to advocate on behalf of and with participants and communities at micro, meso, and macro levels to optimize individual and community outcomes through education, practice, and policy (Toporek & Daniels, 2018).

Because advocacy has become such a critical role within education and social sciences in the new millennium for our multicultural society, the use of qualitative approaches has major implications for social change within professional settings. The role of "action" should be valued in qualitative research. There are qualitative approaches that specifically have action as an integral component to their approach (e.g., participatory action research, feminism, critical race theory), where the researcher collaborates with community partners to answer a question salient to the community. Furthermore, the role of the qualitative researcher itself has an action dimension within it (see Chapter 1).

Qualitative data collection tends to be intimate and relational in nature, so there is also the action involved in the research connecting with participants. Rather than completing a Likert scale, participants reveal their innermost truths to us as qualitative researchers as they share about their daily lived experiences of a phenomenon. In doing so, we must challenge ourselves to not only uphold the utmost integrity as researchers but also recognize (and not minimize) that we as researchers hold significant power in the lives of our participants as they share their experiences with us.

One of our favorite stories about data collection comes from our colleague and friend Dr. Sheneka Williams (see Chapter 6 for her author perspective). She tells the story of her first qualitative data collection, where she was collecting data on African American experiences of education in the South. The participants for this particular study did not have access to significant educational and financial resources and equity. At the time Dr. Williams was a doctoral student at Vanderbilt University. More often than not, her participants wanted to talk about how she as an African American "made it" to Vanderbilt. She became a symbol—whether she wanted it or not—of change to her participants, and she was a source of information and hope for them.

As Dr. Williams's story illustrates, even when we are not looking to "make change" or "take action" as qualitative researchers, we do so. Greenwood and Levin (2005) asserted both the challenges and opportunities that researchers encounter when they decide to value a researcher role that acknowledges the central importance of action. Although the authors are specifically discussing participatory action research (PAR), they also discuss that one of the central barriers to action research that is collaborative with communities is the "ivory tower" of university academia itself. If it is the ivory tower that creates these barriers between the researcher and community individuals and groups, the authors encourage ways that researchers might intentionally transcend these barriers—in addition to discussing the ethical mandates social science researchers have to ensure their research is relevant to the daily lives of people and communities.

Therefore, it is important to honor this in how we engage with the qualitative research process. This is also why we think it is important for current qualitative researchers in education and social sciences to be aware of and identify how their qualitative designs are action research in themselves. Some important questions to ask along the way are:

- What is the influence of participants and communities on the research process?
- What is the influence of the research process on participants and communities?
- How will we interact with participants before, during, and after the research process?
- What will we "leave" with participants, and what do we inevitably "take away" from participants from our mere presence as researchers?

Although we do not think there are simple answers to these questions, we do believe it is important to hold these questions in mind throughout every single step of qualitative research.

In addition, the feminist rallying call of the 1960s and 1970s (i.e., "the personal is political") is an important one to keep in mind as a qualitative researcher: We as researchers have an impact and influence on the phenomena we investigate. Hays (2020) noted that researchers are to continually engage in multicultural and social justice research to identify and work to minimize factors and conditions that might hinder individual, group, and systemic well-being. **Advocacy**, briefly defined, refers to actions that empower a community. Furthermore, advocacy through qualitative research can illuminate individual and community assets and resources to rescript dominant views of education and social science phenomena. To this end, qualitative researchers respond to the call to action by using culturally appropriate research designs, working within the intersection of power, privilege, and oppression within the research relationship and using research as a means of advocacy (Hays & Dahl, 2021; Singh et al., 2013; Toporek & Daniels, 2018).

The term "advocacy" is often used as a general term that encompasses a range of actions for social change. There are three interdependent forms of advocacy that are integral for using qualitative research when engaging in community and legislative action: social advocacy, legislative advocacy, and professional advocacy. **Social advocacy**, sometimes called *social justice advocacy*, is grounded in community-level change and calls attention to inequities across societal institutions, such as educational, legal, and health care. Through social advocacy, educators, practitioners, and other social scientists recognize the impact of privilege, oppression, and discrimination on the social, educational, mental health, and other outcomes of individuals and communities (dickey et al., 2017; Gnilka et al., 2023; Toporek & Daniels, 2018).

The second form of advocacy is legislative advocacy. **Legislative advocacy** is defined as efforts to systemic change carried out by working with legislators and through the legislative process and encompasses lobbying activities; it calls attention to issues that can be addressed through public policy, such as sharing research that could shape a particular public policy (Bond, 2019; Cullerton et al., 2018). The final form, **professional advocacy**, refers to efforts that seek to unify a profession, increase the visibility of the profession within a community, and strengthen the training and licensure standards for that profession (Farrell & Barrio Minton, 2019; Myers et al., 2002). Professional advocacy requires intentional efforts in both social advocacy and legislative advocacy: Advancing the visibility of our respective professions and our own professional identity requires actions aligned with social and public policy change.

Establishing social validity is the cornerstone bridging qualitative researchers' call to action and meaningful social change and public policy. **Social validity** is defined as evidence of research findings being applied to the conduct of everyday life in a timely and socially valued manner. Thus, findings inform what interventions are effective with a specific group, and what was gained has social value to that context. Qualitative research is well-suited for establishing social validity, offering research traditions and methodologies that provide feedback loops among research, practice, and advocacy. Interactions within qualitative research are social and cultural, yielding contextual information on addressing issues and solutions that communities note as important. To maximize social validity, qualitative researchers actively embed participant voice in the research process, including them as a member of the research team as possible (Kozleski, 2017).

Throughout the remainder of this chapter, we describe and provide strategies for how qualitative researchers can address the call to action by conducting and applying research in social and legislative advocacy contexts. Effective advocacy within these two arenas then will strengthen professional advocacy.

## Professional Organizations and Community and Legislative Action

Competency standards available in education and social sciences disciplines are particularly foundational to the call to action for qualitative researchers. In this section, we highlight several competency standards and guidelines available in education and social sciences. These competencies may be applied to qualitative research practice to support the components of the qualitative researcher's role (i.e., equity and advocacy, participant voice, researcher reflexivity, and researcher subjectivity).

### AERA Policy and Advocacy

The American Educational Research Association (AERA) can be a helpful resource for qualitative researchers in both educational and clinical settings. For instance, AERA continuously updates their "Policy & Advocacy" link on their website (see https://aera.net) to include current statements and letters submitted to the government and other entities about educational advocacy. AERA also updates their "Research Policy & Advocacy News" regularly and includes information about research funding advocacy and research policy.

In addition, AERA has standing committees (i.e., Equity and Inclusion Council, Social Justice Action Committee, Special Interest Groups Executive Committee, Committee of Scholars of Color in Education) that help shape AERA policy and advocacy. You can also see the "Position Statements" tab on their website, which has a range of statements about supporting the rights of persons with disabilities, educator preparedness, human rights, academic freedom, high stakes testing, and more. These position statements can help you see how AERA is seeking to shape general advocacy in educational research and beyond. If you are interested in influencing public policy specifically, you can use the AERA Advocacy Toolkit to guide your interactions with lobbying and other efforts with legislators.

### ACA Multicultural and Social Justice Counseling Competencies

The American Counseling Association's (ACA) multicultural and social justice counseling competencies (MSJCCs; Ratts et al., 2015, 2016) can be applied to counseling, psychology, and other related clinical disciplines—but are helpful for those in educational settings as well. As you look at Figure 13.1, you can see that there are quadrants of these competencies that can help you think about to which extent you and the participants you work with hold identities related to privilege and oppression. These quadrants are as follows:

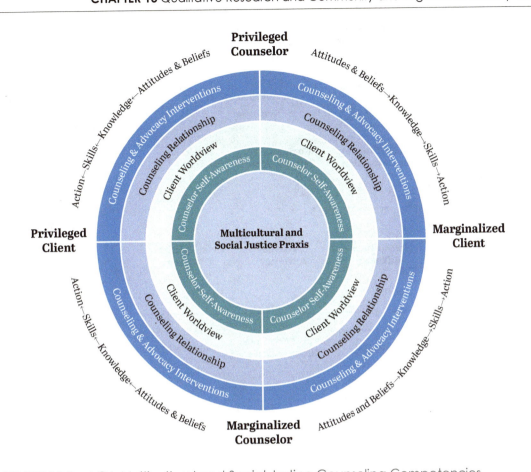

**FIGURE 13.1**   ACA Multicultural and Social Justice Counseling Competencies

- Quadrant I: privileged counselor-marginalized client
- Quadrant II: privileged counselor-privileged client
- Quadrant III: marginalized counselor-privileged client
- Quadrant IV: marginalized counselor-marginalized client

There are also four domains within the MSJCCs that are developmental in that they help guide progressive levels of counselor multicultural and social justice competency: (a) counselor self-awareness, (b) client worldview, (c) counseling relationship, and (d) counseling and advocacy interventions (this latter domain guides counselors to take action on the intrapersonal, interpersonal, institutional, community, public policy, and international/global affairs levels). Throughout each of these development domains, there are aspirational competencies designated across attitudes and beliefs, knowledge, skills, and action.

## ACA Advocacy Competencies

The ACA advocacy competencies (Toporek & Daniels, 2018) can also be applied to qualitative research advocacy in education and social science settings. These advocacy competencies can help guide you as a qualitative researcher to consider, first, whether you are acting with or on behalf of the participants in your research to make change. You can see in Figure 13.2 that next

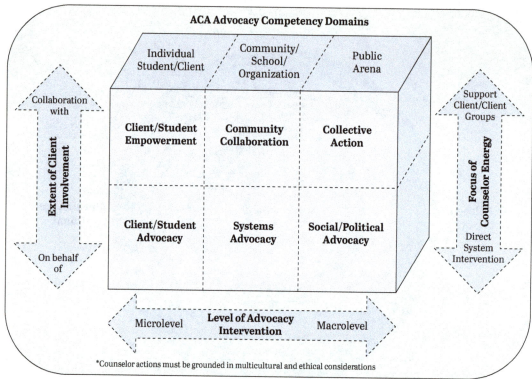

**ACA Advocacy Competency Domains**

Original model by Lewis, Arnold, House & Toporek (2003) updated by Toporek & Daniels (2018)

**FIGURE 13.2** ACA Advocacy Competencies

you can determine the site of change you are making with your research, on a continuum from collaboration with to engagement on behalf of a research partner or participant:

- *micro level:* an individual student/client is the primary research audience. The researcher collaborates with participant to support client/student empowerment to engages on behalf of the participant in client/student advocacy.
- *meso level:* a community/school/organization is the primary research audience. The researcher engages in community collaboration to more extensive involvement (i.e., systems advocacy) during the research process.
- *macro level:* the primary focus or audience for research is the general public. The researcher engages with others in the public for collective action to more extensive involvement (i.e., social/political advocacy) to advance research and/or its findings.

In addition to the helpful figure that portrays these different levels of advocacy, you can read about specific advocacy competencies you can engage in to help you brainstorm potential action and social change and expand possibilities of what advocacy efforts you consider.

## Applying Competency Standards to Qualitative Research

Qualitative researchers interested in engaging in multicultural and social justice advocacy research can translate these competency standards to aspirational researcher qualities and actionable steps in the research process and reporting of findings for advocacy. Hays and Dahl (2021) identified four interdependent researcher qualities as follows: (a) counseling researcher self-awareness, (b) knowledge of research participant worldview, (c) mutually beneficial counseling research relationship, and (d) engagement in research advocacy. While these are written for counselors engaged in research, these may be applied to other disciplines within education and social sciences. Table 13.1 highlights examples of how these researcher qualities translate to the practice of qualitative research as well as community and legislative action.

*Researcher self-awareness* relates to having a high degree of self-awareness as an educator, practitioner, or other social scientist *and* as a qualitative researcher. Qualitative researchers should reflect deeply on how their social identities, their privilege and oppression experiences, and attitudes and beliefs impact their approach to research and their research experiences in general. Further, they seek knowledge and skills to foster self-awareness as an education or social science professional.

*Research participant worldview* can be conceptualized as the values, norms, biases, and assumptions derived from individual social experiences that impact the research process. For example, participants may have previous negative experiences with qualitative researchers or may have not been able to participate often in research. Qualitative researchers also need to be knowledgeable about the history and events that shape how research is conducted today while gauging whether those practices are conducive to culturally competent research.

As qualitative data are collected, interpreted, and reported, it is also useful for qualitative researchers to understand how researcher and participant worldviews, shaped by their respective privilege and oppression experiences, coalesce to develop and sustain a *mutually beneficial research relationship* (i.e., both researchers and participants should gain positive outcomes from the research process). Positive outcomes for participants might include access to much-needed educational, clinical, and/or other interventions or an opportunity to provide input on needs during a focus group interview session. Some positive outcomes for qualitative researchers can include access to data to be used to publish in a journal or to apply for external funding.

*Research advocacy* may be defined as the adoption of research practices that serve to empower both researchers and participants; these practices can result in improved individual and community-based services and/or education and training opportunities for participants, researchers, and those practicing in education and social science disciplines. They conduct research that promotes cultural understanding and participant and community empowerment. By prioritizing empowerment and thus participant and community voice, the community of interest is more likely to benefit from the research.

## Research and Policy Briefs

Before delving into social and legislative advocacy tactics, we highlight two written communications tools that can be used in paper or electronic format to inform your social and legislative advocacy efforts. The first tool is the research brief. A **research brief** is a description of your research; it can be a description of research you are proposing to do or a short overview of

**TABLE 13.1** Applying Qualitative Researcher Qualities to Research and Action

| Researcher qualities | Research process | Community and legislative action |
|---|---|---|
| **Researcher self-awareness** | Reflect on who you are as a practitioner and researcher and how your positionality influences researcher subjectivity. | Identify your personal and professional perspectives on a community concern of interest. Consider how those perspectives are influenced by your own privileged and oppressed statuses and general experiences with research. Collaborate with others in advocacy activities to safeguard against community or participant harm. |
| **Research participant worldview** | Understand who the participant is. Depending on the community in which the research is taking place, the participant might be an individual, family, and/or the entire community. Once the participant group is identified, gain extensive information about the community, and maintain contact with that community before, during, and after the research process. | Ascertain how the constructs of interest are conceptualized and are traditionally explored within a community. Check in with your respective research team and community of interest to ensure findings and reporting align with others' understanding and that any reported data are presented in an empowering manner to the extent possible. |
| **Mutually beneficial research relationship** | At the beginning of the potential research relationship, assess participants' previous experiences with research and the degree of trust with the research process. Work to build trust by being transparent about research design components as well as the benefits and challenges of the research relationship. | Co-create research and advocacy goals with participants, considering them as coresearchers as possible and minimizing the researcher–participant power differential. Solicit their input on how advocacy can be done to address a community concern. |
| **Research advocacy** | Remain an informed consumer of published research and a critical analyst of your own motives for engaging in research. Consider the impact of your research on traditionally marginalized populations. Maximize equitable participation while safeguarding against unnecessary participant harm during data collection, analysis, and reporting. | Coestablish fair evidence-based practices that inform professional practice and future research. |

Sources: Hays & Dahl (2021) and O'Hara et al. (2016)

research you have completed. Sometimes, research briefs include a summary of research in a particular area or topic (e.g., recruitment and retention of Indigenous students, mental health inequities for first-generation college students). An effectively written research brief is one that connects information about a particular topic directly to a community concern.

The components of a research brief may vary depending on the target of advocacy for the research brief. You should keep in mind the target audience for the research brief throughout the writing of it. If you are preparing the research brief for a conference or grant submission, you will follow their particular guidelines in preparing your research brief. If you are preparing the research brief to connect with other researchers, then using the constructs and language of academic disciplines is important. Finally, if you are preparing it to share with community members, then using accessible, everyday language is vitally important to promote community utility of the research brief.

Some essential components of the research brief are as follows:

- *overview/purpose:* What are the aims of the research brief? What do you want the audience to understand about the purpose of your research that you can summarize in 2–4 sentences? For this component, identify any funding sources that will support or have supported the presented research.
- *relevant previous literature:* What are the most pertinent studies related to your study? Outlining previous literature should extend beyond a brief summary of previous scholarship on a particular topic; you should clearly identify research gaps in terms of findings or methodological limitations that warrant the present research.
- *method and study design:* Whether your research is proposed or completed, what are the most critical aspects of your method and study design to share with your audience? In this section, you should note the "big picture" of participant recruitment, selection, and composition as well as procedures and research approaches used. Oftentimes, it is critical to remove methodological jargon to present a streamlined description of the method and overall study design.
- *findings:* What are the most important findings related to the advocacy you are targeting? For this component, write a summary of themes, adding quotes and other supplemental information to maximize the transferability or generalizability of the findings to a reader's local context and experiences.
- *implications:* What are the most critical implications related to your findings? How might these study findings align with or challenge previous literature in this area related to the target of your advocacy? What are community-based recommendations that may be made from the findings? You should outline how the findings have been implemented within the authors' setting(s) as applicable. As information regarding implementation is discussed, you should present ways in which the findings or recommendations from the findings may be readily applied by the reader for advocacy within their own context.

Again, the reference to the label "brief" in research brief can be both helpful and a bit misleading. On the helpful side, you can use the areas listed above to create an outline for a 1-page research brief or a 1-paragraph research brief. Other times, you will be asked to create a research brief that is longer (e.g., 5–10 pages or more). Regardless, you are consistently asking yourself, "What are the most vital components to include related to my advocacy target? What are the components that do not advance my target (and may even distract my audience or move them in a different direction than I intended)?" We encourage you to review Case Example 13.1, which highlights several examples of research briefs that feature qualitative research findings.

## Case Example 13.1. Sample Research Briefs

### A Qualitative Study of the Impact of Peer Networks and Peer Support Arrangements in Project Pilot Schools

Logsdon et al. (2018) highlight the need for students with disabilities to form meaningful peer support networks to foster positive academic and social outcomes within K–12 settings. Qualitative findings from eight school sites highlight beneficial social, academic, and school climate outcomes associated with the University of Kentucky's Peer Support Network Project. In addition, challenges linked to logistical constraints are discussed. As the brief is concluded, the authors update the reader on how the Peer Support Network Project has adapted based on the present study findings.

### Student Experience with the High School Choice Process in Chicago Public Schools

Shyjka (2021) illuminates how 38 eighth-grade students in three Chicago Public Schools experienced the school choice process in Chicago, shortly after Chicago Public Schools implemented an online application platform (i.e., GoCPS). Findings from seven focus group interviews outline three school choice factors: (1) setting—school location, distance from home, and transportation logistics; (2) school—characteristics, reputations, rating, and impressions of school; and (3) students—identities, personally and within social contexts. In addition, the research brief notes findings related to how high school students learned about school choice options as well as their perceptions of using GoCPS. These student experiences offer important considerations about school choice policies and practices for educators, policy-makers, and researchers.

### Veteran Sex Offender Access to Housing and Services after Release from Incarceration: Obstacles and Best Practices

Simmons et al. (2018) highlight the housing and other structural barriers facing sex-offending veterans released from incarceration. Through individuals interviews with 14 men who were convicted of sex offenses as well as 21 stakeholders of the VA Health Care for Reentry Veterans, the authors identified barriers and facilitators to housing and health care. Barriers included social stigma, housing, lack of social support, access to sex offender treatment, and legal barriers. Facilitators included access to treatment during and after prison release; the presence of offender legal knowledge, self-advocacy skills, and hope; and formal and informal social support.

In addition to these general research brief components, there are alternate ways to structure research briefs based on the intended use of those briefs. Anneliese developed and coordinated The Trans Resilience Project, which is comprised of a group of researchers across the United States and globe who engage in research related to trans and nonbinary resilience, resistance, and liberation. She asked for research briefs from those scholars who were interested in participating. Anneliese asked the scholars to submit research briefs that described their scholarship in the following areas:

- *research agenda:* Describe in 2–4 sentences your overarching research agenda.
- *research findings:* Describe in 1–2 paragraphs the most important study findings you have related to trans and nonbinary resilience, resistance, and liberation.
- *advocacy and policy change:* Describe in 1 paragraph any advocacy and/or policy change efforts you are involved in (or have been involved in) and any relevant organizations with whom you work in your advocacy and/or policy change.
- *contact information:* Include email and other social media information.

The areas Anneliese asked for were to tailor a website and contact sharing form, so she also asked researchers to use accessible, everyday language to reach a general trans and nonbinary audience.

Research briefs can also be tailored to inform **policy briefs**, which are communications materials specifically targeted for communicating with legislators. Details about previous research, methodology, and current findings outlined within a research brief must be distilled to clearly communicate how information garnered from research is valuable for shaping policy decisions. In addition, the following strategies can be beneficial to maximize the utility of policy briefs for legislative advocacy: (a) using a descriptive title to capture reader attention; (b) including simple graphs, charts, or text boxes to highlight key information; (c) presenting key statistics, factors, and findings, assuming no previous knowledge of the topic; and (d) sharing success stories regarding how research informed legislation within other areas and regions.

Developing and distributing policy briefs should be an ongoing process to capture and sustain attention of legislative bodies. As an example, the University of Nevada, Las Vegas, College of Education develops policy papers continually on key legislative issues related to education and wraparound services; these papers are presented to Nevada legislators to help inform work concerning education- and mental-health-related issues. Policy briefs are codeveloped by faculty and community members and are based in their respective scholarship and state- and national-level statistics regarding a particular issue. Policy briefs (2015–present) may be found online (https://unlv.edu/education/policy).

## Social Advocacy

**Social advocacy** is taken up by qualitative researchers when we focus our attention on educational, legal, health care, and other societal inequities. We can use social advocacy to highlight issues of privilege, oppression, power, discrimination, and allyship regarding social determinants of academic success and overall health and well-being for historically marginalized individuals and communities (dickey et al., 2017; Toporek & Daniels, 2018). As qualitative researchers, we can consider the connections that exist between social advocacy and qualitative research, the specific steps for social advocacy, and considerations of how we share our findings with community members.

## Social Advocacy and Qualitative Research

The connection between social advocacy and qualitative research rests on the issues of equity and advocacy we have woven in throughout this text. These issues are related to who has the power and privilege to make change (and making sure those who have this power and privilege to make social change use it) and who does not have access to this power and privilege (and then those who have power and privilege seeking to share it). Therefore, right from the beginning of your social advocacy as a qualitative researcher, you are looking to identify the areas of power, privilege, and oppression impacting the participants and communities you work with as well as yourself as a researcher.

This question is an ongoing one throughout your research, especially as you begin to take action, for instance, on the implications of your completed study findings. To illustrate this, let's take Anneliese's longitudinal multisite study (i.e., Atlanta, New York, San Francisco) funded by the National Institutes of Health with trans and nonbinary communities on their experiences of resilience, risk, and identity development. As she was beginning this research with trans and nonbinary participants in 2014, she and her research collaborators across the site did not expect the results of the 2016 presidential election and that this presidential administration would go on to continue trans-antagonistic policies within research and public policy. Only 2 years into the study, she and her collaborators noticed they had regular conversations with their participants about the fear, targeting, and other negative outcomes they had experiences as trans and nonbinary people during the run-up to the election and afterwards. So, they decided to conduct an additional qualitative study on the sociopolitical environment to make this connection between qualitative research and social advocacy examining trans and nonbinary vulnerability and resilience during this time of sociopolitical change (see Bockting et al., 2020). The researchers not only conducted the study but also connected with other researchers in trans and nonbinary health scholarship to find ways to advocate for continued funding of this scholarship and to also support one another in expanding the scholarship base at a time there was an explicit pushback on this work.

Anneliese's example shows how there can be continuously unfolding opportunities for social advocacy during the course of qualitative research, the connection between social advocacy and qualitative research can also be collecting the lived experiences and stories participants have of a particular social justice issue to highlight their voices. Within the scholarship base you are researching, there can be helpful existing literature on your research topic and social advocacy that scholars have called for that is needed. These articles might be conceptual in nature, or social advocacy implications of a study's findings might be included in the discussion sections of journal articles. Sometimes, this connection between social advocacy and qualitative research is even further developed, such as in Table 13.2, where scholars have written about

**TABLE 13.2**   Checklist for Participatory Action Research (PAR) Feminist Researchers Working with Transgender Communities (Singh et al., 2013, p. 97)

- Assess one's intersecting cultural identities (e.g., race/ethnicity, gender identity or expression, etc.) as they related to privilege and oppression and power as a qualitative researcher.
- Clearly articulate a theory on gender and determine how this theory informs methodological choices.
- Reflect on researcher positionality related to transgender concerns.
- Conduct a current transgender literature review informed by both peer-reviewed sources and other nonacademic sources of information (e.g., blogs, advocacy websites, novels, etc.).
- Provide and/or attend presentations or activities at community centers that serve transgender individuals so that a potential PAR relationship can be initiated.
- Determine community needs by working collaboratively with transgender people and communities.
- Identify the opportunity for advocacy associated with the PAR study.
- Work with a research team in order to establish expectations and accountability related to researcher privileges, assumptions, and biases.
- Use sampling practices that ensure a diverse and representative population.
- Share all aspects of the research process and data with informants and communities (stakeholders) and be sure to ask for feedback and input along the way.
- Practice humility about one's knowledge and assumptions, apologize as necessary, and make changes to the study based on this learning.
- Understand historical oppression of transgender people and communities.
- Identify how your personal liberation is connected to the liberation of the informants and participants with whom you work.

Source: Singh, A. A., Richmond, K., & Burnes, T. R. (2013). Feminist participatory action research with transgender communities: Fostering the practice of ethical and empowering research designs. *International Journal of Transgenderism, 14*(3), 93–104. https://doi.org/10.1080/15532739.2013.818516

the connections of power, privilege, oppression, and qualitative research when engaging in PAR with trans and nonbinary communities grounded in feminist theory.

Regardless of how well-developed your area of qualitative research and social advocacy is with regard to your topic, keep in mind you can search in near disciplines for this information. For instance, educators can draw on the multicultural and social justice counseling competencies mentioned earlier to make their case for social advocacy. Mental health practitioners can draw on the AERA policy and advocacy updates and position statements to guide their social advocacy in their qualitative research. In addition, keep in mind that as you deepen your understanding of the connection between qualitative research and social advocacy, you will naturally begin to think about public policy, legislative action, and policy change efforts (which we discuss in the next major section of this chapter).

## Steps for Social Advocacy

Ideally, at the beginning of your research process you have considered the end of your research process and how to connect your study to social advocacy. You can use the ACA advocacy competencies (Toporek & Daniels, 2018) or other scholarly articles on advocacy in your field to help you determine the specific ways you might advocate for the community you have researched. The National Council for the Social Studies (n.d.) has a 10-step process for developing an advocacy plan that we find helpful to shape your social advocacy approach. Their approach was originally designed for professional advocacy, but we have applied their 10-step process for connecting qualitative research and social advocacy below:

1. *Identify an advocacy challenge or opportunity:* Determine the most pressing social advocacy that is needed at this time and consult with others (especially those in the impacted community) to identify the challenges and opportunities that rest with addressing this particular advocacy issue.

2. *Determine the key audiences:* Know who the key stakeholders are for your selected social advocacy. Who are they, and where will you find them? How accessible are these stakeholders? What contacts to them may you already have or need to develop?

3. *Find out what those audiences currently know or perceive:* Consult with those who may be engaged in social advocacy already to understand what your key audiences may or may not know about your social advocacy issue. Will you have to educate them on the value of qualitative research in learning the lived experiences of participants?

4. *Determine how each audience receives its information:* Identify the best ways to communicate with your key audiences (e.g., email, snail mail). Are in-person meetings helpful, or is a social media campaign (or direct messaging them on Twitter, for instance) a more effective approach? Are you the best person to directly engage in the particular social advocacy issue, or is there another stakeholder with a preexisting relationship that might be more effective in delivering this social advocacy message?

5. *Establish measurable objectives for each audience:* Reflect on how you would determine that your message is received successfully. Would the key audiences need a copy of a research brief or some other information relevant to them?

6. *Define message points for each audience:* Craft your primary message and a secondary (and even tertiary) message. What is the most important message you want them to receive (primary message), and what are the messages that back these up (secondary and tertiary messages)?

7. *Determine the communication activities to deliver those messages:* What access do you have to the key audiences? Is it a person, organization, or a mix of both whom you will contact in your social advocacy?

8. *Decide what resources are necessary to complete each activity:* What are the costs related to engaging in this social advocacy with your key audiences? Is this a paid sponsored message in a social media campaign or a free direct message to a stakeholder about your advocacy issue? Are you using a mailing campaign or an in-person meeting where the main resource needed is time to schedule and participate in the meeting?

9. *Establish a timeline and responsible party for each activity:* Just like your research study itself, a timeline can help you organize your approach and make the social advocacy you are engaging real and tangible. A timeline connected to a person (e.g., working alone,

working with others) can also make bring the timeline for your social advocacy alive and make it clearer how you will implement it.

10. *Evaluate whether you have reached your objectives:* Take some time at the end to engage in formative or summative evaluation. In addition, set aside time to reflect personally on the process of engaging in social advocacy related to your qualitative research (it is very helpful to do this step with others) to identify what worked well and what you might change in future advocacy efforts.

## Sharing Findings with the Community

As a qualitative researcher—regardless of how you engage in social advocacy—it is important to share your findings with community members at the conclusion of your research. Qualitative research traditions such as PAR demand this sharing, and we believe this is a critical practice and an ethical issue in order to share power and validate the lived experiences and local knowledge that already exists in communities you may study. In addition, sharing your findings can help highlight new and emerging issues within a community setting and help local, regional, national, and international advocates build your research findings into their own everyday intervention and response work in a particular community.

McDavitt et al. (2016) share four major reasons that researchers concerned about advocacy and participatory approaches to research should share their findings. First, individuals in communities have given a lot of themselves to participate in your study and should have other ways of engaging in your research. Second, community members are able to provide different perspectives of the findings from a localized perspective. Third, advocates and fellow educators and clinicians can utilize your research findings to make immediate, short-term, and long-term changes to enhance services for community members, narrowing the space between you as a researcher and participants. Finally, dialogue with participants in their own community setting helps foster culturally relevant interventions for community members. The authors emphasize that regardless of how and where findings are shared, it is important to have a flow of dialogue back and forth between researcher and participants as opposed to a top-down approach.

In addition, if you have set up a community advisory board (CAB) in your research study, then it is helpful to discuss with your CAB members what the best approach to sharing your study findings would be. Your CAB members can also let you know if there are important people to work with in advance of the meeting and help arrange those meetings (Sevelius et al., 2017). For instance, if you are engaged in a study with Latinx parents of elementary school students, then the school setting may or may not be the best location to have a community meeting to share the findings; instead, possibly a community center or religious community setting might be the most conducive place to hold this sharing, and your CAB members can guide you in this decision-making process.

In addition, your research tradition, theoretical framework, and research question may also help you make the decision about the most helpful way to distribute findings. Another consideration concerns the venue in which you share your findings. You may simultaneously consider using social media and other forms of technology alongside in-person venues to share your research findings (Glazier & Topping, 2021). Regardless of how you make the decision to share your findings, the overarching aim is to take an approach that is intentional and develops trust and transparency: critically important components for community members (Hoover et al., 2016).

## Legislative Advocacy

Educators, practitioners, and other social scientists are "in the trenches" daily and thus have insider knowledge and positional authority regarding the issues that impact communities. They understand how policies and decisions impact things such as educational outcomes for students in a classroom or mental health and social consequences of clients and families. As such, they have sound, practice-based ideas for reform (Bond, 2019). Qualitative researchers, whether conducting research within their professional settings or with those working in professional settings, are critical conduits for informing public policy regarding education, mental health, and/or social reform that benefits communities. Furthermore, legislative advocacy is a professional standard for those in education and social sciences, often documented in the mission statement and ethical guidelines for their respective disciplines.

Because they are removed from the daily environment of education, mental health, and other community settings, policymakers tend to have significantly less knowledge about how policy decisions impact their constituents (Bond, 2019). Legislative advocacy can occur at local, state, or federal levels; however, most advocates focus their work at one of these levels. Floden (2007) noted three primary approaches to research to inform policy: economics, organizational studies, and critical. The *economics approach* refers to research guided by questions that inform expenditures for a profession or setting. Questions might relate to expenditures, productivity, or the general economic structure of a program, initiative, or practice in education and social science settings. An *organizational studies approach* involves research questions surrounding policy implementation; there is an examination of the alignment of policy intent and actual impact. A *critical approach* explicitly explores how policy works to legitimize and reproduce social inequalities within social, educational, and mental health structures and institutions.

The Community Tool Box (n.d.-b) provides several reasons for why you should conduct research to influence policy:

- to show that there is a need for funding and/or an intervention on a particular issue
- to show that a need or issue exists and to assure it is actually addressed
- to assure that what is addressed is, in fact, what needs to be addressed
- to support or discredit a specific method or practice
- to identify and advocate for appropriate policy in a given situation
- to protect the public health and safety
- to provide a solid base for advocacy
- to maintain your professional integrity

Furthermore, qualitative research should be conducted when there is no policy to address a community issue yet there is a need for one. Consider the issue of the need for wrap-around services in educational settings (e.g., mental health services, housing assistance for youth experiencing homelessness). Qualitative research can be employed to highlight the prevalence and experiences of those in need of these services. Qualitative research can help to support or refute current knowledge that is informing a proposed or established policy. Using the wrap-around services example, qualitative researchers might investigate whether a current policy that implements wrap-around services is the most appropriate policy or includes the most relevant wrap-around services for a particular community. Or qualitative researchers may conduct and report on research that helps to highlight how particular wrap-around services are beneficial yet may be presently left out of a proposed policy.

Community members can and should be integral to legislative advocacy. Their experiences with an issue or concern can yield compelling and powerful accounts for legislators. In addition, their participation can empower them, as their voice is included in policy change efforts. In particular, the use of narratives and storytelling is increasingly becoming a powerful method in advocacy efforts to influence policy change. As such, narratives and storytelling can mobilize participants and foster a collective identity. Case Example 13.2 describes how youth storytelling can inform legislative advocacy to dismantle the school-to-prison pipeline (Moyer et al., 2020).

### Case Example 13.2. Combatting the School-to-Prison Pipeline Through Youth Storytelling

In 2013, a group of high school students in Chicago launched a campaign to inform the passage of Senate Bill 100, designed to end zero-tolerance school discipline policies and promote restorative justice practices across the state of Illinois. The campaign was informed by Voices of Youth in Chicago Education (VOYCE), a coalition of five community organizations that worked primarily with lower socioeconomic status Black and Latinx high school youth and their communities. VOYCE was founded in 2007, and Warren et al. (2016) developed a community-engaged project with the coalition. The project involved in-depth interviews with 35 organizational staff members, youth leaders, Illinois policymakers, and other VOYCE allies. In addition, they conducted focus group interviews with 11 VOYCE youth leaders, 15 observations of organization activities, and a review of VOYCE documents, reports, and legislative materials.

Some of the research design components were as follows:

- consultation on research design, participant selection, and data analysis
- continual trust-building with VOYCE staff and participants who were culturally different from the authors
- discussion of how issues of power and privilege could be raised throughout the research process in a safe way
- active listening to feedback and concerns of participants
- shared drafts of the findings for member checking

VOYCE's 2013 legislative proposal required that public schools report their disciplinary statistics by racial/ethnic group as well as reduce the ability of districts to use zero-tolerance discipline and mandated that schools consider alternative restorative justice practices prior to imposing suspensions or expulsions. VOYCE youth leaders traveled weekly to the Illinois statehouse to share their stories in one-on-one legislator visits as well as through testimony at hearings. Through witnessing youth leaders' stories, legislators empathized with how participants had been adversely impacted by harsh school discipline policies. In addition to narratives, youth leaders shared data that reflected that the impact of zero-tolerance policies and their racialized outcomes were widespread across the state.

Source: Moyer, J. S., Warren, M. R., & King, A. R. (2020). "Our stories are powerful": The use of youth storytelling in policy advocacy to combat the school-to-prison pipeline. *Harvard Educational Review, 90,* 172–194.

## Legislative Advocacy Strategies and Steps

What leads to effective legislative advocacy, and what are the strategies and steps in which qualitative researchers should engage? Bond (2019) conducted a multiple case study in which educators identified as advocacy experts highlighted three themes regarding how they successfully engaged in legislative advocacy. First, they noted motives for their involvement in legislative advocacy were grounded in a desire to influence decisions that directly affected their daily work as educators and sought to change negative perceptions held by policymakers and the general public about education and the work of education. Second, they personalized the advocacy process by relying on their subjective experiences and unique knowledge and skills as they presented on an issue. These experiences and competencies were partly based on their research in their discipline. Third, they intentionally collaborated and engaged with policymakers and constituents to have the most impact in their messaging. Some of this engagement involved getting the word out about issues affecting constituents through op-eds in newspapers and community and professional email lists.

Based on Bond's (2019) findings, it is evident that effective legislative advocacy centers around a clear understanding of key issues impacting a community and/or a profession as well as the desire to include multiple stakeholders throughout the process. Even though legislative advocacy can occur at several levels, politics and thus policy change are most successful when they are localized and specific. As qualitative research tends to be a localized and contextualized examination of a phenomenon or issue, you can have considerable impact as legislative advocates by sharing your findings and advocating for change within a specific community or setting.

In the remainder of this section, we highlight several beneficial strategies and steps to maximally inform and affect public policy. Perspectives 13.1 highlights how educator shortages in Nevada were discussed to inform policy change and gain funding to increase educator pathways in the state. Although we present legislative advocacy as a separate section, as we shared earlier in this chapter, it is typical that legislative advocacy and social advocacy are intertwined and share similar goals. As such, qualitative researchers engaged in social advocacy are encouraged to engage with legislators and the legislative process as part of their community empowerment work.

## PERSPECTIVES 13.1. FOSTERING EDUCATOR PATHWAYS IN NEVADA

Since arriving at UNLV, I have been involved in dialogue and action related to improving educator pathways in Nevada; these improvements relate to expanding and diversifying the educator workforce through intentional recruitment and retention efforts. Efforts have been supported by local and national research as well as nonacademic sources (e.g., community forums, state commissions, educator testimony). Living and working within one of the largest and most diverse school districts in the nation, the need for university partnerships with the community and local school district (i.e., Clark County School District) has been critical to advancing the educator workforce. The COVID-19 pandemic only exacerbated what was already a critical educator workforce locally and nationally.

The costs of educator shortages are measurable and significant for students: larger class sizes, fewer teacher aides, fewer extracurricular activities, curricular changes, hiring of less qualified teachers, placement of teachers trained in another field or grade level to teach in an understaffed area, and more extensive use of substitute teachers. These shortages have been particularly problematic in subject areas such as special education, foreign languages, STEM-related fields, English/language arts, and English language learning (ELL)/English as a second language (ESL).

Local scholarship has informed since 2015 legislative action within Nevada regarding educator pathways. Through my college's partnership with schools, district leaders, the state department of education, and community organizations, policymakers have been further informed by our collective work of the pervasive educator shortages and possible remedies. The outcome has been legislative changes that allow paraprofessionals to count their work experience toward student teaching requirements, multi-million-dollar incentives that support current and prospective students of Nevada teacher education programs with substantial scholarships, induction and mentorship programs for educators within their first 3 years in the profession, curricular changes to prepare educators to be more culturally responsive, and tuition support for practicing educators who seek additional endorsements to serve culturally and linguistically diverse students. In the end, research informing social and community advocacy efforts works. Educator enrollments have increased, education curricula are more culturally responsive, and licensed educators are being retained while mentoring the next generation of educators.

—D. G. H.

## Understand the Legislative Environment

One of the first considerations in legislative advocacy is understanding the legislative environment and even connecting with those who are already engaged in lobbying (the latter can be very helpful guides in your legislative advocacy, helping you combine your efforts with existing efforts and/or helping you refine the target of your advocacy). Qualitative researchers are to stay informed about issues that impact their profession, with particular attention to those involved in proposed legislative bills. Professional organizations and community advocacy groups typically include legislation-related sections on their websites and discuss current issues and legislative concerns through email lists and social media. In addition, staying abreast of the latest research on an issue through reading academic journals and newsletters can augment what you are identifying in your own qualitative research. Finally, engaging with advocacy organizations or think tanks related to your discipline can highlight how organizations focused on public policy and community issues work to inform policy decisions across a variety of community concerns.

Understanding professional issues and actual and potential public policy decisions impacting those issues can be a daunting task. Qualitative researchers can concentrate on the limited issues they investigate and seek to become an expert on those issues. Becoming an expert involves privileging participant voice throughout the research process and data reporting.

In addition to being familiar with professional issues as well as existing and potential public policy, qualitative researchers are to be cognizant of the processes and terminology associated with legislation. Engaging in legislative advocacy at the local and state levels is particularly invaluable. States and municipalities play a critical role in determining what projects and issues get funded and what level of funding each receives. Oftentimes, these levels of government are provided federal funds to augment their resources and serve as "laboratories" where innovative practices are developed and evaluated (Albert & Brown, 2007).

## Know Your Legislators

Another initial strategy for linking research with legislative agendas is to know who your legislators are: Understand that you are represented by different legislators at the state and federal levels who address and have influence on different issues. Because you will be contacting each legislator from the perspective of your role in education or social sciences, locate the legislator who represents the geographical area of your work setting. In addition, know the legislative calendar, how long members of the legislature have served, and whether staff are permanent or temporary for a particular legislative session (Albert & Brown, 2007).

Once the legislator is identified, it is important to do your homework and learn about the issues that lawmakers support, their voting record, committees of which they serve and hold influence, along with personal information such as previous careers. Visit your legislator's website, read news articles, and talk to others who have met with the legislator to understand their priorities. Because legislators encounter a broad range of community concerns facing their constituents, they need expertise, research, and information on several issues, particularly those issues currently on a legislative agenda.

Building a relationship with legislators takes time, yet this is critical for communicating an issue of concern in education and social sciences and/or potential solutions for the issue using research. Knowing your legislators is a continual process that involves regular communication: Periodic emails, telephone calls, and visits throughout the year speak volumes about your passion for an issue in education and social sciences. Furthermore, this ongoing communication can lead to a deeper relationship with legislators.

## Build the Case for Change

Qualitative research provides rich, contextual data that can be shared with legislators to make the case about why an issue should be addressed or whether a particular bill should be supported. With qualitative research findings that are easily understandable and localized, qualitative researchers also offer—whenever possible—community anecdotes and powerful personal stories to help the research come alive for legislators. For example, sharing participant quotes about lived experiences and/or a theoretical model based on prolonged engagement within a community can bring to life the issue for the legislator representing that area. It is critical to understand that the "case" that qualitative researchers make is based in resolving a community-based concern that is aligned with legislators' agendas, not a case to support ongoing research that you may want to conduct. For legislators who represent your community, the issue brought forth should be one that directly impacts their constituents in some way.

Part of building the case involves qualitative researchers understanding the real and potential costs of proposed solutions to address a community issue as well as those associated with those not addressing the issue. Because initiatives have financial costs associated with them, it is important that you demonstrate that you are aware of what these costs are and how those costs balance with the benefits of an initiative.

You can highlight examples from your own work or other federally funded education research, but be sure to tie the findings to real-world problems. A particularly effective approach is to relate implications of research to (a) saving or improving lives or (b) saving money. Whenever possible, try to relate your discussion to your member's state or district and the people whose interests they were elected to represent. You can talk about the federal research dollars going to district universities, the impact of research findings on the local economy, or improvements to local programs that are the result of evidence-based policymaking.

As you present your case, consider how the research will be received. Albert and Brown (2007;) provide some questions for reflection:

- What questions can you anticipate about your findings?
- What are people most likely to not understand or misinterpret?
- How do your findings support or refute previous findings?
- How does the research relate more broadly to what is known in a particular area or issue, and how might that relate to public policy concerns? (p. 275)

## Communicate Effectively with Legislators

With a compelling case in hand, communicating the case can be done through social media, op-ed pieces for newspapers or magazines, letters to legislators, public comments at various meetings where decisions are made, policy briefs and papers, professional and community presentations, and face-to-face visits and interactions with legislators. Those within education and social sciences are to make the case for the issue face to face to the extent possible, using written communications tools as possible. To prepare for these interactions, it is important to have a user-friendly one-page handout summarizing key issues, research findings, and proposed solutions. In addition to a one-page handout, prepare longer documents for those who seek additional information about a concern and/or request to see more details about the research methodology and findings.

Furthermore, qualitative researchers are to approach legislators at an appropriate time to maximize legislators' attention to the issue. Face-to-face interactions can include inviting a legislator to an education, clinical, or other setting where they can witness the issue firsthand. Alternatively, it can include inviting them to present in a community or professional forum on their interests relevant to the discipline. Or they can involve you visiting their offices to speak with them or members of their staff. This is where current lobbyists can help guide you in what the best intervention approaches are with particular legislators and particular pieces of legislation. Regardless, practice talking points that convey the primary takeaways summarized further in the handout and ask how you and other professionals can support or inform the legislators' work on a particular issue.

Communication about an issue affecting education and social sciences must be clear verbally and in writing, with information that is widely accessible in terms of user-friendly content and its distribution to a variety of stakeholders. Furthermore, communication should be culturally responsive and consider the input of those particularly from traditionally marginalized identities. Ensure that you communicate with legislators regularly, issuing updates on research and other information germane to a specific community concern.

At times, the most effective way to make the case is to gather broad-based support regarding addressing the issue. Simply put, there is power in numbers. Building support can involve partnering with organizations, schools, or agencies that align with you on an advocacy issue. These partnerships can include having letters of support for your case. Organizational representatives might accompany you to face-to-face visits with legislators or coparticipate in legislative committee meetings.

---

## CHAPTER SUMMARY

In the concluding chapter of this text, we have emphasized the inextricable link among social, legislative, and professional advocacy for qualitative researchers in education and the social sciences. No matter your professional and community organization affiliations, it is very likely that there is attention to community and legislative advocacy to support individuals and communities. Qualitative research is an invaluable resource for that work: The role of the qualitative researcher, which includes a focus on equity and advocacy, aligns well with a call to action to support positive outcomes in education and the social sciences.

The chapter highlighted several examples of how professional organizations provide competency standards, guidelines, and policy and advocacy documents that can guide qualitative research for action. Based on the ACA MSJCCs, we highlighted four interdependent researcher qualities for community and legislative action: (a) researcher self-awareness, (b) knowledge of research participant worldview, (c) mutually beneficial research relationship, and (d) engagement in research advocacy. Furthermore, as qualitative researchers prepare to engage in community and legislative action, developing research briefs and policy briefs is an important step. This chapter defined these briefs, described their typical components, and provided examples.

Next, we described the link between social advocacy and qualitative research more explicitly. We encourage you to apply the 10 steps for social advocacy as well as adapt the checklist (see Table 13.2) provided to inform positive advocacy outcomes. The chapter concluded with a discussion or legislative advocacy, including strategies and steps for success as well as examples of how scholarship and community collaboration have positively influenced public policy.

## Review Questions

1. Why are qualitative researchers called to action in terms of social, legislative, and professional advocacy? Are there particular research approaches more suitable for community and legislative action?
2. How do the four qualities of qualitative researchers inform community and legislative action within your discipline?
3. To what extent are research briefs and policy briefs developed differently based on the intended audience and outcome desired?
4. How can the 10 steps for social advocacy be applied to qualitative research?
5. What are the four major strategies and steps for legislative advocacy, and how might you translate them to your topic of interest?

## Recommended Readings

American Counseling Association Advocacy Resources: https://www.counseling.org/government-affairs/advocacy-tips-tools

American Education Research Association Advocacy Toolkit: https://cqrcengage.com/aeraedresearch/AERAAdvocacyToolkit?o

Community Advocacy: A Psychologist's Toolkit for State and Local Advocacy: https://www.communitypsychology.com/advocacytoolkit/

Ratts, M. J., Singh, A. A., Nassar McMillan, S., Butler, S. K., & McCullough, J. R. (2016). Multicultural and Social Justice Counseling Competencies: Guidelines for the counseling profession.

*Journal of Multicultural Counseling and Development, 44*(1), 28–48. https://doi.org/10.1002/jmcd.12035

Toporek, R., & Daniels, J. (2018). *American Counseling Association advocacy competencies.* American Counseling Association. https://www.counseling.org/docs/default-source/competencies/aca-advocacy-competencies-may-2020.pdf?sfvrsn=85b242c_6

## Image Credits

Fig. 13.1: Copyright © 2015 by Manivong J. Ratts, Anneliese A. Singh, S. Kent Butler, Sylvia Nassar-McMillan and Julian Rafferty McCullough.

Fig. 13.2: Rebecca Toporek and Judy Daniels, "American Counseling Association Advocacy Competencies," p. 2. Copyright © 2018 by American Counseling Association.

# Sample Qualitative Research Proposals and Reports

# Experiences of Gay, Bisexual, Queer, and Questioning Greek Students

*Joseph W. Davis*
*Old Dominion University*

## ABSTRACT

Gay, bisexual, queer, and questioning students who select to become members of Greek organizations at academic institutions often face unique situations in terms of the Greek process (Windmeyer, 2005). The Greek system, particularly for students who identify as male, enculturated to adhere to the masculine stereotype and may involve instances of hazing, alcohol consumption, and hypersexualization. This qualitative proposal includes findings from a pilot study that examined any barriers and benefits in regard to being a gay, bisexual, queer, or questioning member of a Greek organization. Interviews were conducted with two gay, bisexual, queer, or questioning members of Greek affiliation, and a text detailing the experiences of gay men in college fraternities were examined to assist in identifying the barriers and benefits of being a gay, bisexual, queer, or questioning member of a Greek organization. This research proposal also details plans for a larger scale study on a similar topic.

## Experiences of Gay, Bisexual, Queer, and Questioning Greek Students

Gay, bisexual, queer, and questioning (GBQQ) students have a unique perspective of campus life. These students are contending with adapting to a college environment, in addition to negotiating their sexual orientation within the new campus environment (Windmeyer,

2005). To assist with the adaptation to a college setting, one option students often consider is becoming a member of a Greek letter organization. Greek letter organizations provide opportunities for the formation of personal bonds, leadership activities, and community service (Old Dominion University, n.d.). GBQQ students often must decide if and how they wish to disclose their sexual identity. In Gortmaker and Brown's (2006) survey analysis, a majority of participants who had not disclosed their sexual orientation (74%) often perceived the need to hide their sexual identity in an effort to avoid unfair treatment from the university community.

In a grounded theory study of fraternities (Stevens, 2004), the researcher's findings included that these organizations were characterized as being hypermasculine. Within this type of environment, this study found that participants who were GBQQ felt the need to hide their sexual orientation from their organizations due to fear of rejection if they disclose their sexual orientation. Stevens (2004) argued that this conflict and fear might produce a significant amount of stress for an individual. If the concept of brotherhood or sisterhood is taken literally, then the process of disclosure could be likened to that of disclosing to a biological family member. The researcher's findings suggested that a cornerstone to participants' sexual orientation identity development involved finding empowerment. Participants identified finding empowerment as being a personal process that relied on inner strengths. Even though this empowerment was a personal process, other factors such as environmental influences and disclosure to others influenced their experience of empowerment.

## Challenges Faced by GBQQ Fraternity Members

A significant barrier for GBQQ individuals is homophobia that may exist within fraternities. *Homophobia* is defined as the perceived threat to one's self-concept via homosexually oriented ideas (Moradi et al., 2006). Moradi et al. (2006) concluded that increased levels of perceived threat from lesbian and gay individuals were related to increased levels of negative attitudes about the lesbian and gay population. The researchers argued that to retain a firm since of self, some individuals take action against what they deem to be a threatening group. These actions can include acts of violence (Moradi et al., 2006). If fraternities are often seen as hypermasculine (Stevens, 2004), then the fear to disclose or affiliate with a Greek organization might be due to a concern for physical safety.

In addition to homophobia as a barrier, GBQQ fraternity members may also experience internalized homophobia. Kimmel and Mahalik's (2005) survey analysis research suggested that a gay individual's mental well-being could be impacted by negative perceptions of their sexual orientation. An individual could develop a negative sense of self and act out in a potentially destructive manner. Windmeyer and Freeman (1997) suggested that homophobia could be destructive for both straight and GBQQ members of a Greek letter organization, as homophobia may manifest in hypermasculine activities. An individual may feel pressured to consume alcohol and engage in other potentially dangerous activities in order to appear masculine. They argue that this negatively impacts the ideal of fraternal bonds that the organization had worked to create.

Sexual orientation can serve as both an obstacle as well as a positive influence (Dilley, 2005). Dilley's (2005) phenomenological interviews were conducted on nonheterosexual college men and found that college served as both an opportunity and obstacle in terms of personal development. His research resulted in categories of homosexual identification. A person classified as gay would have an open support network of similar individuals. A person classified as parallel would, in essence, be leading two separate lives that did not intersect. While some of the participants in Dilley's research were able to integrate their identity and form positive male bonds in fraternities, others remained undisclosed and disaffiliated from their organization.

To further assess the campus climate for gay and lesbian students, Jurgens et al.'s (2004) mixed methods approach to examining heterosexual students' attitudes toward gay and lesbian people found that gay and lesbian individuals were generally positively viewed in society but were also seen with uncertainty in regard to more personal factors such as identity development. While this finding suggests support for a warmer campus climate, the researchers note that the participants were less supportive in a public discussion group than in private survey submissions. If applied to the concept of Greek letter organizations, then support is lent to Stevens's (2004) idea that gay individuals may be afraid to disclose due to fear of rejection. Even if GBQQ individuals are generally viewed by heterosexual individuals in a positive manner, there might not be adequate visible support to assist with the disclosure decision.

Cass's (1979) model suggests that homosexual identity development occurs through six stages: identity confusion, identity comparison, identity tolerance, acceptance, pride, and synthesis. While there is no concrete time frame for progression of these stages, college may be the first time that some individuals are able to examine their own lives. This coincides with Stevens's (2004) research as individuals evaluate the need for disclosure of their sexual orientation. An individual may not be ready or willing to disclose at earlier stages of the model.

Liang and Alimo's (2005) survey analysis research examined the change in attitudes toward lesbian, bisexual, and gay populations after significant exposure to the population and found a positive correlation. While not a causal relationship, the results do lend support to a notion that increased exposure to the lesbian, bisexual, and gay population can foster a sense of acceptance (Liang & Alimo, 2005). In terms of Greek letter organizations, this could support the idea of familial bonds and acceptance from within the organization if a member was contemplating disclosing their sexual orientation.

In Troiden et al.'s research (as cited in Evans et al., 1998), there is an emphasis on the role of personal support in the development and well-being of a homosexual identity. This support can be found through the bonds with family and friends. These bonds and their assistance with personal development resemble the mission of several Greek letter organizations, as they strive to provide true and lasting bonds for each of their members (Old Dominion University, n.d.). Individuals seeking acceptance and such bonds through a Greek letter organization have the potential to have the positive support to assist in their personal development.

## Purpose and Conceptual Framework of Current Study

In regard to the proposed study, the ontology of this social constructivist approach involved each participant's subjective reality, consisting of varied experiences and personal relationships. Individuals' perspectives regarding sexual orientation and Greek letter organizations were varied. Salience is individualistically based, and each narrative will fluctuate with unique life experience. Epistemologically, knowledge about perspectives of being a GBQQ member of a Greek letter organization will be constructed jointly with the participants and the researcher. While there will be no set end to the amount of knowledge to be gained from individual perspectives, a general working knowledge about the topic can be acquired. In regard to axiology, the voices and experiences of the participants will be of high importance. The study will be designed to examine these perspectives and will respect individual differences. The data gained from this study will be presented via thematic groupings involving the use of participant narrative where appropriate.

The purpose of this grounded theory will be to examine and build theory about the perspectives of GBQQ undergraduate students in Greek letter organizations. The primary research question to be answered involves the depiction of any obstacles and benefits to being a GBQQ member of a Greek letter organization. Additionally, the research team examined what role, if any, disclosure of sexual orientation plays in the Greek letter system. The participants in this study identified as GBQQ. Undergraduate students consisted of students enrolled in a 4-year baccalaureate institution. The term "Greek letter organization" was used to refer to single-sexed and socially based student organizations at baccalaureate institutions. "Disclosure" refers to the process of informing others about one's sexual orientation.

## Method

### Participants

Participants to be involved in this study will be recruited via snowball and criterion sampling and with the requested assistance with the Lambda 10 Project, a national clearinghouse for gay, lesbian, bisexual, and transgendered issues relating to Greek letter organizations. Utilizing the Lambda 10 Project's resources assists the researcher in leading toward a sense of maximum variation in regard to gender and geographical location. Additionally, the researcher will use recruitment methods seeking a broad range of experience levels and time spent inside of Greek letter organizations. These actions will develop trustworthiness, as the sample came from multiple academic institutions in several geographical areas. A total of 25 participants will be recruited in hopes of reaching saturation. Additional participants will be recruited to establish saturation. To be eligible, participants must be undergraduate students in a 4-year baccalaureate institution, identify as GBQQ, and be members of a Greek letter organization at their respective academic institution. There are no age or ethnicity requirements for eligibility. To assist with negative case analysis, five heterosexual members of Greek letter organizations will be recruited via snowball sampling from the 25 participants.

## Research Team

In relation to qualitative research, the issue of researcher bias must be addressed to promote the ideal of trustworthiness. For the proposed study, the primary researcher was be a 25-year-old White individual who identifies as male and who is working toward a doctorate in counselor education. The researcher identifies as gay and is actively involved in a Greek letter organization at his academic institution. He is at a level of complete disclosure within his organization in regard to his sexual orientation. The researcher has been involved with the interest area of GBQQ students in Greek letter organizations for 5 years and has brought a national speaker to his academic institution to present on the subject material. The researcher holds the belief that Greek letter organizations have the potential to be beacons of acceptance for GBQQ individuals. However, this belief exists in that the potential for acceptance has rarely been met. He has experienced homophobic insults and derogatory jokes from within his own fraternity as well as others at his academic institution. These experiences have led to the occasional belief that the Greek system does not represent itself in an acceptable manner to incoming GBQQ students. Along with what he has witnessed, the researcher also recognized the acceptance he has gained from the majority of the other people in his respective organization.

The primary researcher will use a team of at least three other individuals to assist in developing the interview protocol, coding processes, and triangulation for this pilot study. A diverse research team will be recruited to allow for variation in gender, ethnicity, sexual orientation, and Greek letter organization experience. This action will help the researcher further document researcher bias by providing multiple perceptions on the data.

## Data Sources

The primary source of data will be individual interviews. The individuals will each be interviewed once, and the interviews will be semistructured to allow for participant elaboration and exploration. The questions focus on the experiences of perceived obstacles and benefits to being a GBQQ member of a Greek letter organization and the process of sexual identity disclosure from within the same organization. The interviews will be approximately 40 minutes and consist of approximately 10 questions. Due to the wide geographical area range, the interviews will be conducted and recorded via telephone. The primary researcher will transcribe each participant interview verbatim.

Additionally, texts depicting the first hand experiences of GBQQ students in Greek letter organizations will be utilized as a source of data. Windmeyer's (2005) text examined the narratives of gay and bisexual men inside of fraternities. In a separate text, Windmeyer (2001) displayed narratives from lesbian and bisexual women in sororities. Four narratives will be randomly selected from each text and utilized in the proposed study.

## Data Analysis

The research team will recursively immerse themselves in the produced transcripts. Open coding will be conducted after each interview. The initial codebooks will serve as a framework for coding future transcripts. The unit of analysis for the initial set of coding will be at the sentence level. Once open coding has been completed for each interview, the researchers will use axial coding to relate thematic concepts and categories across the data sets. During this process, the researchers will revisit the original transcripts to ensure accuracy in coding. As the cyclical process of constant comparison continues, the researchers will use selective coding to identify core categories and several interacting subcategories. The research team will continue to revisit the original data to search for variation to the core category. The researchers, in regard to the projected sample size, will continue adding data sets until saturation of findings has been reached.

Alongside the interviews, the researchers will use document analysis on the two texts. This process will occur after interview data collection and coding. A similar process of open coding, axial coding, and selective coding will occur with the narrative texts, as the researchers created a separate codebook for the text analysis. Cross coding will occur to search for thematic groupings between the multiple forms of data. Additionally, researchers will code five interviews from non-GBQQ members of Greek letter organizations to provide negative case analysis.

## Strategies for Trustworthiness

Several strategies will be utilized to increase trustworthiness for this proposed study. Negative case analysis will be used to confirm data presented by the participants. In the case of this study, the primary researcher will interview heterosexual Greek letter organization members. In order to further establish confirmability, the research team will engage in member checking and solicit feedback from participants on their transcripts.

The researchers will use reflexive journaling to identify and address researcher bias and to document thought processes as the research progresses. The research team also will use memoing after each data collection in an effort to increase the dependability of the research. As the data are collected, analysis will occur. This will allow for the process of constant comparison between the data sets. The researcher has prolonged engagement with the subject matter. The primary researcher has identified as a gay for over 12 years and has been a member of a Greek letter organization for the past 5 years.

The research team will additionally use triangulation in an effort to increase trustworthiness. Triangulation between the research team will be used to ensure coding validation. Weekly team coding meetings help structure this process. Additionally, a similar process will be used across multiple data sources and allow for a wide range of variance and cross-checking. For this proposed study, an auditor from an unaffiliated academic institution will work with the research team. The enlisted auditor has an interest in the target research populations and is selected on the basis of ensuring that the participants have an accurate voice in the research.

As is the purpose of grounded theory, the focus on this research will be on the development of theory. This will be done via the process of open, axial, and selective coding and will search for a core category (Corbin & Strauss, 2015). Close attention must be paid to the accurate perceptions of the participants and will be replicated until saturation.

# Pilot Study

To further support the proposed study, a pilot study was conducted that observed the perceptions of any obstacles and benefits to being a GBQQ member of a Greek organization.

## Participants

For the pilot study, individual interviews were conducted with two individuals. The participants were recruited via convenience sampling. Each interview lasted between 20 and 25 minutes. The interviews were semistructured and consisted of 10 predetermined questions. The researcher was allowed to ask follow-up or probing questions to further engage the participant and to get a more complete understanding of the participant's experience. Each participant provided informed consent and completed a participant demographic form. After the interviews, both participants were sent their respective transcripts for review. The participants were each given the opportunity to provide feedback and both chose to provide any comments on their transcripts.

The first participant was an 18-year-old White man. He was a freshman communications major at his academic institution and was in the process of becoming a member of his fraternity. He identifies as bisexual. The second participant was a 21-year-old White man. He was an engineering major at his academic institution and held a leadership position in his fraternity. This participant identifies as gay. Both participants came from the same large mid-Atlantic institution.

The second form of data came from Windmeyer's (2005) edited book *Brotherhood: Gay Life in College Fraternities*. Two narratives were randomly selected from the text and were used in data analysis.

## Research Team

The primary researcher for this pilot study was a 25-year-old White man. He was a doctoral student in a counselor education program at a large, mid-Atlantic academic institution. He identified as gay and was a member of a Greek letter organization. His biases are based on his prolonged exposure to both populations. The researcher has had experiences with discrimination via derogatory insults from multiple Greek letter organizations. Even with these negative experiences, he still holds to a positive ideal of what these specific organizations could aspire to become in the future. Additionally, he has had several positive experiences that have facilitated bonding and development from within his own organization.

The research team consisted of three female doctoral-level students enrolled in a qualitative methods course at the same institution as the primary researcher. Their involvement with the pilot study consisted of several meetings throughout the course of the study about the logistics and design of the study. Only the primary researcher was involved in the interviews, coding of the participant interviews, and document analysis.

## Data Analysis

For the pilot study, the researcher created memos after each data collection. Due to the nature of study and instructional design, coding could not be accomplished immediately after transcription. An initial codebook was created via open coding for the first interview of the data collection. The unit of analysis was based on the multiple sentence level. This codebook served as the guide for future codebooks. Upon completion of the initial codebook for the second interview, the first data set was reviewed again to begin the process of constant comparison. With both interviews complete, axial coding began while attempting to observe any emerging core concept or category.

In Windmeyer's (2005) narrative compilation, each of the two stories served as a separate source of data. The unit of analysis for these data sets was on the paragraph level. An initial codebook was created for each narrative using open coding. The codebook from the participant interviews serves as a guide for narrative coding. Upon completion of open coding with the two narratives using constant comparison, axial coding was used to begin the search for thematic categories. Comparison occurred at the between-story level as well as between the written narratives and participant interviews. Three final codebooks were developed over the course of this pilot study. The participant interviews and text-based narratives each maintained their own codebook, as they are separate forms of data. A final codebook that attempted to combine the emerging core categories and potential theory was also produced. A case display was produced to summarize key concepts in relation to each participant. Finally, a concept map was constructed to assist with the organization of project ideas.

## Strategies for Trustworthiness

Trustworthiness was assisted by the use of several methods. Member checking was attempted via soliciting feedback from the interview participants on their transcripts. However, none of the participants returned any comments on their transcripts.

Reflexive journaling was performed by the primary researcher prior to and after several of the data collections to assist in reducing bias and organizing researcher thoughts and opinions. Memos were created for each set of the data to assist in the organization process and to support the process of coding. Constant comparison was available to a limited extent due to the number of data sources and the delay for coding opportunities present within the design.

The role of the research team was not to interact with the collected data. The research team was used to assist in development of the interview protocol and to reduce personal bias in designing the pilot study.

Just as in the proposed study, the researcher established prolonged engagement with the subject material and the population. The researcher has identified as a gay man for over 12 years. Additionally, the researcher has been a member of a Greek letter organization for over 5 years. Furthermore, the interviewer has known one of the participants for over 3 years.

While emerging theory could not be fully developed by the conclusion of the pilot study, emerging core categories could be observed as well as several smaller intervening categories.

## Findings

At the conclusion of the pilot study, several thematic groups were identified as a result of the constant comparison of the data. The idea of acceptance had emerged as a core category. This central category involved two subsets. The acceptance of one's self as a GBQQ man was found across all data sets. Included in this are thoughts about self and admittance to self of GBQQ status. Additionally, these groupings consisted of thoughts related to self-knowledge and adequacy.

> For an example, Participant PA010 noted:

> I guess they do say you know, college is a big time you know, when you discover ... you finally know who you are. And I guess, this is, your views change all the time. You learn new things about yourself and this is just one of those things. Uh, it's been a real growing experience for me, I guess you could say. Um, I guess I feel more. It's not a fact that I try to hide. Kind of. Um, I'm happy with it. I guess, I realize it's nothing to be ashamed of, it's just who I am.

Additionally, the core category of acceptance involves a sense of being accepted within the organization. In the text-based narratives (Windmeyer, 2005), the stories often revolved around a fear of disclosure to their respective fraternities. There was often the concern about how a GBQQ member would be viewed in the fraternity. For one of the text examples, the individual commented that even though he had disclosed his sexual orientation to the entire Greek system, he was still concerned about finding acceptance within the organization.

In both sets of text narratives (Joseph, 2005; Shumake, 2005), acceptance was found only after personal disclosure of sexual orientation had occurred. Disclosure is an intervening category of acceptance. Also of note here is that emphasis was placed on being accepted by the fraternity and the importance of self-acceptance had been marginalized. The text narratives begin with what can be described as internalized homophobia. In Joseph's (2005) story, he commented: "Deep down, I thought, *I could never let my fraternity brothers down. I could never let them see who I really am*" (p. 12). This lends support to the idea that there is not a strong sense of self-acceptance prior to finding acceptance with a fraternity due to disclosure.

Along with the category of acceptance, there also seems to be a community of GBQQ students within the Greek letter organizations. Both interviewed participants as well as the written texts referenced the other GBQQ students involved in the Greek system. The text narratives appeared to reference this community as something to be kept as a secret. While the GBQQ community was referenced as a positive source of support and acceptance in the participant interviews, there was no mention of keeping such connections hidden.

Intervening with the core category of acceptance is the idea of being masculine via a macho stereotype. Appearing across the data sets was the idea that fraternities were to fill the masculine stereotype. One participant (PA010) who identified himself as bisexual claimed that he felt like just another "skirt-chasing guy" when he was with his fraternity. Another participant quickly recognized the hypermasculine stereotype and debunked it within his own organization. However, he did mention that the masculine stereotype was active in other organizations on this campus.

The role of diversity also serves as an intervening category in the participant interviews. Both participants noted diversity as the joining together and the learning that happens between different cultures. Diversity was cited as a dominant motivation for both participants throughout their lives. Inside of this category rests the idea that the participant's home institution values diversity. While both participants lack knowledge of university policies on matters of sexual orientation, they both attribute the positive climate to the academic institution.

## Discussion

The findings of this proposed grounded theory would ultimately lead to a core category that would assist in the development of theory regarding the benefits and obstacles, if any, of being a GBQQ member of a Greek letter organization. In the proposed study, the idea of acceptance could be a recurring theme as a major benefit to being a GBQQ member of a Greek letter organization. As the pilot data showed strong connections to both ideas of acceptance of self and acceptance from the organization, it is expected that the proposed study would expand upon this category. As this proposed study would involve multiple aspects of diversity, such as gender and geographical region, there is the possibility for more negative experiences to be expressed as students search for acceptance of themselves and from their respective Greek letter organizations. An additional area of interest became disclosure strategies, if any, of these students to their respective organizations. The results would likely lend support to the idea of disclosing as a means to seek acceptance. Disclosure, on the other hand, may serve as an obstacle that inhibits the feeling of acceptance.

Additionally, expanding the research to other diverse areas could continue highlighting the inner community of Greek members who are also GBQQ. With this more diverse study, different groups of organizations and individuals could be examined, as sororities, lesbian women, and bisexual women would all be afforded the opportunity to participate. All four data sources in the pilot study were able to express some recognition regarding others in their respective organizations that were of similar sexual orientations.

## Potential Implications of Future Data Collection and Analysis

The issues facing GBQQ populations in Greek letter organizations are often seen as a side result in larger studies regarding college student development and sexual orientation (Dilley, 2005; Gortmaker & Brown, 2006; Jurgens et al., 2004; Stevens, 2004). However, little research has been conducted to examine this exact population. The conducted pilot study lends support to the larger proposed study and can assist in filling the gap in research that had previously only been touched upon. As Windmeyer and Freeman (1997) noted, there are potential negative consequences for both heterosexuals and GBQQ members in Greek letter organizations if homophobia is present.

The central idea of acceptance needs to be expanded upon to fully gain an adequate understanding of its dimensions. The dimensions might possibly include different geographic areas, different Greek letter organizations, gender, and different variations of sexual orientation. This study could assist in further describing how GBQQ individuals make sense of their sense of self as well as well as how Greek letter organizations can work to promote or hinder the developing sense of self through support and understanding.

In terms of supporting and advocating for GBQQ individuals in Greek letter organizations, this research has the potential to provide rational and open discussion within organizations and school settings about acceptance and the traditional stereotypes about Greek letter organizations. Freeman (2005) suggests that bringing these stories out into the open can assist in giving voices to an otherwise invisible issue in society. Perhaps the shame that Joseph (2005) felt in his personal narrative would no longer be a relevant issue. Much like Joseph's (2005) case, suicide can become an option for some individuals who are unable to come to terms with their sexual identity. As consistent with Cass's (1979) model of sexual identity development, these students may need support as they transition toward a state of identity acceptance.

There are several potential limitations with the proposed study. The first potential threat to trustworthiness would come from sampling adequacy. While the initial 25 interviews may be enough to reach saturation on a given topic, it may not be enough to reach saturation across multiple levels, such as both fraternities and sororities. Adequate sampling must also be given to the various forms of sexual identity.

Another possible limitation would be the transferability of the resulting theory. The acceptance described in this study would only be applicable to the Greek system on college campuses. Acute awareness must be paid to ensure that any findings are made specific to the target populations. Along with this notion is the idea of substantive validation. The proposed study may not be considered worthwhile due to the narrow target population. However, the individual voices and chance for life improvement assist this study in becoming worthwhile.

There are ethical limitations to this study. Participants must be willing to disclose their sexual orientation. If they are not at a point of disclosure to others, then the interview has the potential for harming one's sense of security. While including informed consent and making concerted efforts to protect confidentiality can ease this, the individual choice to disclose must be unique. Individuals may not want there to be any possible method of their responses being traced back to their respective Greek organizations or any other individuals. To assist in this process, the names of the individual Greek letter organizations will not be solicited. As seen in the pilot data, participants may not want to represent their experiences within a Greek organization in a negative fashion.

One additional consideration comes in terms of the other forms of sexual identities. The proposed study only covers gay men, lesbian women, and bisexual men and women. No attempts will be made to seek out transgender or asexual individuals. The rationale for this is due to the rarity of these individuals inside of Greek letter organizations.

Cultural considerations also provide another potential limitation. There are several types of fraternities and sororities. There are traditionally African American and multicultural fraternities and sororities that are governed by their own standards. The focus of this proposed study is open to all forms of social Greek letter organizations; however, special attention must be paid to ensure adequate representation is allotted to different forms of fraternities and sororities. Additionally, religious differences must be considered as a cultural difference when analyzing the results. Attention must be given to ensure that religion is given the opportunity to exist as a cultural entity.

By the use of grounded theory, a general understanding it to be developed that depicts any possible obstacles or benefits to being a GBQQ member of a Greek letter organization. Special attention to the idea of acceptance and the disclosure process furthers the understanding of individual perspectives regarding the subject matter. While generating theory on a target population is not destined to cause massive changes in world paradigms, it does have the potential to change lives on an individual level.

## References

Cass, V. (1979). Homosexual identity formation: A theoretical model. *Journal of Homosexuality*, 4(3), 219–235.

Corbin, J., & Strauss, A. (2015). *Basics of qualitative research: Techniques and procedures for developing grounded theory* (4th ed.). Sage.

Dilley, P. (2005). Which way out? A typology of non-heterosexual male collegiate identities. *The Journal of Higher Education*, 76(1), 56–88.

Evans, N. J., Forney, D. D., & Guido-DiBrito, F. (1998). *Student development in college: Theory, research, and practice*. Jossey-Bass.

Freeman, P. (2005). How to use stories as educational tools. In S. Windmeyer (Ed.), *Brotherhood: Gay life in college fraternities* (pp. 261–271). Alyson Books.

Gortmaker, V. J. & Brown, R. D. (2006). Out of the college closet: Differences in perceptions and experiences out and closeted lesbian and gay students. *College Student Journal*, 40(3), 606–619.

Old Dominion University. (n.d.). *Greek life*. http://studentaffairs.odu.edu/osal/greeklife/index.shtml.

Joseph, E. (2005). Cry freedom. In S. Windmeyer (Ed.), *Brotherhood: Gay life in college fraternities* (pp. 10–17). Alyson Books.

Jurgens, J. C., Schwitzer, A. M., & Middleton, T. (2004). Examining attitudes towards college students with minority sexual orientations: Findings and suggestions. *Journal of College Student Psychotherapy*, 19(1), 57–75. https://doi.org/10.1300/J035v19n01_07

Kimmel, S. B., & Mahalik, J. R. (2005). Body image concerns of gay men: The roles of minority stress and conformity to masculine norms. *Journal of Consulting and Clinical Psychology*, 73(6), 1185–1990. https://doi.org/10.1037/0022-006X.73.6.1185

Liang, C. T. H., & Alimo, C. (2005). The impact of white heterosexual students' interactions on attitudes toward lesbian, gay, and bisexual people: A longitudinal study. *Journal of College Student Development, 46*(3), 237–250.

*Matthew's life.* (n.d.). http://www.matthewsplace.org/mattslife.htm.

Moradi, B., van den Berg, J. J., & Epting, F. R. (2006). Intrapersonal and interpersonal manifestations of antilesbian and gay prejudice: An application of personal construct theory. *Journal of Counseling Psychology, 53*(1), 57–66. https://doi.org/10.1037/a0014571

Shumake, T. C. (2005). Change takes time. In S. Windmeyer (Ed.), *Brotherhood: Gay life in college fraternities* (pp. 63–71). Alyson Books.

Stevens, R. A. (2004). Understanding gay identity development within the college environment. *Journal of College Student Development, 45*(2), 185–206.

Windmeyer, S. L., & Freeman, P. W. (1997). *How homophobia hurts the college fraternity.* Campus Pride. https://www.campuspride.org/resources/how-homophobia-hurts-the-college-fraternity/

Windmeyer, S. (Ed.). (2001). *Secret sisters: Stories of being lesbian and bisexual in college sororities.* Alyson Books.

Windmeyer, S. (Ed.). (2005). *Brotherhood: Gay life in college fraternities.* Alyson Books.

## Interview Protocol

1. How do you define "diversity"?
2. What role, if any, has diversity played in your life?
3. Can you describe your personal experiences of being a member of a Greek letter organization?
4. If all of your attributes, sexual orientation included, were made into characters for a play about your life, what would the sexual orientation character's role be like?
5. How, if at all, has your sexual orientation interacted with being a member of a Greek Organization?
6. What perceptions do you have about the climate for GLBT individuals inside of your Greek organization?
7. a) If a new and "out" GLBT student were to express interest in joining a Greek letter organization, what possible obstacles or challenges would they face?
   b) What possible benefits would this same person experience?
8. How would you describe your personal growth while going through the Greek system?
9. What university or fraternity policies are in place about GLBT individuals?
10. Is there anything that you would like to comment on that we did not cover?

# Participant Demographic Sheet

Age: _____

Race/ethnicity: _____

Marital/relationship status: _____

Job: _____

Sexual orientation: _____

Gender: _____

Number of years in college: _____

Years in Greek organization: _____

Annual household income: _____

Religious/spiritual orientation: _____

Please circle the groups of people, if any, with whom you have disclosed your sexual orientation:

Friends          Family          Greek brothers/sisters          Coworkers

Other (please specify): _____

May we contact you for follow up? Circle one:          Yes          No

How do you want to be contacted? Phone, email, other (please specify)

_____

Phone number: _____          Email: _____

Please provide any additional information you would like for us to know about you.

Thank you!

# Final Codebook

## Codebook: Final Codebook

### TEXT ONE AND TEXT TWO

PA005 and PA010

| Code | Meaning | Example (Interview Transcript Lines) |
|---|---|---|
| Disclosure | Talking about disclosing identity | 63: Being gay might not mix with the traditional ideas of fraternal brotherhood.<br>70: None of the brothers had any idea what was going on.<br>14: Solidly slammed my closet door shut<br>16: It felt so good to be coming out of the closet.<br>81: This kind of snuck up on me.<br>91–92: I hadn't really discovered myself until I moved to college. |
| Acceptance—Others | Accepted by organization | 63: The brothers all seemed eager to meet me.<br>71: I knew where I belonged.<br>16: someone who could just listen to me<br>13: Let's not forget the gay 10% rule.<br>215: Brothers are able to look past that.<br>126–127: Candidates are openly gay and it's typically not an issue.<br>146–147: Oh, you're my brother. And no matter what, I'll be here for you.<br>150: I don't think they would care about my orientation. |
| Macho | Masculine stereotyping | 64: a punch on the arm from one, a strong handshake from another<br>69: Fraternity life was no place for an openly gay guy.<br>12: I do not need friends this badly.<br>12: I could never let my fraternity brothers down. I could never let them know who I am.<br>12: fear of being labeled gay by association<br>122: There is a very macho stereotype of Greeks.<br>109: just another skirt-chasing guy |
| Gay community within organization | Depicts gay community within organization | 69: I never suspected that it was Cole.<br>12: Rob was openly bisexual.<br>90: meeting fellow gays of the family<br>119–120: around some of the other brothers who, uh, we of uh, the same orientation as myself |
| Diversity | Working together with people from different backgrounds | 8–9: the collaboration, coordination of different types, groups of people.<br>21: raised to be a more understanding and appreciative person<br>13–14: mixing or intermingling like, a social uh, a social background<br>265–266: Diversity is alive, it is growing. It is just a genuinely good thing. |
| Self-acceptance | Learning about and appreciating self | 39: taught me a lot about myself and others<br>162–163: You learn so much more about yourself.<br>255: a great growing experience for me<br>283-284: Acceptance in my orientation is a huge difference. |

# Cross-Case Display

| Data | Acceptance of self | Acceptance: Organization | Diversity | Disclosure | Macho stereotype | Gay community |
|---|---|---|---|---|---|---|
| PA005 | Accepted, but not integral to identity | Acknowledges that some are not keen, but also lacking understanding. Has acceptance. | Collaboration of many groups of people. Learning environment. Always a part of life. | Ambivalent brothers. Mostly neutral reactions. | Sees some organizations and members subscribing to the fraternity stereotype. | Numerous individuals mentioned within organization and Greek system. |
| PA010 | Conflicted, accepts self but can see as a negative attribute | Brothers as accepting. Goes with the flow. Unsure about candidate class. | Learning of other groups, particularly religious. Growing sense of awareness. | Feels no need to hide, but sees how it can be stressful. Keeping a secret challenging. | Occasionally identifies with the stereotype as "just one of the guys." | Numerous individuals mentioned within own organization. |
| Text 1 | Accepted, but initially low form. Accepts more as organization accepts. | Fear of rejection. Witness of negative remarks. Feeling of belonging. | N/A | Avoidant of disclosure initially. Would rather die than disclose. Disclosure met with acceptance. | Doesn't need friends this badly (hazing). Initial thoughts. | Hidden members mentioned in organization. Outside community referenced. |
| Text 2 | Accepted, but cautious of reactions of others. | Rejected by two organizations before accepted by the first. Earned acceptance. | N/A | Never hidden within Greek system, but never on the front lines of knowledge. | Stereotypical roles. Punch on the arm. Firm handshakes. | Hidden member mentioned within organization. |

# Concept Map

# The Experience of Success for Adolescents Diagnosed with Attention-Deficit/ Hyperactivity Disorder

Anne M. P. Michalek
*Old Dominion University*

## ABSTRACT

This qualitative study describes the experience of success for adolescents with ADHD. For the pilot study, the author used a phenomenological paradigm, tradition, and method of analysis. The primary researcher conducted two semistructured interviews in order to gather data. Results of this pilot study suggest that adolescents with ADHD had negative self-efficacy with regard to success and that their effort is linked to internal level of worth. Implications and future research directions are provided.

## The Experience of Success for Adolescents Diagnosed with Attention Deficit Hyperactivity Disorder

Attention-deficit/hyperactivity disorder (ADHD) is one of the most frequently cited medical/ behavioral conditions and the most common childhood disorder (Barkley, 1997). Barkley (1997) describes ADHD as a developmental disorder affecting a child's ability to regulate behavior, control behavior, or keep future goals and consequences in mind. These deficits are manifested and demonstrated through a variety of behaviors, including an inability to sustain attention, effectively regulate levels of activity according to the situation, and effectively plan and complete tasks.

The specific criteria for diagnosing ADHD in children is outlined in the Diagnostic Statistical Manual-IV (DSM-IV) and divides ADHD into three specific subtypes, including the inattentive type, the hyperactive type, and the combined type. The purpose of these criteria is to ensure that a diagnosis is made based on observable behaviors that are manifested before the age of 7 in two or more settings, thereby impacting the child's ability to function and are not due to another disorder (APA, 2000). These descriptions are meant to ensure the accurate and consistent diagnosis of ADHD in children. Today, between 3% and 5% of children have been diagnosed with a form of ADHD (Schmitz et al., 2003). Although the prevalence of ADHD in the pediatric population is growing, there remains a significant debate regarding the existence and relevance of the ADHD diagnosis (Kendall et al., 2003).

Over the past 10 years, ADHD has been the topic of numerous research articles and news stories. The media has taken the stance that ADHD is grossly overdiagnosed resulting in the irresponsible prescription of the stimulant methylphenidate in young children (Brazelton & Sparrow 2003; LeFever et al., 1999; Vatz, 2001). The evidence for this argument is essentially rooted in prevalence studies, anecdotal stories of misdiagnosis, and passed down misperceptions developed from personal bias and belief systems (Vatz, 2001; Brazelton & Sparrow 2003; LeFever et al., 1999; Scuitto & Eisenberg, 2007). Scholars and researchers contend that ADHD is not overdiagnosed, basing their argument on the same prevalence studies, current diagnostic criteria, and semantic nuances of the word "overdiagnosis" (Scuitto & Eisenberg, 2007; Singh et al., 2006). Regardless of position, researchers and news commentators agree that clinical science continues to recognize ADHD as a serious problem with serious consequences (Barkley, 2000).

Consequences of ADHD are experienced by parents, educators, and the child. Often, quantitative and qualitative studies summarize the effects of ADHD from the perspective of parent, caregiver, and/or educator. Rarely do quantitative or qualitative studies explain or give voice to the child or adolescent diagnosed with ADHD. In 2003, Kendall et al. discussed the consequences of ADHD from the children's perspective. Through this qualitative study, the researchers identified six common themes regarding how ADHD had impacted the lives of the children interviewed. These themes included problems, meaning and identity, pills, mom, and ethnicity. In general, children with ADHD consistently experienced problems with learning, thinking, feeling, and behaving. The children also described ADHD in terms of emotion words (i.e., feeling ashamed, sad, frustrated, and mad). In general, the authors discussed that the children interviewed had developed an ADHD identity that was characterized by the following descriptors: hyper, bad, trouble, and weird. Although the children reported learning problems, the research team did not seek information regarding how the children experience, recognize, and predict failure or success.

Success is a subjective concept that can be defined and described differently depending on the person's profession and point of reference. According to Schindler and Jones (2009), there are three main variables of success. These variables include (a) the internal locus of control, (b) self-acceptance, and (c) orientation toward goal setting (Schindler & Jones, 2009). *Internal locus of control* refers to how an individual orients themselves toward success. That is, does the individual believe that they are able to influence results so that they have control over outcomes or do they believe that things just happen to them? According to Schindler and Jones, self-acceptance is judged according to how well a person likes themselves. The third variable of success, *orientation toward goal setting*, refers to an individual as either failure-avoiding or success-seeking (Schindler & Jones, 2009). These variables, combined, set the internal stage for a person's ability to successfully attain goals.

The purpose of the current pilot study is to develop an understanding of how ADHD impacts an adolescent's ability to recognize and plan for academic success in order to improve service delivery. In addition, the study will identify the overt and covert variables that influence the success of an adolescent with ADHD in the academic setting. The overarching research question guiding this study is: How do adolescents with ADHD experience academic success?

For the purposes of this study, adolescents are defined as between the ages of 13 and 17 years old.

ADHD is operationalized as the DSM-IV criteria: a persistent pattern of inattention or hyperactivity-impulsivity that is more frequent and severe according to a physician or psychologist. *Academic failure* is defined as one or more of the following: a "D" or below in one or more academic subjects, recommended accommodations/modifications/strategies ineffective, few interpersonal relationships, several parental concerns. *Academic success* is defined as one or more of the following: a "C" or above in more than two academic subjects, recommended accommodations/modifications/strategies effective, several interpersonal relationships, and/or few parental concerns.

## Method

This study will use an emergent design within a theoretical framework synthesized from the five philosophies of science. For the purposes of this study, the first philosophy, ontology, recognizes that there are multiple truths regarding how success and failure are experienced. Epistemologically, the research team will recognize that an individual's knowledge of success is unlimited and context specific. With regard to axiology, the research team will recognize that their beliefs and values will impact and influence the research process. Rhetorically, the researchers agree that once multiple individuals share their experiences, an essence of the experience can be categorized and organized (Patton, 2014). With regard to methodology, the researchers will embrace the social constructivism paradigm because multiple realities are constructed through social interactions, thereby generating knowledge of a phenomenon. Based on this paradigm, multiple realities of the phenomenon success exist; therefore, phenomenology will be the tradition used to capture and describe how a distinct group of people (i.e., adolescents) experience the phenomenon of success (Patton, 2014).

### Research Team

The research team for this study will be comprised of five scholars. There will be three doctoral-level students and two professors. The doctoral-level students will have varying educational backgrounds and professional experiences. One student will have a master's degree in counseling and will be working toward her doctorate. A second student will have a master's degree in special education and will be working toward her PhD. The third student will have a master's degree in speech language pathology and will be working toward her PhD. All three students will be White and will be familiar with ADHD. The entire research team is made up of women. There will be one primary researcher responsible for data collection, transcription, and initial analysis. Both professors will oversee the research project and provide support and guidance as necessary. Like the students, the professors have varied areas of expertise. One professor specializes in counseling while the other is an aphasia expert.

A very important step of a qualitative study is to acknowledge and explain researcher bias. Since this is a phenomenological study, these biases will also be bracketed throughout data collection and analysis. Specifically, the primary researcher recognizes that she has had work experiences that have influenced her core beliefs regarding how ADHD impacts an individual's ability to recognize and experience success. In addition, she has witnessed the importance of effective remediation and treatment for children with ADHD. A former patient sustained multiple traumatic brain injuries due to inconsistent and ineffective management of ADHD behaviors resulting in additional long-term cognitive deficits and eventual incarceration.

## Participants

Participants for the study will be selected using criterion sampling of typical cases in order to facilitate a diverse sample. A total of 30–40 adolescents diagnosed with ADHD will be selected for the study if they are also experiencing academic failure. These adolescents may have the following codiagnoses: learning disability, oppositional defiant disorder, and/or conduct disorder.

## Data Collection

This study will be expected to take between a year and a year and a half to complete. Participants will be recruited through word of mouth and flier distributions to schools, other speech-language pathologists, and psychologists. The international review board (IRB) will examine and approve all research methods and materials before the primary researcher will initiate participant recruitment. In addition, before interviewing participants, they will provide their assent as evidenced by signing the assent document. Furthermore, the adolescent's parent and/or caregiver will be required to provide their parental consent by signing the parental consent document. Once the team has received proper consent and assent, the primary researcher will be responsible for conducting individual interviews with each adolescent participant. The interviews will be semistructured and designed using a variety of question types. These types include, but are not limited to, experience/behavior, opinion, knowledge, feeling, and probing questions. The interview protocol will be reviewed and agreed upon by research team members before being administered to participants.

In addition to adolescent interviews, the primary researcher will conduct participant observations in the home and school environments. The primary researcher will thoroughly document her observations using field notes. It should be noted that these observations will only be completed if permission from all parties (i.e., school, parents, adolescents) is granted.

## Data Analysis

The primary researcher will be responsible for transcribing each participant interview individually. Once transcribed, the interviews will be coded. The following coding procedure will be implemented. First, the primary researcher will bracket her assumptions, noting her biases and their influence on the coding process. Second, the primary researcher will use horizontalization. This essentially refers to the researcher identifying direct quotes from the individual transcripts that may answer or provide more information on the research questions. Third, the primary researcher will use textual themes. This means the researcher will thickly describe the identified quotes using key words in order to generate codes. Finally, the primary researcher will use structural themes. This means the researcher will collapse textual themes into patterns. These patterns will be axial coded as either general, typical, or variant.

Throughout this procedure, the primary researcher will be reading and reviewing the transcripts and simultaneously reviewing, comparing, and collapsing themes. This will continue while the research team reviews the generated codes. Coding will be considered conclusive once the team has reached a point of saturation where no other codes or themes emerge and there is 95% agreement on the resulting codebook.

## Strategies for Trustworthiness

For the purposes of this study, trustworthiness will be defined according to four categories: credibility, transferability, dependability, and confirmability. Credibility will be demonstrated through the use of memos, member checking, a thorough audit trail, and prolonged observation. Transferability will be demonstrated through the use of a diverse sample that meets the predetermined criteria and using thick description. Dependability will be demonstrated by having multiple coders and/or readers, triangulating the data sources, and using member checking. Finally, confirmability will be demonstrated by bracketing the researcher's assumptions.

# Pilot Study

In order to generate preliminary information and assess the viability of the research project, a pilot study was completed. Two participants were selected for the pilot study, and one unobtrusive method of data collection was facilitated. From this, several textual and structural themes were identified. These results indicate several potential contributions and suggest that the research project has value.

The pilot study was conducted through a larger research project. Initially, IRB approval had been obtained and several fliers were distributed announcing the recruitment of adolescents diagnosed with ADHD. To date, two participants have provided their assent in addition to parental consent. These participants are siblings. The first participant is described as a White male whose chronological age is 15 years, 6 months. He has a confirmed medical diagnosis of ADHD and was referred to the research project by his guidance counselor due to academic failure. Finally, this participant takes prescription medication to help alleviate ADHD symptomology.

The second participant is described as a White female whose chronological age is 14 years, 7 months. She has a confirmed medical diagnosis of ADHD and was also referred to the research project by her mother due to academic failure. This participant also takes Adderall to help alleviate ADHD symptomology.

The primary research collected data over the course of 2 days. Each research participant was interviewed individually using a semistructured format with varied questions; the interviews were approximately 35–40 minutes in length. The interviews took place at a child study center in a university setting. Once completed, the primary researcher transcribed each interview individually. Once transcribed, the primary researcher bracketed her assumptions, noting her biases and their influence on the coding process. Second, the primary researcher used horizontalization. This essentially refers to the researcher identifying direct quotes from the individual transcripts that may answer or provide more information to the research questions. Third, the primary researcher used textual themes. This means the researcher thickly described the identified quotes using key words in order to generate codes. Finally, the primary researcher generated structural themes. This means the researcher collapsed textual themes into patterns. Throughout this procedure, the primary researcher was reading, reviewing, comparing, and collapsing codes and themes. For the purposes of the pilot study, coding concluded once the primary researcher subjectively determined she had reached saturation. The research team did not reach consensus during this process. The resulting codebook is included toward the end of the proposal.

In order to maintain trustworthiness, the primary researcher aligned selected data collection and analysis procedures with the following four categories: credibility, transferability, dependability, and confirmability. The primary researcher used memos, member checking, and an audit trail to demonstrate credibility and thick description when coding to demonstrate transferability. To demonstrate dependability, the primary researcher used member checking. Finally, the primary researcher bracketed her assumptions in order to demonstrate confirmability.

## Pilot Findings

The primary researcher identified several textual and structural themes in the pilot study test data. The codebook outlines these results. In summary, 34 textual themes were generated and defined according to the communicative purpose they served and the research question they answered. Once identified, these themes were studied for similarities that would allow them to be collapsed into structural themes. From this, six structural themes were identified and defined according to previous literature and/or the meaning gleaned from the interview. These six structural themes serve as the basis of the discussion and potential implications. The structural themes were motivation, self-esteem, language, family connection, hot executive functions, and cold executive functions (Barry & Welsh, 2007). It should be noted that data generated through individual interviews were confirmed when reviewing internet blogs posted by parents and guardians of adolescents with ADHD.

## Discussion

Several interesting, independent, and relevant conclusions were made based on the identified structural themes. With regard to executive functions, the female participant demonstrated deficits with hot executive functions while the male participant demonstrated deficits with cold executive functions. While the researcher is unable to say that this information is generalizable, it is valuable for the participants' educators, counselors, and parents. Recognizing and responding to differences in executive function ability has significant consequences with regard to academic performance and interpersonal relationships. Both participants would benefit from direct and intense instruction to develop insight regarding the impact hot and cold executive functions have on their activities of daily living.

In addition to profiling specific aspects of executive functions, the results support the existing literature that suggests that hot and cold executive functions impacts an individual's ability to use verbal and nonverbal feedback to successfully self-evaluate (Barry & Welsh, 2007). The participants consistently demonstrated a lack of insight regarding how to use environmental cues to change their behavior. In the face of old problems, they continue to make choices that have negative consequences. This continued cycle makes it difficult for individuals to use lessons learned from previous experiences to effectively make choices when confronted with new problems. These deficits are closely related with the ability to plan effectively. That is, individuals use feedback not only to respond differently but also to make accurate, realistic, and concise plans. The results of this pilot study indicate that although cold executive functions impact planning skills, so too do motivation and self-esteem. Unfortunately for our participants, all three of these areas were judged to be weaknesses, making it very difficult for them to plan effectively.

In addition to planning, self-esteem appears to impact the participants' level of motivation. Both participants communicated a decreased level of value for their individual characteristics as evidenced by self-deprecating comments. This, combined with their decreased level of motivation or desire to achieve, gave the general impression of hopelessness. At a young age, these participants already seemed to have waved the white flag and surrendered to their inherent challenges. They have yet to internalize success, making it very difficult for them to embrace challenging or difficult academic tasks. Most importantly, it appears that these participants can recognize consequences but their self-esteem influences their ability to recognize their worthiness for success. That is, they know what will happen if they are successful but do not believe they are good enough to succeed. It appears that these participants believe that they are only good enough for failure, and therefore, their worth has become inextricably linked to their effort.

In the area of language, both participants demonstrated unique and different language profiles. The female participant had average to above average expressive and receptive language skills while the male participant demonstrated average receptive language with significant expressive language deficits. Specifically, the male participant has difficulty elaborating, creating syntactically and semantically complex sentences, and producing narratives. It should be noted that although the male participant had significant language deficits, he demonstrated a decreased level of apathy.

Finally, both participants consistently communicated a poor family connection. This is a structural theme identified and defined by the primary researcher. It refers to the influence immediate family members (i.e., mother, father, siblings) have had on the participants. Both participants communicated a strong desire to avoid their home environment, indicating that their caregivers may not provide adequate support.

## Implications

This study has the potential to contribute to the field of education. Specifically, this research will give a voice to an otherwise voiceless population. It is very rare for researchers to ask adolescents themselves about their experience with success. This research project provides a great starting point for future discussions with adolescents who are diagnosed with ADHD in order to understand their deficits and, more importantly, what academic strategies are functional and beneficial. Finally, this study contributes preliminary information regarding the relationship between executive functions and ADHD.

## Future Research Directions and Limitations

Specifically, the pilot study provided the following as future research topics: the language profile of adolescents with ADHD, the impact of parental interactions on adolescents with ADHD, the characterization of hot and cold executive functions in this population, and the impact of interpersonal relationships on adolescents with ADHD.

This study has several limitations. The language profile of the participants may interfere with effective communication; therefore, provided verbal responses may not be a true representation of individual experiences. The study did not represent various cultures or race/ethnicities.

The primary researcher had a working relationship with the participants, and this may have influenced their responses. In addition, the primary researcher used her knowledge about participants when coding interviews and drawing conclusions. The primary researcher did not account for the impact of comorbidity, specifically depression, on the experience of participants. It is unknown if these participants had another mental health diagnosis. This variable needs to be accounted for since the literature suggests that there is a high rate of comorbidity for this population. Also, this study did not address medication or the impact mediation may have on the participant's level of functioning.

The primary researcher did not interview teachers, which makes it difficult to triangulate results. Some neuropsychological literature argues that there is poor construct validity for executive functions. This information was not discussed during the literature review, making the review limited in its scope. The methods selected to ensure trustworthiness may not be comprehensive or effective. Finally, with regard to cultural limitations, this study is not culturally representative. In addition, a speech-language pathologist completed this research from that perspective.

# References

American Psychiatric Association. (2000). *Diagnostic and statistical manual of mental disorders* (4th ed.).

Barkley, R. A. (1997). *ADHD and the nature of self-control*. Guilford.

Barry, P. G., & Welsh, M. (2007). The BrainWise curriculum: Neurocognitive development intervention program. In D. Romer & E. Walker (Eds.), *Adolescent psychopathology and the developing brain* (pp. 420–440). Oxford University Press.

Kendall, J., Hatton, D., Beckett, A., & Leo, M. (2003). Children's accounts of attention-deficit/hyperactivity disorder. *Advances in Nursing Science, 26*(2), 114–130.

Brazelton, T. B., & Sparrow, J. (2003, April 24). Overdiagnosis is a major problem with ADHD. *Deseret News.* http://www.findarticles.com/p/articles/mi_qn4188/is_20030424/ai_nl1386912.

LeFever, G. B., Dawson, K. V., & Morrow, A. L. (1999). The extent of drug therapy for attention deficit-hyperactivity disorder among children in public schools. *American Journal of Public Health, 89*(9), 1359–1364.

Patton, M. Q. (2014). *Qualitative research and evaluation methods* (4th ed.) Sage.

Scuitto, M. J., & Eisenberg, M. (2007). Evaluating the evidence for and against the overdiagnosis of ADHD. *Journal of Attention Disorders, 11*(2), 106–113.

Schindler, J., & Jones, A. (2009). *A three-factor operational definition of success psychology.* https://web.calstatela.edu/faculty/jshindl/cm/Success%20Psych%201pg.htm

Schmitz, M. F., Filippone, P., & Edleman, E. M. (2003). Social representations of attention-deficit/hyperactivity disorder, 1998–1997. *Culture and Psychology, 9*, 383–406.

Singh, M. K., DelBello, M. P., Kowatch, R. A., & Strakowski, S. M. (2006). Co-occurrence of bipolar and attention-deficit hyperactivity disorders in children. *Bipolar Disorders, 8*, 710–720.

Vatz, R. E., & Weinberg, L. S. (2001, March 1). Problems in diagnosing and treating ADD/ADHD (attention deficit disorder, attention deficit hyperactivity disorder). *USA Today Magazine.* http://www.findarticles.com/p/articles/mi_m1272/is-2670-129/ai-72272577.

## Interview Protocol

1. Describe your typical school day.
2. What would a great school day be like?
3. Describe, if any, a time of success in school.
4. Describe, if any, a time of failure in school.
5. Complete this sentence: Thinking about school makes me _____.
6. Complete this sentence: When I am not doing well in school, I _____.
7. What would I see when you were having a good day at school? What would cause it? What would happen?
8. What would I see when you were having a bad day at school? What would cause it? What would happen?
9. What advice would you give to other kids who might have a bad day at school?
10. Is there anything else you would like to add?

## Codebook

| TEXTURAL THEMES | DESCRIPTION |
|---|---|
| Consequence_success | Participant indicated understanding of what would happen if successful. |
| Recognition_success | Participant recognizes when success happens. |
| Example_success | Participant provided an example of success. |
| Consequence_failure | Participant indicated understanding of what would happen if they failed. |
| Recognition_failure | Participant recognizes failure. |
| Example_failure | Participant provided an example of failure. |
| Incongruent exp_success | Participant identified an example of success that was not indicative of something positive. |
| Self-perception_neg | Participant made a statement that was a "put down" or reflected poor self-acceptance. |
| Incongruent nonverbals | Participant demonstrated nonverbal communication that was not aligned with the verbal message. |
| Congruent nonverbal | Participant demonstrated nonverbal communication that matched the verbal message. |
| Demeanor nonverbals | Participant demonstrated nonverbal communication that gave the impression of being bored, irritated, indifferent, and uninterested. |
| Canned phrase | Participant made a comment that appeared to be repetitive of something heard by another person or adult. |
| Elaboration | Participant had difficulty elaborating. |
| Self-perception nonverbal | Participant demonstrated nonverbal communication that indicated poor self-acceptance. |
| Mean length utterance | Participant produced a sentence that was not the appropriate mean length of utterance for their chronological age. |
| Problem solving | Participant response indicated difficulty with problem solving. |
| Planning | Participant response indicated poor planning. |
| Incongruent response | Participant response did not match something previously said or the question presented. |
| Learning_prob | Participant response evidenced a problem learning or using academic strategies. |
| Appropriate response | Participant answered the question appropriately. |
| Interpersonal_prob | Participant response revealed a problem getting along with peers, siblings, or parents. |
| Clarification | Participant response was in an effort to get or provide clarification. |

*(continued)*

| TEXTURAL THEMES | DESCRIPTION |
|---|---|
| Apathy_other | Participant response communicated a lack of interest or concern regarding something. |
| Apathy_interpersonal | Participant response communicated a lack of interest or concern regarding peers, parents, or siblings. |
| Apathy_school | Participant response communicated a lack of interest or concern regarding school. |
| Avoidance_home | Participant indicated they try to get away from home . |
| Avoidance_school | Participant response indicates they try to get away from school and school-related activities. |
| Avoidance_answer | Participant response indicated they tried to avoid answering the question. |
| Insight_own | Participant response indicated difficulty with understanding their own motives or thought processes. |
| Insight_others | Participant response indicated difficulty understanding someone else's motives or thought processes. |
| Personal account | Participant response described a personal story or situation. |

| STRUCTURAL THEMES | DESCRIPTION |
|---|---|
| Motivation | Desire to achieve; moving them into action |
| Self-esteem | Valuing your individual characteristics; feeling good about those characteristics |
| Language | Expressive language; syntax, semantics, and pragmatics |
| Family connection | Mother, father, siblings, and their influence on you; use of them for support |
| Hot executive functions | Self-monitoring and self-regulation or emotion |
| Cold executive functions | Planning, problem solving, predicting, consequences |

# Sample Qualitative Research Reports

The following represent qualitative research reports published in academic journals by qualitative research tradition.

## Case Study

Goodman-Scott, E. G., Hays, D. G., & Cholewa, B. (2018). "It takes a village": A case study of positive behavioral interventions and supports implementation in an exemplary urban middle school. *The Urban Review, 50*, 97–122. https://doi.org/10.1007/s11256-017-431-z

Jett, S. T., & Delgado Romero, E. A. (2009). Prepracticum service learning in counselor education: A qualitative case study. *Counselor Education and Supervision, 49*(2), 106–121. https://doi.org/10.1002/j.1556-6978.2009.tb00091.x

Saeed, S., & Zyngier, D. (2012). How motivation influences student engagement: A qualitative case study. *Journal of Education and Learning, 1*(2), 252–267.

## Grounded Theory

Hays, D. G., Crockett, S., & Michel, R. (2021). A grounded theory of counselor educators' academic leadership development. *Counselor Education & Supervision, 60*, 51–72. https://doi.org/ 10.1002/ceas.12196

Salvador, K., Paetz, A. M., & Tippetts, M. M. (2020). "We all have a little more homework to do": A constructivist grounded theory of transformative learning processes for practicing music teachers encountering social justice. *Journal of Research in Music Education, 68*(2), 193–215. https://doi.org/10.1177/0022429420920630

Singh, A. A., Urbano, A., Haston, M., & McMahon, E. (2010). School counselors' strategies for social justice change: A grounded theory of what works in the real world. *Professional School Counseling, 13*, 135–145.

## Phenomenology

Farmer, L. B., & Byrd, R. (2015). Genderism in the LGBTQQIA community: An interpretative phenomenological analysis. *Journal of LGBT Issues in Counseling, 9*(4), 288–310. https:/doi.org/10.1080/15538605.2015.1103679

Ghasemi, F. (2021). Exploring middle school teachers' perceptions of factors affecting the teacher–student relationships. *Educational Research for Policy and Practice*, 1–16. https://doi.org/10.1007/s10671-021-09300-1

Gleason, B. K., & Hays, D. G. (2019). A phenomenological investigation of wellness within counselor education programs. *Counselor Education and Supervision, 58*(3), 177–194. https://doi.org/10.1002/ceas.12149

## Heuristic Inquiry

Chang, B., & Delaney, K. (2019). A heuristic inquiry on the role of person environment interaction in suicide risk among transgender youth. *Journal of Child and Adolescent Psychiatric Nursing, 32*(2), 47–50. https://doi.org/10.1111/jcap.12237

Sadat Ahadi, H. (2020). Unveiling the voices of Afghan women in community college. *Journal of Applied Research in the Community College, 27*(2), 81–93.

Sultan, N. (2018). Embodiment and the therapeutic relationship: Findings from a heuristic inquiry. *Journal of Humanistic Counseling, Education, and Development, 47*, 3–8. https://doi.org/10.1002/johc.12052

## Consensual Qualitative Research

Ahn, L. H., Keum, B. T., Meizys, G. M., Choudry, A., Gomes, M. A., & Wang, L. (2021). Second-generation Asian American women's gendered racial socialization. *Journal of Counseling Psychology, 69*(2), 129–145. https://doi.org/10.1037/cou0000575

Caperton, W., Butler, M., Kaiser, D., Connelly, J., & Knox, S. (2020). Stay-at-home fathers, depression, and help-seeking: A consensual qualitative research study. *Psychology of Men and Masculinities, 221*, 235–250. https://doi.org/10.1037/men0000223

Goodrich, K. M., & Luke, M. (2019). Consensual qualitative research of LGB persons' counseling experiences addressing religious/spiritual foci. *Journal of Counseling Sexology & Sexual Wellness: Research, Practice, and Education, 1*, Article 5. https://doi.org/10.34296/01011003

## Life History

Bremner, N. (2020). "Belief-changing" teacher education: Mexican English teachers' experiences. *MEXTESOL Journal, 44*(1), 1–12.

Cazers, G., & Curtner-Smith, M. D. (2017). Robin's story: Life history of an exemplary American female physical education teacher. *Journal of Teaching in Physical Education, 36*(2), 197–208. https://doi.org/10.1123/jtpe.2015-0084

Ezzani, M. D., & King, K. M. (2018). Whose Jihad? Oral history of an American Muslim educational leader and US public schools. *Journal of Educational Administration and History, 50*(2), 113–129. https://doi.org/10.1080/00220620.2018.1448369

## Narratology

Cavanaugh, K. M., & Luke, M. M. (2021). Transgender college student identity development: A narratology of intermediating experiences. *Journal of Humanistic Counseling, 60*(2), 137–156. https://doi.org/10.1002/johc.12161

Haiyasoso, M., & Trepal, H. (2019). Survivors' stories: Navigating parenthood after surviving child sexual abuse. *Journal of Counseling & Development, 97*(3), 281–292. https://doi.org/10.1002/jcad.12268

Mellor, R., Lancaster, K., & Ritter, A. (2021). Recovery from alcohol problems in the absence of treatment: A qualitative narrative analysis. *Addiction*, *116*(6), 1413–1423. https://doi.org/doi:10.1111/add.15288

## Ethnography

Freeman, S., Jr., & Kochan, F. (2019). Exploring mentoring across gender, race, and generation in higher education: An ethnographic study. *International Journal of Mentoring and Coaching in Education*, *8*(1), 2–18. https://doi.org/10.1108/IJMCE-05-2018-0027

Griffin, D. M., & Bryan, J. (2021). A qualitative study of school counseling in Barbados: A focused ethnography. *International Journal for the Advancement of Counselling*, 1–22. https://doi.org/10.1007/s10447-021-09445-x

Woodson, A. (2019). Racial code words, re-memberings and Black kids' civic imaginations: A critical race ethnography of a post-civil rights leader. *Anthropology & Education Quarterly*, *50*(1), 26–47. https://doi.org/10.1111/aeq.12277

## Ethnomethodology

Corsby, C. L., & Jones, R. L. (2020). Complicity, performance, and the "doing" of sports coaching: An ethnomethodological study of work. *The Sociological Review*, *68*(3), 590–605. https://doi.org/10.1177/0038026119897551

Janusz, B., Bergmann, J. R., Matusiak, F., & Peräkylä, A. (2021). Practices of claiming control and independence in couple therapy with narcissism. *Frontiers in Psychology*, *11*, 3779. https://doi.org/10.3389/fpsyg.2020.596842

Maree, N., & van der Westhuizen, G. (2020). How classroom talk contributes to reading comprehension. *Per Linguam*, *36*(2), 1–15. http://dx.doi.org/10.5785/36-2-910

## Autoethnography

Chan, C. D., Harrichand, J. J., Anandavalli, S., Vaishnav, S., Chang, C. Y., Hyun, J. H., & Band, M. P. (2021). Mapping solidarity, liberation, and activism: A critical autoethnography of Asian American leaders in counseling. *Journal of Mental Health Counseling*, *43*(3), 246–265. https://doi.org/10.17744/mehc.43.3.06

Coker, A. D., Martin, C., Culver, J., & Johnson, C. (2018). Black women's academic and leadership development in higher education: An autoethnographic study. *Periferia*, *10*(2), 44–66. https://doi.org/10.12957/periferia.2018.33714

Hughes, S. (2020). My skin is unqualified: an autoethnography of Black scholar-activism for predominantly White education. *International Journal of Qualitative Studies in Education*, *33*, 151–165. https://doi.org/10.1080/09518398.2019.1681552

## Participatory Action Research

Bessaha, M., Reed, R., Donlon, A. J., Mathews, W., Bell, A. C., & Merolla, D. (2020). Creating a more inclusive environment for students with disabilities: Findings from participatory action research. *Disability Studies Quarterly*, *40*(3). http://dx.doi.org/10.18061/dsq.v40i3.7094

Oscós-Sánchez, M. A., Lesser, J., Oscós-Flores, L. D., Pineda, D., Araujo, U., Franklin, B., Hernández, J. A., Hernández, S., & Vidales, A. (2021). The effects of two community-based participatory action research programs on violence outside of an in school among adolescents and young adults in a Latino community. *Journal of Adolescent Health, 68*, 370–377. https://doi.org/10.1016/j.jadohealth.2020.10.004

Shiller, J. (2018). The disposability of Baltimore's Black communities: A participatory action research project on the impact of school closings. *The Urban Review, 50*(1), 23–44. https://doi.org/10.1007/s11256-017-0428-7

## Community-Based Participatory Research

Lamson, A. L., Clark, R. J., Bellamy, R. W., Hodgson, J. L., Knight, S. M., Baugh, E. J., & Flores, J. (2020). Latina sexual health care in the US: Community-based participatory research and her lived experience. *Journal of Feminist Family Therapy, 32*(1–2), 76–96. https://doi.org/10.1080/08952833.2020.1755167

Nieweglowski, K., Corrigan, P. W., Tyas, T., Tooley, A., Dubke, R., Lara, J., Washington, L., Sayer, J., Sheehan, L., & Addiction Stigma Research Team. (2018). Exploring the public stigma of substance use disorder through community-based participatory research. *Addiction Research & Theory, 26*(4), 323–329. https://doi.org/10.1080/16066359.2017.1409890

Pomeranz, J. L. (2014). Creating a tobacco cessation program for people with disabilities: A community-based participatory research approach. *Journal of Addiction Research & Therapy, 5*(4), 1–8. https://doi.org/10.4172/2155-6105.1000204

# Glossary

**abductive analysis:** the qualitative researcher's immersion in and deliberate moving away from inductive and deductive analysis to remain open to new insights and concepts during data analysis.

**action research:** corresponds to the purpose of solving specific problems and engaging individuals in solving those problems. The researcher focuses on a specific site, collaborates with individuals with a relationship to the topic, and works to resolve key issues to improve the lives of those at the site.

**action strategies:** a concept of the grounded theory tradition that refers to the purposeful, goal-oriented activities performed in response to the phenomenon and intervening conditions.

**advocacy:** actions that empower a community; can illuminate individual and community assets and resources to rescript as appropriate dominant views of education and social science phenomena.

**analysis:** a sorting procedure in ethnographic data analysis that involves highlighting specific material introduced in the descriptive phase or displaying findings through tables, charts, diagrams, and figures.

**analytic autoethnography:** a form of autoethnography where a researcher expands the descriptive narrative of evocative autoethnography to apply the description to theory and professional practice.

**analytic generalizability:** a form of transferability where findings are translated to an established construct or theory, even when samples or contexts are different.

**analytic induction:** the process by which qualitative data analysis moves from exploratory to confirmatory or verification methods. Verification involves seeking out cases to disconfirm present codes and themes in order to strengthen emerging models.

**anonymity:** protection of participant identity from the researcher and others.

**applied research:** a type of research where a researcher seeks specialized knowledge about a specific problem in order to intervene in the problem.

**archival data:** an unobtrusive, often secondary data source such as written materials (e.g., case records, data sets, applications, forms) or statistics maintained typically by government or educational institutions. Archival data can be a helpful supplement to primary data collection.

**attributional coding:** analysis of public attributions individuals make during spoken or written discourse; their understanding of the causes of various events of interest.

**audiovisual media:** media that contains sound and/or visual aspects; may be used during data collection and can include photography, drawing and painting, film and video, sculpture, collage, murals, printmaking, craft-making, mixed media, and multimedia as visual methods.

**audit trail:** the physical evidence of systematic data collection and analysis procedures to provide a collection of evidence of the research process for an auditor or any other consumer to review.

**auditor:** individual without a conflict of interest who reviews the audit trail to determine the extent to which the researcher or research team(s) completed a comprehensive and rigorous study.

**authenticity:** a criterion of trustworthiness similar to confirmability in that the researcher strives to represent participant perspectives authentically using theoretical versus methodological criteria.

**autoethnography:** a qualitative research tradition that involves first-person researcher accounts of events, interactions, and relationships within a cultural context.

**autonomy:** a metaethical principle in which qualitative researchers seek to demonstrate consideration for the rights of individuals, groups, and communities by maximizing their agency along with promoting voluntariness of research.

**axial coding:** data analysis in the grounded theory tradition wherein a research refines and examine relationships among open codes. This process collapses open codes into broader categories or codes for theory-building.

**axiology:** a philosophy of science that refers to values in the research process: the role of the qualitative researcher, participant values, values associated with the research design, and the degree to which the research relationship is prioritized.

**background question:** a type of interview question the interviewer seeks about the participant, setting, or phenomenon during the interview itself, typically solicited in written form, such as a demographic questionnaire.

**basic research:** a type of research whereby a researcher serves to expand the scope and depth of knowledge of a case for the sake of contributing knowledge to a particular discipline.

**behavior or experience question:** a type of interview question that seeks to gather a thick description of what occurred by and for the participants rather than why things occurred.

**being-in-the-world:** a phenomenological construct that refers to individuals being embedded in their world and thus having both identifiable and unidentifiable experiences.

**Belmont Report:** a national report attending to three key research ethics: respect for persons (i.e., informed consent, voluntariness of participation), beneficence (i.e., maximizing participant benefits with minimal risk), and justice (i.e., representative and equitable participation and representation in the research process and reports).

**beneficence:** a metaethical principle that refers to the implementation of research that yields benefit outcomes for the intended population.

**blog:** also referred to as "weblog," a type of journal that is either publicly or privately written online. It may involve concise content presented as a microblog.

**blurred genres period:** a historical moment of qualitative research between approximately 1970 and 1986; represented greater attention to the act of writing qualitative reports, with researchers no longer viewing a report as being free from their values; reports were now considered interpretations of interpretations.

**bracketing:** typically viewed as the first step in phenomenological data analysis. The researcher examines and sets aside preconceived beliefs, values, and assumptions about the research topic and proposed research design. Also referred to as "bridling."

**British School:** emerged in the 1920s and 1930s within the field of anthropology and included as part of the traditional period of qualitative research; credited with the fieldwork method, particularly in areas of urbanization and imperialism in England.

**case:** the unit of analysis or object of study; can be an individual or individuals, setting, process, or event within a bounded system (i.e., distinctive boundaries of time, sampling frame, activity, and/or psychical space or setting).

**case display:** qualitative data management tool. A case display is a graphic depiction of reduced (and chunked) data. Case displays are initially created for each individual case (within-case display) and then are later consolidated to examine concepts and variables across cases (cross-case display) for increased understanding of themes and patterns and thus enhance generalizability.

**case study:** a research tradition labeled as the hybrid tradition. Case studies are distinguished from other qualitative traditions because cases are researched in depth and the data are delineated by time period, activity, and place, using multiple data sources and methods.

**categorical aggregation:** a form of case study analysis where a researcher examines several occurrences for critical incidents, concerns, and issues within the data collected.

**causal conditions:** a component of analysis in the grounded theory tradition. Causal conditions are factors influencing the phenomenon you are studying.

**causal network:** a form of case display that allows for explanation and prediction of data. A causal network is a display of the most important variables, showing directions and sequences rather than relationships. For cross-case displays, this allows for a comparative analysis of individual cases, using the most influential variables accounting for a particular outcome as the organizing principle. This display rates antecedents found across cases and links variables and processes.

**chat room:** a social media tool that involves online bound spaces where participants interact with one another around a common topic.

**Chicago School:** an outcome of sociological inquiry and qualitative research that sought to examine "slices of life" in the Chicago area through participant observation; a component of pragmatism and the traditional period of qualitative research.

**co-constitutionality:** a phenomenological construct where phenomenological meanings identified in a study are a blend of researcher and participant meanings.

**code:** a label, tag, or "chunks" of various sizes based on the defined case or unit of analysis; may be referred to by many other terms, including domains, factors, themes, subthemes, and items, to name a few. May be descriptive or interpretive and specifically labeled by participants themselves (emic codes) and/or by the researcher (etic codes).

**codebook:** a document with a listing of codes, subcodes, and patterns; can contain a definition or description of each code, examples from data, and direct quotes or references to aspects of visual data.

**coherence:** a strategy of trustworthiness that refers to the degree of consistency of an epistemological perspective throughout the research design. The researcher is responsible for infusing it throughout the research process and describing it thoroughly in the research report.

**collective autoethnography:** an analysis of multiple autoethnographies to more proudly define a phenomenon using multiple researcher self-narratives.

**collective case study:** a case study design where multiple cases are used to investigate more general or broad phenomenon or population.

**colonial ethnography period:** a historical moment of qualitative research within the 17th, 18th, and 19th centuries; characterized by one camp of researchers who had an interest in studying and colonizing "primitives" and another camp who had an interest in liberating colonized peoples.

**community-based participatory research:** a qualitative research tradition that involves collaborating with participants as coresearchers to establish research question and processes that directly benefit the community; a tradition used to influence social change and entails social justice and liberation components.

**comparative pattern analysis:** a qualitative data analysis technique that involves researchers moving back and forth through chunked data to compare categories; examination of the processing and sequencing of data and attending to where, how, why, and by whom that data occurred.

**comparison memo:** a form of memo that is written after coding is complete in which qualitative researchers extract quotations across data sources for a particular code, then illustrate a code's complexity and "stretchiness" by highlighting how different quotations may indicate various dimensions of that code.

**comparison question:** A type of interview question that can be used to have the participant link information presented in other parts of data collection.

**competence:** the qualitative researcher having the necessary training, skills, professional experience, and education to work with a research population in some capacity.

**complexity of analysis:** a strategy of trustworthiness that involves collecting and analyzing data simultaneously or in close sequence.

**comprehensive sampling:** a purposive sampling method used to represent a sample where the researcher selects an entire group of people by an established set of criteria.

**concept map:** a visual display of an evolving theory and/or researcher assumptions about an area of inquiry, developed before data collection and revised throughout the research process; may be categorized as variance or process maps (display of causal links or relationships between particular constructs or variables and descriptive display of specific events or situations rather than variables, respectively).

**conceptual framework:** a network of concepts, theories, personal and professional assumptions, exploratory studies, and alternative explanations that collectively inform your research topic; includes four major components of a conceptual framework, which are experiential knowledge (researcher assumptions, expectations, and biases); prior theory and research; pilot and exploratory studies; and thought experiments (alternative models or frameworks).

**conceptually ordered case display:** a case display that explores and describes a concept (see "case display"). Conceptually ordered case displays can be created for individual case displays (e.g., thematic conceptual matrix, cognitive map, and folk taxonomy) or several case displays (e.g., content-analytic summary table and the decision tree model).

**confidentiality:** the protection of a research participant's identity during the research process from disclosure; can relate to how data are collected and reported.

**consequences:** a component of analysis in the grounded theory tradition. Consequences are the results of action strategies for participants.

**confirmability:** a criterion of trustworthiness similar to authenticity that refers to the degree from a methodological perspective that findings are genuine reflections of the participants investigated. This concept is most similar to objectivity and neutrality in quantitative research.

**confirming or disconfirming sampling:** a purposive sampling method associated with theory development and verification. As patterns emerge, the researcher looks for confirming cases to add depth to the study and seeks disconfirming cases to look for exceptions that disconfirm the pattern.

**consensual qualitative research:** a research tradition that integrates phenomenological, grounded theory, and other approaches. Consensus is key to this approach, as qualitative researchers use rigorous methods to facilitate agreement in interpretations among themselves, participants, as well as the general audience.

**consensus coding:** use of multiple researchers where each independently code a data source and then reach agreement on a code as a team, discussing and agreeing on an operational definition of a code.

**consequentialism:** an ethics concept related to determining what impact that research actions are likely to have on those directly affected.

**constant comparison:** concurrent data collection and analysis; the continuous process of using earlier coding systems to code future data sources and revise a codebook.

**constructivism:** a research paradigm that assumes that "universal truth" cannot exist because there are multiple contextual perspectives and subjective voices that can label truth in scientific pursuit; construction of knowledge through social interactions.

**contact summary sheet:** a qualitative data management tool that summarizes a single contact with a case and serves as initial step to qualitative data analysis; helps a researcher capture their own reflections about the data, outline initial salient themes based on the interview process, and jot down additional questions to be asked of a participant or setting.

**content analysis:** a process of examining content and themes typically from written documents; process to identify relationships and patterns among words, phrases, and ideas within the data.

**context:** concept in the grounded theory tradition that involves "background" variables influencing an action strategy and/or causal condition.

**convenience sampling:** a purposive sampling method that is viewed as the least representative sampling strategy where researchers sample those to whom they have relatively easy access.

**conversation analysis:** an outgrowth of the ethnomethodological research tradition in which a researcher examines characteristics and structures of personal conversations.

**creative synthesis:** the final qualitative data analysis phase of heuristic inquiry where the researcher seeks the best way to portray the findings as a composite whole, integrating their role and experience with the phenomenon.

**credibility:** a criterion of trustworthiness that refers to the "believability" of a study; somewhat analogous to internal validity in quantitative research. It is one of the major criteria qualitative researchers use to determine if conclusions make sense for a qualitative study.

**crisis of representation:** A historical moment of qualitative research within the mid-1980s characterized by a rise in feminism, constructivism, and critical theory paradigms and a subsequent realization that qualitative researchers may not be representing themselves and their participants in an accurate way; greater examination of the role of gender, class, and race in participants' and researchers' lives.

**criterion sampling:** a purposive sampling method used to describe a phenomenon. Researchers sample participants who meet an important, predetermined criterion. The purpose is to review all cases that meet a criterion.

**critical case sampling:** purposeful sampling method used to describe a phenomenon. The researcher looks for experiences that are particularly significant because of their intensity or irregularity in order to serve as a benchmark of "cut-off score" for other participants.

**critical race theory (CRT):** a research paradigm based on theory borne from legal studies regarding dismantling racism and promoting racial equity. Applied to qualitative research, it assumes participants' experiences and thus constructions of various phenomena may be influenced by social injustices and work to change participant experiences within and outside the research process. It involves strands such as Latino-critical (LatCrit), Asian American critical legal studies, and queer critical legal studies.

**critical reflection:** a major characteristic of participatory action research. It refers to Freire's work that provided a critical analysis of power holders as a way to generate social and systemic change.

**cross-analysis:** the third phase of analysis for the consensual qualitative research tradition. Research team members meet and attempt to research consensus on core ideas. It should result in a separate document that includes a list of domains and within-domains categories common to all participants and any participant data that was not common across participant and/or was not included in another domain or subdomain.

**cross-case synthesis:** a data analysis technique of the case study tradition specific to multiple case study designs; can involve single cases within one study or can consolidate findings across multiple studies.

**data saturation:** a form of saturation where saturation is reached for an individual participant or other data source.

**data triangulation:** a form of triangulation where the researcher uses multiple sources of data (i.e., people, time, and space) and each data source represents different data of the same event and takes place over time.

**deontologicalism:** an ethics concept related to determining whether an action itself in research—no matter its actual consequences—was appropriate within itself.

**demographic question:** a foundational question that the interviewer should seek about the participant, setting, or phenomenon during the interview itself or in some written form, such as a demographic questionnaire.

**dependability:** a criterion of trustworthiness that refers to the consistency of study results over time and across researchers; similar to the concept of "reliability" in quantitative research.

**descriptive field notes:** details of what occurred in a setting during an observation; provides behavioral descriptions of behaviors that are often abstract, such as teaching and clinical work; can include detailed depictions of participants and the physical setting, thick descriptions of specific events, and paraphrases, summaries, or verbatim quotations from participant conversations.

**dialogical analysis:** a qualitative data analysis technique of the narratology tradition, with attention to dialogue in a participant narrative.

**dichotomous question:** a question involving forced-choice responses (i.e., yes/no, true/false) where participants select a response without an opportunity to elaborate on why they responded in a particular way.

**direct interpretation:** a form of case study analysis where the researcher directly interprets the meaning of singular critical incidents, concerns, and issues within the data.

**discussion board:** a social media tool in which participants can post their thoughts about a phenomenon and review and respond to other participant posts.

**document reflection memos:** a form of memo that is developed by examining a data source holistically for meaning, gleaning through repetitive content and initial patterns.

**domain abstraction:** the second phase of analysis for the consensual qualitative research tradition. The research team abstracts core ideas within by reimmersing themselves in the data. They keep an eye out for core ideas that illuminate aspects of domains they have previously selected to examine.

**domain development and coding:** the initial phase of analysis for the consensual qualitative research tradition. Each research team member immerses themselves in all of the data, reading each participant transcript. As they read this data, their analysis begins by identifying independently then collectively a list of large domains, categories, or themes they see in the data.

**duty to warn and protect:** ethical and legal responsibility to warn identifiable victims and protect others from dangerous individuals or, in some instances, danger from themselves.

**dyadic interview:** a type of interview that involves interviewing two participants at a time, and it is an approach that falls between individual interviews and focus group interviews; a relationship-based interviewing style used to facilitate conversation rather than group discussion.

**early ethnography period:** a historical moment of qualitative research within the 15th, 16th, and 17th centuries that involved a comparison of diversity throughout the globe against an established theory of human diversity; characterized by research describing how non-Western societies diverged from the "civilized" European nations.

**effects matrix:** a form of case display that allows for explanation and prediction of data; case display that explains and predicts data. Effects matrices may be developed as individual case displays (e.g., explanatory effects matrix and case dynamics matrix) or for several case displays (e.g., case-ordered effects matrix, case-ordered predictor-outcome matrix, and variable-by-variable matrix).

**epiphany:** stories or critical incidents within the biography tradition.

**episodic narrative interviewing:** an interviewing approach that allows researchers to ask directly for stories and, with the participant, attempt to structure the different happenings into in-depth depictions and episodes of those stories.

**epistemology:** a philosophy of science that involves the process of knowing, or the acquisition of knowledge; the degree to which knowledge is believed to be constructed by the research process in general and in the context of the researcher–participant relationship.

**epoche:** analogous to bracketing, it involves setting aside prior explanations of phenomena found in literature and acknowledging researchers' values and assumptions regarding phenomena. It refers to refraining from judgment and is characteristic of the phenomenological research tradition.

**equity:** absence of avoidable or remediable differences among groups of people with regard to social, cultural, economic, geographical, and other demographic characteristics; lack of evidence of oppressive systems that marginalize individuals or groups of people.

**essence:** a characteristic of the phenomenological research tradition that refers to the delineation of essential features across participants about a lived experience to get at a phenomenological structure.

**ethical validation:** a strategy of trustworthiness that refers to treating all aspects of the qualitative research process as a moral and ethical issue; the practice of engaging in research that provides insights to practical and meaningful real-world problems.

**ethics:** a set of guidelines established within a professional discipline to guide thinking and behavior.

**ethics of practice:** adherence to relevant, professional behaviors when addressing day-to-day ethical issues that occur during the conduct of research.

**ethnography:** a qualitative research tradition in which the researcher describes and provides interpretations about the culture of a group or system; characterized by participant observation and prolonged engagement in order to describe the process and experience of its culture.

**ethnomethodology:** a qualitative research tradition that seeks to study social order and patterns; focus of study is on the informants' perspectives of social order, assessments, and explanations—or "everydayness" of their lives.

**evaluation:** a type of research that refers to assessing the effectiveness of a program or intervention throughout its course. Two common forms of evaluative research, formative evaluation and summative evaluation, involve (a) the examining practices throughout a program or intervention in an effort to improve and shape it and (b) assessing the outcomes at the end of the program or intervention, respectively.

**evaluative research:** See entry for "evaluation."

**evocative autoethnography:** a form of autoethnography in which a researcher provides a first-person narrative of a phenomenon with the primary purpose of connecting to the reader.

**experimental setting:** a characteristic more typical of quantitative research where variables are controlled within the research setting to evaluate differences.

**explanation building:** a specific form of pattern matching within the case study tradition in which the goal is to analyze the case study data by building an explanation of the case. Explaining a case involves describing in narrative form how or why something happened.

**explication:** the fifth phase of heuristic inquiry where the researcher integrates new knowledge to identify themes and patterns; can include focusing (i.e., targeting a significant idea relevant to personal transformation) or indwelling (i.e., turning inward for an active self-dialogue to allow space for new insights about the phenomenon).

**external audit:** a strategy of trustworthiness where an individual suggest alterations, revisions, and/or data that were not addressed within the original design and/or findings; also considered a step of analysis within consensual qualitative research in which a secondary research team comes in to assess the accuracy of the cross-analysis and creation of domains and subdomains common to all participants.

**extreme or deviant sampling:** a purposive sampling method that refers to the selection of participants whose experiences are characterized at either or both extremes.

**feeling question:** a type of qualitative interview question that assesses participant affect regarding a phenomenon.

**feminism:** a research paradigm that places emphasis on gender as an organizing principle for understanding and reporting research findings; involved four waves, with later waves deconstructing and expanding the concept of gender while introducing the impacts of intersectionality on gender and sexism.

**feminist communitarianism:** a rebuttal to utilitarianism that emphasizes the need to balance individual rights and interests with those of the community; a focus on collectivism and the infusion of social values into individual identities.

**feminist standpoint:** centering of voices of traditionally marginalized cultural groups in order to highlight their ways of knowing; notion that narratives "stand" on their own and take into account how gender, race, socioeconomic status, sexual orientation, and other identities intersect.

**fidelity:** a metaethical principle that refers to the qualitative researcher being honest and trustworthy during the research process; establishing a trusting relationship with participants and having integrity regarding the research process.

**field notes:** written records of field activities developed within an observational period (as possible) and continually expanded and revised after the observation has occurred; includes two types: descriptive field notes (i.e., detailed behavioral descriptions of what occurred in a setting) and reflective field notes (i.e., subjective aspects of data collection including assumptions, impressions, attitudes, and ideas).

**fieldwork:** research activities individuals engage in when in a particular setting to gather a thick description of the context and provide a deeper understanding of a particular phenomenon. Fieldwork is often associated with participant observation but can be used with a variety of methods.

**focus group interview:** a type of interview that results in generating data from interactions among participants that share a common experience or are homogenous in some manner; often serves as a catalyst for participant disclosure, connecting with others, and expanding on or challenging perspectives in a synergistic manner.

**focused coding:** specific to constructivist grounded theory, identifying the more significant and/or frequently occurring initial codes to sift through large amounts of data.

**formal grounded theory:** development of a metatheory to maximize generalizability of multiple primary studies or substantive grounded theories.

**frequency analysis:** the final qualitative data analysis technique of the consensual qualitative research tradition where research team members categorize domains into one of three categories: general, typical, and variant. A general domain is one that reflects each of the participants' sharing or does not include one participant. A typical domain is one that was identified for the majority (at least half) of the participants. A variant theme is one that has significance for participants but was common to less than half or fewer of the participants' data.

**frequency counting:** a tally of the number of times a code occurs for a data source.

**gatekeeper:** an individual who grants the researcher access to participants and/or site of study.

**genealogy:** also called "family history," refers to tracing one's family lineage.

**grounded theory:** a qualitative research tradition that seeks to generate theory that is "grounded" in data from participants' perspectives for a particular phenomenon. Characteristics include inductive approach, constant comparison, theoretical sampling, saturation, and theory development. Strands include classic or Glaserian grounded theory, Straussian grounded theory, and constructivist grounded theory.

**hermeneutics:** a historical moment in qualitative research in the early-19th-century tradition that involved interpreting "sacred" texts, such as religious documents, mythology, history, art, and politics; contributed the concept of researcher reflexivity, or the innate drive for humans to interpret and understand; assumption is that texts and others are recorded expressions of human experience.

**heuristic inquiry:** a qualitative research tradition that is a variation of phenomenology in which living rather than lived experience is highlighted; emphasizes the essence of discovering or finding an experience and the person in relation to that experience.

**homogenous sampling:** a purposive sampling method that serves to represent a sample by selection of those who share similarities to one another; common when a researcher is interested in gaining a depth of information about one specific subgroup.

**horizons:** meaning units in phenomenological data sources.

**horizontalization:** a phenomenological data analysis technique where researchers identify nonrepetitive, nonoverlapping statements in participants' transcripts.

**humanness of research:** also referred to as *Verstehen*, the integration of the personal perspectives of qualitative researchers with research skill sets; the notion that the qualitative researcher is an instrument of research itself who can augment technical research skills throughout the qualitative research.

**illumination:** the fourth phase of heuristic inquiry where the researcher has new awareness or modification of previous knowledge related to the phenomenon; may involve data collection from others.

**illustrative question:** an interview question used by interviewers to communicate to respondents that they "have heard it all." Response extremes can be presented to participants to illustrate a range of potential responses.

**immersion:** the second phase of heuristic inquiry where a researcher "lives" the phenomenon and actively self-reflects and interacts with others to identify potential links between these experiences and the phenomenon.

**importance of context:** a qualitative research characteristic that refers to how participants create and give meaning to social experience. Phenomena are created and maintained by those in an environment, and social settings are self-organized in a manner that activities are structured for themselves.

**incubation:** the third phase of heuristic inquiry where the researcher step back from the research process.

**Indigenous ethics:** recognition that Indigenous communities' shared ways of knowing based on a relation to and resistance to colonization. Applied to research ethics, it is the researchers' reflection on who owns, designs, reports, and ultimately benefits from research process and products.

**Indigenous populations:** individuals or groups belonging to developing or underdeveloped regions nationally or internationally, as well as those who have been marginalized by Eurocentric values and/or research methodologies. Applied to qualitative research, it is those who have been affected by cognitive imperialism and thus experience deleterious effects from generated scholarship.

**individual interview:** a type of interview that involves soliciting data from one participant at a time.

**inductive analysis:** a "bottom-up" approach of assessing qualitative data with the assumption that data drive theory or a deeper understanding of an issue or phenomenon; data collection to refine research questions and build theory, not test hypotheses.

**inferential generalizability:** a form of transferability in which the researcher provides enough information to readers to determine the extent to which findings apply from one situation or context to another.

**informed consent:** an ethical and legal concept that clearly identifies and outlines research activity and rights and responsibilities of all parties involved; the process of the researcher describing the purpose and process of research, and providing information about the researcher, the extent of participation, limits of confidentiality, and any foreseeable risks and benefits of participation and nonparticipation and emphasizes the voluntariness of participation; articulation of how and what data will be accessed and presented.

**initial engagement:** the first phase of heuristic inquiry where a researcher identifies a phenomenon of personal significant interest to study.

**insider research:** research where the investigator is not necessarily part of an organization and/or the phenomenon of inquiry but rather has knowledge of the organization and/or phenomenon prior to the study's commencement.

**institutional review board (IRB):** a team of institutional and outside members that review research applications and monitor federal compliance with aspects of the Belmont Report to ensure protection of human subjects.

**instrumental case study:** a case study design where the researcher seeks out cases to assist in an understanding of a particular issue exterior to a specific case.

**intensity sampling:** a purposive sampling method where intense (but not extreme) cases are identified to demonstrate a phenomenon.

**intentionality:** a characteristic of the phenomenological research tradition that relates to actively describing the how and what of individuals' action on an experience and being conscious of the surrounding context of that experience.

**interactive interviewing:** a type of interviewing commonly associated with autoethnography; provides an interpretive process by which participants can share their experiences for joint meaning-making.

**interpretivism:** a philosophical perspective also referred to as "postmodernism" that assumes everything is relative; belief that criteria for determining the trustworthiness of research are socially constructed. This approach for evaluating research is most closely assigned with constructivist, critical race theory, feminist, and queer theory paradigms.

**interrater reliability:** also referred to as "reproducibility reliability," a method for determining consistency or agreement among research team members; a ratio between research team members about the appropriateness for use of each code or pattern in textual or visual data.

**intersectional generalizability:** a form of transferability that refers to the extent to which research is done in order to understand a community and its intersections.

**intervening conditions:** a component of analysis in the grounded theory tradition. Intervening conditions are ways participants address influencing factors.

**interview:** a data collection method that can involve one individual (individual interviews), a pair of informants (dyadic interviews), couples, families, or groups (i.e., focus group interviews); a conversational method between the researcher and participant that can be unstructured, semistructured, or structured.

**interview protocol:** a written document that outlines what will be said before and after interview questions are asked (e.g., informed consent information) and the interview questions.

**intrinsic case study:** a case study design where the researcher as an individual has an internally guided or intrinsic interest in a particular case.

**investigator triangulation:** a form of triangulation that refers to the use of multiple researchers or research teams to participate in data collection, analysis, and/or reporting.

**in vivo codes:** participant-identified concepts and theories that can serve as codes or labels during qualitative data analysis.

**justice:** a metaethical principle related to promoting good and equity for individuals of various groups, circumstanced, and statuses; promotion of participant voice and representation.

**key informant:** an individual who often provides important information that may shape qualitative inquiry.

**key quotation memos:** a form of memo that focuses on an illustrative or evocative quotation or quotations within a data source.

**knowledge question:** a type of interview question that solicits responses from participants about the amount of information they possess about a phenomenon as well as where that knowledge originated.

**leading question:** a type of question that can influence the direction of the respondent's response and thus can limit the openness of the response.

**legislative advocacy:** efforts toward systemic change by working with legislators and through the legislative process and encompasses lobbying activities; calls attention to issues that can be addressed through public policy, such as sharing research that could shape a particular public policy.

**life history:** a qualitative research tradition following the life of an individual within a broader social context, including the cultural norms that shape the person studied, and focuses on using interviews with them as data collection.

**lifeworld:** also referred to as "*Lebenswelt,*" the structural whole of a lived experience that is socially and culturally shared yet individually experienced.

**literal replication:** criterion within the case study tradition that bases selection of case(s) on its potential to contrast findings within the current study of with other studies.

**literature map:** a display (e.g., figure, table, flow chart) that visually organizes themes of prior literature; helps the researcher to organize prior literature to facilitate new ideas about the literature itself or future research directions.

**literature review:** what is already known about the topic and has been published; a snapshot of what studies in a general topic area have been found, summarizing key findings and highlighting major limitations or gaps for a research topic.

**logic model:** a data analysis technique within the case study tradition that consists of matching outcomes of a particular case study against an initial theoretical statement or proposition yet delineates immediate, intermediate, and long-term or ultimate outcomes.

**macrocoding:** a deductive process of coding by which data are first sorted into broad categories.

**macro-level ethics:** ethical decision-making with regard to how knowledge gained from research is used in practice.

**matrix:** a form of case display that involves using rows and columns to portray major concepts or variables.

**maximum variation sampling:** a purposive sampling method that seeks to maximize diversity of characteristics within a sample to help illustrate the central aspects of your research topic.

**member checking:** ongoing consultation with participants to test the "goodness of fit" of developing findings as well as final reports; also termed "transactional validity," the process of consensus building among researchers and participants by which the accuracy of data and analysis is supported.

**memos:** a data collection, management, and analysis tool where extensive thoughts or reflections are jotted down. Memos may be integrated in field notes at a later point in the research process.

**metaethical principles:** a core set of ethical principles that guide professional behavior within research no matter the discipline; includes nonmaleficence, autonomy, beneficence, justice, fidelity, and veracity.

**methodological triangulation:** a form of triangulation where the researcher uses multiple data collection methods to obtain data pertaining to the same research question; can involve triangulating qualitative and/or quantitative data collection methods.

**methodology:** a philosophy of science that involves the actual practice or methods of qualitative research, or the approach used to identify and/or develop knowledge about a phenomenon; involves decisions about research paradigms and traditions, research questions, data collection methods, and type of research design (i.e., qualitative, quantitative, mixed methods).

**microblog:** a concise blog post that can have images, GIFs, links, infographics, videos, and audio clips.

**microcoding:** a process of coding in which inductive analysis is performed within each category to identify further codes, themes, and patterns.

**micro-level ethics:** ethical decision-making with regard to the research design.

**mind maps:** visual diagrams that organize a researcher's ideas about important players in the field and document potential challenges and opportunities related to access and fieldwork.

**mixed methods:** the integration of qualitative and quantitative research approaches that may occur concurrently (i.e., quantitative and qualitative data collection occurs at the same time) or sequentially (i.e., either quantitative or qualitative data first depending on the research purpose and question). When researchers employ qualitative strategies first, the design is referred to as an exploratory design. When they introduce a study with quantitative measures, the design is referred to as an explanatory design.

**modernist phase:** a historical moment in qualitative research that occurred between the 1940s and 1970s; primarily involved the emergence of several new approaches as well as the increased attention to rigor and quality, with particular attention to symbolic interactionism. This period was known as the "golden age of qualitative analysis."

**multiple case study:** investigation of several cases that are similar in nature.

**multiple embedded design:** a type of case study that examines multiple units of analysis across multiple cases.

**multiple holistic design:** a type of case study that examines a single unit of analysis across multiple cases.

**multiple question:** also known as a "double-barreled question," involves asking more than one question within one question so the respondent may not address the question thoroughly or accurately.

**multiple relationships:** having one or more roles with participants; can include prior personal and professional relationships.

**narrative process coding system:** type of narrative data analysis involving three techniques: (a) external narrative sequences, which describe events; (b) internal narrative sequences, which build on a description of clients' subjective experiences and expand these descriptions; and (c) reflexive narrative sequences, which analyze the meaning of client narratives.

**narrative synthesis:** also referred to as a "metanarrative," the collective analysis of multiple narratives; examines across primary narratological studies how human interactions share the construction, meaning, and reconstruction of narratives.

**narratology:** a qualitative research tradition that seeks to understand what stories or narratives reveal about an individual. With origins in social sciences and literature, it extends the hermeneutic approach by examining data sources such as interview transcripts, life history and other historical narratives, and creative nonfiction.

**naturalistic generalization:** evidence of trustworthiness related to the case study tradition whereby the researcher actively interprets the data with an eye toward the ways an audience would be able to transfer or apply the broad categories or findings from the case study to another case(s); the transfer of findings situated in one study context to other similar contexts.

**naturalistic setting:** a characteristic of qualitative research whereby researchers engage in activities within naturally occurring practice and/or social settings; allows opportunities to examine how individuals naturally interact with their environment through symbols, social roles, and social structures, to name a few.

**negative case analysis:** a trustworthiness strategy that involves refining a developing theme as additional information become available. A researcher constantly searches for data that goes against your current findings or searches for cases that may be represented by the same findings yet differ from the population of interest.

**netnography:** a form of fieldwork within online environments (e.g., computer-mediated, network based, audiovisual data) used to understand online social experience or cultural phenomena; also referred to as "virtual ethnography" or "videography."

**network:** a form of case display that refers to points or nodes with links between them; can show causal links or chronology among variables.

**nonmaleficence:** a metaethical principle related to minimizing harm during the research process.

**Nuremberg Code:** The first legal attempt to deal with controversies of research, specifically to those of the Nazi medical experiments. Established in 1947, it was an initial effort to put forth guidelines for social, medial, and behavioral research, with particular emphasis on informed consent.

**observation:** a primary source of qualitative data used to gather sensory information about a context or setting in whole or in part.

**observer bias:** the subjective manner in which you as an observer selectively observe particular individuals, events, and activities within an observation period.

**observer effect:** the unintentional effect an observer has on the research and participants.

**observation protocol:** instructions and rubrics for qualitative researchers to identify indicators of a phenomenon of interest when conducting observations; can be designed to observe a single or multiple target behaviors and to code behaviors by participant role.

**observer role:** one extreme of the observation continuum that refers to having minimal or no interactions with participants. In these cases, participants are often not aware that they are being observed.

**observer-as-participant role:** a point on the observation continuum that involves having a primary role as an observer with some interaction with study participants.

**one-shot question:** a type of interview question popular with opportunistic sampling that refers to preparing one question to ask a key informant should an opportunity to do so present itself.

**online focus groups:** application of the focus group method via the internet. Individuals can share a common experience of a phenomenon that might be rare and/or a difficult subject to discuss in a group of people.

**online media:** a category of data collection that includes textual and visual data, sound files, audiovisual productions, websites, vlogs and blogs, and podcasts.

**ontology:** a philosophy of science that refers to the nature of reality or the degree to which a "universal truth" is sought about a particular construct or process; how broadly a qualitative researcher defines reality of the "known" regarding a phenomenon.

**open coding or initial coding:** the initial data analysis technique of the grounded theory tradition. General domains such as keywords or phrases provided by the participants or the researchers are identified.

**opinion question:** a type of interview question that seeks participants' personal beliefs about a phenomenon.

**opportunistic sampling:** sometimes called "emergent sampling," a purposive sampling method that seeks to capitalize on the appearance of new potential samples as the research process evolves.

**organization of turn-design:** a technique in conversation analysis where the researcher examines the overall structure of conversations.

**otherness:** the degree of relationship between those inside and outside of the research. There are four types of otherness that interact with one another: epistemological otherness, societal otherness, practical otherness, and local otherness. Epistemological and practical otherness refers to the distance between the researcher and the participant within the research context, whereas societal and local otherness refer to the social context that privileges or diminishes people—researchers and participants alike—in terms of social power.

**outsider research:** studies where the investigator has no prior intimate experience with the participants or topic area of interest.

**partially ordered display:** a data management tool used for exploring and describing data during the initial stages of data analysis. Types of partially-ordered displays include context chart, checklist matrix, and the partially ordered metamatrix.

**participant-as-observer role:** a point on the observation continuum that involves becoming more a participant than an observer of others.

**participant observation:** the researcher's active involvement in the setting. Participant observation is often used in interviewing and other activities to negotiate tensions in a setting.

**participant role:** an extreme on the observation continuum that refers to researchers functioning both as a member of a community under investigation and as an investigator. While "going native" is rare, it is most likely to occur with this role.

**participatory action research:** a qualitative research tradition that focuses on change of the participants and researcher in the process of the examination. Goals include emancipation and transformation, and the researcher is required to critically reflect on the power of research as a change agent.

**parts-whole memo:** a form of memo that examines parts of a data source to its whole.

**pattern identification:** a form of case study data analysis where the researcher examines broad categories within the case for their relationships or interactions.

**pattern matching:** a data analysis technique in the case study tradition that refers to the comparison of the identified theory or pattern from your data to a preexisting theory or theories.

**peer debriefing:** a strategy of trustworthiness that refers to consultation with peers as another check outside of a designated research team. Peers can be interested colleagues, classmates, or individuals within the community of which the phenomenon is investigated.

**persistent observation:** a strategy of trustworthiness related to having depth in the data; results from a more focused interaction and exposure to a sample in a setting or context.

**personal documents:** a data source typically solicited to help understand the culture and context of participants' experiences of a phenomenon. Examples of personal documents include letters, books, health care records, diaries or journals, financial records, report cards or grading sheets, homework assignments, legal documents, and any other artifacts that may help elucidate the phenomenon.

**phenomenology:** a historical moment of qualitative research introduced in the early 20th century as well as a qualitative research tradition; purpose to discover and describe the meaning or essence of participants' lived experiences, or knowledge as it appears to consciousness; includes three strands: descriptive phenomenology, hermeneutic phenomenology, and idiography, or interpretive phenomenological analysis.

**phenomenological reduction:** a phenomenological approach where the researcher enters research with curiosity and a fresh perspective of the phenomenon; entering fully in the experience to describe and/or interpret the phenomenon.

**philosophies of science:** five interrelated constructs that help conceptualize the nature of scientific inquiry and how a qualitative researcher views what is science: ontology, epistemology, axiology, rhetoric, and methodology.

**photovoice:** a data collection strategy using photography to document visual information.

**policy brief:** communications materials specifically targeted for communicating with legislators; can include research findings and/or nonacademic material to inform public policy.

**politically important case sampling:** a purposive sampling method that selects a critical case that draws political attention to the phenomenon.

**positionality:** how social and cultural power is distributed in the researcher–participant relationship and recognized when there are power differentials.

**positivism:** a research paradigm common in quantitative research where there is an assumption that researchers may arrive at an objective, universal truth through direct observation and experience of phenomena.

**postpositivism:** a research paradigm common in quantitative research; assertion that universal reality can never fully be realized because one cannot say with complete certainty that a theory fully describes a phenomenon or construct; characterized by concepts such as reliability, validity, and alternative hypothesis testing. It is similar to positivism yet assumes that a theory is strengthened when it is verified and falsified.

**poststructuralism:** philosophical position that systemic structures cannot be fixed in terms of categories or interpretations; highlights that individuals tend to seek structure and categorical descriptions on structures that are constantly in flux and that cannot be fully understood.

**pragmatism:** a historical moment in qualitative research between the 1910s and 1960s; focuses on the outcomes of human behavior and assumes that humans engage in reflective interactions with one another; influenced the Chicago School within sociology.

**presupposition question:** a type of interview question that a researcher uses when it is relevant to assume some experience in a question to encourage participant elaboration.

**privacy:** the basic human right of protecting individual's worth, dignity, and self-determination.

**privacy rule:** a federal law that protects participants' health information and limits who can receive that information.

**privileged communication:** notion that confidential communication is legally protected, unless that right is waived by the individual.

**probing question:** the "who, what, when, where, and how" interview question that helps to expand an interviewee's responses. Probing questions can be verbal, such as elaboration and clarification questions, or can be nonverbal, such as head nods.

**procedural ethics:** a form of ethics involving adhering to a general protocol approved by review boards, such as an institutional review board.

**procedural rigor:** a criterion of trustworthiness referring to how researcher subjectivity impacts all components of the research design.

**process consent:** a component of informed consent where consent is viewed as an ongoing, mutually negotiated and developed activity.

**professional advocacy:** efforts that seek to unify a profession, increase the visibility of the profession within a community, and strengthen the training and licensure standards for that profession.

**prolonged engagement:** a strategy of trustworthiness involving "staying in the field" to build and sustain relationships with participants and settings to be able to accurately describe a phenomenon of interest.

**public documents:** an unobtrusive data source, such as official records, newspapers, newsletters, magazines, meeting minutes, public artifacts, reports, tax records, legal reports.

**purpose statement:** a sentence or sentences within a proposal or report that establish the objectives, intent, and major ideas of a proposal or study.

**purposive sampling:** selection of participants for the amount of detail they can provide about a phenomenon and thus address the research question(s) (i.e., information-rich cases).

**qualitative data management:** a system for tracking data collection and analysis; should begin with a clear plan of who will be collecting and analyzing data and a timeline for completing respective tasks (e.g., data collection, independent analysis, consensus coding).

**queer theory:** a research paradigm that attends to how sexual orientation as a participant characteristic influences experiences of various phenomena; evolved in response to gay identity politics of the 1980s. Asserts that concepts of gender, sexuality, and body are social constructions that are fluid and continually negotiated.

**random purposeful sampling:** a purposive sampling method used to increase the variation of cases within your study; refers to randomly selecting from a purposive sample.

**realism:** a view of science involving the notion that one can only know reality from one's own perspective. This view is also known as "subtle realism" and "modernism."

**recording:** a step in content analysis that refers to storing data in a way that they can be read by multiple coders.

**reducing:** a step in content analysis that involves the actual coding of data.

**referential adequacy:** a strategy of trustworthiness that involves checking preliminary findings and interpretations against archived raw data.

**reflective field notes:** details within an observational record that includes subjective aspects of data collection, including assumptions, impressions, attitudes, and ideas.

**reflexive journal:** a strategy of trustworthiness that includes thoughts of how the research process is impacting the researcher. The researchers reflects in writing upon how the participants, data collection, and data analysis are impacting them personally and professionally.

**repair organization:** a technique within conversation analysis where the researcher evaluates situations when individuals forego taking up an issue within a conversation.

**research brief:** short overview of research completed or in proposal.

**research goal:** a broad plan for achieving a desired result that considers what data need to be obtained based on the needs of all those involved in qualitative inquiry.

**research tradition:** a methodological blueprint for the research process; informed by research paradigms and philosophies of science to inform the research design.

**researcher-practitioner-advocate model:** the perspective of having research, practice, and advocacy inform one another during the qualitative research process. Integration of practical and scholarly knowledge inform how the qualitative researcher understands and addresses social justice needs of a population of interest.

**researcher reflexivity:** a component of the qualitative researcher role that involves active self-reflection throughout the research process; consideration of how personal and professional assumptions, biases, and relationships impact all aspects of the research design.

**rhetoric:** a philosophy of science that refers to the content and voice (first, second, or third person) of qualitative data presentation; involves the degree to which narratives, thematic categories, and/or numbers are presented as findings.

**role-ordered case display:** a data management tool used to explore and describe data. Role-ordered display depicts social interactions for a setting or variable of interest; it provides a "role occupant" view for each key participants. A role X time matrix, contrast table, and a scatterplot display are examples of role-ordered displays.

**role-playing question:** a type of interview question that allows the participant to discuss a topic from a particular role of authority.

**sampling:** a step in content analysis that refers to where and how the units of analysis are located by the researcher.

**sampling adequacy:** a strategy of trustworthiness that refers to using the appropriate sample composition and size based on the research question(s) and research tradition(s).

**sampling plan:** a formal, broadly defined proposal outlining the sampling method(s), sample size, and recruitment procedures.

**saturation:** typically associated with the grounded theory tradition, a point where there are no new data available to refute conclusions and a theory has been fully developed; development of no new concepts, no new properties of those concepts, and/or no new dimensions at an individual unit level.

**scientific method:** an approach in experimental research designs in which a researcher moves from asking a research question, to formulating findings based on observation, experimentation and hypotheses testing, to generalizing any findings to a population of interest.

**selective coding:** a grounded theory analysis technique used to further refine axial codes and/or theoretical codes. Selective coding is the most complex coding process in grounded theory, where patterns, processes and sequences are identified among axial codes to generate a theory about a phenomenon.

**sequence organization:** a technique within conversation analysis where the researcher examines dynamics of individuals initiating topics within a conversation.

**semistructured interview:** a form of interview where an interview protocol serves as a guide and starting point for the interview experience.

**sensory question:** an interview question that uses the five senses (i.e., sight, sound, taste, smell, touch) to seek information from participants about their bodily experiences.

**simulation question:** an interview question that requests that the participant verbally observe a phenomenon for the interviewer. That is, the interviewer will ask the participant to place themselves in a situation.

**single case study:** the examination of one phenomenon that is one case and should meet the criteria for testing a theory with one case.

**single embedded design:** type of case study in which multiple units of analysis are investigated within a single case.

**single holistic design:** type of case study design involving a single unit of analysis within a single case.

**situated freedom:** a phenomenological construct that refers to the notion that humans are inextricably tied to social, cultural, and political contexts.

**situated meanings:** concept of the ethnography tradition in which the researcher examines the ways that a local culture experiences and makes meaning of the events within their group.

**snowball sampling:** a purposive sampling method also called chain or network sampling. This sampling method has a "snowball" or "chain" effect where the researcher solicits participants from previous participants or gatekeepers, stakeholders, or key informants.

**social advocacy:** sometimes called "social justice advocacy," is grounded in community-level change and calls attention to inequities across societal institutions, such as educational, legal, and health care.

**social media:** a form of data collection that involved internet-based applications that allow creation, co-creation, and exchange of user-generated content based in social interactions.

**social validity:** evidence of research findings being applied to the conduct of everyday life in a timely and socially valued manner; when findings inform what interventions are effective with a specific group and what was gained has social value to that context.

**stability reliability:** analogous to test-retest reliability in quantitative research, refers to the extent that the same researcher codes text the same way more than once.

**stakeholder:** an individual or group who has an investment, or "stake," in the findings of your study.

**stratified purposeful sampling:** a purposive sampling method that allows a researcher to demonstrate the distinguishing features of subgroups (or strata) of a phenomenon in which you are interested.

**structural description:** an aspect of phenomenological data analysis whereby the researcher creates a list or visual model that represents a framework of the experiences of participants that are a result of refining the horizontalization of data into a textural description of the phenomenon's essence; may be considered analogous to axial codes in the grounded theory tradition.

**structured interview:** a form of interview that relies on a preestablished sequence and pace of questions that a researcher follows rigidly. Questions are asked exactly as written, and probes, if included, are also standardized.

**subjectivity/virtuous subjectivity:** a component of the role of the qualitative researcher; the internal understandings of the qualitative researcher of their phenomenon that are used to understand the phenomenon more intimately from the researcher perspective; when viewed as a positive aspect of the researcher reflexivity process, referred to as "virtuous subjectivity."

**substantive validation:** a strategy of trustworthiness, also known as "relevance criterion," that relates to the question "Does the research report and other products have "substance?" It is the degree to which research either adds new knowledge or supports existing information about a phenomenon.

**summarizing question:** a type of interview question that signals the conclusion of the interview where the interviewer offers an opportunity for the participant to add final comments or thoughts.

**summary formulation:** a technique in conversation analysis where segments of conversational text are sequentially reviewed to describe the segments as a whole.

**symbolic interactionism:** a characteristic of the modernist Phase of qualitative research that asserts that only through social experience can individuals become self-identified. Thus, individuals interpret their experiences and identities based on social interactions.

**tacit knowledge:** a researcher's internal self-knowledge that is identified through intense immersion and self-exploration during the heuristic inquiry process.

**talking circle:** An Indigenous data collection method that can be considered a form of focus group interview; method by which individuals form a circle and given an opportunity to speak uninterrupted. A common practice in talking circles is to share a sacred object, which is passed around from individuals to individuals as they speak.

**textural description:** a phenomenological analysis to refine data into new categories. Textural description drives to understand the meaning and depth of the essence of the experience.

**thematic analysis:** a narrative data analysis technique where the researcher identifies central themes and their subthemes to note a larger storyline in which these themes and subthemes are subsumed.

**theoretical coding:** a data analysis phase within the grounded theory tradition; process by which qualitative researchers collapse or link focused codes to generate categories and subcategories like axial coding procedures and, later, theoretical relationships parallel to selective coding.

**theoretical replication:** criterion within the case study tradition that bases selection of case(s) on its potential to replicate or support findings within the current study or with other studies.

**theoretical sampling:** a purposive sampling method that assumes the evolving theory of data collection should guide the sampling strategy; commonly used in grounded theory studies.

**theoretical saturation:** a form of saturation where there is the determination that there are no new codes or themes identified from the data.

**theory triangulation:** a form of triangulation that refers to the use of multiple theories to analyze findings; can include a blend of research traditions in the design, known as a "blended design."

**thick description:** a strategy of trustworthiness that refers to creating a detailed account of the research process and outcome, usually evidenced in your qualitative report but may also be included in an audit trail; provision of detail and an auditable file about the research process, participants, context, and participants.

**time-ordered display:** a data management tool that is used to explore and describe data when time is the organizing principle. This display depicts a sequence or flow of events or processes of a phenomenon of interest. Examples of time-ordered displays include event listing, a critical incident chart, an activity record, a decision model, and the scatterplot over time.

**time series analysis:** a data analysis technique within the case study tradition that is used to examine some relevant "how" and "why" questions about the relationship of events over time, not merely to observe the time trends alone.

**traditional period:** a historical moment of qualitative research that extends from the early 1900s to the mid-1940s. Classic ethnography is prevalent at the beginning of this period, slowly shifting to what is known as "modern ethnography." It is characterized by a greater emphasis on conducting fieldwork, taking field notes, and writing theory and includes works from the British School and Chicago School.

**traditionalism:** a perspective of science also known as "positivist realism" and "naïve realism" that represents a lens through which researchers verify for a phenomenon a single truth in science using the five physical senses. Through experimental methods and empirical verification, traditionalists look for rational, objective, and logical explanations to research questions.

**transferability:** a criterion of trustworthiness similar to external validity in quantitative research where researchers provide enough detailed description of the research process to apply findings to other participants or contexts.

**transition question:** a type of interview question that is used when an interviewer moves to a different section of the interview and/or seeks to close the interview; used to elicit further information or check for understanding.

**transnational research:** research typically conducted across multiple nations, societies, or territories that involve researchers from the research sites or areas.

**triangulation:** a strategy of trustworthiness that involves using multiple forms of evidence (e.g., data sources, data methods, investigators, unit of analysis, theories). Triangulation seeks to strengthen evidence that a particular theme exists by looking for inconsistencies among these forms.

**triple crisis:** a historical moment in qualitative research during the mid-1980s to mid-1990s; characterized by the qualitative researcher's struggle to best represent their participants and phenomena, be flexible in how they evaluate the rigor of qualitative design, and determine consider alternative methods beyond writing to disseminate their findings.

**trustworthiness:** degree to which a qualitative study genuinely reflects through its design and report participant perspectives and the context under investigation.

**turn-taking organization:** a technique within conversation analysis where a researcher evaluates dynamics associated with individual turn-taking processes in conversational text.

**typical case sampling:** a purposive sampling method where the researcher attempts to represent who is an average or typical example of the focus of their study.

**typological analysis:** a narrative data analysis technique that involve investigations into the typology of clients' narratives.

**unitizing:** a step in content analysis whereby a researcher identifies the part of whole of a data source that will count as one unit of analysis (e.g., social media posts, advertisements, journal entries, videos), which should align with the research questions and purpose of the overall study.

**unstructured interview:** occurs as part of participant observation and often associated with ethnography and perhaps other "in the field" research traditions. The label "unstructured" is misleading since no interview can truly be unstructured and is more likely a "guided conversation." Unstructured interviews focus a lot on the surrounding context at the time of the interview.

**utilitarianism:** an ethics concept espousing research utility, or the notion that that which produces the greatest good for the greatest number of individuals is the right course of action; acceptance of a universal set of rules (i.e., ethical guidelines in which researcher compliance with those guidelines is values).

**validity:** evidence of authentic, believable findings from a phenomenon; includes internal validity (i.e., likelihood that there is a causal relationship between two variables without interference from other variables or threats) and external validity (i.e., degree to which a study's sample, research design, and findings may generalize to an outside population or setting).

**value question:** a type of interview question where a researcher asks about social norms in relation to individual beliefs.

**values:** principles that are used to evaluate outcomes and actions from research; used to inform ethical decision-making; includes four epistemic principles: truth, justifiability, relevance, and feasibility.

**veracity:** a metaethical principle in which qualitative researchers are truthful to individuals affected by research; a precursor to the metaethical principle of fidelity.

**virtues:** desired personal dispositions that influence the practice of ethical qualitative research.

**visual ethnography:** use of images (e.g., photographs, paintings) to understand a culture-sharing group. The external narrative serves as the context for the image, whereas the internal narrative is the interpretation of the image by those who view it.

**vlog:** a form of blog that uses video to integrate the diary-like component of blogs and is also either in the public or private internet domain.

**whole client narrative analysis:** a narrative data analysis technique where the whole client narrative is evaluated to illuminate the entire "case" of the narrative rather than its diverse parts.

# References

Adams-Santos, D. (2020). "Something a bit more personal": Digital storytelling and intimacy among queer Black women. *Sexualities*, 23(8), 1434–1456. https://doi.org/10.1177/1363460720902720

Addeo, F., Paoli, A. D., Esposito, M., & Bolcato, M. Y. (2020). Doing social research on online communities: The benefits of netnography. *Athens Journal of Social Sciences*, 7(1), 9–38. https://doi.org/10/30958/ajss.7-1-1

Agar, M. (2006). An ethnography by any other name. ... *Qualitative Social Research*, 7(4). https://doi.org/10.17169/fqs-7.4.177

Ahern, K. J. (1999). Ten tips for reflexive bracketing. *Qualitative Health Research*, 9(3), 407–411.

Ahn, L. H., Keum, B. T., Meizys, G. M., Choudry, A., Gomes, M. A., & Wang, L. (2021). Second-generation Asian American women's gendered racial socialization. *Journal of Counseling Psychology*, 69(2), 129–145. https://doi.org/10.1037/cou0000575

Airoldi, M. (2018). Ethnography and the digital fields of social media. *International Journal of Social Research Methodology*, 21(6), 661–673. https://doi.org/10.1080/13645579.2018.1465622

Alaggia, R., & Millington, G. (2008). Male child sexual abuse: A phenomenology of betrayal. *Clinical Social Work Journal*, 36(3), 265-275.

Albert, B., & Brown, S. S. (2007). State your case: Working with state governments. In Melissa K. Welch-Ross & Lauren G. Fasig (Eds.), *Handbook on communicating and disseminating behavioral science* (pp. 267–280). Sage.

Allen, M. (2017). Chat rooms. In *the SAGE encyclopedia of communication research methods*. Sage.

Allen, A. (2019). Intersecting arts based research and disability studies: Suggestions for art education curriculum centered on disability identity development. *Journal of Curriculum Theorizing*, 34(1), 72–82.

Allport, G. W., Bruner, J., & Jandorf, E. (1941). Personality under social catastrophe: An analysis of 90 German refuges life histories. *Character and Personality*, 10, 1–22.

American Association of Marriage and Family Therapy. (2015). *Code of ethics*. https://www.aamft.org/Legal_Ethics/Code_of_Ethics.aspx

American Counseling Association. (2014). *ACA code of ethics*. https://www.counseling.org/resources/aca-code-of-ethics.pdf

American Educational Research Association. (2011). *Code of ethics*. https://www.aera.net/Portals/38/docs/About_AERA/CodeOfEthics(1).pdf

American Psychological Association. (2017). *Ethical principles of psychologists and code of conduct*. https://www.apa.org/ethics/code

American Psychological Association. (2020a). *Publication manual of the American Psychological Association* (7th ed.).

American Psychological Association. (2020b). *Journal article reporting standards: Qualitative research design (JARS-Qual)*. https://apastyle.apa.org/jars/qualitative

American Sociological Association. (2018). *Code of ethics*. https://www.asanet.org/sites/default/files/asa_code_of_ethics-june2018a.pdf

Anderson, L. (2006). Analytic autoethnography. *Journal of Contemporary Ethnography*, 35, 373–395.

Anderson, K. M., & Mack, R. (2019). Digital storytelling: A narrative method for positive identity development in minority youth. *Social Work with Groups*, 42(1), 43-55. https://doi.org/10.1080/01609513.2017.1413616

Angen, M. J. (2000). Evaluating interpretive inquiry: Reviewing the validity debate and opening the dialogue. *Qualitative Health Research*, 10, 378–395. https://doi.org/10.1177/104973200129118516

Angus, L. E., Levitt, H., & Hardtke, K. (1999). The narrative process coding system: Research applications and implications for psychotherapy. *Journal of Clinical Psychology*, 55, 1255–1271.

Anthony-Stevens, V., Mahfouz, J., & Bisbee, Y. (2020). Indigenous teacher education is nation building: Reflections of capacity building and capacity strengthening in Idaho. *Journal of School Leadership*, *30*, 541–564. https://doi.org/10.1177/1052684620951722

Anzaldua, G. (1987/2012). *Borderlands / la frontera: The new mestiza* (4th ed.). Aunt Lute Books.

Arber, A. (2006). Reflexivity: A challenge for the researcher as practitioner? *Journal of Research in Nursing*, *11*(2), 147–157.

Archibald, M. M., Ambagtsheer, R. C., Casey, M. G., & Lawless, M. (2019). Using zoom videoconferencing for qualitative data collection: Perceptions and experiences of researchers and participants. *International Journal of Qualitative Methods*, *18*, 1–8. https://doi.org/10.1177/1609406919874596

Asiamah, N., Mensah, H. K., & Oteng-Abayie, E. F. (2017). General, target, and accessible population: Demystifying the concepts of effective sampling. *The Qualitative Report*, *22*(6), 1607–1622.

Assante, M. K. (2007). *The history of Africa: The quest for eternal harmony*. Routledge.

Association of Internet Researchers. (2019). *Ethics guidelines for internet research 3.0*. https://aoir.org/ethics/

Avdi, E., & Georgaca, E. (2007). Narrative research in psychotherapy: A critical review. *Psychology and Psychotherapy: Theory, Research, and Practice*, *80*, 407–419.

Battiste, M. (2016). Research ethics for protecting indigenous knowledge and heritage: Institutional and researcher responsibilities. In N. K. Denzin & M. D. Giardina (Eds.), *Ethical futures in qualitative research: Decolonizing the politics of knowledge* (pp. 111–132). Routledge

Becker, H. S., Geer, B., Hughes, E. C., & Strauss, A. L. (1961). *Boys in white: Student culture in medical school*. University of Chicago Press.

Belk, R., & Kozinetz, R. (2016). Videography and netnography. In R. Belk & R. Kozinetz, *Formative research in social marketing* (pp. 265–279). Springer.

Beninger, K. (2017). Social media users' views on the ethics of social media research. In L. Sloan & A. Quan-Haase (Eds.), *The Sage handbook of social media research methods* (pp. 57–73). Sage.

Benjamin-Thomas, T. E., Corrado, A. M., McGrath, C., L., Laliberte, D., & Rudman, C. H. (2018). Working towards the promise of participatory action research: Learning from aging research exemplars. *International Journal of Qualitative Methods*, *17*(1). http://doi.org/10.1177/1609406918817953

Bessaha, M., Reed, R., Donlon, A. J., Mathews, W., Bell, A. C., & Merolla, D. (2020). Creating a more inclusive environment for students with disabilities: Findings from participatory action research. *Disability Studies Quarterly*, *40*(3). http://dx.doi.org/10.18061/dsq.v40i3.7094. Retrieved from https://dsq-sds.org/article/view/7094

Bhattacharya, K. (2016). The vulnerable academic: Personal narratives and strategic de/colonizing of academic structures. *Qualitative Inquiry*, *22*, 309–321. https://doi.org/10.1177/1077800415615619

Bhattacharya, K. (2017). *Fundamentals of qualitative research: A practical guide*. Taylor & Francis.

Bingham, A., Pane, J., Steiner, E., & Hamilton, L. (2018). Ahead of the curve: Implementation challenges in the personalized learning movement. *Educational Policy*, *32*(3), 454–489. https://doi.org/10.1177/0895904816637688

Bingham, A. J., & Witkowsky, P. (2022). Deductive and inductive approaches to qualitative data analysis. In C. Vanover, P. Miles, & J. Saldaña (Eds.), *Analyzing and interpreting qualitative research: After the interview* (pp. 133–148). Sage.

Blumer, H. (1969). *Symbolic interactionism*. University of California Press.

Bockting, W., Barucco, R., LeBlanc, A., Singh, A., Mellman, W., Dolezal, C., & Ehrardt, A. (2020). Sociopolitical change and transgender people's perceptions of vulnerability and resilience. *Sexuality Research & Social Policy*, *17*(1), 162–174. https://doi.org/10.1007/s13178-019-00381-5

Boddy, C. R. (2016). Sample size for qualitative research. *Qualitative Market Research: An*

*International Journal, 19*(4), 426–432. https://doi.org/10.1108/QMR-06-2016-0053.

Bogdan, R. C., & Biklen, S. K. (2016). *Qualitative research for education: An introduction to theories and methods* (5th ed.). Pearson.

Bolin, S. T., Hays, D. G., & Foxx, S. (2021). *A grounded theory of research-practice partnerships in counselor education.* Unpublished manuscript.

Bond, N. (2019). Effective legislative advocacy: policy experts' advice for educators. *The Educational Forum, 83*, 75–89. https://doi.org/10.1080/00131725.2018.1505992

Bonomi, C. (2005). Was Freud afraid of flying? *International Forum of Psychoanalysis, 14*, 49–53.

Bouck, E. C. (2008). Exploring the enactment of functional curriculum in self-contained cross-categorical programs: A case study. *Qualitative Report, 13*(3), 495–530.

Brattland, H., Høiseth, J. R., Burkeland, O., Inderhaug, T. S., Binder, P. E., & Iversen, C. (2018). Learning from clients: A qualitative investigation of psychotherapists' reactions to negative verbal feedback. *Psychotherapy Research, 28*(4), 1–15. https://doi.org/10.1080/10503307.2016.1246768

Bremner, N. (2020). "Belief-changing" teacher education: Mexican English teachers' experiences. *MEXTESOL Journal, 44*(1), 1–12.

Bridges, D. (2018). Epistemology, ethics, and educational research. In P. Smeyers & M. Depaepe (Eds.), *Educational research: Ethics, social justice, and funding dynamics* (pp. 109–120). Springer.

Brinkmann, S., & Kvale, S. (2014). *InterViews: Learning the craft of qualitative research interviewing* (3rd ed.). Sage.

Brinkmann, S., & Kvale, S. (2018). *Doing interviews* (Vol. 2). Sage.

Brinkmann, S., Jacobsen, M. H., & Kristiansen, S. (2014). Historical overview of qualitative research in the social sciences. In P. Leavy (Ed.), *The Oxford handbook of qualitative research* (pp. 17–42). Oxford University Press.

Brooks, F., Arminio, J., & Caballero-Dennis, K. A. (2013). A narrative synthesis of addictions, surrender, and relapse: Confirmation and application. *Alcoholism Treatment Quarterly,*

*31*, 375–395. https://doi.org/10.1080/07347324.2013.800427

Burnes, T. R. (2007). Opening the door of a bigger closet: An analysis of sexual orientation identity development for lesbian, bisexual, and queer college women of color. *Dissertation Abstracts International: Section B: The Sciences and Engineering, 67*(7-b), 41300.

Butler, J. (2004). *Undoing gender.* Routledge.

Butler, J. (2011). *Bodies that matter: On the discursive limits of sex.* Taylor & Francis.

Buzan, T. (2018). *Mind map mastery: The complete guide to learning and using the most powerful thinking tool in the universe.* Watkins Publishing.

Campbell, D. T., & Stanley, J. G. (1996). *Experimental and quasi-experimental design for research.* Ran McNally.

Campillo-Ferrer, J. M., Miralles-Martínez, P., & Sánchez-Ibáñez, R. (2021). The effectiveness of using edublogs as an instructional and motivating tool in the context of higher education. *Humanities and Social Sciences Communications, 8*(175). https://doi.org/10.1057/s41599-021-00859-x

Caperton, W., Butler, M., Kaiser, D., Connelly, J., & Knox, S. (2020). Stay-at-home fathers, depression, and help-seeking: A consensual qualitative research study. *Psychology of Men and Masculinities, 221*, 235–250. https://doi.org/10.1037/men0000223

Carpenter, D. (2018). Ethics, reflexivity and virtue. In R. Iphofen & M. Tolich (Eds.), *The Sage handbook of qualitative research ethics* (pp. 35–50). Sage.

Carpenter, J., Tani, T., Morrison, S., & Keane, J. (2020). Exploring the landscape of educator professional activity on Twitter: An analysis of 16 education-related Twitter hashtags. *Professional Development in Education*, 1–22. https://doi.org/10.1080/19415257.2020.1752287

Caretta, M. A., & Pérez, M. A. (2019). When participants do not agree: Member checking and challenges to epistemic authority in participatory research. *Field Methods, 31*(4), 359–374. https://doi.org/10.1177/1525822X19866578.

Carminati, L. (2018). Generalizability in qualitative research: A tale of two traditions. *Qualitative Health Research*, 28, 2094–3101. https://doi.org/10.1177.1049732318788379

Caron, C., Raby, R., Mitchell, C., Théwissen-LeBlanc, S., & Prioletta, J. (2016). From concept to data: Sleuthing social change-oriented youth voices on YouTube. *Journal of Youth Studies*, 20(1), 47–62. https://doi.org/10.1080/13676261.2016.1184242

Carter, D. (2019). *Providing counseling in a rural setting: a new multicultural perspective* [Unpublished doctoral dissertation]. Northern Illinois University.

Carter, S. M., Shih, P., Williams, J., Degeling, C., & Mooney-Somers, J. (2021). Conducting qualitative research online: Challenges and solutions. *The Patient-Centered Outcomes Research*, 11, 1–8. https://doi.org/10.1007/s40271-021-00528-w

Casterline, G. L. (2009). Heuristic inquiry: Artistic science for nursing. *Southern Online Journal of Nursing Research*, 9(4), 1–8.

Cavanaugh, K. M., & Luke, M. M. (2021). Transgender college student identity development: A narratology of intermediating experiences. *Journal of Humanistic Counseling*, 60(2), 137–156. https://doi.org/10.1002/johc.12161

Cazers, G., & Curtner-Smith, M. D. (2017). Robin's story: Life history of an exemplary American female physical education teacher. *Journal of Teaching in Physical Education*, 36(2), 197–208. https://doi.org/10.1123/jtpe.2015-0084

Chan, C. D. (2018). *The lived intersectional experiences of privilege and oppression of queer men of color in counselor education doctoral programs: An interpretative phenomenological analysis* [Unpublished doctoral dissertation]. The George Washington University.

Chan, C. D., & Farmer, L. B. (2017). Making the case for interpretative phenomenological analysis with LGBTGEQ+ persons and communities. *Journal of LGBT Issues in Counseling*, 11(4), 285–300. https://doi.org/10.1080/15538605.2017.1380558

Chan, C. D., Harrichand, J. J., Anandavalli, S., Vaishnav, S., Chang, C. Y., Hyun, J. H., & Band, M. P. (2021). Mapping solidarity, liberation, and activism: A critical autoethnography of Asian American leaders in counseling. *Journal of Mental Health Counseling*, 43(3), 246–265. https://doi.org/10.17744/mehc.43.3.06

Chang, B., & Delaney, K. (2019). A heuristic inquiry on the role of person-environment interaction in suicide risk among transgender youth. *Journal of Child and Adolescent Psychiatric Nursing*, 32(2), 47–50. https://doi.org/10.1111/jcap.12237

Charmaz, K. (2006). *Constructing grounded theory* (1st ed.). Sage.

Charmaz, K. (2014). *Constructing grounded theory* (2nd ed.). Sage.

Chenail, R. J. (1995). Presenting qualitative data. *Qualitative Report*, 2(3), 1–9. https://doi.org/10.46743/2160-3715/1995.2061

Chilisa, B. (2020). *Indigenous research methodologies* (2nd ed.). Sage.

Chowdhury, I. A. (2015). Issue of quality in qualitative research: An overview. *Innovative Issues and Approaches in Social Sciences*, 8(1), 142–162. https://doi.org/10.15929/issn.1855-0541.IIASS-2015-no1-art9

Christians, C. (2017). Ethics and politics in qualitative research. In N. Denzin & Y. Lincoln (Eds.), *The Sage handbook of qualitative research* (5th ed., pp.66–82). Sage.

Christensen, G. (2014). Genealogy and education research. *International Journal of Qualitative Studies in Education*, 29(6), 763–776. https://doi.org/10.1080/09518398.2016.1162871

Chwalisz, K., Shah, S. R., & Hand, K. M. (2008). Facilitating rigorous qualitative research in rehabilitation psychology. *Rehabilitation Psychology*, 53(3), 387-399. https://doi.org/10.1037/a0012998

Clandinin, D. J., Caine, V., & Lessard, S. (2018). *The relational ethics of narrative inquiry*. Routledge.

Coker, A. D., Martin, C., Culver, J., & Johnson, C. (2018). Black women's academic and leadership development in higher education: An autoethnographic study. *Periferia, 10*(2), 44–66. https://doi.org/10.12957/periferia.2018.33714

Colaizzi, P.F. (1978) Psychological research as a phenomenologist views it. In R. S. Valle & M. King (Eds.), *Existential-phenomenological alternatives for psychology* (pp. 48–71). Oxford University Press.

Cole, A. L., & Knowles, J. G. (2008). Arts-informed research. In J. G. Knowles & A. L. Cole (Eds.), *Handbook of the arts in qualitative research* (pp. 55–70). Sage.

Collins, P. H. (2009). *Black feminist thought* (2nd ed.). Routledge.

Community Tool Box. (n.d.-a). *Section 36: Community-based participatory research.* https://ctb.ku.edu/en/table-of-contents/evaluate/evaluation/intervention-research/main

Community Tool Box. (n.d.-b). *Section 10: Conducting research to influence policy.* Retrieved from https://ctb.ku.edu/en

Corbin, J., & Strauss, A. (2015). *Basics of qualitative research: Techniques and procedures for developing grounded theory* (4th ed.). Sage.

Corey, G., Corey, M. S., & Calahan, P. (2018). *Issues and ethics in the helping professions* (10th ed.). Cengage.

Corsby, C. L., & Jones, R. L. (2020). Complicity, performance, and the "doing of sports coaching: An ethnomethodological study of work. *The Sociological Review, 68*(3), 590–605. https://doi.org/10.1177/0038026119897551

Crenshaw, K. (1991). Mapping the margins: Intersectionality, identity politics, and violence against women of color. *Stanford Law Review, 43*, 1241–1299.

Creswell, J. W., & Creswell, J. D. (2018). *Research design: Qualitative, quantitative, and mixed methods approaches* (5th ed.). Sage.

Creswell, J. W., & Plano Clark, V. L. (2017). *Designing and conducting mixed methods research* (3rd ed.). Sage.

Creswell, J. W., & Creswell, J. D. (2017). *Research design: Qualitative, quantitative, and mixed methods approaches* (4th ed.). Sage.

Creswell, J. W., & Poth, C. N. (2017). *Qualitative inquiry and research design: Choosing among five approaches* (4th ed.). Sage.

Crowe, M., & Sheppard, L. (2012). Mind mapping research methods. *Quality & Quantity, 46*(5), 1493–1504. https://doi.org/10.1007/s11135-011-9463-8

Crowell, S. G. (2001). *Husserl, Heidegger, and the space of meaning: Paths toward transcendental phenomenology.* Northwestern University Press.

Cullen, J. E. (2009). "Some friends and I started talking ...": A participatory action research project to deconstruct White privilege among student affairs practitioners. *Dissertation Abstracts International Section A: Humanities and Social Sciences, 69*(8-A), 3057.

Cullerton, K., Donnet, T., Lee, A., & Gallegos, D. (2018). Effective advocacy strategies for influencing government nutrition policy: A conceptual model. *International Journal of Behavioral Nutrition and Physical Activity, 15*(83). https://doi.org/10.1186/s12966-018-0716-y

Dawson, M., McDonnell, L., & Scott, S. (2017). Note on recruitment as an ethical question: Lessons from a project on asexuality. *International Journal of Social Research Methodology, 20*, 255–261. https://doi.org/10.1080/13645579.2017.1277871

de Kok, B. C. (2008). The role of context in conversation analysis: Reviving an interest in ethnomethods. *Journal of Pragmatics, 40*, 886–903.

de Montigny, G. (2020). Engaging ethnomethodology for social work. *Journal of Social Work, 20*, 131–151. https://doi.org/10.1177/1468017318795925

Decker, L. (2020). *The noise from the writing boundaries: Collaboration and tutor identity in writing intensive courses* [Unpublished doctoral dissertation]. University of Nevada, Las Vegas.

Delaney, M. E. (2016). Grant writing for the counseling professional. *Journal of Counselor Preparation and Supervision, 8*(3). http://dx.doi.org/10.7729.83.1135

Delgado, R., & Stefancic, J. (2017). *Critical race theory: An introduction* (3rd ed.). New York University Press.

Denzin, N. K. (1989). *Interpretive biography* (Vol. 17). Sage.

Denzin, N. K. (2012). Triangulation 2.0. *Journal of Mixed Methods Research, 6*, 80–88. https://doi.org/10.1177/1558689812437186.

Denzin, N. K., & Giardina, M. D. (2016). *Ethical futures in qualitative research*. Routledge.

Denzin, N. K., & Lincoln, Y. S. (2011). Introduction: The discipline and practice of qualitative research. In N. K. Denzin & Y. S. Lincoln (Eds.), *The Sage handbook of qualitative research* (4th ed., pp. 1–19). Sage.

Denzin, N. K., & Lincoln, Y. S. (2018). *The Sage handbook of qualitative research* (5th ed.). Sage.

Denzin, N. K., Lincoln, Y. S., & Smith, L. T. (Eds.). (2008). *Handbook of critical and Indigenous methodologies*. Sage.

Derrida, J. (1976). *Of grammarology*. Johns Hopkins University Press.

Derrida, J. (1978). *Writing and difference*. University of Chicago Press.

Derrida, J. (1981). *Positions*. University of Chicago Press.

Dichter, E. (1947). *The psychology of everyday living*. Kessinger Publishing.

Dichter, E. (1964). *Handbook of consumer motivations*. McGraw Hill.

dickey, l. m., Singh, A. A., Chang, S. C., & Rehrig, M. (2017). Advocacy and social justice: The next generation of counseling and psychological practice with transgender and gender-nonconforming clients. In A. Singh & l. m. dickey (Eds.), *Affirmative counseling and psychological practice with transgender and gender nonconforming clients* (pp. 247–262). American Psychological Association.

Dimaggio, G., & Semerari, A. (2001). Psychopathological narrative forms. *Journal of Constructivist Psychology, 14*, 1–23.

Dixon, C. S. (2015). Interviewing adolescent females in qualitative research. *The Qualitative Report, 20*(12), 2067–2077.

Do, P. L., Frawley, P., Goldingay, S., & O'Shea, A. (2021). The use of photovoice in research with people on the autism spectrum: A meta-synthesis of the literature. *Research in Autism Spectrum Disorders, 87*. https://doi.org/10.1016/j.rasd.2021.101828

Dollard, J. (1946). *Criteria for the life history*. Yale University Press.

Donovan, F. R. (1920). *The woman who waits*. RG Badger.

Donovan, F. R. (1929). *The saleslady*. University of Chicago Press.

Drapeau, M (2002). Subjectivity in research: Why not? But … *The Qualitative Report, 7*(3). https://core.ac.uk/download/pdf/51087002.pdf

Drisko, J. W. (1997). Strengthening qualitative studies and reports: Standards to promote academic integrity. *Journal of Social Work Education, 33*(1), 185–197.

Dunbar, C., Jr. (2008). Critical race theory and indigenous methodologies. In N. K. Denzin, Y. S. Lincoln, & L. T. Smith (Eds.), *Handbook of critical and indigenous methodologies* (pp. 85–99). Sage.

Duncan, M. (2004). Autoethnography: Critical appreciation of an emerging art. *International Journal of Qualitative Methods, 3*(4), 28-39.

Dwyer, S. C., & Buckle, J. L. (2009). The space between: On being an insider-outsider in qualitative research. *International Journal of Qualitative Methods, 8*, 54–63.

Edwards, D. D. (2017). An examination of Black women leaders' educational and professional experiences on the path toward the superintendency. *Dissertation Abstracts International Section A: Humanities and Social Sciences, 78*(3-A).

Eisner, E. (1991). *The enlightened eye: Qualitative inquiry and the enhancement of educational practices*. MacMillan.

Eger, K. S. (2008). Powerless to affect positive change for the gifted students in an urban school district as revealed through one teacher's heuristic inquiry. *Dissertation Abstracts International Section A: Humanities and Social Sciences, 69*(3-A), 827.

Elliott, E. (2003). Moving in the space between researcher and practitioner. *Child and Youth Care Forum, 32*(5), 299–303. https://doi.org/10.1023/A:1025839911970

Elliott, A., Salazar, B. M., Dennis, B. L., Bohecker, L., Nielson, T., LaMantia, K., & Kleist, D. M.

(2019). Pedagogical perspectives on counselor education: An autoethnographic experience of doctoral student development. *The Qualitative Report, 24*(4), 648–666.

Ellis, C., Adams, T. E., & Bochner, A. P. (2011). Autoethnography: An overview. *Historical Social Research, 36*, 273–290.

Ellis, C., Kiesinger, C. E., & Tilmann-Healy, L. M. (1997). Interactive interviewing: Talking about emotional experience. In R. Hertz (Ed.), *Reflexivity & voice* (pp. 119–149). Sage.

Emden, C., & Sandelowski, M. (1998). The good, the bad and the relative, part one: Conceptions of goodness in qualitative research. *International Journal of Nursing Practice, 4*, 206–212. https://doi.org/10.1046/j.1440-172X.1998.00105.x

Emerson, R. M., Fretz, R. I., & Shaw, L. L. (1995). *Writing ethnographic fieldnotes.* University of Chicago Press.

Ercikan, K., & Roth, W. (2006). What good is polarizing research into qualitative and quantitative? *Educational Researcher, 35*(5), 14–23. https://doi.org/10.3102/0013189X035005014

Eriksen, E. (1963). *Childhood and society* (2nd ed.). Norton.

Espino, M. (2008). *Seeking the "truth" in the stories we tell: An approach to constructing counter-storytelling in higher education research.* Unpublished manuscript.

Etziono, A. (2009). The common good and rights: A neo-communitarian approach. *Georgetown Journal of International Affairs, 10*(1), 113–119.

Evans, Y. N., Gridley, S. J., Crouch, J., Wang, A., Moreno, M. A., Ahrens, K., & Breland, D. J. (2017). Understanding online resource use by transgender youth and caregivers: A qualitative study. *Transgender Health, 2*(1), 129–139. https://doi.org/10.1089/trgh.2017.0011

Ezzani, M. D., & King, K. M. (2018). Whose Jihad? Oral history of an American Muslim educational leader and US public schools. *Journal of Educational Administration and History, 50*(2), 113–129. https://doi.org/10.1080/00220620.2018.1448369

Farmer, L. B., & Byrd, R. (2015). Genderism in the LGBTQQIA community: An interpretative phenomenological analysis. *Journal of LGBT Issues in Counseling, 9*(4), 288–310. https:/doi.org/10.1080/15538605.2015.1103679

Farrell, I. C., & Barrio Minton, C. A. (2019). Advocacy among counselor leaders: The three-tiered legislative professional advocacy model. *Journal of Counselor Leadership and Advocacy, 6*, 144–159. https://doi.org/10.1080/2326716X.2019.1644254

Fawcett, B., & Hearn, J. (2004). Researching others: Epistemology, experience, standpoints and participation. *International Journal of Social Research Methodology, 7*(3), 201–218. https://doi.org/10.1080/13645570210163989

Finlay, L. (2012). Debating phenomenological methods. In N. Friesen, C. Henriksson, & T. Saevi (Eds.), *Hermeneutic phenomenology in education* (pp. 15–37). Brill/Sense.

Floden, R. (2007). Philosophical issues in education policy research. In S. H. Fuhrman, D. K. Cohen, & F. Mosher (Eds.), *The state of education policy research* (pp. 3–15). Routledge.

Flynn, S. V., & Hays, D. G. (2015). The development and validation of the Comprehensive Counseling Skills Rubric. *Counseling Outcome Research and Evaluation, 6*(2), 87–99. https://doi.org/10.1177/2150137815592216

Foote Whyte, W. (1943). *Street corner society: The social structure of an Italian slum.* University of Chicago Press.

Forman, J. (2010). *The influence of rape empathy and demographic variables on counselor rape myth acceptance* [Unpublished doctoral dissertation]. Old Dominion University, Norfolk, Virginia.

Fossey, E., Harvey, C., McDermott, F., & Davidson, L. (2002). Understanding and evaluating qualitative research. *Australian and New Zealand Journal of Psychiatry, 36*, 717–732. https://doi.org/10.1046/j.1440-1614.2002.01100.x

Foucault, M. (1984). On the genealogy of ethics: An overview of work in progress. In P. Rabinow (Ed.), *The Foucault reader* (pp. 381–390). Pantheon.

Frankel, Z., & Levitt, H. M. (2009). Clients' experiences of disengaged moments in psychotherapy: A grounded theory analysis. *Journal of Contemporary Psychology, 39*, 171–186.

Freebody, P. (2001). Re-discovering practical reading activities in homes and schools. *Journal of Research in Reading, 24*(3), 222–234.

Freeman, S., Jr., & Kochan, F. (2019). Exploring mentoring across gender, race, and generation in higher education: An ethnographic study. *International Journal of Mentoring and Coaching in Education, 8*(1), 2–18. https://doi.org/10.1108/IJMCE-05-2018-0027

Freud, S. (1905/2000). *Three essays on the theory of sexuality*. Basic Books.

Freud, S. (1940/1989). *An outline of psycho-analysis*. W.W. Norton & Company.

Freud, S. (1899/2010). *The interpretation of dreams*. Basic Books.

Friere, P. (1972). *Pedagogy of the oppressed*. Penguin Books.

Fryer, E. M. (2004). Researcher-practitioner: An unholy marriage? *Educational Studies, 30*(2), 175–185. https://doi.org/10.1080/0305569032000159813

Fusch, P., Fusch, G. E., & Ness, L. R. (2018). Denzin's paradigm shift: Revisiting triangulation in qualitative research. *Journal of Social Change, 10*(1), 19–32. https://doi.org/10.5590/JOSC.2018.10.1.02

Gallagher, R. J., Reagan, A. J., Danforth, C. M., & Dodds, P. S. (2018). Divergent discourse between protests and counter-protests: #BlackLivesMatter and #AllLivesMatter. *PloS One, 13*(4), e0195644. https://doi.org/10.1371/journal.pone.0195644

Garcia, C. E. (2020). Belonging in a predominantly White institution: The role of membership in Latina/o sororities and fraternities. *Journal of Diversity in Higher Education, 13*(2), 181–193. https://doi.org/10.1037/dhe0000126

Garcia, C. K., & Vemuri, A. (2017). Girls and young women resisting rape culture through YouTube videos. *Girlhood Studies, 10*, 26–44. https://doi.org/10.3167/ghs.2017.100204

Garfinkel, H. (1967). *Studies in ethnomethodology*. Prentice Hall.

Garfinkel, H. (2002). *Ethnomethodology's program: Working out Durkheim's aphorism*. Rowman & Littlefield.

Gee, J. P. (1991). A linguistic approach to narrative. *Journal of Narrative and Life History, 1*, 15–39.

Geertz, C. (1973). *The interpretation of cultures*. Basic Books.

Geertz, C. (1983). *Local knowledge: Fact and law in comparative perspective*. Basic Books.

Giorgi, A. (1985). *Phenomenology and psychological research*. Duquesne University Press.

Gitlin, L. N., Kolanowski, A., & Lyons, K. J. (2021). *Successful grant writing: Strategies for health and human services professionals* (5th ed.). Springer.

Ghasemi, F. (2021). Exploring middle school teachers' perceptions of factors affecting the teacher–student relationships. *Educational Research for Policy and Practice*, 1–16. https://doi.org/10.1007/s10671-021-09300-1

Gladding, S. T. (2020). *Group work: A counseling specialty* (8th ed.). Pearson.

Gladstone, B. M., & Volpe, T. (2008, April 23). *Qualitative secondary analysis: Asking "new" questions of "old" data* [Paper presentation]. Qualitative Research Interest Group, Athens, GA, United States.

Glaser, B. J. (1978). *Theoretical sensitivity*. University of California San Francisco.

Glaser, B. J. (1992). *Emergence vs. forcing basics of grounded theory analysis*. Sociology Press.

Glaser, B. J., & Strauss, A. (1967). *The discovery of grounded theory: Strategies for qualitative research*. Aldine.

Glaw, X., Inder, K., Kable, A., & Hazelton, M. (2017). Visual methodologies in qualitative research: Autophotography and photo elicitation applied to mental health research. *International Journal of Qualitative Methods, 16*(1). https://doi.org/10.1177/1609406917748215

Glazier, R. A., & Topping, M P. (2021). Using social media to advance community-based research. *PS: Political Science & Politics, 54*(2), 254–258. https://doi.org/10.1017/S1049096520001705

Gleason, B. K., & Hays, D. G. (2019). A phenomenological investigation of wellness within counselor education programs. *Counselor Education and Supervision, 58*(3), 177–194. https://doi.org/10.1002/ceas.12149

Glesne, C. (2014). *Becoming qualitative researchers: An introduction* (5th ed.). Pearson.

Gnilka, P., O'Hara, C., & Chang, C. Y. (2023). Social justice counseling. In D. G. Hays & B. T. Erford (Eds.), *Developing multicultural counseling competence: A systems approach* (4th ed., pp. 82–108). Pearson.

Golden-Biddle, K. G., & Locke, K. (2007). *Composing qualitative research* (2nd ed.). Sage.

Golonka, E. M., Tare, M., & Bonilla, C. (2017). Peer interaction in text chat: Qualitative analysis of chat transcripts. *Language, Learning & Technology, 21*(2), 157–178. https://dx.doi.org/10125/44616

Goodman-Scott, E. G., Hays, D. G., & Cholewa, B. (2018). "It takes a village": A case study of positive behavioral interventions and supports implementation in an exemplary urban middle school. *The Urban Review, 50*, 97–122. https://doi.org/10.1007/s11256-017-431-z

Goodrich, K. M., & Luke, M. (2019). Consensual qualitative research of LGB persons' counseling experiences addressing religious/spiritual foci. *Journal of Counseling Sexology & Sexual Wellness: Research, Practice, and Education, 1*, article 5. https://doi.org/10.34296/01011003

Gordon, R. (2019). "Why would I want to be anonymous?" Questioning ethical principles of anonymity in cross-cultural feminist research. *Gender & Development, 27*, 541–554. https://doi.org/10.1080/13552074.2019.1664044

Gosnell, H. F. (1935). *Negro politicians: The rise of Negro politics in Chicago.* University of Chicago Press.

Granholm, C., & Svedmark, E. (2018). Research that hurts: Ethical considerations when studying vulnerable populations online. In R. Iphofen & M. Tolich (Eds.), *The Sage handbook of qualitative research ethics* (pp. 501–509). Sage.

Grbich, C. (2012). *Qualitative data analysis: An introduction* (2nd ed.). Sage.

Green, J. C., Caracelli, V. J., & Graham, W. F. (1989). Toward a conceptual framework for mixed-method evaluation designs. *Educational Evaluation and Policy Analysis, 11*, 255–274.

Greenwood, D. J., & Levin, M. (2005). Reform of the social sciences and of universities through action research. In N. K. Denzin & Y. S. Lincon (Eds.), *The Sage handbook of qualitative research* (4th ed., pp. 43–64). Sage.

Griffin, D. M., & Bryan, J. (2021). A qualitative study of school counseling in Barbados: A focused ethnography. *International Journal for the Advancement of Counselling*, 1–22. https://doi.org/10.1007/s10447-021-09445-x

Grigorovich, A., & Kontos, P. (2019). A critical realist exploration of the vulnerability of staff to sexual harassment in residential long-term care. *Social Science & Medicine, 238*. https://doi.org/10.1016/j.socscimed.2019.112356

Groves, O. (2021). The diary method and its power to record the routine and forgettable in the language lives of international students. In X. Cao & E. F. Henderson (Eds.), *Exploring diary methods in higher education research: Opportunities, choices and challenges* (pp. 15–25). Routledge.

Gruzd, A., Wellman, B., & Takhteyev, Y. (2011). Imagining Twitter as an imagined community. *American Behavioral Scientist, 55*(10), 1294–1318.

Guba, E. G., & Lincoln, Y. S. (1989). *Fourth generation evaluation.* Sage.

Haiyasoso, M., & Trepal, H. (2019). Survivors' stories: Navigating parenthood after surviving child sexual abuse. *Journal of Counseling & Development, 97*(3), 281–292. https://doi.org/10.1002/jcad.12268

Hall, J. (2020). *Focus groups: Culturally responsive approaches for qualitative inquiry and program evaluation.* Myers Education Press.

Hammersley, M. (2004). Toward a usable past for qualitative research. *International Journal of Social Research Methodology, 7*(1), 19–27. https://doi.org/10.1080/13645570310001640581

Hammersley, M. (2018). Values in social research. In R. Iphofen & M. Tolich (Eds.), *The Sage handbook of qualitative research ethics* (pp. 23–34). Sage.

Hammersley, M., & Atkinson, P. (2007). *Ethnography: Principles in practice* (3rd ed.). Taylor & Francis.

Harding, S. (1991). *Whose science? Whose knowledge? Thinking from women's lives.* Cornell University Press.

Harrison, H., Birks, M., Franklin, R., & Mills, J. (2017). Case study research: Foundations and methodological orientations. *Forum: Qualitative Social Research, 18*(1). https://doi.org/10.17169/fqs-18.1.2655

Hart, D. (2018). Other ways of knowing: The intersection of education when researching family roots. *Genealogy, 2*(2). https://doi.org/10.3390/genealogy2020018

Hartsock, N. (1983). *Money, sex, and power: Toward a feminist historical materialism.* Northeastern University Press.

Haug, F. (2008). Memory work. *Australian Feminist Studies, 23*(58), 537–541. https://doi.org/10.1080/08164640802433498

Haverkamp, B. E. (2005). Ethical perspectives on qualitative research in applied psychology. *Journal of Counseling Psychology, 52*(2), 146–155. https://doi.org/10.1037/0022-0167.52.2.146

Haverkamp, B. E., & Young, R. A. (2007). Paradigms, purpose, and the role of the literature: Formulating a rationale for qualitative investigations. *The Counseling Psychologist, 35*, 265–294.

Hays, D. G. (2020). Multicultural and social justice counseling competency research: Opportunities for innovation. *Journal of Counseling & Development, 98*(3), 331-344. https://doi.org/10.1002/jcad.12327

Hays, D. G., Chang, C. Y., & Dean, J. K. (2004). White counselors' conceptualization of privilege and oppression: Implications for counselor training. *Counselor Education and Supervision, 43*, 242–257.

Hays, D. G., Crockett, S., & Michel, R. (2021). A grounded theory of counselor educators' academic leadership development. *Counselor Education & Supervision, 60*, 51–72. https://doi.org/10.1002/ceas.12196

Hays, D. G., & Dahl, H. (2021). Research and writing. In S. K. Butler, A. F. Locke, & J. M. Filmore (Eds.), *Introduction to 21st century counseling: A multicultural and social justice approach* (pp. 274–297). Cognella.

Hays, D. G., Forman, J., & Sikes, A. (2009a). Use of visual data to explore adolescent females' perceptions of dating relationships. *Journal of Creativity in Mental Health, 4*(4), 295-307.

Hays, D. G., & McKibben, W. B. (2021). Promoting rigorous research: Generalizability and qualitative research. *Journal of Counseling & Development, 99*(2), 178–188. https://doi.org/10.1002/jcad.12365

Hays, D. G., McLeod, A. L., & Prosek, E. A. (2009b). Diagnostic variance among counselors and counselor trainees. *Measurement and Evaluation in Counseling and Development, 42*, 3–14.

Hays, D. G., & Shillingford-Butler, A. (2023). Racism and White supremacy. In D. G. Hays & B. T. Erford (Eds.), *Developing multicultural counseling competency: A systems approach* (4th ed. pp. 110–155). Pearson.

Hays, D. G., & Wood, C. (2011). Infusing qualitative traditions in counseling research designs. *Journal of Counseling & Development, 89*, 288–295.

Hays, D. G., Wood, C., Dahl, H., & Kirk-Jenkins, A. (2016). Methodological rigor in *Journal of Counseling & Development* qualitative research articles: A 15-year review. *Journal of Counseling & Development, 94*(2), 172–183. https://doi.org/10.1002/jcad.12074

Heesen, R., Bright, L. K., & Zucker, A. (2019). Vindicating methodological triangulation. *Synthese, 196*, 3067–3081. https://doi.org/10.1007/s11229-016-1294-7

Hellawell, D. (2006). Inside-out: Analysis of the insider-outsider concept as a heuristic device to develop reflexivity in students doing qualitative research. *Teaching in Higher Education, 11*(4), 483–494. https://doi.org/10.1080/13562510600874292

Hellström, T. (2008). Transferability and naturalistic generalization: New generalizability concepts for social science or old wine new bottles? *Quality & Quantity, 42*, 321–337.

Hempel, S. (2020). *Conducting your literature review.* American Psychological Association.

Hennink, M. M., Kaiser, B. N., & Marconi, V. C. (2017). Code saturation versus meaning saturation: How many interviews are enough?

*Qualitative Health Research, 27,* 591–608. https://doi.org/10.1177/1049732316665344

Heppner, P. P., Wampold, B. E., Owen, J., & Wang, K. T. (2015). *Research design in counseling* (4th ed.). Cengage Learning.

Herman, R. D. K. (2018). Approaching research in Indigenous settings: Nine guidelines. In First Nations of Quebec and Labrador Health and Social Services Commission, Université du Quebec en Abitibi-Témiscamingue, & Université du Quebec en Outaouais (Eds.), *Toolbox of research principles in an aboriginal context: ethics, restrict, fairness, reciprocity, collaboration and culture* (pp. 103–113). https://www.cssspnql.com/docs/default-source/centre-de-documentation/toolbox_research_principles_aboriginal_context_eng16C3D3AF4B658E221564CE39.pdf

Hershkovitz, A. (2016). Editorial: Genealogy and family history through multiple academic lenses: An introduction to the special issue. *Journal of Multidisciplinary Research, 8,* 5–10.

Hill, C. E. (2012). *Consensual qualitative research: A practical resource for investigating social science phenomena.* American Psychological Association.

Hill, S.R., Troshani, I., & Chandrasekar, D. (2020). Signalling effects of vlogger popularity on online consumers. *Journal of Computer Information Systems, 60,* 76-84. https//doi.org/10.1108/ITP-01-2021-0008

Hill, C. E., Knox, S., Thompson, B. J., Williams, E. N., Hess, S. A., & Ladany, N. (2005). Consensual qualitative research: An update. *Journal of Counseling Psychology, 52,* 196–205. https://doi.org/10.1037/0022-0167.52.2.196

Hill, C. E., Thompson, B. J., & Williams, E. (1997). A guide to conducting consensual qualitative research. *The Counseling Psychologist, 25,* 517–572. https://doi.org/10.1177/0011000097254001

Ho, B. S. (2002). Application of participatory action research to family-school intervention. *School Psychology Review, 31*(1), 106–121.

hooks, b. (2000). *Feminist theory: From margin to center.* Pluto Press.

Hoover, M. A., Green, H. D., Jr., Bogart, L. M., Wagner, G. J., Mutchler, M. G., Galvan, F. H., &

McDavitt, B. (2016). Do people know I'm poz?: Factors associated with knowledge of serostatus among HIV-positive African Americans' social network members. *AIDS Behavior, 20*(1), 137–146. https://doi.org/10.1007/s10461-015-1039-5

Horsburgh, D. (2003). Evaluation of qualitative research. *Journal of Clinical Nursing, 12,* 307–312. https://doi.org/10.1046/j.1365-2702.2003.00683.x

Hughes, S. (2020). My skin is unqualified: an autoethnography of Black scholar-activism for predominantly White education. *International Journal of Qualitative Studies in Education, 33,* 151–165. https://doi.org/10.1080/09518398.2019.1681552

Hughes, S. A., & Pennington, J. L. (2017). *Autoethnography: Process, product, and possibility.* Sage.

Huisman, K. (2008). "Does this mean you're not going to come visit me anymore?": An inquiry into an ethics of reciprocity and positionality in feminist ethnographic research. *Sociological Inquiry, 78,* 372–396.

Insch, G. S., Moore, J. E., & Murphy, L. D. (1997). Content analysis in leadership research: Examples, procedures, and suggestions for future use. *Leadership Quarterly, 8,* 1–25.

Ireland, L., & Holloway, I. (1996). Qualitative health research with children. *Children & Society, 10*(2), 155–164. https://doi.org/10.1002/(SICI)1099-0860(199606)10:2<155::AID-CHI15>3.0.CO;2-Q

Iosifidis, P., & Nicoli, N. (2020). The battle to end fake news: A qualitative content analysis of Facebook announcements on how it combats disinformation. *International Communication Gazette, 82*(1), 60–81. https://doi.org/10.1177/1748048519880729

Jacquez, F., Vaughn, L. M., & Wagner, E. (2013). Youth as partners, participants or passive recipients: A review of children and adolescents in community-based participatory research (CBPR). *American Journal of Community Psychology, 51*(1–2), 176–189. https://doi.org/10.1007/s10464-012-9533-7

Janusz, B., Bergmann, J. R., Matusiak, F., & Peräkylä, A. (2021). Practices of claiming control and independence in couple therapy with narcissism. *Frontiers in Psychology, 11,* 3779. https://doi.org/10.3389/fpsyg.2020.596842

Jardine, G. M. (2005). *Foucault & education* (Vol. 3). Peter Lang.

Jett, S. T., & Delgado-Romero, E. A. (2009). Pre-practicum service-learning in counselor education: A qualitative case study. *Counselor Education and Supervision, 49*(2), 106 -121. https://doi.org/10.1002/j.1556-6978.2009.tb00091.x

Johnson, A. S. (2007). An ethics of access: Using life history to trace preservice teachers' initial viewpoints on teaching for equity. *Journal of Teacher Education, 58,* 299–314. https://doi.org/10.1177/0022487107305604

Johnson, C. W. (Ed.). (2018). *Collective memory work: A methodology for learning with and from lived experience.* Routledge.

Johnson, C. W., Singh, A. A., & Gonzalez, M. (2014). "It's complicated": Collective memories of transgender, queer, and questioning youth in high school. *Journal of Homosexuality, 61,* 419–434. https://doi.org/10.1080/00918369.2013.842436

Jones, S. (2006). *Girls, social class, and literacy: What teachers can do to make a difference.* Heinemann.

Jong, S. T. (2017). Netnography: Researching online populations. In P. Liamputtong (Ed.), *Handbook of research methods in health social sciences* (pp. 1321–1337). Springer.

Jordan, J. V. (2010). *Relational–cultural therapy.* American Psychological Association.

Kant, I. (1787). *The critique of practical reason and other writings in moral philosophy.* University of Chicago Press.

Kasturirangan, A., & Williams, E. N. (2003). Counseling Latina battered women: A qualitative study of the Latina perspective. *Journal of Multicultural Counseling and Development, 31,* 161–172.

Kearney, M. (n.d.). *Tweetbotornot.* GitHub. https://github.com/mkearney/tweetbotornot

Kelly, T., & Howie, L. (2007). Working with stories in nursing research: Procedures used in narrative analysis. *International Journal of Mental Health Nursing, 16,* 136–144.

Kendall, M. (2020). *Hood feminism: Notes from the women that a movement forgot.* Viking.

Kennedy, A. C., Meier, E., & Prock, K. A. (2021). A qualitative study of young women's abusive first relationships: What factors shape their process of disclosure? *Journal of Family Violence, 36,* 849–864. https://doi.org/10.1007/s10896-021-00258-5

Kidd, S. A., & Kral, M. J. (2005). Practicing participatory action research. *Journal of Counseling Psychology, 5,* 187–195.

Kirkness, V. J., & Barnhardt, R. (1991). First Nations and higher education: The four R's—Respect, relevance, reciprocity, responsibility. *Journal of American Indian Education, 30*(3), 1–15. https://www.jstor.org/stable/24397980

Kline, W. B. (2008). Developing and submitting credible qualitative manuscripts. *Counselor Education and Supervision, 47*(4), 210–217.

Koelsch, L. E. (2013). Reconceptualizing the member check interview. *International Journal of Qualitative Methods, 12,* 168–179.

Kourgiantakis, T., Sewell, K. M., Lee, E., & Kirvan, A. (2021) MSW students' perspectives on learning in a social work practice in mental health course: A qualitative research study. *Social Work in Mental Health, 19*(2), 141–165. https://doi.org/10.1080/15332985.2021.1894628

Korstjens, I., & Moser, A. (2017). Series: Practical guidance to qualitative research. Part 2: Context, research, questions, and designs. *European Journal of General Practice, 23,* 274–279. https://doi.org/10.1080/13814788.2017.1375090

Kowal, E. (2015). *Trapped in the gap: Doing good in indigenous Australia.* Berghahn.

Kozinets, R. V. (2019). *Netnography: The essential guide to qualitative social media research.* Sage.

Kozleski, E. B. (2017). The uses of qualitative research: Powerful methods to inform evidence-based practice in education. *Research and Practice for Persons with Severe Disabilities, 42,* 19–32. https://doi.org/10.1177/1540796916683710

Krippendorff, K. (2018). *Content analysis: An introduction to its methodology* (4th ed.). Sage

Kross, J., & Giust, A. (2018). Elements of research questions in relation to qualitative inquiry. *The Qualitative Report, 24*(1), 24–30. https://doi.org/10.46743/2160-3715/2019.3426

Ladhari, R., Massa, E., & Skandrani, H. (2020). YouTube vloggers' popularity and influence: The roles of homophily, emotional attachment, and expertise. *Journal of Retail and Consumer Services, 54*. https://doi.org/10.1016/j.jretconser.2019.102027

Ladson-Billings, G., & Tate, W. F. (1995). Toward a critical race theory of education. *Teachers College Record, 97*(1), 47–68.

Lamson, A. L., Clark, R. J., Bellamy, R. W., Hodgson, J. L., Knight, S. M., Baugh, E. J., & Flores, J. (2020). Latina sexual health care in the US: Community-based participatory research and her lived experience. *Journal of Feminist Family Therapy, 32*(1–2), 76–96. https://doi.org/10.1080/08952833.2020.1755167

Lanford, M. (2019). Making sense of "outsiderness": How life history informs the college experiences of "nontraditional" students. *Qualitative Inquiry, 25*(5), 500–512. https://doi.org/10.1177/1077800418817839

Lanford, M., Tierney, W. G., & Lincoln, Y. (2018). The art of life history: Novel approaches, future directions. *Qualitative Inquiry, 25*(5), 459–463. https://doi.org/https://doi.org/10.1177/1077800418817834

Larkin, M., & Thompson, A. R. (2012). Interpretative phenomenological analysis in mental health and psychotherapy research. In D. Harper & A. R. Thompson (Eds.), *Qualitative research methods in mental health and psychotherapy: A guide for students and practitioners* (pp. 101–116). John Wiley & Sons.

Lather, P. (1986). Issues of validity in openly ideological research: Between a rock and a soft place. *Interchange, 17*, 63–84. https://doi.org/10.1007/BF01807017

Lather, P. (2007). *Getting lost: Feminist efforts toward a double(d) science.* SUNY Press.

Lavallée, L. F. (2009). Practical application of an Indigenous research framework and two qualitative Indigenous research methods: Sharing circles and Anishnaabe symbol-based reflection. *International Journal of Qualitative Methods, 8*(1), 21–40. https://doi.org/10.1177/160940690900800103

LeCompte, M. D., & Schensul, J. J. (2012). *Analysis and interpretation of ethnographic data: A mixed methods approach* (Vol. 5). Rowman Altamira.

Lenette, C., & Boddy, J. (2013). Visual ethnography and refugee women: Nuanced understandings of lived experiences. *Qualitative Research Journal, 13*(1), 72–89. https://doi.org/10.1108/14439881311314621

Lestari, I. W. (2020). First experiences in a school-based practicum: Pre-service teachers' emotional and perceived benefits towards the program. *English Journal of Merdeka, 5*(1), 31–40.

Levinson, D. (1978). *The season of a man's life.* Knopf.

Levitt, H. M., Bamber, M., Crewell, J. W., Frost, D. M., Josselson, R., & Suàrez-Orozco, C. (2018). Journal article reporting standards for qualitative primary, qualitative meta-analytic, and mixed methods research in psychology: The APA publications and communications board task force report. *American Psychologist, 73*(1), 26–46. https://dx.doi.org/10.1037/amp0000151

Liedenberg, L. (2018). Thinking critically about photovoice: Achieving empowerment and social change. *International Journal of Qualitative Methods, 17*(1), 1–9. https://doi.org/10.1177/1609406918757631

Lim, J. (2016). Editor's pick: Top qualitative research blogs. *Qual360.* https://qual360.com/editors-pick-top-qualitative-research-blogs/

Lincoln, Y. S., & Guba, E. G. (1995). *Naturalistic inquiry* (2nd ed.). Sage.

Liu, S., & Liu, J. (2021). Public attitudes toward COVID-19 vaccines on English-language Twitter: A sentiment analysis. *Vaccine, 39*, 5499–5505. https://doi.org/10.1016/j.vaccine.2021.08.058

Liu, W. M., Stinson, R., Hernandez, J., Shepard, S., & Haang, S. (2009). A qualitative examination of masculinity, homelessness, and social class among men in a transitional shelter. *Psychology of Men and Masculinity, 10*(2), 131–148.

Llewellyn-Beardsley, J., Rennick-Egglestone, S., Callard, F., Crawford, P., Farkas, M., Hui, A., & Slade, M. (2019). Characteristics of mental health recovery narratives: systematic review and narrative synthesis. *PloS One, 14*(3), e0214678. https://doi.org/10.1371/journal.pone.0214678

Lobe, B., Morgan, D., & Hoffman, K. A. (2020). Qualitative data collection in an era of social distancing. *International Journal of Qualitative Research, 18.* https://doi.org/10.1177/1609406920937875

Lofland, J., Snow, D. A., Anderson, L., & Lofland, L. H. (2005). *Analyzing social settings: A guide to qualitative observation and analysis* (4th ed.). Wadsworth.

Logsdon, P., Samudre, M., & Kleinert, H. (2018). *A qualitative study of the impact of peer networks and peer support arrangements in project pilot schools.* Human Development Institute. https://files.eric.ed.gov/fulltext/ED590603.pdf

Long, B. T., & Hall, T. (2018). Educational narrative inquiry through design-based research: Designing digital storytelling to make alternative knowledge visible and actionable. *Irish Educational Studies, 37*(2), 205–225. https://doi.org/10.1080/03323315.2018.1465836

Love, B. L. (2017). A ratchet lens: Black queer youth, agency, hip hop, and the Black ratchet imagination. *Educational Researcher, 46*(9), 539–547.

Lynd, R. S., & Lynd, H. M. (1929). *Middletown: A study in contemporary American culture.* Harcourt/Brace.

Lynd, R. S., & Lynd, H. M. (1937). *Middletown in transition: A study in cultural conflicts.* Harcourt/Brace.

Lysaker, P. H., Lancaster, R. S., & Lysaker, J. T. (2003). Narrative transformation as an outcome in the psychotherapy of schizophrenia. *Psychology and Psychotherapy: Theory, Research and Practice, 76,* 285–299.

MacDonald, S. (2001). British social anthropology. In P. Atkinson, A. Coffey, S. Delamont, J. Lofland, & L. Lofland (Eds.), *Handbook of ethnography* (pp. 60–79). Sage.

Mackrill, T. (2008). Solicited diary studies of psychotherapy in qualitative research: Pros and cons. *European Journal of Psychotherapy and Counselling, 10*(1), 5–18.

Malinowski, B. (2002). *Argonauts of the Western Pacific: An account of native enterprise and adventure in the archipelagoes of Melanesian New Guinea.* Routledge. (Original work published 1922)

Malone, R. E., Yerger, V. B., McGruder, C., & Froelicher, E. (2006). "It's like Tuskegee in reverse": A case study of ethical tensions in institutional review board review of community-based participatory research. *American Journal of Public Health, 96*(11), 1914–1919.

Mantzoukas, S. (2008). Facilitating research students in formulating research questions. *Nurse Education Today, 28,* 371–377.

Maree, N., & van der Westhuizen, G. (2020). How classroom talk contributes to reading comprehension. *Per Linguam, 36*(2), 1–15. http://dx.doi.org/10.5785/36-2-910

Marshall, C. (1990). Goodness criteria: Are they objective or judgment calls? In E. G. Guba (Ed.), *The paradigm dialog* (pp. 188–197). Sage.

Martin, F. E. (1998). Tales of transition: self-narrative and direct scribing in exploring care-leaving. *Child & Family Social Work, 3*(1), 1–12.

Mayo, E., Roethlisberger, F., & Dickson, W. (1939). *Management and the worker.* Harvard University Press.

Mays, N., & Pope, C. (2000). Qualitative research in health care: Assessing quality in qualitative research. *BMJ, 320,* 50–52. https://doi.org/10.1136/bmj.320.7226.50

Mayton, H. N., & Wester, K. (2019). Understanding the experiences of survivors of a loss by suicide: A photovoice study. *Journal of Creativity in Mental Health, 14*(1), 10–22. https://doi.org/10.1080/15401383.2018.1491814

Maxwell, J. A. (2013). *Qualitative research design: An interactive approach* (3rd ed.). Sage.

Mazzei, L. A. (2009). An impossibly full voice. In A. Y. Jackson & L. A. Mazzei (Eds.), *Voice in qualitative inquiry: Challenging conventional, interpretative, and critical conceptions in qualitative research* (pp. 45–62). Routledge.

Mazzei, L. A., & Jackson, A. Y. (2009). Introduction: The limit of voice. In A. Y. Jackson & L. A. Mazzei (Eds.), *Voice in qualitative inquiry: Challenging conventional, interpretative, and critical conceptions in qualitative research* (pp. 1–14). Routledge.

McDavitt, B., Bogart, L. M., Mutchler, M. G., Wagner, G. J., Green, H. D., Jr., Lawrence, S. J., Mutepfa, K. D., & Nogg, K. A. (2016). Dissemination as dialogue: Building trust and sharing research findings through community engagement. *Preventing Chronic Disease*, 13. http://dx.doi.org/10.5888/pcd13.150473external icon

McFerran, K. S., Hense, C., Koike, A., & Rickwood, D. (2018). Intentional music use to reduce psychological distress in adolescents accessing primary mental health care. *Clinical Child Psychology and Psychiatry*, 23(4), 567–581. https://doi.org/10.11771359104518767231

McKenna, B., Myers, M. D., & Newman, M. (2017). Social media in qualitative research: Challenges and recommendations. *Information and Organization*, 27, 87–99. https://doi.org/10.1016/j.infoandorg.2017.03.001

McKibben, W. B., & Logan-McKibben, S. (2021). A content analysis of counseling organizations' social media usage. *Journal of Technology in Counselor Education and Supervision*, 1(1). https://doi.org/10.22371/tces/0001

McKibben, W. B., Umstead, L. K., & Borders, L. D. (2017). Identifying dynamics of counseling leadership: A content analysis study. *Journal of Counseling & Development*, 95(2), 192–202. https://doi.org/10.1002/jcad.12131

McLeod, J. (2011). Qualitative research in counseling and psychotherapy (2nd ed.). Sage.

McLeod, J., & Lynch, G. (2000). This is our life: Strong evaluation in psychotherapy narrative. *European Journal of Psychotherapy, Counselling and Health*, 3, 389–406.

Mead, G. H. (1934). *Mind, self and society.* University of Chicago Press.

Mead, M. (1928). *Coming of age in Samoa.* William Morrow Paperbacks.

Mead, M. (1930). *Growing up in New Guinea.* Blue Ribbon Books.

Mead, M. (1964). *Continuities in cultural evolution.* Routledge.

Mead, G. H., & Schubert, C. (1934). *Mind, self and society* (Vol. 111). University of Chicago Press.

Mellor, R., Lancaster, K., & Ritter, A. (2021). Recovery from alcohol problems in the absence of treatment: A qualitative narrative analysis. *Addiction*, 116(6), 1413–1423. https://doi.org/doi:10.1111/add.15288

Mertens, D. M. (2017). *Mixed methods design in evaluation.* Sage.

Merton, R. K. (1972). Insiders and outsiders: A chapter in the sociology of knowledge. *American Journal of Sociology*, 78(1), 9–47.

Miles, M. B., Huberman, A. M., & Saldaña, J. (2020). *Qualitative data analysis: A methods sourcebook* (4th ed.). Sage.

Milhas, P. (2022). Memo writing strategies: Analyzing the parts and the whole. In C. Vanover, P. Miles, & J. Saldaña (Eds.), *Analyzing and interpreting qualitative research: After the interview* (pp. 243–257). Sage.

Mishler, E. G. (1986). *Research interviewing: Context and narrative.* Harvard University Press.

Moon, S. (2019). *Three approaches to qualitative research through the arts: Narratives of teaching for social justice and community.* Brill.

Moore, S., & Murphy, M. (2005). *How to be a student: 100 great ideas and practical habits for students everywhere.* Open University Press.

Moore-Lobban, S., O'Leary Wiley, M., & Singh, A. A. (2021). Introduction to the special issue: Integration of practice, advocacy, and research of counseling psychology. *The Counseling Psychologist*, 49(7), 946–957. https://doi.org/10.1177/00110000211019667

Morais, G. M., Santos, V. F., & Gonçalves, C. A. (2020). Netnography: Origins, foundations, evolution and axiological and methodological developments and trends. *The Qualitative Report*, 25(2), 441–455. https://nsuworks.nova.edu/tqr/vol25/iss2/10

Moran, D. (2005). *Edmund Husserl: founder of phenomenology.* Polity.

Morar, N. (Ed.). (2016). *Between Deleuze and Foucault.* Edinburgh University Press.

Morgan, D. L., Ataie, J., Carder, P., & Hoffman, K. (2013). Introducing dyadic interviews as a method for collecting qualitative data. *Qualitative Health Research, 23*(9), 1276–1284. https://doi.org/10.1177/1049732313501889

Morgan, D. L., Eliot, S., Lowe, R. A., & Gorman, P. (2016). Dyadic interviews as a tool for qualitative evaluation. *American Journal of Evaluation, 37*(1), 109–117. https://doi.org/10.1177/1098214015611244

Morrow, S. L. (2005). Quality and trustworthiness in qualitative research in counseling psychology. *Journal of Counseling Psychology, 52*(2), 250–260. https//doi.org/10.1037/0022-0167.52.2.250

Morrow, S. L. (2007). Qualitative research in counseling psychology: Conceptual foundations. *The Counseling Psychologist, 35*, 209–235. https://doi.org/10.1177/0011000006286990

Morse, J. M. (1999). Silent debates in qualitative inquiry. *Qualitative Health Research, 9*, 163–165. https://doi.org/10.1177/104973299129121730

Morse, J. M. (2015). Data were saturated. ... *Qualitative Health Research, 25*(5), 587–588. https://doi.org/10.1177/1049732315576699

Morse, J. M., Barrett, M., Mayan, M., Olson, K., & Spiers, J. (2002). Verification strategies for establishing reliability and validity in qualitative research. *International Journal of Qualitative Methods, 1*(2), 1–19.

Moser, A., & Korstjens, I. (2018). Series: Practical guidance to qualitative research. Part 3: Sampling, data collection and analysis. *European Journal of General Practice, 24*(1), 9–18. https://doi.org/10.1080/13814788.2017.1375091

Mosley, D. V., Hargons, C. N., Meiller, C., Angyal, B., Wheeler, P., Davis, C., & Stevens-Watkins, D. (2021). Critical consciousness of anti-Black racism: A practical model to prevent and resist racial trauma. *Journal of Counseling Psychology, 68*(1), 1–16. https://doi.org/10.1037/cou0000430

Moustakas, C. (1990). Heuristic research: Design and methodology. *Person-Centered Review, 5*(2), 170–190.

Moustakas, C. (1994). *Phenomenological research methods.* Sage.

Moyer, J. S., Warren, M. R., & King, A. R. (2020). "Our stories are powerful": The use of youth storytelling in policy advocacy to combat the school-to-prison pipeline. *Harvard Educational Review, 90*, 172–194.

Mueller, R. A. (2020). Episodic narrative interview: Capturing stories of experience with a methods fusion. *International Journal of Qualitative Methods, 18*, 1–11. https://doi.org/1609406919866044

Myers, J., Sweeney, T. J., & White, V. E. (2002). Advocacy for counseling and counselors: A professional imperative. *Journal of Counseling & Development, 80*, 394–402.

Nastasi, B. K., Chittooran, M. R. M., Arora, P., & Song, S. (2020). Infusing global and intercultural perspectives to transform school psychology and school psychologists. *School Psychology, 35*(6), 440-450. https://doi.org/10.1037/spq0000403

Nastasi, B. K., Schensul, J. J., De Silva, M. A., Varjas, K., Silva, K. T., Ratnayake, P., & Schensul, S. L. (1998). Community-based sexual risk prevention program for Sri Lankan youth: Influencing sexual-risk decision making. *International Quarterly of Community Health Education, 18*(1), 139-155.

Nastasi, B. K., Varjas, K., Schensul, J. J., Schensul, S. L., Silva, K. T., & Ratnayake, P. (2000). The participatory intervention model: A framework for conceptualizing and promoting intervention acceptability. *School Psychology Quarterly, 15*, 207–232.

National Association of Social Workers. (2017). *Code of ethics.* https://www.socialworkers.org/About/Ethics/Code-of-Ethics

National Council for the Social Studies. (n.d.). *Advocacy planning: Your 10-step plan.* https://www.socialstudies.org/advocacy/advocacy-planning-your-10-step-plan-0

National Institutes of Health. (2019). *Guidelines and policies for the conduct of research in the Intramural Research Program at NIH.* https://oir.nih.gov/sites/default/files/uploads/sourcebook/documents/ethical_conduct/guidelines-conduct_research.pdf

Nelson, J. (2017). Using conceptual depth criteria: Addressing the challenge of reaching saturation in qualitative research. *Qualitative Research, 17*(5), 554–570. https://doi.org/10.1177.1468794116679873

Nelson, M. L., & Quintana, S. M. (2005). Qualitative clinical research with children and adolescents. *Journal of Clinical Child and Adolescent Psychology, 34,* 344–356. https://doi.org/10.1207/s15374424jccp3402_14

Neri de Souza, F., Neri de Souza, D., & Costa, A. P. (2016). Asking questions in a qualitative research context. *The Qualitative Report, 21*(13), 6–18. https://doi.org/10.46743/2160-3715/2016.2607

Nieweglowski, K., Corrigan, P. W., Tyas, T., Tooley, A., Dubke, R., Lara, J., Washington, L., Sayer, J., Sheehan, L., & Addiction Stigma Research Team. (2018). Exploring the public stigma of substance use disorder through community-based participatory research. *Addiction Research & Theory, 26*(4), 323–329. https://doi.org/10.1080/16066359.2017.1409890

O'Hara, S. (2018). Autoethnography: The science of writing your lived experience. *Health Environments Research & Design Journal, 11,* 14–17. https://doi.org/10.1177/1937586718801425

O'Hara, C., Clark, M., Hays, D. G., McDonald, C. P., Chang, C. Y., Crockett, S. A., Filmore, J., Portman, T., Spurgeon, S., & Wester, K. L. (2016). AARC standards for multicultural research. *Counseling Outcome Research and Evaluation, 7*(2), 67-72. https://doi.org/10.1177/2150137816657389

Okech, J. E. A., & Kline, W. B. (2004). A qualitative exploration of group co-leader relationships. *Journal for Specialists in Group Work, 30*(2), 173–190.

Okubo, Y., Yeh, C. J., Lin, P. Y., Fujita, K., & Shea, J. M. Y. (2007). The career decision-making process of Chinese American youth. *Journal of Counseling and Development, 85,* 440–448.

O'Malley, M. P., Asher, N., Beck, B. L., Capper, C. A., Lugg, C. A., Murphy, J. P., & Whitlock, R. U. (2018). Asking queer(er) questions: epistemological and methodological implications for qualitative inquirers. *International Journal of Qualitative Studies in Education, 31,* 572–594.

Onwuegbuzie, A. J., & Leech, N. L. (2007). A call for qualitative power analysis. *Quality and Quantity, 41,* 105–121. https://doi.org/10.1007/s11135-005-1098-1

Oscós-Sánchez, M. A., Lesser, J., Oscós-Flores, L. D., Pineda, D., Araujo, U., Franklin, B., Hernández, J. A., Hernández, S., & Vidales, A. (2021). The effects of two community-based participatory action research programs on violence outside of an in school among adolescents and young adults in a Latino community. *Journal of Adolescent Health, 68,* 370–377. https://doi.org/10.1016/j.jadohealth.2020.10.004

O'Shaughnessy, S. & Krogman, N. T. (2017) A revolution reconsidered? Examining the practice of qualitative research in feminist scholarship. *Signs, 37*(2), 493–420.

Park, R. E. (1950). *Race and culture.* Free Press.

Park, R. E. (1955). *Society: Collective behavior, news and opinion, sociology and modern society.* Free Press.

Park, R., Burgess, E. W., & McKenzie, R. D. (1925). *The city.* University of Chicago Press.

Park, R. E., & Doyle, B. (1937). *The etiquette of race relations in the South.* University of Chicago Press.

Parnell, J. (2017). Vlogging: A new phenomenon, but is it a concern for people's health? *Journal of Aesthetic Nursing, 6*(4), 196–198. https://doi.org/10.12968/joan.2017.6.4.196

Patton, M. Q. (1991). Qualitative research on college students: Philosophical and methodological comparisons with the quantitative approach. *Journal of College Student Development, 32,* 389–396.

Patton, M. Q. (2014). *Qualitative research & evaluation methods* (4th ed.). Sage.

Peshkin, A. (1988). Virtuous subjectivity: in the participant observer's I's. In D. Berg & K. Smith (Eds.), *The self in social inquiry: Researching methods* (pp. 267–281). Sage.

Piaget, J. (1964). *Six psychological studies.* Penguin Books.

Piaget, J., & Inhelder, B. (1969). *The psychology of the child.* Basic Books.

Pink, S. (2013). *Doing visual ethnography* (3rd ed.). Sage.

Pitts, M. J. (2007). Upward turning points and positive rapport-development across time in researcher-participant relationships. *Qualitative Research, 7*(2), 177–201.

Poland, B. D. (1995). Transcription quality as an aspect of rigor in qualitative research. *Qualitative Inquiry, 1*(3), 290–210.

Polit, D. F., & Beck, C. T. (2010). Generalization in quantitative and qualitative research: Myths and strategies. *International Journal of Nursing Studies, 47*, 1451–1458.

Polkinghorne, D. E. (1989). Phenomenological research methods. In R. S. Valle & S. Halling (Eds.), *Existential-phenomenological perspectives in psychology* (pp. 41–60). Plenum Press.

Pomeranz, J. L. (2014). Creating a tobacco cessation program for people with disabilities: A community-based participatory research approach. *Journal of Addiction Research & Therapy, 5(4)*, 1–8. https://doi.org/10.4172/2155-6105.1000204

Ponterotto, J. G. (2005). Qualitative research in counseling psychology: A primer on research paradigms and philosophies of science. *Journal of Counseling Psychology, 52*, 126–136. https://doi.org/10.1037/0022-0167.52.2.126

Porter, R. (2007). Why academics have a hard time writing good grant proposals. *The Journal of Research Administration, 38*(2), 37–43.

Porter, S. (2007). Validity, trustworthiness and rigour: Reasserting realism in qualitative research. *Journal of Advanced Nursing 60(1)*, 79–86. https://doi.org/10.1111/j.1365648.2007.04360.x

Powell, P. J. (2005). *The effects of grade retention: Life histories of adults who were retained as children* [Unpublished doctoral dissertation]. Northern Arizona University.

Prasad, P. A. (2005) *Crafting qualitative research: Working in the postpositivist traditions.* Taylor & Francis.

Prescott, J., Gray, N. J., Smith, F. J., & McDonagh, J. E. (2015). Blogging as a viable research methodology for young people with arthritis: A qualitative study. *Journal of Medical Internet Research, 17*(3) e61. https://doi.org/ 10.2196/jmir.3608

Project South. (2008). *As the South goes ... so goes the nation.* https://projectsouth.org/wp-content/uploads/2012/05/ProjectSouth21stAnniversary-Scrapbook.pdf

Protection of Human Subjects, 45 C.F.R. § 46 (2009). https://www.hhs.gov/ohrp/regulations-and-policy/regulations/45-cfr-46/index.html

Quimby, E. (2006). Ethnography's role in assisting mental health research and clinical practice. *Journal of Clinical Psychology, 62*(7), 859–879.

Raby, R., Caron, C., Thévissen-LeBlanc, S., Prioletta, J., & Mitchell, C. (2017). Vlogging on YouTube: The online, political engagement of young Canadians advocating for social change. *Journal of Youth Studies, 21*(4), 495–512. https://doi.org/10.1080/13676261.2017.1394995

Ramello, S. (Ed.). (2020). *Fascination of queer.* BRILL.

Rapley, M. (2012). Ethnomethodology/conversation analysis. In D. Harper & A. R. Thompson (Eds.), *Qualitative research methods in mental health and psychotherapy: A guide for students and practitioners* (4th ed., pp. 177–192). Wiley.

Ratts, M. J., Singh, A. A., Nassar-McMillan, S., Butler, S. K., & McCullough, J. R. (2015). *Multicultural and social justice counseling competencies: Guidelines for the counseling profession.* American Counseling Association. https://www.counseling.org/docs/default-source/competencies/multicultural-and-social-justice-counseling-competencies.pdf?sfvrsn=8573422c_22

Ratts, M. J., Singh, A. A., Nassar-McMillan, S., Butler, S. K., & McCullough, J. R. (2016). Multicultural and social justice counseling competencies: Guidelines for the counseling profession. *Journal of Multicultural Counseling and Development, 44*, 28–48. https://doi.org/10.1002/jmcd.12035

Reason, P. (1994). Three approaches to participative inquiry. In N. K. Denzin & Y. S. Lincoln (Eds.), *Handbook of qualitative research* (2nd ed.; pp. 324–339). Sage.

Reger, J. (2017). Contemporary feminism and beyond. In H. J. McCammon, V. Taylor, J. Reger, & R. L. Einwohner (Eds.), *The Oxford handbook of US women's social movement activism* (pp. 109–128). Oxford University Press.

Reiners, G. M. (2012). Understanding the difference between Husserl's (descriptive) and Heidegger's (interpretive) phenomenological research. *Journal of Nursing & Care*, *1*(5), 1–3. http://dx.doi.org/10.4172/2167-1168.1000119

Reinharz, S. (1992). *Feminist methods in social research*. Oxford University Press.

Reissman, C. K., & Speedy, J. (2012). Narrative inquiry in the psychotherapy professions: A critical review. In D. J. Clandinin (Ed.), *Handbook of narrative inquiry: Mapping a methodology* (2nd ed., pp. 426–456). Sage.

Rennie, D. L., Watson, K. D., & Monteiro, A. (2000). Qualitative research in Canadian psychology. *Forum*, *1*(2). Art 29. https://doi.org/10.17169/fqs-1.2.1098

Richards, J. (2013). *Principal-generated YouTube video as a method of improving parental involvement* [Unpublished doctoral dissertation]. Texas Wesleyan University.

Richards, J. C. (2022). Coding, categorizing, and theming the data: A reflexive search for meaning. In C. Vanover, P. Miles, & J. Saldaña (Eds.), *Analyzing and interpreting qualitative research: After the interview* (pp. 149–167). Sage.

Richardson, L., & Adams St. Pierre, E. (2018). Writing: A method of inquiry. In N. K. Denzin & Y. S. Lincoln (Eds.), *The Sage handbook of qualitative research* (5th ed., pp. 818–838). Sage.

Riggs, D. W., & Treharne, G. J. (2017). Queer theory. In B. Gough (Ed.), *The Palgrave handbook of critical social psychology* (pp. 101–121). Palgrave Macmillan.

Rinehart, E. K. (2020). Abductive analysis in qualitative inquiry. *Qualitative Inquiry*, *27*, 303–311. https://doi.org/1077800420935912

Rodriguez, S. (2020). "You're a sociologist, I am too ...": Seducing the ethnographer, disruption, and ambiguity in fieldwork with (mostly) undocumented youth. *Journal of Contemporary Ethnography*, *49*(2), 257–285. http://dx.doi.org/10.1177/0891241619882075

Rogers, C. (1961). *On becoming a person: A therapist's view of psychotherapy*. Constable and Robinson.

Rolfe, G. (2006). Validity, trustworthiness, and rigour: Quality and the idea of qualitative research. *Journal of Advanced Nursing*, *53*(3), 304–310. https://doi.org/10.1111/j.13652648.2006.03727.x

Roulston, K. (2013). *Reflective interviewing: A guide to theory & practice*. Sage.

Roulston, K. (2019). Using archival data to examine interview methods: The case of the former slave project. *International Journal of Qualitative Methods*, *18*, 1–13. https://doi.org/10.1177/1609406919867003

Rowan, J. (2000). Research ethics. *International Journal of Psychotherapy*, *5*(2), 103–111.

Sacks, H. (1995). *Lectures on conversation*. Blackwell Publishing.

Sadat Ahadi, H. (2020). Unveiling the voices of Afghan women in community college. *Journal of Applied Research in the Community College*, *27*(2), 81–93.

Saeed, S., & Zyngier, D. (2012). How motivation influences student engagement: A qualitative case study. *Journal of Education and Learning*, *1*(2), 252–267.

Salas, R. (2019). Latino critical race theory (Latcrit). In K. T. Han & J. Laughter (Eds.), *Critical race theory in teacher education: Informing classroom culture and practice* (pp. 59–70). Teachers College Press.

Saldaña, J. (2016). *The coding manual for qualitative researchers* (3rd ed.). Sage.

Salinas, C. S., Fránquiz, M. E., & Rodríguez, N. N. (2016). Writing Latina/o historical narratives: Narratives at the intersection of critical historical inquiry and LatCrit. *The Urban Review*, *48*, 264–284.

Salvador, K., Paetz, A. M., & Tippetts, M. M. (2020). "We all have a little more homework to do": A constructivist grounded theory of transformative learning processes for practicing music teachers encountering social justice. *Journal of Research in Music Education*, *68*(2), 193–215. https://doi.org/10.1177/0022429420920630

Sandelowski, M. (1993). Rigor or rigor mortis: The problem of rigor in qualitative research revisited. *Advances in Nursing Science, 16*(2), 1–8.

Sandelowski, M. (1995). Sample size in qualitative research. *Research in Nursing & Health, 18*(2), 179–183.

Sands, R. G., Bourjolly, J., & Roer-Strier, D. (2007). Crossing cultural barriers in research interviewing. *Qualitative Social Work, 6*(3), 353–372. https://doi.org/10.1177/1473325007080406

Sanjari, M., Barhamnezhad, F., Fomani, F. K., Shoghi, M., & Cheraghi, M. A. (2014). Ethical challenges of researchers in qualitative studies: The necessity to develop a specific guideline. *Journal of Medical Ethics and History of Medicine, 7,* 14–19.

Saunders, B., Sim, J., Kingstone, T., Baker, S., Waterfield, J., Bartlam, B., Burroughs, H., & Jinks, C. (2018). Saturation in qualitative research: Exploring its conceptualization and operationalization. *Quality and Quantity, 52,* 1893–1907. https://doi.org/10.1007/s11135-017-0574-8

Schroeder, W. R. (2004). *Continental philosophy: A critical approach.* Wiley.

Schwandt, T. A. (2001). *Dictionary of qualitative inquiry* (2nd ed.). Sage.

Seidman, I. (2019). *Interviewing as qualitative research: A guide for researchers in education and social sciences* (5th ed.). Teachers College Press.

Sevelius, J., dickey, l. m., & Singh, A. A. (2017). Engaging in TGNC-affirmative research. In Singh, A. A. & dickey, l. m. (Eds.), *Trans affirmative counseling and psychological practice.* American Psychological Association.

Shaw, C. R. (1930). *The jack-roller: A delinquent boy's own story.* University of Chicago Press.

Shaw, C. R. (1938). *Brothers in crime.* University of Chicago Press.

Shaw, C. R., & Moore, M. E. (1931). *The natural history of a delinquent career.* University of Chicago Press.

Shelburne, S., Curtis, D., & Rockwell, D. (2020). Spontaneous transformation and recovery from problematic eating: A heuristic inquiry. *Journal of Humanistic Psychology.* https://doi.org/10.1177/0022167820945803

Sherrell, R. S., & Lambie, G. W. (2016). A qualitative investigation of college students' Facebook usage and romantic relationships: Implications for college counselors. *Journal of College Counseling, 19,* 138–153. https://doi.org/10.1002/jocc.12037

Shiller, J. (2018). The disposability of Baltimore's Black communities: A participatory action research project on the impact of school closings. *The Urban Review, 50*(1), 23–44. https://doi.org/10.1007/s11256-017-0428-7

Shordike, A., Hocking, C., Bunrayong, W., Vittayakorn, S., Rattakorn, P., Pierce, D., & Wright-St. Clair, V. A. (2017). Research as relationship: Engaging with ethical intent. *International Journal of Social Research Methodology, 20,* 285–298. https://doi.org/10.1080/13645579.2017.1287874

Shyjka, A. (2021). *Student experience with the high school choice process in Chicago public schools.* UChicago Consortium on School Research. https://files.eric.ed.gov/fulltext/ED614999.pdf

Silverman, D. (1993). *Interpreting qualitative data: Methods for analyzing talk, text and interaction.* Sage.

Silvester, J. (1998). Attributional coding. In G. Symon & C. Cassell (Eds.), *Qualitative methods and analysis in organizational research: A practical guide* (pp. 73–93). Sage.

Sim, J., Saunders, B., Waterfield, J., & Kingstone, T. (2018). Can sample size in qualitative research be determined a priori? *International Journal of Social Research Methodology, 21*(5), 619–634. https://doi.org/10.1080/13645579.2018.1454643

Simmons, M., Kim, B., Hyde, J., Lemon, T., Resnick, K., & McInnes, D. K. (2018). *Veteran sex offender access to housing and services after release from incarceration: Obstacles and best practices.* VA National Center on Homelessness Among Veterans. https://www.va.gov/HOMELESS/nchav/resources/docs/justice-involved/convicted-of-sexual-offenses/Veteran-Sex-Offender-Access-To-Housing-Services-May-2018-508.pdf

Singh, A. A., Hays, D. G., Chung, Y. B., & Watson, L. (2010a). South Asian immigrant women who have survived child sexual abuse: Resilience and healing. *Violence Against Women, 16*(4), 444–458. https://doi.org/10.1177/1077801210363976

Singh, A. A., Hays, D. G., & Watson, L. S. (2011). Strength in the face of adversity: Resilience strategies of transgender individuals. *Journal of Counseling & Development, 89*(1), 20–27. https://doi.org/10.1002/j.1556-6678.2011.tb00057.x

Singh, A. A., Hofsess, C. D., Boyer, E. M., Kwong, A., Lau, A. S., McLain, M., & Haggins, K. L. (2010b). Social justice and counseling psychology: Listening to the voices of doctoral trainees. *The Counseling Psychologist, 38*(6), 766–795. https://doi.org/10.1177/0011000010362559

Singh, A. A., & Lukkarila, L. (2017). *Successful academic writing: A complete guide for social and behavioral scientists.* Guilford Press.

Singh, A. A., & McKleroy, V. S. (2011). "Just getting out of bed is a revolutionary act" the resilience of transgender people of color who have survived traumatic life events. *Traumatology, 17*(2), 34-44. https://doi.org/10.1177/1534765610369261

Singh, A. A., Richmond, K., & Burnes, T. R. (2013). Feminist participatory action research with transgender communities: Fostering the practice of ethical and empowering research designs. *International Journal of Transgenderism, 14*(3), 93–104. https://doi.org/10.1080/15532739.2013.818516

Singh, A., Truczczinski, L., Estevez, R., White, L., LeBlanc, A., & Bockting, W. (under review). "I was always silenced, and I refused to be silent:" The development of resilience in Black trans and nonbinary people. *The Counseling Psychologist.*

Singh, A. A., Urbano, A., Haston, M., & McMahon, E. (2010b). School counselors' strategies for social justice change: A grounded theory of what works in the real world. *Professional School Counseling, 13,* 135–145.

Slovin, L. J., & Semenec, P. (2019). Thinking/writing within and outside the IRB box. *Reconceptualizing Educational Research Methodology, 10*(1), 14–27.

Smeyers, P., & Depaepe, M. (2018). Educational research: A tale of tensions and constraints. In P. Smeyers & M. Depaepe (Eds.), *Educational research: Ethics, social justice, and funding dynamics* (pp. 1–10). Springer.

Smith, L. T. (2012). *Decolonizing methodologies: Research and indigenous peoples* (2nd ed.). Zed Books.

Smith, J. A., Flowers, P., & Larkin, M. (2012). *Interpretative phenomenological analysis.* Sage.

Snelson, C. (2013). Vlogging about school on YouTube: An exploratory study. *New Media & Society, 17*(3), 321–339. https://doi.org/10.1177/1461444813504271

Snow, K. C., Hays, D. G., Caliwagan, G., Ford, D. J., Jr., Mariotti, D., Mwendwa, J. M., & Scott, W. E. (2016). Guiding principles for indigenous research practices. *Action Research, 14*(4), 357–375.

Snow, M. S., Hudspeth, E. F., Blake, G., & Seale, H. A. (2007). A comparison of behaviors and play themes over a six-week period: Two case studies in play therapy. *International Journal of Play Therapy, 16,* 147–159. https://doi.org/10.1037/1555-6824.16.2.147

Solórzano, D. G., & Delgado Bernal, D. (2001). Examining transformational resistance through a critical race and LatCrit theory framework: Chicana and Chicano students in an urban context. *Urban Education, 36*(3), 308–342.

Solórzano, D. G., & Yosso, T. J. (2002). Critical race methodology: Counter-storytelling as an analytical framework for education research. *Qualitative Inquiry, 8,* 23–44.

Sommers, I., & Baskin, D. (2006). Methamphetamine use and violence. *Journal of Drug Issues, 36,* 77–96.

Spall, S. (1998). Peer debriefing in qualitative research: Emerging operational models. *Qualitative Inquiry, 4*(2), 280–292.

Spooner, M. (2019). A life history of place: A future place for life histories? *Qualitative Inquiry, 25*(5), 513–522. https://doi.org/10.1177/1077800418817840

Stake, R. E. (1995). *The art of case study research.* Sage.

Stake, R. E. (2006). *Multiple case study analysis.* Guilford.

Stake, R. E. (2013). *Multiple case study analysis* (2nd ed.). Guilford.

Staller, K. M. (2018). Stitching tattered cloth: Reflections on social justice and qualitative inquiry in troubled times. *Qualitative Inquiry, 26*(6), 559–566. https://doi.org/10.1177/1077800418786900

Starman, A. B. (2013). The case study as a type of qualitative research. *Journal of Contemporary Educational Studies, 1*, 28–43.

Stoecker, R. (2018). Participatory action research and social problems. In A. J. Treviño (Ed.), *The Cambridge handbook of social problems* (pp. 39–56). Cambridge University Press.

Stone, L. (2018). Research ethics and a case for positionality. In P. Smeyers & M. Depaepe (Eds.), *Educational research: Ethics, social justice, and funding dynamics* (pp. 55–72). Springer.

Strauss, A., & Corbin, J. (1990). *Basics of qualitative research: Techniques and procedures for developing grounded theory* (1st ed.). Sage.

Strauss, A., & Corbin, J. (1998). *Basics of qualitative research: Techniques and procedures for developing grounded theory* (2nd ed). Sage.

Subrahmanyam, K., Greenfield, P. M., & Tynes, B. (2004). Constructing sexuality and identity in an online teen chat room. *Journal of Applied Developmental Psychology, 25*(6), 651–666. https://doi.org/10.1016/j.appdev.2004.09.007

Sultan, N. (2018). Embodiment and the therapeutic relationship: Findings from a heuristic inquiry. *Journal of Humanistic Counseling, Education, and Development, 47*, 3–8. https://doi.org/10.1002/johc.12052

Sultan, N. (2020). Heuristic inquiry: Bridging humanistic research and counseling practice. *Journal of Humanistic Counseling, 59*, 158–172. https://doi.org/10.1002/johc.12142

Sutherland, E. H. (1937). The professional thief. *Journal of Criminal Law and Criminology (1931–1951)*, 161–163.

Swensen, M. S. (2019). *Finding a job: A descriptive qualitative study of challenges of female refugees resettled in the United States* [Unpublished doctoral dissertation]. Grand Canyon University.

ten Have, P. (2007). *Doing conversation analysis: A practical guide* (2nd ed.). Sage.

Thomas, D. R. (2017). Feedback from research participants: Are member checks useful in qualitative research? *Qualitative Research in Psychology, 14*(1), 23–41. https://doi.org/10.1080/14780887.2016.1219435

Thomas, W. I., & Znaniecki, F. (1927). *The Polish peasant in Europe and America* (2nd ed.). Knopf.

Tinker, C., & Armstrong, N. (2008). From the outside looking in: How an awareness of difference can benefit the qualitative research process. *The Qualitative Report, 13*(1), 53–60.

Tobin, G. A., & Begley, C. M. (2004). Methodological rigour within a qualitative framework. *Journal of Advanced Nursing, 48*(4), 388–396. https://doi.org/10.1111/j.1365-2648.2004.03207.x

Toporek, R., & Daniels, J. (2018). *American Counseling Association Advocacy Competencies.* https://www.counseling.org/docs/default-source/competencies/aca-advocacy-competencies-may-2020.pdf?sfvrsn=85b242c_6

Turner, D. (2022). Coding system design and management. In C. Vanover, P. Miles, & J. Saldaña (Eds.), *Analyzing and interpreting qualitative research: After the interview* (pp. 117–132). Sage.

U.S. Department of Health and Human Services. (2013). *Summary of the HIPAA privacy rule.* https://www.hhs.gov/hipaa/for-professionals/privacy/laws-regulations/index.html

Valdes, F. (2005). Legal reform and social justice: An introduction to LatCrit theory, praxis and community. *Griffith Law Review, 14*(2), 148–173.

van Kaam, A. L. (1959). The nurse in the patient's world. *The American Journal of Nursing, 59*(12), 1708–1710.

van Kaam, A. L. (1966) *Existential foundations of psychology.* Duquesne University Press.

Varjas, K., Meyers, J., Henrich, C. C., Graybill, E. C., Dew, B. J., Marshall, M. L., Williamson, Z., Skoczylas, R. B., & Avant, M. (2006). Using a participatory culture-specific intervention model to develop a peer victimization intervention. *Journal of Applied School Psychology, 22*(2), 35–57. https://doi.org/10.1300/J370v22n02_03

Varpio, L., Ajjawi, R., Monrouxe, L. V., O'Brien, B. C., & Rees, C. E. (2016). Shedding the cobra effect:

Problematising thematic emergence, triangulation, saturation and member checking. *Medical Education, 51,* 40–50.

Varpio, L., & MacLeod, A. (2020). Philosophy of science series: Harnessing the multidisciplinary edge effect by exploring paradigms, ontologies, epistemologies, axiologies, and methodologies. *Academic Medicine, 95,* 686–689.

Vidich, A. J., & Lyman, S. M. (2001). Qualitative methods: Their history in sociology and anthropology. In N. K. Denzin & Y. S. Lincoln (Eds.), *The landscape of qualitative research* (2nd ed., pp. 55–129). Sage.

Vidourek, R. A., & Burbage, M. (2019). Positive mental health and mental health stigma: A qualitative study assessing student attitudes. *Mental Health & Prevention, 13,* 1–6. https://doi.org/10.1016/j.mhp.2018.11.006

Wahesh, E., Fulton, C. L., Shannonhouse, L. R., McKibben, W. B., & Kennedy, S. D. (2018). A content analysis of CSI chapter efforts to promote counselor leadership development. *Journal of Counselor Leadership and Advocacy, 5*(1), 82–94. https://doi.org/10.1080/2326716X.2017.1422997

Waldrop, D. (2004). Ethical issues in qualitative research with high-risk populations: Handle with care. In D. K. Padgett (Ed.), *The qualitative research* experience (pp. 240–253). Thomson Brooks/Cole.

Wall, S. (2008). Easier said than done: Writing an autoethnography. *International Journal of Qualitative Methods, 7*(1), 38–53.

Wanat, C. L. (2008). Getting past the gatekeepers: Differences between access and cooperation in public school research. *Field Methods, 20,* 191–208.

Wang, C., & Burris, M. A. (1994). Empowerment through Photo Novella: Portraits of participation. *Health Education Quarterly, 21,* 171–186.

Warren, M. R., Oh, S., & Tieken, M. (2016). The formation of community-engaged scholars: A collaborative approach to doctoral training in educational research. *Harvard Educational Review, 86,* 233–260. https://doi.17763.0017-8055.86.2.233

Watt, D. (2007). On becoming a qualitative researcher: The value of reflexivity. *The Qualitative Report, 12*(1), 82–101.

Weber, R. P. (1990). *Basic content analysis.* Sage.

Wells, P. C., & Hunt, B. (2020). A qualitative research study of counseling students' journeys through internship using photovoice. *Journal of Creativity in Mental Health,* 1–12. https://doi.org/10.1080/15401383.2020.1790455

Welton, D. (1999). *The essential Husserl: Basic writings in transcendental phenomenology.* Indiana University Press.

Werle, G. D. (2004). The lived experience of violence: Using storytelling as a teaching tool with middle school students. *The Journal of School Nursing, 20,* 81–87. https://doi.org/10.1177/10598405040200020501

Wertz, F. J., Charmaz, K., McMullen, L. M., Josselson, R., Anderson, R., & McSpadden, E. (2011). *Five ways of doing qualitative analysis.* Guilford.

Wester, K. L. (2011). Publishing ethical research: A step-by-step overview. *Journal of Counseling & Development, 89*(3), 301–307. https://doi.org/10.1002/j.1556-6678.2011.tb00093.x

Whittemore, R., Chase, S. K., & Mandle, C. L. (2001). Validity in qualitative research. *Qualitative Health Research, 11*(4), 522–537. https://doi.org/10.1177/104973201129119299

Wiersma, W., & Jurs, S. G. (2009). *Research methods in education* (9th ed.). Pearson.

Williams, G. T., & Ellison, L. (2009). Duty to warn and protect. In the American Counseling Association (Ed.), *The ACA encyclopedia of counseling* (pp. 163–165). American Counseling Association.

Wilson, E., Kenny, A., & Dickson-Swift, V. (2015). Using blogs as a qualitative health research tool: A scoping review. *International Journal of Qualitative Methods, 14*(5), 1–12. https://doi.org/10.1177/1609406915618049

Wolcott, H. F. (2008). *Writing up qualitative research* (3rd ed.). Sage.

Wood, L. (2019). *Participatory action learning and action research: Theory, practice and process.* Routledge.

Woodbridge, L., & O'Beirne, B. R. (2017). Counseling students' perceptions of journaling as a tool for developing reflective thinking. *The Journal of Counselor Preparation and Supervision*, 9(2). http://dx.doi.org/10.7729/92.1198

Woodson, A. (2019). Racial code words, re-memberings and Black kids' civic imaginations: A critical race ethnography of a post-civil rights leader. *Anthropology & Education Quarterly*, *50*(1), 26–47. https://doi.org/10.1111/aeq.12277

World Health Organization. (n.d.). *Equity.* https://www.who.int/health-topics/health-equity#tab=tab_1

Yazan, B. (2015). Three approaches to case study methods in education: Yin, Merriam, and Stake. *The Qualitative Report*, 20(2), 134–142. http://www.nova.edu/ssss/QR/QR20/2/yazan1.pdf

Yeh, C. J., Inman, A. G., Kim, A. B., & Okubo, Y. (2006). Asian American families' collectivistic coping strategies in response to 9/11. *Cultural Diversity and Ethnic Minority Psychology*, 12, 134–148. https://doi.org/10.1037/1099-9809.12.1.134

Yin, R. K. (2000). Rival explanations as an alternative to "reforms as experiments." In L. Bickman (Ed.), *Validity & social experimentation: Donald Campbell's legacy* (pp. 239–266). Sage.

Yin, R. K. (2017). *Case study research and applications: Design and methods* (6th ed.). Sage.

# Author Index

Lau, A. S., 368, 409–411
Lavallée, L. F., 49
Lawless, M., 331
Lawrence, S. J., 499
LeBlanc, A., 296, 341
LeCompte, M. D., 357, 363
Lee, A., 487
Lee, E., 257
Leech, N. L., 213, 268
LeFever et al., 1999, 529
Lemon, T., 494
Lenette, C., 335
Leo, M., 529
Lessard, S., 136, 422
Lesser, J., 148
Lestari, I. W., 337
Levin, M., 486
Levina, E., 70
Levinson, D., 134
Levinson, D., 134
Levitt, H. M., 423, 446–448, 454, 467, 483
Liedenberg, L., 335
Lin, P. Y., 420–421
Lincoln, Y. S., 11, 13, 39, 41, 43, 46–48, 50, 53, 56, 134, 138, 147, 234–235, 237, 244–247, 260–261, 359, 375, 446, 463
Liu, J., 325
Liu, S., 325
Liu, W. M., 420
Llewellyn-Beardsley, J., 136–137
Lobe, B., 331
Locke, J., 39
Locke, K., 449
Lofland, J., 375
Lofland, L. H., 375
Logan-McKibben, S., 371–372
Logsdon, P., 494
Long, B. T., 137
López, I. H., 59
Lowe, R. A., 310
Lugg, C. A., 61
Luke, M., 131
Lukkarila, L., 186
Lyman, S. M., 39, 41–43, 47
Lynch, G., 423
Lynd, H. M., 46
Lynd, R. S., 46
Lyons, K. J., 480–482
Lysaker, J. T., 423
Lysaker, P. H., 423

M
MacDonald, S., 43
Mack, R., 137
Mackrill, T., 338
MacLeod, A., 49–52

Mahfouz, J., 77
Malinowski, B., 43
Malone, R. E., 84–85
Mandle, C. L., 268
Mantzoukas, S., 186
Marconi, V. C., 216
Marcuse, H., 44
Mariotti, D., 62–63
Marshall, C., 235
Marshall, M. L., 146
Martin, F. E., 136
Marx, K., 71
Maslow, A., 44
Massa, E., 331
Maxwell, J. A., 36–37, 159, 165, 178, 181, 183, 235, 243, 274–275, 357, 445
Mayan, M., 238
Mayo, E., 292
Mays, N., 267
Mayton, H. N., 334
Mazzei, L. A., 6–7
McCullough, J. R., 147, 488
McDavitt, B., 499–500
McDermott, F., 267
McDonagh, J. E., 328
McDonald, C. P., 492
McDonnell, L., 79, 99
McFerran, K. S., 189
McGrath, C. L., 26
McGruder, C., 84–85
McInnes, D. K., 494
McKenna, B., 325
McKenzie, R. D., 46
McKibben, W. B., 122, 142, 236, 245–246, 266, 371–372
McKleroy, V. S., 274–275
McLain, M., 368, 409–411
McLeod, A. L., 349, 351–354, 357–360
McMahon, E., 368, 409–411
McMullen, L. M., 123–124
McSpadden, E., 123–124
Mead, G., 43–46
Mead, M., 43
Meier, E., 176–177
Meiller, C., 122
Mellman, W., 296
Mensah, H. K., 202
Merleau-Ponty, M., 44, 123
Mertens, D. M., 38
Merton, R. K., 10
Meyers, J., 146
Michel, R., 30, 257, 264, 358, 408
Middleton, T., 512, 519
Miles, M. B., 6, 178
Miles, M. B., 6, 178, 204, 206, 208, 215, 243, 315, 349,

354, 357, 363–364, 374–375, 380, 382, 384–385, 389, 396
Milhas, P., 351–352
Mill, J. S., 70
Millington, G., 257
Mills, J., 112, 114
Miralles-Martínez, P., 328
Mishler, E. G., 375
Mitchell, C., 327, 331
Monrouxe, L. V., 241, 254–255
Monteiro, A., 47
Montoya, M., 59
Moon, S., 332
Mooney-Somers, J., 332
Moore, J. E., 368–371
Moore, M. E., 45, 134
Moore, S., 169
Moore-Lobban, S., 19
Moradi, B., 511
Morais, G. M., 321
Moran, D., 123
Morar, N., 71
Moreno, M. A., 328
Morgan, D., 310, 312, 331
Morrison, S., 329
Morrow, S. L., 12–13, 35, 38
Morse, J., 217, 238, 262
Moser, A., 184, 204–205, 212–213, 217, 224
Mosley, D. V., 122
Moustakas, C. 44, 123–124, 126–128, 413–416, 418, 438, 458, 461
Moyer, J. S., 501
Mueller, R. A., 308, 310
Murphy, J. P., 61
Murphy, L. D., 368–371
Murphy, M., 169
Mutchler, M. G., 499–500
Mutepfa, K. D., 499
Mwendwa, J. M., 62–63
Myers, J., 487
Myers, M. D., 325

N
Nassar-McMillan, S., 147, 488
Nastasi, B. K., 146–147, 433
Nelson, J., 217
Nelson, M. L., 105
Neri de Souza, D., 183
Neri de Souza, F., 183
Ness, L. R., 240, 259
Newman, M., 325
Nicoli, N., 325
Nielson, T., 143–144
Nietzsche, F., 71
Nogg, K. A., 499

# Subject Index

# About the Authors

**Danica G. Hays, Ph.D.**, is Professor and Dean of the College of Education at the University of Nevada, Las Vegas. She earned a doctorate in counselor education and supervision, with an emphasis in multicultural research, from Georgia State University. She has published more than 125 journal articles and book chapters in her areas of research expertise, which include research methodology and program evaluation, leadership development, domestic violence prevention, assessment and diagnosis, and multicultural and social justice issues in community mental health and counselor preparation. In addition to authoring this text, she is coeditor of *Developing Multicultural Counseling Competence: A Systems Approach* (4/e, Pearson); *A Counselor's Guide to Career Assessment Instruments* (6/e, National Career Development Association); *Corona Chronicles: Necessary Narratives in Uncertain Times* (1/e, Dio Press); and *Corona Chronicles: On Leadership, Processes, Commitments, and Hope in Uncertain Times* (1/e, Dio Press). She is also an associate and content editor of the *American Counseling Association Encyclopedia of Counseling* (1/e, ACA), author of *Assessment in Counseling: Procedures and Practices* (6/e, ACA), and coauthor of *Mastering the NCE and CPCE* (3/e, Pearson). She has extensive leadership history in the Association for Assessment and Research in Counseling (AARC) and the Association for Counselor Education and Supervision (ACES), including serving as AARC President and Governing Council Representative to ACA, ACES journal editor for *Counselor Education and Supervision*, founding editor for the *Counseling Outcome Research and Evaluation* journal, and President of an ACES region. The American Counseling Association has recognized her nationally as an ACA Fellow, as well as presented her awards for her research and advocacy as a counselor educator. She also received the ACES Legacy Award. Dr. Hays is @drdghays on Twitter.

**Anneliese A. Singh, Ph.D., LPC** (she/they) serves as Associate Provost for Diversity and Faculty Development/Chief Diversity Officer at Tulane University, where she is also a professor in social work with a joint appointment in psychology. Her scholarship and community organizing explores racial healing and racial justice, as well as National Institutes of Health-funded work with trans and nonbinary people. She is the author of several books, including *The Racial Healing Handbook: Practical Activities to Help You Challenge Privilege, Confront Systemic Racism, and Engage in Collective Healing*; *The Queer and Trans Resilience Workbook: Skills for Navigating Sexual Orientation and Gender Identity*; *Successful Academic Writing: A Complete Guide for Social and Behavioral Scientists* (with Lauren Lukkarila); and the *Clinician's Guide for Gender-Affirming Care* (with Sand Chang and lore m. dickey). She has edited the *Affirmative Counseling and Psychological Practice with Transgender and Gender-Nonconforming Clients* (with lore m. dickey) and *Social Justice in Group Work: Practical Interventions for Change* (with Carmen Salazar). Dr. Singh has written extensively on qualitative methodology and multicultural and social justice competency development in the counselor education, psychology, and the larger helping professions (*ACA Multicultural and Social Justice Counseling Competencies, ACA Transgender Counseling Competencies, ACA LGBQIQA Counseling Competencies, ACA Multiracial Counseling Competencies, ASGW Multicultural and Social Justice Group Work Principles, APA Guidelines for Psychological Practice with Transgender and Gender Nonconforming Clients, APA Guidelines for Prevention*). She has served as President for SAIGE (formerly ALGBTIC) and SACES within ACA and President of Counseling Psychology within APA. She is a Fellow within both ACA and APA and has received numerous awards for her scholarship and community organizing, including the inaugural SAIGE Anneliese Singh Award, Queer and Trans People of Color Award, and the ACES Legacy Award. Dr. Singh is @anneliesesingh on Twitter and Instagram.

CPSIA information can be obtained
at www.ICGtesting.com
Printed in the USA
LVHW060837280223
740531LV00011B/42